NINTH EDITION

Communication Works

Teri Kwal Gamble
College of New Rochelle

Michael Gamble
New York Institute of Technology

McGraw Hill

Boston   Burr Ridge, IL   Dubuque, IA   Madison, WI   New York   San Francisco   St. Louis
Bangkok   Bogotá   Caracas   Kuala Lumpur   Lisbon   London   Madrid   Mexico City
Milan   Montreal   New Delhi   Santiago   Seoul   Singapore   Sydney   Taipei   Toronto

Higher Education

COMMUNICATION WORKS

Published by McGraw-Hill, a business unit of The McGraw-Hill Companies, Inc., 1221 Avenue of the Americas, New York, NY, 10020. Copyright © 2008, 2005, 2002, 1999, 1996, 1993, 1990, 1988, 1984 by The McGraw-Hill Companies, Inc. All rights reserved. No part of this publication may be reproduced or distributed in any form or by any means, or stored in a database or retrieval system, without the prior written consent of The McGraw-Hill Companies, Inc., including, but not limited to, in any network or other electronic storage or transmission, or broadcast for distance learning. Some ancillaries, including electronic and print components, may not be available to customers outside the United States.

This book is printed on acid-free paper.

1 2 3 4 5 6 7 8 9 0 WCK/WCK 0 9 8 7 6

ISBN: 978-0-07-353422-0
MHID: 0-07-353422-6
AIE ISBN: 978-0-07-326621-3
AIE MHID: 0-07-326621-3

Vice President and Editor-in-Chief: *Emily Barrosse*
Publisher: *Phillip A. Butcher*
Sponsoring Editor: *Suzanne S. Earth*
Senior Developmental Editor: *Jennie Katsaros*
Editorial Assistant: *Erika Lake*
Senior Marketing Manager: *Leslie Oberhuber*
Managing Editor: *Jean Dal Porto*
Senior Project Manager: *Rick Hecker*
Senior Designer: *Kim Menning*
Photo Research Coordinator: *Natalia C. Peschiera*
Media Project Manager: *Stacy Bentz*
Senior Media Producer: *Nancy Garcia*
Production Supervisor: *Janean A. Utley*
Composition: *Techbooks*
Printing: *45# Pub Matte, Quebecor World*

Credits: The credits section for this book begins on page C-1 and is considered an extension of the copyright page.

Library of Congress Cataloging-in-Publication Data

Gamble, Teri Kwal.
   Communication works / Teri Kwal Gamble, Michael Gamble. — 9th ed.
      p. cm.
   Includes index.
   ISBN-13: 978-0-07-353422-0 (softcover : alk. paper)
   ISBN-10: 0-07-353422-6 (softcover : alk. paper)
   ISBN-13: 978-0-07-326621-3 (annotated instructor's edition, softcover : alk. paper)
   ISBN-10: 0-07-326621-3 (annotated instructor's edition, softcover : alk. paper) 1.
Communication.   I. Gamble, Michael,   1943–   II. Title.
   P90.G299 2006
   302.2—dc22   2006019497

The Internet addresses listed in the text were accurate at the time of publication. The inclusion of a Web site does not indicate an endorsement by the authors or McGraw-Hill, and McGraw-Hill does not guarantee the accuracy of the information presented at these sites.

www.mhhe.com

For Matthew Jon and Lindsay Michele, our children,

who grew up with this book and who have had more influence

on its eight revisions than they can imagine. Wonderful

students of life and always there when it matters, they

embody communication at its best.

For Martha and Marcel Kwal and Nan and Wesley Gamble,

our parents, who live on in our memories and were

instrumental in helping us learn how and why

communication works.

ABOUT THE AUTHORS

Teri Kwal Gamble and Michael W. Gamble both earned PhDs in communication from New York University. They are full professors of communication and award-winning teachers, with Teri at the College of New Rochelle and Michael at the New York Institute of Technology in Manhattan. As co-founders of Interact Training Systems, a communication consulting firm, they have conducted seminars, workshops, and short courses for numerous business and professional organizations across the United States.

The Gambles are co-authors of several textbooks and training systems, including *Public Speaking in the Age of Diversity; Interpersonal Communication in Theory, Practice and Context;* and *Literature Alive!* Their trade books include *Sales Scripts That Sell, Phone Power,* and *The Answer Book.*

Teri and Michael live in New Jersey and spend much of their time exploring how and why communication works. Their personal favorite communicators are their children—their son, Matthew Jon, who has his doctorate in biochemistry and is now a scientist, and their daughter, Lindsay Michele, who recently received her MBA in marketing.

Teri and Michael Gamble with son Matthew and daughter Lindsay.

BRIEF CONTENTS

ONLINE UNIT
Mass Communication and Media Literacy

This section is found on the book's Online Learning Center Web site at www.mhhe.com/gamble9

CONTENTS

Chapter 3
Communication and the Self-Concept: Who Are You? 46

Chapter 4
Communication and Perception: I Am More Than a Camera 74

Chapter 5
Language and Meaning: Helping Minds Meet 104

PART TWO
Interpersonal Communication

**Chapter 9
Person to Person:
Relationships in
Context   240**

**Chapter 10
Person to Person:
Interviewing   274**

PART THREE
Communicating in the Small Group

Chapter 11
Groups and Teams: Strategies for Decision Making and Problem Solving 306

Chapter 18
Persuasive Speaking   498

ONLINE UNIT
Mass Communication and Media Literacy   A-1

This section is found on the book's Online Learning Center Web site at www.mhhe.com/gamble9

NINTH-EDITION HIGHLIGHTS: WHAT'S NEW AND REVISED

The response to the preceding eight editions of *Communication Works* has been very gratifying. While our basic approach remains the same, we have worked diligently to incorporate the suggestions and comments of users to improve the text's ninth edition in ways that meet the needs of both instructors and students:

1. We updated and **streamlined the content** and enhanced the text's friendly language to promote ease of readability and usability, to help students focus on the most relevant aspects of communication, and to allow them to apply their knowledge using a range of practical skill-building exercises and experiences.

2. Responding to user interest, we **enhanced the text's service learning component** by making this unique exercise series a marginal callout.

3. We **incorporated new part-ending case studies** designed to help students assess their understanding of chapter concepts and improve their ability to apply theory to the kinds of real-life situations they face every day.

4. We improved the integration of ethics and civility, gender and culture, media and technology, workplace communication, and critical thinking issues into our discussions of communication theory and skill-building activities.

5. Even more than in prior editions, we **emphasize pedagogy that is interactive;** it involves students in self-reflections as well as stimulating dyadic, group, and class discussions. In addition, it invites enhancement through the use of boxed applications and through the integration of media and technology.

6. We **added an Idioms in Translation feature** to facilitate understanding of the content by students whose native language is not English.

7. We **integrated discussions on popular culture, technology, and media** throughout the text, stressing those issues of most concern to students, such as privacy, online disclosures, and dating.

8. We again expanded our discussion of contemporary ethical concerns, including the effects that lying and deception have in both the private and public arenas of our lives.

9. We updated the songs, films, and reading suggestions contained in the Listen to Me, View Me, and Read Me features located in the Wrap-Up section at the end of each chapter.

10. We worked to create activities that are adaptable to both large lecture and traditional class settings and that speak to students of diverse ages and backgrounds.

11. In addition to revising all the Web site features, we added the *Mass Communication and Media Literary Appendix* to the book's Online Learning Center.

Even more than in prior editions, we emphasize pedagogy that is interactive.

SIGNATURE FEATURES AND THEMES

Our approach and organization reflect our commitment to helping students actively explore how and why communication works.

Skill Builders

Because we believe that people learn best when they participate, we continue to offer a wide selection of Skill Builders—learning activities that appear in the text, online, and in the instructor's resources—for use in or out of class. Skill Builders encourage students to observe and consider communication, to assess its effects, and to experience the insights and practice they need to become skillful communicators. Instructors report that these exercises make *Communication Works* a complete teaching and learning package and make the study of communication active, exciting, involving, and rewarding. We do not expect any instructor to use in a single course or semester all the Skill Builders or other exercises, or even all the chapters in the text. We purposely have built flexibility into the text so that each instructor may easily choose those elements that fit the needs of his or her students and the available time frame.

Exploring Diversity, Ethics & Communication, and Thinking Critically

To reflect the needs and interests of an increasingly diverse student audience and to encourage critical inquiry, we continue to pay significant attention to the influence of culture and the importance of communication ethics. Content related to culture and ethics is represented comprehensively throughout the narrative as well as in the Exploring Diversity boxes, the Ethics & Communication boxes, and the Thinking Critically exercises, all of which appear throughout the text.

Media Wise and Resources for Further Inquiry and Reflection

Because of the myriad ways in which communication and technology are linked, we have continued and improved the Media Wise boxes. We also have updated the Listen to Me, View Me, Read Me, and Tell Me features. The Resources feature encourages students to demonstrate and apply their understanding of chapter content to popular media, such as music, movies, and books. All the features in the book are designed to create a pedagogical environment that compels students to ask questions and become involved and that launches individual assignments or group or class discussions. The text's special features—Skill Builder, Exploring Diversity, Ethics & Communication, Media Wise, Thinking Critically, and Resources for Further Inquiry and Reflection—are clearly identified in the table of contents so that instructors and students can locate them easily.

ORGANIZATION

We have made every effort to design and produce a book that students will enjoy reading, because we believe that student interest and information presentation are equal partners. Thus, we were devoted to creating a book that exhibits clarity of language and encourages reader participation, and does so in a lively, colorful

To reflect the needs and interests of an increasingly diverse student audience, and to encourage critical inquiry, we continue to pay significant attention to the influence of culture and to the importance of communication ethics.

All the features in the book are designed to create a pedagogical environment that compels students to ask questions and become involved.

format. We have tested the text materials with students of different ages, cultures, and ethnic groups. On the basis of that feedback we received, we have retained several popular pedagogical features from prior editions.

Each chapter begins with behavioral objectives, which illuminate the material, establish goals, and prepare the readers for the concepts that will be introduced. Within the chapters, students are periodically expected to complete self-assessment scales to evaluate their attitudes and reactions and to measure their mastery of skills. The marginal comments and questions, which juxtapose key content, are written to arouse curiosity and encourage thinking and questioning. The running glossary is meant to make terminology accessible. The Wrap-Up, which concludes each chapter, comprises a summary that reflects the chapter's behavioral objectives and recapitulates key content and skill building; a list of key chapter terminology and Idioms in Translation, and instructions for the Test Your Understanding self quizzes.

COMMUNICATION WORKS CD-ROM AND ONLINE LEARNING CENTER WWW.MHHE.COM/GAMBLE9

The Communication Works CD-ROM and Online Learning Center are integral parts of this text. Both extend the concepts and pedagogical methods of the book and were produced to appeal to a variety of learning styles.

The Communication Works CD-ROM and Online Learning Center are integral parts of this text. Both extend the concepts and pedagogical methods of the book and were produced to appeal to a variety of learning styles. In the book itself, icons in the text margin and in the end-of-chapter Wrap-Up sections prompt readers to view relevant video clips and to use relevant interactive tools. The CD-ROM is packaged free with every new copy of the book, and the Online Learning Center does not require students to use a password. The enthusiastic reaction of instructors and students who used these media resources with the previous edition of this text has been gratifying. Thanks to feedback from many of those students and instructors, both media have been revised and improved.

The Communication Works CD-ROM and Online Learning Center feature the following:

Self quizzes with feedback

Key terminology flash cards

Communication Concepts videos

Speech videos

Outline tutor

Outline exercises

Checklist for preparing and delivering a speech

Topic helper

Speech critique

PowerPoint tutor

Mass communication and media literary appendix

We are especially proud of this edition and hope you enjoy its new information and features. We would love to hear from you. Please know we value your suggestions. You can reach us via e-mail at gamble@carroll.com.

ACKNOWLEDGMENTS

The ninth edition of *Communication Works* finds us approaching the third decade in the text's evolution. We are astutely aware of how changes in our world, our lives, and the lives of our readers have led to changes in this book. The contributions of many people, including past and present students, the instructors who have been so loyal over the years, and the wonderful professionals at McGraw-Hill, demonstrate that *it takes a team to produce a text*. We are so grateful to all these people for the attention, nurturing, and care they have given *Communication Works*. They have contributed in untold ways to the text's continued relevance and success.

We want to recognize the extremely talented editing team at McGraw-Hill. We are especially thankful to Phil Butcher for his friendship and trust; Suzanne Earth for her continued belief in *Communication Works*; Jennie Katsaros, our tireless development editor, for taking this book under her artful wing, understanding it and us, and providing keen insight into the market; and Nanette Giles for having been a delight to work with. We also want to thank Rick Hecker, the text's project manager, who has an uncanny ability to stay on schedule; Kim Menning for the text's fresh design; and Natalia Peschiera for the wonderful photos that help bring the text's words to life.

We especially thank our reviewers for their loyalty and for their insightful advice that has resulted in this edition's improvements:

Titi Ufomata, *Kentucky State University*

Barbara Antonicka, *North Virginia CC*

Jane Sullivan, *Jefferson College*

Amy Lenoce, *North Virginia CC*

Judy Sims, *Georgia Highlands College*

Dana Pergrem, *Georgia Highlands College*

Rob Craig, *Central Piedmont CC*

Donna Munde, *Mercer County Community College*

Anne McIntosh, *Central Piedmont Community College*

We also want to thank our respective colleges, colleagues, and students for being sounding boards, for helping us refine the text, and for seeing the impact of our efforts.

Finally, once again, we have so much to thank Matthew and Lindsay, our children, for their insights, support, and laughter complete our understanding of how and why communication works. When all is said and done, they are our reasons for loving life!

Teri Kwal Gamble
Michael W. Gamble

Visual Preview

The ninth edition of *Communication Works* continues its tradition of helping students explore how and why communication works. Throughout the text, questions in the margins, boxes, headings, and picture captions encourage students to become actively involved with the course.

Skill Building and Critical Thinking

A focus on development and practice of communication and critical thinking skills is evident throughout the text.

Skill Builder

Skill Builder boxes help students become stronger communicators. Box topics include problem solving in organizations, relationship skills, group culture, and conflict resolution.

Skill Builder

Let's Get Tough

Human relations consultant and interviewer trainer Justin Menkes helps employment recruiters learn how to gather a lot of information in a brief period of time. To accomplish this, he suggests they ask questions like those identified in the text. Try your hand at answering one of those questions: You have two very important responsibilities that both have deadlines that are impossible to meet. You cannot accomplish both. How do you handle that situation?

Which of the following possible responses does your answer most resemble?

1. I'd focus on the project I'm most comfortable with and give it my all.

2. I'd plan carefully, assign segments of the project to others, and multitask so that I could complete both.

3. I'd ask my supervisor which project is most important to the company.

According to Menkes, the first response suggests that the interviewee's focus is on himself or herself, the second response does not answer the question asked, and the third response reveals an interest in the needs of the company and an interest in developing a collaborative relationship.[24]

Thinking Critically

Reflect and Respond

On the basis of your understanding of leadership and the value of conflict and conflict management, agree or disagree with this excerpt from Deborah Tannen's *Talking from 9 to 5*. Supply reasons and examples from both research and your own life that support the stance you are taking.

When decisions are made by groups, not everyone has equal access to the decision-making process.

Those who will take a position and refuse to budge, regardless of the persuasive power or intensity of feeling among others, are far more likely to get their way. Those who feel strongly about a position but are inclined to back off in the face of intransigence or very strong feeling from others are much less likely to get their way.[51]

Thinking Critically: Reflect and Respond

Thinking Critically exercises promote higher-order thinking and class discussion about issues related to the text content. Examples include perception, conflict and conflict management, self-concept, and nonverbal cues.

Diversity

Thoughtful, balanced integration of diversity prepares students to meet the challenges of communicating in today's complex societies.

Exploring Diversity

Exploring Diversity boxes prompt students to consider the effects of diversity on communication, and facilitate classroom discussions of topics such as culture, gender, and global teams; multicultural communication classes; and persuasion and assumed similarity.

Exploring Diversity

When Is a Kiss Not a Kiss?

When the Middle Eastern version of the reality show *Big Brother* was aired in the Arab world, one segment had a handsome Saudi kiss a Tunisian beauty. Viewers already perceived unrelated men and women sharing a house as abhorrent. The kiss complicated things, leading to protests and accusations of moral depravity. Critics called the show an assault on traditional values. As far as some viewers were concerned, the two might as well have had sex. In short order, the show was taken off the air, pleasing those opposed to it.[87]

Can reality television be transferred easily from one nation to another? Is reality for one country's audience necessarily another country's reality as well? Do you believe the globalization of programming concepts promotes or undermines cultural diversity?[88] Explain.

Because of the way they are socialized, men and women may share their feelings differently.

instance, when flirting. According to one educator, flirting is "a verbal power struggle between men and women."[29] For men "it is a form of foreplay," while for women it is more often "a way of making a connection."[29]

Researchers also affirm that women place a higher value on emotionally close relationships than do men, whose friendships frequently seem to lack emotional depth.[30] Because of the ways men are socialized, they often feel uncomfortable expressing their feelings directly with words, preferring instead to express them through shared activities such as sports.[31] Thus, women use personal and disclosive talk to develop and sustain their relationships to a greater extent than do men. While women bond through talk, men bond through doing things together.[32]

In addition, women focus on the maintenance of relationships more than men do. Women are eager to acquire personal information about their relational partners. They desire a partner who demonstrates care and concern and who is empathetic. As a result, they use more maintenance strategies than do men.[33]

This is not to imply that men and women do not share any commonalities in their views regarding relationships, because they do. Both men and women value same-sex friends and desire friends they can trust, who accept them and help them.

Culture and Relationships

Attitudes toward self and others influence the effectiveness of the relationships persons from different cultures share. Acceptance, for instance, is one necessary factor for relationship satisfaction. Researchers report that, to be satisfied in their relationships with Whites, both African Americans and Mexican Americans need to feel that Whites respect, confirm, and accept them.[34] Asians also practice the positive exchange of ideas, demonstrating care for the other person during the exchange. They value harmony as a means of relationship nurturance. Conformity and group well-being are especially important to them. Generally, they do not reach out to strangers, and they make great efforts to conceal unfavorable information about members of the group to which they belong from those whom they perceive to be outsiders.[?] Latinos, in contrast, tend to focus on relational support.[?]

While some cultures emphasize social relationships and interpret individuals to give preference to the interests of others over their own private interests, other cultures, including American culture, stress individualism. While Americans find

Integrated Diversity

Cultural diversity is woven into discussions throughout the text and is consistently included in examples and sample speeches.

Ethics

Coverage of ethics throughout the text examines how ethics has an impact on communication in families, social groups, the workplace, and more.

Ethics & Communication

Ethics & Communication boxes present a range of the ethical quandaries communicators face as they work to define what the expression "ethical communication" means. Topics covered include self-concern and concern for others, résumé padding and résumé poaching.

Ethics & Communication

Avoiding Problems

Group members face a number of problems that can influence the effectiveness of the decisions they make. How would you respond when faced with each of the following situations? What do your responses reveal about the nature of groups?

1. What consequences might your group face if instead of handling a problem, the members opted to run away from the problem, rationalize it, or otherwise avoid confronting it directly? Is running away from a problem ever a viable alternative to solving the problem?

2. Put yourself in the place of the character, Jim, in the following situation. What advice would you offer Jim?

Jim is, at heart, an investigative journalist who has considerable talent but who has been earning a living by writing restaurant reviews for a major magazine, which pays him very well, enabling him to support his wife and three young children. Despite this, Jim longs to return to his real vocation. Recently, he was offered a freelance position with a well-known newspaper, which asked Jim to resign from his present position and go undercover in an effort to determine if there is collusion between U.S. government agencies and major companies that seek to influence policy decisions being made by the administration. If Jim is successful in his investigation, it could make his journalistic career. If he is unsuccessful, however, he will have expended considerable time and energy, possibly ruining his reputation and ending his journalistic career. Should Jim give up his current job to take the new assignment? Check the lowest probability that you would consider acceptable for Jim to take the new assignment?

_____ 1 in 10	_____ 6 in 10
_____ 2 in 10	_____ 7 in 10
_____ 3 in 10	_____ 8 in 10
_____ 4 in 10	_____ 9 in 10
_____ 5 in 10	_____ 10 in 10

PEANUTS reprinted by permission of United Features Syndicate, Inc.

Media and Technology

Media and technology play a role in shaping the world. Communication Works examines how mediated and mass communication influence our interactions in all communication contexts.

Media Wise

Media Wise boxes are designed to develop media literacy skills and an understanding of issues such as the influence of media and the ethics of media practitioners. Topics include talk radio, stereotypes on film and TV, and what our choice of clothing reveals about us.

Media Wise

Frames of Reference

1. Intermittent reports of terrorist threats distort perceptions of risk, inducing an experience of fear that is out of proportion with actual danger. The more attention the media pay to a particular risk factor, the worse we assume the risk to be. For example, Dr. Baruch Fischoff, a psychologist at Carnegie Mellon University and a leader in the study of risk perception, reports: "If scientists are studying it and the news reports it, people assume it must be worth their attention."[41] Another risk researcher, Dr. Paul Slovic, reports that adding to this effect is the finding "that people put more stock in reports of bad news than in reports that might increase their trust."[42]

   Give an example of a media report that caused you to perceive a risk as greater than it was in reality. Did it involve weather? Traffic? Crime? Environmental issues? Political issues?

   Films perpetuate inaccurate perceptions that induce fear in viewers. View one of the following films: *Collateral Damage, The Siege, True Lies, Rules of Engagement, Executive Decision,* or *Not Without My Daughter.* In what ways, if any, does the film perpetuate bias against Arabs? In your opinion, is the "Arab as terrorist" stereotype responsible for increasing our fear and arousing our suspicion regarding who may or may not be a potential terrorist?

2. The popular media are also reflecting a crossing of cultures. An increasing number of films, such as *The Matrix Reloaded,* feature a rainbow cast, that is, a cast of all colors. Leon Wynter, author of *American Skin: Pop Culture, Big Business, and the End of White America,* suggests that commercial transracial representations sell because they "present a vision of the American dream in which we are liberated from the politics of race to openly embrace any style, cultural trope or image of beauty that attracts us regardless of its origin."[43] Others suggest such films sell because of the disproportionate representation of minorities in the audience; for example, market studies reveal that Black people buy movie tickets at higher rates than those of other ethnic groups.[44] To what extent, if any, do you find that rainbow casting is helping change perceptions of who in society is fit to occupy positions of power? Explain.

Like any relationship tool, laughter has a downside too. The opposite of joyful laughter is jeering, malicious laughter, laughter that is designed to punish, belittle, or exclude rather than include another. In this case, laughter, rather than expressing our sociability, signals our disdain for and power over another person.

When it comes to the use of humor in our relationships, there are wide laughter variations based on sex. A man talking with a male listener laughs only marginally more than his interaction partner. A woman talking with a woman listener laughs somewhat more than her partner. And a male speaker with a female listener laughs less often than does the woman. However, when a woman speaks to a man, she laughs much more than her male partner.[68] Why do you think that is so?

Laughter is a relationship tool. What role does it play in the relationship you share?

TECHNOLOGY AND OUR RELATIONSHIPS

Technology and the Internet are enabling men and women alike to initiate, sustain, and end relationships in new ways. We now have different options when it comes to developing or terminating our relationships. In fact, while we still have singles bars, singles cruises, parties, and personal ads, many friendships and romantic relationships now begin on the Internet. In addition to an abundance of chat rooms, there are many commercial Web sites focused on helping people meet. The online dating business is booming, with revenues surpassing $300 million.[69] The popularity of sites such as Match.com and Yahoo Personals is a testament to the fact that online services are changing the way people find others today. Such sites are especially popular with busy people who do not have to leave home to develop relationships that gel.[70]

In addition, newsgroup users form friendships or relationships with persons they meet online. Approximately 25 percent of the people in one newsgroup study reported that they communicated with their partners a minimum of three or four times weekly.[71] While women are more likely than men to form personal relationships online, persons of both sexes establish both friendships and romantic relationships in cyberspace.[72] Although the computer probably will not replace face-to-face interaction, the relationships begun in cyberspace may transfer to real space. In fact, a number of relationships begun in cyberspace develop into extended friendships, romances, and marriage.[73] Thus, the computer presents us with different options when it comes to developing or terminating our relationships.

A number of key differences between face-to-face and online communication can impede relationship development. First, unless we exchange photographs or

Integrated Media and Technology

Media and technology are featured in each chapter. Topics include technology and the communication of emotion, groups in cyberspace, and virtual neighborhoods and communities.

Media Resources for the Student

Two new CD-ROMs and the Online Learning Center are designed to appeal to a variety of teaching and learning styles by extending course content into interactive and multimedia formats. Icons in the text guide readers to specific applications on both resources.

For Content Review and Test Preparation

Self Quizzes—Self-scoring quizzes allow students to assess their understanding of chapter concepts.

Audio Flash Cards—Students can hear how key terms are pronounced and study for exams.

Crossword Puzzles—Students use key words and definitions to solve these chapter-specific puzzles.

For Visualization of Concepts and Practice

Video Clips—Seventeen brief video clips illustrate important chapter concepts. Nine clips focus on sample student speeches (two informative and two persuasive speeches, and five clips that cover the use of statistics, examples, and images in a presentation).

For Critical Thinking and Reflection

Self Inventories—Chapter-related surveys challenge students to examine their attitudes and feelings. Responses are included for each survey.

Internet Activities—These activities provide students with a variety of Internet resources to further their understanding of chapter topics, such as culture and diversity, nonverbal communication, and conflict resolution.

For Building Confidence in Public Communication and Managing Speech Projects

Video Clips—Brief clips illustrate a number of communication concepts and offer sample student speeches.

PowerPoint Tutor—The tutorial presents the basic steps in effectively creating and using a PowerPoint presentation.

Outline Tutor—This interactive program and outlining template shows the various parts of an outline and makes it easy for users to insert appropriate content into the parts.

Speech Preparation Checklist—A list of steps helps students manage and prepare their speeches.

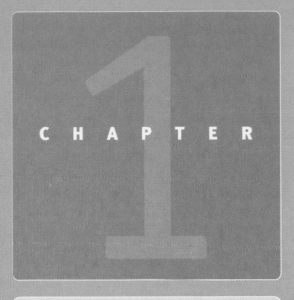

CHAPTER 1

Communication: The Starting Line

After finishing this chapter, you should be able to

1. Define *communication*.

2. List and explain the essential elements of communication.

3. Describe and explain representative models of communication.

4. Describe the characteristics and functions of communication.

Whether clear or garbled, tumultuous or silent, deliberate or fatally inadvertent, communication is the ground of meeting. . . . It is, in short, the essential human connection.

—Ashley Montagu and Floyd Matson

A college student. A corporate vice president. A teenager. An octogenarian. Two people in love. A doctor and a patient. A native and a foreigner. Parents. Children. Friends. Enemies. Decision makers. Speakers. You. All these people share at least one thing: a need to communicate.

This book is about you, about your need to communicate and how communication can help you relate more effectively to others. Possessing or developing the ability to communicate effectively with others is essential not only for your own success but also for the success of any organizations you work for, any groups you become part of, and any relationships you develop with people you come to know. In today's world, job-specific talent, technical expertise, and graduation from a prestigious school do not carry any guarantees for upward mobility or attainment of goals. Many of us get our jobs because of our social capital, that is, our social connections or social networks—whom we know—rather than our human capital—what we know.[1] Our workplaces are prime environments for connecting with others. The Internet has democratized information. Anyone with a modem can gather nearly as much intelligence as the CIA, access virtually as much data as exists in the Library of Congress, and contact people around the world at any hour.[2] One factor shared by people who are able to ascend both the professional and the personal ladders of success is superior communication skills. These people are promoted rapidly, are happy in their marriages and other relationships, and in general view their lives as being rich and fulfilling. That is why this book can be of value to you. The topics we cover will help you as you go about your usual business of making friends, informing and persuading others, solving problems, falling in or out of love, and making your personal and professional relationships work. From birth to death, many types of communication are an integral part of your life. Whether you are 18 or 80, female or male, married or single, employed or unemployed, it is never too late to learn skills that will enrich and improve the quality of your life. Interpersonal, small-group, organizational, and public communication skills are not inborn. You have to develop them, a process that will continue throughout your life. That is why this book is designed to provide you with a program for lifelong learning. If you want to improve your ability to relate

Identify people you know personally or people you know of who have attained their positions because of their social capital and/or their human capitial. Which form of capital do you believe is more important? Why?

to people in your social life, your job, or your academic life, now is the time to start making communication work.

■ ■ ■

WHO IS A COMMUNICATOR?
WHAT IS COMMUNICATION?

A communicator is a person who enters into relationships with other people. During the course of a single day we interact with others to share information and beliefs, exchange ideas and feelings, make plans, and solve problems. Sometimes this interaction is done interpersonally, sometimes in a team or small group, sometimes in a public forum, and sometimes through the media or via computer. However communication occurs, it is essential in helping us initiate, develop, control, and sustain our contacts with others.[3]

We all engage in intrapersonal (we communicate with ourselves), dyadic (one-to-one), small-group (one-to-a-few), public (one-to-many), and mass communication (communication that is shared across great distances with potentially large audiences through a technological device or mass medium). Many of us also participate in computer-assisted or online communication. Every time we knowingly or unknowingly send a verbal or nonverbal message to a friend, lover, relative, stranger, audience, acquaintance, supervisor, employee, co-worker, or group, communication takes place.[4] We can define **communication** as the deliberate or accidental transfer of meaning. It is the process that occurs whenever someone observes or experiences behavior and attributes meaning to that behavior. It doesn't matter whether the observed or experienced behavior is intentional or accidental, conscious or unconscious. As long as what someone does or says (his or her symbolic behavior) is interpreted as a message—as long as the behavior of one person affects or influences the behavior of another—communication is occurring. From birth to death our lives are dependent on and affected by our communication skills, especially the ability to create and

communication

the deliberate or accidental transfer of meaning

 ## Skill Builder

Contacts!

Identify five people with whom you recently had a sustained communication contact. (Note: The contact need not have been initiated by you.) For each contact, indicate the nature of your communication (the subject or message), the context or environment in which it occurred (classroom, office, home, voice mail, online, etc.), the type of interaction experienced (interpersonal, virtual, small-group, or public), and the outcome (what happened as a result of the interaction). Finally—and this is important—as an assessment of your communication effectiveness, rate each contact on a scale of 1 (extremely ineffective) to 5 (extremely effective), and give your rationale for each rating.

Extremely ineffective   1   2   3   4   5   Extremely effective

Now, how would you replay each contact if you were given the opportunity? If possible, would you prefer to increase or decrease the percentage of contacts you have that are virtual as opposed to face-to-face? Why?

interpret symbolic messages or behavior. Since we spend more time communicating than doing anything else, our communication skills help shape our personal, social, work, and professional relationships. Communication is our link to the rest of humanity.

The following examples illustrate the prevalence and importance of communication.

> On September 11th, the dramatic potential of communication became apparent—cell phone calls from the World Trade Tower and from airplanes, e-mail messages reassuring the families of survivors, Web pages listing missing persons, videophone images of bombs in Afghanistan, and "embedded reporters" on the way to Baghdad. However, just as important are the day-to-day interactions we have with our loved ones, friends, and co-workers.
>
> —www.decadeofbehavior.org

> Communication is the vehicle which allows humans to recall the past, think in the present, and plan for the future.
>
> —ROY BERKO

> It's a mark of real leadership to take the lead in getting to know people. . . .
> It's always a big person who walks up to you and offers his/her hand and says hello.
> —DAVID J. SCHWARTZ, *The Magic of Thinking Big*

> Computers don't just do things for us, they do things to us, including to our ways of thinking about ourselves and other people.
>
> —SHERRY TURKLE, *Life on the Screen*

Which of these observations do you agree with? Which do you find most applicable to your own communication experiences?

hyper-competitiveness
the contention that one needs to defeat another to achieve one's goals

Media Wise

Does Reality TV Reflect Reality?

In reality-type television programs, such as *The Amazing Race, Fear Factor, The Apprentice* (Donald Trump or Martha Stewart), *Survivor, American Idol, The Bachelor, America's Next Top Model,* and *Big Brother,* people may be thrown together, filmed continuously, and isolated from or permitted to have only limited contact with the outside world as they compete against each other in an effort to win money, fame, and/or love. Such programs are definitely a pop-culture trend, with the ratings to prove that huge numbers of people view them. Critics ask whether shows like these, which emphasize wealth, beauty, and popularity, are "in reality" promoting the worst in human behavior. What is more, they ask, do programs that place people in unusual situations—situations that exist in a setup environment and deviate from most of the everyday experiences that the vast majority of us have—reflect reality at all?[5]

Consider these questions: Does reality television reflect reality? What values do your most and least favorite reality television shows promote? What do your most and least favorite shows suggest about human nature? What do they reveal about our competitiveness and the role competition plays in our lives? In your opinion, are shows like these symptomatic of an emerging **hyper-competitiveness,** the belief that one needs to defeat another in order to achieve one's goals? And what do they reveal about our communication ethics? Will people do anything to win? Do these shows encourage us to live in the here and now? Do they fuel our materialistic greed and our desires for what is superficial by making us eager to sacrifice privacy, relationships, commonsense, and morality in the drive to acquire great wealth, fame, and beauty? And what do they suggest about us as viewers? Have we become, as author Clay Calvert suggests, a "voyeur nation"?

HOW GOOD A COMMUNICATOR ARE YOU?

When has insensitivity caused problems for you or others, on the job or at home?

Simply communicating frequently or having many person-to-person contacts each day does not mean that you are as effective a communicator as you could be. We frequently neglect problems that plague our communicative relationships—even though these issues are crucial in our lives. When we lack sensitivity and fail to consider the feelings of others, for example, our relationships suffer. There is no such thing as being too effective at establishing, maintaining, and controlling personal and public contacts with others.

We can all improve our communication skills. In the Skill Builder on page 4, you evaluated your proficiency during a variety of interpersonal, small-group, public, or computer-assisted communication experiences. Now let's consider steps you can take to improve or enhance your ability to relate to others in a variety of communication settings.

First, use the scale of 0 (totally ineffective) to 100 (totally effective) to rate your overall effectiveness as a communicator. Next, using the same scale, rate the communication skills of your best friend, an older relative, a fellow student, a boss or an instructor, and a boyfriend, girlfriend, or spouse.

Totally ineffective   0   10   20   30   40   50   60   70   80   90   100   Totally effective

According to your evaluations, whose communication skills do you consider better than, equal to, or inferior to yours? Why?

Now set a goal that indicates the extent to which you would like this course to help you improve your effectiveness as a communicator. If you are to realize this improvement, there are probably a number of skills you should work to maintain or master, and a number of ineffective behaviors you should work to eliminate. To function effectively in interpersonal, small-group, public, mass, or computer-assisted communication, you will need to acquire certain skills and perceptions:

1. the ability to understand and communicate with yourself
2. knowledge of how and why you and those with whom you relate see things the way you do
3. an appreciation of the extent to which gender, culture, the media, and new technologies affect communication
4. the capacity to listen and then process the information you receive
5. sensitivity to silent messages that you and others send
6. knowledge of how words affect you and those with whom you relate
7. an understanding of how relationships develop
8. an understanding of how feelings and emotions affect relationships
9. the ability to handle conflict by learning how to disagree without being disagreeable
10. an understanding of the behaviors that contribute to successful group decision making, leadership, and team building
11. an understanding of how beliefs, values, and attitudes affect the formulation and reception of messages and the development of speaker–audience relationships
12. the desire to apply all these skills and perceptions to each communication experience and arena

As we continue exploring and investigating what it means to experience effective interpersonal, small-group, mass, online or machine-assisted, and public communication, you will realize that the objectives just provided describe, in brief, the method and purpose of this book.

TYPES OF COMMUNICATION

Because our focus is communication, it makes sense to define and distinguish among the types of communication we use. During **intrapersonal communication,** you think about, talk with, learn about, reason with, and evaluate yourself. In contrast, when you engage in **interpersonal communication,** you interact with another, learn about him or her, and act in ways that help sustain or terminate your relationship. When you participate in **group communication,** you interact with a limited number of others, work to share information, develop ideas, make decisions, solve problems, offer support, or have fun. Through **public communication,** you inform and persuade the members of an audience to hold certain attitudes, values, or beliefs so that they will think, believe, or act in a particular way; on the other hand, you can also function as a member of an audience, in which case another person will do the same for you. During **mass communication,** the media entertain, inform, and persuade you. You, in turn, have the ability to use your viewing and buying habits to influence the media. During **online, or machine-assisted, communication,** you navigate cyberspace as you converse, research and exchange ideas, and build relationships with others using computers and the Internet. Whatever the nature or type of communication, however, the communicative act itself is characterized by the interplay of certain elements.

Elements of Communication

All communication interactions have certain common elements that together help define the communication process. The better you understand these elements, the easier it will be for you to develop your own communicative abilities. Let's begin by examining the **essentials of communication,** those components present during every interpersonal, small-group, public, and mass communication event.

PEOPLE

Obviously, human communication involves people. Interpersonal, small-group, and public communication encounters take place between and among all types of **senders** (persons who encode messages) and **receivers** (persons who decode messages). Senders and receivers, respectively, are individuals who give out and take in messages. Although it is easy to picture an interpersonal, small-group, public, media, or computer-assisted communication experience beginning with a sender and ending with a receiver, it is important to understand that during communication the role of sender does not belong exclusively to one person and the role of receiver to another. Instead, the processes of sending and receiving are constantly being reversed. Reflecting this fact, in *That's Not What I Meant!* linguist Deborah Tannen writes, "Communication is a continuous stream in which everything is simultaneously a reaction and an instigation, an instigation and a reaction."[6] Thus, when we communicate with one or more people, we simultaneously send and receive.

---

intrapersonal communication
communication with the self

interpersonal communication
the relationship level of communication

group communication
interaction with a limited number of persons

public communication
communication designed to inform, persuade, or entertain audience members

mass communication
the transmission of messages which may be processed by gatekeepers prior to being sent to large audiences via a channel of broad diffusion

online, or machine-assisted, communication
the building of relationships using computers and the Internet

Which type of communication do you use most? Least? Which do you enjoy most? Least? Why?

essentials of communication
those components present during every communication event

senders
persons who formulate, encode, and transmit a message

receivers
persons who receive, decode, and interpret a message

MESSAGES

During every interpersonal, small-group, or public communication encounter, we all send and receive both verbal and nonverbal messages. What you talk about, the words you use to express your thoughts and feelings, the sounds you make, the way you sit and gesture, your facial expressions, and perhaps even your touch or your smell all communicate information. In effect, a **message** is the content of a communicative act. Some messages we send are private (a kiss accompanied by "I love you"); others are public and may be directed at hundreds or thousands of people. We send some messages purposefully ("I want you to realize . . .") and others accidentally ("I had no idea you were watching . . . or 'lurking'"). Everything a sender or receiver does or says is a potential message as long as someone is there to interpret the behavior. When you smile, frown, shout, whisper, or turn away, you are communicating, and your communication is having some effect.

message
the content of a communicative act

CHANNELS

We send and receive messages with and through all our senses; equally, messages may be sent and received through verbal and nonverbal modes, or **channels.** Thus, we are multichannel communicators. We receive sound messages (we hear noises from the street), sight messages (we see how someone looks), taste messages (we enjoy the flavor of a particular food), smell messages (we smell the cologne a friend is wearing), and touch messages (we feel the roughness of a fabric). Which channel are you most attuned to? Why? To what extent do you rely on one or more channels while excluding or disregarding others? Effective communicators are adept at switching channels. They recognize that communication is a multichannel experience.

channels
media through which messages are sent

The following dialogue between a husband and a wife illustrates the multi-channel nature of communication:

Inventory each message you receive during a two-minute period, and note the channel through which it came.

> *Wife:* What's the matter with you? You're late again. We'll never get to the Adamses' on time.
>
> *Husband:* I tried my best.
>
> *Wife:* (Sarcastically) Sure, you tried your best. You always try your best, don't you? (Shaking her finger) I'm not going to put up with this much longer.
>
> *Husband:* (Raising his voice) You don't say! I happen to have been tied up at the office.
>
> *Wife:* My job is every bit as demanding as yours, you know.
>
> *Husband:* (Lowering his voice) OK. OK. I know you work hard too. I don't question that. Listen, I really did get stuck in a conference. (Puts his hand on her shoulder) Let's not blow this up. Come on. I'll tell you about it on the way to Bill and Ellen's.

What message is the wife (the initial source–encoder) sending to her husband (the receiver–decoder)? She is letting him know with her words, her voice, and her physical actions that she is upset and angry. Her husband responds in kind, using words, vocal cues, and gestures in an effort to explain his behavior. Both are affected by the nature of the situation (they are late for an appointment), by their attitudes (how they feel about what is occurring), and by their past experiences.

NOISE

In the context of communication, **noise** is anything that interferes with or distorts our ability to send or receive messages. Although we are accustomed to thinking of noise as a particular sound or group of sounds, the perceptive communicator realizes that noise can have both internal and external causes. Internal noise is attributed to the psychological makeup, intellectual ability, or physical condition of the communicators. External noise is attributed to the environment. Thus, noise includes distractions such as a loud siren, a disturbing odor, and a hot room; personal factors such as prejudices, daydreaming, and feelings of inadequacy; and semantic factors such as uncertainty about what another person's words are supposed to mean.

noise
anything that interferes with or distorts the ability to send and receive messages

CONTEXT

Communication always takes place in a **context,** or setting. Sometimes a context is so natural that we hardly notice it. At other times, however, the context makes such an impression on us that it exerts considerable control over our behavior. Consider the extent to which your present environment influences the way you act toward others or determines the nature of the communication encounters you share with them. Consider as well the extent to which certain environments might cause you to alter your posture, manner of speaking, attire, or means of interacting. Take into account the fact that sometimes conditions of place and time—that is, context—can affect our communications without our consciously realizing it.

context
the setting

FEEDBACK

Whenever we communicate with one or more persons, we receive information in return. The verbal and nonverbal cues that we perceive in reaction to our communication function as **feedback.** Feedback tells us how we are coming across. A smile, a frown, a chuckle, a sarcastic remark, a muttered thought, or simply silence in response to something we did or said can cause us to change, continue, or end a transaction. Feedback that encourages us to continue behaving as we are is **positive feedback;** it enhances whatever behavior is in progress. In contrast, **negative feedback** extinguishes a behavior; it serves a corrective rather than a reinforcing function. Thus, negative feedback can help eliminate unwanted, ineffective behaviors. Note that the terms *positive* and *negative* should not be interpreted as "good" and "bad"; these terms simply reflect the way the responses affect behavior.

feedback
information returned to a message source

positive feedback
a behavior-enhancing response

negative feedback
a response that extinguishes behavior in progress

Skill Builder

Contact in Context

Compare and contrast the types of communication that would be most likely to occur in each of the following contexts. Include a description of the nature of each interaction, the probable attire of each person, and his or her demeanor.

1. the first few minutes of a party
2. a business meeting
3. a coffeehouse
4. a funeral home
5. a college classroom
6. a political rally
7. a football stadium
8. a computer chat room

internal feedback

a response you give yourself

external feedback

a response from another

What positive and negative feedback have you recently given to others? What positive and negative feedback have you received?

effect

the commmunication outcome

Both positive and negative feedback can emanate from internal or external sources. **Internal feedback** is feedback you give yourself as you monitor your own behavior or performance during a transaction. **External feedback** is feedback from others who are involved in the communication event. To be an effective communicator, you must be sensitive to both types of feedback. You must pay attention to your own reactions as well as the reactions of others.

EFFECT

As people communicate, they are changed in some way by the interaction, which in turn influences what follows. In other words, communication has an **effect** and can be viewed as an exchange of influences. This means that communication always has some effect on you and on the person or people with whom you are interacting.

An effect can be emotional, physical, cognitive, or any combination of the three. An interpersonal, small-group, or public communication contact can elicit feelings of joy, anger, or sadness (emotional); communication can cause you to fight, argue, become apathetic, or evade an issue (physical); or it can lead to new insights, increased knowledge, the formulation or reconsideration of opinions, silence, or confusion (cognitive). The result of a communication encounter can also be any combination of the three effects just mentioned. Since effects are not always visible or immediately observable, there is obviously more to a communication reaction than meets the eye, or the ear.

COMMUNICATION PRINCIPLES

Besides considering the elements at play during communication, we also need to keep the following communication principles in mind.

Communication Is Dynamic

When we call communication a dynamic process, we mean that all its elements constantly interact with and affect each other.[7] Since all people are interconnected, whatever happens to one person determines in part what happens to others.

Can you think of an interpersonal, small-group, or public communication encounter you had that affected a later encounter?

Like the humans who compose them, relationships constantly evolve. Nothing about communication is static. Everything is accumulative. We communicate as long as we are alive, and thus every interaction we engage in is part of connected happenings. All our present communication experiences may be thought of as points of arrival from past encounters and as points of departure for future ones. (This is well illustrated by a spiral model of communication developed by Frank Dance, which is discussed in the section "Models of Communication" on page 14.) Do your experiences support this premise?

Communication Is Unrepeatable and Irreversible

Can you describe a work-related or personal situation in which the irreversibility of communication caused difficulties for you?

Every human contact you experience is unique. It has never happened before, and never again will it happen in just the same way. Our interpretation of the adage "You can never step into the same river twice" is that the experience changes both you and the river forever. Similarly, a communication encounter affects and changes people so that the encounter can never happen in exactly the same way again. Thus, communication is both unrepeatable and irreversible. We can neither take back something we have said nor erase the effects of something we have done. And although we may be greatly influenced by our past, we can never reclaim it. In the words of a Chinese proverb, "Even the emperor cannot buy back one single day." Do you think this proverb is accurate?

Communication Has No Opposite

It is not uncommon to assume that communication is purposeful and that we communicate only because we want to communicate. While this is sometimes true, it is also true that sometimes we communicate without any awareness of doing so—and just as often even without wanting to.

Whenever we are involved in an interaction, we respond in some way. Even if we choose not to respond verbally, even if we maintain absolute silence and attempt not to move a muscle, our lack of response is itself a response, constitutes a message, influences others, and communicates. We can never voluntarily stop behaving—because behavior has no opposite. No matter how hard we try, we cannot *not* communicate, because all behavior is communication and therefore is a message.

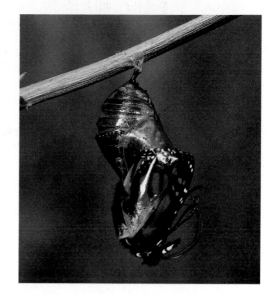

Experience changes us forever.

Communication Is Affected by Culture

As we will learn in Chapter 2, how we formulate and interpret messages depends on our culture. Cultural diversity, including race, ethnicity, gender, and age, influences the meanings we attribute to communication. Cultural differences exist not only between persons who speak different languages but between persons who speak the same language as well. Every cultural group has its own rules or preferences for interaction. When these are ignored or unknown, we are likely to misinterpret the meaning of messages received and miscalculate the impact of messages sent.

Communication Is Influenced by Ethics

Every time we communicate, we decide implicitly or explicitly whether we will do so ethically. Ethics are the moral principles, values, and beliefs that the members of society use to guide behavior. Since communication has consequences, it involves judgments of right and wrong. When the agreed-upon standards of behavior are violated, the behavior is judged unethical. For example, most of us expect those with whom we interact to be honest, play fair, respect our rights, and accept responsibility for their actions.

Communication Is Competence-Based

According to communication scholar Osmo Wiio, if communication can fail, it will.[8] The problem we face is determining how we can prevent communication from failing.

What does the following observation by Koji Yanase, a Japanese bar-association official, suggest about the nature of communication?

If an American is hit on the head by a ball at the ballpark, he sues. If a Japanese person is hit on the head, he says, "It's my honor. It's my fault. I shouldn't have been standing there."

—Newsweek, February 26, 1996

Can you identify an experience in which the understanding or misunderstanding of culture contributed to your communication effectiveness or ineffectiveness?

Can you identify a communication experience in which, looking back, you believe communication between you and another person was effective or ineffective because of the presence or absence of ethical behavior on your part?

Can you cite an example of how improving a specific communication skill enabled you to resolve a problem in your personal, academic, or professional life?

While we all have different communication strengths and weaknesses, we can all benefit from getting better at communicating. When we add to our knowledge and make a commitment to develop the skills to apply that knowledge across an array of communication situations or contexts, we gain communication competence. For example, included among the skills necessary for effective communication is the ability to think critically. When we can think critically, we have the ability to examine ideas reflectively and to decide what we should and should not believe, think, or do, given a specific set of circumstances.[9]

Communication Is Being Transformed by Media and Technology

As media critic Marshall McLuhan cautioned, "The medium is the message."[10] In McLuhan's view, different channels of communication affect the way a sender encodes a message and the way a receiver responds to a message. The same words delivered face-to-face, on paper, or via radio or television do not constitute the same message. The channel of communication changes things. For example, terminating a relationship via an answering machine or e-mail is very different from delivering such news in person. What channel would you use, for example, to say "good-bye"? Which channel would you use to tell someone "I'm sorry"? What about "I love you"?

Not just the medium, but also its content, changes communication. The content of books, newspapers, radio, television, and film, for example, also influence our cultural values, often reinforcing the stereotypes we have of gender, race, and ethnicity and contributing to the perceptions we have of various people and groups in society, including ourselves.

New forms of communication also alter our communication experiences. According to media scholar Neil Postman, a new technology does not merely add or subtract something; it changes everything. Postman contends that our culture is now a **technopoly**—a culture in which technology monopolizes the thought-world.[11] Technology continues to speed up communication as it brings the world into our living rooms and bedrooms, offices and automobiles. Instead of valuing sequential understanding and careful logic, we now value immediate gratification and emotional involvement. Technology has also given us the ability to interact in more ways, more quickly, and with more people than ever before. For example, we experienced the tsunami in Southeast Asia, Hurricane Katrina, and the war on terror as these events occurred. E-mail and digital cameras make it possible for us to see, interact with, and visit with people across the country and around the world.

technopoly
a culture in which technology monopolizes the thought-world

Is technology increasing or undermining social contact? As Postman fears, are we becoming tools of our tools? Are technological innovations overwhelming us with information or underwhelming us with a lack of credibility? Are they freeing us or complicating our lives? Are they bringing us closer together or keeping us apart? What do you think?

MODELS OF COMMUNICATION

Now that we have examined the basic elements of communication, we are ready to see how our understanding can be reflected in a picture, or model, of the communication process.

Through communication, we share meaning with others by sending and receiving messages—sometimes intentionally and sometimes unintentionally.

Communication thus includes every element that could affect two or more people as they knowingly or unknowingly relate to one another.

At this point, we need to reiterate that communication occurs whenever one person assigns significance or meaning to the behavior of another. But, you might ask, will knowing this enable us to understand or establish better and more satisfying relationships with our friends, spouse, employer, parents? The answer is yes. If you understand the processes that permit people to contact and influence each other, if you understand the forces that can impede or foster the development of every kind of effective communication, then you stand a better chance of communicating effectively yourself. Models of communication, like the ones in Figures 1.1 and 1.2, explain and help you visualize the process we employ to initiate and maintain communicative relationships with others. You will find these models useful tools in discovering how communication operates and in examining your own communication encounters.

The model in Figure 1.1 shows that communication is a circle and that the sending and receiving responsibilities are shared by the communicators. A message or messages may be sent through one or more channels, and the interaction occurs in and is affected by a definite context. Note that noise can enter the interaction at any point and can affect either the sending or the receiving abilities of the communicators. Furthermore, noise can be caused by the context, can be present in the channel, or can pop up in the message itself.

Another model of communication, devised by communication theorist Frank Dance[12] (see Figure 1.2), depicts the communication process in a more abstract way. Dance's spiral, or helix, represents the way communication evolves or progresses in a person from birth to the present moment. This model emphasizes the fact that each person's present behavior is affected by his or her past experience and, likewise, that present behavior will have an impact on future actions. Thus, Dance's helix indicates that communication has no clearly observable beginning and no clearly observable end.

By playing with Dance's model, we can picture two communication spirals as meeting in a number of different ways, one of which is shown in Figure 1.3.

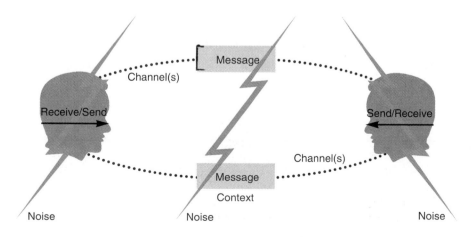

FIGURE 1.1

Gamble and Gamble's Model of Communication.

The point where the spirals touch is the point of contact; each time a contact occurs, messages are sent and received by the interactants. Some helical spirals touch each other only once during a lifetime, whereas others crisscross or intertwine in a pattern that indicates an enduring relationship. Furthermore, the spirals (interactants) may sometimes develop in similar ways (grow together) and sometimes develop in different ways (grow apart; see Figure 1.4).

The understanding you now have should provide you with some of the background you will need as you work to increase your effectiveness as a communicator.

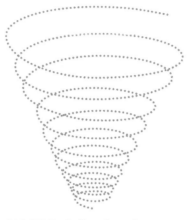

FIGURE 1.2   Dance's Communication Helix.

Source: From *Human Communication Theory: Original Essays* by Frank E. X. Dance. Holt, Rinehart & Winston. Copyright © 1967 by Frank E. X. Dance. Used by permission of the author.

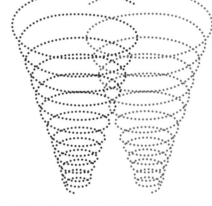

FIGURE 1.3   Meeting of Helixes.

FIGURE 1.4

Model of Communication in Relationships.

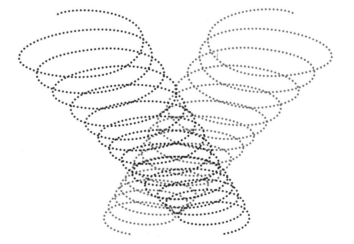

FUNCTIONS OF COMMUNICATION: WHAT CAN IT DO FOR YOU?

Every communication experience serves one or more functions. For example, communication can help us discover who we are, help us establish meaningful relationships, or prompt us to examine and try to change either our own attitudes and behaviors or the attitudes and behaviors of others.

Understanding and Insight

One key function of communication is self–other understanding: insight into ourselves and others. When you get to know another person, you also get to know yourself; and when you get to know yourself, you learn how others affect you. We depend on communication to develop self-awareness.

We need feedback from others all the time, and others are constantly in need of feedback from us. Interpersonal, small-group, public, and media communications offer us numerous opportunities for self–other discovery. Through communication encounters we are able to learn why we are trusting or untrusting, whether we can make our thoughts and feelings clear, under what conditions we have the power to influence others, and whether we can effectively make decisions and resolve conflicts and problems.

Meaningful Relationships

In building relationships, we cannot be overly concerned with ourselves but must consider the needs and wants of others. It is through effective communication that our basic physical and social needs are met.

Psychologists tell us that we need other people just as we need water, food, and shelter. When we are cut off from human contact, we become disoriented and maladjusted, and our life itself may be placed in jeopardy. People who are isolated from others—people who lack satisfying social relationships—are more likely to experience health problems and to die early than people who have an abundance of satisfying relationships.

Communication offers each of us the chance to satisfy what psychologist William Schutz calls our "needs for inclusion, control, and affection."[13] The **need for inclusion** is our need to be with others, our need for social contact. We like to feel that others accept and value us, and we want to feel like a full partner in a relationship. The **need for control** is our need to feel that we are capable and responsible, that we are able to deal with and manage our environment. We also like to feel that we can influence others. The **need for affection** is our need to express and receive love. Since communication allows each of these needs to be met, we are less likely to feel unwanted, unloved, or incapable if we are able to communicate meaningfully with others.

In today's world, it is a given that we will need to interact with persons who are culturally different from us. To attempt to insulate ourselves from such intercultural contacts is virtually impossible, nor is it desirable. It is through communication that we can reveal to others what is important to us and what we stand for, as well as learn what is important to them and what they stand for.

Communication also gives us the chance to share our personal reality with people from our own culture, as well as people from different cultures. Whether

The one thing that unites all human beings, regardless of age, gender, religion, economic status or ethnic background is that deep down inside, we all believe that we are above-average drivers.

—Dave Barry

In your opinion, are there other characteristics that unite us? If so, what are they?

need for inclusion
the need for social contact

need for control
the need to feel we are capable and responsible

need for affection
the need to express and receive love

Exploring Diversity

"I Hate Him"

Over 24 years ago, researcher Gordon Allport wrote the following in his now-classic *The Nature of Prejudice*:

> See that man over there?
> Yes.
> Well, I hate him.
>   But you don't know him.
> That's why I hate him.

Why does lack of knowledge or familiarity breed hate? Why might we experience hate when encountering people from a new or unfamiliar culture or group? Although Allport was writing over two decades ago, his comments remain true today. Why? To what extent do you believe that enhanced self–other understanding can help resolve this predicament? Explain.

we live in an East Coast urban area, a southern city, a desert community, a home in sunny California, a village in Asia, a plain in Africa, or a town in the Middle East, we all engage in similar activities when we communicate. We may use different symbols, rely on different strategies, and desire different outcomes, but the processes we use and the motivations we have are strikingly alike. Equally significant is the fact that insensitivity to another's needs and preferred ways of interacting can hamper our ability to relate effectively.

Influence and Persuasion

During interpersonal, small-group, public, mediated, and online communication, people have ample opportunities to influence each other subtly or overtly. We spend much time trying to persuade one another to think as we think, do what we do, like what we like. Sometimes our efforts meet with success, and sometimes they do not. In any case, our experiences with persuasion afford each of us the chance to influence others so that we may try to realize our own goals.

Career Development

How could the attitude by the employer or employee affect their relationship and ability to work together?

There is a positive relationship between the ability to communicate and career success. Employers seek to hire people who know how to make communication work. If you develop the abilities to speak so that others listen, listen when others speak, critically evaluate what you read and hear, adapt to differences in cultural perspectives, handle conflicts and solve problems, and make sound decisions, then you will exhibit skills valued by employers.[14]

COMMUNICATING IN A DIGITAL AGE

The nature of our communication experiences is changing. Media content influences our thoughts and feelings about the world we live in. Large numbers of us no longer rely merely on the more traditional media of television, music, radio, film, and print for information about ourselves, each other, and our world; millions of us now also interact with each other in "cyberia," or **cyberspace**[15] (the digital world of computers and online communication; the term was first used in the science fiction novel *Neuromancer* by William Gibson). Thus, the media and

cyberspace

the digital world of computers and online communication

Cell phones and personal digital assistants keep us connected. In your opinion, are they facilitating or impeding human interaction?

emerging technologies are bringing us new ways of discovering ideas and information, new ways of relating with friends and strangers, and new ways of learning about our world, our identities, and our futures.

The media and technology are also causing us to reexamine our relationships and redefine our notions of effective and meaningful communication. Because of their presence in our lives, we may think differently about ourselves, each other, and society in general.[16] Media and computers have the ability to influence our perceptions of communication, alter our interaction preferences, and reformulate our ways of thinking and knowing. As we expand our real and virtual communication repertoires, we need to continually ask the following questions: What changes are the media and technology creating in us? How are they influencing our social and emotional lives and cultural sensibilities? How are they altering our desire to relate to others—that is, our desire to communicate? In other words, what does it mean to be a communicator in a digital age?

Like television in the 1950s, both the Internet and cell phones are society-altering devices affecting personal interaction. While the Internet, e-mail, and text messages have increased some forms of human interaction, they may be limiting other forms of interaction. For example, 13 percent of Internet users say they spend less time with friends and family, 59 percent spend less time viewing television, 34 percent spend less time reading newspapers, and 25 percent spend more time

To what extent, if any, has your use of the Internet affected the time you have available for family and friends? How has it had an impact on your personal and professional relationships?

working as a result of the time they spend online. (See Figures 1.5 and 1.6.) The question of whether the innovations of the digital age are bringing us together or contributing to social isolation is worthy of our attention.

What would visitors from another planet say about us as communicators both in and out of the e-culture of cyberspace? They would likely observe that online experiences are now central to our lives. They would notice that we spend

FIGURE 1.5

Connected.

Source: Figure from New York Times, February 16, 2000, p. A-1. Based on data from the Stanford Institute for the Quantitative Study of Society. Used by permission of The New York Times Graphics.

Connected

A survey at the outset of this century concluded that 55% of Americans have access to the Internet. Of those, 36% said they were online at least five hours a week. Where do you fit into the graphs below?

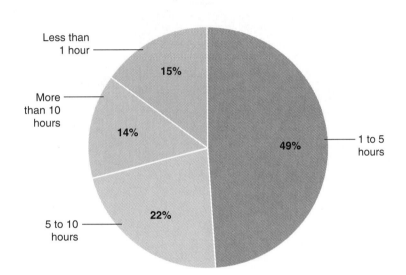

FIGURE 1.6

The Wired Life.

Source: Figure from New York Times, February 16, 2000, p. A-18. Based on data from the Stanford Institute for the Quantitative Study of Society. Used by permission of The New York Times Graphics.

Toll

The Wired Life

According to researchers who conducted a survey, the more people use the Internet, the less time they spend with real people. Of the 20% who are online five or more hours a week...

13% spend less time with family and friends

8% attend fewer social events

34% spend less time reading the newspaper

59% spend less time watching television

25% spend less time shopping in stores

25% are working more at home (without any decline in work at the office)

Thinking Critically

Reflect and Respond

Agree or disagree with each of the following statements, supplying reasons and examples for each position you take.

1. Communication is communication. If you can communicate effectively with persons who are similar to you, you can also communicate effectively with persons who are different from you. If you can communicate effectively with others when face-to-face, you can communicate equally well with them when online. In other words, neither the gender nor the nationality of the communicators, nor the means used to interact with others, should influence the satisfactions derived from or the outcomes of a communication experience.

2. Too many observers of our new, technologically wired society spout **cyberbole**—exaggerated claims about the effect the new technology has on society. In reality, the problems of social division in our society far outweigh what the Internet can bring to us. In the end, according to skeptic Steve Woolgar, the Internet will probably be like the telephone—"this huge new revolution that didn't make much difference to existing social structures."[17]

significant blocks of time connected to spaces and time zones that we occupy mentally but not physically. They would probably also say, however, that whether we are on- or offline, we display an interest in people and making connections. And with regard to self-expression, the visitors would probably find that when we are online, many of us become more willing to speak up or to discuss topics often considered taboo offline. On the other hand, they would also observe that a number of enjoyable, offline communication-enhancing activities, such as aromatherapy, eating, and dancing, cannot be experienced online.

A question to consider is: Does what happens online stay online, or do our online experiences affect our offline realities?[18] Another fact worthy of our attention is that cell phones are not just for making calls any more. Text messaging is altering how we communicate, leading us to ask what effect the diffusion of cell phones with texting capabilities is having on our personal, social, and work lives.[19] The cell phone is no longer just a means of social interaction; it is also a source of news and public information, as well as a medium through which we express our social identity.[20]

cyberbole

exaggerated claims about the effects new technologies have on society

IMPROVING YOUR EFFECTIVENESS AS A COMMUNICATOR

The major purpose of this book is to help you gain an understanding of communication and to assist you in developing your skills at interpersonal, small-group, public, mass, and online communication. To achieve these goals, you will need to accomplish the following preliminary tasks.

Become Actively Involved in the Study of Communication

Focus on Service Learning

Develop a two- to three-minute presentation promoting the importance of communication for delivery to an elementary, junior, or senior high school class and/or the parents and teachers. In addition to a review of the value of communication and the reasons it is fundamental to our lives, the tasks required include confirming a school's participation, securing a date and time, developing the content of your presentation, and delivering it. For online help in completing this assignment, you may want to visit the Web site of the National Communication Association at www.natcom.org.

The materials in this book will benefit you only if you make a commitment to try out and experience the principles discussed. First, each chapter opening lists targets, or objectives, that specify what you should have learned after completing your study of the chapter. Use these lists to clarify your personal communication objectives as you make your way through the book. Next, a plethora of boxes— Skill Builder, Exploring Diversity, Ethics & Communication, Media Wise, and Thinking Critically—are included to help you explore communication and become aware of what you must know and do to become a more effective communicator. A number of these features contain self-analysis and assessment scales. Together, they give you an opportunity to process and apply your new knowledge to actual communication experiences. If you use them as directed, you will increase your opportunities to grow, because you will be actively using your own learning and diagnosing your own needs for self-improvement.

Believe in Yourself

Above all else, you must believe that you are worth the time and effort needed to develop your communication skills. You must also believe that developing these skills will immeasurably improve the quality of your life. We think you are worth it. And we know that communication works. Do you?

The Wrap Up

Revisiting Chapter Objectives

1. **Define *communication*.** Communication is the deliberate or accidental transfer of meaning. Human communication takes place interpersonally (one to one), in small groups (one to a few), in public forums (one to many), via the media, or online.

2. **List and explain the essential elements of communication.** The essential elements of communication are people, messages, channels, noise, context, feedback, and effect.

3. **Describe and explain representative models of communication.** Models of communication have been developed to illustrate the communication process in action.

   Communication reflects a number of general principles. First, since communication is a dynamic process, each interaction is part of a series of interconnected communication events. Second, every communication experience is unique, unrepeatable, and irreversible. Third, culture influences communication. Fourth, communication has no opposite. Fifth, it is influenced by ethics. Sixth, it is competence-based. Seventh, communication is being transformed by media and technology.

4. **Describe the characteristics and functions of communication.** Communication serves a number of essential functions in our lives. It promotes self–other understanding, helps us establish meaningful relationships, enables us to examine and attempt to change the attitudes and behavior of others and enhances career development.

Developing communication skills is a lifelong process. This book explains the strategies you can use to assess your own communication abilities, improve the effectiveness of your communication relationships, and enhance the quality of your life.

Resources for Further Inquiry and Reflection

To apply your understanding of how the principles in Chapter 1 are at work in our daily lives, consult the following resources for further inquiry and reflection. Or, if you prefer, choose any other appropriate resource. Then connect the ideas expressed in your chosen selection with the communication concepts and issues you are learning about both in and out of class.

 ### Listen to Me

"You Oughta Know" (Alanis Morrisette)
"Bohemian Rhapsody" (Queen)
"Cry Me a River" (Justin Timberlake)
"The Greatest Love of All" (Whitney Houston)
"Dance with My Father" (Luther Vandross)

What message is the speaker sending regarding both the functions and the effects of communication?

 ### View Me

Traffic   *When a Man Loves a Woman*
Million Dollar Baby   *The Truth about Cats and Dogs*
Cast Away   *Sideways*

What do the main characters in the selected film reveal about the nature of communication and how it has an impact on others?

 ### Read Me

Edmond Rostand. Anthony Burgess, trans. *Cyrano de Bergerac*. New York: Applause Books, 1998.
Toni Morrison. *Beloved*. New York: Knopf, 1998.
John Twelve Hawks. *The Traveler*. New York: Doubleday, 2005.

These authors identify certain understandings we must internalize if we are to be successful communicators. Identify and discuss the understandings conveyed by your selected author.

 ### Tell Me

Share with the class the insights you gained from your chosen Listen to Me, View Me, or Read Me selection.

React to the following statement with reasons justifying your stance: *More communication does not always make things better.*

Communication
Works

online learning center

www.mhhe.com/gamble9

Key Chapter Terminology

Use the Communication Works CD-ROM and the Online Learning Center at www.mhhe.com/gamble9 to further your knowledge of the following terminology.

channels 8

communication 4

context 9

cyberbole 19

cyberspace 16

effect 10

essentials of communication 7

external feedback 10

feedback 9

group communication 7

hyper-competitiveness 5

internal feedback 10

interpersonal communication 7

intrapersonal communication 7

mass communication 7

message 8

need for affection 15

need for control 15

need for inclusion 15

negative feedback 9

noise 9

online, or machine-assisted, communication 7

positive feedback 9

public communication 7

receivers 7

senders 7

technopoly 12

Idioms in Translation

ascend the professional and personal ladder of success—achieve professional and personal goals

blow this up—exaggerate

e-culture—online culture

human capital—what we know

tied up—detained

Communication
Works

online learning center

www.mhhe.com/gamble9

Test Your Understanding

Go to the *Self Quizzes* on the Communication Works CD-ROM and the book's Online Learning Center at www.mhhe.com/gamble9.

Notes

1. Robert D. Putnam. *Bowling Alone: The Collapse and Revival of American Community*. New York: Simon & Schuster, 2000.
2. Alan Murray. *The Wealth of Choices*. New York: Crown Business, 2000.
3. For a discussion of how the computer is altering communication, see David H. Rothman. *Networld!* Rocklin, CA: Prima, 1996.
4. See, for example, Stephen R. Covey. *The 7 Habits of Highly Effective People*. New York: Simon & Schuster, 1989, pp. 236–260.
5. See, for example, www.theworldjournal.com/2003/realitycheck.htm.
6. See Deborah Tannen. *That's Not What I Meant!* New York: Morrow, 1986.

7. See, for example, Alan E. Ivey and James C. Hurse. "Communication as Adaptation." *Journal of Communication* 21, 1971, pp. 199–207. Ivey and Hurse reaffirm that communication is adaptive, like biological evolution—not an end in itself, but a process. For a more recent discussion of this topic, see J. F. Nussbaum, ed. *Life-Span Communication: Normative Processes.* Hillsdale, NJ: Erlbaum, 1989.

8. O. Wiio. *Wiio's Laws—and Some Others.* Espoo, Finland: Welin Goos, 1978.

9. C. Wade and C. Tarvis. *Learning to Think Critically: The Case of Close Relationships.* New York: HarperCollins, 1990.

10. Marshal McLuhan. *Understanding Media.* Cambridge, MA: MIT Press, 1994.

11. Neil Postman. *Technopoly: The Surrender of Culture to Technology.* New York: Vintage, 1992.

12. Frank E. X. Dance. "Toward a Theory of Human Communication." In Frank E. X. Dance, ed. *Human Communication Theory: Original Essays.* New York: Holt, Rinehart & Winston, 1967.

13. William Schutz. *The Interpersonal Underworld.* Palo Alto, CA: Science & Behavior Books, 1966.

14. National Association of Colleges and Employers. *Job Outlook 2003.*

15. William Gibson. *Neuromancer.* New York: Ace, 1984.

16. For a discussion of identity in the age of the Internet, see Sherry Turkle. *Life on the Screen.* New York: Simon & Schuster, 1995.

17. John Markoff. "A Newer, Lonelier Crowd Emerges in Internet Study." *New York Times*, February 16, 2000, p. 1.

18. See, for example, Hector José Huyke. "Technologies and the Devaluation of What Is Near." *Techne* 6:3, 2003, pp. 57–70.

19. See, for example, Janet Kornblum. "Cellphones Do a New Number with 'Texting.'" *USA Today*, June 3, 2003, p. 7D.

20. J. E. Katz and M. Aakhus. *Perpetual Contact: Mobile Communication. Private Talk, Public Performance.* Cambridge, UK: Cambridge University Press, 2002.

Communicating in a Multicultural Society and World

After finishing this chapter, you should be able to

1. Assess your ability to communicate effectively with persons from different cultures.

2. Discuss the kinds of problems the culturally confused face.

3. Define *intercultural communication*.

4. Compare and contrast culture and co-culture, ethnocentrism and cultural relativism, melting pot philosophy and cultural pluralism.

5. Compare and contrast the following: individualism and collectivism, high-context communication cultures and low-context communication cultures, high power distance cultures and low power distance cultures, masculine and feminine cultures.

6. Identify techniques you can use to reduce the strangeness of strangers.

7. Discuss how technology is bringing diversity into our lives.

If we don't speak out when people behave in a discriminatory manner, we are partly responsible for the consequences.

—William Gudykunst

Prejudice is the child of ignorance.
—William Hazlitt

Ours is an age of globalization. We define globalization as the increasing economic, political, and cultural integration and interdependence of diverse cultures—the worldwide integration of humanity. Globalization requires that we pay attention to a related concept—**diversity**—the recognition and valuing of difference, encompassing such factors as age, gender, race, ethnicity, ability, religion, education, marital status, sexual orientation, and income.

An early observer of how the mass media affect behavior and thinking, theorist Marshall McLuhan predicted many years ago that our world would become a global village.[1] He was right. We are now linked physically and electronically to people around the globe. In addition to using the Internet with increasing frequency, most of us move for personal or professional reasons—an average of five times during our lives.[2] We also travel regularly to other countries, some of us to visit relatives (one in five Americans was born abroad or has one or more parents who were); others, to represent an employer; and still others, to vacation.

Digital technology has helped erase the notion of territorial boundaries between countries, gradually eroding the idea of the term *nation* as it does so. People we once considered strangers are now friends and co-workers, creating the need for people who are **multiculturalists**—persons respectful of and engaged with people from distinctly different cultures. This reality is also causing colleges and universities to emphasize the importance of diversity education in curricula offerings. The practice has its critics and its supporters. While some people believe that understanding diversity and engendering respect for difference can help erase the tensions globalization creates, others believe that by emphasizing our differences we fuel potential conflicts. Which do you believe? Some people say we need to spend more time learning about other cultures, while others believe that we are better served spending our time focusing on American values.[3] Which of these beliefs is closest to your own? Some believe that globalization enriches cultures; others say it destroys them. What do you think?

Effective communication and the ability to understand cultural differences are skills that are too frequently deficient both in students and in educators.[4] With that in mind, answer these questions:

- Do you feel prepared to communicate in a society that is a nation of minorities?

diversity
the recognition and valuing of difference

multiculturalists
persons respectful of and engaged with people from distinctly different cultures

- Do you have the understandings and sensitivity you need to interact in a global community in which other persons may look, act, and think differently than you do?
- Are you ready to embrace diversity?

■ ■ ■

PREPARING TO COMMUNICATE ACROSS CULTURES

Assess your personal preparedness to communicate effectively with persons of different cultures by labeling each of the following statements as true or false.

1. I enjoy communicating with persons unlike me as much as with persons like me.
2. I am equally sensitive to the concerns of all groups in our multicultural society.
3. I can tell when persons from other cultures do not understand me or are confused by my actions.
4. I do not fear interacting with persons from minority groups any more than I fear interacting with persons from the dominant culture.
5. Persons from other cultures have a right to be angry at members of my culture.
6. Persons from other cultures who don't actively participate in a conversation, dialogue, or debate with others may act that way because of their culture's rules.
7. How I handle disagreements with persons from other cultures depends on the situation and the culture(s) they are from.

Go to the Online Learning Center at www.mhhe.com/gamble9 and answer the questions in the *Self Inventory* to evaluate your understanding of cultural diversity.

Developing insights into persons from different cultures facilitates communication. What steps have you taken to enhance your intercultural IQ?

8. My culture is not superior to other cultures.
9. I am knowledgeable of how to behave with persons of different cultures.
10. I respect the communication rules of cultures other than my own.

The greater the number of statements you labeled true, the more prepared you are to enrich your communication arena by welcoming people from different cultures into it.

Virtually every day, we find ourselves in situations that require us to communicate with persons culturally different from ourselves. Whether we are aware of it or not, culture influences communication.[5] According to researchers, the effectiveness of the United States in the global arena depends on our ability to communicate competently with people from other cultures.[6]

THE COST OF CULTURAL IGNORANCE

Communicators who fail to realize that persons from different cultures may not look, think, or act as they themselves do run the risk of having those with whom they interact judge them to be insensitive, ignorant, or **culturally confused.** The culturally confused pay a high price. Cultural misunderstandings often lead to lost opportunities and increased levels of tension between people. The following examples demonstrate the extent to which cultural ignorance affects communication:

- Showing the sole of a shoe means nothing to observers in the United States or Europe. As a result, when visiting Saudi Arabia, the American and European delegates to a conference thought nothing about crossing their legs and pointing their shoes toward the speaker while listening to his presentation. The speaker, however, was horrified. In Muslim cultures, the gesture is perceived as insulting.[7] Similarly, while crossing your legs in the United States indicates you are relaxed, in Korea it is a social faux pas.

- John, who represented the interests of an American multinational corporation, and Yu-Chen, his Taiwanese counterpart, had difficulty establishing a working relationship. John's eyeblink rate increased as he became more and more nervous, fearing that his efforts to resolve their misunderstanding had reached an impasse. This only made things worse. Blinking while another person talks is considered normal to North Americans; to Taiwanese it is considered impolite.[8]

- McDonald's fast-food chain unintentionally offended thousands of Muslims when it printed an excerpt from the Koran on its throwaway hamburger bags.[9] Muslims saw this as sacrilegious. The mistake could have been avoided if McDonald's had displayed greater sensitivity and awareness.

- The Japanese view the business card as an extension of a person, while Americans view it as a business formality and a convenience. Consequently, while the Japanese handle business cards with great care, making certain to put them in safe places, Americans are quick to put them away and thus often end up insulting the Japanese.[10]

- Arabs typically adopt a direct body orientation when communicating. Americans employ a stance that is somewhat less direct and thus often find the communication of Arabs aggressive and unnerving. Arabs and South

In Japan, the word for "different" is the same as the word for "wrong." Compare and contrast a culture in which the goal is to become as much like others as possible with a culture in which the goal is to distinguish oneself from others. Which cultural attitude are you most comfortable with?

culturally confused
lacking an understanding of cultural difference

How do you adapt when in the company of people who are more at home with an alternative cultural convention?

Describe a cultural misunderstanding in which you or someone you know was involved. Was it resolved?

Do you believe any of the following cultural practices are unethical?

- *cockfighting*
- *the withholding of medical intervention, such as a blood transfusion*
- *female circumcision*
- *the stoning of a rape victim*

If you answer yes to any, explain why. If you answer no to any, explain why not. To what extent do your answers support or negate the belief that every culture has a right to its own customs and beliefs?

cultural imperialism

the expansion of dominion of one culture over another culture

Americans also tend to gesture vigorously when speaking to others, causing the less physical Americans to construe their behavior as inappropriate and unmannerly. It is common in Middle Eastern cultures for both males and females to physically exaggerate responses, while in the United States emotions are more likely to be suppressed. In Japan, individuals may try to hide or mask certain emotions. It is common among Asian cultures to exhibit reserve and emotional restraint.

- Eye contact preferences also differ across cultures. Americans place a high value on eye-to-eye communication and tend to distrust those who fail to look at them directly. The Japanese, in contrast, believe eye contact over a sustained period of time shows disrespect. Among Asian cultures, too much eye contact is deemed intrusive. Arabs, on the other hand, maintain direct eye contact with those they interact with for prolonged periods.

- Americans tend to value personal achievement and individualism. In contrast, Asian and Native American cultures stress group cohesion and loyalty, placing greater emphasis on group rather than individual achievement.

Failing to develop insights into cultural nuances and differences can be costly. Recognizing and responding to differences among cultures allows for more meaningful relationships. At the same time, we need to be mindful that not everyone from a particular culture exhibits the same characteristics and communication traits.

Ethics & Communication

Seeing Our Culture through the Eyes of Others

Since 9/11/01, Americans have been moved to ask, "Why don't people in other countries like us more?"[11] Global public opinion surveys reveal that, in increasing numbers, persons from foreign countries perceive Americans to be overbearing, aggressive, and domineering. While some blame such perceptions on foreign policy, others, such as communication researchers Melvin and Margaret DeFleur, blame the media. The DeFleurs surveyed 1,259 teenagers from 12 countries whose main contact with Americans was through the television programs and movies they watched and the music they listened to. Based on these vicarious experiences, in their judgment, Americans were violent, materialistic, sexually loose, disrespectful of people unlike them, unconcerned about the poor, and prone to criminal activity. The DeFleurs concluded that the exporting of American commercialized popular culture contributes to cultural imperialism and the creation of anti-Americanism.[12]

If imperialism is the expansion of dominion of one country over another country, then **cultural imperialism** is the expansion of dominion of one culture over another culture. Cultural imperialism's critics assert that the news,

entertainment, and products of an industrialized country such as the United States overwhelm the national cultures of other countries. They contend that our ethnocentricity leads us to promote our way of life as superior.

On the other hand, there are some signs that the reign of American pop culture is beginning to erode. Foreign film successes such as "Crouching Tiger, Hidden Dragon," a film set in China starring Chinese actors speaking in Chinese, was wildly successful in the United States. U.S. music charts regularly feature vocalists from other countries who speak in Spanish or another language, and foreign news services such as al Jazeera are influencing coverage of the war on terrorism. Cross-fertilization of ideas inevitably leads to more diversity.

However, in order to consider how exposure to popular culture in the United States is affecting the opinions that people in other countries have of the United States and its people, try this: Select an issue of *TV Guide*. Imagine that you live in the Middle East, Africa, or any other Third-World country. Based on your perusal of our prime-time programming, what characteristics would you attribute to Americans? How many of your listed characteristics would you consider positive? Negative?

This chapter will sensitize you to the ways cultural values and habits influence interaction. Learning about such differences will help you (1) appropriately respond to varied communication styles, (2) recognize the need to expand your choices as a communicator, and (3) increase the effectiveness of your interactions with persons of different cultures.

The challenge facing us today is clear: to learn to accept cultural, and therefore communication, differences. Those of us who insist on clinging to the notion of a melting pot, who refuse to take cultural diversity into account, will simply not be able to meet the communication needs of our society and our world. Most likely, we will not only fail to share meaning with others but also not understand why we fail. When we view the world myopically, we distort our ability to respond appropriately.

Intercultural communication is nothing new. It has been practiced for as long as persons of different cultures have interacted with one another.[13] In this age of increased global contact, however, it is essential that we become even more interculturally aware and competent.

DEFINING INTERCULTURAL COMMUNICATION

Whenever cultural variability influences the nature and the effects of communication, **intercultural communication** is at work. Thus, when we speak about intercultural communication, we are concerning ourselves with the process of interpreting and sharing meanings with individuals from different cultures.[14] In actuality, intercultural communication comprises a number of forms. Among its many variations are **interracial communication** (which occurs when interactants are of different races), **interethnic communication** (which occurs when the communicating parties have different ethnic origins), **international communication** (which occurs between persons representing political structures), and **intracultural communication** (which includes all forms of communication among members of the same racial, ethnic, or other co-culture groups).[15]

Cultures and Co-Cultures

To become more adept at communicating with persons who are culturally different from ourselves, we need to learn not only about their cultures but also about our own. A **culture** is the system of knowledge, beliefs, values, customs, behaviors, and artifacts that are acquired, shared, and used by its members during daily living.[16] Within a culture as a whole are **co-cultures;** these are composed of members of the same general culture who differ in some ethnic or sociological way from the parent culture. In our society, African Americans, Hispanic Americans, Japanese Americans, the disabled, gays and lesbians, cyberpunks, and the elderly are just some of the co-cultures belonging to the same general culture.[17]

Have you ever felt like an outsider? Persons who believe they belong to a *marginalized group*—that is, a group whose members feel like outsiders—have a number of options to choose from regarding how they want to interact with members of the dominant culture or even if they want to interact with them at all. Have you or has anyone you know used any of the following strategies?

intercultural communication
interaction with individuals from different cultures

interracial communication
the interpreting and sharing of meanings with individuals from different races

interethnic communication
interaction with individuals of different ethnic origins

international communication
communication between persons representing different nations

intracultural communication
interaction with members of the same racial or ethnic group or co-culture as yours

culture
a system of knowledge, beliefs, values, customs, behaviors, and artifacts that are acquired, shared, and used by members during daily living

co-cultures
groups of persons who differ in some ethnic or sociological way from the parent culture

assimilation
the means by which co-culture members attempt to fit in with members of the dominant culture

accommodation
the means by which co-culture members maintain their cultural identity while striving to establish relationships with members of the dominant culture

separation
the means co-culture members use to resist interacting with members of the dominant culture

Were you ever the only person of your age, race, ethnicity, or sexual preference in a group? How did the experience make you feel?

Compare and contrast the lessons taught you by your culture with the lessons taught peers by other cultures.

Co-culture members who use the strategy of **assimilation** attempt to fit in, or join, with members of the dominant culture. They converse about subjects that members of the dominant group talk about, such as cars or sports, or they dress as members of the dominant culture dress. They give up their own ways in an effort to assume the modes of behavior of the dominant culture. In comparison, co-culture members who use the strategy of **accommodation** attempt to maintain their cultural identity even while they strive to establish relationships with members of the dominant culture. A gay or lesbian who takes his or her partner to an occasion in which members of the dominant culture will be present, such as a company or family celebration, is using the strategy of accommodation. On the other hand, when members of a co-culture resist interacting with members of the dominant culture, they employ the strategy of resistance, or **separation.** Because these persons, such as Hassidic Jews, prefer to interact with each other rather than have contact with persons they perceive to be outsiders, they tend to keep to themselves.

Members of co-cultures can practice *passive, assertive, aggressive,* or *confrontational communication* approaches in their efforts to accomplish their objectives relative to the dominant culture. Co-culture members who practice passive communication may use avoidance strategies as they seek to have as little to do as possible with the dominant group's members. They do not attempt to interact with or have contact with those outside their own group. They passively accept their position in the cultural hierarchy. In contrast, co-culture members who employ an assertive communication approach seek to realize their objectives as well as meet the objectives of those with whom they interact. One assertive technique is relating to the dominant group via liaisons, persons who share the same cultural identity or trusted members of the dominant group. In contrast, some co-culture members choose to exhibit a more aggressive communication approach whereby they become "hurtfully expressive" and "self-promoting" and attempt to control the choices the persons they are interacting with make.[18] Co-culture members who use a confrontational approach seek to make dominant culture members hear them, recognize them, and react to them by making it impossible for them to ignore their presence or pretend they do not exist.

In summary, co-culture members who opt for separation from the dominant culture typically use a passive communication approach (such as going to lunch alone, living in an area with similar people), those who seek accommodation use an assertive approach (such as wearing a yarmulke at work, wearing a sari to a party), and those who choose assimilation use an aggressive approach, often becoming confrontational, belligerent, or disruptive (such as the staging of a protest by a group such as Act Up—a group committed to direct action to combat the AIDS crisis) in their effort to demarginalize themselves and enter the world known to members of the dominant culture. See Table 2.1.

Many theorists believe that an understanding of both the general culture and its co-cultures is essential if one is to communicate effectively. Merely knowing another's language, jargon, or argot or sharing some but not all of a group's values does not necessarily ensure understanding. It is also necessary to become aware of the norms and rules of the culture or co-cultures that might influence the nature of interactions you have with its members, whether those interactions occur in public or in private.

Whenever a message generated by a member of one culture or co-culture needs to be processed by a member or members of another culture or co-culture, the interactants are communicating interculturally.[19] Thus, when you and the individuals with whom you are interacting belong to different cultures, for you to understand each other, you each need to consider the role culture plays in shaping your communication. According to cultural anthropologist Edward T. Hall, culture is communication and communication is culture.[20] It is your culture that teaches

TABLE 2.1 Preferred Strategies and Communication Approaches of Marginalized Groups

Strategy	Communication Approach	Example
Separation	Passive	Lunching alone, living in an area with similar people
Accommodation	Assertive	Wearing a yarmulke to work, wearing a sari to a party
Assimilation	Aggressive, confrontational	Staging a protest

you how to think and what to think about. It is your culture that teaches you what is beautiful or ugly, helpful or harmful, appropriate or out of place. Culture is the lens through which you view the world; it is the mirror you use to reflect and interpret reality.[21]

Culture Guides Communication

Among the lessons taught by culture are how to say "hello" and "good-bye," when to speak or remain silent, how to act when you're angry or upset, where to focus your eyes when functioning as a source or receiver, how much to gesture during speech, how close to stand to another, and how to display happiness or rage at another's actions. By teaching you lessons like these, culture guides behavior and communication. It tells you who you are, how to act, how to think, how to talk, and how to listen.[22]

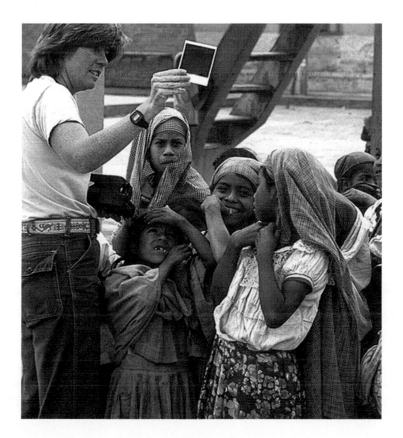

Culture is the lens through which we see the world. Can you provide an example of how your culture has influenced your view of events?

Skill Builder

Ethnocentrism versus Cultural Relativism

Evaluate the extent to which you display culturally ethnocentric or culturally relativistic tendencies by labeling the following statements true or false. For each statement, provide an example of behaviors you used when interacting with or attempting to avoid interacting with a member of another culture. Be specific.

1. I would rather communicate with someone like me than with someone unlike me.
2. I can cooperate with people like me, but I find it difficult to cooperate with people unlike me.
3. I trust those who are like me more freely than I trust those who are different from me.
4. I am less fearful when I am around people like me than when I am around people unlike me.
5. I go out of my way to be with people like me.
6. I go out of my way to maintain my distance from people unlike me.
7. I am much more apt to blame people unlike me for causing trouble than I am to blame people like me.
8. I use my frame of reference to assess the rightness of the behaviors of people like and unlike me.
9. I believe that people unlike me threaten my ability to succeed.
10. I believe that people unlike me should make an effort to become more like me.

What do your answers and examples tell you about the extent to which you and others practice ethnocentrism or cultural relativism? Are there some cultures different from your own that you are more comfortable with than others? Why do you think that is so? Are you content with your responses? Why or why not? What steps are you willing to take, if any, to minimize the potentially negative effects of ethnocentrism?

Identify the extent to which ethnocentrism and/or cultural relativism affects you or those you know.

ethnocentrism
the tendency to see one's own culture as superior to all others

cultural relativism
the acceptance of other cultural groups as equal in value to one's own

When cultures meet, when we interact with persons whose values are different from ours or whose behavioral norms differ from our own, we must first recognize and acknowledge our differences. We must come to accept diversity if we are to be able to process other cultures' influences and communicate with each other in a meaningful way. **Ethnocentrism,** the tendency to see your own culture as superior to all others, is a key characteristic of failed intercultural communication efforts. Persons who are ethnocentric experience great anxiety when interacting with persons from different cultures. Quick to utter statements like "They take our jobs," "They're everywhere," and "They're just not like us," those who embrace ethnocentrism lack cultural flexibility and are particularly unprepared to meet the challenges posed by our society and our world today.[23] The more ethnocentric you are, the greater your tendency is to view groups other than your own as inferior. As a result, you tend to blame others for problems and seek to maintain your distance from them.[24]

Cultural relativism is the opposite of ethnocentrism. When you practice cultural relativism, instead of viewing the group to which you belong as superior to all others, you work to try to understand the behavior of other groups on the basis of the context in which the behavior occurs rather than from your own frame of reference.

TAKING THE DEMOGRAPHIC PICTURE: DIVERSITY IN FOCUS

The United States is the most demographically diverse country in the world. Have you taken advantage of the opportunities you have to interact with persons from different cultures?

To what extent has the amount of contact you have with persons of diverse cultural backgrounds changed since you were a child? When you were younger, you were more apt to interact with persons just like yourself. Your experience today most likely is different. Continuing developments in technology and changes in demography are influencing the nature of our interactions.

Intercultural communication is fast becoming the norm. In fact, living in the United States gives you an incredible opportunity to interact interculturally without having to pay for international travel. But it hasn't always been that way. Years ago, the United States embraced a **melting-pot philosophy.** According to that theory, when individuals from other countries came here, they lost or gave up their original heritage and became Americans. The national motto, *E pluribus unum*—a Latin phrase meaning "one out of many"—reflected this way of thinking. It was believed that diverse cultural groups should be assimilated into the parent, or dominant, culture. Cultural differences were submerged and eradicated as quickly as possible rather than accepted by the parent culture and allowed to thrive.

Over time, this philosophy was replaced by one that stresses **cultural pluralism.** Cultural pluralists advocate respect for uniqueness, tolerance for difference, and adherence to the principle of cultural relativity. In a multicultural society, every group, it is believed, will do things differently, and that's OK.

Demographers tell us that diversity will shape our country's future. According to U.S. Census Bureau statistics, the five largest ethnic groups are composed of people who identify themselves as White (207.7 million), African-American (36.6 million), Hispanic (38.8 million), Asian-American (12.7 million), and Native American (3.5 million). Hispanics are now the largest minority group, followed by African Americans, Native Americans, and Hawaiian Pacific Islanders.[25]

The United States is now the most demographically diverse country in the world. Because of this and because of advances in communications and transportation, we will continue to experience an increasing number of contacts with members of other cultures. This alone makes it especially important for us to be able to understand and interact with persons of different backgrounds, nationalities, and lifestyles. We are truly interconnected with all of humanity.

THE INTERCULTURAL COMMUNICATION IMPERATIVE: REDUCE THE STRANGENESS OF STRANGERS

While intercultural communication is inevitable, we are neither as effective nor as successful at it as we could be. The reason is clear: Not all of us work hard enough to understand or to be understood by those with whom we differ.

According to intercultural communication theorists Larry A. Samovar and Richard E. Porter, there are too many of "us" who do not work as hard as we should at intercultural communication simply because we do not wish to live or interact with "them."[26] Too many of us have adopted an "us versus them" mentality, which prevents us from effectively meeting the challenges cultural diversity presents. To counter this, we need to conduct ourselves in a manner designed to reduce the strangeness of strangers; that is, we need to open ourselves to differences by adding to our storehouse of knowledge, by learning to cope with uncertainty, and by developing an appreciation of how increasing our cultural sensitivity will positively affect our communication competence.

We take a giant step toward improving intercultural communication by accepting the fact that our culture is not superior to others. Nor should we base our behavioral expectations for the members of other cultures on our own culture's

melting-pot philosophy
the view that different cultures should be assimilated into the dominant culture

cultural pluralism
adherence to the principle of cultural relativism

Statistics tell us an interesting story about diversity. The growth rate of the Caucasian population is lower than the growth rates for Asians, Hispanics, and African Americans. It is estimated that by 2025, the Hispanic population will be about 25 percent of the total population. By 2025, the age distribution will also shift. More people will be very young (there will be a 21 percent increase in the people 14 or younger), fewer people will be middle-aged (there will be a 4 percent decrease in the people age 35–49), and more people will be very old (there will be a 14 percent increase in the number of people over 80). It is also expected that race and ethnic mixing will accelerate. What effects do you imagine that changes like these will have on the social and cultural landscape? How do you imagine they will personally affect you?

What steps have you taken to reduce the strangeness of strangers?

Have you ever considered your culture superior to another culture? How did your feelings influence your relationship with members of that culture?

Exploring Diversity

How Hard Do You Work?

Make a list of individuals whose cultural backgrounds differ from your own and with whom you have recently communicated. How many of the following questions can you answer with respect to each person on your list?

1. How do the individual's feelings about socialization differ from your own?
2. How does the individual's concept of self compare with yours?
3. To what extent do the individual's values and attitudes differ from yours?
4. Which of your behaviors did the individual have difficulty understanding or accepting? Which of his or her behaviors did you have difficulty with?

5. Which of the individuals you interacted with did you find most like you? Most unlike you? Can you identify your points of similarity and difference?
6. To what extent was the individual more cooperative or competitive than you?
7. In what ways did the individual's use of verbal language differ from your own?
8. In what ways did the individual's nonverbal behavior differ from your own?
9. How did the individual's treatment of time and space differ from your own?
10. In what ways did the individual's thinking processes differ from yours?

For those questions you cannot answer, take the time to conduct research; then answer them.

norms. To do so would cause us to label the responses of those who belong to other cultures as foreign or strange. To the extent that we are able to use our understanding of another's culture to reduce the number of misunderstandings between us, to the extent that we do not interpret the behavior of others on the basis of our own frames of reference, we take further steps toward reducing the strangeness of strangers.

Exploring Cultural Dialectics

Let's continue by focusing on four variables used to distinguish cultures: (1) individualism versus collectivism, (2) high-context versus low-context communication, (3) high power distance versus low power distance, and (4) masculine or feminine culture. Identified by Hofstede, Kluckhohn and Strodtbeck, and Hall, these dialectics reveal a culture's values and help us make comparisons across cultures.[27]

INDIVIDUALISM VERSUS COLLECTIVISM

individualistic cultures
cultures in which individual goals are stressed

collectivistic cultures
cultures in which group goals are stressed

What roles or rituals are used to celebrate the achievements of persons belonging to an individualistic culture? To a collectivistic culture? Which culture would feature a "salesperson of the year" award? Which would reward the achievements of the team?

The cultural dimension of individualism versus collectivism reveals how people define themselves in their relationships with others. **Individualistic cultures,** such as those of Great Britain, the United States, Canada, France, and Germany, stress individual goals, whereas **collectivistic cultures,** represented by many Arab, African, Asian, and Latin American countries, give precedence to group goals. Individualistic cultures cultivate individual initiative and achievement, while collectivistic cultures tend to nurture group influences. This means that, while the "I" may be most important in individualistic cultures, the "we" is the dominant force in collectivistic ones. While in collectivistic cultures the individual is expected to fit into the group, in individualistic cultures emphasis is placed on developing a sense of self.

HIGH CONTEXT VERSUS LOW CONTEXT

A second way cultures vary in communication style is in their preference for high-context or low-context communication. Cultures with **high-context communication** systems are tradition-bound; their cultural traditions shape the behavior and lifestyle of group members, causing them to appear to be overly polite and indirect in relating to others. In contrast, cultures with **low-context communication** systems generally encourage members to exhibit a more direct communication style. Members of low-context cultures tend to gather background information when meeting someone for the first time. Thus, they will ask people they have just met where they went to college, where they live, and who they work for, while persons from high-context cultures are much less likely to ask such questions.[28] In addition, persons from low-context cultures are apt to feel that they have to explain everything rather than rely on nonverbal, contextual information as demonstrated by those who display a preference for high-context communication. In contrast, persons who believe that most messages can be understood without direct verbal interaction reveal their preference for high-context communication. Asian cultures typically emphasize high-context communication, whereas Western cultures typically represent low-context communication systems. For example, the Japanese have traditionally valued silence, believing that a person of few words is thoughtful, trustworthy, and respectable. Thus, the Japanese spend considerably less time talking than do people in the United States. This orientation also helps explain why the Japanese often perceive self-disclosures during interaction as socially inappropriate.

high-context communication
a tradition-bound communication system which depends on indirectness

low-context communication
a system that encourages directness in communication

HIGH POWER DISTANCE VERSUS LOW POWER DISTANCE

Power distance measures the extent to which individuals are willing to accept power differences. Individuals from **high power distance cultures,** such as Saudi Arabia, India, and Malaysia, view power as a fact of life and are apt to stress its coercive or referent nature. Superiors and subordinates in these countries are likely to view each other differently; subordinates are quick to defer to superiors. In contrast, individuals from **low power distance cultures,** such as Israel, Sweden, and the United States, believe power should be used only when it is legitimate; thus, they are apt to employ expert or legitimate power. Superiors and subordinates from low power distance countries emphasize their interdependence by displaying a preference for consultation; subordinates will even contradict their bosses when necessary.[29]

high power distance cultures
cultures based on power differences in which subordinates defer to superiors

low power distance cultures
cultures that believe that power should be used only when legitimate

MASCULINE VERSUS FEMININE CULTURE

Cultures differ in their attitudes toward gender roles.[30] In highly masculine cultures, members value male aggressiveness, strength, and material symbols of success. In highly feminine cultures, members value relationships, tenderness in members of both sexes, and a high quality of life. Among highly **masculine cultures** are Japan, Italy, Germany, Mexico, and Great Britain. Among highly feminine cultures are Sweden, Norway, the Netherlands, Thailand, and Chile. Masculine cultures socialize members to be dominant and competitive. They tend to confront conflicts head-on and are likely to use a win–lose conflict strategy. In contrast, the members of **feminine cultures** are more apt to compromise and negotiate to resolve conflicts, seeking win–win solutions.

masculine cultures
cultures that value aggressiveness, strength, and material symbols of success

feminine cultures
cultures that value tenderness and relationships

What assumptions do the following proverbs lead you to make about the identified culture's members? How can understanding the proverbs a culture embraces help enhance communication with that culture's members?

God helps those who help themselves.

The squeaky wheel gets the grease.

—(American)

When spiderwebs unite, they can trap a lion.

It takes a whole village to raise a child.

—(African)

No need to know the person, only the family.

—(Chinese)

It's the nail that sticks out that is hammered.

—(Japanese)

Interpreting Cultural Differences

Where a culture falls on the individualistic-collectivistic, low-context–high-context communication, and power distance scales affects the interactional preferences of its members. In Japanese and Chinese societies, for example, individuals tend to understate their own accomplishments and successes, while members of North American cultures typically are taught to be assertive and take credit for their personal achievements. It appears that individualistic cultures tend to use low-context communication, while high-context communication tends to predominate in collectivistic cultures. Thus, whereas members of low-context communication cultures interact in a direct way with each other, members of high-context communication cultures interact indirectly. For example, North Americans tend to speak directly on an issue, whereas individuals from Japan, Korea, and China prefer to avoid confrontation, to preserve a sense of harmony, and to make it possible for the individuals with whom they are speaking to save face, or maintain self-esteem. Similarly, rarely will one Saudi Arabian publicly criticize another; to do so would label the individual as disloyal and disrespectful.[31] When persons from diverse power distance cultures interact, unless these differences in orientation are acknowledged, interactions may well result in misunderstandings.

IDENTIFYING INFLUENCES ON CULTURAL IDENTITY

We all belong to a number of groups, including gender, age, racial and ethnic, religious, socioeconomic, and national. Our cultural identity is based on these group memberships.

How we define *gender roles*, for example, affects the way males and females present themselves, socialize, work, perceive their futures, and communicate. U.S. men tend to adopt a problem-solving orientation, while women tend to be relationship-oriented.[32] We also have ideas regarding the meaning and significance of *age*, including how persons our age should look and behave. In the United States, large numbers of people place great value on looking youthful and appear to be younger than they are. In contrast, in Muslim, Asian, and Latin American cultures, people respect, rather than deny, aging. Our *racial and ethnic identities* are similarly socially constructed. Some racial and ethnic groups, for example, share experiences of oppression. Their attitudes and behaviors may reflect their struggles, influencing their attitudes toward contemporary issues such as affirmative action. *Religious identity* is at the root of countless contemporary conflicts occurring in the Middle East, India and Pakistan, and Bosnia-Herzegovina. The proselytizing that occurred at the U.S. Air Force Academy by Evangelical cadets and officers illustrates the strength and influence of religious identity. Similarly, *socioeconomic identify* frames how we respond to issues of our day. The widening gap between the ultrawealthy and the middle and lower classes in the United States is contributing to their developing different attitudes on a wide array of issues. *National identity* refers to our legal status or citizenship. People from different countries have been U.S. citizens for generations, yet some still perceive them as foreigners. Do you? The reality is that approximately 32 million people (or 11.5 percent of the total population of the United States) were born in another country.[33]

The Storyteller: Seeing through the Eyes of the Stereotyped

Over the years, some media producers have made the effort to remove stereotypes from films and television programs. Disney, for example, changed the sound of the original Bad Wolf in the *Three Little Pigs* from that of a heavy Jewish accent to a falsetto voice. Similarly, the lyrics to the opening song in *Aladdin* were revised after complaints by the American-Arab Anti-Discrimination Committee. In the film, however, both Jasmine and her father, though Arabian, speak unaccented, standard American English, while the "bad guys" speak with foreign accents.[34] If you were of Middle Eastern descent, how would you feel about having an accent associated with evil?

Latino advocates report that, while Black men seem to be getting meatier roles on television shows, they, Native Americans, and Asian-Americans are not. They criticize the networks for a lack of racial and ethnic diversity in their schedules. Joining forces with the NAACP, the Asian Pacific American Media Coalition, and the American Indians in Film and Television, they negotiated agreements with the major networks to increase minority participation both on and off the screen.[35] The problem isn't only minority representation, however. It's portrayal as well. Latino actor Martin Sheen (real name Ramon Estevez) played a Caucasian character on TV's *The West Wing*. When minority representation is glaringly absent in media offerings, the roles minorities do appear in have more impact. The parts given Latinos, for example, often are reminiscent of pre–civil rights African-American portrayals such as the entertainer, the criminal, the crime victim, or the maid, or they are secondary roles with nonprofessional jobs. Were you to see yourself portrayed as a victim, or as subservient to the dominant Anglo society, how do you imagine that would affect your perceptions of the options that exist for you? How would they affect your view of your culture?

Like film, television has been called a cultural storyteller, an agent of norms and values. Watch a week's prime-time programming on a particular station. Count the number of characters in each program that are from another culture. What did you learn from each character about his or her culture? In your opinion, were cultural stereotypes used to develop each character from another culture? If so, describe them. To what extent, if any, did what you viewed reinforce and/or alter your existing attitudes toward members of that culture? What emotional reactions, if any, were triggered in you by each character? Did you find that the shows contributed to your having predominantly positive or negative attitudes toward the members of another culture? Finally, using one or two words, identify the key value of each show viewed. For example, the message of one show may focus on materialism, the message of another on force and violence.

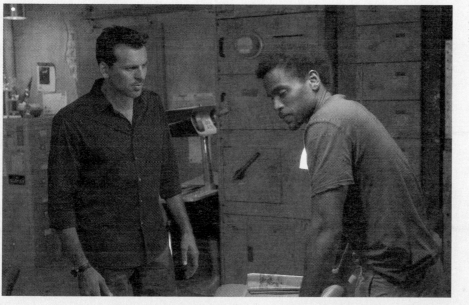

Which character do you believe was stereotyped? Why?

IDENTIFYING THE IMPACT OF STEREOTYPES AND PREJUDICE

stereotypes

mental images; shortcuts
that guide reactions

Stereotypes are mental images or pictures we carry around in our heads; they are shortcuts, whether positive or negative, that guide our reactions to others.[36] When attached to the way we view the world, stereotypes generate unrealistic pictures of others and prevent us from distinguishing an individual from a group. Racial profiling is just one example of how stereotyping affects worldview.

prejudice

a positive or negative
prejudgment

    Prejudice describes how we feel about a group of people whom, more likely than not, we do not personally know. A negative or positive prejudgment, prejudice arises either because we want to feel more positively about our own group, or because we feel others present a threat, real or not.[37] Prejudice leads to the creation of in-groups and out-groups, with out-group members becoming easy targets for discrimination. Because of the negative expectations that stereotypes and prejudices produce, we may try not to interact with people who are the objects of our prejudices. (We discuss stereotypes and prejudice again in Chapter 4).

TECHNOLOGY AND INTERCULTURAL COMMUNICATION

The Internet permeates national boundaries and erodes the connection between location and experience. It enables us to interact more easily with people who have different worldviews than we do. Although a minority of the world's population currently uses the Web, computer connectivity is changing things. With a few clicks, you can locate a group of people and form associations with a Web "tribe" or group independent of geography.[38]

**virtual neighborhoods
and communities**

online, surrogate communities

    Technology and computer networks are also changing the traditional definition of a community. When we speak of a communication community today, no longer are we limited to real neighborhoods. Our concept of community has widened. **Virtual neighborhoods and communities** now also populate the communication landscape. Perhaps the neighborhoods in which we actually live are not delivering the person-to-person contact we seek. Seeking surrogate neighborhoods, millions of people communicate online. For many of us, the Internet, with its worldwide reach, has become an integral part of our communication lives.[39] However, some critics contend that, rather than bringing us together, computer networks are isolating us. What is missing from online communities, they assert, is that which constitutes the essence of a real neighborhood, including a sense of location and a feeling of permanence and belonging. They also believe that the culture of computing, especially when it comes to the Net's Newsgroups, attracts extreme political positions and contributes to long-standing international conflicts.[40]

    Being able to reach so many different people who live in so many different places so quickly gives us a new sense of communication power. Wherever we live, the Internet may also help bring diversity and new cultures into our lives. Over time, the Internet may help change our social and business lives. Through it, we may meet a wider array of people. It has the capacity to introduce us to new friends and contacts and to allow us to network with persons around the world. The question for us to ponder, however, is the form that these new alliances will take: Will they be shallow and short-lived or deep and enduring? Will we commit ourselves emotionally to them or keep our online interactions superficial? What kinds of relationships will we develop by conversing with diverse individuals in distant lands without actually meeting them? Will all voices really be heard? Will we be more or less tolerant of each other? Will we be aware that words posted to global online groups have consequences, just as they do when delivered in person?

Our Western version of the Net is loaded with Western culture and advertising. Even most of us complain about the pop-ups and the advertising glut. How this emphasis on consumerism is interpreted around the world is a source of controversy.

We also need to face the fact that in some cultures and religions, technology is considered evil. Even in our own culture, we have over 100 million Americans who have no desire to get connected.[41] In the past five years, over 30 million Americans chose to stop using the Internet. Why? Because they desired to lead a more simple life, asserting that technology was making their lives too complicated. These people are part of the digital backlash.[42]

There also is the question of who is represented on the Internet. Will we really be able to interact with diverse groups of people? Currently, African Americans, the elderly, and the poor are still underrepresented online. In time, however, increased access via libraries and schools may help change this trend.

If the trend continues, however, the **digital divide** (information gap) will widen. Those who are financially able to afford Internet service and the purchase of new technologies will have an advantage over those who are not. (Typically, affluent neighborhoods are the first to be wired to receive new services.) The "information haves" will have access to social and educational services and will be in position to acquire knowledge and skills that the "have nots" will not have available, creating what some civil rights leaders call a "technological apartheid." The information gap is especially evident along racial, ethnic, age, geographic, and income lines.[43] What steps, if any, do you think we should take to democratize access to new technologies?

digital divide
information gap

HOW TO IMPROVE YOUR ABILITY TO COMMUNICATE INTERCULTURALLY

Having the desire to relate more effectively with persons of different cultures is critical to improving your ability to communicate interculturally. Also important is limiting your reliance on stereotypes that can diminish your success when you interact with others. In addition, you need to be able to reduce your uncertainty levels regarding the persons of different cultures with whom you communicate. Since you do not necessarily share the same communication rules, the degree of ambiguity you feel when interacting with them increases as your ability to predict their responses decreases. The following guidelines should help you increase your tolerance for ambiguity, enhance your ability to handle

Focus on Service Learning

Attend a local continuing education session for persons from other countries who want to learn English. Keep a log in which you identify and analyze your reactions to the persons attending, including any stereotypes you have about them. Develop a proposal for teaching an English as a Second Language (ESL) course for adults on-site at a local factory.

Thinking Critically

new situations, and better prepare yourself to meet the communication challenges of today and tomorrow:

- Refrain from formulating expectations based solely on your own culture.

When those you interact with have diverse communication styles, it is critical that you acknowledge the differences and accept their validity. By not isolating yourself within your own group or culture, you allow yourself to be more fully a part of a multicultural society and thus a better communicator.

- Recognize how faulty education can impede understanding.

It is important to identify and work to eliminate any personal biases and prejudices you have developed over the years. Determine, for example, the extent to which your family and friends have influenced your feelings about persons from other cultural groups. Do those you have grown up with appear comfortable or uncomfortable relating to persons of different cultural origins? To what extent have their attitudes affected your intercultural communication competence?

- Make a commitment to develop communication skills and abilities appropriate to life in a multicultural world.

While culture is a tie that binds, the creation of the global village makes it essential that you leave the comfort of your cultural niche, become more knowledgeable of other cultures, and strive to be culturally aware.

It is important to familiarize yourself with the communication rules and preferences of members of different cultures so that you can increase the effectiveness of your communication encounters. Your ability to develop intercultural communication skills depends in large part on how many of the following promises you are willing to make:

I will make a commitment to seek information from persons whose cultures are different from my own.

I will try to understand how the experiences of persons from different cultures leads them to develop perspectives that differ from mine.

I will pay attention to the situation and the context when I communicate with persons from different cultures.

I will make every effort to become a more flexible communicator.

I will not insist that persons from other cultures communicate with me on my terms.

Intercultural communication will become increasingly important in the coming years. We hope you feel better prepared to meet your future.

Revisiting Chapter Objectives

1. **Assess your ability to communicate effectively with persons from different cultures.**   Ours is an age of increased global contact and diversity. Consequently, assessing and developing an understanding of and sensitivity to cultural differences is an essential component in each of our communication repertoires. To the extent we are able to reduce cultural ignorance and enhance cultural awareness, we increase our personal preparedness to communicate effectively.

2. **Discuss the kinds of problems the culturally confused face.**   By taking steps to eliminate cultural misunderstandings, we also facilitate the development of more meaningful relationships between persons from different cultures whether these relationships occur face-to-face or online.

3. **Define *intercultural communication.***   Intercultural communication is the process of interpreting and sharing meanings with individuals from different cultures.

4. **Compare and contrast culture and co-culture, ethnocentrism and cultural relativism, melting pot philosophy and cultural pluralism.**   A culture is a system of knowledge, beliefs, values, customs, behaviors, and artifacts that are acquired, shared, and used by members. A co-culture is a group of persons who differ in some ethnic or sociological way from the parent culture. Ethnocentrism is the tendency to see one's own culture as superior to all others. Cultural relativism is the acceptance of other cultural groups as equal in value to one's own. The melting pot philosophy advocates the assimilation of different cultures into the dominant culture. Cultural pluralism acknowledges that other cultural groups are equal in value to one's own.

5. **Compare and contrast the following: individualism and collectivism, high-context communication cultures and low-context communication cultures, high power distance cultures and low power distance cultures and masculine and feminine cultures.**   Individualistic cultures stress individual goals. Collectivistic cultures stress group goals. High-context communication cultures are tradition-bound, valuing indirectness. Low-context communication cultures encourage directness in communication. High power distance cultures view power as a fact of life with subordinates deferring to superiors. Low power distance cultures believe power should only be used if legitimate. Masculine cultures value aggressiveness, strength, and material success. Feminine cultures value relationships, tenderness, and a high quality of life.

The Wrap Up

6. **Identify techniques you can use to reduce the strangeness of strangers.** Although the lessons taught by culture influence our communication style preferences, there are techniques we can use to reduce the strangeness of strangers, adding to the storehouse of knowledge that underscores our communication competence and, as a result, increasing our ability to handle the communication challenges of today and tomorrow.

7. **Discuss how technology is bringing diversity into our lives.** For many of us, the Internet is facilitating this task. Enabling us to interact with people who have different world views, the Internet brings diversity and culture into our lives.

Resources for Further Inquiry and Reflection

To apply your understanding of how the principles in Chapter 2 are at work in our daily lives, consult the following resources for further inquiry and reflection. Or, if you prefer, choose any other appropriate resource. Then connect the ideas expressed in your chosen selection with the communication concepts and issues you are learning about both in and out of class.

 ### Listen to Me

"Born in the U.S.A." (Bruce Springsteen)
"Land Down Under" (Men at Work)
"My Woman from Tokyo" (Deep Purple)
"Colors of the Wind" (Vanessa Williams)
"Al Otro Lado del Rio" (Antonio Banderas)

What do the views of the song's speaker or speakers suggest about the ability they have to meet diversity's challenges?

 ### View Me

Bend It Like Beckham   *Dances with Wolves*
Boys Don't Cry   *The Joy Luck Club*
Mississippi Burning   *Jungle Fever*
La Cage aux Folles   *Lost in Translation*
The Gods Must Be Crazy

How does culture influence the interaction of the characters in the film? What lessons about the effects of culture can be taught through the film?

 ### Read Me

Harper Lee. *To Kill a Mockingbird*. Philadelphia: Lippincott, 1960.
Wen Ho Lee. *My Country versus Me: The First-Hand Account by the Los Alamos Scientist Who Was Falsely Accused*. New York: Hyperion, 2002.
Khaled Hosseini. *The Kite Runner*. New York: Riverhead Books, 2003.
Sherman Alexie. *Reservation Blues*. New York: Atlantic Monthly, 1995.

Discuss how age, gender, ethnic affiliation, family ties, education, beliefs and religion, and/or nationality influence and shape attitudes.

 ### Tell Me

Share with the class the insights you gained from your chosen Listen to Me, View Me, or Read Me selection.

Choose a side and discuss the arguments for or against using English as a universal language.

Key Chapter Terminology

Use the Communication Works CD-ROM and Online Learning Center at www.mhhe.com/gamble9 to further your knowledge of the following terminology.

Communication
Works

online learning center

www.mhhe.com/gamble9

accommodation 30	individualistic cultures 34
assimilation 30	intercultural communication 29
co-cultures 29	interethnic communication 29
collectivistic cultures 34	international communication 29
cultural imperialism 28	interracial communication 29
cultural pluralism 33	intracultural communication 29
cultural relativism 32	low power distance cultures 35
culturally confused 27	low-context communication 35
culture 29	masculine cultures 35
digital divide 39	melting-pot philosophy 33
diversity 26	multiculturalists 26
ethnocentrism 32	prejudice 38
feminine cultures 35	separation 30
high power distance cultures 35	stereotypes 38
high-context communication 35	virtual neighborhoods and communities 38

Idioms in Translation

get connected—communicate digitally or via the Internet

save face—maintain self-esteem

storehouse of knowledge—information

Test Your Understanding

Go to the *Self Quizzes* on the Communication Works CD-ROM and the book's Online Learning Center at www.mhhe.com/gamble9.

Communication
Works

online learning center

www.mhhe.com/gamble9

Notes

1. M. McLuhan. *The Medium Is the Message*. New York: Bantam Books, 1967; M. McLuhan. *Understanding Media*. New York: Mentor, 1964.
2. *Christian Science Monitor*.
3. H. J. Whitlock Gyory and Diana D. Q. Tran. "Walking in Another's Shoes: A Reflective Diversity Exercise." *Journal of College Student Development* 43:1, January/February 2002, p. 133–136.
4. Gail L. Thompson. "Teachers' Cultural Ignorance Imperils Student Success." *USA Today*, May 29, 2002, p. 13A.
5. William B. Gudykunst. *Bridging Differences: Effective Intergroup Communication*, 3rd ed. Thousand Oaks, CA: Sage, 1998, p. 40.
6. Guo-Ming Chen and William J. Starosta. "A Review of the Concept of Intercultural Sensitivity." *Human Communication* 2, 1997, p. 5.

7. As reported in Larry A. Samovar and Richard E. Porter. *Communication between Cultures*. Belmont, CA: Wadsworth, 1991, p. 154.

8. William B. Gudykunst. *Bridging Differences: Effective Intergroup Communication*, 4th ed. Thousand Oaks, CA: Sage, 2004, pp.12–13.

9. "Unhappy Meal for Muslims." *The Record*, June 8, 1994, p. C-3.

10. Wendy Griswold. *Cultures and Societies in a Changing World*. Thousand Oaks, CA: Pine Forge, 1994, p. 1.

11. Nicholas D. Kristof. "Why Do They Hate Us?" *New York Times*, January 15, 2002, p. A21.

12. Margaret H. DeFleur and Melvin L. DeFleur. "The Next Generation's Image of Americans: Attitudes and Beliefs Held by Teen-Agers in Twelve Countries." www.bu.edu/news/releases/2002/defleur/report.pdf, October 3, 2002.

13. Larry A. Samovar and Richard E. Porter. *Intercultural Communication: A Reader*, 9th ed. Belmont, CA: Wadsworth, 2000.

14. William B. Gudykunst and Young Yun Kim, eds. *Readings on Communicating with Strangers*. New York: McGraw-Hill, 1992.

15. Larry A. Samovar and Richard E. Porter, *Communication between Cultures*, 4th ed. Belmont, CA: Wadsworth, 2001, pp. 5, 46–47.

16. Judith Cornelia Pearson and Paul Edward Nelson. *Understanding and Sharing: An Introduction to Speech Communication*, 6th ed. Dubuque, IA: Brown & Benchmark, 1994, p. 193.

17. Griswold, p. 57.

18. M. P. Orbe. "Laying the Foundation for Co-Cultural Communication Theory: An Inductive Approach to Studying 'Nondominant' Communication Strategies and the Factors That Influence Them." *Communication Studies* 47, 1996, pp. 157–176.

19. Samovar and Porter, *Communication between Cultures*, pp. 2, 46.

20. Edward Hall. *The Silent Language*. New York: Fawcett, 1959.

21. Griswold, pp. 22–24.

22. Carley H. Dodd. *Dynamics of Intercultural Communication*, 3rd ed. Dubuque, IA: Brown, 1991, p. 3.

23. Thomas Keneally. "Racism's as Human as Love." *The Sunday Record*, February 6, 1994, p. R-1.

24. William B. Gudykunst. *Bridging Differences*, 3rd ed. Thousand Oaks, CA: Sage, 1998, pp. 106–110.

25. U.S. Census Bureau; Haya El Nasser, "39 Million Make Hispanics Largest Minority Group." *USA Today*, June 19, 2003, pp. 1A, 2A.

26. Samovar and Porter, *Intercultural Communication: A Reader*, p. 5.

27. See, for example, G. Hofstede. *Culture's Consequences: International Differences in Work-Related Values*, 2nd ed. Beverly Hills, CA: Sage, 2001; F. R. Kluckhohn and F. L. Strodtbeck. *Variations in Value Orientations*. New York: Row & Peterson, 1960; and E. T. Hall. *Beyond Culture*. New York: Doubleday, 1976.

28. See Judith N. Martin and Thomas K. Nakayama. *Intercultural Communication in Contexts*, 2nd ed. Mountain View, CA: Mayfield, 2000, pp. 265–266.

29. G. Hofstede. *Cultures and Organizations*. London: McGraw-Hill, 1991.

30. See G. Hofstede. *Masculinity and Femininity: The Taboo Dimension of National Cultures*. Thousand Oaks, CA: Sage, 1998.

31. Robert R. Harris and Robert T. Moran. *Managing Cultural Differences*, 3rd ed. Houston: Gulf, 1991.

32. Deborah Tannen. *You Just Don't Understand: Women and Men in Conversation*. New York: Morrow, 1990.

33. Sam Roberts. "Forming a More Diverse Union." *New York Times*, June 29, 2003, p. WK2.

34. Fred E. Jandt. *Intercultural Communication: An Introduction*. Thousand Oaks, CA: Sage, 1998, pp. 90–91. See also F. Delgado. "Mass-Mediated Communication and Intercultural Conflict." In J. N. Martin, T. K. Nakayma, and L. A. Flores, eds. *Readings in Cultural Contexts*. Mountain View, CA: Mayfield, 1998, pp. 442–449.

35. Paul Shepard. "Latinos Seek More Featured TV Roles." *The Record*, July 4, 2000, p. A-10.

36. W. Lippmann. *Public Opinion*. New York: Macmillan, 1922.

37. For more on prejudice, see M. L. Hecht, ed. *Communicating Prejudice*. Thousand Oaks, CA: Sage, 1998.

38. Josh Meyrowitz. "Media Theory." In Erik P. Bucy, ed. *Living in the Information Age*. Belmont, CA: Wadsworth, 2002, p. 32.

39. Clifford Stoll. *Silicon Snake Oil: Second Thoughts on the Information Highway*. New York: Doubleday, 1995, pp. 8–11.

40. Clifford Stoll. "Further Explorations into the Culture of Computing." In Erick P. Bucy, ed. *Living in the Information Age*. Belmont, CA: Wadsworth, 2002, pp. 210–215.

41. Edward Iwata. "Tech's Tyranny Provokes Revolt." *USA Today*, August 21, 2000, p. 1A.

42. Jan Samoriski. *Issues in Cyberspace*. Boston: Allyn & Bacon, 2002, p. 37.

43. See Jan Samoriski. *Issues in Cyberspace*. Boston: Allyn & Bacon, 2002.

CHAPTER

Communication and the Self-Concept: Who Are You?

After finishing this chapter, you should be able to

1. Define and explain the nature of the self-concept.

2. Identify how different factors, including popular culture, help shape your self-concept.

3. Define *self-fulfilling prophecy* and explain how a self-fulfilling prophecy can influence behavior.

4. Compare and contrast the ways males and females as well as people from different cultures see themselves.

5. Identify the purposes and functions of the Johari window as a model of self-disclosure.

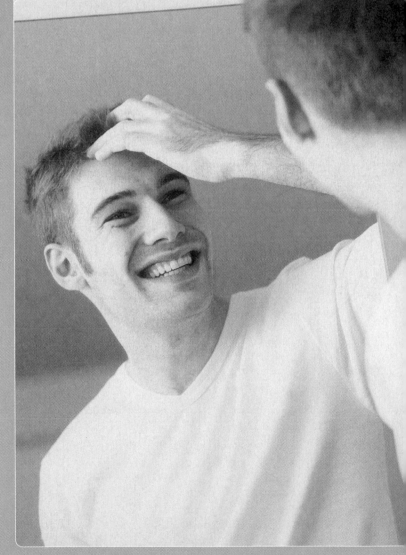

There are three things extremely hard, Steel, a Diamond, and to know one's self.

—Benjamin Franklin

. . . the self is not something that one finds. It is something that one creates.

—Thomas Szasz

Do you talk to yourself? Of course you do! Intrapersonal communication, as we learned in Chapter 1, is thinking, or self-talk; it is the communicating we do with ourselves, the basis for all other communication, and communication's most important element. How we see and talk to ourselves today is a result of all our communication experiences. It also expresses our relationship with ourselves. What words would you use to describe the relationship you have with yourself? Do the words you chose suggest that you feel good about yourself? If so, to what do you attribute your feeling good about yourself? if you do not feel good about yourself, what is it that keeps you from doing so? Let's find out.

WHAT IS THE SELF-CONCEPT?

How we communicate with ourselves and how others communicate with us builds in us a sense of self. Our sense of self evolves as we interact with different people, find ourselves in new situations, and form new relationships. It is important that you spend some time considering who you are and what you intend to do with the rest of your life. The question, Who am I? is a serious one. How you answer it is extremely significant, since who you think you are to a large extent determines what you choose to do, how you choose to act, whom you choose to communicate with, and even whether you desire to communicate. If someone were to ask you on 10 separate occasions, "Who are you?"—and if each time you had to supply a different answer—what types of responses would you offer? Would you be able to group your responses into categories? For example, you might see yourself in reference to your sex (male or female), your gender (masculine or feminine), your religion (Buddhist, Jewish, Muslim, Christian), your race (African, Hispanic, Caucasian, Asian), your nationality (U.S. citizen, Turkish, German), your physical attributes (fat, thin), your roles (wife, son, student, employee), your attitudes and emotions (hopeful, pessimistic, personable), your mental abilities (smart, slow), and your talents (musically or artistically gifted). The words you use to describe yourself reveal both to yourself and to others what you think you are like.

The self is a social product—a composite of who we think we are, who other people think we are, and who we think others think we are. Some of us are more self-aware than others; this developed **self-awareness** (the ability to reflect on

self-awareness

the ability to reflect on and monitor one's own behavior

self-concept

everything one thinks and feels about oneself

self-image

the sort of person one perceives oneself to be

self-esteem

how well one likes and values oneself

and monitor one's own behavior) facilitates a fuller understanding of the self, including the attitudes, beliefs, and values we hold as well as the strengths and weaknesses we have.[1]

How we think about ourselves, the **self-concept** (your self-identity—your perceived self—the rather consistent and organized image you form of yourself) is composed of two parts—self-image and self-esteem. **Self-image** is your mental picture of yourself; it is the kind of person you perceive yourself to be. Self-image includes the roles you see yourself performing, the categories you place yourself within, the words you use to describe or identify yourself, and your understanding of how others see you. **Self-esteem,** on the other hand, is your self-assessment; it is your evaluation of your ability and worth and indicates how well you like and value yourself. Self-esteem usually derives from your successes and/or failures and colors your self-image with a predominantly positive or negative hue. According to researcher Chris Mruk, self-esteem has five dimensions, which affect your feelings about yourself and your communication with others: competence (your beliefs about your ability to be effective), worthiness (your beliefs about the degree to which others value you), cognition (your beliefs about your character and personality), affect (how you evaluate yourself and the feelings generated by your evaluation), and stability or change.[2]

Our self-concepts significantly affect our behavior, including what we think is possible. How the self-concept affects communication is the focus of the remainder of this chapter.

EXPLORING THE SELF-CONCEPT AND BEHAVIOR CONNECTION

Self-concept concerns us all. One sports coach, for example, notes, "If I single some out for praise, I would kill the others' self-esteem." One person praises another for a job that wasn't very well done, observing that "I didn't want to hurt his self-esteem."[3] Some school systems even believe that the promotion of self-esteem should be a central goal of education.[4] Others challenge the merit of a "feel-good curriculum" and distain the fact that we walk around on eggshells to avoid hurting another person's self-esteem.[5] Why is self-esteem considered so critical?

Have you ever been teased? How did it affect your sense of self?

Some believe that an overemphasis on reinforcing self-esteem, especially in persons whose self-esteem is already high, has precipitated bullying in some segments of our culture. Why do people tease or bully others? What motivates one person to want to belittle another person? What is bullying? Who is a bully? Bullying is persistent teasing, name-calling, or social exclusion. A bully is likely to be among the most popular people, admired by others, and high among those persons others want to "hang" with.[6] Some researchers say the behavior of a person who bullies can be attributed to a self-appraisal that is unrealistically inflated.[7] A prime contributor to aggression in person-to-person interaction appears to be unusually high self-esteem combined with a sense of arrogance and narcissistic tendencies.[8] Consider the adulation in our society that is accorded our icons of popular culture, including professional athletes, and music and movie stars. Our behavior helps precipitate the self-centered, egomaniacal characteristics they too often exhibit. Balance is needed in how much praise we give people,

In your opinion, is self-control more important than self-esteem?

Ethics & Communication

Self-Concern and Concern for Others

In her book *The New Peoplemaking*, Virginia Satir notes:

Every person has a feeling of worth, positive or negative; the question is, Which is it?

Every person communicates; the question is, How, and what happens as a result?

Every person follows rules; the question is, What kind, and how well do they work for her or him?

Every person is linked to society; the question is, In what way, and what are the results?[14]

How would you answer each of these questions with regard to yourself? Your parents? Your friends? The people you work with? What does each set of answers reveal about self-concern and concern for others? How is this an ethical issue?

---

lest we help create in them a perception of their own self-importance that is out of whack with reality.

People with very low self-esteem define themselves primarily by their limitations and tend to be negative about a lot of things. In comparison, people with high self-esteem tend to be significantly happier than their low–self-esteem counterparts.[9] If their self-esteem is undeservedly high, they also are likely to ignore their own weaknesses. People in this category suffer from an inflated sense of their worth, displaying an inappropriate overconfidence in their abilities. This may be because they were overpraised by those around them and told that they did "a great job" whether that was true or not. These people are unprepared for the criticism of supervisors; they quickly fall apart if told that they are wrong or lacking in some ability.[10] People in both the extremely high and extremely low self-esteem groups also have something in common: They tend to be self-absorbed. In contrast,

Our self-concept is shaped by our experiences.

Exploring Diversity

Describe Yourself

Is it possible to define yourself in just a single word? Try it.

When a *New York Times*/CBS News poll asked 1,136 adults to describe themselves in only one word, interviewers received a multitude of answers.[15]

Generally, the respondents seemed to resist labeling themselves as members of a special interest group or easily identifiable minority group; avoiding stereotyping, they chose instead either a broader affiliation or a narrower, more personal response.

For example, none of the 97 Black respondents said "Black," and none of the 967 Whites said that being White was the defining fact of their lives. Instead, the word given most often in the survey was *American.*

For those who answered, it was certainly a challenge. "You cannot reduce yourself to one word. It is too complicated," said Suzanne Keller, a sociologist at Princeton University. "People really feel multiple. They have multiple poses and attitudes and roles and one is no more important than the next. If they're forced to choose between family and work and leisure roles, which are not even roles but personas, they can't, really, because they live a multifaceted, multitudinous life, not a single track."

Author Margaret Atwood seemed to feel the same way when asked to define herself in one word. She picked *indescribable,* warning that "one must always resist the tyranny of adjectives."

Now ask 10 people to describe themselves in one word. How do their responses compare with the ones in the study?

Part of knowing who we are is knowing we are not someone else.

—Arthur Miller,
Incident at Vichy

people with healthy self-esteem do not have an inflated sense of their abilities and are not awash in "unwarranted self-regard;"[11] instead, they are in touch with both their strengths and their weaknesses, and are able to tolerate feelings of frustration. Expecting a positive outcome, they persist when at first they fail. They are both confident and resilient, traits necessary for success.[12] Researchers now believe that high self-esteem rather than causing good performance is its result. According to J. D. Hawkins, president of the National Self-Esteem Association (NSEA), "self-esteem is more than just feeling good about yourself. It's about being socially and individually responsible."[13]

HOW IS YOUR SELF-CONCEPT FORMED?

How did your self-concept develop? The day you recognized yourself as separate from your surroundings, life began to change as you strove to fit into the world as you saw it. Your concept of self—that relatively stable set of perceptions you attribute to yourself—became your most important possession.

While you are not born with a self-concept, you certainly do play a key role in building one.[16] Even though you are constantly undergoing change, once built, the theory or picture you have of yourself is fairly stable and difficult to alter. For example, have you ever tried to revise your parents' or friends' opinions about themselves? Did you have much luck? Our opinions about ourselves grow more and more resistant to change as we become older and presumably wiser. The statements we make are more or less accurate maps of the territory that is ourselves, but some of us map ourselves better than others do—that is, some of us have a more accurate mental picture of our personal strengths, weaknesses, and needs than others do.[17]

A number of forces converge to help create your self-concept. Among them are the image that other people have of you, which helps guide the way they relate to you; the way you experience and evaluate yourself; the roles you perform; the media messages you absorb; the expectations you and others have for you; and the gender, cultural, and technological messages you internalize.

To a large extent, your self-concept is shaped by your environment and by the people around you, including your parents, relatives, teachers, supervisors, friends, and co-workers. If people who are important to you have a good image of you, they probably make you feel accepted, valued, worthwhile, lovable, and significant, and you are likely to develop a positive self-concept as a result. On the other hand, if those who are important to you have a poor image of you, more than likely they make you feel left out, small, worthless, unloved, or insignificant, and you probably develop a negative self-concept as a consequence.

It is not difficult to see how people you value influence the picture you have of yourself and help determine the ways you behave. Nineteenth-century poet Walt Whitman recognized this:

How do your employer and your friends picture you?

There was a child went forth every day,
And the first object he look'd upon, that object he became,
And that object became part of him for the day or a certain part of the day,
Or for many years or stretching cycles of years.

ROLES, SELF-EVALUATIONS, BEHAVIOR, AND THE SELF-CONCEPT

Self-concept, besides being your own theory of who and what you are, is a mental picture you have of yourself. This mental image is easily translated into the faces or masks you wear, the roles you play, and the ways you behave. If you feel you have little worth, you probably expect to be taken advantage of. When you expect the worst, you usually get the worst. Similarly, if you feel you have significant worth, you probably expect to be treated fairly, supported, and otherwise held in esteem by others. When you expect to succeed, you usually find success.

The nature of the self at any given moment is a composite of all the factors that interact in a particular environment. Thus, how you look at yourself is affected by how you look at other people, how other people actually look at you, and how you imagine or perceive that other people look at you. We might say that self-concept is derived from experience and projected into future behavior. Of course, your self-concept may be realistic or unrealistic. Unfortunately, we never really come to know all there is to know about ourselves, so we keep searching for clues.

The language we use, the attitudes we display, and the appearances we present also change as we vary the masks we wear and the roles we perform. We become different selves as we move from one set of conditions to another. The more we attempt to be ourselves, the more selves we find. Conditions and circumstances affect the nature of the self.

Pessimism is self-fulfilling. Pessimists don't persist in the face of challenges, and therefore fail more frequently—even when success is attainable.

—Martin P. Seligman

Developmental psychologist Jean Piaget notes that the construction of the self occurs as a person acts on his or her environment and figures out what he or she can and cannot do.[18] In cyberspace, for example, if you don't like how you are

Ethics & Communication

Age, Physical Challenges, and Self-Esteem

Self-esteem may be related to age and physical ability. According to researchers Justine Coupland, John F. Nussbaum, and Nikolas Coupland, "elderly people are prone to assimilate society's devalued appraisals of their own social group, and so lower their self-esteem."[19] Similarly, researchers note that persons who are physically challenged often face myriad social barriers, primarily because they feel isolated from their peers and believe that their futures are limited and that their lives are less meaningful because of their disabilities.[20] On the other hand, in *Old Is Not a Four-Letter Word: A Midlife Guide,* author Ann E. Gerike notes that aging has advantages, bringing with it a more reliable inner voice, an acceptance that life is not always fair, and a willingness to shoulder responsibility instead of blaming others for what happens.[21] How do you feel about aging? What messages have you received from parents and older friends and relatives regarding their sense of self as they age? What messages do you send older or physically challenged people with whom you relate regarding your estimations of their worth and abilities?

How might online interactions with peers be used to transform the nature of self-

concepts and lives? For example, if a person imagines that others view him or her negatively, low self-esteem can result. In contrast, when a person imagines that others find him or her interesting, self-esteem may be improved. Log on to *Ability Online.* Describe the extent to which sites such as this one can facilitate the strengthening of self-esteem by helping reduce the effect of a person's disability on his or her self-concept.

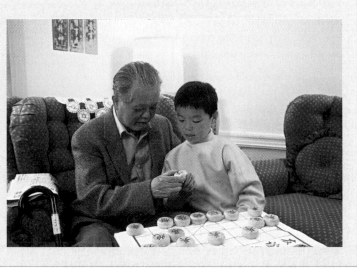

characterized or treated, you can change. Interacting online lets you reinvent yourself by morphing into different identities. This type of transformation is far different from being a student part of the day, an athlete another part of the day, an employee during the evening, and a child at home. In cyberspace you can have parallel identities or parallel selves and use them to develop better relationships and to manage more effectively the many selves that exist within you.[22] Technological innovations not only encourage us to reinvent ourselves to find success or happiness but also provide us the tools to do so.

When it comes to thinking about the self and who we want to be today, some of us categorize ourselves as optimists. If we suffer a defeat, we view it as a temporary setback brought about by circumstances, bad luck, or other people. Optimists are resilient; they do not view defeat as their own fault. Psychologist Albert Bandura tells us that an optimistic belief in our own possibilities and competence endows us with feelings of **self-efficacy.** (Note: We are talking about optimism, not unrealistic optimism based on overconfidence.) When we have strong feelings of self-efficacy, we are more persistent, less anxious, and less depressed. We don't dwell on our inadequacy when something goes wrong;

self-efficacy

an optimistic belief in one's own competence

instead, we seek a solution. Those of us who are persistent are apt to accomplish more. As we do so, our belief in ourselves grows.[23] Some of us categorize ourselves as pessimists. Unlike optimists, pessimists lack resilience and believe that bad events are their own fault, will last, and will undermine whatever they do. Instead of believing they can control their own destiny, pessimists believe that outside forces determine their fate. In effect, they "can't because they think they can't," in contrast to optimists, who "can because they think they can." Psychologist Martin Seligman tells this story:

> We tested the swim team at the University of California at Berkeley to find out which swimmers were optimists and which were pessimists. To test the effects of attitude, we had the coach "defeat" each one: After a swimmer finished a heat, the coach told him his time—but it wasn't his real time. The coach had falsified it, making it significantly slower. The optimists responded by swimming their next heat faster; the pessimists went slower on their next heat.[24]

Clues to self-understanding come to you continually as you interact with others and with your real-world or online environments. To understand yourself, you need to be open to information that other people give you. Just as we tend to categorize ourselves and others, so others tend to categorize themselves and us. For better or worse, the categorization process is a basic part of interpersonal communication. We classify people according to their roles, their status, their material possessions, their personality traits, their physical and vocal qualities, and their skills and accomplishments. Which of these categories are most important to you? Which do you think are most important to the people who are significant in your

According to the psychologist Martin P. Seligman, pessimists can learn to be optimists. How do you think optimism would enhance the self-concept?

Are you the person you think you are, the person someone else thinks you are, or the person you think someone else thinks you are? Why?

life? How do others help shape your image of yourself? How do they enhance or belittle your sense of self?

POPULAR MEDIA AND TECHNOLOGY: SEEING OURSELVES IN THE ELECTRONIC OR ONLINE LOOKING GLASS

What cultural values does advertising convey? Who is highlighted in the ads? How many ads focus on how people look and the lifestyles they have? Are there differences between the advertising messages aimed at women and those aimed at men? Are the messages different for members of cultural groups different from the one to which you belong?

Thus far we have established that your self-image is made up partly of information and feelings drawn from past experiences and partly from your interactions with others. At least five other important sources affect your opinion of who you are: television, film, radio and music, the print media (especially advertisements), and the Internet. We are all influenced by media images, including the personalities and characters that populate the media, to a greater extent than we may realize. Subtly but effectively, these visual and aural media shape our views of ourselves and our relationship to our world.

Let's consider some ways the popular media and the experience of growing up digitally affect the picture you have of yourself. First, many media and Internet offerings expose us to a standard of living few of us can expect to achieve. Thus, our evaluation of ourselves as providers—or even as successful—may be seriously colored by what we see. Second, media and online offerings may affect the ways parents and children perceive themselves and each other. After all, both parents and children are exposed to a steady succession of media counterparts who appear either so perfect that even their mistakes become the raw material of a closer relationship or so absurd that their foibles can only constitute charming comedy. Third, the visual media fill our need for a bigger, better, smarter, prettier, stronger personal image. When we were younger, it was easy and fun to try on television and film images. For example, we could become Harry Potter, a Power Ranger, Daredevil, Lara Croft, a Hobbit, Hermione Granger, Triple X, or Xena. As we mature, however, this process becomes more subtle. As adolescents, we attempt to become like popular idols or heroes by imitating their fashions, adopting their speech mannerisms, and copying their movements and gestures. Thus, we communicate the picture we have of ourselves, or the picture we would like to have, through the way we dress, move, speak, and so on. When you put on a certain outfit, comb your hair in a new style, walk or speak in a particular way, or choose to wear a certain artifact, you are telling other people something about who you think you are, whom you would like to resemble, and how you would like to be treated. Fourth, today's teenagers and young adults are often smarter on cyber issues and have more digital expertise than those for whom they work or learn. You are users, not just viewers or listeners, as were your parents. You have new, powerful tools for self-expression. Among teenagers, being online is now on a par with dating and partying. The parting line "Call me" has been replaced by "Send me an e-mail," or "T-M" or "I-M me."[25]

If you could trade places with any television or film star or character, who would you be? What does this person, real or fictional, "do" for you? Do you have a more positive image of this person than you have of yourself? Why? Would you like to be more like the media image, or would you like the image to be more like you?

The way the media depict the physically challenged can affect their self-concept and the way persons without disabilities relate to them. Some years ago, the Mattel corporation introduced the first disabled fashion doll, Share a Smile Becky, as a new friend for Barbie. According to a Mattel marketing manager, "Some kids want a doll that looks like them, and we wanted to make that

Media Wise

possible for kids in wheelchairs. But we hope all kids play with her."[26] Hopefully, the new doll helped break down barriers for children and others with disabilities, and children who played with this new doll became more comfortable interacting with persons who were physically challenged.[27] However, Drew Browning, an expert on portrayals of people with disabilities in the media, sees the introduction of such a doll differently. According to Browning, "It's telethon phraseology, implying people with disabilities need cheering up because they're so pitiful. It makes her sound like a Barbie poster child."[28] Browning believes that Beckie should have been Barbie, not merely her friend. What do you think?

Media and online offerings can support us or deflate us. They can cause us to feel good, adequate, or inferior.

EXPECTATIONS: THE SELF-FULFILLING PROPHECY AND THE PYGMALION EFFECT

Consider the following excerpt from *The People, Yes*, by poet Carl Sandburg:

> Drove up a newcomer in a covered wagon. "What kind of folks live around here?" "Well, stranger, what kind of folks was there in the country you come from?" "Well, they was mostly a lowdown, lying, gossiping, backbiting lot of people." "Well, I guess, stranger, that's about the kind of folks you'll find around here." And the dusty grey stranger had just about blended into the dusty grey cottonwoods in a clump on the horizon when another newcomer drove up. "What kind of folks live around here?" "Well, stranger, what kind of folks was there in the country you come from?" "Well, they was mostly a decent, hardworking, law-abiding, friendly lot of people." "Well, I guess, stranger, that's about the kind of people you'll find around here." And the second wagon moved off and blended with the dusty grey.[29]

The speaker in this passage understands the significance of the self-fulfilling prophecy. A **self-fulfilling prophecy** occurs when an individual's expectation of

self-fulfilling prophecy
a prediction or an expectation that comes true simply because one acts as if it were true

FIGURE 3.1

**The Self-Fulfilling Prophecy
in Action.**

Source: From "Self-Fulfilling
Prophecy: Better Management by
Magic" by Len Sandler in *Training:
The Human Side Of Business,*
February 1986. Copyright 1986 by
VNU Business Publications USA.
Reproduced by permission of VNU
Business Publications via the
Copyright Clearance Center.

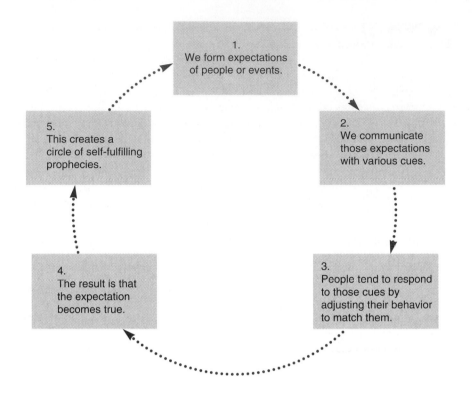

an event helps create the very conditions that permit that event to happen (see
Figure 3.1). In other words, your predictions can cause you and others to behave
in ways that increase the likelihood of an initially unlikely occurrence. For example, have you ever anticipated botching a presentation and then did so? Have you
ever assumed you wouldn't like someone and you turned out to be correct? Did it
occur to you that you might have acted in a way that caused your prediction to
come true?

Perhaps the most widely known example of the self-fulfilling prophecy is
the **Pygmalion effect.** The term comes from the Greek myth of Pygmalion, a
sculptor, who falls in love with a beautiful statue of his own creation. The god-
dess Aphrodite, moved by Pygmalion's obsession with the statue, comes to
his rescue and brings it to life. George Bernard Shaw adapted the story to a
more modern setting, and Shaw's version in turn served as the basis for the
stage and film musical *My Fair Lady.* In this version, Henry Higgins
(Pygmalion) seeks to transform a flower seller, Eliza Doolittle, into a refined,
well-spoken lady of the upper class. The play illustrates the principle that we
live up to labels. We, like Eliza Doolittle, learn to act like the sorts of people
others perceive us to be.

A real-life example of the startling effects of self-fulfilling prophecies is a classroom experiment described by psychologist Robert Rosenthal.[30] In the experiment,
teachers were notified that certain of their students were expected to bloom—that
is, to do exceptionally well—during the course of the school year. What the teachers did not know was that there was no real basis for this determination. The
experimenters had simply selected the names of the "bloomers" at random. Do you
think the selected students actually bloomed? If you said yes, you are quite right.

Pygmalion effect

the principle that we fulfill
the expectations of others

*Do you have any beliefs that
cause you to function in ways
that are self-defeating? What
are they? What can you do to
eliminate them?*

Those students did perform at a higher level than would otherwise have been expected and did improve their IQ scores.

Why did this happen? First, the teachers' expectations apparently influenced the way they treated the selected children. The teachers gave those students extra positive verbal and nonverbal reinforcement, waited patiently for them to respond if they hesitated, and did not react negatively when they offered faulty answers. Second, the way the teachers treated the students had a marked impact on the way the students perceived themselves and their own abilities. The bloomers responded to the prophecy that had apparently been made about them by fulfilling it.[31]

This treatment of students, choosing certain ones to succeed, continues. Researchers Myra and David Sadker describe their view of education in the book *Failing at Fairness: How America's Schools Cheat Girls:*

> Sitting in the same classroom, reading the same textbook, listening to the same teacher, boys and girls receive very different educations. From grade school through graduate school female students are more likely to be invisible members of classrooms. Teachers interact with males more frequently, ask them better questions, and give them more precise and helpful feedback. Over the course of years the uneven distribution of teacher time, energy, attention, and talent, with boys getting the lion's share, takes its toll on girls. Since gender bias is not a noisy problem, most people are unaware of the secret sexist lessons and the quiet losses they engender.
>
> Girls are the majority of our nation's schoolchildren, yet they are second-class educational citizens. The problems they face—loss of self-esteem, decline in achievement, and elimination of career options—are at the heart of the educational process. Until educational sexism is eradicated, more than half of our children will be shortchanged and their gifts lost to society.[32]

The self-fulfilling prophecy has important implications, not only for education but also for our personal lives. Have you ever joined a group of people you were convinced would not like you? What happened? Very likely you were proved right. What you probably did was act in a way that encouraged them to dislike you. The self-fulfilling prophecy also plays itself out in families. If a parent tells a child that he or she cannot do anything right, the child will soon incorporate this idea into his or her self-concept and fail at most of the tasks he or she attempts. In contrast, if a parent repeatedly demonstrates to a child that he or she is lovable or capable, the child will probably live up to that expectation as well.[33]

The Pygmalion effect is also at the root of many business problems.[34] Apparently, some managers treat employees in ways that precipitate superior performance, while many others unconsciously treat workers in ways that precipitate inferior performance. High expectations tend to result in increased productivity, whereas low expectations result in decreased productivity. Thus, subordinates more often than not confirm the expectations of their superiors. For this reason, when you assume a leadership role, you have the potential to function as both a positive and a negative Pygmalion. Which would be more effective?

What about the messages you send yourself? A variation of the Pygmalion effect is the **Galatea effect.** (Galatea is the name Pygmalion gave his statue once it was brought to life.) The Galatea effect refers to the expectations we have for ourselves rather than the expectations others have for us. We tend to realize the expectations we have for ourselves. We react to the internal mes-

Identify people who have functioned as positive or negative "Pygmalions" in your life. Then complete these sentences: I work best for people who . . . ; I work least for people who . . . .

Media are drawing attention to a new gender crisis: many colleges now admit and graduate more women than men. Some place the blame for this new gender gap on "feminized pedagogy" that emphasizes collaboration not competition. Are boys and men becoming the new "victims"? What do you think?

Biologists have determined that, technically speaking, the bumblebee cannot fly. Fortunately, the bumblebee doesn't know this. Remember: People rise no higher than their expectations.

Galatea effect
the principle that we fulfill our own expectations

sages we continuously send ourselves. Our feelings about our own competence and ability can exert an influence on our behavior in much the same way that our performance can be influenced by others' high or low expectations for us. Thus, how we and others answer the question, Who are you? affects how we behave.

GENDER: DO MALES AND FEMALES SEE THEMSELVES DIFFERENTLY?

Do you think you would feel differently about yourself if you were of the opposite sex? If you answered yes, is it because you believe that others would treat you differently? Would they encourage you to exhibit certain behaviors while at the same time discouraging you from exhibiting others?

Research tells us that others do treat us differently because of our gender. For example, we dress male and female babies in different colors and styles. For the most part, our prevalent conceptions of masculinity and femininity are reinforced in the television shows we view, the films we watch, the books we read, the toys we play with, and the online sites we frequent. For instance, young girls are given Barbies that say, "Let's go shopping," while young boys are given G.I. Joes that say, "Attack." A group calling itself the Barbie Liberation Organization attempted to call attention to such sexual stereotyping and make a statement about the way toys can influence behavior by switching G.I. Joe voice boxes with Barbie voice boxes, thereby altering the dolls to say the unexpected. The result? "A mutant colony of Barbies-on-Steroids who roar things like 'Attack!' 'Vengeance is mine!' and 'Eat lead, Cobra!' The emasculated G.I. Joes meanwhile twitter, 'Will we ever have enough clothes?'"[35] The point is that the experiences we have during our formative years influence our later views of masculinity and femininity, thus affecting our identities.

As soon as our gender becomes integrated into our self-concept, we form a gender identity. Once we learn the attributes of maleness and femaleness, our perceptions of self are affected by what we have come to believe about our gender. When asked to describe their characteristics, for example, males mention qualities such as initiative, control, and ambition. Females, in contrast, lead with qualities such as sensitivity, concern for others, and consideration. Appearance plays a major role in the self-image of a woman but is not nearly as integral to the self-image of a man.

Others may treat us differently because of our gender.

Why is this so? Can it be because, since infancy, greater emphasis is placed on a female's looks? Can it be because women, more than men, are teased about how they look and how much they weigh?[36]

Many women develop a less positive self-concept than men do. Our society expects those who are feminine to be nurturing, unaggressive, deferential, and emotionally expressive. Because of this expectation, young women are rewarded for having a pleasing appearance, revealing their feelings, being forgiving, and being helpful to others. While women of all ages appear to value relationships, adolescent girls become so preoccupied with pleasing others that they metaphorically "bend themselves into pretzels."[38] Girls are more likely to be self-critical and self-doubting than are boys. Men are more apt to develop an independent sense of self. Since men are expected to be strong, resilient, ambitious, in control of their emotions, and successful and, unlike women, are reinforced for displaying these qualities, independence is central to their lives.[39] Male characteristics typically are more highly valued by our society than are female characteristics. Thus, men often feel better about themselves than do women. And that may be why many women try harder and harder to attain success by attempting to be and do it all.[40] As Carol Leifer, a standup comic, expresses it: "I just had a baby an hour ago and I'm back at work already. While I was delivering, I took a course in tax-shelter options."

In one of his columns aptly titled "Beauty and the Beast," Miami Herald columnist and humorist Dave Barry reported that, for men, being considered average-looking is just fine; for women, being average is not good enough.[37] To what extent, if any, do your experiences support such findings and observations?

No one can make you feel inferior without your consent.

—Eleanor Roosevelt

DIVERSITY AND THE SELF-CONCEPT: HOW IMPORTANT IS THE "I"?

Diversity influences person-to-person interactions in both subtle and overt ways. It affects the way we look at the self, the expectations we have for ourselves and others, and our behavior. Our notion of self is shaped by our culture. Who we are, at least in part, emerges from participation in a culture.

In North American and Western European cultures, the self is considered paramount. People from these cultures tend to reflect the importance placed on individuals as they set and work toward the realization of personal goals. In contrast, people from Asia, Africa, and Central and South America, places where collectivistic cultures are dominant, are more likely to downplay their own goals, emphasizing instead goals set or valued by the group as a whole.[41] Japanese parents, for example, do not lavish praise on their children because they are concerned that, if they do, the children will end up thinking too much about themselves and not enough about the group.[42] In Western cultures, the assumption is that your life will be enriched if you are able to define who you are—all your possible selves. Stress is placed on the power of personal control. There is an intra-individual focus.[43] Even in popular culture, the focus is on self-reliance ("I Did It My Way"), self-realization ("I Gotta Be Me"), and self-love ("The Greatest Love of All"). In the United States, for example, we emphasize self-determination. In contrast to the independence emphasized in Western cultures, the emphasis in collectivistic cultures is on the interdependent self. Identity is not defined individually, but rather, in relation to others. Thus, the focus is extra-individual.[44]

For members of collectivistic cultures, the self is not of prime importance. In their view, the group, not the individual, is the primary social unit. Thus, whereas individualistic cultures link success with personal achievement,

online learning center

Go to the Online Learning Center at www.mhhe.com/gamble9 and answer the questions in the *Self Inventory* to evaluate your understanding of individualistic and collectivistic orientation.

collectivistic cultures link it to group cohesion and loyalty. This basic difference is symbolized by the fact that the "I" in the Chinese written language looks very much like the word for *selfish*.[45] While Western cultures emphasize self-promotion, Asian cultures decry self-importance and reward cooperation with the group. No one is singled out; members share credit and blame. Members of collectivistic cultures gain a sense of identity via their group memberships, not by stressing their self-importance, as members of Western cultures tend to do.[46] Loyalties in collectivistic cultures are directed at others instead of the self. For members of those cultures, the "we" takes precedence over the "I"; the self is not developed at the expense of the group. Thus, culture influences our whole notion of self.

idiocentric

exhibiting an individualistic orientation

allocentric

exhibiting a collectivistic orientation

distinctiveness theory

the theory stating that a person's own distinctive traits are more salient to him or her than are the more prevalent traits possessed by others in the immediate environment

Researchers use the terms **idiocentric** to refer to an individualistic point of view and **allocentric** to mean a primarily collectivistic way of thinking and behaving.[47] Which term would you use to describe your standpoint?

As you can see, your self-concept—how you define yourself—is influenced by your unique personal experiences as well as by your membership in a group or groups. Together with culture, these influences play integral parts in helping you formulate a sense of self. According to **distinctiveness theory,** a person's own distinctive traits (red-headed, minority group member, left-handed) are more salient to him or her than are the more prevalent traits (Caucasian, brunette, right-handed) possessed by other people in the immediate environment. For example, persons who are members of groups that are a numeric minority in the United States are more mindful of their ethnicity. For this reason, a White person is much less apt than a minority group member to mention his or her ethnicity when asked to define himself or herself. As a result, an African-American woman in a large group of Caucasian women will probably be well aware of her race. When the same woman is with a large group of African-American men, she is more conscious of her gender and less conscious of her race.[48]

 Exploring Diversity

Idiocentric versus Allocentric

Assess the extent to which you exhibit an individualistic (idiocentric) or collectivistic (allocentric) orientation by evaluating the following statements. If the statement is very important to you, rate it a 5; somewhat important, a 4; neither important nor unimportant, a 3; somewhat unimportant, a 2; and very unimportant, a 1.

I Matter

___ 1. I desire to prove my personal competency.

___ 2. I've got to be me.

___ 3. I want others to perceive me as having stature.

___ 4. I need to achieve personal fulfillment.

___ TOTAL

We Matter

___ 1. If I hurt you, I hurt myself.

___ 2. I desire harmony at all costs in my relations with others.

___ 3. My goal is to preserve the welfare of others, even if it is at my expense.

___ 4. I am loyal to tradition.

___ TOTAL

To determine your score, total the numbers you entered for each category. Which score is higher? A higher "I Matter" score indicates greater idiocentric tendencies. A higher "We Matter" score indicates greater allocentric tendencies.

Your culture also feeds your self-concept. For example, African-American girls tend to have higher overall self-esteem during their adolescent years than do Caucasian or Latina girls. According to Peggy Orenstein, Latina girls experience the most serious self-esteem crisis. She notes that between the ages of 9 and 15, the number of Latina girls who are happy with the way they are plunges by 38 percentage points.[49] Despite basic differences in orientation, however, young people throughout the world still share many attitudes regarding the self. Most are concerned about developing and maintaining social relationships, especially with their peers, and most are confident in their ability to assume responsibility for themselves in the future. However, despite this apparent optimism, about 25 percent of the teenagers described themselves as sad and lonely, emotionally empty, and overwhelmed by life's problems; these youngsters are burdened with the weight of poor self-images.

Young people are not the only group that describes themselves as lonely. The 2000 U.S. Census found that 27 million Americans live by themselves—more than twice the number of single-person households reported in 1970. Singles, including seniors, now constitute the largest census group. An editorial in the *New York Times* noted that although solitary living cannot be equated with loneliness, it may certainly involve some loneliness:

> If [individuals are] elderly, they may take great pleasure in having the wherewithal to live on their own, especially if they remember when the old depended on relatives for meals and a bedroom off the hall. If they're young, they may rejoice that the pressure's off, that marriage is no longer regarded as the ceremony that separates the desirable from the unwanted. On the other hand, they may not. To some of them, a home empty of companions may be synonymous with an empty life.[50]

In fact, more and more people are reporting that they experience transitory, if not persistent, bouts of loneliness.[51] People who describe themselves as lonely typically have difficulty making connections with other people. The loneliness they experience seems attributable to a gap between what they want and what they achieve in their social relationships.

If men define situations as real, they are real in their consequences.

—W. I. Thomas

DEVELOPING SELF-AWARENESS

To enhance our ability to communicate with others, we need to use ourselves as a resource. By focusing on and acknowledging ourselves, we become more aware of ourselves and more sensitive to our own thoughts and feelings.

Viewing Ourselves and Others: The Johari Window

Self-understanding is the basis of self-concept. To understand yourself, you must understand your own way of looking at the world. To understand others, you must understand how they look at the world.

Psychiatrist Eric Berne believes that we enact identity scripts—the rules for living we learned growing up that spell out our roles and how to play them.[52] He finds that we sometimes pattern our transactions in such a way that we repeatedly enact the same script with a different set of players. In other words, it is not

Focus on Service Learning

Choose an organization such as the American Cancer Society or a homeless shelter. Do some preliminary research about the organization, including but not limited to visiting its Web site before approaching it. Identify issues related to the purposes of the agency that could adversely affect the self-concept of the agency's clients. What strategies can you suggest the organization use to ameliorate harm to the clients' self-image?

FIGURE 3.2

The Johari Window

Source: From *Group Processes: An Introduction to Group Dynamics* by Joseph Luft. Copyright ©1984, 1970, 1963 by Joseph Luft. Reprinted by permission of The McGraw-Hill Companies.

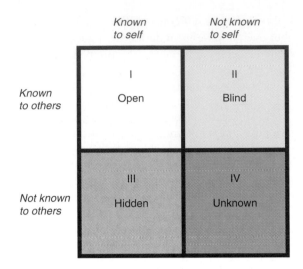

Johari window

a model containing four panes that is used to explain the roles that self-awareness and self-disclosure play in relationships

open area

the part of the self containing information known to both the self and others

blind area

the part of the self known to others but not known to oneself

hidden area

the part of the self that contains information about the self known to oneself but that is hidden from others

uncommon for us to attempt to "stage" dramas with casts of characters drawn from different phases of our lives. We might, for example, repeatedly enact life scenes in which we express the belief that others are out to get us or that they are jealous of us. This urge to repeat transactions can become a problem if it leads us to failure rather than to success. The remedy is to become aware of the scripts we enact, identify those that are not productive, and rewrite them. Once we are in control of the scripts we use, taking part as an active and not a passive player, we put ourselves in position to script our own lives.

At one time or another, we all wish that we knew ourselves or others better. The concept of self-awareness, basic to all functions and forms of communication, can be explored through a psychological testing device known as the **Johari window.** Joseph Luft and Harrington Ingham developed an illustration of a paned window to help us examine both how we view ourselves and how others view us.[53] Before proceeding further, let's look at the window (see Figure 3.2).

Pane I, the **open area,** represents information about yourself that is known to you and another. For example, your name, age, religious affiliation, and food preferences might all be found in this pane. The size and contents of the quadrant vary from one relationship to another, depending on the degree of closeness you share with that other person. Do you allow some people to know more about you than others?

Pane II, the **blind area,** contains information about you that others, but not you, are aware of. Some people have a very large blind area and are oblivious to their own faults and virtues. At times, people may feel compelled to seek outside help, such as therapy, to reduce the size of their blind area. Do you know something about a friend that he or she does not know? Do you feel free to reveal this information to your friend? Why? What effect do you think your revelation would have on your friend's self-image?

Pane III, the **hidden area,** represents your hidden self. It contains information you know about yourself but do not want others to find out for fear they will reject you. John Powell, author of *Why Am I Afraid to Tell You Who I Am?*

expresses the fear of rejection this way: "If I tell you who I am, you may not like who I am, and it is all that I have."[54] Sometimes it takes a great deal of effort to avoid becoming known, but at one time or another each of us feels a need to have people important to us know us well and accept us for what we are.

When we move information from Pane III to Pane I, we engage in the process of **self-disclosure.** Self-disclosure occurs when we purposely reveal to another person information about ourselves that he or she would not otherwise know. None of this is to suggest that the hidden area should not be allowed to exist within each of us. It is up to you to decide when it is appropriate for you to share your innermost thoughts, feelings, and intentions with others; it is also up to you to decide when complete openness is not in your best interest.

While self-disclosure is a process we normally control, what happens when this process is taken out of our control? What happens when another party, without our permission, takes information from our hidden area and reveals it in public? While anyone who knows us well can do this, some media practitioners have made a business out of forced disclosures. The late tennis star Arthur Ashe, for example, was forced to reveal he had AIDS, although he and his family preferred to keep it private, because otherwise the story of his condition would have appeared in a well-known tabloid. Florida Governor Jeb Bush's daughter had to deal with her drug problem under the scrutiny of the public eye. And because gay and lesbian groups threatened to go public with the news, David Hope, the Bishop of London, felt it necessary to announce his homosexuality.

Pane IV of the Johari window is the **unknown area** in your makeup. It contains information about which neither you nor others are aware. Eventually, education and life experience may help bring some of the mysteries contained in this pane to the surface. Only then will its content be available for examination. Have you ever done something that surprised both you and the people close to you? Did you and a friend ever exclaim together, "Wow! I didn't know I could do that!" "I didn't know you could do that!"

People commonly develop a style that is a consistent and preferred way of behaving interpersonally. Figure 3.3 illustrates four representative styles. Style A is characteristic of people who adopt a fairly impersonal approach to interpersonal relationships. Dominated by their unknown areas, these people usually withdraw from contacts, avoid personal disclosures or involvements, and thus project an image that is rigid, aloof, and uncommunicative. In Style B, the hidden area, or facade, is the dominant window. Here we find people who desire relationships but also greatly fear exposure and generally mistrust others. Once others become aware of the facade, they are likely to lose trust in these people. Style C is dominated by the blind area. People who are characterized by this style are overly confident of their own opinions and painfully unaware of how they affect others or are perceived by others. Those who communicate with such people often feel that their own ideas or insights are of little concern. In Style D, the open area, or area of free activity, is dominant. Relationships involve candor, openness, and sensitivity to the needs and insights of others.

Communication of any depth or significance is difficult if the people involved have little open area in common. In any relationship you hope to sustain, your

self-disclosure

the process of revealing to another person information about the self that this person would not otherwise know

What policy would you advocate the media follow regarding the disclosure of private information? Which in your opinion is more harmful: the media revealing a personal fact to the public that an individual did not want disclosed or someone whom you trusted revealing a personal fact about you to someone to whom you did not want to reveal the information?

unknown area

the part of the self that is unknown to oneself and others

The media have participated in a number of "outings"—that is, exposing the homosexuality of persons who until then had kept their sexual preferences a secret. In effect, the media have moved information from the hidden area of these persons into the open area without the permission of the persons being "outed." In your opinion, should anyone other than you ever be in control of what you reveal to or conceal from others?

Which style appears to be most characteristic of you and the people you interact with?

goal should be to increase the size of the open area while decreasing the size of the hidden, blind, and unknown areas. As human beings we are thinking about others and what they think about us. The question is whether we are able and willing to share what we are thinking.

FIGURE 3.3

Interpersonal Styles, in Terms of the Johari Window.

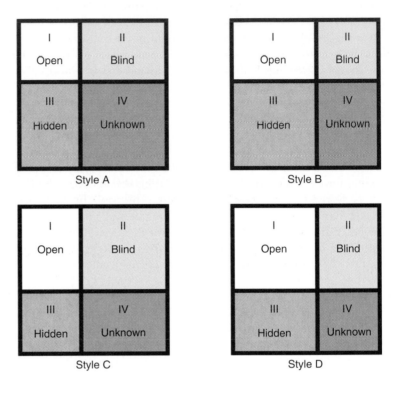

Style A

Style B

Style C

Style D

Skill Builder

Symbolizing the Self

Take four objects to class. The first object should reveal something about the way you see yourself, something you believe everyone recognizes about you. In other words, it should represent an aspect of your open area. The second object should reveal something about you that up until this point you believe resided in your hidden area. This second object could symbolize an attitude, feeling, desire, or fear that you had hoped to keep from others but are now willing to move into the open pane. The third object you bring to class should represent how you believe another person sees you. For example, do you believe that a friend or relative sees you

as you see yourself? How do you think your perceptions are similar? How are they different?

Finally, after selecting these three objects, ask someone else to choose an object that represents his or her perception of you. Take this fourth object to class along with the other three. Be prepared to discuss how your perceptions of yourself and the other person's perception of you conflict or coincide. For example, did the object selected by the other person help you move information from the blind area to the open area? To what extent has each phase of the experience altered the appearance of your Johari window?

MANAGING IMPRESSIONS

It is normal for us to want to present ourselves to others in desirable ways. However, this leads us to ask some questions: When we say something publicly, do we always feel it privately? Do we present a different self than we feel?

When we create a positive image of ourselves to influence what others think of us and how they view us, we are practicing **impression management.** Among the strategies we use to manage the impressions others have of us are *self-enhancement* (we bolster our own image) and *other-enhancement* (we bolster the image of others).

While the **perceived self** is the self we believe ourselves to really be, according to sociologist Erving Goffman, we use **facework** to present a public image, our *presenting self*, that is as favorable as possible to others. Oftentimes, we show different sides of ourselves to different people. Sometimes this choice is conscious and our communication is strategic—designed to accomplish a specific purpose. Other times, this choice is unconscious—in effect, we are on automatic pilot. What matters most is if the side we show is authentic, that is, a true reflection of our self-concept. If it is not, then as Goffman suggests, our front-stage behavior may contrast with our back-stage behavior or the behavior we exhibit when we are alone.[55] Do your experiences support this?

Human beings are unique in being able to observe their own behavior. **High self-monitors** are people who are highly attuned to their impression management efforts. **Low self-monitors** pay little attention to the responses others have to their messages. Still others believe that it is unethical to attempt to artificially control a communication by trying to present to others a version of you that is idealized; they believe it is disingenuous to treat relating to others like a performance. To which, if any, of these groups do you belong?

SELF-CONCEPT AND TECHNOLOGY

If you're interested in improving the impression you make on others, computer-mediated communication might give you an advantage. After all, the computer gives you more control over the information you choose to reveal to others as well as the information you choose to keep hidden. For example, e-mail enables you to edit the messages you send until you create one that will succeed in communicating the impression you desire. It gives you the ability to correct what you say and take back a message by not sending it. "Some communicators just do better when they can push the delete key."[56] Online you can also deliver messages that it might be too difficult to deliver, were you face-to-face, especially if you are shy. And if the receiver doesn't like the message you send, he or she can ignore it rather than have to walk away or insult you, were she or he in your presence.

The Internet may also be a factor in influencing the way we think of ourselves. If we have a positive self-concept, we are probably better able to adapt to both the rapid changes and the technological innovations of our world. Some use the Internet to see themselves differently. Do you? The Internet makes it possible for us to inhabit virtual worlds, participate in simulations, and assume different personae. A Pew Internet and American Life Project survey revealed, for example, that teenagers in the United States typically have more than one e-mail

---

impression management
the creation of a positive image designed to influence others

perceived self
the self we believe ourselves to be

facework
the means used to present a public image

high self-monitors
people highly attuned to impression management efforts

low self-monitors
people who pay little attention to responses others have to them

The following line is from T. S. Eliot's poem "The Love Song of J. Alfred Prufrock":

Prepare a face to meet the faces that you meet.

To what extent, if any, do you behave as the line advises?

Do you ever find yourself doing things in private, such as making faces at yourself in a mirror, that you would never think about doing in front of other people?

What if you were given the opportunity to design a personal Web site with the function of communicating you to all who accessed the site? The persons who open your site might be friends you already know or faceless, anonymous strangers. What aspects of yourself would you focus on? What facets would you ignore? How much would you reveal about yourself on the site? Would you include pictures or leave them out? To what extent, if any, do you think that having a personal Web site would enhance your ability to manage the identity you present to others?

"On the Internet, nobody knows you're a dog."

address or screen name. Many adopt multiple personae to hide their real identity from friends or strangers. A large number of people experiment online by pretending to be those whom they are not. They provide fake personal data in their e-mails or instant messages. In effect, they use the Internet to try out new identities.[57] By constructing a number of imaginary selves and experimenting with different kinds of social relationships, they are able to explore unexplored aspects of themselves. They might, for example, pretend to be the opposite sex, conceal their culture or where they live, and gloat as they hide any number of physical or psychological characteristics. Who we are online can simply be who we want to be for the moment. Instead of playing the roles we play in real life, when online, we might simultaneously play a number of varied roles that facilitate our thinking about ourselves in different ways. Because we are able to remain anonymous, we feel freer to cycle through many selves in an effort to construct and reconstruct our identity and assume roles that we otherwise would consider not part of our "real self."[58] Psychologist Sherry Turkle notes that, in an online world, "The obese can be slender, the beautiful plain, the 'nerdy' sophisticated."[59] Thus, for some people, communicating online gives them an opportunity to feel more positive about themselves.[60] In addition, some researchers believe that online interaction can affect psychological health. While some researchers believe Internet use correlates positively with depression and loneliness, others contend that it decreases them and actually enhances self-esteem.[61] In your opinion, is an online persona an extension of who you are in real life? Is it part of the real you or completely separate and distinct from your real-life self? Consider the following

Have you ever been anyone but yourself online? If so, what prompted you to adopt an alternative identity? If you spoke with people online who you later discovered were not who they represented themselves to be, how did you feel? What did you do?

comment by a woman who is about to come face-to-face with a man whom she met online:

> I didn't exactly lie to him about anything specific, but I feel very different online. I am a lot more outgoing, less inhibited. I would say I feel more like myself. But that's a contradiction. I feel more like who I wish I was. I'm just hoping that face-to-face I can find a way to spend some time being the online me.[62]

Blogs (Web logs) are another way people are using technology by creating online journals (virtual diaries) that define and reveal to others how they see themselves and their world. Using Google's Blogger.com, Diaryland.com, or Live-Journal.com, you can start a blog and receive feedback delivered via postings or even voice messages from its visitors. Visit the blogs of both someone you know and someone who is a relative stranger to you. What does each person's blog reveal to you about his or her self-concept and willingness to reveal him- or herself to others? What clues did you use to make your judgments?

To what extent, if any, is the computer changing the way you think and feel about yourself? In which environment, real or virtual, do you feel freer to experiment with who you are and who you can be? Why? What about that environment causes you to feel that way? Be specific. In your opinion, is the Internet an effective social laboratory for self-discovery? Explain with reference to specific sites and personal experiences.

IMPROVING SELF-AWARENESS AND AWARENESS OF OTHERS

Throughout this chapter, we have stressed that we all carry figurative pictures of ourselves and others with us wherever we go. Together, these pictures form a mental collage of past, present, and future images of ourselves—alone or interacting with other people. If you closely examine your various images, you probably will discern that how you look in each is related to when the picture was taken, what environment you were in, and with whom you were communicating. Each picture reveals a somewhat different you, because you change and grow from moment to moment, situation to situation, and year to year.

We sometimes forget that our self-image and our images of others can change. Keeping "self-pictures" updated and current is a challenge. Sharpening a fuzzy image, refocusing an old image, and developing a new image can help you discard worn-out perceptions of yourself and others. Use the following guidelines to improve the "picture-taking" skills you have gained while working your way through this chapter.

Take Pictures of Yourself and Others

You can increase your self-awareness by continuing to examine your self-image and your relationship to others. Developing a clear sense of who you are is one of the most worthwhile goals you can set for yourself. Be willing to watch yourself in action. Periodically examine your own self-perceptions—and your self-misconceptions.

Study the composite picture that emerges from your reflections. How close are you to becoming the person you would like to be?

Encourage Others to Take Pictures of You

How others perceive you may be very different from how you perceive yourself. Obtaining information from others can help you assess how realistic your

Thinking Critically

Reflect and Respond

First, agree or disagree with the following statement; state the reasons for your response.

I may not be what I think I am. I may not be what you think I am. I may well be what I think you think I am.

Then, consider this: Each of your friends, relatives, and co-workers probably sees you as a somewhat different person. Write a paragraph that describes your perception of how one person from each of these groups sees you. Who has the most positive view of you? Whose view, in your opinion, is most accurate? Why?

self-concept is. Others who come to know you may observe strengths you have overlooked, traits you undervalue, or weaknesses you choose to ignore. However, you do not have to accept all the pictures other people take of you.

No one can prevent you from adhering to your own beliefs and rejecting the opinions of others. Looking at other people's pictures of you does mean, however, that you are at least opening yourself to the possibility of change by attempting to see yourself as others see you.

Refocus, Refocus, Refocus

Carl Sandburg wrote, "Life is like an onion; you peel off one layer at a time." As you move from yesterday through today and into tomorrow, your self is in constant transition. Try not to let your view of yourself today prevent you from adapting to meet the demands of changing circumstances and conditions. Continually formulating new answers to the question, Who am I? will allow you to discover the vibrant, flexible, and dynamic qualities of your self.

The Wrap Up

Revisiting Chapter Objectives

1. **Define and explain the nature of the self-concept.** Self-concept is the entire collection of attitudes and beliefs you hold about who and what you are. It is the mental picture you have of yourself. It can be positive or negative, accurate or inaccurate. Your self-concept influences all aspects of your communicative behavior—with whom, where, why, and how you choose to communicate.

2. **Identify how different factors, including popular culture, help shape your self-concept.** You are not born with a self-concept. Rather, your self-concept is shaped by your environment, by its technology, and by those around you, including your parents, relatives, instructors, supervisors, friends, and co-workers. In addition, television and films, self-expectations and other people's expectations, gender, and culture can shape your opinion of who you are.

3. **Define *self-fulfilling prophecy* and explain how a self-fulfilling prophecy can influence behavior.** A self-fulfilling prophecy occurs when prior expectations of an event help create the very conditions that permit the event to occur. The prediction leads to the behavior. The media, as well as other people, help determine which self-fulfilling prophecies you experience.

4. **Compare and contrast the ways males and females as well as people from different cultures see themselves.** Once we learn the attributes of maleness and femaleness, what we believe about gender affects our perceptions of self. Males, for example, believe they display initiative, control, and ambition while females see themselves as sensitive, concerned for others and considerate. Culture similarly shapes people, determining whether they emphasize self-determination or interdependence, and whether they have an intra-individual or extra-individual focus.

5. **Identify the purposes and functions of the Johari window as a model of self-disclosure.** You can change and improve your self-concept by developing greater self-awareness and self-understanding. The Johari window can help you identify the open, blind, hidden, and unknown areas of your self.

Resources for Further Inquiry and Reflection

To apply your understanding of how the principles in Chapter 3 are at work in our daily lives, consult the following resources for further inquiry and reflection. Or, if you prefer, choose any other appropriate resource. Then connect the ideas expressed in your chosen selection with the communication concepts and issues you are learning about both in and out of class.

 Listen to Me

"Beautiful" (Christina Aguilera)
"I'm a Loser" (Beck)
"Human Nature" (Madonna)
"Eleanor Rigby" (The Beatles)
"Hands" (Jewel)
"Kim" (Eminem)
"Unpretty" (TLC)
"Lose Yourself" (Eminem)

The speaker or speakers in these songs express beliefs about how communication affects the self. Choose a song, and use it to explain the interaction between communication and self-concept.

 View Me

Beautiful
Girl Fight
Hoop Dreams
The Talented Mr. Ripley
Monster
The Truth about Cats and Dogs
American Beauty
Shrek

How do the incidents described in the film enhance your understanding of self-concept and its influence on person-to-person interaction?

"I know I'm wrong, but I'm sure you can make me more wrong."

 ### Read Me

What do the two cartoons above suggest about the self-concepts of males and females? Which do you believe is more accurate? Why?

 ### Tell Me

Share with the class the insights you gained from your chosen Listen to Me, View Me, or Read Me selection.

Women and men spend more on cosmetics and body alterations today than was spent in 1970, yet the number of women and men unhappy with their appearance has increased and will probably continue to do so. In a brief presentation, agree or disagree with this statement, and state the reasons for your position.

Key Chapter Terminology

Communication **Works**

online learning center

www.mhhe.com/gamble9

Use the Communication Works CD-ROM and the Online Learning Center at www.mhhe.com/gamble9 to further your knowledge of the following terminology.

allocentric 60
blind area 62
distinctiveness theory 60
facework 65
Galatea effect 57
hidden area 62
high self-monitors 65
idiocentric 60
impression management 65
Johari window 62
low self-monitors 65

open area 62
perceived self 65
Pygmalion effect 56
self-awareness 48
self-concept 48
self-disclosure 63
self-efficacy 52
self-esteem 48
self-fulfilling prophecy 55
self-image 48
unknown area 63

Idioms in Translation

growing up digitally—maturing in the Internet age

kill another person's self-esteem—cause his or her self-esteem to decrease

on automatic pilot—acting without deliberate effort or awareness

walk around on eggshells—be extraordinarily careful

Test Your Understanding

Go to the *Self Quizzes* on the Communication Works CD-ROM and the book's Online Learning Center at www.mhhe.com/gamble9.

Communication Works

online learning center

www.mhhe.com/gamble9

Notes

1. K. G. Wilson and S. C. Hayes. "Why It Is Crucial to Understand Thinking and Feeling: An Analysis and Application to Drug Abuse," *Behavior Analyst* 23, Spring 2000, pp. 25–43.

2. C. Mruk. *Self-Esteem: Research, Theory, and Practice*. New York: Springer, 1995.

3. See Maureen Stout. *The Feel-Good Curriculum: The Dumbing Down of America's Kids in the Name of Self-Esteem*. New York: Perseus Books, 2000; and Mary Amoroso. "Is Self-Esteem Overrated?" *The Record*, April 27, 2000, pp. HF-1, HF-3.

4. Adam Bryant. "America's Latest Fad: Modesty It's Not." *New York Times*, February 9, 1997, p. E-3.

5. Roy F. Baumeister, Jennifer D. Campbell. Joachim I. Krueger, and Kathleen D. Vohs. "Exploding the Self-Esteem Myth." *Scientific American*, January 2005, pp. 84–91.

6. Michele Orecklin. "Beware of the In Crowd." *Time*, August 21, 2000, p. 69.

7. R. Baumeister, L. Smart, and J. Boden. "Relation of the Threatened Egotism to Violence and Aggressions: The Dark Side of High Self-Esteem." *Psychological Review* 103, 1996, pp. 5–33.

8. B. Bushman and R. Baumeister. "Threatened Egotism, Narcissism, Self-Esteem, and Direct and Displaced Aggression: Does Self-Love or Self-Hate Lead to Violence?" *Journal of Personality and Social Psychology* 75, 1998, pp. 219–229.

9. Roy F. Baumeister, Jennifer D. Campbell, Joachim I. Krueger, and Kathleen D. Vohs. "Does High Self-Esteem Cause Better Performance, Interpersonal Success, Happiness, or Healthier Lifestyles?" *Psychological Science in the Public Interest* 4:1, May 2003, pp. 1–44.

10. Sharon Jayson. "Yep, Life 'll Burst That Self-Esteem Bubble." *USA Today*, February 16, 2005, pp. 1D, 2D.

11. Marlene Zuk. "A Case of 'Unwarranted Self-Regard,'" *The Record*, May 30, 2005, p. L-7.

12. See Rosabeth Moss Kanter. *Confidence: How Winning Streaks and Losing Streaks Begin and End*. New York: Crown, 2004.

13. Sharon Begley. "Real Self-Esteem Builds on Achievement, Not Praise for Slackers." *The Wall Street Journal*, April 18, 2003, p. B1.

14. Virginia Satir. *The New Peoplemaking*, 2nd ed. Palo Alto, CA: Science and Behavior Books, 1988.

15. See James Baron. "Who Are You? If You Had to Choose One Word That Best Defined You and Your Life, What Word Would It Be?" *New York Times*, February 13, 1994, sec. 9, pp. 1, 7.

16. See D. Hamacheck. *Encounters with the Self*, 3rd ed. Fort Worth: Holt, Rinehart & Winston, 1992, pp. 5–8.

17. S. I. Hayakawa and Alan R. Hayakawa. *Language in Thought and Action*, 5th ed. San Diego: Harcourt Brace Jovanovich, 1990, pp. 217–218.

18. See Jean Piaget. *The Construction of Reality in the Child.* New York: Free Press, 1954.

19. Justine Coupland, John F. Nussbaum, and Nikolas Coupland. "The Reproduction of Aging and Ageism in Intergenerational Talk." In Nikolas Coupland, Howard Giles, and John Wiemann, eds. *Miscommunication and Problematic Talk.* Newbury Park, CA: Sage, 1991, p. 85.

20. Don Tapscott. *Growing Up Digital: The Rise of the Net Generation.* New York: McGraw-Hill, 1998, p. 90.

21. A. Gerike. *Old Is Not a Four-Letter Word: A Midlife Guide.* Watsonville, CA: Papier Mache, 1997.

22. See also Sherry Turkel. *Life on the Screen.* New York: Simon & Schuster, 1995.

23. See A. Bandura. *Self-Efficacy: The Exercise of Control.* New York: Freeman, 1997.

24. Martin E. P. Seligman. Interview in *Success,* July–August 1994, p. 41. Used by permission of *Success* magazine.

25. Tapscott.

26. Linda Temple. "Is Barbie's Pal an Insult or an Inspiration?" *USA Today,* May 30, 1997, p. 7D.

27. Janelle Carter. "Barbie's Newest Friend Uses a Hot-Pink Wheelchair." *The Record,* May 22, 1997, p. A-17.

28. Temple.

29. Carl Sandburg. *The People, Yes.* New York: Harcourt Brace Jovanovich, 1936.

30. Robert Rosenthal and Lenore Jacobson. *Pygmalion in the Classroom.* New York: Holt, Rinehart & Winston, 1968.

31. R. Rosenthal. "The Pygmalion Effect and its Mechanisms," In J. Aronson, ed. *Improving Academic Achievement: Impact of Psychological Factors on Education.* San Diego: Academic, 2002, pp. 25–36.

32. Myra Sadker and David Sadker. *Failing at Fairness: How America's Schools Cheat Girls.* New York: Scribner's, 1994, p. 1.

33. See, for example, P. Watzlawick. "Self-Fulfilling Prophecies." In J. O'Brien and P. Kollock, eds. *The Production of Reality,* 3rd ed. Thousand Oaks, CA: Pine Forge, 2001, pp. 411–423.

34. J. Sterling Livingston. Cited in video, *The Self-Fulfilling Prophecy.* CRM Films, 1992.

35. David Firestone. "While Barbie Talks Tough, G.I. Joe Goes Shopping." *New York Times,* December 31, 1993, p. A-12.

36. T. F. Cash. "Development Teasing about Physical Appearance: Retrospective Descriptions and Relationships with Body Image." *Social Behavior and Personality* 23, 1995, pp. 123–130.

37. Dave Barry. "Beauty and the Beast," *Miami Herald,* January 30, 1998.

38. Diane Hales. *Just Like a Woman.* New York: Bantam, 1999, p. 136.

39. Julia T. Wood. *Gendered Lives: Communication, Gender and Culture.* Belmont, CA: Wadsworth, 1994, p. 21.

40. See Sally Quinn. "Look Out, It's Superwoman." *Newsweek,* February 15, 1993, pp. 24–25.

41. Richard Breslin. *Understanding Culture's Influence on Behavior.* Orlando, FL: Harcourt Brace Jovanovich, 1993, p. 47.

42. "Hey, I'm Terrific." *Newsweek,* February 17, 1992, p. 48.

43. Steven J. Heine. "Self as Cultural Product: An Examination of East Asian and North American Selves." *Journal of Personality* 69:6, December 2001, pp. 881–906.

44. Ibid.

45. Larry Samovar and Richard Porter. *Communication between Cultures.* Belmont, CA: Wadsworth, 1991, p. 91.

46. W. B. Gudykunst and S. Ting Toomy. *Culture and Interpersonal Communication.* Newbury Park, CA: Sage, 1988.

47. H. C. Triandis, K. Leung, and F. Clark. "Allocentric v. Idiocentric Tendencies." *Journal of Research in Personality* 19, pp. 395–415.

48. O. Appiah. "Americans Online: Differences in Surfing and Evaluating Race-Targeted Web Sites by Black and White Users." Paper presented at the annual meeting of the Association for Education in Journalism and Mass Communication. Miami, FL, August 2002.

49. P. Orenstein. *School Girls: Young Women, Self-Esteem, and the Confidence Gap.* New York: Anchor Books, 1994.

50. "In Truth, Most of Them May Not Be Lonely." *New York Times,* May 9, 1991, p. A-24. Copyright © 1991 by the New York Times Co. Reprinted with permission.

51. Robert A. Bell and Michael E. Roloff. "Making a Love Connection: Loneliness and Communication Competence in the Dating Marketplace." *Communication Quarterly* 39: 1, winter 1991, p. 58.

52. See Eric Berne. *Games People Play.* New York: Grove, 1964.

53. Joseph Luft. *Group Processes: An Introduction to Group Dynamics,* 2nd ed. Palo Alto, CA: Mayfield, 1970.

54. John Powell. *Why Am I Afraid to Tell You Who I Am?* New York: Tabor, 1982.

55. See E. Goffman. *The Presentation of Self in Everyday Life.* Garden City, NY: Doubleday, 1959, and *Relations in Public.* New York: Basic Books, 1971.

56. A. Markham. *Life Online: Researching Real Experience in Virtual Space.* Walnut Creek, CA: Alta Mira, 1998, pp. 202–203.

57. A. Lenhart, L. Rainie, and O. Lewis. *Teenage Life Online.* Washington, DC: Pew Internet and American Life Project, 2001.

58. Turkle, pp. 14, 178.

59. Turkle, p. 12.

60. John A. Bargh, Y. A. Katelyn McKenna, and Grainne M. Fitzsimons. "Can You See the Real Me? Activation and Expression of the 'True Self' on the Internet." *Journal of Social Issues* 58:1, January 2002, pp. 33–49.

61. See, for example, Larry M. Gant. "In Defense of the Internet: The Relationship between Internet Communication and Depression, Loneliness, Self-Esteem, and Perceived Social Support." *CyberPsychology and Behavior* 5:2, April 2002, pp. 157–172.

62. Turkle, p. 179.

CHAPTER 4

Communication and Perception: I Am More Than a Camera

After finishing this chapter, you should be able to

1. Explain why a person is more than a camera.

2. Define and explain how the following affect perception: the figure–ground principle, selective exposure, selective perception, closure, stereotyping, open and closed orientation, and first impressions.

3. Describe how past experience, gender, cultural background, the media, and technology can influence perception.

4. Define and provide examples of allness, blindering, and facts and inferences.

5. Identify ways to increase the accuracy of your perceptions.

If, to people, crickets appear to hear with their legs, it is possible that to crickets, people appear to walk on their ears.

—Anonymous

As I am, so I see.
—Ralph Waldo Emerson

Little Red Riding Hood Uncloaked: Sex, Morality and the Evolution of a Fairy Tale takes a look at the childhood fairy tale about the little girl who sets off to visit her grandmother only to find herself interrupted by a big bad wolf who seeks to eat both her and her granny. Over the centuries, the Little Red Riding Hood story has been interpreted and rewritten. In some versions, a hunter saves Little Red Riding Hood; in others, she saves herself. Critics, similarly, have different views of the tale. One critic sees it as a parable of rape, while another sees it as a parable of retribution. The moral in some versions stresses the dangers of promiscuity, while in others, it speaks of the danger of trusting strangers, or the importance of obedience to a parent. What does Little Red Riding Hood represent for you? What do the different versions tell us about the nature of perception?

What is the relationship between perception and communication? As we will see, perception and communication are connected to, interact with, and influence each other. Perception influences how we understand situations, other people, and ourselves. We do not, for example, perceive our friends and those we label strangers in the same way. Similarly, communication influences all our perceptions. The meanings we form and the messages we send to others about what we see and how we think shape their understanding of events and us.

Why is it that we develop different meanings for the same events? How can we account for perceptual and communication gulfs? Is it because the media have segmented themselves, appealing to members of different co-cultures? Is it because Republicans and Democrats, Middle Easterners and Westerners are spoken about and to as if they live on different planets?[1] People living in different countries, the members of different generations, and the members of different genders, races, religions, or classes (just to name a few groups) are likely to perceive things differently. So are the members of the media. On a single day, for example, the three largest newspapers in the United States had three different headlines concerning drugs and AIDS: "Vaccine for AIDS Shows Promise" (*USA Today*), "Large Trial Finds AIDS Vaccine Fails to Stop Infection" (*The New York Times*), and "Steep Price of Roche AIDS Drug May Put It Out of Patients' Reach" (*The Wall Street Journal*).[2] Whether we are talking about drugs, politics, international relations, a fairy tale, other people, or ourselves, interpretation mirrors ideology.

Can we ever experience or see the same things? Can we ever believe our own eyes?

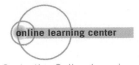

Go to the Online Learning Center at www.mhhe.com/gamble9 and answer the questions in the *Self Inventory* to evaluate your understanding of perceptual differences.

In this chapter, we will attempt to answer questions about perception as we explore how we perceive our world and the people in it. By learning more about the process of perception, we will prepare ourselves to better handle the continuing problems posed by perceptual variations. By exploring why stimuli appear different to each of us, we will better understand why we think and act differently as well. Only by getting behind the "I" of the eye do we put ourselves in a position to understand why "where we stand depends on where we sit."[3]

■ ■ ■

WHAT IS PERCEPTION?

Perception is a complex process. Certainly we use our senses to perceive, but perception includes more than just the eye alone, the ear alone, the nose alone, the skin alone, and the tongue alone. What occurs in the "real world" may be quite different from what we perceive to occur. During perception, we make experience our own. We define **perception** as the process of selecting, organizing, and subjectively interpreting sensory data in a way that enables us to make sense of our world.

perception

the process by which we make sense out of experience

Perceiving Stimuli: The "Eye" and the "I"

We all inhabit different worlds. We view reality from different angles, or vantage points. Our physical location, interests, personal desires, attitudes, values, personal experiences, physical condition, and psychological states interact to influence our judgments or perceptions.

What if you woke up tomorrow as a person of a race or ethnicity different from your own? How do you imagine your view of your life and the world would change? Would a change in age affect you the same way? What about a change in gender?[4]

How do you absorb information from the world around you? Do you look and listen? Do you touch, taste, and smell your environment and those who interact in it? Certainly. Your senses function as perceptual antennae and gather information all the time.

However, it is impossible for you to process all the stimuli available to you. Without realizing it, you take steps to select or limit what you perceive. You will see this for yourself if you try the following test:

1. For the next 60 seconds, attempt to internalize everything that exists in the room you now inhabit. Make an effort to react to each sound, sight, smell, touch, and taste that is present in your environment.
2. Were you able to focus simultaneously on each stimulus or sensory experience, or did you find yourself skipping from one stimulus to another and back again?

How do you imagine your perception would change were it necessary for you to move around in a wheelchair? Besides making you feel shorter, how would your new height affect what you would be able to see and access easily?

Most probably, you found yourself switching between stimuli; thus, you are aware that you simply cannot effectively handle, or process, all the sensory experiences that compete for your attention. Information theorists tell us that the eye can process about 5 million bits of data per second; they also tell us that the brain can utilize only some 500 bits per second. We are therefore forced to identify or select those stimuli we will attend to or experience. By exhibiting **selective perception**—an aspect of the perceptual process that includes both selective exposure and selective attention—you expose yourself to and attend to particular stimuli while ignoring others. Selective perception enables you to create a more limited but more coherent and meaningful picture of the world, one that conforms to the beliefs, expectations, and convictions you hold.

Perceptual processes are not only highly selective but also personally based. For this reason, different people experience the same cues in very different ways. Thus, we never really come into direct contact with reality.[5] Instead, everything we experience is manufactured by the nervous system.

Organizing Stimuli: The "I" of the Beholder

We have said that perception provides each of us with a unique view of the world—a view sometimes related to, but not necessarily identical with, that held by others. Since we cannot actually become one with the world out there, we are forced to use our senses to help create a personal picture of the people and objects that surround us. How do we make sense of our world? How do we process the stimuli that compete for our attention?

During the perception process, we are active, not passive, participants. We do not simply relax and absorb stimuli available to us, the way a sponge absorbs liquid. We select, we organize, and we evaluate the multitude of stimuli that bombard us, so that what we focus on becomes figure and the rest of what we experience becomes ground.[6] This is how the **figure–ground principle** functions.

selective perception
the means of interpreting experience in a way that conforms to one's beliefs, expectations, and convictions

figure–ground principle
a strategy that facilitates the organization of stimuli by enabling us to focus on different stimuli alternately

Do different people perceive you differently? Why?

"Wernock, here, sees your suit as half empty, but I see it as half full."

FIGURE 4.1

Figure and Ground. Do you see a vase or two people?

To experience the concept of figure and ground, examine Figure 4.1. What do you see? At first glance, you probably see a vase—or you may see two people facing each other. When stimuli compete for your attention, you can focus on only one, because it is simply impossible to perceive something in two ways at once. Although you may be able to switch your focus rapidly, you will still perceive only one stimulus at any given time. The same holds true for Figure 4.2. When you look at Figure 4.2(a), you may see a duck, a rabbit, or both alternately. In Figure 4.2(b), you may see the profile of an Indian, the back of an Eskimo walking away, or both alternately.

In addition to using the principle of figure–ground as an organizing strategy, we also use **closure**—the tendency to fill in missing perceptual pieces. Look at the stimuli pictured in Figure 4.3. What do you see? Most see a dog rather than a collection of inkblots and a rectangle, triangle, and circle rather than some lines and an arc. Because we seek to fill in gaps, we mentally complete the incomplete figures. We fill them in on the basis of our previous experiences and our needs. We make sense of relationships and events in much the same way. We fill in what is

closure

the tendency to fill in missing perceptual pieces to perceive a complete world

FIGURE 4.2

Figure-Ground Illustrations: (a) Duck or Rabbit? (b) Eskimo or Indian?

Source: Mitsuko Saito-Fakunage, "General Semantics and Intercultural Communication," *ETC,* Vol. 46, no. 4, Winter 1989, p. 27. Reprinted by permission of the International Society for General Semantics.

(a)

(b)

FIGURE 4.3
Test for Closure.

not there by making assumptions, or inferences—some of which are more accurate and valid than others.

Processing Stimuli: The "I's" Memories

As we see, perception involves a series of stages: (1) the selecting stage, during which we attend to only some stimuli from all those to which we are exposed; (2) the organizing stage, during which we give order to the selected stimuli; and (3) the interpreting/evaluating stage, during which we make sense of or give meaning to the stimuli we have selected and organized based on our life experiences (see Figure 4.4). Perception also involves a fourth stage, the responding stage, during which we decide what to think, say, or do as a result of what we have perceived. How we interpret and respond to selected stimuli also determines whether or not a particular person or experience enters our memory. If a perception does enter our memory, we can retrieve it at another point in time. Whether or not our memory is reliable, however, depends on whether our reconstruction of experience is accurate and clear. Our perceptual abilities influence how we interpret and remember events. For example, many Americans have vivid memories of September 11, 2001. In interviews, when asked to recall those memories, people spoke of watching television all morning, riveted to the TV by images of the two planes striking the twin towers. Their memory of what they think they witnessed is false. There was no video that day of the first plane hitting the North Tower of the World Trade Center. Despite this, 76 percent of New Yorkers surveyed said they saw it on September 11, as did 73 percent of people nationwide. What is more, they were confident about their memories. Memories of events that did not actually happen the way we remember them are at the root of countless disputes; they are reminiscent of these lines from an old Lerner and Lowe song: "We met at nine,"

FIGURE 4.4
Stages of Perception.

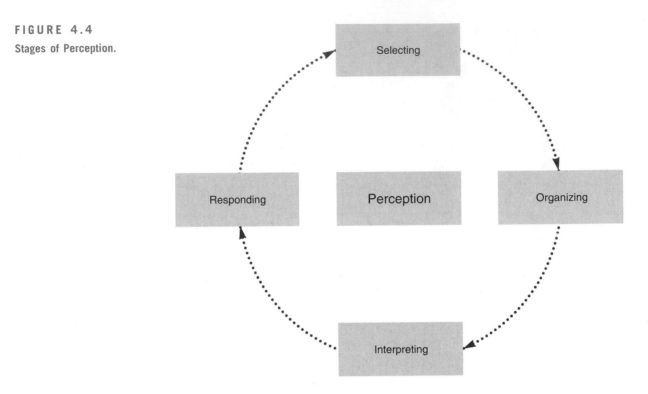

"We met at eight," "I was on time," "No, you were late." "Ah yes, I remember it well!"* What we remember depends on what we believe, even if what we believe never happened or is based on misinformation that subsequently was retracted.[7] Memory is a human construct, an amalgam of what we experience, read, piece together, and want to be true. A number of reasons account for our misremembering events: (1) Memories are transient and tend to fade over time; (2) we remember aspects of an event but are likely to misattribute them; and (3) our biases distort our recollections. In other words, our memories are fallible.[8] When it comes to memory, there is little correlation between confidence and accuracy.

Skill Builder

Memories in Conflict

Despite our best efforts to interpret and recollect the past accurately, sometimes transience, misattribution, and bias keep us from doing so. Identify examples from your own experiences, from history, or from the legal system that illustrate the problems that can develop if recollections of an event conflict. What steps can we take to help remedy the reality that our expectations color our memories?

---

*"I Remember it Well." Words and Music by Alan Jay Lerner and Frederick Loewe © 1957, 1958 Chappell & Co. Copyrights Renewed. All rights reserved. Used by permission.

CULTURE, GENDER, AND PERCEPTION: INTERPRETING THROUGH DIFFERENT "I"S

There is more to perception than meets the eye. We see the world not necessarily as we are but as we have been conditioned to see it. Our culture, our gender, and our past experiences precipitate in us a preference for **perceptual constancy**—the desire to see exactly as we have seen in the past. Thus, many of our perceptions are learned. The more similar our life experiences, the more similarly we will perceive the world. The more dissimilar our life experiences, the wider the gap between us and others with respect to the way we view things.[9] Not everyone perceives things the same way we do. Cultural habits or selectivities see to that.

perceptual constancy
the desire to perceive experience exactly as we have perceived it in the past

Culture and Perception

Culture teaches us how to perceive. For example, when looking at configurations created by the craters on the moon, North Americans see a man, while Native Americans report a rabbit, the Chinese a lady fleeing her spouse, and Samoans a woman weaving.[10] Whether we are judging beauty, describing snow, or evaluating a child's behavior, our culture influences our assessment of reality. Individuals from different cultures are simply trained to regard the same cues differently; they interpret what they perceive through a cultural lens. Some years ago, researchers used a binocular-like apparatus to compare the perceptual preferences of Native Americans and Mexicans. Each subject was shown 10 pairs of photographs—in each pair, one photo displayed a picture from U.S. culture and the other photo, a picture from Mexican culture. After viewing the paired images through the binocular-like device, the subjects reported their observations. Results showed that both the Native Americans and the Mexicans were more likely to report having seen a picture from their own culture.[11] Similarly, most of us find it easier to interpret the emotions communicated via the verbal and nonverbal facial expressions of members of our own culture than those expressed by members of other cultures. We also tend to be more perceptually accurate in recognizing and interpreting the expressions of emotion sent by members of our own culture.[12]

Have you ever considered why the United States almost always appears in the center in our maps of the world? Is there any geographical reason for this? Or could it be an example of ethnocentrism on the part of mapmakers and users?

Additionally, culture teaches us to expect others to behave in certain ways when faced with specific conditions. Misunderstandings can result, however, when each party in an interaction is operating according to different assumptions and rules. For North Americans, talk is desirable and is perceived as a tool used to achieve goals or to complete tasks. They view the opposite of talk, silence, more negatively. Because North Americans tend to value directness and honesty, they are likely to perceive someone who fails to "tell it like it is" as either vague or cowardly. In contrast, members of Asian cultures value silence, believing that one who understands need not speak. From the Asian perspective, a person who states the obvious is merely showing off. Can you see how not understanding the perceptions of the members of both cultures could lead to difficulties in communicating?

We have not all experienced the same lessons, and thus we do not attribute the same meanings to similar behavioral cues. When we fail to understand this concept, we exhibit **cultural nearsightedness**. We misread cues and miss opportunities to use the differences between us as a means to help ourselves perceive each other more clearly.

cultural nearsightedness
the failure to understand that we do not all attribute the same meanings to similar behavioral clues

Gender and Perception

Like ethnicity, gender influences the interpretation of experience. Men and women have different standpoints, perceive different realities, have different expectations set for them, and exhibit different communication styles. Beliefs regarding gender-appropriate behavior not only influence how men and women see each other but also affect how they relate to each other. From childhood on, both men and women are conditioned to use behaviors that conform to their gender: While men are rewarded for displaying strength and independence, women are reinforced for expressing their feelings and being nice to others. While women are categorized as emotional, men are classified as rational.[13]

Through interaction with parents, teachers, peers, and others, we internalize the lessons of appropriate male and female behavior. These lessons frame our perceptions and teach us how society expects us to behave. These constructs, however, can limit the way each gender is perceived and may lead to males' and females' being judged on the basis of gender expectations rather than observed cues. Perceived differences between male and female behavior develop as a result of others' expectations, the behavior role models exhibit, the traditional educational institutions that promote stereotyped notions of sex roles, and the media that send repeated confirmation of male and female stereotypes.[14] If we want to change the perception of the kinds of behavior appropriate for males and females, then we need to change the way society categorizes them.

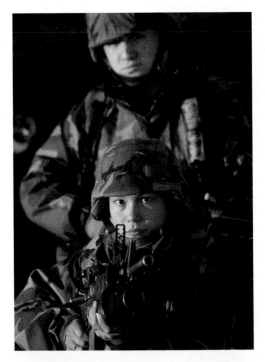

Are these women redefining a gender prescription? Will their behavior change how others perceive them?

As we perceive, we sort stimuli, selecting some and rejecting others. What we select and store in our internal database determines our view of reality and gives our lives a sense of stability. If, for example, we conclude that men are more dominant than women, then we feel we can more readily predict their actions and thus recategorize them as such. When expectations lead to misperceptions, undesirable consequences can result. All too frequently, rigid categorizing creates communication problems. For example, a recent *New York Times Magazine* contained a series of full-page photographs depicting women soldiers. Titled "Warrior Women," the series acknowledged the change in the Pentagon's perception regarding the types of positions in which women could serve.[15] Although still barred from roles that have specific physical requirements and from units primarily involved with frontline battle, because modern warfare may have no perceptible front line at all, women can come under attack and easily become casualties. Thus, the list of women injured or killed in combat situations is likely to rise. Are you perceptually ready for this change? Why or why not?

Similarly, criticisms of mass media productions often include a discussion of how women and minorities are systematically excluded and/or relegated to minor roles or roles that are consistent with traditional stereotypes. These portrayals reinforce perceptions that perpetuate racism and sexism.[16]

Individual men and women, however, can reject cultural prescriptions, and when they do so, they elicit changes in the behavior of others toward them. As we defy a gender-based definition, we also help redefine it. When, for example, one woman encourages another to be more independent, she may help her friend expand her definition of behavior appropriate for women. As women change their behavior and roles, men may perceive them and themselves differently and may change as well. As we widen our perceptions of each other by experiencing a greater variety of situations and people, we may alter our expectations for each other and revise our views of what males and females can do as well. In the process, we recast what masculinity and femininity mean.

Which gender-based definitions, if any, have you helped redefine?

BARRIERS TO PERCEPTION

Many variables affect us during the perceptual process, interacting to guide us in making our perceptual selections. Some of these constitute barriers to perception.

Perceptual Sets: Is Your Past Following You?

Past experiences often provide us with expectations, or **perceptual sets,** that affect how we process our world. To better understand the concept of a perceptual set, quickly read the statements written in the triangles in Figure 4.5. Then examine the words more carefully. During your first reading, did you miss anything that you now perceive? Many people fail to see the second *the* or *a* in the statements on the first reading. Did you? Why? We are so accustomed to seeing words in familiar groups, or clusters, that often we simply fail to perceive a number of single words when we see them in such phrases. Faster, more accomplished readers make this mistake more readily than slower, less skillful readers.

Past experiences create perceptual sets in numerous ways. Sometimes culture is a factor. In Saudi Arabia, for example, the way women are raised influences how people both within that culture and outside it perceive them. In Saudi Arabia, women have few legal rights, are usually not permitted to drive a car, and need a man's permission to obtain a passport; clearly, the Saudis and Americans perceive women very differently.[17]

Motivation is another variable affecting our perceptual sets and thus our perception. Both hunger and poverty, for instance, can alter the way we interpret experience. In one study, researchers showed sailors some ambiguous pictures and asked them to describe what they saw. Sailors who were hungry "saw with the

perceptual sets

expectations that produce a readiness to process experience in a predetermined way

FIGURE 4.5
Test for Perceptual Sets.

Barefoot
in the
the park

Snake
in the
the grass

Busy
as a
a beaver

stomach"—to them, an elongated smudge looked like a fork, and a swirl looked like a fried onion. In a second study, rich and poor children were shown circles of various sizes and were asked which ones were the same size as certain coins. The poor children consistently chose circles that were much too large. Why? A quarter looks bigger to the poor than to the rich.[18]

Obviously, education is also an important part of our past experience. How much education and what kind of education we have had affect the way we process and perceive information.[19] For instance, you may find that your views of television and other media have changed since you were in grade school and that they will change again as you acquire additional education. (Young children, for example, view television commercials as absolute truths.) At times, education can become a barrier rather than a facilitator of or aid to perception. When asked to interpret a stimulus as simple as a nursery rhyme or as complex as a world event, a sociologist, an economist, a political scientist, or a biologist might bring her or his specific professional bias to the assignment, which could blind each person to other possible interpretations.

As is apparent, perceptual sets are the result of unique experiences. The lessons life has taught you necessarily differ from those life has taught others. As a result, people can perceive the same stimulus differently.

Exploring Diversity

What Do You See? What Do You Think?

1. Patricia Williams, the author of *Seeing a Color-Blind Future,* asks: "How can it be that so many well-meaning white people have never thought about race when so few blacks pass a single day without being reminded of it?" How would you answer her? In your opinion, is color blindness a legitimate hope for the future? Why or why not?

2. If education influences perception, do you think that Congress should pass an Academic Bill of Rights to ensure that a diversity of dissenting viewpoints are heard in all your classes? Why or why not?

Which man looks guilty? If you picked the man on the right, you're wrong. Wrong for judging people based on the color of their skin. Because if you look closely, you'll see they're the same man. Unfortunately, racial stereotyping like this happens every day. On America's highways, police stop drivers based on their skin color rather than for the way they are driving. For example, in Florida 80% of those stopped and searched were black and Hispanic, while they constituted only 5% of all drivers. These humiliating and illegal searches are violations of the Constitution and must be fought. Help us defend your rights. Support the ACLU. www.aclu.org **american civil liberties union**

Exploring Selectivities: Are You Open or Closed? Are You a Distorter?

Four types of selectivity concern us: (1) **selective exposure**—the tendency to expose ourselves to information that reaffirms existing attitudes, beliefs and values; the tendency to close oneself to new experiences; (2) **selective attention**—the tendency to focus on certain cues and ignore others; (3) *selective perception*—the tendency to see, hear, and believe only what we want to; and (4) **selective retention**—the tendency to remember those things that reinforce our way of thinking and forget those that oppose our way of thinking.

A key factor in how we view our world is the extent to which we open ourselves to experiences. Although numerous sensory stimuli compete for our attention, we tend to practice selective exposure; we select only those experiences that reaffirm our existing attitudes, beliefs, and values. We likewise tend to ignore or diminish the significance of those experiences that are incongruent with our existing attitudes, beliefs, and values. Just as children sometimes place their hands over their ears to avoid hearing what a parent is saying, so we select what we will perceive by deciding whether to expose ourselves to a variety of types and sources of information. When driving through poverty-stricken areas, for example, people often roll up their automobile windows. They tell themselves that they are doing this for self-protection, but rolling up the windows is also a means of self-deception that helps them avoid contact with some of the depressing sights and sounds of their society. How difficult is it for you to expose yourself to certain new ideas, places, or experiences? As for selective attention, you are more apt to overhear someone seated near you speak of wanting to buy a home if you are a real estate agent than if you are in computer sales. Selective perception is a related concept. When it comes to selective perception, we tend to overlook negative qualities in persons we like, just as we tend to deemphasize the negative policies of institutions we support. We see what we want to see and hear what we want to hear. As a result of selective perception, different people may interpret the same message or event differently.

Finally, our memories aid us in this process by enabling us to engage in selective retention—we recall better the positive qualities of persons we like and the negative qualities of persons we dislike. Perception is subjective. What we think about as well as what we think about one another are powerful forces. The reality is that we can bias the selection process and end up with quite a distorted view of the people in our lives as well as the world. For example, think about a relationship that has soured and that you are planning to terminate. Since making this decision, have you become more aware of qualities the person has that you do not like? Why do you suppose this is so? When we like or love someone, we tend to perceive primarily his or her positive qualities. This is called the **halo effect.** However, when our perception of another changes for the worse, we are more likely to see only his or her negative qualities. This is called the **horn effect.**

First Impressions: Do You Freeze Your Perceptions of Others?

How important are **first impressions**? Do the snap judgments we make about people matter? According to a study by researchers Artemio Ramirez and Mike Sunnafrank,

selective exposure

the tendency to expose oneself to information that reaffirms existing attitudes, beliefs and values

selective attention

the tendency to focus on certain cues and ignore others

selective retention

the tendency to remember those things that reinforce one's way of thinking and forget those that oppose one's way of thinking

Try viewing the same news broadcast with someone whose political views differ sharply from your own. How similar do you imagine your interpretations of the delivered information will be? Why?

Can you cite instances when you chose not to expose yourself to a certain stimulus or idea? Are there some subjects you would prefer not to know about? Are there some people you would just as soon avoid?

halo effect

the perceiving of qualities that are primarily positive

horn effect

the perceiving of qualities that are primarily negative

first impressions

initial judgments about people

"You're not at all like your answering machine."

assessments made during the first few minutes of meeting someone strongly influence the nature of a relationship. Ramirez and Sunnafrank randomly paired 164 college freshmen in a communications class, let them chat for 3, 6, or 10 minutes, and then asked them to predict the kind of relationship they would share, ranging from casual acquaintance to close friend. At the end of the course, students were again asked to assess their predictions. Results revealed that students who reported a positive impression were more likely to have developed a friendly relationship even if they were given only 3 minutes to make their assessment. The results support the predicted outcome value theory developed by Sunnafrank, which says that when we first meet another person, we predict the probable outcome of our relationship and try the hardest to develop relationships we expect to be rewarding.[20]

On what basis do you make initial judgments about the people you meet? What makes you decide if you like or dislike someone? Is it his or her economic status? Is it the job he or she holds? Perceiving others and the roles they play is

Skill Builder

What's on First?

Person A. Read the following list of A's character traits to another person, in the order given:

1. intelligent 4. critical
2. industrious 5. stubborn
3. impulsive   6. envious

Ask that person to choose one word to represent his or her impression of A.

Person B. Next, read this list of B's character traits to another person, in the order given:

1. envious   4. impulsive
2. stubborn   5. industrious
3. critical   6. intelligent

Then, ask the person to choose one word to represent his or her impression of B.

an essential part of the communication process. In this section, we will explore how we form first impressions and why we sometimes stereotype other people. We will attempt to determine why we often feel it is necessary to "freeze" our perceptions of people to conform to our expectations.

If you analyze the responses you obtain for the Skill Builder entitled "What's on First?" (adapted from an experiment conducted by Solomon Asch[21]), you'll find that people usually attribute positive qualities to person A, selecting a descriptive word with very positive connotations. In contrast, person B is often perceived as possessing negative qualities, and for this reason the word chosen to describe B also has negative connotations. Why? The answer seems to be simply that the first list begins with positive traits and the second begins with negative traits; otherwise, each list is precisely the same. Thus, first impressions can dramatically affect perception. In addition, a first impression—or **primacy effect,** as it is sometimes called—can even affect the result of communication efforts. Trial lawyers, for example, depend to some degree on the primacy effect when selecting jurors. The first impression that potential jurors make on attorneys will often determine whether the attorneys accept them or use peremptory challenges to remove them from consideration.

primacy effect
the ability of one's first impression to color subsequent impressions

Even if our first impressions are wrong, we tend to hold on to them. Doing this can cause a number of problems. For example, if the opinion we have of someone is erroneous, we can sustain our inaccurate perception by clinging to it and reshaping the conflicting information available to us until it conforms to the image we hold. Thus, we may never come to experience the real person—only our faulty conception of him or her. And it is this faulty conception that will influence the way we respond to that person. Suppose, for instance, you make a new friend, Kevin, at work. You tell an old friend about him. Your old friend tells you, "Yeah. I know that guy. Worked with him two years ago. He's nothing but trouble. Always looking to use people. He'll bleed you of your ideas, pass them off as his own, and leave you far behind as he makes his way to the top. Did it to me. And he'll do it to you. Watch and see." The danger here is that this evaluation may be unfair, biased, or simply wrong. Kevin might have changed during the past two years, or your friend's initial assessment of him might be incorrect. But your friend's words will probably influence the way you interact with Kevin, and you will probably find reasons to substantiate your first impression, whether or not such reasons are actually present. You simply may not be able to avoid a basic stumbling block to accurate perception—closing your mind after forming a first impression.

In a communication interaction, receivers' psychological states can affect their first impressions of senders. Sometimes receivers use cues provided by senders, mix those cues with their own preconceptions, and create perceptions based partly on myth or fiction. When such perceptions involve dividing people into groups, it is called stereotyping.

Stereotypes: Do You Squeeze Others into Niches?

A **stereotype** is a generalization about people, places, or events that many members of a society hold. For example, when we go into a physician's waiting room for the first time, we carry with us a general idea, or stereotype, about what to expect and how to behave in that environment. In other words, we have developed an ability to identify and generalize about what we consider appropriate in a physician's office. While waiting to be examined, we would not expect to find flashing laser lights or people dancing to loud music.

stereotype
a generalization about people, places, or events held by many members of a society

The stereotypes we hold affect how we process stimuli around us. For one thing, while we remember more favorable information about in-groups, we retain more unfavorable information about out-groups. Our stereotypes also cause us to disregard any differences individuals may have that set them apart from the stereotyped group. When we stereotype, instead of responding to the communication or cues of individuals, we create expectations, assume they are valid, and behave as if they had occurred. Thus, when we stereotype, we judge persons on the basis of what we believe about the group in which we have placed them. We emphasize similarities and overlook discrepancies. Stereotyping leads us to oversimplify, overgeneralize, and grossly exaggerate what we observe. Lazy perceivers develop prejudices; **prejudice** involves making a negative prejudgment based on membership in a social category. Lazy perceivers also rely on stereotyping as their key perceptual process. Because it discourages careful observation and encourages pigeonholing, it discourages the noting of differences and encourages categorization.

Sports reporter Jerry Bembry reports the following incident:

> At a basketball media day at the Naval Academy, a ranking Navy official was greeting the news media. Each journalist received a gracious hello, but when the Navy man got to me, I was asked a question.
>
> "So," the official said, extending his hand. "Where did you play ball at to get this job?"
>
> His assumption: Because I'm an athletic-looking African American male, my education must have come in combination with an athletic scholarship. It's a question I'm often asked, although I've never played collegiate sports.
>
> No matter how many times such instances happen to me, it's unsettling.[22]

In your opinion, what accounts for such behavior? What can we do to prevent ourselves and others from making such assumptions?

Experts believe stereotyping can be as big an issue among groups of minorities as it has been between Whites and minorities. In other words, stereotypes, unfortunately, are everywhere. In fact, a variety of ethnic groups share the same

prejudice

a biased, negative attitude toward a particular group of people; a negative prejudgment based on membership in a social category

Ethics & Communication

For Your Eyes Only

What we see in other people's faces depends on what we know, or think we know, about people. When researcher Paul Chance showed subjects a set of photographic portraits and asked them to set aside those of Jews, the guesses were not very accurate. He reported that the subjects who were anti-Semitic were not any better at the task than the other subjects, but they set aside more photographs. To their prejudiced eyes, more people looked Jewish.[23]

Why do you think the prejudiced subjects saw more faces as "Jewish"? How might this affect their ability, for example, to hire people to work for them?

Using the images you carry around in your head, list the traits you believe are most characteristic of the members of each of the following groups: Afghans, Pakistanis, North Koreans, Israelis, and the French.

1. Do you believe it is possible to identify characteristics for groups with whom you have had little, if any, personal contact? Why or why not?

2. How do you imagine that your list would influence future communication with members of these groups?

stereotypes as Whites.[24] Commonly held stereotypes about Hispanics include that they are foreign-born, have a lot of children, and speak only Spanish. Existing stereotypes about Asians include that they are inscrutable and disloyal and that they own restaurants and laundries. Americans are likely to be stereotyped as being boisterous and loud. African Americans are stereotyped as being good dancers and good athletes.

Stereotypes are dangerous because, even at best, they are oversimplifications and overgeneralizations; often, they are gross exaggerations and misrepresentations. Stereotypes based on half-truths and derived from invalid premises pose major problems. Ralph Ellison, an African American and author of the book *Invisible Man,* noted:

> I am an invisible man. No, I am not a spook like those who haunted Edgar Allan Poe . . . I am a man of substance, of flesh and bone, fiber and liquid . . . and I might be said to possess a mind. I am invisible, understand, simply because people refuse to see me. Like the bodiless heads you see sometimes in circus sideshows, it is as though I have been surrounded by mirrors of hard, distorting glass. When they approach me they see only my surroundings, or figments of their imagination— indeed, everything and anything except me.[25]

Stereotypes do a special kind of harm when groups believe their own caricatures. If, for example, African Americans believe the stereotype and think that they are good only at sports, music, and dance, then it is entirely possible for some group members to exhibit "internalized oppression," act on the stereotype, and harass achievers in the group who do not fit that stereotype.[26]

Stereotypes also promote racial profiling.[27] For too many years, police have stopped drivers on the basis of their skin color rather than on how they were driving. In a similar situation, Aquil Abdullah, an American rowing champion, was denied permission to board his plane at Newark's Liberty International Airport because he had a common Muslim name.[28] Although most Caucasian Americans perceive themselves to be unbiased, when unconscious stereotypes are measured, approximately 90 percent link African Americans with negative traits. (To examine a test of unconscious stereotyping, go to https://implicit.harvard.edu/implicit/.) If, however, individuals make a conscious attempt to see someone as unique, race-based stereotypes diminish.[29]

The term *stereotype* is derived from a printing practice in which the typesetter repeatedly uses the same type to print text. In effect, when we stereotype, we repeatedly use the same thoughts, or fixed mental images, to "print" the same judgment repeatedly. We use our knowledge, beliefs, and expectancies about a human group to make judgments about people and our potential interaction with them. We apply the judgment to all members of the group, failing to acknowledge the uniqueness of what we are describing. We use the stereotype as a means of rationalizing our behavior in relation to members of that group. As media theorist Peter Orlik notes:

> When ages, occupations, genders, religions, or racial groups are represented in stereotypical ways, the treatment becomes potentially more dishonest the longer it is allowed to remain on microphone or on camera. All Texans, all Native Americans, all Baptists, or police officers are not the same; and to depict each member of such groups as exactly the same is to be functionally dishonest and insincere . . . to the concept of individual human dignity.[30]

The practice of stereotyping can be extremely harmful. At one time or another, almost everyone forms fixed impressions of a racial, ethnic, religious,

Has anyone ever stereotyped you? How did his or her doing so affect your relationship with that person?

occupational, or socioeconomic group.[31] When we stereotype, we project our attitude toward a group of people onto one particular member of that group. By ignoring individual differences, persons who stereotype create perceptual inaccuracies.

What should be emphasized, of course, is that we are all individuals. Whenever we interact with another person, we must realize that we are communicating with a person, not with a stereotype. Furthermore, we need to understand that our stereotype of any group is necessarily based on incomplete information and that, although stereotypes may be partly true, they are never completely true. In fact, when we stereotype, categorize, or pigeonhole others, we are really stereotyping, categorizing, or pigeonholing ourselves.

To improve our perceptual capabilities, we must make an effort to see differences as well as similarities among people. To paraphrase communication expert Irving J. Lee, the more we are able to discriminate among individuals, the less we will actively discriminate against individuals.[32] We can be aware of stereotypes but reject them.

Allness: Do You Assume That's All There Is?

allness

the erroneous belief that any one person can know all there is to know about anything

Knowledge of everything about anything is certainly an impossibility. In his book *Science and Sanity,* Alfred Korzybski coined the term **allness** to refer to the erroneous belief that any one person can possibly know all there is to know about everything.[33] Even if we are wise and do not assume that our favorite newscaster (or even our favorite friend) is telling us all there is to know about a topic, we often persist in believing that he or she is telling us all that is important about the topic. Did you ever ask someone to fill you in on the content of a class session you missed? Did you assume that the person was giving you all the important information? Did a later exam prove you wrong?

How can we avoid allness? We can begin by recognizing that, because we can focus on only a portion of a stimulus or an event, we necessarily neglect other aspects of that stimulus or event. Another safeguard is to refrain from thinking of ourselves as the center of the world.

Allness can impede the development of effective relationships. To counteract allness, try to end every assessment you make with the words *et cetera* ("and others"). You can never know everything there is to know about anything, and these words remind you that you should not pretend to know it all.

Blindering: Is Your Focus Too Narrow?

blindering

the process by which one unconsciously adds restrictions that limit one's perceptual capabilities

We can illustrate the concept of **blindering** as a factor in perception with the following exercise: Attempt to draw four straight lines that will connect each of the dots in Figure 4.6. Do this without lifting your pencil or pen from the page or retracing a line.

Did you find the exercise difficult or impossible? Most people do. Why? The problem imposes only one restriction—that you connect the dots with four straight lines without lifting your pencil or pen from the page or backtracking over a line. Most of us, however, add another restriction: After examining the dots, we assume that the figure to be formed must be a square. Actually, no such restriction exists, and once you realize this, the solution becomes clear. (Check the answer in the Answer Key at the back of the text.) In effect, the image of a square "blindered" you in your attempts to solve the problem.

FIGURE 4.6
Test for Blindering.

Just as we put blinders on a horse to reduce the number of visual stimuli it receives, we can also put blinders on ourselves. Blinders may help a horse, but they can drastically hinder human beings. Because it is a habit that forces us to see only certain things or to see things only in certain ways, blindering can lead to undesirable actions or prevent us from finding solutions. It can also impede needed actions or decisions.

Inferences: Do You Confuse What You Infer with What You Observe?

Another factor that affects our perception and evaluation of people and events is the inability to distinguish what we have inferred from what we have observed. For example, if you plan to leave your home to drive to a friend's house about a mile away, you probably make some inferences: that when you put the key into the ignition, your automobile will start; that you will not have a flat tire; and that no construction will block your approach to the friend's home. Likewise, when a traffic light turns green, you usually infer that it is safe to cross the street.

Ethics & Communication

Mind Reader? Soothsayer?

1. How often do you assume you understand what another person is feeling or thinking? Indicate which, if any, of the following statements you can see yourself making about people you know, where X or Y represents that person:

   I know X is angry.

   I can't tell Y the truth because she'll hold it against me.

   X just doesn't want to be friends.

   Y is uncaring.

   X is a nurturer.

   Y is uninterested in politics.

2. Indicate which of the following statements are facts and which are inferences.

   a. Jason would not make a good detective.

   b. Birth control leads to promiscuity.

   c. There are 50 stars in the U.S. flag.

   d. Theo earned $25,000 this year in dividends.

   e. Political candidates who fail to complete their taxes on time are lazy.

   f. The president is wearing a red tie.

3. How does the act of mind reading blur the difference between facts and inferences? What dangers does the merging of fact and fiction present for interpersonal relationships? What dangers does it present for journalists?

fact

that which is known to be true based on observation

inference

an assumption with varying degrees of accuracy

It is important to distinguish facts from inferences. A **fact** is something that you know to be true on the basis of observation. You see a woman walking down the street, carrying a briefcase. The statement "That woman is carrying a briefcase" is a fact. If the woman with the briefcase has a frown on her face, you may state, "That woman is unhappy." This second statement is an **inference,** since it cannot be verified by observation. Facts are not always easy to come by, and sometimes we mistakenly believe we have facts when we actually have inferences. Failing to recognize this distinction can be embarrassing or dangerous. For example, when actor and concert pianist Dudley Moore began flubbing lines, walking unevenly, and having difficulty playing the piano, he was mistakenly accused by entertainment industry insiders of being drunk, when in reality he was suffering from an incurable neurological disease.[34]

Acting as if an assumption is a certainty is risky. When we confuse facts with inferences, we are likely to jump to conclusions. Test your ability to distinguish facts and inferences by completing the Skill Builder below, "The Detective." How did you do? (Check your answers against the Answer Key at the back of the text.) This test is not designed to discourage you from making inferences. Of necessity, we live our lives on an inferential level. It is designed, however, to discourage you from making inferences without being aware of doing so. It is also designed to help you stop operating as if your inferences were facts.

Are you aware of the inferences you make? As semanticist S. I. Hayakawa noted, the real question is not whether we make inferences but whether we are cognizant of the inferences we make. One of the key characteristics of a mature relationship is that neither party to it jumps to conclusions or acts on inferences as if they were facts.

He laughed because he thought that they could not hit him; he didn't imagine that they were practicing how to miss him.

——Bertolt Brecht

Skill Builder

The Detective

Read the following story. Assume that the information contained in it is true and accurate. Then assess each statement that follows the story. On a sheet of paper, indicate whether you think the statement is definitely true by writing *T,* definitely false by writing *F,* or questionable by writing a question mark. (Note: A question mark indicates that you think the statement could be true or false, but on the basis of the information in the story, you cannot be certain.) Respond to the statements in the order given. Do not go back to change any of your responses.

A tired executive had just turned off the lights in the store when an individual approached and demanded money. The owner opened the safe. The contents of the safe were emptied, and the person ran away. The alarm was triggered, notifying the police of the occurrence.

1. An individual appeared after the owner had turned off the store's lights.
2. The robber was a man.
3. The person who appeared did not demand any money.
4. The man who opened the safe was the owner.
5. The owner emptied the safe and ran away.
6. Someone opened the safe.
7. After the individual who demanded the money emptied the safe, he sped away.
8. Although the safe contained money, the story does not reveal how much.
9. The robber opened the safe.
10. The robber did not take the money.
11. In this story, only three persons are referred to.

The following lists summarize the essential differences between facts and inferences:

Facts	Inferences
1. may be made only after observation or experience	1. may be made at any time
2. are limited to what has been observed	2. extend beyond observation
3. can be offered by the observer only	3. can be offered by anyone
4. may refer to the past or to the present	4. may refer to any time—past, present, or future
5. approach certainty	5. represent varying degrees of probability

THE MEDIA AND PERCEPTION

The media also play a role in determining how we perceive experience. According to the book *Glued to the Set: The 60 Television Shows and Events That Made Us Who We Are Today,* we are defined by and, thus, become like what we watch.[35]

Judging the Accuracy and Inaccuracy of Media Perceptions

More and more ads on television contain examples of multicultural socializing, showing Americans playing and living together regardless of race. In an effort to reach a diverse range of consumers, the ads present racially mixed scenarios in which ethnic communities in the United States mesh effortlessly. But do these ads represent reality? Unfortunately, according to sociologist Charles Gallagher, they do not. Gallagher reports that only about 7 percent of all marriages are interracial, 80 percent of Whites live in neighborhoods in which more than 95 percent of their neighbors are White, and most Americans have few close friends of another race. However, marketing professor Sonya Grier believes that in suggesting "multiculturalism is socially desirable," the ads reflect aspirations of what life could be, not what life is.[36] Such ads play a part in determining how we perceive experience.

Television programs face similar challenges. For example, the Council on American-Islamic Relations expressed concern that Muslims are the media's new "bad guys." In television and cable offerings, Muslim extremists are no longer portrayed as antisocial fanatics hiding in seedy places; the new stereotype presents Muslims as neighbors who are terrorists.[37] If most viewers get their knowledge of Muslims from the media, what messages do such portrayals send? Muslims are not alone in protesting stereotypical depictions. Representatives of Italian Americans, African Americans, Mexican Americans, older Americans, and women, just to name a few, also have protested offensive depictions of the members of their groups. Why? Because the more television people watch, the more accepting they become of social stereotypes, and the more likely they are to help perpetuate the unrealistic and limiting perceptions shown them. According to **cultivation theory,** a theory propounded by George Gerbner and colleagues focusing on the mass

cultivation theory

a theory propounded by George Gerbner and colleagues focusing on the mass media's ability to influence users' attitudes and perceptions of reality media's ability to influence users' attitudes and perceptions of reality, television is the primary means through which we form perceptions of society and people. The theory proposes that heavy television viewers develop perceptions that are inconsistent with facts.[38]

What are some of the specific perceptual lessons we learn from the media? In part, because women and older people are underrepresented in the media, we come to believe that they are unimportant or invisible. A review of prime-time television programming, for example, determined that viewers see three times as many White men as women.[39]

The media can limit our perceptions of males and females in other ways as well. Whereas the media often present men as active, independent, powerful, and virile, it portrays women as passive, dependent, and incompetent, and as the objects of male sexual desires. Whereas men are shown taking care of business, women are more typically shown taking care of their looks and other people, especially family members. From the point of view of the media, then, males dominate and females are subservient.[40] Males are providers. Females are caregivers.

For similar reasons, we might also come to perceive minorities inappropriately. Minorities have even less of a media presence than do women. For the most part, minorities occupy supporting rather than leading roles and often, instead of being depicted in complimentary ways, they are depicted as lazy, law-breaking, or dumb.

MediaWise

Frames of Reference

1. Intermittent reports of terrorist threats distort perceptions of risk, inducing an experience of fear that is out of proportion with actual danger. The more attention the media pay to a particular risk factor, the worse we assume the risk to be. For example, Dr. Baruch Fischoll, a psychologist at Carnegie Mellon University and a leader in the study of risk perception, reports: "If scientists are studying it and the news reports it, people assume it must be worth their attention."[41] Another risk researcher, Dr. Paul Slovic, reports that adding to this effect is the finding "that people put more stock in reports of bad news than in reports that might increase their trust."[42]

   Give an example of a media report that caused you to perceive a risk as greater than it was in reality. Did it involve weather? Traffic? Crime? Environmental issues? Political issues?

   Films perpetuate inaccurate perceptions that induce fear in viewers. View one of the following films: *Collateral Damage, The Siege, True Lies, Rules of Engagement, Executive Decision,* or *Not Without My Daughter.* In what ways, if any, does the film perpetuate bias against Arabs? In your opinion, is the "Arab as terrorist" stereotype responsible for increasing our fear and arousing our suspicion regarding who may or may not be a potential terrorist?

2. The popular media are also reflecting a crossing of cultures. An increasing number of films, such as *The Matrix Reloaded,* feature a rainbow cast, that is, a cast of all colors. Leon Wynter, author of *American Skin: Pop Culture, Big Business, and the End of White America,* suggests that commercial transracial representations sell because they "present a vision of the American dream in which we are liberated from the politics of race to openly embrace any style, cultural trope or image of beauty that attracts us regardless of its origin."[43] Others suggest such films sell because of the disproportionate representation of minorities in the audience; for example, market studies reveal that Black people buy movie tickets at higher rates than those of other ethnic groups.[44] To what extent, if any, do you find that rainbow casting is helping change perceptions of who in society is fit to occupy positions of power? Explain.

As a result of media depictions, our perceptions of Native Americans also may be inaccurate. For example, the print media too frequently present an image of them that is negative and degrading, suggesting that "all American Indians are poor, greedy, corrupt alcoholics, who just cannot seem to succeed in American society."[45] Representing Native Americans in this way undermines their ability to act effectively or be taken seriously.

On the other hand, Leon E. Wynter, author of the book *American Skin: Pop Culture, Big Business and the End of White America*, notes that we are now witnessing the browning of mainstream commercial culture. In addition to superstars like LeBron James, Oprah Winfrey, and Tiger Woods, we also have former heavyweight champ George Foreman as an affable pitchman, and ads like the Budweiser "Whassup?!" commercial that feature basically anonymous Black men talking Black street talk. It appears that American pop culture is becoming increasingly transracial. Products that aspire to be perceived as "all-American" depict a racially diverse image. According to Wynter, America wants to perceive itself as a unified multiracial society.[46] To this end, Hollywood has been using more of a color-blind approach to casting actors, giving audiences multiracial casts with the implied message that differences in skin color amount to "no big deal."[47] This is in line with the new "postethnic" reality that reveals ethnic labels are becoming less important to large numbers of teenagers whose personal identity is shaped more by cultural preferences than by skin color or ethnic heritage.

TECHNOLOGY AND PERCEPTION

According to social psychologist Kenneth Gergen, as new communication technologies continue to spread our relationships across the globe and as our knowledge of other cultures continues to revitalize our attitudes, depriving us of firm behavioral norms, we tend to exist in a state of flux, in which perceptions are partial and negotiated rather than complete and fixed.[48] As a result, perceptions derived from information received over the Internet may be both accurate and inaccurate, depending on whether the goal of the information provider is clarity or distortion. As with other media, the information we receive via the Internet is only as reliable as the source.

Computer-mediated communication raises a variety of perception-based issues involving the nature of communication and identity. We tend to perceive and interact with people differently when we relate to them online than when we talk to them face-to-face. A number of researchers even refer to communication that occurs in the world of cyberspace as unreal in order to differentiate it from communication that occurs in real life, also known as IRL, and without the aid of computer mediation.[49] Fantasy and playfulness play significant roles in online interactions, allowing people to experiment in ways that may be uncomfortable for them in real life. Thus, the Internet is precipitating perceptual revisions of the self and others.[50]

The Internet inspires some of us to feel larger than ourselves. In addition, the availability of the computer and **virtual reality** allows many of us to spend more time in our dreams. As sociologist Sherry Turkle reminds us, "In film and photography, realistic-looking images depict scenes that never took place between people who never met."[51] Anyone can create an image, import sections

virtual reality
an environment that exists as data in a computer system

"Here you are—I've been all over the Internet looking for you."

of pictures, and blend them into a new whole. Image processing and synthesis enable us to create illusions of reality. In effect, with digital media you never know what is real, what is the truth. As a result, Web users must develop the ability to look critically at what they perceive rather than simply accept what is on the screen as a given; it is imperative for them to analyze, weigh, probe,

Ethics & Communication

Image Making

Before digital photography, people perceived photos as truthful. In fact, a decision by *Jet Magazine*'s publisher John H. Johnson to print the gruesome photograph of the brutally murdered and mutilated African-American teenager Emmett Till, revealing to the nation the level of brutality and inhumanity that led to his death, is credited with having sparked the civil rights movement.[52] Today, however, what you see in photographs or in the media is not necessarily what is really there. Digital manipulation lets users tinker with reality, changing the "taking" of a photo to the "making" of a photo. Today, products can be digitally inserted into the background

of films postproduction without viewer knowledge. Separate pictures can be combined to make it appear as if people who were never actually together are standing or seated next to each other. The appearance of people can also be altered, making them more or less attractive, slimmer or heavier than they actually are. Type the words "fake pictures" into an Internet search engine and you'll find people willing to alter any photo.

In your opinion, should the Federal Communications Commission require disclaimers when counterfeit images are shown on TV? What measures, if any, should be taken to protect consumers from "phony reality"? What measures should consumers take to protect themselves?

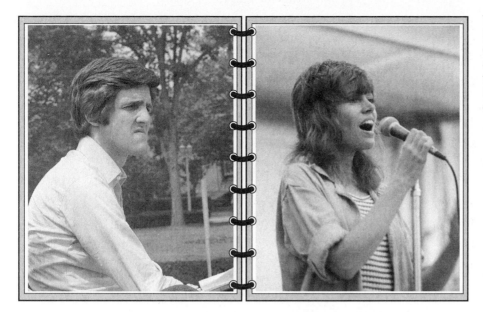

These pictures of John Kerry and Jane Fonda were combined to make it seem as if the two had been together at a war protest leading receivers to draw an erroneous conclusion.

and take stock of what they perceive. This practice differs from the experiences of the members of earlier generations, who would rarely perceive a picture and feel it was a fake. Back then, it was felt that a fact was a fact. Today, we all know better. We now see a photograph and realize that it could be a total fabrication.[53]

For example, during the Iraqi war, a photo that appeared in the *Los Angeles Times* of a British soldier standing over a group of Iraqi civilians near Basra was actually a combination of two photographs taken moments apart. How was this discovered? A reader noticed that some of the figures in the background appeared twice. Why did the journalists choose to merge the photos and deceive the public? One photo featured a dramatic pose of a British soldier, while the other photo featured an Iraqi man carrying a child. In the more powerful merged version, the soldier and the civilian appeared to be interacting. While the *Los Angeles Times* fired the journalist for his deception, what is noteworthy is that this kind of deception continues. During the 2004 presidential campaign, separate pictures of Senator John Kerry and former anti–Vietnam War activist and actress Jane Fonda were combined to make it appear as though they were together at an antiwar rally. The resulting image was circulated on the Internet. How long will it be before we consider real photos to be fake?[54]

We also need to understand how other factors, such as race, influence our attention to Web sites. For example, recent research reveals that African Americans are more attentive when visiting a Black-targeted site, while Caucasians are equally attentive to White- and Black-targeted sites. It appears that race or ethnicity may be of more interest to people whose racial or ethnic group is in the minority of their social environment than to people of the majority group. Since they are in the majority, Caucasians may be less mindful of their race when browsing a Web site.[55]

We are also faced with a number of questions: Will emerging technologies help us become more flexible and resilient? Or will they cause us to think strictly logically and constrain us to prescribed, more conventional thought channels? Will they facilitate our ability to use our virtual experiences to enrich our real experiences? Or will they contribute to our losing our sense of reality by enabling us to lose ourselves in a virtual world that disappears when we disconnect our modems?

HOW TO INCREASE THE ACCURACY OF YOUR PERCEPTIONS

Although our effectiveness as communicators is determined in part by our perceptual abilities, we rarely consider ways to increase our perceptual accuracy. Let's examine some suggestions for improving perceptual skills.

Focus on Service Learning

Visit a Web site on teaching the dangers of stereotyping, such as www.du.edu/ctir/ pubs_culture.html or http://school.discovery. com/lessonplans/programs/ stereotypes. Then, on the basis of information you find there, other research you conduct, and the knowledge you now have, prepare to conduct a workshop for an audience of your own choosing (young children, parents, members of the police force, physicians, lawyers) that uses a series of case studies you create to help the audience members avoid drawing the wrong conclusions from perceptions.

Be Aware That Your Perceptual Processes Are Personally Biased

By becoming aware of your role in perception, by recognizing that you have biases, by acknowledging that you do not have a corner on the truth market, you can increase the probability that your perceptions will provide you with accurate information about the world around you and the people who are a part of it.

Take Your Time

Effective communicators are not in a hurry; they take the time they need to process information fairly and objectively. When we act too quickly, we often make careless decisions that reveal poor judgment. In our haste, we overlook important clues, make inappropriate or unjustified inferences, and jump to conclusions. Delaying a response instead of acting impulsively gives us an opportunity to check or verify our perceptions.

Thinking Critically

Reflect and Respond

Discuss how the excerpts that follow help amplify our understanding of the nature of perception. Then agree or disagree with each selection; supply reasons and examples that support your position.

What I set down here is true until someone else passes that way and rearranges the world in his own style.

—John Steinbeck

It is with our judgments as with our watches; no two go just alike, yet each believes his own.

—Alexander Pope

Try to Be More Open

Frequently, we act like robots or computers that have been programmed to look at the world in a set way. But a person is neither a robot nor a computer. We can take steps to become more observant and broaden our expectations. We need to become willing to expect the unexpected and to expand the size of our perceptual window. This will happen if we recognize that our reality is subjective, incomplete, and unique. Thus, if we want to cultivate a fuller, more valid perception of our world, we must be willing to review, revise, and update our view of the world.

Develop Your Ability to Empathize

Differing perceptions lie at the heart of an array of interpersonal and global communication challenges. If we can experience the world from a perspective other than our own—in effect, recreating it from the other party's perspective—we can help facilitate mutual understanding. Both cognitive and emotional behaviors are integral components of empathy. The cognitive component, perspective taking (the ability to assume the viewpoint of another person) requires that we take on the opinions of another, setting our own opinions away until we understand theirs. The second component of empathy, emotional understanding, requires that we step into the shoes of the other person and feel what they are feeling. The third component, caring, is "the icing on the cake." When you genuinely care about the welfare of another person and you combine this with the personal realization of what their situation is like, that is, you have made their experience your own thinking and feeling as they feel, at least temporarily, you gain a greater appreciation of what the world looks like through their eyes. The ability to empathize can make a difference in life.

 ## Ethics & Communication

Through the Eyes of the Beholder

The defendant, 12-year-old Raymond Thomas, had shot 16-year-old Reggie Haines. How do you teach a 12-year-old defendant a lesson he will never forget? One judge devised a novel sentence in an effort to accomplish that objective. Circuit Judge Lynn Tepper imposed a sentence that required 12-year-old Thomas to get a feel for what life was now like for his gunshot victim. As punishment for shooting Haines point-blank in the forehead, Judge Tepper ordered that Thomas first serve time in a wheelchair, then that he use a walker, and finally that he walk with a cane. The judge told Thomas:

"You're going to be moving around in Reggie's world, which you created. You will go to the

bathroom in a wheelchair. You will get in and out of bed, eat, try to drink from the water fountain in a wheelchair." The judge continued, "Perhaps you will appreciate what Reggie had to go through to get where he is today, which is a miracle."[56]

What message is the judge's sentence designed to communicate? In your opinion, is the punishment ethical? Why or why not? Do you believe that Raymond Thomas will perceive the judge's message as intended? In addition, will the sentence enable Raymond Thomas to perceive what Reggie is really going through?

Revisiting Chapter Objectives

1. **Explain why a person is more than a camera.**   Perception is the process of selecting, organizing, and interpreting sensory data in a way that enables us to make sense of our world. Perceptions are personally based. They are affected by the perspective we adopt, our sensory capabilities, our past experiences, and our level of motivation.

2. **Define and explain how the following affect perception: the figure–ground principle, selective exposure, selective perception, closure, stereotyping, open and closed orientation, and first impressions.**   The accuracy of our perceptions is affected by our inability to perceive two stimuli simultaneously (figure–ground principle). It is also influenced by our tendency to close ourselves to new experiences (selective exposure), our inclination to distort our perceptions of stimuli to make them conform to our need for internal consistency (selective perception), our desire not to open ourselves to unfamiliar experiences, and our need to perceive a complete world (closure).

   How we perceive another person is a key determinant of the kind of relationship we will share with that person. Thus, perceiving others and the roles they play is an essential part of the communication process. In this regard, a number of factors can prevent accurate perceptions. We frequently evaluate others on the basis of first impressions, and we tend to stereotype people—to divide them into groups and place them in niches. Stereotyping can be especially harmful by promoting prejudice, since it encourages us to emphasize similarities and ignore differences. Prejudice is an unfair or biased extension of stereotyping, which we must guard against.

3. **Describe how past experience, gender, cultural background, the media, and technology can influence perception.**   Past experience, culture, gender, the media, and technology influence how we perceive and interpret people and events. By serving as perceptual filters, they guide us in giving meaning to both our real and virtual experiences.

4. **Define and provide examples of allness, blindering, and facts and inferences.**   Other barriers to perceptual accuracy are allness (the habit of thinking we know it all), blindering (the tendency to obscure solutions to problems by adding unnecessary restrictions), and confusion of facts with inferences (the inability to distinguish between observations and assumptions).

5. **Identify ways to increase the accuracy of your perceptions.**   Working to increase the validity of your perceptions is important. As a first step, you need to recognize the role you play in the perceptual process.

Resources for Further Inquiry and Reflection

To apply your understanding of how the principles in Chapter 4 are at work in our daily lives, consult the following resources for further inquiry and reflection. Or, if you prefer, choose any other appropriate resource. Then connect the ideas expressed in your chosen selection with the communication concepts and issues you are learning about both in and out of class.

Listen to Me

"Theme From the Bottom" (Phish)
"Hurricane Eye" (Paul Simon)
"I've Seen It All" (Bjork)
"If I Could Turn Back Time" (Cher)
"Suspicious Minds" (Elvis Presley)
"Jenny from the Block" (Jennifer Lopez)
"Wonderful World" (Louis Armstrong)

These songs explore one or more aspects of perception. Choose a song and discuss how the speaker's perception affects his or her relationship with one or more other people.

 View Me

Oleanna	*The Constant Gardener*
Big	*American History X*
Dancer in the Dark	*Shallow Hal*
The Doctor	*The Cider-House Rules*
Groundhog Day	*Remember the Titans*
Life Is Beautiful	*A Beautiful Mind*
Rashomon	*Crash*
A History of Violence	*Freaky Friday*

In each of these films, perception plays a key role in the plot. Choose one film and identify the lessons we learn regarding how perception can alter one's reality and life experiences.

 Read Me

James Thurber. "The Secret Life of Walter Mitty." In *The Works of James Thurber*. New York: Longmeadow, 1986.

Mark Medoff. *Children of a Lesser God*. New York: Dramatists Play Service, 1980.

Ralph Ellison. *The Invisible Man*. New York: Random House, 1989.

Laura Z. Hobson. *Gentleman's Agreement*. New York: Simon & Schuster, 1947.

How does the perception of the main character or characters in the work affect both their experiences and their interaction with others? To what extent, if any, does stereotyping play a role in limiting perception?

 Tell Me

Share with the class the insights you gained from your chosen Listen to Me, View Me, or Read Me selection.

Find examples that enable you to support or negate the following: Once you have a belief, it influences your perception of all other relevant information. Once you call a country hostile, you will interpret ambiguous actions on the part of its leaders as indicative of that hostility.

Key Chapter Terminology

Use the Communication Works CD-ROM and the Online Learning Center at www.mhhe.com/gamble9 to further your knowledge of the following terminology.

allness 90	perception 76
blindering 90	perceptual constancy 81
closure 78	perceptual sets 83
cultivation theory 93	prejudice 88
cultural nearsightedness 81	primacy effect 87
fact 92	selective attention 85
figure–ground principle 77	selective exposure 85
first impressions 85	selective perception 77
halo effect 85	selective retention 85
horn effect 85	stereotype 87
inference 92	virtual reality 95

Communication
Works

online learning center

www.mhhe.com/gamble9

Idioms in Translation

absorb stimuli—take in information

pigeonholing—categorizing based on stereotypes

saw with the stomach—let hunger guide interpretation

Communication
Works

online learning center

www.mhhe.com/gamble9

Test Your Understanding

Go to the *Self Quizzes* on the Communication Works CD-ROM and the book's Online Learning Center at www.mhhe.com/gamble9.

Notes

1. David Brooks. "All Cultures Are Not Equal." *The New York Times,* August 11, 2005, p. A23.
2. Al Neuharth. "Why Your News Is Sometimes Slanted." *USA Today,* February 28, 2003, p. 15A.
3. Steven R. Covey. *7 Habits of Highly Effective People.* New York: Simon & Schuster, 1990, p. 28.
4. For an in-depth discussion of how race affects perception, see M. L. Hecht, R. L. Jackson II, and S. A. Ribeau. *African American Communication,* 2nd ed. Mahwah, NJ: Erlbaum, 2003.
5. William V. Haney. *Communication and Organizational Behavior.* Homewood, IL: Irwin, 1973, p. 55.
6. E. Rubin. "Figure and Ground." In D. Beardslee and M. Wertheimer, eds. *Readings in Perception.* Princeton, NJ: Van Nostrand, pp. 194–203.
7. Sharon Begley. "People Believe a 'Fact' That Fits Their Views Even If It's Clearly False." *The Wall Street Journal,* February 4, 2005, p. B1.
8. See, for example, Steve Freiss. "Memory Does Not Always Serve, and That's No Lie." *USA Today,* September 14, 2004, p. 9D; and Daniel L. Schacter. "The Fog of War." *The New York Times,* April 5, 2004, p. A21.
9. Marshall Singer. "Culture: A Perceptual Approach." In Larry A. Samovar and Richard E. Porter, eds. *Intercultural Communication: A Reader,* 4th ed. Belmont, CA: Wadsworth, 1985, pp. 62–69.
10. Larry A. Samovar and Richard E. Porter. *Communication between Cultures.* Belmont, CA: Wadsworth, 1994, p. 105.
11. J. W. Bagby. "A Cross-Cultural Study of Perceptual Predominance in Binocular Rivalry." *Journal of Abnormal and Social Psychology* 54, 1957, pp. 331–334.
12. H. A. Elfenbein and N. Ambady. "Is There an In-group Advantage in Emotion Recognition?" *Psychological Bulletin* 128, pp. 243–249; M. D. Weathers, E. M. Frank, and I. A. Spell. "Differences in the Communication of Affect: Members of the Same Race versus Members of a Different Race." *Journal of Black Psychology* 28, p. 66–77.
13. Julia T. Wood. *Gendered Lives.* Belmont, CA: Wadsworth, 1994, pp. 21, 131.
14. See Judy Cornelia Pearson. *Gender and Communication.* Dubuque, IA: Brown, 1985.
15. Dan Winters. "Warrior Women." *New York Times Magazine,* February 16, 2003, pp. 23–34.
16. J. Long. "Symbolic Reality Bites: Women and Racial Ethnic Minorities in Modern Film." *Sociological Spectrum* 22:3, July–September 2002, pp. 299–335.
17. Samovar and Porter, *Communication between Cultures,* p. 81.
18. Paul Chance. "Seeing Is Believing," *Psychology Today,* January–February 1989, p. 26.
19. See Charles G. Russel. "Culture, Language and Behavior: Perception." *ETC.* 57:2, Summer 2000, pp. 189–218.
20. M. Sunnafrank, A Ramirez, and S. Metts. "At First Sight: Persistent Relational Effects of Get Acquainted Conversations." *Journal of Social and Personal Relationships* 21:3, February 2005, pp. 361–379.
21. Solomon Asch. *Social Psychology.* New York: Oxford University Press, 1987.
22. Jerry Bembry. "The Pain That Whites Don't See." *The Record,* January 23, 1994, p. E-3. From Jerry Bembry, "Blacks Anguish Gives 'Rage' its Strength," Baltimore Sun, 12/30/93 p. 8D. © 1993, reprinted by permission of the Baltimore Sun.
23. Chance.
24. Maria T. Padilla. "Studying Stereotypes among Minority Groups." *The Record,* July 19, 1998, p. L-1.
25. Ralph Ellison. *Invisible Man.* New York: Random House, 1989.

26. Padilla, p. L-3.

27. See, for example, I. V. Blair. "The Malleability of Automatic Stereotypes and Prejudice." *Personality and Social Psychology Review* 6:3, 2002, pp. 242–262; P. C. Hughes and J. R. Baldwin. "Communication and Stereotypical Impressions." *Howard Journal of Communication* 13, pp. 153–171.

28. Ira Berkow. "Rower with Muslim Name Is an All-American Suspect." *New York Times,* February 21, 2003, pp. D1, D4.

29. Sharon Begley. "Racism Studies Find Rational Part of Brain Can Override Prejudice." *The Wall Street Journal,* November 19, 2004, p. B1.

30. Peter B. Orlik. *Electronic Media Criticism: Applied Perspectives.* Boston: Focal, 1994, p. 23.

31. See, for example, Gordon W. Allport. *The Nature of Prejudice.* Garden City, NY: Double day, 1958.

32. Irving J. Lee. *How to Talk with People.* San Francisco: International Society for General Semantics, 1982.

33. Alfred Korzybski. *Science and Sanity,* 4th ed. San Francisco: International Society for General Semantics, 1980.

34. As told on *20/20,* ABC Television, June 30, 2000.

35. See Steven D. Stark. *Glued to the Set: The 60 Television Shows and Events That Made Us Who We Are Today.* New York: Free Press, 1997.

36. Erin Texeira. "Multicultural Socializing in Ads Doesn't Reflect Reality in U.S.," *The Record,* February 18, 2005, p. A24.

37. V. Rohan. "Defining the Face of Evil." *The Record,* January 23, 2005, p. E1.

38. G. Gerbner, L. P. Gross, M. Morgan, and N. Signorielli. "The 'Mainstreaming' of America: Violence Profile No. 11." *Journal of Communication* 30, pp. 10–29; J. Shanahan and M. Morgan. *Television and Its Viewers: Cultivation Theory and Research.* New York: Cambridge University Press, 1999.

39. S. A. Basow. *Gender: Stereotypes and Roles,* 3rd ed. Pacific Grove, CA: Brooks/Cole, 1992, p. 159.

40. Wood, p. 238.

41. See Daniel Goleman. "Hidden Rules Often Distort Ideas of Risk." *New York Times,* February 1, 1994, pp. C-1, C-10.

42. Goleman.

43. Joel Kotkin and Thomas Tseng. "The New Post-Ethnic Reality." *The Record,* July 13, 2003, pp. O1, O4.

44. Michael Medved. "Hollywood Finally Moves beyond Race Obsession," *USA Today,* June 10, 2003, p. 13A.

45. Autumn Miller and Susan Dente Ross. "They Are Not Us: Framing of American Indians by the *Boston Globe.*" Paper delivered at the annual convention of the Association for Education in Journalism and Mass Communication in Miami, FL, August 7–10, 2002.

46. Leon E. Wynter. *American Skin: Pop Culture, Big Business and the End of White America.* New York: Crown, 2002.

47. Medved.

48. Kenneth Gergen. *The Saturated Self: Dilemmas of Identity in Contemporary Life.* New York: Basic Books, 1991, p. 6.

49. Andrew F. Wood and Matthew J. Smith. *Online Communication: Linking Technology, Identity, and Culture.* Mahwah, NJ: Erlbaum, 2001, p. 18.

50. Susan B. Barnes. *Online Connections: Internet Interpersonal Relationships.* Cresskill, NJ: Hampton, 2001, p. 102.

51. Sherry Turkle. *Life on the Screen: Identity in the Age of the Internet.* New York: Simon & Schuster, 1995, p. 267.

52. Lawrence Aaron. "Paying Tribute to a Courageous Publisher." *The Record,* August 17, 2005, p. L9.

53. Don Tapscott. *Growing Up Digital: The Rise of the Net Generation.* New York: McGraw-Hill, 1998, p. 100.

54. Russell Frank. "Altered Picture's Worth a Thousand Lies." *The Record,* April 9, 2003, p. L11.

55. Osei Appiah. "Americans Online: Differences in Surfing and Evaluating Race-Targeted Web Sites by Black and White Users." Paper presented at the annual convention of the Association for Education in Journalism and Mass Communication, Miami, FL, August 2002.

56. "Boy Who Shot Teen Ordered to Spend Time in Wheelchair." *The Sunday Record,* January 9, 1994, p. A16.

CHAPTER 5

Language and Meaning: Helping Minds Meet

After finishing this chapter, you should be able to

1. Define *language*.

2. Describe and explain the triangle of meaning.

3. Distinguish between connotative and denotative meanings.

4. Discuss how culture and gender influence language use.

5. Provide examples of bypassing and intensional and extensional orientation.

6. Identify two strategies to improve oral language abilities.

7. Explain how technology is affecting language use.

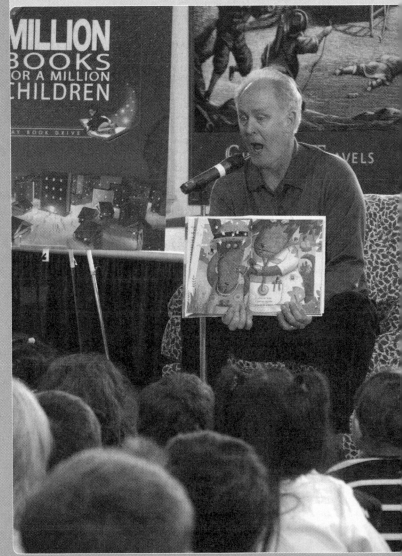

Whatever we call a thing, whatever we say it is, it is not. For whatever we say is words, and words are words and not things. The words are maps, and the map is not the territory.

—Harry L. Weinberg, "Some Limitations of Language"

Tact is . . . a kind of mind reading.

—Sara Orne Jewett

Have you ever considered not speaking for a day? What about for a week? A month? How about a year? What if you were not allowed to use any words to make yourself understood? The words that constitute language are so much a part of our lives that many of us cannot imagine not being able or allowed to use them.

Like so many other things of importance, however, the ability to communicate is frequently appreciated only when it is threatened or lost. We depend on language to help us share meaning with others. By understanding how language works, we will become better able to use words to do just that. The sharing of meaning is what communication is all about.

■ ■ ■

WHAT LANGUAGE IS

Language is a unified system of symbols that permits the sharing of meaning. A **symbol** stands for, or represents, something else. Words are symbols, and thus words represent things. Notice the words *represent* and *stand for* rather than *are*. This is a very important distinction. Words stand for, or represent, things but are not the things they stand for. Words are spoken sounds or the written representations of sounds that we have agreed will stand for something else. Thus, by mutual consent, we can make anything stand for anything.

The process of communication involves using words to help create meanings and expectations. However, as important as words are in representing and describing objects and ideas, meaning is not stamped on them. Meanings are in people, not in words. Even a common word such as *cat* can bring to mind meanings ranging from a fluffy Angora to a sleek leopard. Your goal in communicating with another person is to have your meanings overlap, so that you can each make sense out of the other's messages and understand each other. Thus, to communicate, you translate the meaning you want to express into language, so that the other person will respond to it by forming a meaning similar to yours. Although language is obviously intended to aid communication, far too often language serves as its obstacle.

Ethics & Communication

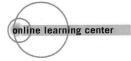

Go to the Online Learning Center at www.mhhe.com/gamble9 and answer the questions in the *Self Inventory* to evaluate your understanding of communication terms.

language

a unified system of symbols that permits the sharing of meaning

symbol

that which represents something else

triangle of meaning

a model that explains the relationship which exists among words, things, and thoughts

HOW LANGUAGE WORKS: WORDS, THINGS, AND THOUGHTS

Language fulfills its potential only if we use it correctly. The **triangle of meaning,** developed by two communication theorists—C. K. Ogden and I. A. Richards—helps explain how language works (see Figure 5.1).[2] In Ogden and Richards' triangle of meaning, the three points are *thought, word,* and *thing.* The broken line connecting *word* (a symbol) and *thing* (a referent, or stimulus) indicates that *the word is not the thing* and that there is no direct connection between the two. Thus, when you use words, you need to remind yourself that the only relationships between the words you use and the things they represent are those that exist in people's thoughts (including, of course, your own). Frequently, even the existence of an image (a physical object) does not establish meaning. Some years ago, a public service commercial depicting a rat and a child living in a tenement was shown on television. The child was seen beckoning to the rat as she repeated, "Here, kitty, kitty! Here, kitty, kitty!" Although this example may seem somewhat bizarre, its meaning is really quite clear: It is possible for two of us to look at the same object but give it different meanings, because the meaning of anything is inside each person who experiences it.[3] If you are to be a successful communicator, you should understand the relationships that exist between words and people's thoughts and reactions.[4]

FIGURE 5.1

Triangle of Meaning.

Skill Builder

The Triangle of Meaning at Work

Situation 1. "Congratulations. You've just given birth to a 3.5-kilogram baby." How do you respond? Your joy is momentarily muted if you don't know what a kilogram is. There is no information in bare facts; information comes from what you do with the facts and what you bring to them. If you've never stored a mental image of a kilogram, you can't generate a mental image of the baby's weight from the data.[5]

Situation 2. Imagine that you're at an old Western Union telegraph office. The telegraph operator hears a message on the wire and bursts into tears. You hear the same dots and dashes but have no reaction at all. Why not?

If you don't know Morse code, the information means nothing, even if you hear it quite clearly. Meaning is not in the cues reaching our senses, but in the associations we attach to them.

Situation 3. Instead of referring to North Korea as "the imperialist aggressor," U.S. government officials have been instructed to refer to it as a "superpower of concern."[6] Then President George W. Bush included North Korea in the "axis of evil." Will this make a difference in how we perceive and behave toward the North Korean people?

Situation 4. Provide your own example of the triangle of meaning at work.

THE COMMUNICATION OF MEANING

The communication of meaning from one person to another is a key function of language. The factors identified in this section relate to problems in the sharing of meaning.

Word Barriers

In talking to others, we often assume too quickly that they understand what we mean. There are many reasons, however, we may not be understood as we want to be and why the words we use can create barriers. In Lewis Carroll's *Through the Looking Glass*, Humpty Dumpty and Alice have the following conversation:

> "I don't know what you mean by 'glory,'" Alice said.
> Humpty Dumpty smiled contemptuously, "Of course you don't—till I tell you. I meant, 'There's a nice knock-down argument for you!'"
> "But 'glory' doesn't mean 'A nice knock-down argument,'" Alice objected.
> "When I use a word," Humpty Dumpty said in a rather scornful tone, "it means just what I choose it to mean—neither more nor less."

We can make words mean whatever we want them to mean. Nothing stops us—except our desire to share meaning with others.

Words, like eyeglasses, blur everything that they do not make more clear.

— Joseph Jourbert

Meanings Are Both Denotative and Connotative

We may experience a problem in communication if we consider only our own meaning for a word. Although *we* know what we mean, the crucial question is, What does our word bring to mind for those with whom we are communicating? When we think about what language means, we must think in terms of both **denotative** (objective, or dictionary) **meaning** and **connotative** (subjective, or personal) **meaning.**

denotative meaning
dictionary meaning; the objective or descriptive meaning of a word

connotative meaning
subjective meaning; one's personal meaning for a word

John and Judy spent their Saturday waxing.

MEANING AND TIME

Every noteworthy event, particularly catastrophes, catapult words into everyday speech and dictionaries. September 11, 2001, is no exception. When the American Dialect Society met to decide the top or newly reconditioned words of the previous year, *9/11* was voted the expression most likely to last. Also recognizing this, the editors of the *American Heritage College Dictionary's* fourth edition went back in after their editorial deadline and added an entry for *9/11*.

Words come and go from dictionaries. For example, the word *wilding*, meaning the action or practice by a gang of youths of going on a protracted and violent rampage in a street, a park, or another public place, attacking or mugging people at random along the way, was included in the fourth edition of *The American Heritage Dictionary*, released in 2000. The word became popular after being used by suspects in the rape of a Central Park jogger to describe their behavior: "We were going wilding," one of them told police. The use of the word has since faded because it was intrinsically linked with that attack. When issues fade from consciousness, some words fade with them.[7]

Bad now has a new definition—"good." The word *gay*, now an acceptable term for "homosexual," has lost its former primary meaning of "happy," "bright," or "merry." Until the creation of the Apple computer, when people heard the word

Skill Builder

A Time Capsule for Words

1. Briefly define each of the following terms:

   Net _____

   Pot _____

   Hooking up _____

   Straight _____

   Crack _____

   Kicks _____

   Mud _____

   Blunt _____

   Happy ending _____

   AIDS _____

   Spam _____

   Cookies _____

2. Show the list, without definitions, to your parents, older relatives, or older friends, and ask them to write their definitions for the words.

3. Compare your meaning for each term with the meanings given by others. Why do you suppose their meanings differed from yours?

4. Pretend it is now the year 2020. On a separate sheet of paper, create a new meaning for each word listed.

apple, they probably thought of the fruit. That's probably not the first thing you think of today when someone refers to an apple. (To get a good sense of how time affects meaning, try the Skill Builder "A Time Capsule for Words" above.)

Time, then, is certainly an important element in determining meaning. Consequently, when we use a word that referred to a particular object at a particular time, we should attempt to determine if it still means the same thing now. Many "old" words acquire vivid new meanings every decade or so. It is often necessary to remember this when speaking with people who are older or younger than we are. Viruses today are not just germs spread from person to person, but malicious programs that can spread instantaneously from one computer to millions of other computers globally.[8]

MEANING AND PLACE

Words change meaning not only over time, but also from one region of the country to another. For example, what would you envision having if you were to stop for a soda? For an egg cream? What each word brings to mind probably depends on the region of the country you grew up in. In some parts of the United States, *soda* refers to a soft drink, but in others it refers to a concoction of ice cream and a soft drink. In some sections of the country, *egg cream* refers to a mixture of seltzer, syrup, and milk, but elsewhere it conjures up the image of an egg mixed with cream.

MEANING AND EXPERIENCE

The meanings we assign to words are based on our past experiences with the words and with the things they represent. Consider the word *cancer*, for example. If you were dealing with three people in a hospital—a surgeon, a patient, and a statistician—how do you imagine each would react to this word? The surgeon might think about operating procedures or diagnostic techniques, or about how to tell a patient that he or she has cancer. The patient might think about the odds for recovery and might well be frightened. The statistician might see cancer as an important factor in life expectancy tables.

Unlike denotative (dictionary) meanings—which are generally agreed to and are objective, abstract, and general—connotative (personal) meanings are individual, subjective, and emotional. Thus, your own experiences influence the meanings you assign to words; that is, your connotative meanings vary according to your own feelings for the object or concept you are considering.

Whether Language Is Concrete or Abstract Influences Meaning

The language we use varies in its specificity. Consider this family pet. We could call it:

> dog
> domesticated canine
> small, domesticated canine
> a toy Poodle
> Lucy

In each instance, our description becomes somewhat more specific. Alfred Korzybski and S. I. Hayakawa devised an abstraction ladder to describe this process.[9] The ladder is composed of a number of descriptions of the same thing. Lower items focus specifically on the person, object, or event, while higher items are generalizations that include the subject as part of a larger class. As the words we use move from abstract (less specific) to concrete (more specific), they become more precise in meaning and are more likely to appeal to our senses and conjure up a picture. Specific words clarify meaning by narrowing the number of possible images a person pictures. Were we to talk, for example, about our children's academic experiences, we could say that one of our children is in graduate school and the other is working at a university (rather high levels of abstraction), or we could get more concrete and say that our daughter is an MBA candidate at a New York college and our son has a postdoctoral fellowship at an Ivy League university. What would we need to do to make these statements even more concrete?

Lucy is a poodle with personality.

Using high-level abstractions serves a number of functions. First, because high-level abstractions function as a kind of verbal shorthand, they enable us to generalize, and our communication becomes easier and faster.

Second, when we believe it is necessary, because they also enable us to be deliberately unclear, high-level abstractions allow us to limit understanding and avoid confrontations. When, for example, a friend asks you what you think of a new outfit or your boss asks you what you think of a new corporate strategy, if telling the truth appears too risky to you, you can offer an abstract answer to the question and avoid being put on the line. On the other hand, relying on high-level abstractions can also cause meaning to become fuzzy—primarily because the words you use can be interpreted ambiguously. Thus, becoming aware of levels of abstraction reduces the likelihood of misunderstandings. For example, if individuals do not have a reservoir of shared experiences or interpretations, using more concrete language can enhance understanding between them. The goal is to use the level of abstraction that meets the needs of your communication objectives and the situation.

CULTURE AND LANGUAGE

Since culture influences language use, communication between members of diverse cultures can be a challenge.

Culture Influences the Words Used

Both the **dominant culture** (the culture in power, the mainstream culture composed of people who share the same values, beliefs, and ways of behaving and communicating and who pass them on from one generation to another) and co-cultures (groups of people such as African Americans, Hispanics, Asians, musicians, athletes, environmentalists, and drug users, who have a culture of their own outside the dominant culture) have different languages. Hence, usages vary from culture to culture. If a concept is important to a culture, there will be a large number of terms to describe it. For example, in our culture, the word *money* is very important and we have many words to describe it: *Wealth, capital, assets, backing, resources,* and *finance* are just a few. Similarly, the Inuit, or Eskimos, have a number of words for snow, because they need to be able to make fine distinctions when speaking of it. While English is somewhat lacking when it comes to individual words for snow (we have words like *sleet, slush, blizzard,* and *powder*), Inuktitut, the Inuit language, has different words for snow that is falling (*quanniq*), snow on the ground (*aput*), snow that is blowing (*pirsiriug*), snow that is drifting (*natiruvaaq*), wet snow (*masak*), wet and compact snow (*kinirtaq*), fresh and wet, soggy snow (*aquilluqaaq*), the first snowfall of autumn (*apigiannagaut*), encrusted snow that gives way underfoot (*katakarktariaq*), and snow causing crunchy sounds when you walk (*qeqergranaartoq*), to name just a few.[10] In contrast to the Inuit, Arabs have only one word for snow—*talg*—and it refers to either ice or snow. The Arabs are simply not very interested in snow, since it rarely affects them. Similarly, Mandarin (a Chinese language) reflects the interests and concerns of the Chinese people. There are, for example, at least 19 Chinese words for silk and 8 for rice. And because the Chinese care deeply for their families, there is a plethora of words for relations. The Chinese have 5 words they can use for uncle, depending on whose brother he is.[11]

The world we experience helps shape the language we speak, and the language we speak helps sustain our perception of reality and our view of our world. This idea is contained in the **Sapir–Whorf hypothesis,** which holds that the labels we use help shape the way we think, or our habits of thinking; our worldview, or

dominant culture
the culture in power; the mainstream culture

Some cultures encourage minimal verbal communication. A Japanese proverb says, "By your mouth you shall perish." What do you think this proverb means?

Sapir–Whorf hypothesis
the belief that the labels we use help shape the way we think, our worldview, and our behavior

the way we perceive the world; and our behavior. According to the Sapir-Whorf hypothesis, people from different cultures perceive stimuli and communicate differently, at least in part because of their language differences. For this reason, you should not assume that the words you use and the words people from other cultures use mean the same thing, nor should you assume that you even see the same reality when viewing the same stimulus. Language and perception are intertwined.[12]

linguistic determinism
the belief that language influences how we interpret the world

linguistic relativity
the belief that persons who speak different languages perceive the world differently

The Sapir-Whorf hypothesis has two threads: linguistic determinism and linguistic relativity. **Linguistic determinism** suggests that our language influences how we interpret the world. **Linguistic relativity** suggests that, since language affects thought, persons who speak different languages will perceive the world differently. In *When Cultures Collide*, Richard Lewis explains why the Zulu language has 39 words for green, while English has but 1. According to a Zulu chief, before their national highway system exisited, the Zulu were required to make long trips across the savannah, or grasslands. Since no signposts or maps existed to facilitate their journeys, they had to rely on the descriptions of those who traveled the road before. Thus, the Zulu devised different words for tree leaves, bush leaves, leaves vibrating with the wind, river greens, pool greens, tree trunk greens, crocodile greens, and so on. The different greens functioned much as a map would in alerting the travelers to important route signposts.[13]

Cultural Differences Can Lead to Confused Translations

Translating ideas from one language to another can lead to problems. Sometimes the situation produced by a bungled translation, while costly, is still amusing. For example, an English-speaking representative of an American soft drink company could not understand why Mexican customers laughed when she offered them free samples of Fresca soda. In Mexican slang, the word *fresca* can be translated as "lesbian." Similarly, Beck's beer has been translated into Chinese as *Bei Ke*, which means "shellfish overcome."[14] Along the same lines, Dr Pepper no longer runs its "I'm a Pepper" ads in the United Kingdom, because *pepper* in British slang means "prostitute."

Other times, however, a poor translation can insult and confuse recipients. For example, one Spanish-language letter sent to welfare recipients about changes in New Jersey's welfare program contained numerous grammatical errors, suggesting a lack of multicultural competency. Referring to the recipient's ability to support himself or herself, the letter uses the word *soportarse*. But the common translation of the verb *support* in Spanish is *sostener* or *mantener*. In Spanish, *soportarse* means "to tolerate oneself." Another section translated *parole violator* as "rapist under oath."[15]

Poorly translated reports can have economic as well as political repercussions. For example, a badly translated version of a Chinese tourism reporter's speculative musings on how an appreciation of the Chinese currency might play itself out not only made the reporter's story much more concrete, but its garbled English also triggered a trading panic and the potential reevaluation of world currencies. The translator blamed the reporter for putting too many vague sentences in the story, thereby causing the mistranslation.[16] How can such problems be avoided?

Culture Influences Communication Style

Because members of Asian cultures practice the principles of *omoiyari* (listeners need to understand the speaker without the speaker's being specific or direct) and *sassuru* (listeners need to use subtle cues to infer a speaker's meaning), they are apt to keep their feelings to themselves and use language more sparingly and carefully than do Westerners.[17] Because Westerners value straight talk, prefer to speak explicitly, and use inductive and deductive reasoning to make points, they may interpret the roundabout expressions of Asians as evasive, manipulative, or misleading.

The way parents in both Western and Asian cultures handle a request from a child to whom they do not want to accede provides a prime example of the cultural differences in directness. When confronted with such a situation, most U.S. parents would simply say no. In Japan, however, the parent would give reasons for denying the child's request but will not say no directly.[18] Every culture teaches its members its preferred style. Whereas in the United States we prefer to be up-front and tell it like it is, many Asian cultures stand by the value of indirectness because it helps people save face and avoid being criticized or contradicted in public.

Prejudiced Talk

Sometimes members of a dominant culture use derogatory terms or racist language to label members of a co-culture, disparage them as inferior or undesirable, and set them apart from the mainstream group. **Linguistic prejudice** or the use of **prejudiced language** reflects the dominant group's desire to exert its power over other groups. Such language stresses the differences between people of different groups, downplays any similarities, claims that the persons who are different do not make an effort to adapt, and notes that they are involved in negative acts and that they threaten the interests of in-group members.[19]

The courts have ruled that managers who use **racial code words** (words that are discriminatory but are not literally racist), such as "you people" and "one of them," help create a racially hostile environment. As a result of this ruling, many businesses are banning the use of such phrases.[20] Additionally, corporate advertisers and educational institutions have long used Native American names such as "redskins" "braves," "Seminoles," and "Crazy Horse," as well as logos and images including severed heads, tomahawk chops, and a Native American princess to sell products and events.[21] There is a significant degree of economic and emotional investment in "playing Indian."[22] In your opinion are such practices and representations racist? Should they be eliminated? The National Collegiate Athletic Association (NCAA) thinks they should be. In 2005, the NCAA banned the use of Indian imagery and nicknames from postseason tournaments unless the named American Indian tribe gave its approval for their use, as the Seminole tribe of Florida did to Florida State University.[23] The ban means that without the express permission of an affected Indian tribe, no mascots will perform at tournament games, and beginning in 2008, Indian images on uniforms will also be prohibited.

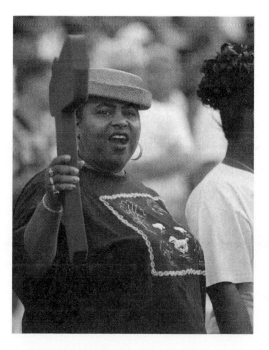

linguistic prejudice
the use of prejudiced language

prejudiced language
sexist, ageist, or racist language; language disparaging to the members of a co-culture

racial code words
words that are discriminatory but not literally racist

Exploring Diversity

Language in Thought and Action

Those who favor the use of Indian names, mascots, and rituals in sports and society dismiss calls to prohibit such use. They assert that those who oppose such use are oversensitive and humorless. Those who oppose the use counter by saying that supporters are unwilling to grant Indians full and participatory citizenship, as indicated by their objectifying them, relegating Indians to the role of mascot or caricature.[25]

How would you react if a sports team were named the "Fighting Whites" and had a white man in a suit as its mascot? To protest an opposing team's use of the name

"Fighting Reds," one multiracial team in Colorado made an attempt to promote a national debate over the stereotyping of American Indians and did just that.

What about the U.S. military's use of equipment such as the Apache, Chinook, and Black Hawk helicopters? What about the names of popular vehicles such as Jeep Cherokee and Pontiac? In your opinion, could carmakers market a car named the "Wandering Jew" effectively?[26] Do you believe there is a double standard when it comes to the contemporary use of racial slurs, products, and mascots? If so, what, if any, action should we take?

What do you think of the NCAA's decision? Can you imagine a team today being called the "Cleveland Africans," the "Cleveland Asians," or the "Cleveland Hispanics"?[24] Why or why not?

Globalization Influences Language Use

Because of free trade, and the popularity of Hollywood and the Internet, the use of English around the world is growing. With globalization, more and more companies, such as the French telecommunications company Alcatel, use English as their internal language.[27] Not everyone is pleased with this side effect of globalization, however. The fear among non-English-speaking nations is that, if their citizens use English, the use of their native languages will disappear, threatening national identity. For example, so many young Germans mix their language with English so freely that their speech is called Denglish, a blend of *Deutsch* (meaning "German") and *English*.[28]

The adoption of English or English-sounding words is common for persons within the United States for whom English is not their first language. When people from different groups converge, they begin to straddle cultural worlds, with language acting as the bridge. For example, the influence of English on New York Spanish produced Spanglish, a blend of Spanish and English. This may suggest that Latinos who speak Spanglish think of themselves less as members of national groups than they did in the past and more as members of a wider community. Spanglish is also used in TV programs such as *¡Mucha Lucha!* and in Hallmark greeting cards, signifying its growing prominence.

In an effort to find new ways to reach Hispanics, now the largest minority group in the United States, at one Grammy awards ceremony Crest, Procter & Gamble's (P&G) oral care brand, became the first P&G consumer product to air a Spanish-language advertisement during a nationally broadcast television event that reaches a general audience. The tag (last line) for the Crest spot, entitled "Good-Bye Kiss" was in English.[29]

Hip-Hop and Rap Talk

Hip-hop is a social community that uses rap, a special language, to help express its culture.[30] Rap is a celebration of language that speaks to both the body and

Rap is a language that speaks to both the body and the brain. Some critics malign it while others praise it. What do you think of it?

the brain. Since its introduction about a quarter of a century ago, critics have maligned and praised, condemned and lauded rap. Rap is blamed for promoting violence and misogyny, praised for promoting peace and minority influence. The U.S. government even broadcasts raps on the airwaves of Radio Sawa in an effort to win over Arab youth.[31] U.S. soldiers serving in Iraq also turn to rap to express and relieve their fears, aggression, and exhaustion. For some, rap is the defining pulse for the Iraq war, enabling soldiers to share with others what it is like there.[32]

The rapper's words arrive in syncopated speech, peppered with both rapid-fire rhymed boasts and taunts. The subjects of rap range from sex, money, and guns to love, politics, the minutiae of our lives, and the American social experience. Rappers redefine the meanings of words. When someone attuned to the hip-hop culture says, "I'm keeping it ghetto," he or she means "I'm keeping it real." The words in a rap mean something different from what most Americans have come to understand. Rap is an influence on American popular culture in music, fashion, and language, and it can be difficult to keep up with all the new words that hip-hop adds to the national vocabulary. Consequently, journalist Alonzo Westbrook wrote *The Hip Hoptionary: The Dictionary of Hip Hop Terminology*. Westbrook traveled the United States from coast to coast to capture the language as it is used around the country. Sometimes the meaning of a word is coded for the rapper to hide behind it. For example, according to Westbrook, hip-hop artists code the word *nigger* as an acronym to mean "never ignorant, getting goals accomplished." They flipped the word's meaning purposefully to make it less hurtful to African Americans.[33]

Some say that the ambiguous nature of rap reveals that rappers are using a coded language so that they can better juggle multiple constituencies. What do you think?

GENDER AND LANGUAGE

Language influences the attitudes we hold about males and females, as well as the way that males and females perceive each other.

Sexism in Language

Sexist language perpetuates negative stereotypes and negatively affects our communication. Past use of male generics, such as *mankind, chairman, spokesman, manpower,* and *Man of the Year,* are blamed for causing men to be perceived as more important or significant than women. To counter this perception, many companies and individuals stopped using male generics or other kinds of sexist language, and used gender-neutral language instead.

Another way that language use may be sexist is the way words are used to address women. "Women, much more than men, are addressed through terms of endearment such as honey, cutie, and sweetie, which function to devalue women by depriving them of their name while renaming them with trivial terms."[34]

Finally, while the English language has more masculine terms than feminine terms, it has more negative feminine terms than masculine ones.[35]

Gender and Speech Style

qualifiers
tentative phrases

Sometimes the sex of communicators affects not only the meaning we give to their utterances but also the very structure of those utterances. Women, for example, tend to use more tentative phrases, or **qualifiers,** in their speech than men do. Phrases like "I guess," "I think," and "I wonder if" abound in the speech patterns of women but not in those of men. This pattern is also passed on to the very young through their favorite cartoon characters. Just as their real-life counterparts are apt to do, female cartoon characters, more than male characters, use verbs that indicate lack of certainty ("I suppose") and words judged to be polite.[36] Is art mirroring life, or vice versa? When students were shown cartoon characters and asked

pop language
words and phrases used to
sell oneself as hip or cool

MediaWise

What's Said? Who's Wed?

1. In the book *Slam Dunks and No-Brainers: Language in Your Life, the Media, Business, Politics, and, Like, Whatever,* author and media critic Leslie Savan complains about the growing use of **pop language,** words and phrases used to sell oneself as hip or cool. Savan asserts that phrases such as "Saddam is toast," "Don't go there," "Get over it," "I don't think so," "You've got that right," "bling," and "duh," constitute a new subdivision of the English language, one that projects both an attitude and a vocabulary derived from television and advertising. She contends that such phrases click into place without the user's needing to think, displace the use of more complex thoughts, and effectively turn users into corporate pawns. What do you think? Keep a count of the number of pop phrases that you and

people you know use during a typical day. What purposes do you think they serve? What words could have been spoken in their place that might have been more expressive of personal thoughts?

2. Three decades ago, a survey of news stories revealed that a woman's marital status was mentioned 64 percent of the time, while a male's marital status was mentioned in only 12 percent of the stories.[37]

Pick up a copy of a recent English-language newspaper or magazine. Identify five male-centered and five female-centered news stories in it. Count the number of times the marital status of each person is referred to in each story. To what extent, if any, do the percentages of sexist references appear to have changed during the past three decades?

to identify a character's sex on the basis of the words spoken by the character, students assigned the logical, concise, and controlling captions to male characters and the emotional, vague, and verbose captions to female characters.[38] Are cartoons helping to perpetuate stereotypes?

Men and women rely on different conversational strategies. Women, for example, tend to turn statements into questions more than men do, saying something like "Don't you think it would be better to send them that report first?" Men, in contrast, typically respond with a more definitive "Yes, it would be better to send them that report first." According to Robin Lakoff, a researcher on language and gender, women do not "lay claim to" their statements as frequently as men do. In addition, women use more **tag questions** than men do. A tag is midway between an outright statement and a yes–no question. For instance, women often make queries like these: "Joan is here, isn't she?" "It's hot in here, isn't it?" By seeking verbal confirmation for their perceptions, women acquire a reputation for tentativeness. Similarly, women use more **disclaimers** than men do, prefacing their remarks with statements like "This probably isn't important, but . . ." While male speech tends to be dominant, straightforward, and attention-commanding, female speech tends to be gentle, friendly, and accommodating.[39] Such practices weaken the messages women send to others.

According to communications researcher Patricia Hayes Bradley, even if men use tag questions, the perceptual damage done to them by this weaker verbal form is not as great as the damage done to women. Bradley found that when women used tag questions and disclaimers or failed to support their arguments, they were judged to be less intelligent and knowledgeable—but men were not. Simply talking "like a woman" causes a woman to be judged negatively.[40] Researchers Nancy Henley and Cheris Kramarae believe, females face a disadvantage when interacting with males: "Females are required to develop special sensitivity to interpret males' silence, lack of emotional expression, or brutality, and to help men express themselves. Yet it is women's communication style that is often labeled as inadequate and maladaptive."[41]

Compile a list of differences you believe exist between men's and women's uses of language. Why do you think these differences have developed?

tag questions
questions that are midway between outright statements and yes–no questions

disclaimers
remarks that diminish a statement's importance

Exploring Diversity

Language in Action
Interview five males and five females—if possible, from diverse cultural backgrounds. For each interviewee, in addition to identifying his or her sex, also identify his or her age, race, ethnicity, and social class. Ask each interviewee these questions:

1. In general, who tends to take turns more frequently when interacting, males or females?
2. In general, who tends to make reference to the comments of preceding speakers, males or females?
3. In general, who uses language more cooperatively, males or females?
4. In general, who makes more supportive comments, males or females?
5. In general, who is more polite, males or females?

To what extent, if at all, were the answers affected by sex? To what extent, if at all, were they affected by variables other than sex?

Gender-Lects

gender-lects

Deborah Tannen's term for language differences attributed to gender

Gender affects how men and women use and process language in a number of other ways as well. According to linguist Deborah Tannen, men and women speak different **gender-lects.** While women speak and hear a language of connection and intimacy, Tannen finds that men speak and hear a language of status and independence.[42] As a result, when conversing with men, women tend to listen attentively rather than interrupt or challenge what a man is saying. Why? Tannen holds that it is because challenging the man could damage the established connection that most women believe must be preserved at all costs.

In addition, men and women tend to speak about different topics. Monica Hiller and Fern Johnson conducted a topic analysis of conversations held in two coffee shops, one frequented by young adults and the other by middle-aged and older customers. Their research revealed that, whereas men and women both talked about work and social issues, women talked about personal issues and the older men virtually never discussed personal issues.[43] Although men and women frequently talk to each other, their cross-gender talk differs topically from man-to-man or woman-to-woman talk. Women talk about their doubts and fears, personal and family problems, and intimate relationships, while, in general, men talk more about work and sports.

LANGUAGE AND POWER

Some people seem to announce their powerlessness through their language. Because they speak indirectly, people perceive that they lack self-confidence and power. In contrast, persons perceived to be "powertalkers" make definite statements, such as "Let's go out to dinner tonight." Powertalkers direct the action; they assume control.

Typically, powertalkers also hesitate less in their speech. Instead of making statements filled with nonfluencies, such as "I wish you wouldn't, uh, keep me waiting so long," powertalkers enhance their sense of self-worth by projecting their opinions with more confidence. They eliminate fillers, such as "er," "um," "you know," "like," and "well," which serve as verbal hiccups and make a speaker appear weak.

Powerful talk is talk that comes directly to the point. It does not contain disclaimers ("I probably shouldn't mention this, but . . .") or tag questions like those described in the section "Gender and Speech Style." If you speak powertalk, your credibility and your ability to influence others will increase. Changing the power balance may be as simple as changing the words you use.

Talking powerfully may also be less risky. According to Deborah Tannen, speaking indirectly in specific situations can precipitate problems. She cites the following conversation about de-icing between a pilot and a copilot as an example of its dangers:

Copilot: Look how the ice is just hanging on his, ah, back, back there, see that? . . .

Copilot: See all those icicles on the back there and everything?

Captain: Yeah . . .

Copilot: Boy, this is a, this is a losing battle here on trying to de-ice those things . . .

Flight crews are trained to express themselves in direct ways.

Copilot: Let's check these tops again since we've been here awhile.

Captain: I think we get to go here in a minute.[44]

Less than a minute later, the plane crashed. While the copilot, probably because of his lower status, had tried to warn the pilot indirectly, the pilot failed to act on the cues. Indirectness, it seems, is easier for higher-status persons to ignore. As a result, flight crews today are trained to express themselves in more direct ways, and pilots are taught to pick up on indirect hints.

Has indirectness ever caused problems for you? What prevented you or the person you were speaking with from being more direct?

PROBLEMS WITH MEANING: PATTERNS OF MISCOMMUNICATION

If we do not make an attempt to analyze how people's backgrounds influence them in assigning meaning, we may have trouble communicating with them. For most of us, words have more than a single meaning. In fact, a commonly used word can frequently have more than 20 definitions. We know that a strike in bowling is different from a strike in baseball. We know that striking a match is not the same as striking up the band. For this reason, we must pay careful attention to the context of a message. Unfortunately, we frequently forget that words are rarely used in one and only one sense, and we assume when we speak to others that our words are being understood in only the way we intend them to be understood. Our receivers, however, may assume that their interpretation of our words is the meaning we intended. Let's explore what happens when this occurs.

If you cry "Forward" you must be sure to make clear the direction in which to go. Don't you see that if you fail to do that and simply call out the word to a monk and a revolutionary, they will go in precisely opposite directions?

—Anton Chekhov

Bypassing: Confusing Meanings

> All someone said was "Hi, Jack!" but at a suburban Detroit airport, those two words precipitated a crisis.
>
> A microphone happened to be open when an individual aboard a corporate jet greeted the co-pilot. Air traffic controllers in the airport's control tower equated those words with "hijack." The police, the SWAT team, and the FBI were alerted. The plane was ordered to return to the tower.[45]

Sometimes people think they understand each other, when, in fact, they are really missing each other's meaning. This pattern of miscommunication is called **bypassing,** because the interactants' meanings simply pass by one another.

We can identify two main kinds of bypassing.[46] The first occurs when people use different words or phrases to represent the same thing but are unaware that they are both talking about the same thing. For example, two urban politicians once argued vehemently over welfare policies. One held that the city's welfare program should be "overhauled," whereas the other believed that "minor changes" should be made. Far too much time passed before it was realized that the first politician's overhaul was actually equivalent to the second politician's minor changes. How many times have you argued unnecessarily because you were unaware that another person was simply using a different word or phrase to mean the same thing you were saying?

The second, and more common, type of bypassing occurs when people use the same word or phrase but give it different meanings. In such cases, people appear to be in agreement when they substantially disagree. Sometimes this type of bypassing is harmless. Semanticists tell a tall, but otherwise useful, story about a man who was driving on a parkway when his engine stalled. He managed to flag down another driver, who, after hearing his story, consented to push the stalled car to get it started. "My car has an automatic transmission," the first man explained, "so you'll have to get up to 30 or 35 miles an hour to get me moving." The other driver nodded in understanding, and the stalled motorist then climbed back into his own car and waited for the other car to line up behind him. After much more waiting, he turned around—to see the other driver coming at him at 30 miles per hour.

Developing an awareness that bypassing can occur when you communicate is a first step in preventing it from interfering with or needlessly complicating your relationships. If you believe it is possible for your listener to misunderstand you, then be willing to take the time needed to ensure that your meanings for words overlap. To avoid bypassing, you must be "person-minded" instead of "word-minded." Remind yourself that your words may generate unpredictable or unexpected reactions in others. Trying to anticipate those reactions will help you forestall communication problems.

Labeling: Confusing Words and Things

Sometimes we forget that it is people, not words, who make meanings. When this happens, we pay far too much attention to labels and far too little attention to reality. We can approach this phase of our study of meaning by considering the problem of labels and how strongly they can influence us.

How important are labels in our culture? A judge ruled that an individual could not change his name to a number because a number was totalitarian and

bypassing

miscommunication that occurs when individuals think they understand each other but actually miss each other's meaning

Think of instances when being "word-minded" rather than "person-minded" caused problems for you.

What type of behavior would you exhibit around vats labeled "Gasoline Drums"? You would probably be careful not to light any matches; if you smoked, you would be certain not to toss away any cigarette butts. Would you change your behavior if the labels on the containers read "Empty Gasoline Drums"? Chances are, you might relax a bit and give less thought to the possibility of starting a fire—although empty drums are actually more dangerous because they contain explosive vapor.

an offense to human dignity. What does a number, as opposed to a name, signify? Would we change if our names were changed?[47] In *Romeo and Juliet*, Shakespeare offered some thoughts on the significance of names when he had Juliet, of the Capulet family, say these words to Romeo, a Montague:

'Tis but thy name that is my enemy;
Thou art thyself, though not a Montague.
What's Montague? It is nor hand, nor foot,
Nor arm, nor face, nor any other part
Belonging to a man. O! be some other name;
What's in a name? that which we call a rose
By any other name would smell as sweet;
So Romeo would, were he not Romeo call'd.

What's in a name? Is who you are affected by what you are called? Do the names of your friends affect your opinions of them?

Evasive and Emotive Language

Frequently, our reaction to a person or event is totally changed by words. If we are not vigilant, we can easily be manipulated or conned by language.

Analyze the following sets of words to see how your reactions may change as the words used change:

1. coffin	casket	slumber chamber
2. girl	woman	broad
3. backward	developing	underdeveloped
4. the corpse	the deceased	the loved one

A few years ago, the organization People for the Ethical Treatment of Animals asked the Federal Trade Commission to revise the fur label term "animal producing the fur" to read "animal slaughtered for the fur."[48] The word **euphemism** is derived from the Greek term meaning "to use words of good omen." When we use a euphemism, we substitute a pleasant term for a less pleasant one. Euphemisms can help conceal a communicator's meaning by making the message delivered appear more congenial than it actually is. Employees who lose their jobs are "dehired," undergo a "vocational relocation," are left "indefinitely idling," or experience a "realignment" or "constructive dismissal."[49] When was the last time someone was fired? Since the environment became an issue in practical campaigns, strategist Frank Luntz advised candidates to use the term *climate change* in place of *global warming* because "while global warming has catastrophic communications attached to it, climate change sounds a more controllable and less emotional challenge."[50] He also suggested they use *conservationist* instead of *environmentalist* because the former conveys a "moderate, reasoned, common sense position," while the latter has the "connotation of extremism."[51] Euphemisms, according to one expert on corporate doublespeak, are the "language of nonresponsibility."[52] The coiner of the term *doublespeak*, William Lutz, equates it with "linguistic fraud and deception."[53] Lutz believes that former president Ronald Reagan used doublespeak when he called the invasion of Grenada a "predawn vertical insertion," named the MX missile the "Peacemaker," and referred to taxes as "revenue enhancement." In a move to change perception of the privatization of Social Security, some used the words *personal accounts* in place of *private accounts*.[54] And, because the thinking is that everybody fears the word *cloning*, people who oppose cloning research tend to use the word, while people who support it call it something else. Such was the case with South Korean scientists who recently announced that they had used

euphemism

a pleasant word that is substituted for a less pleasant one

"somatic cell nuclear transfer" to produce "human NT blastocysts," from which they extracted "hESC," meaning they had cloned human embryos.[55] Should people use words to disguise reality? The Walt Disney Corporation did some verbal somersaults to make its Mr. Magoo character politically correct. Under fire by the National Federation of the Blind for resuscitating the nearsighted cartoon figure, a Disney spokesperson countered that Mr. Magoo isn't blind but, rather, "visually limited."[56]

Thus, if we like an old piece of furniture, we might refer to it as an antique; if we don't like it, we might well call it a piece of junk. Words broadcast attitude.

Politically Correct Language

The following definitions appear in Henry Beard and Christopher Cerf's tongue-in-cheek guide, *The Official Politically Correct Dictionary and Handbook*:

lazy: motivationally deficient

wrong: differently logical

ugly: cosmetically different

prostitute: sex-care provider

fat: horizontally challenged[57]

What is politically correct language? Is it sensitive speech or censored speech? In what ways, if any, does its use sustain, or violate, our right of free speech? According to Diane Ravitch, author of *The Language Police*, words that might offend feminists, religious conservatives, multiculturalists, ethnic activists, or members of other groups are routinely deleted from the textbooks read in U.S. schools because they are believed to be politically incorrect. For example, one textbook author rewrote Bob Dylan's folk song "Blowin' in the Wind," which had asked, "How many roads must a man walk down before you call him a man?"* to read "How many roads must an individual walk down before you can call him or her an adult?"[58]

Like so many other words, politically correct language means different things to different people. For some of us, being politically correct means making the effort not to offend by selecting words that demonstrate our respect for and sensitivity to the needs and interests of others. Politically correct language is meant to take the sting out of confrontations by blunting the sharpness of the words we use. For example, in the United States, over a period of time, the word *slow* was replaced by the word *retarded*, which was changed to *challenged* and then to *special*. Similarly, over a half century, the defining term for persons of African ancestry has shifted from *colored* to *Negro* to *Black* to *Afro-American* to *people of color* to *African American*.[59] When we use politically correct language, we adapt our language to reveal our sensitivity to the preferences of those we are conversing with.

For others, however, political correctness means that we feel compelled by societal pressures not to use some words—oftentimes referred to as taboo words—because we believe that doing so could cause others to label us as racist, sexist, homophobic, or ageist. For example, some years ago, a student at one Ivy League university was thought to be racist when he yelled, "Shut up, you water buffalo!" out a window at a noisy group of African-American women. Still others view political correctness and sensitivity training as a danger to free speech. Which of these three positions comes closest to the one you hold?

Each of us has learned to see the world not as it is, but through the distorting glass of our words. It is through words that we are made human, and it is through words that we are dehumanized.

—Ashley Montagu,
The Language of Self-Deception

Disparaging remarks are made about civil rights icons Rosa Parks and Martin Luther King in the film Barbershop. *Rosa Parks became the mother of the civil rights movement when she refused to give up her seat on a segregated Montgomery, Alabama, bus. In the film, the character Eddie says Parks did that only because she was tired. Eddie also refers to King as "a ho." Do you think these remarks should have been cut from the film? Explain.*

---

*Copyright © 1962 by Warner Bros. Inc. Copyright renewed 1990 by Special Rider Music. All rights reserved. International copyright secured. Reprinted by permission.

PROFANITY AND OBSCENITY: INCIVILITY AND THE COARSENING OF LANGUAGE

When he won for the fifth time at Talladega, NASCAR driver Dale Earnhardt Jr. told an interviewer that his victory "don't mean s—— right now."[60] Has it become acceptable to utter obscenities in public, including in the media? The use of insults, vulgar expressions, and speech that degrades and encourages hostility in others is on the rise.

A female employee of a major construction company recently complained to the company's director of human resources about the cursing used in the company's facilities. The use of profanity distressed workers. The company countered by publishing "A Language Code of Ethics," separate and apart from its sexual harassment policy guide. It defined inappropriate language as "unwanted, deliberate, repeated, unsolicited profanity, cussing, swearing, vulgar, insulting, abusive or crude language." The company is now a cuss-free workplace. Workers who violate the policy are subject to disciplinary action.[61]

Profanity has become common, especially in high-stress jobs. Some policies differentiate between "casual" and "causal" swearing. Casual swearing is bad language we use for the fun of it, because we are too lazy to use other words and we think we can get away with it. Causal swearing is profanity produced by the inability to control an aroused emotion, such as anger, frustration, or impatience.[62]

Why are we so comfortable using profanity? Might it be because profanity and speech that degrades have become so much a part of our mediated language landscape, used in virtually every crime-adventure television or cable program or film, that we hardly notice when a profane or an obscene expression occurs in real life?[63] Commonplace profanities now function as fillers—they slide off the tongue much as the words *you know* and *like* do. They have become part of the speech pattern—and not just for teenagers and adults. Even elementary school children use four-letter words when in and out of school. For some, this kind of speech is normative; it identifies them as a member of a group.

Students of popular culture observe that profanity has been increasing since the 1960s, when protesters used it to demonstrate their disdain for the establishment. Then, it was perceived as a liberating factor. Many of today's students are swearing, in part, because their parents did. A display of profanity used to be perceived as "macho." Women, for example, began to adopt it as they fought for equality of the sexes.

Entertainment media keep pushing the profanity envelope further and further, making it a challenge to draw the line in either educational settings or the workplace.

Sometimes pejorative words that are used to stigmatize or degrade the members of a group are reclaimed by the group and redefined by group members as positive in nature. For example, gays and lesbians now use the term *queer* to make positive statements about who they are. Some women proudly refer to themselves as girls. And some African Americans, in an effort to invalidate the meaning that bigots attached to it, now use the racial epithet *nigger* among themselves.[64] The use of the n-word, once strictly taboo, has undergone a transformation and is common in popular culture. In video games such as "Grand Theft Auto: San Andreas," for example, Black characters use the word repeatedly. It is also a staple in the stand-up routines of comics such as Chris Rock.[65] In your opinion, does the reappropriation of words that were once used as slurs by members of the very groups

What do you think? Has profanity become an acceptable part of life, or should we develop the skill and discipline not to swear but to interact in a more civil manner?

that were the targets of the offensive language help limit the damage done by those who used the same words in particularly offensive ways?

THINKING CRITICALLY ABOUT LANGUAGE: HOW TO MAKE LANGUAGE WORK FOR YOU

Whenever we communicate, we consciously or unconsciously select the level of language we will use. Normally, the words we select depend on the person with whom we are communicating and the situation in which we are communicating.

A Call for Common Sense

Just as particular styles of apparel and behavior are appropriate for certain situations, so certain styles of language are appropriate at certain times and in certain places. Consider slang—a style of language used by special groups but not considered proper by society at large. Although we may use slang when conversing with our friends, it is inappropriate and unwise when speaking to an instructor or when delivering a speech to the town council.

What kind of language do you find personally offensive? How does your language use change from person to person? Would you feel comfortable using obscenities with any of the following people: your best friend, your instructor, your employer? Why or why not?

"It's only fair to warn you that my conversation contains adult language that you may find offensive."

A Call for Clarity

There is a new language for jurors in California—plain English. For example, the phrase "willfully falsified" is now read or is said as, simply, "lied."[66] Why did officials believe that such an action was necessary? Because in day-to-day communication, in legal or ordinary settings, far too often we use language that others cannot easily understand. It does not matter how accurately a selected word or phrase expresses your ideas if the receivers cannot comprehend it. If you want to be understood, you must make every attempt to select words with meaning for your listeners.

A good rule to follow to achieve clarity is to keep jargon to a minimum unless your receiver is schooled in the jargon. In other words, speak the same language as your listener. Most of us who live in the United States share a common language, but many of us also frequently use one or more sublanguages. A sublanguage is simply a special language used by members of a particular co-culture. We all belong to several co-cultures—a national group, an occupational group, an educational group, an ethnic group, and perhaps a religious group. Having a common sublanguage helps members of the group attain a sense of identity. It also helps them come across as part of the in-crowd or as being in the know.[67]

However, since all sublanguages are intended to enable communication only within a particular group, a sublanguage is probably not readily understood by outsiders. Consider the following brief dialogue between two doctors:

Doctor 1: How's that patient you were telling me about?

Doctor 2: Well, she's improving. But now she's suffering from cephalagia complicated by agrypnia.

You would probably not immediately guess that *cephalagia* is the medical term for a headache and that *agrypnia* refers to insomnia. People schooled in the technical

Jargon functions as shorthand for people who understand the use. In the war in Iraq, weapons of mass destruction were referred to in briefings the military had for the press and public as WMDs. Would you have understood this use?

Using language to facilitate understanding can be a challenge. Too frequently, clashes in cultural style precipitate misunderstandings.

language of a particular group should guard against the temptation to impress others rather than to communicate. In short, if we want our receivers to understand us, we must always ask ourselves, Who am I talking to?

TECHNOLOGY AND LANGUAGE USE

onlinespeak

the informal communication style that marks electronic communication

Internet user Andrew Walker sometimes lapses into **onlinespeak** when writing offline: In one school paper, he wrote, "Surplus is an excess. But surplus can also mean 2 much." His instructor deducted 10 points. The protocol of informality that marks electronic communication for Andrew and millions of others has led to our using language in ways we never would have before and has set off a debate regarding whether the Internet invigorates language or strips it of its expressive power.[68]

When linguists talk of dialects, by tradition, they are referring to the spoken word. The Internet, however, appears to have spawned a new written dialect, one in between speech and writing, in which punctuation is abandoned, uppercasing is used primarily if you are "shouting," and an array of acronyms substitute for phrases. Knowing and using the dialect allows us to develop a sense of belonging to the group—a group that exists in cyberspace.

Educators believe that we should know where to draw the line between formal and conversational writing. Unthinkingly, "Generation Text" members mix rapid-fire Internet English and schoolwork.[70] Do you ever do this?

Currently, millions of us are writing letters, exchanging thoughts, and sharing meaning in a networked world.[69] As members of a cybercommunity, however, we probably share a special language, the equivalent of online jargon, as a strategy of connection. During our communications, for example, we may use truncated speech and acronyms for phrases, including *BTW* for "by the way," *TTFN* for "ta-ta for now," and *IMHO* for "in my humble opinion."

In addition to online truncation, the language of expedience has spread from the Internet to cell phones.[71] Like the Internet, mobile phone text messaging has its share of short hand expressions, including *RUOK* (Are you OK?), *CUL8R* (see you later), *BHL8* (be home late), *TAH* (take a hint), *A3* (anytime, anywhere, anyplace), *SPST* (same place, same time), *XLNT* (excellent), *U4E* (yours forever), and *YTLKIN2ME* (You talking to me?).

netiquette

rules of the Internet

Rules of the Internet—also known as **netiquette**—continue to evolve. Usually, the participants themselves work out conversational ground rules. The word *flame*, for example, is used to describe what occurs when one person verbally attacks or denigrates another online. Flaming, like intemperate speech during face-to-face interaction, is generally frowned upon.

The online style of writers (how they say something) is equally as important as their message (what they say). When it comes to the sound, or tone, of online messages, e-mail writers frequently experience problems. Because of the volume of e-mail messages we send and receive, and the speed with which we fire them off, we may operate under the mistaken impression that we do not need to edit closely what we write. We should concern ourselves with tone, however, because what we write could end up being read by multiple readers. To this end, we should do our best to edit our e-mails for unintended meanings before clicking on Send.[72]

Why has text messaging become so popular? It appears that people longing for private conversations enjoy communicating silently, especially in public places. Many use text messaging while at movies, at sports events, or on subways. Are you one of the many?

Instant messaging (IM) has also gone corporate, spreading to the workplace. It is helping reverse a trend attributed to e-mail and voice mail that had made it difficult for anyone to determine if businesspeople were in the office. It also facilitates telecommuting, because it can verify who is really working at home or at least is logged in. Since failing to respond quickly to an IM message is considered rude, workers typically sign out when they leave their office or show themselves as "too busy to chat" when they know their reply will be delayed.[73]

Since members of online communities tend to be more concerned with what others think rather than what they look like, the presence of sexist and racist language tends to be rare. Nonetheless, one admonition warned: "We would like to remind the frequent posters here that what we say is going out to a potential readership of between 25,000 and 40,000 individuals . . . So words do have meaning and what you write in haste or in anger may have more influence than you realize."[74]

Technological developments are leaving their mark on language. Being uninstalled means being fired. Doing a bit flip means experiencing a disturbing personality alteration. Engaging in nonlinear behavior (NLB) means acting irrationally. Taking a bio-break means taking a trip to the bathroom. Can you offer other examples of technology's impact on language?

GUIDELINES FOR DEVELOPING LANGUAGE SKILLS

Throughout this chapter we have stressed that mastery of certain language skills will improve your ability to communicate effectively with others. Use the following guidelines to ensure that your words work *for* you rather than *against* you.

Identify How Labels Affect Your Behavior

Words are not the things they represent. Always remember that words are nothing more than symbols. No connection necessarily exists between a symbol and what people have agreed that symbol represents. In other words, symbols and their representations are independent of each other.

All of us at times respond as if words and things were one and the same. Think of how often you buy a product such as Intimate, Brut, Bold, Caress, Secret, or Angel because of what the label seems to promise. How many times have you turned against a person because he or she is called liberal, conservative, feminist, chauvinist, intellectual, or brainless? Examine your behavior with others. Make certain that you react to people, not to the categories in which you or others have placed them.

Identify How the Words You Use Affect Your Feelings and Attitudes

Few of the words you select to describe things are neutral. As S. I. Hayakawa and Alan R. Hayakawa, authors of *Language in Thought and Action*, noted:

> We are a little too dignified, perhaps, to growl like dogs, but we do the next best thing and substitute series of words, such as "You dirty double-crosser!" "The filthy scum!" Similarly, if we are pleasurably agitated, we may, instead of purring or wagging the tail, say things like "She's the sweetest girl in all the world."[75]

We all use *snarl words* (words with highly negative connotations) and *purr words* (words with highly positive connotations). These words do not describe the people or things we are talking about; rather, they describe our personal

Count the number of times you use purr words and snarl words each day. What do they reveal about your likes and dislikes? How do your words give you away?

Thinking Critically

Reflect and Respond

Language expert Wendell Johnson was fond of noting that the language we use puts not only words in our mouths but also notions in our heads.

On the basis of your personal understanding of language use and misuse, discuss the kinds of notions that language may promote.

Focus on Service Learning

First, use the Web to investigate the kinds of language problems that a local health clinic or another local service organization of your own choosing confront daily. Next, visit the local health clinic or service organization. Then, using the knowledge you have gained from researching the subject and reading this chapter, meet with representatives of the clinic or service organization. Share with them how an understanding of differences in language and meaning could benefit the clinic's or organization's staff by enabling them to avoid creating or compounding a language-based barrier.

feelings and attitudes. When we make statements like "He's a great American," "She's a dirty politician," "He's a bore," "She's a radical," we should not delude ourselves into thinking that we are talking about anything but our own preferences.

It is also important to realize that a word that does not function as a snarl or purr word for you may function that way for someone else, even if you do not intend it to be given such an interpretation. Therefore, become conscious of how others react to the words you use. Listen to people around you, and attempt to read their responses to your words. Which words that incite them would not incite you? Which words do you find unacceptable or offensive? Why?

Identify How Experience Can Affect Meaning

Since we assign meaning on the basis of our experience, and since no two people have had exactly the same set of experiences, it follows that no two people have exactly the same meanings for the same word.

Too frequently, we let our words lead us away from where we want to go; we unwittingly antagonize our families, friends, or co-workers. We are infuriated, for example, when an important business deal collapses because our position has not been understood, or we are terrified when the leaders of government miscommunicate and put their countries on a collision course.[76] To avoid such problems, we must remember that meanings can change as the people who use words change.

Be Sure That Meanings Are Shared

As John Condon, author of Semantics and Communication, advises, "Learning to use language intelligently begins by learning not to be used by language."

Since intended meanings are not necessarily the same as perceived meanings, you may need to ask people with whom you are speaking such questions as "What do you think about what I've just said?" and "What do my words mean to you?" Their answers serve two important purposes: They help you determine whether you have been understood, and they permit the other people to become involved in the encounter by expressing their interpretations of your message. If differences in the assignment of meaning surface during this feedback process, you will be able immediately to clarify your meanings by substituting different symbols or by relating your thoughts more closely to the background, state of knowledge, and experiences of your receivers.

Revisiting Chapter Objectives

1. **Define language.**   Language is a unified system of symbols that permits a sharing of meaning. Language allows minds to meet, merge, and mesh. When we make sense out of people's messages, we learn to understand people.

2. **Describe and explain the triangle of meaning.**   There is no direct relationship between words and things, as Ogden and Richards' triangle of meaning illustrates. Words do not "mean"; people give meaning to words.

3. **Distinguish between connotative and denotative meanings.**   A serious barrier to communication occurs when we forget the fact that words have both generally agreed upon denotative—objective, or dictionary—meanings and highly individualized connotative—subjective, or personal—meanings. As a result, different people give different meanings to the same words.

4. **Discuss how culture and gender influence language use.**   Culture and gender influence the ways men and women experience, process, and use language. In part because language and perception are intertwined, language use varies from culture to culture. Words change over time and from place to place according to individual experience. Language also influences the attitudes we hold about males and females, as well as how males and females perceive each other.

5. **Provide examples of bypassing.**   A communication problem that results from confusing meanings is bypassing (when people think they understand each other but in fact do not).

6. **Identify two strategies to improve oral language abilities.**   First, we can use common sense to recognize that certain styles of language are appropriate at certain times and in certain places. Second, we can seek to make ourselves as clear as possible by selecting words with meaning for our listeners, taking into account their educational level and the sublanguages they understand.

7. **Explain how technology is affecting language use.**   How we communicate online frequently differs from how we communicate in person. Some believe the Internet is invigorating language, while others believe it is stripping language of its expressive value.

Resources for Further Inquiry and Reflection

To apply your understanding of how the principles in Chapter 5 are at work in our daily lives, consult the following resources for further inquiry and reflection. Or, if you prefer, choose any other appropriate resource. Then connect the ideas expressed in your chosen selection with the communication concepts and issues you are learning about both in and out of class.

The Wrap Up

Listen to Me

"Woman Is the Nigger of the World" (John Lennon)
"Wake Me Up When September Ends" (Green Day)
"Because of You" (Kelly Clarkson)
"Sweet Talkin' Guy" (The Chiffons)
"Snoop Dogg" (Snoop Dogg)

Discuss the extent to which word choice influences listener attitudes toward the song or the extent to which it influences the nature of a relationship described in the song.

View Me

In Her Shoes	*Bulworth*
The Terminal	*Nell*
The Stepford Wives	*What Women Want*
Clueless	*Windtalkers*

In each of these films, the use of words either interferes with or facilitates a character's objective. Choose one film and discuss the role language plays in it to advance or impede the character's goals.

Read Me

Khaled Hosseini. *The Kite Runner*. New York: Riverhead, 2004.
Amy Tan. *Saving Fish from Drowning*. New York: Putnam's, 2005.
William Gibson. *The Miracle Worker*. New York: Bantam Books, 1975.
George Bernard Shaw. *Pygmalion*. New York: Dover, 1994.

Discuss how one of the preceding works illustrates the concept "meaning is in people, not in words."

Tell Me

Share with the class the insights you gained from your chosen Listen to Me, View Me, or Read Me selection.

Consider the following two statements made by one person: "I value freedom of speech." "I find hate speech and racist, sexist, and ageist speech objectionable." How do you reconcile the two positions? In your opinion, should any of the objectionable kinds of speech have First Amendment protection? In a brief presentation, explain why or why not.

Key Chapter Terminology

Communication
Works

online learning center

www.mhhe.com/gamble9

Use the Communication Works CD-ROM and the Online Learning Center at www.mhhe.com/gamble9 to further your knowledge of the following terminology.

bypassing 120
connotative meaning 107
denotative meaning 107
disclaimers 117
dominant culture 111
euphemism 121
gender-lects 118
language 106
linguistic determinism 112
linguistic prejudice 113
linguistic relativity 112

netiquette 126
onlinespeak 126
pop language 116
prejudiced language 113
qualifiers 116
racial code words 113
Sapir–Whorf hypothesis 111
symbol 106
tag questions 117
triangle of meaning 106

Idioms in Translation

collision course—dangerous path

inspect the territory—look closely at what is in front of your eyes

macho—very masculine

save face—avoid being the object of criticism or embarrassment

transfer meaning—communicate meaning

Test Your Understanding

Go to the *Self Quizzes* on the Communication Works CD-ROM and the book's Online Learning Center at www.mhhe.com/gamble9.

Communication
Works

online learning center

www.mhhe.com/gamble9

Notes

1. Michael Agar. *Language Shock: Understanding the Culture of Conversation*. New York: Morrow, 1994.

2. C. K. Ogden and I. A. Richards. *The Meaning of Meaning*. Orlando, FL: Harcourt Brace Jovanovich, 1993.

3. Charles F. Vich and Ray V. Wood. "Similarity of Past Experience and the Communication of Meaning." *Speech Monographs* 36, pp. 159–162.

4. For a discussion of how the mindless use of language affects behavior, see Ellen Langer. "Interpersonal Mindlessness and Language." *Communication Monographs* 59:3, September 1992, pp. 324–327.

5. Loretta Breuning. "Networking with Yourself: How the Brain Uses Information (Part 1)." *ETC.* 47:2, summer 1990, p. 106.

6. Steven Lee Myers. "A Kinder, Gentler Rogues' Gallery." *New York Times*, June 25, 2000.

7. Robert F. Worth. "Horrific Crime Is Captured in One Word." *New York Times*, December 6, 2002, p. B4.

8. Michiko Kakutani. "When the Greeks Get Snide." *New York Times*, June 27, 2000, p. E1.

9. See, for example, S. I. Hayakawa and Alan R. Hayakawa. *Language in Thought and Action*, 5th ed. Orlando, FL: Harcourt Brace Jovanovich, 1990.

10. John Zeaman. "There's Way Too Much Katakarktanaq." *The Record*, February 15, 2004, pp. F1, F4.

11. Nicholas D. Kristof. "Chinese Relations." *New York Times Magazine*, August 18, 1991, pp. 8–10.

12. B. L. Whorf. "Science and Linguistics." In M. J. B. Carroll, ed. *Language, Thought, and Reality*. Cambridge: Massachusetts Institute of Technology Press, 1956; and Paul Kay and Willet Kempton. "What Is the Sapir-Whorf Hypothesis?" *American Anthropologist* 86, 1984, pp. 65–79. Also, for a discussion of cultural diversity and political correctness, see Irving H. Bucher. "The Politics of Race, Gender and Sexual Orientation: Implications for the Future of America." *Equity and Excellence* 25:2–4, winter 1992, pp. 222–227.

13. R. Lewis. *When Cultures Collide: Managing Successfully across Cultures*. London: Nicholas Brealey, 1996, p. 16.

14. Liz Sly. "In China, the Right Name Is Crucial." *The Record*, October 6, 1996, p. A-31.

15. Elizabeth Llorente and Ovetta Wiggins. "Human Services Agency to Correct Letter." *The Record*, February 7, 1997, p. A-3.

16. Andrew Browne. "How a News Story, Translated Badly, Caused Trading Panic." *The Wall Street Journal*, May 12, 2005, pp. A1, A8.

17. See, for example, Deborah Tannen. *Talking from 9 to 5: How Women's and Men's Conversational Styles Affect Who Gets Heard, Who Gets Credit, and What Gets Done at Work*. New York: Morrow, 1994.

18. Tannen.

19. See, for example, Carolyn Calloway-Thomas, Pamela J. Cooper, and Cecil Blake. *Intercultural Communication: Roots and Routes.* Boston: Allyn & Bacon, 1999, pp. 154–155: and William B. Gudykunst. *Bridging Differences: Effective Intergroup Communication,* 2nd ed. Thousand Oaks, CA: Sage, 1994, p. 83.

20. "Work Week." *The Wall Street Journal,* p. A1.

21. J. J. Hemmer, Jr. "Exploitation of Native American Symbols: A First Amendment Analysis." Paper presented at the National Communication Association annual convention, New Orleans, LA, November 22, 2002.

22. Pauline Turner Strong. "The Mascot Slot." *Journal of Sport and Social Issues* 28:1, February 2004, pp. 79–87.

23. Associated Press. "NCAA: Tribes Must OK Use of Their Names." www.msnbc.msn.com/id/9939557/, August 19, 2005.

24. Strong, p. 81.

25. See, for example, S. M. Huhndorf. *Going Native: Indians in the American Cultural Imagination.* Ithaca, NY: Cornell University Press, 2001; J. W. Kasson. *Marble Queens and Captives: Women in Nineteenth-Century American Sculpture.* New Haven, CT: Yale University Press, 1990; and A. Ong. "Cultural Citizenship as Subject-Making: Immigrants Negotiate Racial and Cultural Boundaries in the United States." *Current Anthropology* 37, 1996, pp. 737–762.

26. See, for example, R. J. Coombe. *The Cultural Life of Intellectual Properties: Authorship, Appropriation, and the Law.* Durham, NC: Duke University Press, 1998.

27. Suzanne Daily. "In Europe, Some Fear National Languages Are Endangered." *New York Times,* April 16, 2001, pp. A1, A10.

28. Steven Komarow. "Some Germans Fear Language Is Being Infected by English." *USA Today,* May 16, 2001, p. 6A.

29. See www.hispanicprwire.com/release_Crest_Ad_ENG.htm,

30. B. Kitwana. *The Hip Hop Generation: Young Blacks and the Crisis in African American Culture.* New York: Basic Books, 2002.

31. Jody Rosen. "Rap: A Celebration of Language." *The Record,* December 2, 2002, p. L15.

32. Monica Davey. "Fighting Words." *New York Times,* February 20, 2005, pp. AR1, 34.

33. National Public Radio. Interview of Alonzo Westbrook by Tavis Smiley, November 5, 2002.

34. K. L. Schmidt. "Exit, Voice, Loyalty, and Neglect: Responses to Sexist Communication in Dating Relationships." Unpublished doctoral dissertation. Arizona State University, 1991, p. 30.

35. A. Nilsen. "Sexism as Shown through the English Vocabulary." In A. Nilsen, H. Bosmajian, H. Gershuny, and J. Stanley, eds. *Sexism and Language.* Urbana, IL: National Council of Teachers of English, 1977.

36. A. Mulac, J. Bradac, and S. Mann. "Male/Female Language Differences and Attributional Consequences in Children's Television." *Human Communication Research* 11, 1985, pp. 481–506.

37. K. G. Foreit, T. Agor, J. Byers, J. Larue, H. Lokey, M. Palazzini, M. Paterson, and L. Smith. "Sex Bias in the Newspaper Treatment of Male-Centered and Female-Centered News Stories." *Sex Roles* 6, 1980, pp. 475–480.

38. C. Kramer. "Stereotypes of Women's Speech: The Word from Cartoons." *Journal of Popular Culture* 8, 1974, pp. 624–630.

39. C. Kramer. "Male and Female Perceptions of Male and Female Speech." *Language and Speech* 20, 1978, pp. 151–161.

40. Patricia Hayes Bradley. "The Folk-Linguistics of Women's Speech: An Empirical Examination." *Communication Monographs* 48, pp. 73–90.

41. Nancy M. Henley and Cheris Kramarae. "Gender, Power and Miscommunication." In Nickolas Coupland, Howard Giles, and John Weimann, eds. *Miscommunication and Problematic Talk.* Newbury Park, CA: Sage, 1991, p. 42.

42. Deborah Tannen. *You Just Don't Understand.* New York: Ballantine, 1991, p. 42.

43. M. Hiller and F. L. Johnson. "Gender and Generation in Conversational Topics: A Case Study of Two Coffee Shops." Paper presented at the annual meeting of the Speech Communication Association, San Diego, CA, November 1996.

44. Cited in Craig Johnson and Larry Vinson. "Placement and Frequency of Powerless Talk and Impression Formation." *Communication Quarterly* 38:4, fall 1990, p. 325.

45. "'Hi, Jack' Greeting to Co-Pilot Causes Stir." *The Record*, June 8, 2000, p. A-13. Used by permission of The Associated Press. Copyright © 2000. All rights reserved.

46. See William V. Haney. *Communication and Organizational Behavior*, 3rd ed. Homewood, IL: Irwin, 1973, pp. 247–248.

47. For a discussion of names and how they affect us, see Mary Marcus. "The Power of a Name." *Psychology Today*, October 1976, pp. 75–76, 108.

48. "Washington Wire." *Wall Street Journal*, October 14, 1994.

49. Louis Lavelle. "Canning the Gibberish." *The Record*, January 21, 2000, p. B-1.

50. Stancavish; William Lutz. *The New Doublespeak: Why No One Knows What Anyone's Saying Anymore*. New York: HarperCollins, 1996.

51. Jennifer Lee. "A Call for Softer, Greener Language." *New York Times*, March 2, 2003, p. 24.

52. Ibid.

53. See William Lutz. *Doublespeak Defined*. New York: Harper Resource, 1999; and National Council of Teachers of English. "The 1999 Doublespeak Awards." *ETC* 56:4, winter 1999–2000, p. 484.

54. Jonathan Chait. "A New Language: Partisan English." *The Record*, April 26, 2005, p. L15.

55. Gina Kolata, "Name Games and the Science of Life," *New York Times*, May 29, 2005, p. WK12.

56. Lisa Bannon. "The Vision Thing." *The Wall Street Journal*, July 31, 1997, p. A1.

57. Henry Beard and Christopher Cerf. *The Politically Correct Dictionary and Handbook*. New York: Villard Books, 1992.

58. Diane Ravitch. "You Can't Say That." *The Wall Street Journal*, February 13, 2004, p. W15.

59. Donald G. McNeil, Jr. "Like Politics, All Political Correctness Is Local." *New York Times*, October 11, 1998, p. WK-5.

60. "Improper Words." *USA Today*, October 7, 2004, p. 20A.

61. Rachel Emma Silverman. "On-the-Job Cursing: Obscene Talk Is the Latest Target of Workplace Ban." *The Wall Street Journal*, May 8, 2001, p. B12.

62. See, for example, James O'Connor. *Cuss Control: The Complete Book on How to Curb Your Cursing*. New York: Three Rivers, 2000.

63. J. B. Rusher. *Prejudiced Communication: A Social Psychological Perspective*. New York: Guilford, 2001.

64. Randall Kennedy. *Nigger: The Strange Career of a Troublesome Word*. New York: Pantheon, 2002.

65. Paul H. Johnson. "N-Word Painful Even If Playful." *The Record*, February 14, 2005, pp. A1, A13.

66. Dean E. Murphy. "The New Language of Jurors in California: Plain English." *New York Times*, August 28, 2005, p. 12.

67. Teresa M. McAleavy. "Downsize Jargon!" *The Record*, February 1, 2005, pp. L9, L16.

68. Amy Harmon. "Internet Changes Language for :-) & :-(." *New York Times*, February 20, 1999, p. B-7.

69. T. K. Bikson and C. W. A. Panis. "Computers and Connectivity: Current Trends." www.rand.org/publication/MR/MR650/index.html, 1996.

70. Jennifer Lee. "I Think, Therefore IM." *New York Times*, September 19, 2002, pp. C1, C4.

71. Lini S. Kadaba. "4GET SPLLG & STRT MSGing!" *The Record*, August 25, 2002, pp. F1, F2.

72. Philip Vassallo. "Beware the Seven Deadly Sins of Tone." *Etc: A Review of General Semantics* 57:1, spring 2000, pp. 100–114.

73. William M. Bulkeley. "Instant Message Goes Corporate; 'You Can't Hide.'" *The Wall Street Journal*, September 4, 2002, pp. B1, B4.

74. Margaret L. McLaughlin, Keery K. Osborne, and Christine B. Smith. "Standards of Conduct on Usenet." In Steven G. Jones, ed. *Cybersociety*. Thousand Oaks, CA: Sage, 1995, p. 103.

75. Hayakawa and Hayakawa.

76. For more information, see Richard Lacayo, "Mixed Signals on Sanctions." *Time*, December 17, 1990, p. 114.

Nonverbal Communication: Silent Language Speaks

After finishing this chapter, you should be able to

1. Define and distinguish among the following terms: *nonverbal communication*, *kinesics*, *paralanguage*, *proxemics*, *chronemics*, *haptics*, and *olfactics*.

2. Explain why the face is an important source of information.

3. Explain how artifactual communication can affect interaction.

4. Distinguish among the following terms: *intimate distance*, *personal distance*, *social distance*, and *public distance*; and *informal space*, *semi-fixed-feature space*, and *fixed-feature space*.

5. Explain why territoriality is an important concept in communication.

6. Identify the ways gender, diversity, and technology influence nonverbal behavior.

7. Explain the role nonverbal cues play in deception and truth telling.

8. Identify how you can improve your nonverbal communication effectiveness.

What you are speaks so loudly that I cannot hear what you say.

—Ralph Waldo Emerson

It is easy to be wise after the event.

—Arthur Conan Doyle's
Sherlock Homes

Some years ago, a youth by the name of Peter Reilly was convicted of a crime he did not commit. The court subsequently reversed Reilly's conviction because his written confession to police had not been videotaped. The lack of video substantiation of Reilly's written confession made it impossible to ascertain if his nonverbal cues would have supported or undermined the written message. The court recognizes that nonverbal communication is a requisite part of the sharing and understanding of meaning. Whereas we can plan what we want to say before we write it, most nonverbal messages are neither planned nor deliberate.[1] The court's position confirmed that *how* an individual says something provides a vital part of a message.

More recently, customs inspectors at John F. Kennedy Airport carefully watched hundreds of passengers get off a flight from South America. As people moved past them, they looked for telltale body language indicative of exceptional nervousness. One man caught their attention. His lips were so chapped and dry they appeared white and "his carotid artery was jumping out of his neck." They took the man aside and discovered that he had paid cash for a business-class ticket, even though he was a low-paid service worker. X-rays revealed that the man had swallowed several bags of heroin pellets.

Since 9/11, the science of spotting nervous or threatening behavior has gained respect. According to one security consultant, "well-trained body language profilers might have spotted and questioned some of the September 11th hijackers" using basic behavior pattern recognition work. In fact, security personnel positioned at airports and in office buildings are now trained to watch for darting eyes and hand tremors in addition to identifying other cues of suspicious behavior. For example, they are being taught that our lips get thinner when we become angry, and our blink rate increases when we become nervous. They now know that our nostrils flare when we are aroused, and our blood flow increases, reddening our skin when we prepare for a physical or mental fight.[2]

■ ■ ■

COMMUNICATING WITHOUT WORDS

Do you know people who have had trouble establishing and maintaining good relationships at work and in their personal lives, but neither they nor you can figure out why? The answer may be that they lack the nonverbal communication

FIGURE 6.1

Communication of Social
Meaning.

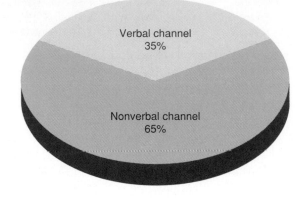

skills essential for social success.[3] Some of us, it appears, have trouble picking up on social cues that others of us use regularly and take for granted. The nonverbally skill-less are, for all practical purposes, communication clueless. For example, many gay men and lesbians possess the ability to identify other homosexuals accurately after only very limited interpersonal contact. They rely on eye contact, clothing style and fit, jewelry, facial expressions, posture, body type, and walk, as well as the types and frequencies of gestures to provide them with needed information.[4] Given the vulnerability gays and lesbians face because of homophobia, their perceptual accuracy offers self-protection. Being able to understand and use nonverbal language is essential for developing and maintaining healthy, productive relationships.[5]

The founder of psychoanalysis, Sigmund Freud, once wrote: "He that has eyes to see and ears to hear may convince himself that no mortal can keep a secret. If his lips are silent, he chatters with his fingertips; betrayal oozes out of him at every pore."

We all communicate nonverbally. In a normal two-person conversation, the verbal channel carries less than 35 percent of the social meaning of a message; this means that more than 65 percent of the meaning is communicated nonverbally (see Figure 6.1).[6] By analyzing nonverbal cues, we can enhance our understanding of what is really being said when people talk. The nonverbal level can also help

Go to the online
learning center at
www.mhhe.com/gamble9
and answer the questions
in the *Self Inventory* to
evaluate your understanding
of nonverbal communication.

Exploring Diversity

The Magic of Sign Language

Marilyn Daniels's book *Dancing with Words*[7] is an exploration of the dynamics of language acquisition through a special form of nonverbal communication. Daniels contends that the use of sign language not only makes hearing students bilingual but also increases the vocabulary learning, reading, and spelling skills of students in all subjects. She also believes that signing positively influences the self-assurance of hearing students, enhancing their ability to interpret and express ideas as well.

According to Daniels, sign language is a natural language that, while strongly rooted in deaf communities throughout the world, also fulfills the diverse communicative needs of daily life, including facilitating communication in the home by allowing babies and young children to express their needs without becoming frustrated.

Should we all be required to take a course in sign language? If so, why? If not, why not? Can you think of how the use of sign language might enhance your communication with hearing persons?

us define the nature of each relationship we share. With practice, we can learn to use the nonverbal mode to provide us with "ways of knowing" that would not otherwise be available to us.[8]

CHARACTERISTICS OF NONVERBAL COMMUNICATION: CUES AND CONTEXTS

What is nonverbal communication? The term **nonverbal communication** designates all the kinds of human messages and responses not expressed in words.

The twinkle in his eye, the edge in her voice, the knowing look of his smile, the rigidity of her posture, the confidence in his walk, her dress, his hairstyle, where she sits, how closely he stands in relation to another, her eagerness to arrive early—each of these cues contains clues regarding the attitudes, feelings, and personality of the displayer. Often, however, we are virtually unaware of what we do with our body, our voice, or the space around us when we interact with others. We simply act and react without considering how the way we act and the way we react modifies, reinforces, or distorts the messages we are communicating.

Sometimes we consciously use nonverbal cues to send specific messages. Our use of nonverbal cues is then purposeful. For example, some years ago, during the Olympic games held in Mexico, some African-American athletes raised clenched fists to protest racial discrimination and symbolize Black power. It is all too common for professional athletes to make obscene gestures at officials, members of the opposing team, or fans. Even more to the point, one college basketball player, Toni Smith, elected to symbolize her displeasure with U.S. foreign policy by turning her back on the flag of the United States and looking down at the floor during the playing of the national anthem before games. Others in Smith's presence signaled their support for U.S. policy and expressed their patriotism by choosing to use different nonverbal cues: Some carried flags onto the court to counter Smith's actions. Others wore American flag lapel pins. Still others indicated their support

nonverbal communication
the kinds of human messages and responses not expressed in words

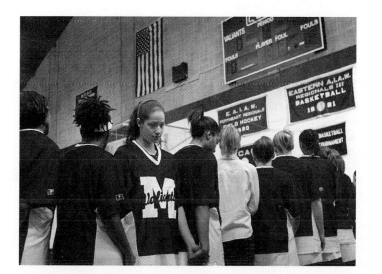

Toni Smith, the basketball player with her back to the flag, used her nonverbal behavior to express her attitude toward U.S. foreign policy.

For the next two minutes, face another person and try not to communicate anything to him or her. What happened? Did you look at each other? Look away? Giggle? Smile? Fidget?

mixed message

message that occurs when words and actions contradict each other

Say, "I am really glad to be here," but meanwhile do everything you can to indicate the opposite. What means did you use? Tone of voice? Posture? Facial expressions?

or opposition to Smith's behavior with their cheers or boos.[9] Although U.S. laws enforcing freedom of speech protect the use of nonverbal cues, school and airline officials have required students and passengers to remove clothes featuring anti-U.S. messages.[10]

If, at this very moment, someone were to photograph you, what could others surmise by examining the photograph? How are you sitting? Where are you sitting? How are you dressed? What would your facial expression reveal about your reaction to this chapter?

Like verbal communication, nonverbal communication is ambiguous. (Think about the example we just gave—the photograph of yourself reading this chapter. Would different people interpret the photograph the same way?) Like words, nonverbal messages may not mean what we think they do. Thus, we have to be careful not to misinterpret them. Don't be surprised if you find that the real reason a person glanced at a clock, left a meeting early, or arrived late for class is quite different from what you assumed. All nonverbal communication must be evaluated or interpreted within the context in which it occurs.

Furthermore, verbal and nonverbal messages can be—and often are—contradictory. When we say one thing but do another, we send an incongruent, or **mixed message.** As you become aware of the nonverbal cues you and others send, you will begin to recognize contradictory messages that impede communication. Whenever you detect an incongruity between nonverbal and verbal (word-level) messages, you will probably benefit by paying greater attention to the nonverbal messages. Researchers in communication believe that nonverbal cues are more difficult to fake than verbal cues—hence the importance of examining the nonverbal dimension. (Remember the case of Peter Reilly.)

FUNCTIONS OF NONVERBAL COMMUNICATION

Nonverbal communication serves an array of communicative functions that can work both independently of and in conjunction with verbal messages to clarify meaning. Knapp and Hall identify a number of these functions.[11]

Message Reinforcement or Complementation

Nonverbal cues reinforce the verbal message by adding redundancy. The woman who says, "I love you," to her fiancé and covers her partner's face with kisses. When an instructor asks, "Did you complete the assignment?" and you reply, "Sure did!" and make an OK sign with your fingers. Message reinforcement occurs when the nonverbal and verbal messages complement each other.

Message Negation

Nonverbal cues can also contradict or negate a verbal message—such as a man who says to his lover, "I need us to spend more time apart," as he moves closer with each word spoken. Such a message is contradicted or canceled by the communicator's nonverbal cues. The interaction represents a double message—the nonverbal cues and the words spoken are at odds with each other. Remember, the nonverbal message is usually the more accurate reflection of meaning.

Message Substitution

Nonverbal cues can replace or substitute for verbal cues. A hand gesture lets everyone know you're OK. A shrug of the shoulders lets others know when someone doesn't care about something. Placing your finger over your lips can indicate that you'd like everyone in the room to stop talking. In each case, instead of words being spoken, an action is performed.

Message Accentuation or Intensification

Nonverbal cues also can be used to underscore or intensify parts of a verbal message. Slowing down speech to stress the meaning and importance of key words, smiling when you say, "It's nice to meet you," and clutching your hair when you say, "I'm so angry I could pull my hair out!" are nonverbal cues that accent or emphasize the verbal messages sent.

Message Regulation

Finally, nonverbal cues help regulate the back-and-forth flow of person-to-person interaction. We direct conversational turn taking with nonverbal cues. With eye contact, posture, gestures, and voice, we signal that we have finished speaking or indicate who should talk next. Nonverbal cues help us manage and control communication. They provide the traffic signals for verbal exchanges.

If we are going to use nonverbal cues effectively, we must understand them. The following section considers the important features of nonverbal communication.

ASPECTS OF NONVERBAL COMMUNICATION

Whereas we use language to communicate explicit information and message content, we use nonverbal communication to convey relational messages, including how we feel about another person, as well as status, power, and deception.[12] To arrive at a better understanding of communication and develop skills that will permit us to both send and receive cues more accurately, we will examine the following areas:

body language (kinesics)
clothing and artifacts
voice (paralanguage)
space and distance (proxemic and environmental factors)
colors (meanings and associations)
time (communicative value of chronemics)
touch (haptics)
smell (olfactics)

The types of messages that fall within these categories do not occur in isolation; they interact, sometimes supporting and sometimes contradicting one another.

Body Language: Kinesics

kinesics
the study of the relationship between human body motion, or body language, and communication

Kinesics is the study of the relationship between body motion, or body language, and communication. Body language includes facial expression (particularly eyebrows, forehead, eyes, and mouth), posture, and gestures. Thus, hand movements, a surprised stare, drooping shoulders, a knowing smile, and a tilt of the head are all part of kinesics. The role of signing and gestures in learning garnered attention when it was reported that infants and toddlers who learn to use and read gestures may learn to read faster and do better on future IQ tests than children who do not.[13] Consciously using multiple channels facilitates communication.

FACIAL EXPRESSIONS

Did you know that the 80 muscles in the face can create more than 7,000 expressions?

Picture this: You play soccer. You have suffered a serious injury and have had a CAT scan. You are meeting with the doctor to discuss your prognosis for a full recovery. You search the doctor's face, looking for clues. Or consider this: You are returning home 24 hours late from a business trip. Your significant other meets you at the door. As you approach, your eyes focus on the expression of the awaiting face. Within a very short span of time, each of these faces can move us to tears of happiness or sadness, put us at ease, or arouse our rage. To a large extent, we send messages with our facial muscles. Why is the face so important? First, it is our main channel for communicating our own emotions and for analyzing the feelings and sentiments of others. This is one reason motion picture and television directors use so many close-ups. The face is relied on to reinforce or contradict what is being communicated through dialogue. Likewise, in your personal relations, your face and the faces of those around you broadcast inner feelings and emotions.

The face is the single most important broadcaster of emotions. What message is your face sending right now?

How well do you read faces? Research has shown that many people are able to decipher facial cues with great accuracy, but others lack this ability. Unpopularity, poor grades, and a variety of other problems that plague schoolchildren may be attributed to an inability to read the nonverbal messages of teachers and peers. According to psychologist Stephen Norwicki, "Because they are unaware of the messages they are sending, or misinterpret how other children are feeling, unpopular children may not even realize that they are initiating many of the negative reactions they receive from their peers."[14] Your ability to read someone's face increases when you know the person, understand the context of the interaction, and are able to compare and contrast the person's facial expressions with others you have seen him or her make.

Of all the nonverbal channels, the face is the single most important broadcaster of emotions. Since we cannot put the face away, we take great pains to control the expressions we reveal to others.

facial management techniques
the means we use to control the expressions we reveal to others

How do we do this? We use the following **facial management techniques**: intensifying, deintensifying, neutralizing, and masking. When we intensify an emotion, we exaggerate our facial responses to meet what we believe to be the expectations of others who are watching us. Have you ever pretended you loved a gift so as not to disappoint the giver, when in reality you couldn't stand it? When we deintensify an emotion, we deemphasize our facial expressions so that others will judge our reactions to be more appropriate. Were you ever very angry with a professor but were compelled to restrain yourself because you feared the professor's response if you let your anger show? When we neutralize an emotion, we avoid displaying it at all. Sometimes neutralization is an attempt to display strength, as when we are saddened by the death of a relative but want to appear brave. In U.S. culture, men neutralize fear and sadness more frequently than women do. Finally, when we mask an emotion, we replace it with another to which we believe others will respond more favorably. Thus, we sometimes conceal feelings of jealousy, disappointment, or rage.

Your facial appearance also influences judgments of your attractiveness.[15] In addition, it affects others' assessment of you as being dominant or submissive.[16] Thus, we speak of a baby face, a face as cold as ice, a face as strong as a bulldog's, and so on. What words would you use to describe your own face?

By now you are probably beginning to realize the importance of observing facial expressions. But what should you watch for? For purposes of analysis, a person's face can be divided into three general areas: (1) the eyebrows and forehead, (2) the eyes, and (3) the mouth. Let us focus on each area separately.

Eyebrows and Forehead   If you raise your eyebrows, what emotion are you showing? Surprise is probably most common, but fear may also be expressed by raised eyebrows; when you are experiencing fear, the duration of the movement will probably be longer.

The brows help express other emotions as well. Right now, move your brows into as many configurations as you can. With each movement, analyze your emotional response. What do the brows communicate?

The forehead also helps communicate your physical and emotional state. A furrowed brow suggests tension, worry, or deep thought. A sweating forehead suggests nervousness or great effort.

Eyes   The second of the three areas is the eyes. Ralph Waldo Emerson noted, perceptively, "The eyes of men converse at least as much as their tongues." What do your eyes reveal to others?

Many expressions refer to the eyes—"shifty eyes," "the look of love," "the evil eye," "look me in the eye." Various eye movements are associated with emotional expressions: A downward glance suggests modesty; staring suggests coldness; wide eyes suggest wonder, naivete, honesty, or fright; and excessive blinking suggests nervousness and insecurity. Researchers have also shown that as we begin to take an interest in something, our blinking rate decreases and our pupils dilate.

The direction of eye gaze also provides interesting insights. For example, have you considered in what direction people look when they are not looking directly at you—and what that might signify? Richard Bandler and John Grinder, two of the founders of neurolinguistic programming, have developed a number of interesting theories. They suggest that people look in one direction when they try to remember something and in another direction when they try to invent something. To test their hypothesis, try this with a partner. Face each other. One person asks the following series of questions; the other person thinks of a response to each. When asking the questions, watch for any patterns in the direction your partner looks while thinking of a response.

Questions That Evoke Visually Remembered Images
What color are the carpets in your car?
What color are your mother's eyes?
What color is your instructor's hair?

How can you use facial cues to determine if others—including your boss, co-workers, and friends—are being honest with you?

When the face assumes an expression of anger, fear, or sadness, the heart rate increases. According to psychologist Robert Levenson, this is because emotions are often associated with a need to behave in a certain way on very short notice. For example, anger and fear are associated with either fighting or fleeing—both of which start the heart pumping.

How does eye contact or lack of eye contact affect your interactions with others? You can explore this by using the following experimental conditions when talking to others: (1) Keep your eyes on the floor. (2) Glance around continually. (3) Stare at the other person's face. (4) Look at the other person's waist. (5) Maintain comfortable eye contact. Report your findings to the class.

Questions That Evoke Visually Invented Images
How would you look from my point of view?
How would you look in purple and green hair?
What would your home look like after it had been ravaged by fire?

Questions That Evoke Auditorily Remembered Images
Can you hear your favorite music?
Can you hear music you dislike?
What are the first four notes of Beethoven's Fifth Symphony?

Questions That Evoke Auditorily Invented Images
How would your dog sound singing "Mary Had a Little Lamb"?
What would King Kong sound like tiptoeing through the tulips?

Bandler and Grinder suggest that a right-handed person will look in the directions shown in Figure 6.2. Do your experiences confirm their findings? Could a lawyer or negotiator ask questions and then use these findings to determine whether the person answering had invented the reply? Could a CIA agent use the technique to determine if an informant was telling the truth? If the findings are valid, presumably the answer is yes. The agent, for example, could inquire about where hostages were being held: "What does the house look like? Did you see terrorist members there?" If the informant looked up and to the right, he or she might be creating images rather than actually remembering; in other words, the informant might be lying.

Whatever your conclusions about the direction of eye gaze, it is important to maintain eye contact with others to recognize not only when others are not looking at you but where they are looking. Because these cues are not consciously controlled, they will seldom mislead us.

How long we look or gaze at a person or thing also communicates a message. In our culture, it is deemed acceptable to stare at animals and inanimate objects, such as paintings or sculptures, but rude to stare at people. Instead of staring at others, we are supposed to practice **civil inattention,** avoiding sustained eye contact and letting our eyes rest only momentarily on people (in other words, keeping our eyes to ourselves). Although it is permissible to look at someone we do not know for one or two seconds, after that we are expected to move our eyes along. Notice your own eye behavior the next time you walk down a street. Your eyes will probably wander from face to face. However, if you and a stranger happen to make eye contact while approaching one another from opposite directions, at least one of you will redirect his or her gaze before you actually get close. If we look at people for a long time, it may make them fidgety and uncomfortable or may seem to imply that we are challenging them. Have

civil inattention
the polite ignoring of others so as not to infringe on their privacy

FIGURE 6.2

How Direction of Gaze Varies According to the Nature of the Item under Consideration.

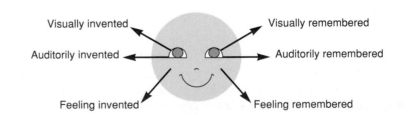

you ever innocently rested your eyes on a stranger who then demanded, "What are you staring at? You want to start something?"

Despite civil inattention, in any gathering, the first thing most people do is eye one another. Eye contact gives us feedback on how we are coming across to others in interpersonal and public situations. It can indicate whether the communication channel is open. It is much easier to avoid talking or listening to people if we have not made eye contact with them. Eye contact between people also offers clues to the kind of relationship they share. For one thing, it can signal a need for inclusion or affiliation. People who have a high need for affiliation will frequently return the glances of others. There is a high degree of eye contact between people who like each other. We also increase eye contact when communicating with others if the physical distance between us is increased.

For others to find us persuasive, we need to refrain from excessive blinking. We should maintain a steady gaze—that is, neither look down nor away from the individuals we are trying to influence nor exhibit eye flutter. In general, we judge persons who look us in the eye as more honest and credible than those whose eyes do not directly meet ours. When individuals avoid meeting our eyes or avert their gaze, we often assume that they have something to hide, that they lack confidence, or that they are unknowledgeable.[17] Visual dominance correlates with increased levels of looking, while increases in the frequency of eye aversions create an impression of submissiveness. Humans, like apes, can stare down each other to establish dominance. Look away first, and you may well find that you have unknowingly agreed to be the less powerful player in the interaction.

Of course, we must keep in mind that eye contact is influenced by culture. Some cultures use eye contact more than we do; other cultures use it less. Arabs engage in more direct eye contact and the Japanese in less eye contact than is typical of Americans. The Japanese, in fact, believe that prolonged eye contact is a sign of disrespect. Japanese children learn at an early age to avoid direct eye contact and to direct their gaze to the area of the Adam's apple instead.[18]

The fact is, the eyes have much to tell us.

The presence or absence of eye contact indicates whether a communication channel is open or closed. What does the eye contact of these people suggest about their relationship?

What is communicated if eye contact is missing? Lack of eye contact can cause others to think that we are trying to hide something or that we do not like them. It can also suggest that two people are in competition with each other. Others may interpret its absence as signifying either boredom or simply a desire to end an interaction. How do you rate your own eye contact? When are you a looker and when are you a nonlooker?

Mouth People who do not smile are perceived to be unfriendly, uninterested in others, or bored. People respond more favorably to those who smile.[19]

Like the eyes, the lower facial area has much to communicate. For example, some people smile with just the mouth and lips. For others, the smile appears to consume the entire face. As a child, were you ever told to "wipe that smile off your face"? Why? Besides happiness, what can a smile communicate?

How does your face look when you are not smiling—when it is at rest? Some faces have a neutral expression; others have a frown, snarl, or habitual smile—that is, the corners of the mouth seem to turn up naturally.

Cathy © 1997 Cathy Guisewite. Reprinted with permission of Universal Press Syndicate. All rights reserved.

When you choose to smile, how do people react to your smile? People often find that others will return a smile to those who smile at them but will look away from, or avoid stopping to speak to, a person whose lips are pursed in a frown. To what extent do your experiences confirm this?

Both men and women tend to smile when seeking approval, but in general, women smile more frequently than men do. Women tend to smile even when given negative messages. Why do you think this is so?

Recently, marketers for products such as Yahoo and cappuccino machines began using the images of women sticking out their tongues in ads. According to nonverbal communication researcher Maureen O'Sullivan, "the mouth is a sexual orifice," and the gesture of "sticking out one's tongue can have multiple meanings. It can be an act of rudeness, disgust, playfulness, or outright sexual provocation." She believes we are seeing more tongues in ads because marketers are running out of body parts to expose.[20] What do you think?

POSTURE

How many times have you heard the following admonitions?

"Stand up straight!"

"Why are you hunched over that desk?"

What kinds of nonverbal messages does your posture send to others? The way we hold ourselves when sitting or standing is a nonverbal broadcast, giving others information that they use to assess our thoughts and feelings.

Describe the posture you consider appropriate for a corporate president.

Research provides enough information for us to draw some general conclusions about how others are likely to interpret our posture. Nancy Henley, in her book *Body Politics*, suggests that "the bearing with which one presents oneself proclaims one's position in life."[21] Television and film support this premise by frequently contrasting the upright bearing of a wealthy person with the submissive shuffle of a servant or the slumped demeanor of a nobody. In line with this, researcher Albert Mehrabian notes that when people assume inferior roles, they reflect this by lowering their heads. In contrast, when they assume superior roles, people often raise their heads.

Recall an instance when posture affected your perception of someone else.

Each of us has certain expectations regarding the postures we expect others to display. For instance, we might expect a high-ranking military officer to adopt an extremely straight and somewhat official posture. Henley suggests that standing tall, in and of itself, helps a person achieve dominance.

Ethics & Communication

Facework

The way *The Wall Street Journal* portrayed Martha Stewart during her trial and prior to her conviction changed over time. At the trial's outset, Stewart was depicted as young and preppy. Two days later, her face was drawn wrinkled and scowling, and she appeared to be much older. Four days later, after Stewart complained that she did not look good or young enough, her face was drawn again—reworked—this time more flatteringly.

Like Martha Stewart, more and more people are concerned by the messages their faces sends to others. Some, such as salespersons, lawyers, bankers, and stockbrokers, want to improve their ability to succeed in their professions, and because they fear that betraying an emotion might cost them a sale, a jury verdict, or a deal, growing numbers of them are using Botox (a drug that temporarily paralyzes muscles) to freeze or sculpt their faces into semipermanent poker faces. With the drug's injection, they also eliminate any telltale frowns, signs of anger and fatigue, and clues to their age. Botox helps people turn back the clock. It also helps them conceal their true feelings. If the ability to express true emotions is taken away, how can you gauge a person's sincerity? What statement is the desire to show less expression really making?

Cosmetic surgery is similarly on the increase. Programs such as *The Swan* and *Extreme Makeover* show us what happens when people undergo cosmetic surgery, getting chin implants, brow lifts, and rubber-doll lip jobs. Critics observe that postsurgery subjects have an "eerie Stepford-spouse similarity," leading some to wonder if we will all end up with the same face.[22] In your opinion, what effect is cookie-cutter cosmetic surgery having on the notion of personal identity? How dangerous is it to believe that self-worth is dependent on physical appearance?

As a communicator, you will want to develop a posture appropriate to and supportive of your goals and aspirations. Stooped shoulders can indicate that you are heavily burdened or submissive; raised shoulders suggest that you are under a great deal of stress. To Americans, square shoulders usually suggest strength. Our emotions or moods and physical bearing are closely related. This relationship is expressed through the verbal idioms that have developed through the years. It is said that we "shoulder a burden," have "no backbone," keep our "chin up," or "shrug off problems." The way we carry ourselves can affect the way we feel and the way others perceive us, just as much as the way we feel can affect the way we carry ourselves.

The last aspect of posture we will consider is how we lean, or orient ourselves, when we communicate. If you were speaking to someone who suddenly turned or leaned away from you, would you consider that a positive sign? Probably not. We usually associate liking and other positive attitudes with leaning forward, not withdrawing. When you are communicating with others, a slight forward tilt of your upper body may indicate that you are interested in what they have to say. Mehrabian found that we lean either left or right when communicating with a person of lower status than ourselves. This right or left leaning is a part of our more relaxed demeanor.[23]

Try on various postures and see what you feel like in each. To what degree does each posture affect your emotional state?

Leaning forward communicates liking and interest. Are you aware when you do this? Is it always a conscious move?

GESTURES

The filmmaker Michael Britto has documented hundreds of different handshakes that New Yorkers use to say hello. He discovered that the kind used sometimes depends on where someone lives. For example, the 1-4-5 is a three-part greeting consisting of a finger to the nose, four placed on the chest near the heart, and a five-finger slap. Another has greeters clasping wrists, and another, touching the knuckles of their clenched fists. What kind of handshake do you use? What does it suggest to others?

The movements of our arms, legs, hands, and feet constitute important nonverbal data. For instance, the way you position your arms transmits information about your attitudes. Cross your arms in front of you. Do you feel closed off from the world? Stand up and put your hands on your hips. How does this stance make you feel? (You may remind yourself of the old stereotype of an army sergeant.) Next, clasp your arms behind your back in a self-assured manner. Then, hold your arms stiffly at your sides, as if you were a nervous speaker or a wooden soldier. Finally, dangle your arms at your sides in a relaxed fashion. Become aware of the arm positions that you habitually use. What message does each of these positions communicate?

Our legs also convey information about us. Try standing as a model would stand. Next, sit down and put your feet up on a desk or table. Then stand with your feet wide apart. Does this last stance make you feel more powerful? Why? The distribution of body weight and the placement of legs and feet can broadcast stability, femininity, masculinity, anger, happiness, or any number of other qualities. For a communication encounter, choose the stance that most accurately reflects your goals. Keep in mind that crossing one's legs does not necessarily play well from country to country. In fact, it is perceived as highly offensive in Turkey and Ghana.

Gestures, however, do not have universal meanings. Consider, for example, our "OK" gesture made by forming a circle with the thumb and forefinger. In Japan, the thumb and forefinger making a circle is used as a symbol for money. To most Americans, this joining of thumb and forefinger signifies that all is positive; the French and Belgians, in contrast, would interpret the gesture as meaning "you're worth zero."[24]

A lack of universality in gesturing can create problems for global advertisers. For years, in its advertisements for insurance, Allstate implied that it offers consumers security and protection by using the image of a person holding out his or her hands while a voice-over intones, "You're in good hands with Allstate." The ad failed in Germany, however, because in that country hands held out symbolize begging rather than security and protection.[25]

ATTRACTIVENESS

Do you notice how people look? Do their looks influence your perception of them? Appearance communicates—making general attractiveness an important aspect of body communication. When it comes to height, for example, tall people tend to "come out on top" whether in elections or job interviews.[26] When it comes to weight, a cold shoulder and brusque treatment are routinely given to people who are perceived as obese.[27] People judged to be attractive date more, earn higher grades, and are rated as more persuasive and likable than others.[28] Obsessing on being attractive may cause men to engage in bodybuilding, women to diet, and both men and women to turn to plastic surgery as a solution to feeling unattractive.[29]

Judgments of race are also based on clues the face and body provide. For marketers, ethnic ambiguity—the multiracial face of youth—is becoming the new American beauty. Advertisers judge a face whose heritage is hard to determine as most desirable. Ethnic mixing is changing the face of attractiveness—and influencing casting choices in advertisements and films.[30]

Clothing and Artifacts

Since people make inferences about our age, social and economic status, educational level, group membership, athletic ability, personality, and relationships to others by the way we dress, our use of **artifactual communication** (the use of personal adornments, such as clothing, jewelry, makeup, hairstyles, and beards) provides important nonverbal cues.

How we dress is extremely important in creating a first impression. What kinds of clothing or jewelry do you like to wear? What do your appearance, hairstyle, and mode of dress suggest to others about who you are and what you are like? Are your choices of clothing or bodily adornments appropriate? To what extent do your choices meet with or disappoint the expectations of those with whom you interact?[31] From Sarah Jessica Parker's Carrie Bradshaw on *Sex and the City,* with her name necklaces and large flower pins, to David Caruso's Horatio Caine on *CSI: Miami,* with his sunglasses, television also influences the way we dress and present ourselves to others. What impression would you like to create when you first meet someone? As the role you enact changes, your dress and chosen image often change as well.

How we dress influences how we behave. Consider singer Gwen Stefani. Does Stefani's dress support her behavior? Given the kind of music she sings, could she just as easily wear more prim and proper attire? Why or why not?

artifactual communication
the use of personal adornments

Have you ever found yourself extremely overdressed or underdressed for an occasion? How did you feel? Were you able to augment your outfit or take off part of it to fit in with what everyone else was wearing? Have you ever been to a posh restaurant that requires men to put on ill-fitting jackets and out-of-style ties in order to partake of the food?

MediaWise

Clothes Talk

People today use clothing to advertise their positions on or interest in issues, their views about religion, and their status.[32] For example, the Tiffany and Hermes labels suggest one's financial status; FCUK, Armani Exchange, and Diesel say something about lifestyle consciousness. T-shirts that picture Jesus and the message "Put Down the Drugs and Come Get a Hug" reveal an attitude about religion or spirituality, while those that feature sayings such as "War Is Not the Answer" attest to a wearer's position on political matters. Articles of clothing are the billboards or picket signs of the twenty-first century.

Inventory the clothing and accessories you have. Do any prominently display or advertise a message like those identified above? If so, what does the item reveal about you? Has it contributed to others' labeling you in some way? What message-driven clothing do celebrities you admire or other people you know own? To what extent do you support or find objectionable the use of message-themed clothing?

What message does the appearance of Gwen Stefani of No Doubt send?

What is your reaction to Molloy's advice? Would this kind of attire be appropriate for you in your present job? In the future? To what extent is his advice contradicted by the casual attire practices of some major corporations? Use the exercise in item (2) of the Skill Builder on page 150 to assess how the clothes you wear affect others.

While Gwen Stefani purposefully wears such clothing to her job, could you wear the same or similar clothing to yours? Unless you are a singer or dancer, you probably answered this question with "Are you kidding?" or "No way." The clothing we wear to work should support the job roles and functions we perform.

John T. Molloy, author of *Dress for Success* and *The Woman's Dress for Success Book,* gathered data from numerous studies in which people offered their first impressions of the attire of others. Molloy identified the kinds of clothing he claims should be worn by people who want to become managers or executives. For men, he suggests dark blue pinstriped suits to add a feeling of authority. Dark gray is also acceptable as executive attire. Molloy also created a uniform for women in business. The basic outfit is summed up in this statement, which many of the women in Molloy's seminars adopted:

> I pledge to wear a highly tailored, dark-colored, traditionally designed, skirted suit whenever possible to the office.[33]

It is clear that we react to people on the basis of their clothing. In the early stages of a relationship, clothing and appearance affect first impressions and exert influences that lead to acceptance or rejection. In addition, judgments regarding our success, character, dominance, and competence are made on the basis of the type of clothing and jewelry we wear.[34] Typically, we respond more positively to those we perceive to be well dressed than we do to those whose attire we find questionable or unacceptable. We are also more likely to respond to requests from or follow the lead of well-dressed individuals, including persons in uniform, than we are to listen to or emulate those whose dress suggests lower status or lack of authority.[35]

Voice: Paralanguage

Your friend asks you a question, and you matter-of-factly reply, "Mm-hmm." Another person shares a revealing piece of gossip with you, and you shout, "Huh!" Reading about the ethical lapses of some politicians, you click your tongue: "Tsk, tsk, tsk." These elements of speech that are not standard words are a part of **paralanguage.** How good you are at using paralanguage determines whether or not you will be able to do your part to convey the meaning of a message to others.[36]

In many ways, you either play your voice—like a musical instrument—or are a victim of your voice. Would you ever advise someone to get a new voice? What about yourself? Are you happy with the sound of yours? Have you ever heard how you sound on a tape of a meeting or on your answering machine? Does you tone go up and down, or do you speak in a monotone? Can you tell a good story, or do your words fall flat? If a new hairstyle and a new outfit are part of the job search, why aren't we similarly concerned with the sound of our voice? According to voice expert Thomas Murry, depth of knowledge and impact of voice are equally important in who gets hired and who succeeds in business.[37] Albert Mehrabian estimates that 38 percent of the meaning of a

paralanguage
vocal cues that accompany spoken language

"You're right. It does send a powerful message."

message delivered during face-to-face conversation is transmitted by voice or vocal cues.[38] Frequently, *how* something is said is *what* is said.

Among the elements of paralanguage are pitch, volume, rate, and pauses. Let us examine these elements of paralanguage more closely.

Pitch is the highness or lowness of the voice; it is the counterpart of pitch on a musical scale. We tend to associate higher pitches with female voices and lower pitches with male voices. We also develop vocal stereotypes. We associate low-pitched voices with strength, sexiness, and maturity and high-pitched voices with helplessness, tenseness, and nervousness. Although we all have what is termed a characteristic, or **habitual, pitch,** we have also learned to vary our pitch to reflect our mood and generate listeners' interest.

Some people tend to overuse one tone to the exclusion of others. These people have monotonous voices characterized by too little variety of pitch. Other people speak at or near the upper end of their pitch scale, producing very fragile, unsupported tones. One way to discover a pitch that is not overly high is simply to yawn. Try it now. Permit yourself to experience a good stretch; extend your arms to shoulder level and let out a vocalized yawn. Do it again. Now count to 10 out loud. To what extent does the pitch of your voice appear to have changed?

pitch
the highness or lowness of the voice

habitual pitch
the characteristic pitch one uses

When playing tennis, players like Maria Sharapova and Serena Williams shriek and grunt when hitting the ball. What functions do you think these sounds serve?

Skill Builder

Something Different

1. Do people judge you on the basis of your clothes? The National Basketball Association (NBA) has long had a dress code for coaches, requiring them to wear a jacket and tie during games. Now the commissioner of the NBA, David Stern, is requiring players and all other personnel to wear a jacket and tie when traveling to or from a game, home and away. The thinking is that clothes will remake the players' image, if not the players. Among the items players are prohibited from wearing are T-shirts, chains or pendants, sunglasses when indoors, headphones (other than on a bus or plane or in a locker room), and jerseys and baseball caps. Some basketball players objected to the new rules, observing that the way you dress has nothing to do with the kind of person you are, even nothing that lots of people who wear suits and dress well are felons. A number of critics even suggested that racism and the desire to move away from the hip-hop generation was the motive.[39] What do you think? Do dressing down and wearing "bling" send the wrong message? Will playing "dress-up" make a real difference? If you were the basketball commissioner, what dress code, if any, would you enforce?

2. Tomorrow wear something different to school or work. Your change in dress style should be noticeable to others. For instance, if you feel you are usually sloppily dressed, appear as meticulous as possible.

Assess the results. How did people respond to you? Did anyone seem surprised? Did anyone ask you questions about your appearance? If so, what kinds of questions were you asked? Does changing your clothing style make a difference?

Is it more resonant? It should be. If you indulge yourself and yawn once or twice before stressful meetings or occasions, you will be able to pitch your voice at a more pleasing level.

volume

the degree of loudness of the voice

Volume, or degree of loudness, is a second paralinguistic factor that affects perceived meaning. Some people cannot seem to muster enough energy to be heard by others. Others blast through encounters. Have you ever sat in a restaurant and heard more of the conversation at a table several feet away than you could hear at your own table? Volume frequently reflects emotional intensity. Loud people are often perceived as aggressive or overbearing. Soft-spoken people are often perceived as timid or polite.

rate

speaking speed

The **rate,** or speed at which we speak, is also important. Do you, for example, expect high-pressure salespeople to talk rapidly or slowly? Most often, they speak very quickly. Similarly, those who are selling gadgets in department stores or on television also speak at a quick clip to retain the audience's interest and

"I think I've finally found my own voice."

involvement. With regard to persons from other cultures, increased rate enhances judgments of credibility.[40]

Of course, more stately or formal occasions require slower speaking rates broken by planned pauses or silences. (Politicians at rallies typically punctuate their speeches with pauses that function almost as applause signs.) Goldman-Eisler, a communications researcher, has concluded that two-thirds of spoken language comes to us in chunks of fewer than six words.[41] Therefore, knowing when to pause is an essential skill. Pauses slow the rate of speech and give both sender and receiver a chance to gather their thoughts. Unfortunately, many people feel that all pauses must be filled and consciously or unconsciously seek ways to fill them. Frequently, we fill a pause with meaningless sounds or phrases: "Er—huh—uh—"; "You know? You know?" "Right! Right!" "OK! OK!" Such **nonfluencies** disrupt the natural flow of speech. Since pauses are a natural part of communication, we should stop trying to eliminate them. Instead, we should give pauses a chance to function.

Silence, the absence of both paralinguistic and verbal cues, also serves important communicative functions.[42] Silence, for example, can allow you time to organize your thoughts. It can also be used to alert receivers that the words you are about to share are important. In addition, choosing not to speak to someone at all can be a forceful demonstration of the indifference one person feels toward another and can be a very powerful message of disconfirmation. Silence can also be used as a form of punishment after an argument or as a conflict to indicate that one person is still angry with the other. Silence, as we see, can communicate a number of meanings. It can indicate that two people are so comfortable with each other that they do not feel a need to talk, or in a

According to psychologist Dr. Gordon G. Gallup, voices rated highest in attractiveness belong to people who have more active sex lives. Why do you think this is so?

nonfluencies

meaningless sounds or phrases that disrupt the flow of speech

silence

the absence of both paralinguistic and verbal cues

different context, it can reveal a person's shyness, by suggesting discomfort or the inability to keep a conversation moving. On the other hand, silence may simply indicate that you, at the moment, agree with what is being said or simply have nothing to say.

Besides communicating emotional content, the voice also communicates personal characteristics. Listening to a voice can sometimes help you identify the speaker's individual characteristics. For instance, on the telephone we are frequently able to determine a speaker's sex, age, vocation, and place of origin even though we have never met him or her. We also tend to associate particular voice types with particular body or personality types. For example, what type of appearance would you expect in a person who has a breathy, high-pitched voice? How do you think a person who has a throaty, raspy voice would look? As a communicator, you should be aware that your voice suggests certain things about you.

How do the voices of 4-year-olds and teenagers differ? The voices of college-age men and retired men? Are there differences in vocal characteristics between, say, a corporate executive and a construction worker?

Space and Distance: Proxemic and Environmental Factors

proxemics

the study of the use of space

How much of the space on our planet do you call your own? How much space do you carry around with you? Are there times when people encroach on your space? In his book *The Hidden Dimension*, Edward Hall uses the term **proxemics** for human beings' "use of space."[43] *Proxemics* is the study of the space that exists between us as we talk and relate to each other, as well as the way we organize the space around us in our homes, offices, and communities. Architects and interior designers, for example, are using proxemics to humanize hospitals. In hospitals with soft lighting, single rooms, relaxing gardens, and artwork, patients heal more quickly, nurses remain more loyal to employers, and doctors perform better. By adding therapeutic touches to a typically sterile environment, such as providing patients with views of trees from their windows and more accessibility for family and friends to visit, patients have speedier and fuller recoveries.[44] Seating patterns, for example, influence our communicative behavior. How might another environment, such as a school, use an understanding of proxemics to encourage learning?

DISTANCES—INTIMATE, PERSONAL, SOCIAL, PUBLIC

Hall identified four distances that we keep between ourselves and other people, depending on the type of encounter and the nature of the relationship:

> intimate distance: 0 to 18 inches
> personal distance: 18 inches to 4 feet
> social distance: 4 to 12 feet
> public distance: 12 feet to limit of sight

intimate distance

a distance ranging from the point of touch to 18 inches from a person

Intimate distance ranges from the point of touch to 18 inches from the other person. At this distance, physical contact is natural. We can wrestle, and we can make love. Our senses are in full operation. They are easily stimulated but also easily offended if we find ourselves in an uncomfortable situation. Have you ever had someone come too close to you and wanted that person to back off? Did you yourself back away? Sometimes we are forced to endure intimate distance between

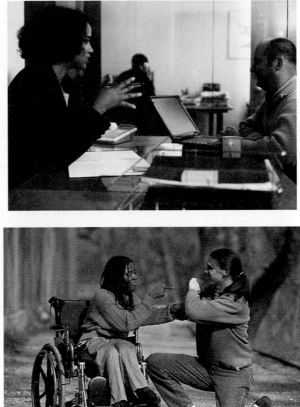

The amount of distance between us depends on the nature of our encounter and our relationship to each other. What do the distances between each of these interactants communicate to you about this relationship?

ourselves and strangers in crowded buses, trains, and elevators. How do you feel and respond in such situations?

Hall's **personal distance** ranges from 18 inches to 4 feet. When communicating at this distance, you can still hold hands or shake hands with another person. This is the most common distance between people talking informally in class, at work, or at parties, and we are apt to conduct most of our conversations within this range. If you reduce personal distance to intimate distance, you are likely to make the other person feel uncomfortable. If you increase it, the other person is likely to begin to feel rejected.

Hall's **social distance** ranges from 4 feet to 12 feet. At the social distance—in contrast to the personal distance—we are not likely to share personal concerns. By using social distance, we can keep people at more than arm's length. Thus, this is a safer distance, one at which we would communicate information and feelings that are not particularly private or revealing. Many of our conversations at meals and at business conferences or meetings occur within this space. In business, the primary protector of social space is the desk. Of course, the greater the distance between people, the more formal their encounters. (At a social gathering, you can normally tell how well people know one another by examining how close they stand to each other.)

personal distance

a distance ranging from 18 inches to 4 feet from a person

social distance

a distance ranging from 4 feet to 12 feet from a person

public distance

a distance of 12 feet and farther from a person

Can you tell how interested people are in you by where they stand in relation to you? Explain. Think of an instance when you unconsciously expressed an interest in someone else by where you stood in relation to him or her.

Public distance (12 feet and farther) is commonly reserved for strangers with whom we do not wish to have an interaction. Distances at the farther end of the range are well beyond the area of personal involvement and make interpersonal communication very unlikely. People waiting in an uncrowded lobby for an elevator frequently use public distance. It can be assumed that if a person opts for public distance when he or she could have chosen otherwise, that person does not care to converse.

What happens when we violate distance norms? Researchers tell us that the outcomes of such violations can be positive. For example, if the approaching person is perceived to be attractive or is viewed as a high-reward source, our evaluation of the approacher may become more favorable, especially if the distance violation is accompanied by other behaviors, such as compliments.[45]

SPACES—INFORMAL, SEMI-FIXED-FEATURE, AND FIXED-FEATURE

The nature of our environment affects the amount of distance we are able to maintain between ourselves and others. Researchers in nonverbal communication divide environmental spaces into three classifications: informal, semi-fixed-feature, and fixed-feature. These categories are based on the perceived permanence of any physical space.

informal space

space that is highly mobile and can be quickly changed

semi-fixed-feature space

space in which objects are used to create distance

Mentally redesign your classroom to promote interaction. Next, redesign it to inhibit interaction. Then consider how you could design an office to promote— or inhibit—interaction.

Informal space is a highly mobile, quickly changing space that ranges from intimate to public (from no space between us and others to 25 feet or more). Informal space functions as a personal bubble that we can enlarge to keep people at a distance or decrease to permit them to get closer.

In contrast to the high mobility of informal space, **semi-fixed-feature space** uses objects to create distance. Semi-fixed features include chairs, benches, sofas, plants, and other movable items. (Some office walls and partitions can be classified as semi-fixed features, since they are designed to be relocated as spatial requirements change.) Researchers find that barriers such as desks reduce interaction. One study of doctor–patient relationships found that patients were more at ease speaking with a physician seated in a chair across from them than they were when the physician was sitting behind a desk.[46] Why do you think this was so? In many public places, if interaction is desired, the space will usually contain chairs facing each other. Such arrangements are found in bars, restaurants, and lounges. In contrast, the chairs in waiting rooms at airports and bus terminals are often bolted together in long parallel rows.

fixed-feature space

space that contains relatively permanent objects

How are the chairs in your classroom arranged? Are they arranged in neat rows? Is the instructor partially hidden by a desk or lectern? Does he or she speak from a raised area or platform?

Fixed-feature space contains relatively permanent objects that define the environment around us. Fixed features include immovable walls, doors, trees, sidewalks, roads, and highways. Such features help guide and control our actions. For example, most classrooms are rectangular, with windows along one side, usually to the students' left. The window location also determines the front of the room. Shopping malls and department stores rely on fixed features to help route pedestrian traffic in certain directions that will increase sales. The next time you shop in a carefully designed store, examine its fixed features. Can you walk, unimpeded, to any department, or are you carefully "directed" through the perfumes, lingerie, and knickknacks? Why?

TERRITORIALITY AND PERSONAL SPACE

Another aspect of proxemics is our need for a defined territory. Some animals mark their territory by urinating around its perimeter and will defend their area against invaders. Human beings also stake out space, or territory, and territoriality

"Honest, Martha, I don't mean to crowd you."

Why do you think people would rather stand than occupy the middle seat in a train? The transit system has a solution to this problem: Order coaches with two seats, not three. What does the behavior of people in elevators reveal about the need for personal space? Most people stare at floor buttons. Many contemplate their feet or stare at other objects. Others gaze at the ceiling. Diverting eye contact decreases feelings of involvement.

is an important variable in interpersonal communication. What examples of **territoriality**—the need to demonstrate a possessive or ownership relationship to space—can you remember encountering? Are you familiar with "Dad's chair"? "Mom's bureau"? How do you feel when someone invades your room—your territory? What happens when someone stands too close to you? How are you treated when you enter another person's territory?

To establish territory, we use **markers,** items that reserve our space, set boundaries that help distinguish space, or identify a space as ours. At the library, for instance, you may spread your things out, over, and across the table, so that others will not find it easy to enter your territory. In large corporations, a

territoriality
the need to demonstrate a possessive or ownership relationship to space

markers
items that reserve one's space

Ethics & Communication

Guarded Territory and the New Need for Security

A majority of persons living in the United States would like to live in a gated community.[47] Gated communities require that someone allow you to enter or that you have a permit that affords you the right of entry. They are typically protected by armed guards, gates, walls, or fences. As in Robert Frost's poetic line "Good fences make good neighbors," security devices and details in gated communities keep their members feeling safe by keeping out those whom the community does not want let in. Sometimes tire-piercing or other antiterrorist devices are used to guard against false entry into the community.

The prime motivator for living in a gated community is the desire for personal safety. On the other hand, because gated communities signal that outsiders should stay out, critics contend that social fragmentation is the cost society pays to allow those living inside them to feel secure. Thus, the fear is that gated communities precipitate in-groups and out-groups who compete for rights to use the same space.

Where do you stand? Are gated communities a good idea? Are there other kinds of living arrangements that could produce security without closing off a community to the outside world?

person's status is often reflected by the size of his or her space. Thus, the president may be accorded a large top-floor territory, while a clerk is given a desk in a second-floor room amid a number of other desks and office machines. Regardless of the size of our location, however, we identify with it and frequently act as if we own it.

Colors: Meanings and Associations

Colors seem to have more than a passing effect on us. It has been found that color affects us emotionally and physiologically.

Max Luscher, in his book *The Luscher Color Test*, claims that, when people look at pure red for a long time, their blood pressure, respiration rate, and heartbeat all increase.[48] This is because red tends to excite the nervous system. In contrast, when researchers examined the effect of dark blue, they found just the opposite: Blood pressure, respiration rate, and heartbeat decreased, and people tended to become calmer.

In the past decade, an increasing number of U.S. companies have chosen to be associated with the color blue: "Big Blue" (IBM), JetBlue (an airline), BlueKite (a wireless technology company), Blue Martini (a software company), and Blue Nile, to name just a few. According to the executive director of the Pantone Color Institute, "Blue is invariably connected with sky and water. The sky has never fallen and water has never gone away. It has dependability and constancy."[49]

How do various colors make you feel? If you were a color consultant, what colors would you choose for a fast-food operation? An airline? Your classroom? Why?

During the uncertain, tension-filled times following 9/11, green became a hot color. Green, we are told, is safe and serene, and it makes people feel better. Even the Department of Homeland Security put green at the bottom of the terrorist alert code, meaning we're safe.[50]

Diverse, top-selling, global brands such as Campbell's soup, Colgate toothpaste, and Coca-Cola are all packaged in red. A stroll down a supermarket aisle reveals an array of products, among them Kellogg, Nabisco, Del Monte, Jell-O, and Band-Aid, with red logos or names. According to John Steel, a senior executive at Colgate-Palmolive, "Red is warm and bright. It's not intimidating. . . . And red, of course, is the lifeblood."[51] Theories abound on why consumers are drawn to red. Some contend that red evokes feelings of warmth, passion, and sensuality. Others observe that people eat more often in the presence of red. Red provides a lift not only to human consumers; according to a report circulated over the World Wide Web, a company that markets red contact lenses for animals contends that chickens that spend the day wearing its lenses are happier and eat less food, and they have more time for laying eggs.[52] On the other hand, some people perceive red to be dangerous, associating it with stop signs and police car lights. Many teachers are also working at "getting the red out" when grading student papers. Because of its association with negativity, parents found papers graded in red "stressful." Now papers are more commonly being graded in less stressful colors such as blue or purple—colors that are perceived as more gentle and do not have the same derogatory connotations as red. Color specialists also believe that using a color not used in a traditional way increases your chances of capturing attention.[53]

Keeping your own reactions in mind, examine the color schemes used in several public areas, including fast-food chains, stores, and terminals. What colors are used? Do they make you want to move quickly? Do the colors excite you, or are they designed to help you relax?

Color also helps persuade. Law enforcement officials, for example, know that when suspects are questioned under green light, they talk more freely; green helps get people to confess.

Time: Communicative Value of Chronemics

Chronemics is the study of how we use time to communicate. The meaning of time differs not only around the United States but also around the world.[54] While some people are preoccupied with time, others regularly waste it. While some are typically early, others are chronically late. While some travel through life with a sense of urgency, others amble through it at a more leisurely pace. Some people function best in the morning (the early birds), while others perform best at night (the night owls). Chronemics expert Robert Levine notes that clock addiction is difficult to break. Because the West is becoming more devoted to the clock by the minute, altering the pace of your life poses numerous challenges.

chronemics
the study of the use of time

Do you have enough time for most of your activities? Are you usually prepared for exams or assignments? Do you arrive for appointments on time, early, or late? Recent surveys reveal that tardiness is a chronic problem among chief executive officers of corporations who arrive late for 6 in 10 meetings.[55] Edward Hall says that "time talks."[56] What does your use or misuse of time say about you? To what extent do others communicate with you by their use of time?

Many jobs demand that the worker be on time. To a military officer, being on time really means arriving 15 minutes early. Thus, the armed forces are characterized by the "hurry up and wait" mentality familiar to anyone in basic training. That is, everyone rushes to arrive, but then everyone stands around for a period of time with nothing to do.

Would you make real estate tycoon Donald Trump wait for a meeting with you, or would you arrive on time or even early? When negotiating a real estate transaction, a group of Chinese millionaires once made Trump wait for them—close to an hour. Do you feel that they were sending a message?

Some students have a habit of always being 15 minutes late to class—even when their previous class was just down the hall. What cues does such habitual lateness transmit to an instructor? Should the instructor conclude that the student is not interested in the class? That the student does not like the instructor? That the student is unable to organize activities to accomplish even the simplest goal?

We are expected to structure time in certain ways to ensure that our activities and tasks are accomplished efficiently. U.S. businesspeople, for instance, seek the greatest return on their time investment. In other countries, however, time is treated differently. In some cultures, people are accustomed to waiting several hours for a meeting to begin. In others, the meeting begins whenever the second party arrives.

Even within the United States, people structure time differently. People from the Northeast, for example, usually walk and talk more quickly, provide change more quickly in shops, and are more likely to wear a watch than are people from other parts of the country.

How long we wait for something or someone is related, first, to the value we place on whatever it is we are waiting for and, second, to our own status. We are taught to value what we wait for. In fact, if something is too readily available, we may decide we do not want it after all. Status determines who waits. If we are "important," others usually have access to us only by appointment; thus, it is easier for us to make others wait—and difficult or impossible for others to make us wait.

How well do you structure your time? In his book *The Time Trap*, Alex MacKenzie lists several barriers to the effective use of time:

attempting too much (taking on too many projects at once)

estimating time unrealistically (not realizing how long a project will take)

procrastinating (putting it off, and off, and off . . .)

allowing too many interruptions (letting yourself be distracted by telephone calls, friends, and so on)[57]

Do any of these apply to you? How might you go about improving your use of time?

Touch: Haptics

haptics
the study of the use of touch

You cannot shake hands with a clenched fist.

—Golda Meir

Another category of nonverbal communication is touch, also referred to as **haptics.** According to researchers, touch is "one of the most provocative, yet least well understood" of nonverbal behaviors.[58] Yet all humans need to touch and be touched.[59] Research reveals that a hug and 10 minutes of hand-holding with a romantic partner greatly reduce the harmful physical effects of stress. It appears that, because touch lowers stress hormones, such loving contact protects us throughout the day.[60] Especially for women, hugs, by buffering women from stress, do their hearts good.[61]

How accessible are you to touch?

The amount of touching we do or find acceptable is, at least in part, culturally conditioned. Where do you touch your father? Your mother? Your brother? Your sister? A friend of the same sex? A friend of the opposite sex? In general, women are more accessible to touch than are men. Touch also correlates positively with openness, comfort with relationships, and the ability to express feelings.[62] Both men and women will often kiss women in greeting; men who meet usually shake hands. Usually, men touch women more than women touch men.[63] Physical contact between males is often limited to contact sports, such as football and soccer.

The kind of touch believed appropriate depends upon the kind of relationships individuals share and the situation they find themselves in. One system of analysis identifies the following touch categories: functional-professional (touch that is impersonal or businesslike, such as the kind of touch that occurs when a doctor examines a patient); social-polite (touch used to acknowledge another person, such as a handshake); friendship-warmth (touch that expresses appreciation or warm feelings for another person, such as a pat on the back); love-intimacy (touch occurring in romantic relationships, such as a hug or kiss); and sexual arousal (the most intimate kind of personal contact used to express physical attraction).[64]

Touch can also reflect status. High-status people touch others and invade their space more than do people with lower status.[65] The person who initiates touch is usually the one with the higher status. Nancy Henley points out that we are unlikely to go up to our boss and pat him or her on the shoulder.[66] Would you put your arm around the president of your college or university? Why? Would your behavior change if you met the president at a party? Probably not. The president, however, might well put an arm around you or another student. The person who initiates touching usually also controls the interaction.

Touch, of course, functions importantly in sexual communication. If people hold hands, we assume they have a romantic interest in one another. Are we right? Most American women shave their legs and underarms and use a variety of lotions to keep their hands soft to the touch.

How we use touch sends many messages about us. It reveals our perceptions of status, our attitudes, and even our needs. In his book *The Broken Heart*, psychologist James L. Lynch establishes a correlation between many diseases—particularly heart disease—and loneliness.[67] Lynch tells the story of one man,

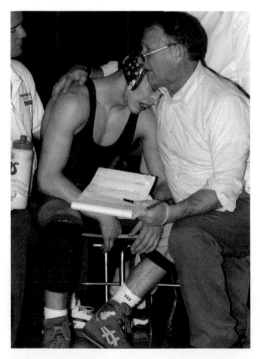

Touch facilitates the expression of feelings.

hooked up to heart-monitoring devices, who was in a coma and near death. When a nurse would walk into his room and hold his hand for a few moments, his heartbeat would change from fast and erratic to slow and smooth.

Different cultures value touch differently. In Asian cultures, for example, very little touching behavior occurs because the members of Asian cultures adhere to norms that forbid public displays of intimacy or affection.[68] For the most part, cultures that encourage outward displays of affection touch more than cultures that stress emotional restraint and rigid status differences. Thus, typically, German, Japanese, and English people touch less than people from the Middle East and Latin America. As a result, when a member of a culture that values touch interacts with a member of a culture that practices touching restraint, the person who is used to touching may perceive the person who rarely touches as aloof or cold, while he or she may be perceived by the other person as aggressive or overly familiar.[69]

Smell: Olfactics

What do happiness and contentment smell like? **Olfactics,** the study of the sense of smell could help us find the answer. Industries are based around our preoccupation with smells and odors. We put on perfumes or colognes and deodorants, clean ourselves with scented soaps, freshen our breath with mouthwash, spray our homes with scented sprays, and burn scented candles in an effort to increase perceptions of attractiveness by enhancing our smell as well as the smell of our home or surroundings.

What kinds of messages does smell send? While some cultures consider the natural smells of both people and the environment to be normal, large numbers of Americans are obsessed with masking natural odors and substituting what they perceive to be more pleasant ones. Aromatherapy even tries to connect smell and well-being, with vanilla being a smell generally accepted as positive and calming.

Smells are associated with attraction, often triggering our emotions or romantic feelings. What smell triggers what emotion depends on our associations, memories, and to some degree, culture. For example, in the United Kingdom, the smell of root beer is reviled whereas people in the United States think it smells good. In England, sarsaparilla and wintergreen, ingredients in root beer, are also used in medicine.[70] Researchers have also studied how smell, specifically pheromones, chemicals emitted by one individual to evoke behavior in another individual, contributes to sexual arousal. Women, research reveals, prefer men whose smell resembles their own.[71] Recently, researchers have also shown that homosexual and heterosexual men respond differently to two odors that may play a part in sexual arousal, with gay men responding similar to women.[72]

TRUTH, DECEPTION, AND NONVERBAL COMMUNICATION

Actors and actresses use nonverbal cues to encourage us to suspend our disbelief and accept them as persons whom they are not. They carefully rehearse the parts they play, down to the smallest gestures and artifacts. As a result, they are able to control the nonverbal cues they exhibit, so that they present the characters being performed in exactly the way they desire.

Marasmus, a Greek word meaning "wasting away," was the term used in the nineteenth and early twentieth centuries to describe a disease babies placed in orphanages or hospitals died from. These infants suffered from a lack of physical contact. Today, in part because of the threat of sexual harassment, teachers refrain from touching students, and employers refrain from touching people with whom they work. Is such a lack of touch contributing to people's thinking that the corporations they work for are cold and uncaring? Should warm and healing, as opposed to sexual, touching be put back into our schools and workplaces? What should be the rules of touch?

olfactics
the study of the sense of smell

What about the rest of us? We, too, may use nonverbal cues to create false impressions in others. While the aim of some deceptive communication is to help receivers save face (we try to appear calm when we are nervous) or to protect oneself from the embarrassment that bluntness can cause (" Yes, I love your new hairstyle," we say when we hate it), the goal of too many deceivers is to take advantage of those with whom they are interacting. Most of us, however, do not rehearse for every one of our person-to-person encounters. Our lives are not that plotted or planned. We do not map out the nonverbal cues we will use during our continuing interactions with others. But what if we could, and what if we did? Would others be able to discern our intentions? Would they be able to tell that we were not really feeling what we were expressing?

In general, people tend to pay closer attention to the nonverbal cues of persons whom they do not trust or whom they suspect may be lying than they do to the rest of the people with whom they interact.[73] Those who plan and rehearse the deceptive messages they are sending tend to be self-confident and experience no guilt about their deception. They are least likely to be suspected by others and, therefore, least likely to be uncovered as liars. This, to be certain, is not necessarily a good thing for those of us trying to detect deceptiveness in others.

Some of us are better at nonverbal deception than others. For example, persons whose occupations require that they sometimes act differently than they feel are most successful at deception. Included in this group are lawyers, diplomats, and salespersons.[74] Researchers also tell us that, as we age, most of us become better liars.[75] Those among us who are high self-monitors are also usually better dissemblers than those of us who possess less self-awareness.

Those of us who are better at nonverbal detection than others are more watchful. Unsuccessful liars are vulnerable to leakage, deception clues that careful observers pick up. Sometimes, it is a change in expression on the face, a movement of the body, a vocal inflection, a deep or shallow breath, a long pause, a slip of the tongue, a microfacial expression, or an ill-timed or inappropriate gesture.[76] How do you protect yourself from being lied to? While there are no specific nonverbal clues that indicate someone is lying, one book went so far as to provide readers with 46 clues to deception.[77] Although the context of the behavior must always be considered, among the nonverbal behaviors typically exhibited by deceivers are increased eye blinking, hand fidgeting, posture shifts, the making of speech errors, rising pitch, and hesitations.[78]

Researchers report the development of a facial imaging device that detects heat patterns in the skin of deceivers. Like the polygraph "lie-detector" test, however, the invention appears to measure anxiety rather than pure deception.[79] Being anxious and not being truthful are not the same things. Do you pride yourself on being a deception detector? What are the clues you rely on?

GENDER AND NONVERBAL BEHAVIOR: MASCULINE AND FEMININE STYLES

The ways men and women use nonverbal communication often reflect societal practices. While men, for example, are expected to exhibit assertive behaviors that demonstrate their power and authority, women are expected to exhibit more reactive and responsive behaviors. Thus, men often talk more than women and interrupt women more frequently than they are interrupted by women.[80]

During interactions, men also tend to be more visually dominant than women. **Visual dominance** is measured by comparing the percentage of looking while speaking with the percentage of looking while listening. When compared with women, men display higher levels of looking while speaking and lower levels when listening. Thus, the visual dominance ratio of men is usually higher than that of women and, again, reflects the use of nonverbal cues to reinforce perceptions of social power.[81]

Men can use space and touch to assert their dominance over women. They are much more likely to touch women than women are to touch them. Again, women are more typically the recipients of touching actions, rather than the initiators. Men also tend to claim more personal space than women usually do, and they more frequently walk in front of women than behind them. Thus, in general, males are the touchers, not the touchees, the leaders rather than the followers.

What kinds of nonverbal cues do women display more than men? According to body language experts, whereas power posture was in vogue in the 1990s, women now do more slouching, using it to express rebelliousness, boredom, and wealth. In fact, what has come to be known as "the sultry slouch" has become a virtual fashion accessory for women.[82] In contrast to their posture of noninvolvement, women tend to smile and show emotion more often than men do. In general, they are more expressive than men are and exhibit higher levels of involvement when engaged in person-to-person interaction than men do. Women stand closer to one another than men do. Women also use nonverbal signals to draw others into conversations to a greater extent than men do. While women demonstrate an interest in affiliation, men generally are more interested in establishing the strength of their own ideas and agendas.[83] In addition, when tests are given to assess nonverbal decoding ability, including the ability to read another person's feelings by relying on vocal or facial cues, females usually outperform males.[84]

visual dominance
a measure calculated by comparing the percentage of looking while speaking with the percentage of looking while listening

DIVERSITY AND NONVERBAL BEHAVIOR: CULTURAL PATTERNS

People throughout the world use nonverbal cues to help them express themselves. In large measure, the culture of a people modifies their use of such cues. People who belong to **contact cultures**—that is, cultures that promote interaction and encourage displays of warmth, closeness, and availability—tend to stand close to each other when conversing, seek maximum sensory experiences, and touch each other frequently. This is not the case, however, among members of **low-contact cultures,** where such behaviors are discouraged. Saudi Arabia, France, and Italy are countries with contact cultures; their members relish the intimacy of contact when conversing. In contrast, Scandinavia, Germany, England, and Japan are low- or lower-contact cultures, whose members value privacy and maintain more distance from each other when interacting.[85]

In similar fashion, people from different cultures may not display emotion or express intimacy in the same ways. Among the members of Mediterranean

contact cultures
cultures that promote interaction and encourage displays of warmth, closeness, and availability

low-contact cultures
cultures that maintain more distance when interacting

Do you think you can teach nonverbal communication, the way you can teach a foreign language? Why or why not?

The U.S. military provides soldiers serving in Iraq "smart cards" with facts like these: In Iraq it is considered unclean to use your left hand for contact with others. It is similarly considered rude to back away from someone during conversation. Could knowing such facts help win the hearts and minds of the people?

cultures, for example, it is normal for emotive reactions to be uninhibited. Thus, it is common for the cultures' members to express a feeling like grief or happiness together with open facial displays, magnified gestures, and vocal cues that support the feeling. On the other hand, neither the Chinese nor the Japanese readily reveal their inner feelings in public, preferring to display less emotion, maintain more self-control, and keep their feelings to themselves; for these reasons, they often appear to remain expressionless.[86] In contrast, persons in the United States are likely to be emotionally expressive and to smile freely.

The cultural background of the individuals communicating also affects their use of personal space and touch. Americans stand farther apart when conversing than do persons from Middle Eastern cultures. Whereas Americans expect persons who live next door to them to be friendly and to interact with them, this expectation is not shared by the Japanese. Consequently, whereas the Japanese may view Americans as overly friendly, the Americans may conclude that the Japanese are unfriendly, cold, and distant. Middle Easterners are apt to do a significant amount of touching; they walk with their arms around each other and are apt to touch each other during conversations a lot more than are persons from noncontact cultures.

Even when the nonverbal cues displayed in different cultures are the same, they do not necessarily convey the same meaning. In the United States, for example, a head nod symbolizes agreement or consent, while in Japan it means only that a message was received. Hand signals can be confusing to those not tuned in to the culture. For example, people in the United States use their hand pointing at their chest when they talk about themselves. The Japanese use their forefinger pointed at their nose. Similarly, diverse cultures feel differently about silence. Whereas in the United States we are apt to perceive another person's silence as a negative and to infer that he or she is too self-absorbed, is not listening, is not interested, or has nothing of value to add to a conversation, other cultures interpret silence in a more favorable light. In Japan, for example, silence is frequently preferred to speech.

What kind of statement does a tatoo or a tongue or belly button ring make? Do you believe such artifacts signal defiance, independence, or something else? What inferences are persons who do not use such personal adornments likely to make about those who do?

Exploring Diversity

When Is a Kiss Not a Kiss?

When the Middle Eastern version of the reality show *Big Brother* was aired in the Arab world, one segment had a handsome Saudi kiss a Tunisian beauty. Viewers already perceived unrelated men and women sharing a house as abhorrent. The kiss complicated things, leading to protests and accusations of moral depravity. Critics called the show an assault on traditional values. As far as some viewers were concerned, the two might as well have had sex. In short order, the show was taken off the air, pleasing those opposed to it.[87]

Can reality television be transferred easily from one nation to another? Is reality for one country's audience necessarily another country's reality as well? Do you believe the globalization of programming concepts promotes or undermines cultural diversity?[88] Explain.

Culture also affects the treatment of space. In an effort to enhance the relationships between the external environment and the inner self, the Chinese, and now others, use feng shui (pronounced "fung-SHWAY"), the ancient Chinese art of placement, to add harmony and balance to living spaces. Feng shui introduces the five elements in nature into design: earth, fire, water, wood, and metal. For example, it uses green plants to bring the outdoors inside, and red candles and fabrics to increase energy.[89] The goal is to arrange space, furniture, walls, colors, and objects to promote blessings and to harness the life force (chi).

For us to experience more effective interaction with people from different cultures, we must make the effort to identify and understand the many ways each culture shapes nonverbal communication. We need to acknowledge that our communication style is not intrinsically better than others, that awareness will contribute to more successful multicultural exchanges.

TECHNOLOGY AND NONVERBAL COMMUNICATION

Nonverbal communication is alive and well in cyberspace. Just as those who communicate in cyberspace rely on established netiquette guidelines for the standards of behavior acceptable during their online interactions, so they have also evolved a system of written symbols to help reinforce those standards. These symbols, called **emoticons,** replace physical gestures and facial expressions, substitute for nonverbal cues, and help those engaged in online dialogues convey action, emotion, and emphasis.[90]

Emoticons, or relational icons, help add personalization and more expressive emotional exchanges to computer-mediated communication as a way to approximate the warmth and intimacy of face-to-face interactions. Thus, emoticons, are used also at times to indicate subtle mood changes.[91] For example, a symbol called the smiley face looks like :-) and indicates the humorous intent of the sender. It may wink mischievously, ;-), or frown, :-(, depending on whether the online comment is to be interpreted humorously or sarcastically. Similarly, capitalizations and asterisks, such as GREAT and ***, convey a user's emphasis and enthusiasm.

The following list contains other emoticons that can be used to describe a communicator's physical or emotional condition or to depict feelings and actions

Focus on Service Learning

Applying the knowledge you have gained from this chapter, together with research you conduct online using the resources of your college library, and other sources, such as http://nonverbal.ucsc.edu/ or www.csupomona.edu/~tassi/ gestures.htm, develop a presentation on cultural norms of nonverbal communication in the United States. Arrange to share your presentation with at least one of the following: an instructor who teaches English as a Second Language (ESL) at a local community school to recent immigrants, the ESL teacher and his or her students at a local high school, or specialists in ESL and those they teach at your own college.

emoticons

symbols that replace nonverbal cues during machine-assisted communication

Do you think jokes play as well online as they do when delivered by someone in person? How does the loss of nonverbal cues influence the impact of a joke? How could you use emoticons to compensate for the loss of such cues?

that straight text alone could not depict. These symbols are commonly understood by online users.

:-P	someone sticking out the tongue
:-O	someone screaming in fright, their hair standing on end
:-&	someone whose lips are sealed
!#!^*&:-	a schizophrenic![92]

Of course, persons unfamiliar with online culture would more than likely be confused by the use of emotions. Lacking more conventional social context cues, they would not be able to use the symbols to achieve understanding.

Since online communicators probably are not able to hear each other, they have also created a shorthand to describe their reactions. For instance, they may describe themselves as "rolling on the floor laughing" with the abbreviation ROFL.

Technological changes are affecting our nonverbal communication in other ways as well. According to Nelson Thall, the president and chief executive officer of the Marshall McLuhan Center on Global Communication, the current variety in fashion is an outgrowth of the electronic technological revolution. According to Thall, "Our clothing is an extension of our skin, just like a hammer is a technological extension of our hand."[93] Thall contends that since computers and the Internet allow people to be nationless, sexless, and ageless, fashion now reflects that option. We now dress similarly across borders and wear clothing that is technologically friendly, with room for cell phones, beepers, PDAs, and so on. We even have a wearable computer, also known as a personal optical mobile appliance or personal multimedia appliance. It has been predicted that more than 60 percent of the U.S. population ages 15 to 50 will carry or wear a wireless computing and communications device at least six hours a day by the year 2007.[94] Do you carry or wear such a device now?

In addition, in our security-conscious age, technology is also being called into play to aid in person identification and behavior analysis by helping with the reading of nonverbal cues. The CIA, for example, has commissioned two research

Has technology become an accessory? Is it now a regular part of your wardrobe? Does wearing it help enhance your credibility?

centers, the Salk Institute and Carnegie-Mellon University's Robotics Institute, to try to teach computers to watch for detailed facial-language clues. Hidden computers are also used to pick up stress in the speech patterns of travelers when they check in at airports.[95]

ASSESSING YOUR EFFECTIVENESS AS A NONVERBAL COMMUNICATOR

Nonverbal communication includes body language (facial expressions, posture, and gestures), clothing, voice, distances and spaces, colors, time, touch and smell—all of which can either support or contradict the meaning of the words we speak. Use your knowledge of these variables to help you react to interactions you observe and to appropriate pictures in this text. For each picture you select, answer the following questions about the interactants and identify the cues that influenced your response:

1. Who is more trustworthy?
2. Who is more dynamic?
3. Who is more credible?
4. Who has more status?
5. Who is older?
6. Who is more intelligent?
7. Who is more powerful?
8. Who is more friendly?
9. What is their relationship to each other?
10. What can you predict about the course of their relationship?

Discussing your observations will be valuable, since many of our judgments and decisions are based on nonverbal cues.

The following guidelines should prove helpful as you continue to develop your ability to make valid judgments and decisions on the basis of nonverbal communication.

Examine the Environment

For any nonverbal interaction, ask yourself if any environmental stimuli are likely to affect it. Determine if other people present could influence the communicators. Attempt to determine whether colors and decor will have an impact on the nature and tone of the communication. Analyze the amount of space available to the interactants. Determine whether architectural factors might alter the outcome. Where are chairs, tables, passageways, and desks situated? Why did the interactants situate themselves as they did? What type of behavior would we expect to see in this environment?

Observe the Communicators

Ask yourself if the sex, age, or status of the communicators will exert an influence on their relationship. Assess to what extent, if any, attractiveness, clothing, or physical appearance should affect the interaction. Determine if, in your own mind, the communicators' dress is appropriate to the environment. Decide if the communicators appear to like each other and to have similar goals.

Observe Body Language

What does each communicator's facial expression reveal? Are his or her facial expressions relatively consistent or fleeting? Do these expressions tend to fluctuate drastically? Assess the extent to which you believe the facial expressions are genuine.

Analyze significant bodily cues. Attempt to decide if hand or foot movements suggest honesty or deception. Decide if either of the interactants moves too much or too little. Ask yourself if both are equally involved in the exchange. Is one more eager to continue the communication than the other? Would one prefer to terminate the communication? How do you know?

Assess the extent to which the interactants mirror each other's posture. Ask yourself how posture supports or contradicts their status relationship. Do the interactants appear to be relaxed or tense? Why? Determine if they have used their bodies to include or exclude others from their conversation. Analyze when and why the communicators alter their postures.

Watch the eye behavior of the participants. Determine if one looks away more than the other. Determine if one stares at the other. To what extent, if any, does excessive blinking occur? When is eye contact most pronounced? How does the eye contact of one participant appear to affect the other?

Listen for Vocal Cues

Assess whether the communicators are using appropriate vocal volumes and rates of speaking, given their situation. Determine if and how the way something that is said verbally supports or contradicts what is being said nonverbally. Analyze how and when silence is used. Be responsive to signals of nervousness and changes in pitch.

Observe Touching

Watch to see if the participants touch each other at all. Determine, if you can, why they touched. How did touching or being touched affect the interactants? Was the contact appropriate or inappropriate to the situation? Why?

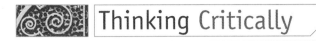 Thinking Critically

Reflect and Respond

Agree or disagree with the following statement; supply reasons and examples that support your position.

Because of the important implications of nonverbal cues—in interviews, in advertising, and in interactions in general—the impressions we form are due more to the nonverbal signals displayed than to the words spoken by the communicators.

Revisiting Chapter Objectives

1. **Define and distinguish among the following terms: *nonverbal communication, kinesics, paralanguage, proxemics, chronemics, haptics, and olfactics.*** Nonverbal communication includes all the human responses that are not expressed in words. Over 65 percent of the social meaning of the messages we send to others is communicated nonverbally. Perceiving and analyzing nonverbal cues can help us understand what is really happening during a conversation.

   Nonverbal messages fall into eight main categories: (1) body language, or kinesics (facial expressions, posture, eye gaze and eye contact, and gestures); (2) clothing and artifactual communication; (3) voice, or paralanguage (including pitch, volume, rate, and pauses); (4) space and distance, or proxemic factors (including both the space that exists between us when we talk to each other and the way we organize space in our homes, offices, and communities); (5) colors; (6) time, or chronemics; (7) touch, or haptics; and (8) smell, or olfactics.

2. **Explain why the face is an important source of information.** Since the face cannot be easily hidden, it is an important source of nonverbal information and communicates a variety of emotions. In addition, eye contact, pupil size, and the smile provide additional cues to informed observers.

3. **Explain how artifactual communication can affect interaction.** Artifactual communication, another category of nonverbal cues, is an integral part of the nonverbal package. It includes the use of personal adornments, such as clothing, jewelry, makeup, hairstyles, and beards. People are apt to make inferences about us based on the way we dress.

4. **Distinguish among the following terms: *intimate distance, personal distance, social distance, and public distance; and informal space, semi-fixed-feature space, and fixed-feature space.*** Proxemic cues, including the treatment of space and territory, influence interaction and help define the communication experience. According to Edward Hall, there are four distances that we keep between ourselves and other people: intimate distance—0 to 18 inches; personal distance—18 inches to 4 feet; social distance—4 to 12 feet; and public distance—12 feet to the limit of sight. In addition, researchers divide environmental spaces into three categories—informal, semi-fixed-feature, and fixed-feature—based on the perceived permanence of the physical space.

5. **Explain why territoriality is an important concept in communication.** Typically, human beings stake out space, or territory. Territoriality is the need to demonstrate a possessive or ownership relationship to space. Markers are used to reserve space and set boundaries that help identify the space as belonging to someone.

6. **Identify the ways gender, diversity, and technology influence nonverbal behavior.** The use of nonverbal cues is affected by variables such as gender, culture, and technology. The ways men and women use nonverbal cues reflects societal practices. To a large degree, people modify their use of nonverbal cues depending on the culture they belong to or identify with. Nonverbal communication is also affected by whether communication is occurring online or offline.

The Wrap Up

7. **Explain the role nonverbal cues play in deception and truth telling.**   If we are watchful, we can identify deception cues that leak out when a person lies. High self-monitors emit fewer cues, making detection more difficult.

8. **Identify how you can improve your nonverbal communication effectiveness.** You can improve your effectiveness as a nonverbal communicator by observing and analyzing the physical environment of interactions as well as the appearance, body language (facial expressions, gestures, posture, and so on), vocal cues, and touching behavior of the participants.

Resources for Further Inquiry and Reflection

To apply your understanding of how the principles in Chapter 6 are at work in our daily lives, consult the following resources for further inquiry and reflection. Or, if you prefer, choose any other appropriate resource. Then connect the ideas expressed in your chosen selection with the communication concepts and issues you are learning about both in and out of class.

 ### Listen to Me

"Hung Up" (Madonna)
"Green Eyes" (Coldplay)
"Good Vibrations" (The Beach Boys)
"Your Body Is a Wonderland" (John Mayer)
"Superman" (Eminem)
"The Sound of Silence" (Simon and Garfunkel)
"You've Lost That Lovin' Feeling" (The Righteous Brothers)

Each song describes the effects of one or more nonverbal cues on an individual and/or a relationship. Identify and discuss the cue or cues emphasized, being certain to explain the impact on communication.

 ### View Me

Mother-in-Law	*Don't Say a Word*
The Mask	*Look Who's Talking*
Edward Scissorhands	*Elizabethtown*
Hitch	

The characters in these films have a prime nonverbal channel either masked or unmasked. Discuss the extent to which the character is affected by his or her ability or inability to use a nonverbal cue effectively.

 ### Read Me

Joan Didion. *The Year of Magical Thinking*. New York: Knopf, 2005.
Arthur Conan Doyle. *Sherlock Holmes*. New York: Knopf, 1996.
Sister Souljah. *The Coldest Winter Ever*. New York: Pocket Books, 2000.
David L. Lieberman. *Never Be Lied to Again*. New York: St. Martin's, 1998.

On the basis of your reading of one of these books, discuss how nonverbal cues can be used to help identify someone who is guilty, select a jury, identify a real friend, or hire a business associate.

Tell Me

Share with the class the insights you gained from your chosen Listen to Me, View Me, or Read Me selection.

According to baseball legend Yogi Berra, "Sometimes you can observe a lot by watching." Give an example of what you think Yogi meant.

Key Chapter Terminology

Use the Communication Works CD-ROM and the Online Learning Center at www.mhhe.com/gamble9 to further your knowledge of the following terminology:

Communication
Works

online learning center

www.mhhe.com/gamble9

artifactual communication 147	nonfluencies 151
chronemics 157	nonverbal communication 137
civil inattention 142	olfactics 159
contact cultures 161	paralanguage 148
emoticons 163	personal distance 153
facial management techniques 140	pitch 149
fixed-feature space 154	proxemics 152
habitual pitch 149	public distance 154
haptics 158	rate 150
informal space 154	semi-fixed-feature space 154
intimate distance 152	silence 151
kinesics 140	social distance 153
low-contact cultures 161	territoriality 155
markers 155	visual dominance 161
mixed message 138	volume 150

Idioms in Translation

adam's apple—larynx

baby face—young-looking face

bling—ostentatious jewelry

clock addiction—obsession with time

give a cold shoulder to—ignore

have no backbone—act cowardly

jumping out of his neck—pulsating

keep your chin up—stay optimistic

read a face—search for nonverbal clues

shoulder a burden—be burdened by a problem

shrug off a problem—ignore a problem

stare down—confront, challenge

turn back the clock—return to an earlier time

Communication
Works

online learning center

www.mhhe.com/gamble9

Test Your Understanding

Go to the Self Quizzes on the Communication Works CD-ROM and the book's Online Learning Center at www.mhhe.com/gamble9.

Notes

1. M. T. Palmer and K. B. Simmons. "Communicating Intentions through Nonverbal Behaviors: Conscious and Nonconscious Encoding of Liking." *Human Communication Research* 22, 1995, pp. 128–160.

2. Ann Davis, Joseph Pereira, and William M. Bulkeley. "Security Concerns Bring New Focus on Body Language." *The Wall Street Journal*, August 15, 2002, pp. A1, A6.

3. See, for example, H. A. Elfenbein and N. Ambady. "Predicting Workplace Outcomes from the Ability to Eavesdrop on Feelings." *Journal of Applied Psychology* October 2002, pp. 963–972.

4. See, for example, L. Carrol and P. J. Gilroy. "Role of Appearance and Nonverbal Behaviors in the Perception of Sexual Orientation among Lesbians and Gay Men." *Psychological Reports*, 9:1, August 2002, pp. 115–122.

5. "Feeling 'Out of It' at Work and Socially?" *USA Today Magazine*, November 2002, p. 8.

6. Ray Birdwhistell. *Kinesics and Context*. Philadelphia: University of Pennsylvania Press, 1970; Mark L. Knapp and Judith A. Hall. *Nonverbal Communication in Human Interaction*, 3rd ed. Orlando, FL: Harcourt Brace Jovanovich, 1992; Albert Mehrabian. *Silent Messages*. 2nd ed. Belmont, CA: Wadsworth, 1981.

7. Marilyn Daniels. *Dancing with Words: Signing for Hearing Children's Literacy*. Bergin & Garvey, Westport, CT: 2001.

8. For some practical advice, see Dale G. Leathers. *Successful Nonverbal Communication: Principles and Applications*. New York: Macmillan, 1992.

9. Tom Pedulla. "Spurning Anthem Creates Rancor." *USA Today*, February 26, 2003, p. 4C.

10. Tamar Lewin. "High School Tells Student to Remove Antiwar Shirt." *The New York Times*, February 26, 2003.

11. Knapp and Hall.

12. See, for example, Judith N. Martin and Thomas K. Nakayama. *Intercultural Communication in Contexts*, 2nd ed. Mountain View, CA: Mayfield, 2000, p. 181.

13. Kathleen Fackelmann. "Look Who's Talking with Gestures." *USA Today*, July 5, 2000, p. 7D.

14. Quoted in Daniel Goleman. "Sensing Silent Cues Emerges as Key Skill." *The New York Times*, October 10, 1989.

15. M. D. Licke, R. H. Smith, and M. L. Klotz. "Judgments of Physical Attractiveness: The Role of Faces and Bodies." *Personality and Social Psychology Bulletin* 12, 1986, pp. 381–389.

16. D. S. Berry. "What Can a Moving Face Tell Us?" *Journal of Personality and Social Psychology* 58, 1990, pp. 1004–1014.

17. See C. L. Kleinke. "Gaze and Eye Contact: A Research Review." *Psychological Bulletin* 100, 1986, pp. 78–100.

18. Helmut Morsbach. "Aspects of Nonverbal Communication in Japan." In Larry Samovar and Richard Porter, eds. *Intercultural Communication: A Reader*, 3rd ed. Belmont, CA: Wadsworth, 1982, p. 308.

19. V. Richmond. "Teacher Nonverbal Immediacy: Use and Outcomes." In J. L. Chesebro and J. C. McCroskey, eds. *Communication for Teachers*. Boston: Allyn & Bacon, 2002, pp. 65–82.

20. Warren St. John. "They're Not Just Saying Ah." *The New York Times*, October 2, 2005, p. 13.

21. Nancy Henley. *Body Politics: Power, Sex and Nonverbal Communication*. New York: Simon & Schuster, 1986.

22. Alex Kuczynski. "A Lovelier You, with Off-the-Shelf Parts." *The New York Times*, May 2, 2004, WR1, WR12.

23. For a summary of Mehrabian's work in this area, see his article "Significance of Posture and Position in the Communication of Attitude and Status Relationship." *Psychological Bulletin* 71, 1969, pp. 359–372.

24. Paul Ekman, W. V. Friesen, and J. Baer. "The International Language of Gestures." *Psychology Today*, May 1984, pp. 64–69.

25. L. Samovar and R. Porter. *Communication between Cultures*, 4th ed. Belmont, CA: Wadsworth, 2001.

26. See L. K. Guerrero, J. A. DeVito, and M. L. Hecht, eds. *The Nonverbal Communication Reader: Classic and Contemporary Readings*, 2nd ed. Prospect Heights, IL: Waveland, 1999; and Joseph Kahn. "Chinese People's Republic Is Unfair to Its Short People." *The New York Times*, May 21, 2004, p. A13.

27. "Cold Shoulder for Fat Customers." *The New York Times*, April 5, 2005, p. F6.

28. V. Ritts, M. L. Patterson and M. E. Tubbs. "Expectations, Impressions, and Judgments of Physically Attractive Students: A Review." *Review of Educational Research* 62, 1992, pp. 413–426.

29. See, for example, J. Kilbourne. "The More You Subtract, The More You Add: Cutting Girls Down to Size." In J. Spade and C. Valentine, eds. *The Kaleidoscope of Gender*. Belmont, CA: Wadsworth, 2004, pp. 234–244.

30. Ruth La Ferla. "Generation E. A.: Ethnically Ambiguous." *The New York Times*, December 28, 2003, pp. ST1, ST9.

31. S. Kaiser. *The Social Psychology of Clothing: Symbolic Appearances in Context*, 2nd ed. New York: Macmillan, 1990.

32. Ruth La Ferla. "Wearing Their Beliefs on Their Chests." *The New York Times*, March 29, 2005, p. B7.

33. John T. Molloy. *New Dress for Success*. New York: Warner, 1990.

34. Molloy.

35. See, for example, M. S. Singer and A. E. Singer. "The Effect of Police Uniforms on Interpersonal Perception." *Journal of Psychology* 119, 1985, pp. 157–161.

36. See, for example, Scott Shane. "Language Help from, Um, Almost-Words." *The Sunday Record*, September 12, 1999, pp. L3, L7.

37. Thomas Murry. In Peter Jaret, "My Voice Has Got to Go." *The New York Times*, July 21, 2003, p. G1.

38. Mehrabian.

39. Steve Adamek. "Doctor of Style." *The Record*, October 21, 2005, p. S3; Christine Brennan. "Stern Rightly Trying to Tailor New NBA Image." *USA Today*, October 20, 2005, p. 2C; Janie McCauley. "Richardson Against NBA's New Dress Code." abcnews.go.com/Sports/wireStory?id=1232360.

40. For background on how culture affects rate, see Hyun O. Lee and Franklin J. Boster. "Collectivism-Individualism in Perceptions of Speech Rate: A Cross-Cultural Comparison." *Journal of Cross-Cultural Psychology* 23:3, September 1992, pp. 377–388.

41. F. Goldman-Eisler. "Continuity of Speech Utterance. Its Determinance and Its Significance." *Language and Speech* 4, 1961, pp. 220–231.

42. Adam Jaworski. *The Power of Silence: Social and Pragmatic Perspective*. Thousand Oaks, CA: Sage, 1993.

43. Edward Hall. *The Hidden Dimension*. New York: Doubleday, 1969.

44. Lizette Alvarez. "Where the Healing Touch Starts with the Hospital Design." *The New York Times*, pp. F5, F10.

45. See J. K. Burgoon. "Privacy and Communication." In M. Burgoon, ed. *Communication Yearbook 6*. Beverly Hills, CA: Sage, 1982, pp. 206–249; J. K. Burgoon and L. Aho. "Three Field Experiments on the Effects of Violations of Conversational Distance." *Communication Monographs* 49, 1982, pp. 71–88; J. K. Burgoon and J. B. Walther. "Nonverbal Expectations and the Evaluative Consequence of Violations." *Human Communication Research* 17:2, 1990, pp. 232–265.

46. See, for example, A. G. White. "The Patient Sits Down: A Clinical Note." *Psychosomatic Medicine* 15, 1953, pp. 256–257.

47. D. Diamond. "Behind Closed Gates." *USA Today*, January 31, 1997, pp. 4–5.

48. Max Luscher. *The Luscher Color Test*. New York: Simon & Schuster, 1980. See also Luscher. *The Four-Color Person*. New York: Simon & Schuster, 1980.

49. Susan Carey, "More U.S. Companies Are Blue, and It's Not Just the Stock Market." *The Wall Street Journal*, August 30, 2001, pp. A1, A2.

50. Craig Wilson. "Serene Color Gets the Green Light in Uncertain Times." *USA Today*. March 7, 2003, p. D1.

51. Meera Somasundaram. "Red Symbols Tend to Lure Shoppers Like Capes Being Flourished at Bulls." *The Wall Street Journal*, September 18, 1995, p. A9.

52. Jennifer Steinhauer. "The Color Red Takes on a Youthful Look." *The New York Times*, June 30, 1996, p. 42.

53. Ben Feller. "Teachers Getting the Red Out." *The Record*, April 4, 2005, p. A6.

54. Robert Levine. *A Geography of Time, or How Every Culture Keeps Time Just a Little Differently.* New York: Basic Books: 1997.

55. Del Jones. "I'm Late, I'm Late, I'm Late." *USA Today*, November 26, 2002, p. B1.

56. Hall.

57. Alex MacKenzie. *The Time Trap*. New York: McGraw-Hill, 1975.

58. J. Burgoon, J. Walther, and J. Baesler. "Interpretations, Evaluations, and Consequences of Interpersonal Touch." *Human Communication Research* 19, pp. 237–263.

59. Marilyn Elias. "Study: Hugging Warms the Heart, and Also May Protect It." *USA Today*, March 10, 2003, p. 7D.

60. An especially persuasive argument is made by Ashley Montagu in *Touching: The Human Significance of the Skin*. New York: Harper & Row, 1971.

61. Marilyn Elias. "Hugs Can Do a Heart Good." *USA Today*, March 8, 2004, p. 7D.

62. See D. F. Fromme, W. E. Jaynes, D. K. Taylor, E. G. Harold, J. Daniell, J. R. Roundtree, and M. Fromme. "Nonverbal Behaviors and Attitudes toward Touch." *Journal of Nonverbal Behavior* 13, 1989, pp. 3–14.

63. Barbara Bales. *Communication and the Sexes*. New York: Harper & Row, 1988, p. 60.

64. See, for example, R. Heslin and T. Alper. "Touch: A Bonding Gesture." In J. M. Wiemann and R. P. Harrison, eds. *Nonverbal Interaction*. Beverly Hills, CA: Sage, 1983, p. 47–75.

65. See, for example, J. T. Wood. *Interpersonal Communication: Everyday Encounters*, 2nd ed. Belmont, CA: Wadsworth, 2002.

66. Henley.

67. James L. Lynch. *The Broken Heart*. New York: Basic Books, 1979. See also James L. Lynch. *The Language of the Heart*. New York: Basic Books, 1986.

68. M. S. Kim. "A Comparative Analysis of Nonverbal Expression as Portrayed by Korean and American Print-Media Advertising." *Howard Journal of Communication* 3, 1992, pp. 320–324.

69. Carolyn Calloway-Thomas, Pamela J. Cooper, and Cecil Blake. *Intercultural Communication: Roots and Routes*. Boston: Allyn & Bacon, 1999, p. 166.

70. Jim Beckerman. "A Whiff of Vanilla Seems to Please Us All." *The Record*, September 16, 2003, pp. F1, F2.

71. N. Wade. "Scent of a Man Is Linked to a Woman's Selection." *The New York Times*, January 22, 2002, p. F2.

72. Nicholas Wade. "For Gay Men, Different Scent of Attraction." *The New York Times*, May 10, 2005, pp. A1, A14.

73. M. G. Millar and K. U. Millar. "The Effects of Suspicion on the Recall of Cues to Make Veracity Judgments." *Communication Reports* 11, 1998, pp. 57–64.

74. R. G. Riggio and H. S. Freeman. "Individual Differences and Cues to Deception." *Journal of Personality and Social Psychology* 45, 1983, pp. 899–915.

75. D. B. Buller and J. K. Burgoon. "Deception: Strategic and Nonstrategic Communication." In J. Daly and J. M. Wiemann, eds. *Interpersonal Communication*. Hillsdale, NJ: Erlbaum, 1994.

76. Paul Ekman and Mark G. Frank. "Lies That Fail." In Michael Lewis and Carolyn Saarni, eds. *Lying and Deception in Everyday Life*. New York: Guilford, 1993, pp. 184–200.

77. David J. Lieberman. *Never Be Lied to Again*. New York: St. Martin's, 1998.

78. See, for example, T. H. Feeley and M. A. Turck. "The Behaviorial Correlates of Sanctioned and Unsanctioned Deceptive Communication." *Journal of Nonverbal Behavior* 22, 1998, pp. 189–204; A. Vrij, L. Akehurst, and P. Morris. "Individual Differences in Hand Movements during Deception." *Journal of Nonverbal Behavior* 21, 1997, pp. 87–102; and L. Anolli and R. Ciceri. "The Voice of Deception: Vocal Strategies of Naïve and Able Liars." *Journal of Nonverbal Behavior* 21, 1997, pp. 259–285.

79. J. Pavlidis, N. L. Eberhardt, and J. A. Levine. "Seeing through the Face of Deception." *Nature* 415, 2002.

80. B. Veland. "Tell Me More: On the Fine Art of Listening." *Utne Reader*, 1992, pp.104–109; A. Mulac. "Men's and Women's Talk in Same Gender and Mixed Gender Dyads: Power or Polemic?" *Journal of Language and Social Psychology* 8, 1989, pp. 249–270.

81. J. F. Dovidio, S. L. Ellyson, C. F. Keating, K. Heltman, and C. E. Brown. "The Relationship of Social Power to Visual Displays of Dominance between Men and Women." *Journal of Personality and Social Psychology* 54, 1988, pp. 233–242.

82. Shelly Branch. "Forget Standing Tall, Female Models Make Slouching Look Good." *The Wall Street Journal*, pp. A1, A9.

83. Julia T. Wood. *Gendered Lives*. Belmont, CA: Wadsworth, 1994, p. 154.

84. N. G. Rotter and G. S. Rotter. "Sex Differences in the Encloding and Decoding of Negative Facial Emotions." *Journal of Nonverbal Behavior* 12:2, 1998, pp. 139–148.

85. Peter Anderson. "Exploring Intercultural Differences in Nonverbal Communication." In L. Samovar and R. Porter, eds. *Intercultural Communication: A Reader*, 3rd ed. Belmont, CA: Wadsworth, 1982, pp. 272–282.

86. Edwin R. McDaniel. "Japanese Nonverbal Communication: A Review and Critique of Literature." Paper presented at the annual meeting of the Speech Communication Association, Miami Beach, FL, November 18–21, 1993.

87. Neil MacFarquhar. "A Kiss Is Not Just a Kiss to an Angry Arab TV Audience." *The New York Times*, March 5, 2004, p. A3.

88. See Alan Riding. "Unesco Adopts New Plan against Cultural Invasion." *The New York Times*, October 21, 2005, p. E3.

89. Kaet Saks. "In Perfect Harmony." *The Record*, August 19, 1999, pp. HF1, HF3.

90. Steven G. Jones. *Cybersociety: Computer-Mediated Communication and Community*. Thousand Oaks, CA: Sage, 1995, p. 116.

91. C. Consstantin, S. Kalyanaraman, C. Stavrositu, and N. Wagoner. "To Be or Not to Be Emotional: Impression Formation Effects of Emoticons in Moderated Chatrooms." Paper presented at the annual meeting of the Association for Education in Journalism and Mass Communication, Miami Beach, FL, August 7–10, 2002.

92. Jones, p. 172.

93. Karen De Witt. "So, What Is That Leather Bustier Saying?" *The New York Times*, January 1, 1995, p. 2-E.

94. Edward C. Baig. "This 'Wearable Computer' Fits Like a Glove." *USA Today*, April 3, 2002, p. 6D.

95. Bret Lortie. "Your Lying Eyes." *Bulletin of the Atomic Scientists* 58:6, November/ December 2002.

CHAPTER 7

Listening, Feedback, and Critical Thinking

After finishing this chapter, you should be able to

1. Define *hearing*, *listening*, and *critical thinking*.

2. Compare and contrast helpful and harmful listening and thinking habits.

3. Explain and use the HURIER model.

4. Define *feedback*, distinguish among and use different types of feedback, and explain how each type affects communication.

5. Set appropriate listening goals.

6. Explain how gender, culture, and media and technology influence listening.

To get what you want in your career, stop talking and start listening.

—Anonymous

Listening is not just hearing what someone tells you word for word. You have to listen with a heart.

—Anna Deavere Smith

Nothing new ever entered the mind through an open mouth.

—The Sperry Corporation
(now part of UNISYS)

Do you know someone whose attention never wavers when talking with you, whose eyes lock on yours, whose facial expressions announce interest in you, and whose questions and ability to paraphrase demonstrate an understanding of you? If you do, then you know a person who knows what it means to be an effective listener.[1]

The Chinese character for "listening" (see Figure 7.1) combines a number of symbols representing the ears, the eyes, and the heart, suggesting that when we listen, we need to give our undivided attention and should not rely on our ears alone but should use our eyes and our hearts as well. In your opinion, do most of the people you know accomplish this goal? Do you?

Famed American author Ernest Hemingway is said to have spoken the following words: "I like to listen. I have learned a great deal from listening. Most people never listen." On the basis of your personal experiences, do you think Hemingway's conclusion is right? Do most people never listen?

One college student, Brett Banfe, convinced that he had failed miserably in listening to others, vowed to correct his failing by remaining silent for a year: "I noticed I wasn't really listening to people. I was just waiting for people to stop talking so I could chime in," Banfe said.[2] "I'd wait for them to stop talking, then I'd start talking. Because . . . my opinion was the right one anyway. It was like, 'Thanks a lot for your input, but here's how it really happened.'"[3] While you may think that the action taken by Brett Banfe seems extreme, far too often listening is something we take for granted. However, listening is a difficult, intricate skill and, like other skills, it requires training and practice.

■ ■ ■

LISTENING AND COMMUNICATION

Consider the following excerpt from Hannah Merker's book *Listening*:

> I noticed the world was getting quieter . . . a silence, a soundlessness was softening the edges of my sometimes strident life. The noticing did not appear in a single startling revelation. No, it was a slow astonishing surprise that I sensed the increasing hush around me, with no glimmer yet of the stunning reality: only my world was growing quieter. I was becoming deaf.

> When we are used to things, familiar with their presence, we often cease to see them. Or hear them. And silence was something I was becoming used to, an atmosphere once sought in retreat from a large noisy family. Now silence came unbidden, softly, unnoticed, creeping close and staying with me. I noticed the absence of things. My mini-house seemed hushed with the stillness present in a storm when power is cut off. We never hear the heating unit simmering slowly, the whirrings of refrigerators. Machinery around us never really registers in our minds as heard.[4]

Listening affects all kinds of communication. From the time the alarm clock rings until the late news winds up, we are inundated with things to listen to. As we proceed through our day and as we move from person to person, from class to lunch, from formal discussions to casual conversations, we are constantly called on to listen. We are expected to listen to others whenever we interact face-to-face with friends and acquaintances, use the telephone, attend meetings, participate in interviews, take part in arguments, give or receive instructions, make decisions based on information received orally, and generate and receive feedback.

The Ethics of Listening

While all of us continually engage in activities that require us to listen, some of us fail to pay enough attention to the role listening plays in these activities. The tragic shootings at educational institutions such as Columbine High School in Littleton, Colorado, and at Santana High School in Santee, California, however, should put us on notice that we need to listen to each other. Listening, as well as the failure to listen, has an impact on our relationships.

HOW RESPONSIVE A LISTENER ARE YOU?

Effective listeners focus their attention. What difficulties do you have when attempting to focus?

Although we expect others to listen to us, we sometimes ignore our ethical responsibility to listen to them. We fake listening or do not listen as carefully as we could. Consequently, problems due to ineffective listening occur.

"I'm sorry, dear, I wasn't listening.
Could you repeat what you've said since we've been married?"

At one time, a poll of American teenagers indicated that as many as half of them believed that communication between themselves and their parents was poor—and that a primary cause was poor listening. Parents, too, often feel that communication is failing. One woman was convinced that her daughter must have a severe hearing problem and took her to an audiologist. The audiologist tested both ears and reported back to the distraught parent: "There's nothing wrong with her hearing. She's just tuning you out."

A leading cause of the high divorce rate (approximately half of all marriages in the United States end in divorce) is the failure of husbands and wives to interact effectively. They don't listen to each other or respond to each other's messages.

Similarly, political scientists report that a growing number of people believe that their elected and appointed officials are out of touch with the constituents they are supposedly representing. Why? They don't believe these officials listen to them. In fact, it seems that sometimes our politicians don't even listen to themselves. Consider this true story: At a national legislative conference held in Albuquerque some years ago, a senator—Joseph Montoya—was handed a copy of a press release by a press aide shortly before he got up to deliver a speech. When he rose to speak, to the horror of his aide and the amusement of his audience, Montoya began reading the press release rather than his speech. He began, "For immediate release. Senator Joseph M. Montoya, Democrat of New Mexico, last night told the National Legislative Conference at Albuquerque . . . ." Montoya read the entire six-page release, concluding with "Montoya was repeatedly interrupted by applause."

Presidents of major companies also identify listening as one of their major communication problems.[5] One nationwide survey revealed that 14 percent of each workweek is wasted as a result of poor listening. That amounts to about seven weeks of work per year.[6] A survey of personnel managers also identified listening as the skill most needed at work if work teams are to succeed.[7]

online learning center

Go to the Online Learning Center at www.mhhe.com/gamble9 and answer the questions in the *Self Inventory* to evaluate your understanding of critical thinking.

It is almost impossible to state a dollar value for the cost of poor listening. But since there are more than 100 million workers in the United States, just one $10 mistake by each of them in a single year would cost over $1 billion.

ARE YOU PREPARED TO LISTEN?

Think back over the years you have spent as a student. Did you receive training in writing? Reading? Speaking? The answer to each of these questions is probably yes. In fact, many children now learn to read and write before they start school, and reading and writing skills are taught and emphasized throughout our educational careers. In addition, courses in writing and speed reading are popular in adult-oriented programs. We often take public speaking courses, and oral presentations are required in many of our classes. But what about listening? How much training have you actually received in listening? It is true that an International Listening Association now exists, and listening is taught in some schools and colleges. Still, of the four communication skills—reading, writing, speaking, and listening—listening has received the least attention from educators, yet listening is the fundamental process through which we initiate and maintain relationships, and it is the primary process through which we take in information. We need to learn to treat listening as if our very existence depends on it, because in many ways it does.[8]

HOW WELL DO YOU USE YOUR LISTENING TIME?

Studies show that, on average, we spend between 42 and 53 percent of our communicative time listening, 16 to 32 percent speaking, 15 to 17 percent reading, and only 9 to 14 percent writing.[9] Thus, we spend more time listening than engaging in other forms of communication. This holds true on the job as well. In fact, employees of Fortune 500 companies spend the majority of their day—approximately 60 percent of it—listening.[10] Despite these figures, we are not born knowing how to listen, or how to listen well. How efficient are your listening skills? Estimate the percentage of information you retain when you listen. This figure represents how good a listener you think you are. How good a listener are you really?

Take a moment to review your personal listening situation. Think of interactions you have had that were complicated because you or someone else failed to listen effectively. For example, when was the last time you jumped to a wrong conclusion? Missed an important word? Failed to realize you were not being understood? Reacted emotionally or let yourself become distracted? Far too often, instead of listening, we daydream our way through our daily contacts—we take side trips or otherwise tune out what is said to us. In other words, we adopt destructive "unlistening" behaviors.

Most people estimate that they listen with 70 to 80 percent accuracy. This means they believe that they can listen to others and accurately retain 70 to 80 percent of what is said. However, researchers like Ralph Nichols tell us that most of us actually listen at only 25 percent efficiency—that is, instead of retaining 75 percent of what we hear, we lose 75 percent.[11]

HOW MUCH OF A ROLE DO YOU PLAY IN ENSURING THE INTEGRITY OF A MESSAGE?

serial communication
a chain-of-command transmission

Although most of us have supposedly had many years of practice in listening, errors are extremely common. According to communication theorist William Haney, we frequently run into problems when we use **serial communication,** or chain-of-command transmissions, to relay messages (see Figure 7.2 on p. 180). In serial communication, person 1 sends a message to person 2; person 2 then communicates his or her perception of person 1's message (not person 1's message itself) to person 3, who continues the process.

Ethics & Communication

Asking Directions

Is it possible that men do not like to put themselves into a listening mode? Can it be that the male need for independence and control actually makes it harder for men to listen? What are the chances that women, used to seeking help from others, are better than men at listening to advice?

According to Deborah Tannen, author of *You Just Don't Understand: Women and Men in Conversation,*

men desire dominance so strongly that they would prefer to drive right past a police officer than to stop and ask for directions. For men, listening to directions implies inferiority. But, according to Tannen, American women are so used to asking for help that they tend to ask strangers for directions even when they are well aware of where they are going.

What do you think? Do men and women listen differently? Should they? Explain.

"Are you telling me you won't even ask the computerized navigational system for directions?"

Whenever one person speaks or delivers a message to a second person, the message occurs in at least four different forms:[12]

1. message as it exists in the mind of the speaker (his or her thoughts)
2. message as it is spoken (actually encoded by the speaker)
3. message as it is interpreted (decoded by the listener)
4. message as it is ultimately remembered by the listener (affected by the listener's personal selectivity and rejection)

According to sociologist Deborah Tannen, "Boys learn to hold center stage by talking; girls learn to listen." Do you agree or disagree? Why?

FIGURE 7.2

Serial Communication.

Source: William Haney
*Communication and Organizational
Behavior.* Homewood, IL: Irwin, 1973.

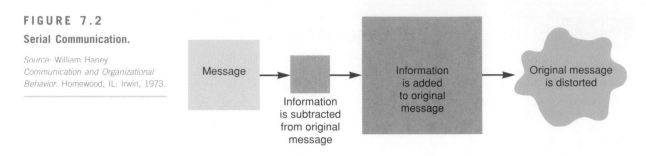

In traveling down this unwieldy chain of command from person to person, ideas can become distorted by as much as 80 percent. Several factors are responsible. First, because passing along complex, confusing information poses many problems, we generally like to simplify messages. As a result, we unconsciously (and consciously) delete information from the messages we receive before transmitting these messages to others. Second, we like to think the messages we pass along to others make sense. (We feel foolish if we convey a message we ourselves do not understand or deliver a message that appears illogical.) Thus, we try to make sense of a message before communicating it to someone else. We do this by adding to, subtracting from, or otherwise altering what we have heard. Unfortunately, as we see in Figure 7.2, once we make sense of the message, it may no longer correspond to the message originally sent. Such errors occur even though we have had years of practice in listening. Estimates are that a 20-year-old person has practiced listening for at least 10,000 hours; a 30-year-old, at least 15,000 hours; and a typical 40-year-old, 20,000 or more hours.[13] These figures are mind-boggling, but have we in reality been practicing listening or unlistening? Research suggests that we have been practicing unlistening.

Listening requires us to make an active, conscious effort to comprehend and remember what we hear.

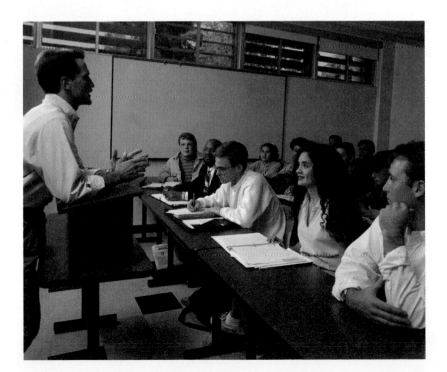

By listening accurately and ethically, you help avoid communication difficulties and breakdowns and increase your chances of being well liked and
appreciated by others.[14] Who has the primary responsibility for clear and effective communication—the speaker or the listener? An old proverb says, "Nature
gave us two ears and one mouth so that we can listen twice as much as we
speak." The effective communicator is not afraid to be two parts listener and
one part speaker. Actually, since everyone functions as both sender and
receiver, everyone must assume 51 percent of the responsibility for communication. This practice might not be mathematically sound, but it would certainly
increase the effectiveness of our interpersonal, small-group, public, and mediated communication.[15]

Are You Ready to Collaborate with the Speaker?

There is a relationship between a speaker's acts and a listener's responses. Typically, speaker gaze coordinates this relationship. While listeners usually look more
at the speaker than the reverse, at key points a speaker will look directly at the
listener, signaling that the speaker is seeking a response. If the listener is attentive, this creates a period of mutual gaze known as "the gaze window." When this
occurs, the listener responds with a nod, a "mhm," or another verbal or nonverbal reaction that lets the speaker know she or he is listening and collaborating in
the dialogue or conversation.[16]

*Comedian George Burns once
said, "I can't help hearing, but
I don't always listen." Describe
an occasion when this statement might have been applied
to your own behavior. What
happened as a result?*

Ethics & Communication

Do We Need Listening and Noise Policies?

How do you answer the following questions?

Do you find yourself becoming more selective about
what you are willing to listen to? For example, do you use
Caller I.D. to screen out callers with whom you do not
want to speak?

Are you concerned that others might overhear a private conversation? Would you like to be able to make
your voice unintelligible to eavesdroppers? Would you use
a voice disguiser to realize this objective?

Do you think there should be cell-free zones, just as
we have no-smoking zones?[17] Should cell phone users
in public places be required to wear headgear, as cyclists
and bikers are, only in this case the headgear would be
a see-through hood with air holes so that their talk would
be muffled?

Is your workplace too noisy? Because of the increasing number of cell phones, speaker phones, and fax
machines, both the number of conversations and the
noise level of offices have gone up. Often, it is a challenge for employees not to overhear very personal

conversations. Recognizing that the modern workplace
has gotten very loud, and in an effort to preserve
"acoustical privacy," some employers are trying to sub-
due the noise by installing white noise machines, which
produce low-level whooshing sounds akin to the hum of
an air conditioner to help mute the noise.[18]

What do you think of using white noise to create a
semblance of quiet? Some who oppose it do so because
they fear that such sound masking may make it possible
for the corporation to send workers subliminal messages.
Others counter that low-tech solutions, such as creating
small rooms that workers can frequent when they need
to escape the noise and have a private conversation, are
more appropriate. Others advise not pinning too many
photographs or notices on cubicle walls, because doing
so raises the decibel level by multiplying the number of
surfaces that sound can bounce off of. Others simply
snap their fingers or throw a crumpled piece of paper at
the offending noisemaker.

After considering each of these problems, identify the
policies that you think should be put into place.

Listening versus Hearing

hearing

the involuntary, physiological process by which we process sound

listening

the deliberate, psychological process by which we receive, understand, and retain aural stimuli

Self-talk—listening to what you say to yourself—can help you make sense of the way you listen to and react to the people in your life.

Listening and hearing are not the same thing. Most people are born with the ability to hear. **Hearing** is a process that occurs automatically and requires no conscious effort on your part. If the physiological elements within your ears are functioning properly, your brain will process the electrochemical impulses received, and you will hear. However, what you do with the impulses after receiving them belongs to the realm of listening.

What is listening? **Listening** is a deliberate process through which we seek to understand and retain aural (heard) stimuli. Unlike hearing, listening depends on a complex set of skills that must be acquired. Thus, whereas hearing simply happens to us and cannot be manipulated, listening requires us to make an active, conscious effort to comprehend and remember what we hear. Furthermore, who we are affects what we listen to. In your environment, from minute to minute, far too many sounds bombard you for you to be able to pay attention to each one. Thus, in listening, you process the external sounds of your environment to select those that are relevant to you, your activities, and your interests. This is not to say that listening is just an external process. It is also an internal process. We listen to the sounds we hear, and we listen to what others say, but we also listen to what we say aloud and what we say to ourselves in response. (Do you ever talk to yourself? Are you your own best listener? Most of us are.)

Besides listening to ourselves talk, what are the various kinds of listening that we engage in? Why are they important?

TYPES OF LISTENING

appreciative listening

listening for enjoyment or relaxation

comprehensive listening

listening to gain knowledge

critical listening

listening to evaluate the worth of a message

empathic listening

listening to help others

Do you spend time listening to music on your iPod, on your CD player, or at concerts? Why? Is it because you enjoy it? When our primary motivation for listening is pleasure or relaxation—to unwind, to escape, or to be entertained—we listen appreciatively. Listening to music, a movie, or a comedy routine are just a few examples of the kinds of **appreciative listening** we engage in. Courses in music or film appreciation teach us how to listen appreciatively. Unlike the next three types of listening we will define, appreciative listening usually does not require us to focus on organizing or remembering what we have listened to. In contrast to appreciative listening, when we listen to gain knowledge, we listen comprehensively. Examples of **comprehensive listening** include listening to directions, a lecture, a job description, or a person's position on an issue of concern, such as whether abortion should be legal. Often, however, we seek not only to gain knowledge, but also to evaluate the worth of what we have listened to. When we listen critically, we listen to determine the usefulness, soundness, and accuracy of messages. During **critical listening** our critical thinking skills also come into play as we decide whether to accept or reject a message. We will talk more about comprehensive and critical listening later in this chapter.

The last type of listening, and the focus of this section, is **empathic listening**. The goal when we listen empathically is to understand the feelings and point of view of another person. Perhaps you serve as a relative's sounding board, listen to the troubles of a friend, or help a co-worker talk through problems. You also help restore that person's sense of emotional balance because you understand him or her as he or she desires to be understood, interpreting the situation he or she is facing as if it were your own.

According to author Daniel Goleman, empathic listeners are effective at *decentering*—placing the focus on others rather than on themselves. They listen from the speaker's point of view, using three different skills to accomplish this: *empathic responsiveness* (the experiencing of an emotional response that corresponds to the emotions of another person),[19] *perspective taking* (placing yourself in another person's shoes);[20] and *sympathetic responsiveness* (feeling concern and compassion for the situation the other person faces). If you use only sympathetic responsiveness, however, your listening will fall short of empathic listening. If you only *feel for* a person, without using perspective taking and empathic responsiveness, you cannot succeed in *feeling with* the person.[21]

Empathic listeners rely heavily on two communication skills: the ability to read the nonverbal cues of others, including their eye contact, physical contact (touching), and facial expressions; and the ability to use the active listening tool—*the paraphrase*—to let those they listen to know that they care enough to listen, understand what is said, and respond to the expressed feelings. When you paraphrase, you engage in listening actively, which means you put yourself in the speaker's place in an effort to understand the speaker's feelings and send back to the speaker what you believe the speaker communicated when delivering his or her total message; that is, you internalize and reflect the message's verbal content as well as the speaker's feelings.

How do you paraphrase? **Paraphrasing** is a three-step process in which you do the following:

paraphrasing
restating in your own words what another person has said

1. make a tentative statement that invites correction—for example, "If I'm not mistaken . . ."
2. repeat the basic idea or ideas in your own words.
3. check your interpretation with the other person, saying something like, "Is that correct?"

For example:

Person 1: *I am so mad at my professor. He's making me rework my entire paper. I worked forever on it.*

Person 2: *If I'm not mistaken, your professor is asking you to rewrite the paper you turned in. You're feeling frustrated because you worked hard. Is that right?*

or

Person 1: *I can't believe my boss is trying to fire me.*

Person 2: *If I understand you, you believe your boss is going to replace you. You're confused and upset. Do I have it straight?*

When we empathize and listen actively, we do more than tune in to the experiences of others cognitively. We also tune in emotionally, putting ourselves in the other person's shoes. Thus, we go beyond expressing what they are going through; we also feel it.[22]

Empathic communication and paraphrasing have roles to play in both our personal and our professional lives. Research reveals that listening to family stories and reminiscing about the past may be both physically and emotionally healing for both the teller and the listener, contributing to their sense of overall well-being.[23] Findings from medical research also underscore the importance of effective listening. Medical school curricula now include courses that teach medical

Skill Builder

Can You Feel What I Feel?

The elderly and the physically challenged face problems that younger and more physically abled people do not. Our attitudes toward the aged and physically challenged shape both our perspectives and our behavior. Age and physical condition function as means of categorization, creating co-cultural groups. Enhancing communication with the members of such groups is a worthwhile goal.

To develop your ability to empathize with the members of these groups, try the following activities. Be sure that no one other than a partner knows what you are doing.

1. Walk around for an hour with your shoes filled with uncooked rice. How did people react to your new way of walking? What kinds of looks did they give you? What did they say or do? How did you feel as a result?

2. Place cotton in your ears and conduct a series of conversations with others, some face-to-face and some on the cell phone or telephone. How did your conversational partners respond? How did their responses make you feel?

3. Keeping your eyes closed and wearing dark glasses so that others are not aware your eyes are closed, have a partner lead you on a walk across your college campus. How did others react as you passed them?

Identify the lessons to be learned from each experience. What do we need to understand about ageism and reactions to the physically challenged to enhance interaction with the members of these groups?

---

students how to listen, ask open-ended questions, and establish productive, caring, and empathic relationships with patients.[24] Doctors who do not practice empathic listening frequently interrupt their patients. This keeps them from eliciting relevant background on the patient's life circumstances and symptoms. The result? Costly mistakes.[25] Far too often doctors fail to paraphrase what a patient says, cutting off the patient's words after allowing only a scant 18 seconds for the patient to reveal what is troubling him or her.[26]

As we make our way through this chapter, we will see that, in addition to being a tool used in empathic communication, the paraphrase is of value in other listening venues as well.

THE STAGES OF LISTENING: MORE THAN MEETS THE EAR

HURIER model

a model of listening focusing on six skill areas or stages

A model of listening developed by listening researcher Judi Brownell, called the **HURIER model**, takes a behavioral approach to listening, suggesting that listening is composed of both mental processes and observable behaviors.[27] The model focuses on six skill areas, or listening stages: *h*earing, *u*nderstanding, *r*emembering, *i*nterpreting, *e*valuating, and *r*esponding (see Figure 7.3).

The Hearing Stage

As the model indicates, the first stage of the listening process is *hearing*. Sounds fill our world and compete to be noticed. Usually, however, we hear what we listen for, meaning that we choose to attend to some aspects of what we hear while the

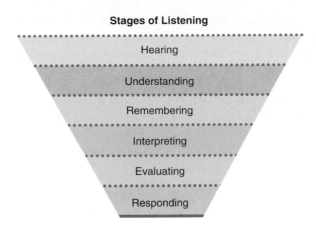

Stages of Listening

Hearing

Understanding

Remembering

Interpreting

Evaluating

Responding

remainder "falls on deaf ears." Once we *attend* to a message—demonstrate our willingness to organize and focus on what we are hearing—if the message holds our attention, we will also seek to understand it.

The Understanding Stage

During stage two, *understanding,* or listening comprehensively, we relate what we have listened to, to what we already know. We do not judge the message until we are certain we comprehend it. We might, for example, ask questions about or paraphrase what we believe another person said during the understanding stage.

According to Ralph Nichols and Leonard Stevens, the authors of *Are You Listening?* words that cause listeners to react emotionally interfere with understanding. Nichols calls these red-flag words. **Red-flag words** produce emotional deafness, sending listening efficiency down to zero.[28] Among the words known to function as red flags for some listeners are *AIDS, spastic,* and *income tax.* Once individuals sensitized to these words hear them, they abandon efforts to understand, take side trips, and dwell on their own feelings and associations. Their emotional eruptions cause listening disruptions.

Other factors that interfere with understanding are the environment (for example, it could be too hot, too cold, too messy) and people themselves (speaking too fast, too slow, too loudly, or too softly). We also think faster than others speak. This is called the **speech–thought differential.** A person usually speaks at a rate of 125 to 150 words per minute. We think, however, at over 500 words per minute, meaning that we have time left over to take mental excursions and to daydream. To use the speech–thought differential to enhance understanding, we need to internally summarize, question, and paraphrase what is being said.

red-flag words
words that trigger emotional deafness, dropping listening efficiency to zero

speech–thought differential
the difference between speaking and thinking rates

The Remembering Stage

Once our brain assigns meaning to a message, the next stage is *remembering,* in which we try to retain what we have listened to for future use. We personally decide how much of what we have listened to is worth storing in memory and how much we can forget. Intense feelings or the reinforcement of a message increases our chances of remembering. Once we remember a message, we should be able to recall it when necessary. On the other hand, we cannot possibly remember everything. Some forgetting is necessary for mental health.

We have two kinds of memory, short-term memory and long-term memory. Most of what we listen to we store briefly in our short-term memory. Unless we use and apply what is stored in short-term memory, we forget it before being able to transfer it into long-term memory. This helps explain why we remember only 50 percent of a message immediately after listening to it, and approximately 25 percent after a period of time has passed. Long-term memory, our more permanent memory bank, plays a key listening role by connecting new experiences to past ones. For example, you probably remember the phone numbers of people important to you, as well as where you were when you found out about the terrorist attacks of 9/11.

We use three key tools to enhance recall. The first is *repetition*. The more we repeat an idea, the more likely we are to recall it later. The second tool is the now-familiar three-step *paraphrase*. By restating in your own words what a person just told you, you not only check on your understanding of what was said, but also help yourself recall it. The third tool is *visualization*. By picturing what someone has said to you—connecting a visual image to a name, a place, or numbers—you can help improve your recall. For example, you might picture a person named John Sanderson as standing atop a large sand pile. Many memory problems are due not to faulty memory, but rather to people's losing their ability to pay attention. Attention and focus build memory.[29]

The Interpreting Stage

During the fourth stage, *interpreting*, we make sense of a message, using *dual perspective taking*—considering the message from the sender's perspective as well as our perspective. If we are successful, we do not impose our personal meaning onto another person's message.

The Evaluating Stage

During stage five, *evaluating*, we weigh the worth of a message and critically analyze it. (Evaluating is a type of listening referred to earlier in this chapter as critical listening.) During the evaluating stage we distinguish facts from inferences, weigh the evidence provided, and identify any prejudices or faulty arguments that could slant meaning. We stay mindful rather than mindless, listening between the lines and being careful not to jump to conclusions.

The Responding Stage

During the last stage, *responding*, we react to what we have listened to and offer feedback to let the speaker know our thoughts and feelings about the message. We become the speaker's radar. (We will cover feedback in more depth later in this chapter.)

The HURIER model provides a foundation for us to consider key aspects of the listening process and our own listening behavior.

Listening versus Unlistening: Exploring the Unethical Behaviors of Ineffective Listeners

Of course, we do not—probably, we cannot—listen at full capacity all the time. But we should be aware of our ineffective listening behaviors if they prevent us from understanding what could be important to us or to someone else. Many factors contribute to ineffective listening, and the following kinds of ineffective listeners are certainly not the only ineffective listeners we can identify. However, we have probably interacted with most of those identified here at some point in the past.

FRAUDULENT LISTENERS

Fraudulent listeners are pseudolisteners; they are also nodders. Persons who practice fraudulent listening and engage in nodding pretend that they are listening. They look at the speaker, nod their heads appropriately in agreement or disagreement, and utter remarks such as "mm" or "uh-huh" that imply they are paying attention. In actuality, the words are falling on deaf ears.

Fraudulent listeners adopt the outward appearances of listeners, but they are counterfeiters—pretenders who let no meaning through. Perhaps they fail to listen because they are thinking their own private thoughts, are bored with the conversation, or are otherwise occupied. Whatever their motivation, the outcome is similar—no listening occurs.

MONOPOLISTIC LISTENERS

Monopolistic listeners want you to listen to them, but they have neither the time nor the desire to listen to you. Frequently egocentric, and as a result, intrigued and obsessed with their own thoughts and ideas, monopolizers deny your right to be listened to while defending their right to express themselves, no matter what the cost.[30]

How many of the ineffective listener categories are you familiar with? Would you ever place yourself in any of the groups?

According to researcher Alfie Kohn, men are more likely than women to be monopolistic listeners, or "ear hogs." Kohn finds that men interrupt women's statements more frequently than women interrupt men's statements; in fact, in his research 96 percent of the interruptions in male–female interactions were initiated by men.[31]

COMPLETERS

Completers are gap fillers; they never quite get the whole story when they listen. To make up for what they have missed or misinterpreted, they manufacture information to fill in the gaps. While the impression is that they got it all, nothing could be farther from the truth.

SELECTIVE LISTENERS

Selective listeners are like bees going after the honey in a flower; they zero in on only those portions of a speaker's remarks that interest them or have particular importance to them. Everything else the speaker says is considered irrelevant or inconsequential and thus is rejected. Selective listeners, in their search for just the honey, often miss the flower.

AVOIDERS

Avoiders figuratively wear earmuffs; they close their ears to information they would rather not deal with. Sometimes they pretend not to understand what you

MediaWise

Talk, Talk, Talk

Talk radio, a mediated form of interpersonal communication that is growing in influence, allows callers a higher level of psychological comfort than does face-to-face interaction, because they can remain relatively anonymous while interacting with another person. Programs featuring argumentative hosts, such as Guardian Angels founder Curtis Slewa and pundits Rush Limbaugh, Al Franken, and Bill O'Reilly, often become either yelling matches between the host and a caller who openly disagrees with an espoused position the host has taken or love fests between the host and a caller who support each other's views.

Listen to a talk radio program. What views did the host espouse? How many on-air callers shared and how many opposed the expressed opinions of the host? Determine whether the host gave the caller's comments an honest hearing or prejudged what the caller was saying. Count the number of times a host became loud and belittled or otherwise insulted a guest who did not agree with his or her views. How did the guest respond? Identify both the ineffective and effective listening behaviors of the host. How do you account for the talk show's popularity?

We wear earmuffs when we close our ears to information we would rather not listen to.

In The Argument Culture: Moving from Debate to Dialogue, *linguist Deborah Tannen discusses how the mind-sets of people living in the United States predispose them to attack rather than listen effectively to others.*[32] *Do you find this is true when it comes to relationships you share in your social and career life?*

tell them or act as if they did not hear you at all. Sometimes they simply forget, in short order, what you have told them.

DEFENSIVE LISTENERS

Defensive listeners tend to perceive the remarks of other persons as personal affronts or attacks. Usually insecure, they are apt to pounce when another person asks a simple question, or they are likely to perceive a threat in the comments of another, when none actually exists. When we listen defensively, we assume others are going to criticize or belittle us; we assume that they do not like, trust, or respect us. As a result, an innocent question, such as, "Did you file your expense account?" may be interpreted as criticism for having spent too much on a business trip.

ATTACKERS

Attackers wait for you to make a mistake, so that they can undercut and challenge what you have to say. They lie in wait, hoping to gather ammunition they can use to diminish your effectiveness. They also are not above distorting your words to advance their personal goals. Attacking listeners are apt to precipitate defensiveness in the person they are listening to. Rather than working to understand your meaning and conducting a discussion with you that is open and fair, they compete with you in an effort to outdo you.

Feedback: A Prerequisite for Effective Listening

The feedback process is intimately connected with the listening process. Developing an understanding and appreciation of the way feedback works is essential to improving your listening skills.

WHAT IS FEEDBACK?

The term *feedback* implies that we are feeding someone by giving something back to him or her. Feedback consists of all the verbal and nonverbal messages that a person consciously or unconsciously sends out in response to another person's communication. As students, you continually provide your instructors with feedback. Many of you, however, are probably not completely honest when you send feedback. At times when you are confused or bored, you may nevertheless put on an "I'm interested" face and nod smilingly, indicating that you understand and agree with everything your instructor is saying. Unfortunately, such behavior tends to encourage the sending of unclear messages.

Whatever the circumstances, we must recognize that the nature of the feedback we give people will affect the communicative interactions we share with them.

TYPES OF FEEDBACK

We constantly provide others with feedback, whether we intend to or not. Everything we do or fail to do in a relationship or interaction with others can be considered feedback. Sometimes we send feedback consciously, intending to evoke a particular response. For example, if you laugh or chuckle at a speaker's joke or story, you may be doing so because you want the speaker to feel that you enjoyed the story and hope he or she will tell more jokes. In contrast, some of the feedback we transmit is sent unconsciously and evokes unintended or unexpected responses. Often, when our words or behaviors prompt a reaction that we never intended, we respond with useless phrases such as "That's not what I meant!" or "I didn't mean it that way!" or "What I meant was . . ."

What we intend to convey by feedback, then, may not be what others perceive. Sometimes others intentionally choose not to perceive our messages. At other times, confusion results because feedback that we mean to be nonevaluative in tone is interpreted as evaluative. Distinguishing between these two categories of feedback will help us use both types effectively and appropriately.

Evaluative Feedback   When we provide another person with **evaluative feedback**—that is, an evaluative response—we state our opinion about a matter being discussed. For example, "How did you like my speech?" will almost always evoke a response that will be perceived as evaluative. A slight hesitation before the words "I loved it" might be perceived as a negative response. When we give evaluative feedback, we make judgments—either positive or negative—based on our own system of values. As we go about the business of daily life, judgments about the relative worth of ideas, the importance of projects, and the classification of abilities are a necessity. By its very nature, the effect of evaluative feedback is either positive and rewarding or negative and punishing.

Positive Evaluative Feedback   Positive evaluative feedback tends to keep communication and its resulting behaviors moving in the direction they are already heading. If a company places an advertisement and achieves a tremendous growth in sales, the company will tend to place the same or a very similar ad in the same or very similar media in the future. If a person wearing a new hairstyle is complimented, he or she will tend to keep that hairstyle. If you are speaking to an instructor who appears receptive to your ideas and suggestions, you will tend to continue offering ideas and suggestions in the future. Thus, positive evaluative feedback makes us continue behaving as we are already behaving and enhances or reinforces existing conditions or actions.

Imagine someone who writes 50 love letters but receives no answer. Has this person received feedback?

evaluative feedback
a positive or negative judgment

Negative Evaluative Feedback Negative evaluative feedback serves a corrective function in that it helps extinguish undesirable communicative behaviors. When we perceive feedback as negative, we tend to change our performance accordingly. For example, if you were to tell a number of off-color stories that your listeners found in bad taste, they might send you negative responses. They might turn away, attempt to change the subject, or simply maintain a cold, lengthy silence. Each cue would indicate that your message had overstepped the bounds of propriety; as a result, you would probably discontinue your anecdotes.

formative feedback

timed negative feedback

Formative feedback Formative feedback is timed negative feedback. Don Tosti, an industrial psychologist, used timed negative feedback with some interesting results.[33] Tosti discovered that, in a learning situation, it is best to provide positive feedback immediately after someone has displayed a desired behavior. Thus, comments such as, "You did a good job" and "Keep up the good work" should be offered immediately, because these responses give people a sense of pride and pleasure in themselves and their work. However, Tosti suggests that what he calls "formative negative" feedback should be given only just before an undesired behavior (or a similar behavior) is about to be repeated. Tosti believes that withholding negative feedback until the person can use it constructively makes the feedback seem more like coaching than criticism. Comments such as "OK, team, let's eliminate the errors we made last time" and "When you go out there today, try to . . ." reduce the extent to which negative feedback is perceived as harmful rather than helpful. Thus, giving formative feedback just before an activity is to be performed again can help eliminate the feelings of rejection that sometimes accompany negative feedback. (In contrast, it should be remembered that immediate positive feedback can do wonders for people's self-image and morale.)

Tosti's findings have many implications for communication. For example, if you handed in a paper to your instructor, following Tosti's guidelines, the instructor would hand you a list containing only positive observations. Not until the instructor had made the next assignment would you be offered formative or negative feedback in the form of a list containing errors to avoid. Formative feedback

Exploring Diversity

Feedback in Japan

Are you culturally sensitive when giving feedback? For example, many Japanese—unlike Americans—use an indirect style of communication. Thus, when interacting with someone from Japan, if you give feedback directly (for example, telling someone outright, "You are not working hard enough"), the feedback, instead of being viewed as helpful, might be viewed as a threat. And if it is perceived as a threat, it could well be ineffective. An American giving feedback to another American, however, can give feedback more directly.

Do you believe we ought to change the way we provide feedback to conform to the preferences of another culture? Explain.

can also be used as a memory refresher or as a motivational tool to improve performance. With formative feedback, it is the timing that counts.

Unlike traditional negative feedback, formative feedback does not tend to discourage an individual from attempting to perform an activity again. Nor does it tend to demoralize the person. Test the theory behind formative feedback by using it in your own communication. Whenever you send evaluative feedback messages, whether positive or negative, preface your statements so as to make it clear that what you are offering is your opinion only. Such phrases as "It seems to me," "In my opinion," and "I think" are usually helpful, because they show your awareness that other interpretations and options are possible. Avoid using phrases like "You must" or "That's stupid." Such comments almost always elicit a certain amount of defensiveness. Expressing either positive or negative feedback in less than adamant terms tends to create a more favorable and receptive climate for the relationship.

Nonevaluative Feedback   In contrast to evaluative feedback, **nonevaluative feedback,** or nondirective feedback, makes no overt attempt to direct the actions of a communicator. Thus, we use nonevaluative feedback when we want to learn more about a person's feelings or when we want to help another person formulate thoughts about a particular subject. When we offer nonevaluative feedback, we make no reference to our own opinions or judgments. Instead, we simply describe, question, or indicate an interest in what the other person is communicating to us.

Despite its nonjudgmental nature, nonevaluative feedback is often construed as being positive. That is, other people's behaviors may be reinforced when we probe, interpret their messages, and offer support as they attempt to work through a problem. Nonevaluative feedback actually reaches beyond positive feedback, however, by providing others with an opportunity to examine their own problems and arrive at their own solutions. For this reason, carefully phrased nonevaluative feedback can be enormously helpful and sustaining to people who are going through a difficult period.

We will consider four kinds of nonevaluative feedback. Three—probing, understanding, and supporting—were identified by David Johnson. The fourth—"I" messages—was identified by Thomas Gordon.[34]

Probing   **Probing** is a nonevaluative technique in which we ask people for additional information to draw them out and to demonstrate our willingness to listen to their problems.[35] Suppose that a student is concerned about his or her grades in a particular course and says to you, "I'm really upset. All my friends are doing

nonevaluative feedback
nondirective feedback

probing
a nonevaluative technique in which we ask for additional information

better in geology than I am." If you use probing, you might ask, "Why does this situation bother you?" or "What is there about not getting good grades that concerns you?" or "What do you suppose caused this to happen?" Responding in this way gives the other person the chance to think through the overall nature of the problem while providing him or her with an opportunity for emotional release. In contrast, comments like "So what? Who cares about that dumb class?" or "Grades don't matter. What are you worrying about?" or "You really were dumb when you stopped studying" would tend to stop the student from thinking through and discussing the problem and, instead, would probably create defensiveness.

Understanding   A second kind of nonevaluative response is what Johnson calls **understanding.** When we offer understanding, we seek to comprehend what the other person is saying to us, and we check ourselves by restating what we believe we have heard. Doing this shows that we care about other people and the problems they face.

Examine the following paraphrases to develop a feel for the nature of this kind of response:

> *Person 1:* I don't think I have the skill to be picked for the team.
> *Person 2:* You believe you're not good enough to make the team this year?
> *Person 1:* I envy those guys so much.
> *Person 2:* You mean you're jealous of the people in that group?

If we use understanding early in a relationship, in effect, we communicate that we care enough about the interaction to want to be certain we comprehend what the other person is saying to us. Such a response strengthens the relationship because it encourages the other person to describe and detail his or her feelings. By delivering understanding both verbally and nonverbally, we also provide support by showing that we are sensitive to the other person's feelings and are really willing to listen.

Supportive Feedback   A third kind of nonevaluative feedback is what Johnson calls **supportive feedback.** This response indicates that a problem the other person deems important and significant is also viewed by the listener as important and significant.

Suppose a friend comes to you with a problem she feels is extremely serious. Perhaps your friend has worked herself into a state of extreme agitation and implies that you cannot possibly understand the situation. In offering supportive feedback, you would attempt to calm your friend down by assuring her that the world has not ended and that you do understand the problem.

Offering supportive feedback is difficult. We have to be able to reduce the intensity of other people's feelings while letting them know that we consider their problems real and serious. Such comments as "It's stupid to worry about that" and "Is that all that's worrying you?" are certainly not supportive. A better approach might be to say, "I can see you are upset. Let's talk about it. I'm sure you can find a way to solve the problem." A friend who is upset because he or she has just failed an exam needs supportive feedback: "I can see you are worried. I don't blame you for being upset." This is certainly not the time to suggest that there is no valid reason for being upset or that your friend's feelings are inappropriate. It would be foolish to say, "Next time you'll know better. I told you that not studying wouldn't get you anywhere." When we use supportive feedback, we judge the problems to be important, but we do not attempt to solve them ourselves; instead, we encourage people to discover their own solutions.

understanding
a nonevaluative response that uses restatement to check comprehension

supportive feedback
a nonevaluative response indicating that the receiver perceives a problem as important

According to Doris Iarovici, a medical student at Yale, "One of the best things you can do for any patient is to listen and show that you care."[36] This, in a nutshell, is supportive feedback.

"I" Messages   Certain nonevaluative feedback messages are called **"I" messages,** a term coined by Thomas Gordon. When we deliver an "I" message, we do not pass judgment on the other person's actions but simply convey our own feelings about the nature of the situation.

According to Gordon, when people interact with us, they are often unaware of how their actions affect us. We have the option of providing these people with either evaluative or nonevaluative feedback. Neither type is inherently good nor bad. However, far too often, the way we formulate our evaluative feedback adversely affects the nature of our interactions and the growth of our relationships. For example, do any of these statements sound familiar? "You made me angry!" "You're no good!" "You're in my way!" "You're a slob!" What do these statements have in common? As you have probably noticed, each one contains the word *you.* Each also places the blame for something on another person. When relationships experience difficulties, people tend to resort more and more to name-calling and to blaming others. Such feedback messages create schisms that are difficult and sometimes even impossible to bridge.

To avoid this situation, Gordon suggests that we replace **"you" messages** with "I" messages. If, for example, a parent tells a child, "You're pestering me," the child's interpretation will probably be "I am bad," and this interpretation will evoke a certain amount of defensiveness or hostility toward the parent ("I am not bad!"). But if the parent tells the child, "I'm really very tired and I don't feel like playing right now," the child's reaction is more likely to be "Mom is tired." Such an approach is more likely to elicit the type of behavior the parent desires than would name-calling and blaming ("You are a pest"). Which of the following messages do you believe would be more likely to elicit a favorable response?

> *Supervisor to Workers:* You lazy bums! We'll never meet the deadline if you don't work faster!
>
> *Supervisor to Workers:* I'm afraid that if we don't work faster, we'll miss the deadline, and the company will lose a lot of money.

Obviously, the second statement would not produce the defensiveness that would be engendered by the first.

"I" messages have one other aspect you should be aware of. It is quite common to say "I am angry" to another person. Anger, however, is a secondary emotion. We are angry because of a stimulus or stimuli. In actuality, we develop anger. For example, if your child or a child you are watching ran into the street, your first response would probably be fear. Only after the child was safe would you develop anger, and then you would probably share your anger—rather than your fear—with the child. When formulating an angry "I" message, be certain to look beyond or beneath your anger and ask yourself why you are angry. Try to identify the forces that precipitated your anger—these are the feelings that should be expressed. Thus, if someone says something that hurts you, find ways to express the initial hurt rather than the resulting anger.

Using "I" messages as feedback will not always evoke the behavior you want from the other person, but it will help prevent the defensive, self-serving behaviors that "you" messages frequently elicit. At this point, ask yourself which of the

---

"I" messages

nonevaluative responses that convey our feelings about the nature of a situation

"you" messages

responses that place blame on another person

Focus on Service Learning

Choose one of the following activities:

Research the work conducted by on-site personnel at a local crisis center. Visit the center's Web site as well as Web sites such as www.suicidehotline.com *or* www.rapecrisiscenter.org. *Then visit the local crisis center itself. Observe and listen to the persons who answer the phones at the site. On the basis of your knowledge and research, develop a workshop designed to enhance the skills of current phone personnel.*
or
Visit a nursing home and research the special needs of the elder people who live there. This experience can help you more fully understand the importance of listening and of empathy. Familiarizing yourself with Web sites such as www.paservicelearning.org/ Reach/Reach7.htm *can add to your knowledge. Once you have completed your information gathering, volunteer to visit with, listen to, and read to residents at a local nursing home.*

types of feedback seem best. Which do you feel are most important? As you probably realize, the categories and types of feedback we have discussed are not necessarily good or bad. Each type can be put to good use. Thus, whether you choose to offer evaluative or nonevaluative responses depends on the person with whom you are interacting and on the nature of the situation in which you find yourself.

EFFECTS OF FEEDBACK

How do you think feedback affects communication? Suppose that someone is telling you a funny story. What would happen if you should consciously decide to treat this person politely but neither smile nor laugh at the story? Such a reaction—polite but somber—can cause the best of storytellers to stop communicating. Sometimes in the middle of a story, the teller will notice that the listener is not amused. At this point, in an attempt to determine if the receiver has heard what was said, the sender will repeat or rephrase key parts of the story: "Don't you understand? What happened was . . ." or "You see, what this means is . . ." The feedback given by the respondent in any encounter strongly influences the direction and outcome of the interaction.[37] You might want to try the "no laugh" procedure the next time

Skill Builder

Now You Have It; Now You Don't

Choose a partner. You and your partner should each draw on a card or slip of paper three designs consisting of a random series of straight, interconnecting lines (like the sample below). Do not show the diagrams to each other. The purpose of the exercise is to give verbal instructions that will enable your partner to reproduce your diagrams.

Deliver your instructions under three conditions:

1. *Zero feedback.* When you explain your first design, turn your back to your partner and neither watch nor comment on his or her efforts. Your partner is not allowed to speak to you or look at you during this phase. This situation approximates a zero feedback (no feedback) condition.

2. *Limited feedback.* When you describe the second design, you may turn and watch your partner work. You may comment on what he or she is drawing, but your partner may not speak to you or look at you. This approximates a limited feedback condition.

3. *Free feedback.* Finally, when you describe your third design to your partner, you may interact openly with each other. You may observe and comment on your partner's efforts, and your partner may interact with you by facing you and asking you questions to check on the accuracy of his or her drawing. This approximates a free feedback condition.

Next, if time permits, you and your partner should reverse roles and repeat the three steps.

Which condition produced the fastest replication? Why? Which condition produced the most accurate replication? Why? During which phase of the experience were you most confident? Least confident? Why? How did functioning as sender or receiver alter your feelings during each phase of the experience?

someone begins to relate a humorous incident or tale to you. If you do, note how not laughing affects the sender's ability to formulate a message.

The Skill Builder on page 194, adapted from an experiment designed by Harold Leavitt and Ronald Mueller, demonstrates how feedback affects the development of our relationships.[38] Feedback usually increases the accuracy with which information is passed from person to person. However, it also increases the amount of time required to transmit information. Under the "zero feedback" condition (phase 1 of the exercise), the speaker requires less time to transmit the information to the receiver than he or she would under either the "limited feedback" condition (phase 2) or the "free feedback" condition (phase 3). Still, most communicators feel that the added time is more than compensated for by the increased accuracy of the replications. In other words, under the free feedback condition, time is not wasted.

THE ROLE OF CRITICAL THINKING: ASSESSING THE CREDIBILITY OF WHAT YOU LISTEN TO

While you listen to information, you interpret and assign meaning to the spoken words. When you go the next step and engage in **critical thinking,** you think carefully about what another person has said to you, and you evaluate the believability of the spoken message. Just as speakers can get carried away with their message's urgency and importance, so listeners can end up believing false or dangerous ideas that have been made to appear reasonable. Consequently, it is essential for you as a listener to stay alert, so that you are ready to challenge and raise questions about what you are listening to. When functioning as a critical thinker, you make a commitment to think for yourself.

critical thinking
the careful and deliberate process of message evaluation

What Critical Thinkers Think About

What do critical thinkers think about? As a critical thinker, you determine if there is a logical connection between ideas and feelings. Rather than falling prey to strong emotional appeals, you examine the evidence on which conclusions are based and establish if they are valid or contain weaknesses and inconsistencies. Critical thinkers listen carefully in an effort to determine if what they are listening to makes sense and is worth retaining or acting upon.[39]

The Critical versus the Uncritical Thinker

The following characteristics differentiate a critical thinker from an uncritical one.

The Critical Thinker

1. knows what he or she does not know
2. is open-minded and takes time to reflect on ideas
3. pays attention to those who agree and disagree with him or her
4. looks for good reasons to accept or reject expert opinion
5. is concerned with unstated assumptions and what is not said, in addition to what is stated outright
6. insists on getting the best evidence
7. reflects on how well conclusions fit premises and vice versa

The Uncritical Thinker

1. thinks he or she knows everything
2. is closed-minded and impulsive; jumps to unwarranted conclusions
3. pays attention only to those who agree with him or her
4. disregards evidence as to who is speaking with legitimate authority
5. is concerned only with what is stated, not with what is implied
6. ignores sources of evidence
7. disregards the connection or lack of connection between evidence and conclusions[40]

Critical thinkers do not rush to judge another's words. Instead of prejudging or evaluating the words of another prematurely, they exhibit a willingness to reexamine ideas. Thus, they withhold their evaluation until they have had sufficient opportunity to assess the information being given to them.

Questions to Facilitate Critical Thinking

You can ask yourself a number of questions to facilitate the critical-thinking process:

1. Is the speaker's message plausible? Could it have reasonably occurred? Does it have a high probability of being true?
2. Does the support provided by the person speaking back up his or her claims? Are the claims he or she makes verifiable?
3. What do I know of the speaker's credibility or authority? Is the speaker reliable; that is, is she or he someone I should trust?
4. Is the speaker's message free of inconsistencies or contradictions?

When you think critically about what other people say to you, you do much more than merely hear their words.

GENDER AND LISTENING STYLE

Women and men are likely to exhibit different listening styles. Women tend to search for relationships among message parts; they rely more on their feelings and intuition. They listen to enhance their understanding as well as to establish personal relationships. Women also demonstrate a greater ability to switch between competing messages; unlike men, who tend to focus on their reactions to only one speaker at a time, women appear able to split their focus. They are more receptive, in general, than are men to what is happening around them. Thus, women are more likely than men to be engaged in conversation with one person and still pick up on the words of another person who is conversing with someone else nearby. In contrast to men, women listen to confirm the relationship as well as the person.[41] They also use head nodding and facial expressions to indicate their interest in a conversation. Because they view talk as a relationship developer, women also provide more vocal and verbal feedback when speaking with others. Women consider it important that others perceive them as receptive and open.[42] Thus, they use more listening cues than men and excel at empathizing and at identifying moods.

Men, in comparison, are more at home with comprehensive listening and less at home with the emotional content of messages. Men are more likely to focus on a message's structure or pattern. Their tendency is to direct their listening efforts

"With your kind permission, I've taken the liberty of putting Marvin on 'mute.'"

toward a goal. Men listen to solve problems.[43] As a result, they listen primarily to get the facts; they want to get to the bottom line. Men will also play up their expertise and use it to control or dominate conversations. Their goal is to have others respect them. In addition, in contrast to women, who exhibit more eye contact when listening than men do, men are more likely than women to survey the environment and direct their gaze away from the person they are conversing with.[44] While past research reported that men did not listen to provide emotional support, more recent research finds that men and women alike place a value on this listening style.[45]

Of course, gender differences continue to be redefined. In your experience, have the observations made above changed? Which do you believe are still valid?

CULTURE'S INFLUENCE ON LISTENING

As the psychological distance between people who live in different countries shrinks, our need to listen to others who neither live in the country we live in nor have the same native language increases. The globalization of business and our personal thirst for traveling to diverse geographical locations demands that we become more aware of cultural differences in listening styles and behavior.

In what ways, if any, do you adjust your listening style to take cultural differences into account?

According to C. Y. Cheng, the Chinese place greater emphasis on the receiving process and less emphasis on the sending process, reflecting the East Asian concern for interpretation and anticipation.[46] In Japan anticipatory communication is the norm. Speakers rarely tell or ask directly for something they want, leaving receivers to guess and accommodate speakers' needs. This communication style helps speakers and receivers save face in case what the speaker wants done cannot be accomplished.[47] Thus, the Japanese and the Chinese use an indirect style of conversation and could be offended by the direct confrontations people in the United States are prone to engage in. In comparison, Germans practice action-oriented listening. They are inquisitive and exhibit a direct style. Israelis, who carefully analyze information, prefer the content style of listening. Collective in orientation, they tend to deemphasize the personal aspects of interactions. The individually oriented Americans, on the other hand, exhibit a people-oriented style, focusing more on the feelings and concerns of the people involved in an interaction and emphasizing the interaction's social aspects. At the same time, however, they are focused on the time that interaction consumes—a time-oriented style.[48]

dialogic listening

listening that focuses on what happens to people as they respond to each other

Dialogic listening focuses on what happens between people as they respond to each other, work toward shared understanding, and build a relationship.[49] Too frequently, life's pressures keep us from adopting open-ended, tentative approaches to conversation. We seem to prefer certainty, closure, and control. Whereas persons from Eastern cultures practice more speculative, metaphoric thinking, believing that people should listen more than they talk, members of Western cultures are less open and tentative in their listening behaviors, preferring specifically focused and concrete thinking instead.[50]

Within the United States, listening rules vary depending on the racial group to which you belong. African Americans, in general, display a more participative listening style than do European Americans. When listening to a speaker, African Americans are likely to shout out responses as a means of demonstrating their interest and involvement.

MEDIA AND TECHNOLOGY'S INFLUENCE ON LISTENING AND THINKING

How are media and technology changing the listening landscape? What roles are they playing in challenging our abilities to listen?

Media's Influence

Is television viewing shortening attention spans? If young children watch more than an hour of television each day, research reveals they are at risk for developing attention deficit problems, as compared with children who watch less TV. Blame is placed on television's quickly changing visual images, which researchers believe may overstimulate and permanently rewire a brain in the process of developing.[51]

Television and radio together account for significant amounts of what we listen to. Increasingly, segments on both television and radio programs are being shortened for fear we will not pay attention to them if they are long, discuss complicated information, or contain descriptions of complex feelings. In the place of complex information, television substitutes more and more graphics. Radio fills in with music and talk shows with guests who, too often, shout over each other, unwilling to listen to another person's point of view, and denying the show's listeners the opportunity to listen to and/or participate in a meaningful discussion.

Technology's Influence

Although they have been working on it for about two decades, scientists have yet to devise a computer that functions as a virtual best friend—one that is able to listen sensitively and empathically to a user.[52] Diametrically opposed to the efforts of these scientists are people who believe that our connections to computers, e-mail, and the Internet are impeding our ability to listen. Focusing our attention on the visual rather than the aural, critics contend, causes us to emphasize the eye over the ear. Despite this perceived failure of the scientists (we wonder if not succeeding is really a benefit) and the objections of critics, our technological listening landscape continues to evolve rapidly.

Today we listen globally—to radio, television, CDs, cellular telephones, videoconferences, beepers, personal message systems, and our computers. Indeed, our appetite for traditional media as well as for the computer and the Internet is eating into time spent listening to other people in face-to-face settings. In fact, even when we are face-to-face with another person, perhaps when at lunch, on a walk, or out for a drive, one of us may be conversing with a third person on a cell phone. Interpersonal etiquette appears to be at an all-time low. The world has become our phone booth. Perhaps we need cell-free zones, so that we can listen more attentively to the person we are with.[53] Perhaps we need cell-free zones for other reasons as well. More and more state legislatures have passed bills restricting car cell-phone use to headphone rather than handheld models. Although multitasking may seem like a necessity, it is hard to drive and speak on a cell phone at the same time. Using a headphone instead of a handheld phone is probably as much of a distraction.

In addition to being surrounded by cell-phone users, according to David Shenk, author of *Data Smog*, we are being inundated with information: e-mail, net-to-phone, cell phones, pagers operating virtually nonstop, enveloping us within a toxic environment of continuous overstimulation.[54] According to the Institute

Media Wise

Listening Gains and Losses

New technologies are changing our listening landscape. Online users spend less time listening to the radio, for example, than do nononline users. They also spend less time watching television. Consider this: How much more reading do you do today than in years past? Are you now reading more and listening less than you used to? In your opinion, what are the chances that e-mail use ultimately will wipe out voice contact?

On the other hand, we can now listen to radio over the Internet or via podcasts. We can now personalize our listening stimuli. In effect, we direct our own listening experiences. Is being able to control what you listen to a good thing? Or did having your listening experience determined for you by others make it impossible for you to filter out what you didn't want to listen to and enable you to develop skills that will now deteriorate? Explain your responses.

for the Future, the typical American worker handles 201 messages a day.[55] It is probable that one outcome of this overload is a decrease in listening effectiveness.

Technology makes it possible for us to multitask when listening outside of our cars as well. How many of us check e-mail while talking to friends on the phone? When we multitask when interacting with another, we do not focus exclusively on one communication channel. As a result, we fail to give the other person our full attention.

Advances in technology will continue to add listening wrinkles. For example, in the past when we listened, we were generally face-to-face with the speaker; we engaged in real-time, synchronous listening. Then came the telephone, and we had the option of not having to share the same space when we exchanged a real-time conversation. Finally, we are in the era of voice mail; we can now have serial conversations (asynchronous listening) with a person who is in a different location and does not hear our words as we speak them. More and more of our conversations are occurring asynchronously.[56] Continuing advances add to the listening challenge. We can now be more selective about our willingness to listen at all. Caller ID allows us to see who is calling and thus to decide who we want to listen to, while call waiting makes it possible for us not to miss a call from someone important to us. We can now line up our listeners.

Thus, we have to ask the following questions: While we may be listening more to the sounds of new media, are we listening less to each other? How actively can we listen to another human being in our immediate environment when technological advances are absorbing our attention and propelling us across national boundaries and into settings far removed from the ones with which we are most familiar?

The real-time transmission of voice is possible over the Internet. Internet phones enable you to use your computer as a telephone. You can talk with another person anywhere in the world for as long as you want without the cost of a long-distance phone call. It is also possible to chat across the Internet using video-conferencing programs. Such programs make it possible for individuals to both hear and see each other.[57]

In addition, with the exception of films shown in theaters, media or computer-generated messages are usually processed by individuals viewing or listening to them alone or in small groups. Because we now process messages, CDs, and videos from around the world, our ears, habitually crossing national boundaries and opening wider and wider, are helping to erase cultural, informational, and personal barriers.

Although new technology presents listening challenges, we also should not forget the listening challenges posed by radio and television. So much of what comes to us via radio and television is delivered in very abbreviated segments; consider, for example, the music videos MTV offers, as well as the average length of radio and TV news reports (shorter than 30 seconds). The fear is that such brevity keeps us from practicing the skills of concentration and focused attention, skills which must be honed for effective listening.

Exploring Diversity

Online Listeners

Is having someone listen to you online the same as having someone listen to you in person? Even when cyber-communicators are using the same online language, because of the Internet's global reach, that language may not be their native language. As a result, the meanings given to the words used may differ drastically. As in face-to-face interaction, not all online listeners receive the same message. As you interact with persons from different cultures in cyberspace, ask yourself these questions:

1. Do they favor a direct or indirect style?
   While some cultures, including those in the United States, tend to exhibit a direct style in communicating—communicators tell it like it is—many Asian cultures use an indirect style, preferring to emphasize politeness and face-saving strategies rather than truth telling. Which style do you prefer?
2. Do they offer hard evidence or tell stories?
   In the United States, our decision making is

influenced by logical reasons and credible testimony. In contrast, members of other cultures tend to be influenced by stories other sources tell convincingly. What kind of substantiation do you tend to offer? Receive?
3. What kind of feedback do they offer?
   In the United States, we expect to receive honest feedback that reveals the feelings of those with whom we communicate. In Asian cultures, however, communicators believe it is more important to offer positive reactions than truthful ones. Not every culture perceives feedback the same way. What kind of feedback do you prefer?
4. How do opportunities for anonymity influence online listening behavior?
   Because we may remain anonymous, some of us tend to exhibit less ego involvement when listening online than when interacting face-to-face. How does the change in ego involvement affect you?

Thinking Critically

Reflect and Respond

Agree or disagree with the father's thinking in the following excerpt from Steven R. Covey's *The 7 Habits of Highly Effective People.* Be sure to supply reasons and examples that support your stance.

A father once told me, "I can't understand my kid. He just won't listen to me at all."

"Let me restate what you just said," I replied. "You don't understand your son because he won't listen to you?"

"That's right," he replied.

"Let me try again," I said. "You don't understand your son because he won't listen to you?"

"That's what I said," he impatiently replied.

"I thought that to understand another person, you needed to listen to him," I suggested.

"Oh!" he said. There was a long pause. "Oh!" he said again, as the light began to dawn. "Oh, yeah! But I do understand him. I know what he's going through. I went through the same thing myself. I guess what I don't understand is why he won't listen to me."[58]

Looking Back and Ahead
Consider This Case: First Impressions

Stacey couldn't believe her luck. She'd been offered the summer internship of her dreams, working for Ángel de la Música, a new, independent record label with offices downtown. The company was small but growing, and Rick Sanchez, the founder and president, hadn't wasted any time setting up a company Web site in Spanish and English and contacting music distributors in Latin America. Rick had told Stacey that one of her assignments as a summer intern would be to help him and the marketing manger choose a list of 10 U.S. cities in which to hold promotional events over the next year, such as contests sponsored by local radio stations, music store appearances by the label's newest artists, and even a couple of free concerts. It all sounded exciting, and Stacey couldn't wait to begin.

"*Hola*, Stacey!" Rick greeted her cheerfully on her first day. "I was hoping I could introduce you to everyone, but I'm going to be gone most of the day meeting with some agents and promoters. There's a couple of new bands I want to sign, and I've got to get to them before anyone else does." He grinned at Stacey as he grabbed his jacket and headed for the door. "Listen, can you take a tour of the office, meet everybody, and then check in with me around four? I'll be back by then and we'll talk, OK?"

"Sure," said Stacey, hiding her surprise. "Perfect!"

"Great—thanks!" said Rick, and he was gone.

Stacey stood in the middle of Rick's office for a minute, thinking. Finally, she flung her coat over a chair and headed back to the reception area.

"*¿Puedo ayudarle?*" the receptionist asked.

"Hi," Stacey replied. "I don't speak Spanish very well; I'm sorry. I'm Stacey and I'm the new summer intern." She held out her hand. "How do you do?"

The young man at the desk shook hands. "I'm Luis," he said. "Rick run out on you already?"

"Oh!" said Stacey. "No, not really. That is, he had a meeting to go to, and . . ."

"Yeah," said Luis. "But you're still wondering what to do with yourself today, aren't you?"

"Well," said Stacey, "I'm not, actually. I want to meet everyone, introduce myself." She tried to smile.

"OK," said Luis, smiling back. "Maybe I can help you with that. Here's the company telephone list. This will tell you who everybody is. See how it's organized by department, with everybody's title next to their name?"

"Hey, thanks! This looks great," said Stacey in relief. She studied the list for a minute while Luis took a phone message in Spanish for Rick. "Where would I find María Lopez? She's the head of marketing."

"Down the hall to the left," said Luis as the phone rang again. Stacey waved her thanks and set off to find the marketing manager. Given her assignment for the summer, she figured María was someone it would be important to meet. She was already imagining herself giving Rick a brief but impressive account of her day when she felt herself bump hard into someone coming quickly around a corner.

"Oh! I'm so sorry!" Stacey cried. The middle-aged woman she'd walked into sighed, adjusted her glasses, and walked away without a word. As Stacey turned the corner to the left, she heard Luis greet the woman in Spanish. Stacey understood only one word, the woman's name. *María*.

Red-faced, Stacey scurried around the corner and buried herself in the phone list, looking for someone else she could meet.

By four that afternoon she was exhausted but pleased. Sitting in Rick's office waiting for him to return, she mentally reviewed her day. She'd met Lourdes, who managed the contracts department; Joe, the head designer for the label; Tina, Rick's part-time assistant; and Timotéo, who was Ángel de la Música's tech expert and Webmaster. Stacey had expected the company's tech people to be young, but Tim had pictures on his desk that he proudly pointed out were of his grandchildren. Tim had shown her the company's Web site for music downloads and asked her opinion about the pricing strategy the company was considering. Victoria, the financial officer, had found Stacey in Tim's office and offered to take her to lunch, where she teased Stacey for not knowing much Spanish and then talked endlessly about her boyfriend.

Stacey hadn't seen Maria again, but she had met Greg, the advertising manager, and the heads of manufacturing and the warehouse, who had both been expecting to find Rick in the office. All in all, thought Stacey, smoothing out her crumpled phone list, it had been a day well spent. Suddenly she heard voices speaking Spanish outside Rick's office.

"Sorry, María," Luis, the receptionist, was saying. "Rick's not back yet. I haven't heard from him all day."

"That son of mine!" María exclaimed. "Late again! I'll wait for him in his office."

DISCUSSION QUESTIONS

1. How do you think Stacey's self-concept changed throughout the day? Why?
2. Do you think Stacey's poor Spanish skills will be a handicap during her internship? What does she have to offer Ángel de la Música?
3. Did Stacey make any prejudgments about the staff of Ángel de la Música? How well do you think she dealt with them on her first day?
4. Are there any potential self-fulfilling prophecies at work in this case? How can Stacey avoid them?
5. How can Stacey use communication skills to ensure that her internship is a success for her and for Ángel de la Música?

Revisiting Chapter Objectives

1. **Define *hearing, listening,* and *critical thinking.*** Listening is a deliberate process through which we seek to understand and retain aural (heard) stimuli. Unlike hearing, which occurs automatically, listening depends on a complex set of acquired skills, including critical thinking. When you engage in critical thinking, you think carefully about what another person is telling you, and you evaluate the believability of the message. You also seek to determine if there is a logical connection between ideas and feelings.

2. **Compare and contrast helpful and harmful listening and thinking habits.** The average person listens at only 25 percent efficiency, losing 75 percent of what is heard. A graphic illustration of the results of inefficient listening is distortion of a message in serial communication (when a message is passed from one person to another in a series). A principal reason for poor listening is failure to determine the involvement level appropriate in a particular situation. Various behaviors we adopt cause us to unlisten—that is, they impede true understanding and critical reflection.

3. **Explain and use The HURIER Model.** The HURIER model takes a behavioral approach to listening. Using it can help develop our listening skills. The model focuses on the six key areas or stages of listening: hearing, understanding, remembering, interpreting, evaluating, and responding.

4. **Define *feedback,* distinguish among and use different types of feedback, and explain how each type affects communication.** A prerequisite of effective listening is effective feedback. Feedback consists of all the verbal and nonverbal messages that a person consciously or unconsciously sends out in response to another person's communication. Through feedback, we either confirm or correct the impressions others have of us and our attitudes. There are two main types of feedback. (1) Evaluative feedback gives an opinion, positive or negative, and attempts to influence the behavior of others. (2) Nonevaluative feedback

The Wrap Up

gives emotional support. Probing, understanding (or paraphrasing), supportive feedback, and "I" messages are all forms of nonevaluative feedback that help sustain interpersonal relationships. When listening and giving feedback to people from other cultures, we must be extremely sensitive to cultural norms.

5. **Set appropriate listening goals.**   You can improve your listening skills by learning to focus your attention while listening and by setting appropriate listening goals. Listening to understand ideas, to retain information, to analyze and evaluate, and to empathize require skills different from those used for listening appreciatively.

6. **Explain how gender, culture, and media and technology influence listening.** Recognizing how gender, culture, and media and technology influence listening skills may further enhance our ability to develop more effective listening practices. New technological advances, while giving us the ability to listen globally, also compete for our listening time.

Resources for Further Inquiry and Reflection

To apply your understanding of how the principles in Chapter 7 are at work in our daily lives, consult the following resources for further inquiry and reflection. Or, if you prefer, choose any other appropriate resource. Then connect the ideas expressed in your chosen selection with the communication concepts and issues you are learning about both in and out of class.

 Listen to Me

"Wake Me Up When September Ends" (Green Day)
"Teary Eyed" (Missy Eliot)
"Bridge over Troubled Water" (Simon and Garfunkel)
"The Reason" (Celine Dion)
"Janie's Got a Gun" (Aerosmith)
"Don't Waste Your Time" (Mary J. Blige)
"She's Leaving Home" (The Beatles)
"The Sound of Silence" (Simon and Garfunkel)

Each of these songs describes a listening problem or skill. Choose one and use it to explain the role deficient or helpful listening plays in life.

 View Me

In Her Shoes	*Analyze That*
Elizabethtown	*Analyze This*
Flightplan	*First Wives Club*
The Ring	*Good Will Hunting*
The Negotiator	*Jerry McGuire*

Listening, effective and/or ineffective, plays a central role in each of these films. Choose one, and discuss how the ability or inability to listen complicates or facilitates the life of one or more of the film's characters.

 Read Me

Ashley Smith. *Unlikely Angel*. New York: Morrow, 2005.
Jennifer Weiner. *In Her Shoes*. New York: Pocket Books, 2002.
Edward Albee. *Who's Afraid of Virginia Woolf?* New York: Pocket Books, 1975.
Hannah Merker. *Listening*. New York: HarperCollins, 1995.

Discuss how the work contributes to our understanding of the role of listening in relationships and in other life experiences.

Tell Me

Share with the class the insights you gained from your chosen Listen to Me, View Me, or Read Me selection.

Who is your best listener? Explain what this person has done to earn this title.

Key Chapter Terminology

Use the Communication Works CD-ROM and the Online Learning Center at
www.mhhe.com/gamble9 to further your knowledge of the following terminology.

Idioms in Translation

at home with—comfortable with

be out of touch—fail to understand

listening wrinkle—listening problem

multitasking—engaging in more than one task at a time

play up—emphasize

tuning you out—not listening to you

zero in on—focus on

Test Your Understanding

Go to the *Self Quizzes* on the Communication Works CD-ROM and the book's Online
Learning Center at www.mhhe.com/gamble9.

Notes

1. Karen Arenson. "The Fine Art of Listening." *New York Times Education Life*, January 13, 2002, pp. 34–35.
2. Cesar G. Soriano. "News Flash: Teen Stops Speaking!" *USA Today*, August 9, 2000, p. 1D.
3. Brendan Schurr. "Teenager Vows Not to Speak for a Year." *The Record*, August 16, 2000, p. A-5.
4. From Hannah Merker. *Listening.* New York: HarperCollins, 1995.
5. See Jane Allan. "Talking Your Way to Success (Listening Skills)." *Accountancy*, February 1993, pp. 612–663; and John W. Haas and Christina L. Arnold. "An Examination of the Role of Listening in Co-Workers." *Journal of Business Communication*, April 1995, pp. 123–139.
6. The Office Team Survey, 2000, was cited in *Sssh! Listen Up!* HighGain, Inc. Newsletter, June 2000, p. 4.
7. K. W. Hawkins and B. P. Fullion. "Perceived Communication Skill Needs for Work Groups." *Communication Research Reports* 16, 1999, pp. 167–174.
8. See, for example, Wendell Johnson. "Do You Know How to Listen?" *ETC: A Review of General Semantics* 56, Spring 1999, p. 109.

9. See Tory Rankin. "The Measurement of the Ability to Understand Spoken Language." Ph.D. dissertation, University of Michigan, 1926, p. 43; Larry Barker, R. Edwards, C. Gaines, K. Gladney, and F. Hally. "An Investigation of Proportional Time Spent in Various Communication Activities by College Students." *Journal of Applied Communication Research* 8, 1981, pp. 101–109.

10. See A. D. Wolvin and C. G. Coakley. "A Survey of the Status of Listening Training in Some Fortune 500 Corporations." *Communication Education* 40, 1991, pp. 152–164.

11. For a detailed discussion, see Ralph G. Nichols and Leonard A. Stevens. *Are You Listening?* New York: McGraw-Hill, 1956. See also K. Watson and L. Barker. "Listening Behavior: Definition and Measurement." In R. Bostrom, ed. *Communication Yearbook* 8. Beverly Hills, CA: Sage, 1985, pp. 178–197; and Andrew Wolving and Carolyn Gwynn Coakly. *Listening*, 4th ed. Dubuque, IA: Brown, 1988.

12. John R. Freund and Arnold Nelson. "Distortion in Communication." In B. Peterson, G. Goldhaber, and R. Pace, eds. Chicago: Science Research Associates, 1974, pp. 122–124.

13. Gerald Goldhaber. *Organizational Communication*, 4th ed. Dubuque, IA: Brown, 1988.

14. See L. Wheeless, A. Frymier, and C. Thompson. "A Comparison of Verbal Output and Receptivity in Relation to Attraction and Communication Satisfaction in Interpersonal Relationships." *Communication Quarterly*, spring 1992, pp. 102–115.

15. See, for example, Judi Brownell. *Listening: Attitudes, Principles, and Skills*. Boston: Allyn & Bacon, 1996.

16. Janel Beavin Bavelas, Linda Coates, and Trudy Johnson. "Listener Responses as a Collaborative Process: The Role of Gaze." *Journal of Communication* 52:3, September 2002, pp. 566–579.

17. For example, see Sharon White Taylor. "Wireless and Witless." *The New York Times*, July 5, 2000, p. A17.

18. Motoko Rich. "Shut Up So We Can Do Our Jobs!" *The Wall Street Journal*, August 29, 2001, pp. B1, B8.

19. B. L. Omdahl. *Cognitive Appraisal, Emotion, and Empathy*. Mahwah, NJ: Erlbaum, 1995.

20. T. Holtgraves. *Language As Social Action: Social Psychology and Language Use*. Mahwah, NJ: Erlbaum, 2002.

21. See, for example, J. B. Weaver III and M. B. Kirtley. "Listening Styles and Empathy." *Southern Communication Journal* 60, 1995, pp. 131–140.

22. Anahad O'Connor. "Brain Senses the Pain of Someone Else's 'Ouch!'" *The New York Times*, February 24, 2004, p. F5.

23. Karen S. Peterson. "Sharing Memorable Moments Can Calm the Soul, Heal the Body." *USA Today*, February 15, 1999, p. 4D.

24. Angela Delli Santi. "N.J. Doctors to Learn Cultural Sensitivity." *The Record*, April 11, 2005, p. A3.

25. Nissa Simon. "Can You Hear Me Now?" *Time*, September 2003; Kim Painter. "Getting Bad Reception?" *USA Today*, October 3, 2005, p. 6D.

26. C. Crosen. "Blah, Blah, Blah," *The Wall Street Journal*, July 10, 1997, pp. 1A, 6A; and Betsy A. Lehman. "Getting an Earful Is Just What the Doctor Needs." *The Record*, March 21, 1994, p. B4.

27. See also Judi Brownell. *Listening Attitudes, Principles and Skills*, 2nd ed. Boston: Allyn & Bacon, 2004.

28. Ralph G. Nichols and Leonard A. Stevens. *Are You Listening?* New York: McGraw-Hill, 1956.

29. Harry Jackson, Jr. "Fear of Forgetting." *The Record*, April 5, 2005, pp. F1, F12.

30. See A. Vangelisti, M. Knapp, and J. Daly. "Conversational Narcissism." *Communication Monographs*, December 1990, pp. 251–271.

31. Alfie Kohn. "Girl Talk, Guy Talk." *Psychology Today*, February 1988, pp. 65–66.

32. D. Tannen. *The Argument Culture: Moving from Debate to Dialogue*. New York: Ballentine, 1998.

33. Don Tosti. "Operant Conditioning." Speech presented at Operant Conditioning Seminar, New York, fall 1983.

34. David W. Johnson. *Reaching Out: Interpersonal Effectiveness and Self-Actualization.* Englewood Cliffs, NJ: Prentice-Hall, 1972; and Thomas Gordon. *Leader Effectiveness Training.* New York: Wyden, 1977.

35. For a discussion of the benefit of questioning, see John F. Monoky. "Listen by Asking." *Industrial Distribution,* April 1995, p. 123.

36. Doris Iarovici. Quoted in "Making TLC a Requirement." *Newsweek,* August 12, 1991, p. 56.

37. For a discussion of the kinds of information conveyed by verbal and nonverbal feedback, see Dale G. Leathers. "The Informational Potential of the Nonverbal and Verbal Components of Feedback Responses." *Southern Speech Communication Journal* 44, 1979, pp. 331–354.

38. H. Leavitt and R. Mueller. "Some Effects of Feedback on Communication." *Human Relations* 4, 1951, pp. 401–410.

39. See R. Boostrom. *Developing Creative and Critical Thinking.* Lincolnwood, IL: National Textbook, 1992.

40. Teri Gamble and Michael Gamble. *Public Speaking in the Age of Diversity.* Boston: Allyn & Bacon, 1994, p. 18.

41. D. Tannen. *You Just Don't Understand: Women and Men in Conversation.* New York: Morrow, 1990.

42. S. Petronio, J. Martin, and R. Littlefield. "Prerequisite Conditions for Self-Disclosing: A Gender Issue." *Communication Monographs* 51, 1984, pp. 282–292.

43. See also Michael Purdy and Deborah Borisoff. *Listening in Everyday Life: A Personal and Professional Approach,* 2nd ed. Lanham, MD: University Press of America, 1997.

44. J. Brownell. *Listening: Attitudes, Principles, and Skills,* 2nd ed. Boston: Allyn & Bacon, 2002.

45. B. R. Burleson. "Emotional Support Skills." In J. O. Green and B. R. Burleson, eds. *Handbook of Communication and Social Interaction Skills.* Mahwah, NJ: Erlbaum, 2003.

46. C. Y. Cheng. "Chinese Philosophy and Contemporary Communication Theory." In D. I. Kincaid, ed. *Communication Theory: Eastern and Western Perspectives.* New York: Academic Press, 1987.

47. Documented by T. S. Lebra in *Japanese Patterns of Behavior.* Honolulu: University Press of Hawaii, 1976.

48. C. Kiewitz, J. B. Weaver III, H. B. Brosius, and G. Wiemann. "Cultural Differences in Listening Style Preferences: A Comparison of Young Adults in Germany, Israel, and the United States." *International Journal of Public Opinion Research* 9:3, Fall 1997, p. 233.

49. John Stewart and M. Thomas. "Dialogic Listening: Sculpting Mutual Meanings." In J. Stewart, ed. *Bridges Not Walls: A Book about Interpersonal Communication,* 6th ed. New York: McGraw-Hill, 1995, pp. 184–201.

50. Larry A. Samovar and Richard E. Porter. *Communication between Cultures.* Belmont, CA: Wadsworth, 1995, pp. 211–212.

51. D. A. Christakis, F. J. Zimmerman, D.L. DiGuiseppe, and C. A. McCarty. "Early Television Exposure and Subsequent Attentional Problems in Children." *Pediatrics* 113, 2004, pp. 707–713.

52. See, for example, "Personality Typing." *Wired,* July 1999, p. 71.

53. Sharon White Taylor. "Wireless and Witless." *The New York Times,* July 5, 2000, p. A-17; and "Cell Phone Rage: Helpful Hints." *The New York Times,* July 8, 2000, p. A-14.

54. David Shenk. *Data Smog.* New York: Harper-Edge, 1997.

55. *The Commercial Appeal,* October 1, 1999, p. A-1.

56. Sheila C. Bentley. "Listening in the 21st Century." Paper presented at the annual convention of the National Communication Association, Chicago, November 1999.

57. Cynthia B. Leshin. *Internet Investigations in Business Communication.* Upper Saddle River, NJ: Prentice Hall, 1997, pp. 53–56.

58. Stephen R. Covey. *The 7 Habits of Highly Effective People.* New York: Simon & Schuster, 1990, pp. 239–240.

CHAPTER 8

Understanding Relationships

After finishing this chapter, you should be able to

1. Explain why we need interpersonal relationships.

2. Define and discuss the following terms: *inclusion, control,* and *affection.*

3. Explain and distinguish among social penetration, cost–benefit/social exchange theory, and relational dialectics theory.

4. Identify and describe the 10 stages of relationships.

5. Discuss how deception, gender, and technology affect interpersonal communication.

6. Identify ways to enhance your satisfaction with your relationships.

People meet and separate. But funny things happen in between.
—Mark L. Knapp

. . . when you start out with someone, you're essentially driving a strange car for the first time and none of the controls are labeled.
—Jerry Seinfeld

Media offerings such as *Survivor, The Apprentice, The Real World, The Amazing Race, Supernanny, Three Wishes,* and *The Bachelor* or *The Bachelorette* present us with an array of men and women who for love and/or money play out their personal and/or professional problems and relationships before our eyes. What accounts for the longevity and high ratings of shows like these? Are some popular because they are mean-spirited? Are others popular because they fulfill the wishes and dreams of participants? Do we view them because we enjoy watching people humble themselves or have miracles transform lives?[1] Or is it because we want to see people begin relationships, figure out

the ground rules, share conversations with or about each other, and then negotiate the level at which their relationship stabilizes or terminates? Do these shows depict what we really want and expect from our friends, family members, significant others, co-workers, or society? However you answer these questions, for many of us, nothing is more important than our interpersonal relationships.

An **interpersonal relationship** is a meaningful, dyadic, person-to-person connection in which two interdependent people engage in communication of a personal nature, develop a shared history, and try to meet each other's social needs. By definition, a dyad is indivisible. During our life span, we share a variety of social connections, some more complicated, meaningful, and/or important to us than others. A number of our relationships succeed and will last for

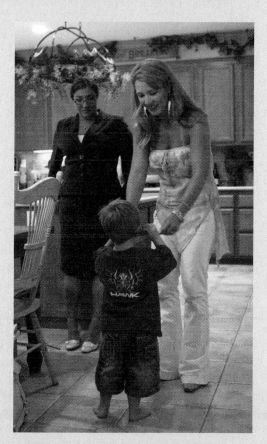

How would having the interactions of your close interpersonal relationships televised affect you?

Skill Builder

One Relationship, Indivisible

Make two lists of relationships. The first list should contain all the interpersonal relationships in which you have participated during the past month that you consider successful and likely to endure for at least another five years. The second list should contain the interpersonal relationships you experienced during the same time period that you expect will not continue much longer. Identify the differences that led you to draw your conclusions about each relationship's future. What do these differences tell you about the qualities necessary to sustain a relationship?

interpersonal relationship

a meaningful connection, such as friendship, between two persons

Go to the Online Learning Center at www.mhhe.com/gamble9 and answer the questions in the *Self Inventory* to evaluate your understanding of relationship building.

autistic society

a society at home with computers but disadvantaged when it comes to establishing human intimacy

high-tech–high-touch society

a technologically advanced society that values interpersonal relationships

years, perhaps even a lifetime. Others fail or are short-lived. According to Virginia Satir, author of both *Peoplemaking* and *The New Peoplemaking*, communication is the largest single factor determining the kinds of relationships people have with each other.[2] This chapter explores the nature of our relationships, our satisfaction or dissatisfaction with them, and the steps we can take to improve them.

■ ■ ■

THE ROLE OF RELATIONSHIPS

How important to you are your relationships? As society places more and more emphasis on technology, some fear we will place less and less emphasis on personal relationships. Linguist John L. Locke, for example, argues that modern technology is robbing us of the inclination to speak meaningfully to one another. He believes that our social voices are disappearing, leaving us isolated. He argues that, while technologies such as e-mail increase the amount of functional information we have access to, they lack the capacity for intimate talking. From his point of view, we live in an **autistic society,** a society that is at home with computers but disadvantaged when it comes to establishing human intimacy.[3] Locke's critics, however, note that his fears may be unfounded. They believe that, while e-mail may strip away some of the intimacy of face-to-face conversation, it also strips away some of the fear, guilt, anger, and self-consciousness.[4] Other theorists reason that, to compensate for the alienation machine-made barriers foster, we internalize a greater need to develop warm, personal relationships. As a result, a major theme of our time is the desire for closer, more personal ties. It appears that forecaster John Naisbitt was right: Our high-tech society has precipitated in us an increasingly prevalent desire for "high-touch" contacts.[5] Technology is not eliminating our need for relationships but is helping foster friendships, even love. Thus, critics contend that we do not live in an autistic society but, rather, in a **high-tech–high-touch society.**[6] In our society, traditional barriers of time and space no longer exist. Relationships begin across time zones and international borders.[7] Instant and text messages vie with phone calls as social glue.[8] In our technologically advanced world, meaningful relationships, while more difficult to maintain, become even more precious.[9] Indeed, social contacts have a positive effect on mortality.[10]

Functions of Relationships: Three Basic Needs

A vast body of research spurred by the work of William Schutz demonstrates that we attempt to meet our needs for inclusion, control, and affection through friendships, work, and romantic relationships.[11]

Inclusion has to do with the varying degrees to which we all need to establish and maintain a feeling of mutual interest with other people—a sense that we can take an interest in others and that others can take an interest in us. We want others to pay attention to us, to take the time to understand us. Wanting to be included is normal. We all remember how it feels to be left out—to be the last person asked to join a team, to not be invited to an important party, or to be ignored during a mealtime conversation. When our need for inclusion is met, we tend to feel worthwhile and fulfilled. If it goes unmet, we tend to feel lonely, and our health may even suffer.

Loneliness is an all too common affliction of our age.[12] Research reveals, for example, that men aged 50 and older who have no close friends or relatives are three times as likely to die after suffering high levels of emotional stress than are persons whose lives are less lonely.[13] What exactly is **loneliness?** Loneliness begins with a recognition that the interpersonal relationships we have are not the kinds we would like to have.[14] Thus, loneliness results from a perceived discrepancy between desired and achieved social relationships.[15] Lonely people find it difficult to connect with others. When our person-to-person contacts are deficient, we feel alone, and we seek substitutes for these contacts—sometimes, for example, opting for the company of professional contact people, such as radio talk show hosts and physicians. To help their patients handle feelings of isolation, physicians are spending course time learning how to deal with the more personal needs of patients.[16] Inclusion is so interconnected with our well-being that some years ago the California State Department of Mental Health mounted an advertising campaign designed to convince people that social relationships could enhance their physical and mental health and increase their life span.

Control deals with our need to establish and maintain satisfactory levels of influence and power in our relationships. To varying degrees, we need to feel that we can take charge of a situation, whereas at other times we need to feel comfortable assuming a more submissive role. When our control need goes unmet, we may conclude that others do not respect or value our abilities and that we are viewed as incapable of making a sound decision or of directing others' or our own future.

Finally, **affection** involves our need to give and receive love and to experience emotionally close relationships. If our need for affection goes unfulfilled, we are likely to conclude that we are unlovable and that therefore people will remain emotionally detached from us (that is, they will try to avoid establishing close ties with us). In contrast, if our experiences with affection have been more pleasant, we are probably comfortable handling both close and distant relationships, and most likely we recognize that not everyone we come into contact with will necessarily care for us in the same way.

These three basic needs differ from each other in a significant way. Inclusion comes first; that is, it is our need for

inclusion
the need for social contact

loneliness
the perceived discrepancy between desired and achieved social relationships

control
the need to feel we are capable and responsible and are able to exert power and influence in our relationships

affection
the need to experience emotionally close relationships

Feelings of inclusion or loneliness can affect our health and the way we view ourselves.

How do you navigate this duality in your own life? That is, how do you balance your need for individuality with your need for social contact?

Do you think men and women differ in their need for inclusion, control, or affection? Do they differ in the way they express their needs? Why or why not?

phatic communication
communication designed to open the channels of communication

grapevine
a type of informal, conversational network existing in organizations

inclusion that impels us to establish a relationship in the first place. By comparison, our needs for control and affection are met through the relationships we have already established. Thus, as psychologist William Schutz notes, "Generally speaking, inclusion is concerned with the problem of in or out, control is concerned with top or bottom, and affection with close or far."[17]

Building Relationships Using Verbal and Nonverbal Conversations

In a news article on flirting, the author observes: "Woman spots man. Man spots woman. Woman smiles. Man looks away. Woman looks away. Man looks back." Will they speak to each other?[18] According to Robert E. Nofsinger, author of *Everyday Conversation*, "Almost everything we do that concerns other people involves us in conversation."[19] We talk to relate; we converse our way through our lives. Talking is fundamental to every relationship—whether it is beginning, ending, or continuing.[20]

Typically, the more time we spend speaking with our relationship partners about our day, the healthier is the relationship we share.[21] Nofsinger also reminds us, "Our family life is created and enacted each day through conversation. And, in large part, we find employment (or fail to) through our everyday talk."

Conversations with friends, co-workers and romantic partners have outcomes; they produce results. Thus, as our conversations progress from **phatic communication,** surface clichés that are designed to open the channels of communication (like "What's up?" and "How are you doing?"), to statements of fact (like "Geography is my worst subject"), to statements of opinion (like "I really support PETA"), to statements of feelings (like "I think Juana likes Joe and I'm jealous"), the better able we are to keep a conversation going, use self-disclosure techniques to draw others into conversation with us, and thereby increase the likelihood that we will develop friendships.[22] Thus, by taking turns or refusing to take turns—that is, through reciprocal turn taking or the lack of reciprocal turn taking—we influence the direction of our relationships. For this reason, some of our relationships go nowhere, while others are particularly effective—usually because we have worked to make them that way.

Following are two special conversational environments we want to explore: the grapevine and the gossip mill.

THE GRAPEVINE
When people perceive a threat or feel insecure at work, and no formal communications from management are forthcoming to guide them or ease their minds, they may use the **grapevine** (a type of informal, conversational network existing in organizations) to communicate key messages that relate to personal or professional matters of importance. Whenever you pass a message to someone in the organizational network, it is wise to assume that what you pass along will be repeated to others. Although research reveals the grapevine to be uncannily speedy and accurate, the messages carried over it are not necessarily delivered unscathed, but often emerge distorted or incomplete.[23] By tapping into the grapevine, however, you may discover clues regarding what is happening in organizational or social circles that could affect you. People report that the grapevine is especially active during times of crisis or change. Do your experiences confirm this?

THE GOSSIP MILL

The **gossip mill** is the network through which unverified information is spread. When we converse with one person about another person who is not present, though we may believe we are only making small talk, we are actually spreading gossip. Why do humans spend so much time gossiping? Perhaps it is because gossip is so prevalent in society. Gossip fills the lifestyle pages of newspapers, is the subject of whole magazines, and has numerous television and cable programs devoted to it. Additionally, gossip is a staple of conversations, promoting social bonding and helping its users feel socially relevant and powerful.[24] Gossipers also typically get to hear more gossip fueling the gossip mill.

What do men and women who gossip talk about? Men tend to gossip about the people they work with, work-related issues, or politics and sports. Women tend to gossip about their social relationships and neighbors. A percentage of what both men and women gossip about involves more than perception checking or the harmless announcement of an event such as a marriage or a birth. In the spirit of *Desperate Housewives,* their gossip also contains conjectures about what friends, politicians, movie stars, famed athletes, or family members are up to. The gossiper frequently hypothesizes about the behavior of an absent party, spreads malicious rumors or false information about the person, and muses about such topics as whether the person is cheating on a significant other or is about to be fired. Thus, though gossip may endow people who gossip with transient feelings of importance, it is also likely that gossiping contributes to others' perceiving those who gossip more negatively.[25] As a result, gossiping can be a risky business.

gossip mill
the network through which unverified information is spread

What kinds of messages have you sent and/or received via the gossip mill? Does gossip function as a form of social glue, cementing relationships, or does it function as a type of interpersonal toxin, ruining relationships instead?

GENDER, CULTURE, AND RELATIONSHIPS

Both gender and culture influence how we form and maintain relationships. Although we all have a need to connect with people, we may do so in different ways. When we don't know how to connect with others from diverse cultures, we may be left feeling that we remain unconnected strangers. Relationship misunderstanding can keep us apart.[26] Thus, it is important to recognize that people who grow up in different cultures have different ideas about what is natural and important in their relationships. Those who do not conform to gender or culture expectations can meet with negative responses.

Gender and Relationships

How do young men and women view the relationships they are likely to share in the future? In one recent poll of teenagers, responses revealed that the sexes hold different attitudes regarding their future relationships: Males, for example, are much more traditional than females regarding the kind of family life they hope to share. While 86 percent of teenage girls surveyed expect to combine work and family and are committed to having careers, only 58 percent of the boys said that they expected their wives to work outside the home. Male respondents expressed a desire for a traditional 1950s-style relationship in which the wife stays home, raises the children, and is a homemaker, while the husband is responsible for paying the bills and mowing the lawn. One teenage girl commented, "If [the male respondents] say they want their wives at home, I think it's because they want more power in the relationship."[27]

Males and females differ not just in their expectations of future relationships but also in their behavior during the preliminary stages of a relationship—for

Because of the way they are socialized, men and women may share their feelings differently.

instance, when flirting. According to one educator, flirting is "a verbal power struggle between men and women."[28] For men "it is a form of foreplay," while for women it is more often "a way of making a connection."[29]

Researchers also affirm that women place a higher value on emotionally close relationships than do men, whose friendships frequently seem to lack emotional depth.[30] Because of the ways men are socialized, they often feel uncomfortable expressing their feelings directly with words, preferring instead to express them through shared activities such as sports.[31] Thus, women use personal and disclosive talk to develop and sustain their relationships to a greater extent than do men. While women bond through talk, men bond through doing things together.[32]

In addition, women focus on the maintenance of relationships more than men do. Women are eager to acquire personal information about their relational partners. They desire a partner who demonstrates care and concern and who is empathetic. As a result, they use more maintenance strategies than do men.[33]

This is not to imply that men and women do not share any commonalities in their views regarding relationships, because they do. Both men and women value same-sex friends and desire friends they can trust, who accept them and help them.

Culture and Relationships

Attitudes toward self and others influence the effectiveness of the relationships persons from different cultures share. Acceptance, for instance, is one necessary factor for relationship satisfaction. Researchers report that, to be satisfied in their relationships with Whites, both African Americans and Mexican Americans need to feel that Whites respect, confirm, and accept them.[34] Asians also practice the positive exchange of ideas, demonstrating care for the other person during the exchange. They value harmony as a means of relationship nurturance. Conformity and group well-being are especially important to them. Generally, they do not reach out to strangers, and they make great efforts to conceal unfavorable information about members of the group to which they belong from those whom they perceive to be outsiders.[35] Latinos, in contrast, tend to focus on relational support.[36]

While some cultures emphasize social relationships and instruct individuals to give preference to the interests of others over their own private interests, other cultures, including American culture, stress individualism. While Americans find it natural to begin and end relationships, Asian cultures believe that relationships should be long-lasting, characterized by loyalty and the fulfillment of obligations.

Not all cultures treat all relationships similarly. Some cultures, for example, have different rules for heterosexual relationships and same-sex relationships, while others have men and women performing different roles in relationships. While Western culture values heterosexual marriage, in the United States some states have given legal status to domestic partnerships enabling gays and lesbians and unmarried heterosexuals to have the same rights as married heterosexuals. Many Scandinavian countries have done the same. In some countries, however, same-sex couples face ostracism or severe consequences—including being arrested or put to death. When it comes to the roles men and women perform in relationships, in the United States, both men and women can begin and end their romantic relationships. In other cultures, parents select relationship partners for their children. Sometimes their goal is to bring two families together; other times, it is to reap a financial reward. In the United States, we typically believe that any person has the right and ability to dissolve a relationship that makes him or her unhappy.

DIMENSIONS OF RELATIONSHIPS: BREADTH AND DEPTH

We can describe every relationship—whether with a friend, a family member, a lover, or a co-worker—in terms of two concepts: breadth and depth. **Breadth** has to do with how many topics you discuss with the other person. **Depth** has to do with how central the topics are to your self-concept and how much you reveal.

The relationship theory of social psychologists Irwin Altman and Dalmas Taylor can be schematized as shown in Figure 8.1.[37] Central to their **social penetration theory** is the idea that relationships begin with relatively narrow breadth (few topics are spoken about) and shallow depth (the inner circles are not penetrated) and progress over time in intensity and intimacy as both breadth and depth increase. Thus, our relationships develop incrementally as we move from discussing few to many topics, and from superficial topics (the periphery of the circle) to intensely personal topics (the center of the circle). Figure 8.2 is an exercise using these concepts.

breadth
the number of topics you discuss with another person

depth
a measure of how central the topics you discuss with another person are to your self-concept

social penetration theory
the theory that states that our relationships begin with relatively narrow breadth and shallow depth and develop over time

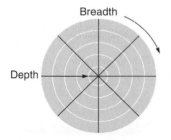

FIGURE 8.1 **Breadth and Depth in Relationships.**

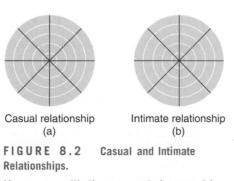

Casual relationship
(a)

Intimate relationship
(b)

FIGURE 8.2 **Casual and Intimate Relationships.**

Use arrows with the segmented concentric circles to show the contrast between one of your casual relationships and one of your more intimate relationships.

The breadth of topics we discuss may be wide for casual as well as for intimate relationships, but the depth of penetration usually increases as a relationship becomes more intimate. Consequently, a highly intimate relationship probably has both considerable breadth and considerable depth as the people involved extend the range of topics they discuss and reveal more about how they feel about those topics.

The social penetration model is useful for a number of reasons. First, it helps us visualize the nature of our relationships by indicating the range of topics we communicate about and the extent to which we reveal ourselves through our discussions. Second, the model helps explain why certain relationships seem stronger than others. For example, is there one person to whom you reveal more about a particular topic than you would reveal to anyone else? Is there someone with whom you would not even consider discussing a particular topic? Do you reveal more of yourself to some people at work than to others? Is the same true for members of your family? What about your friends? Although we may behave in ways that limit some people's access to certain portions of our relationship circle, others may have access to its entire scope; although we may keep some from straying too far from the periphery, we may let others venture close to the center. When your communication with another person lacks breadth, depth, or both, it should not surprise you that you feel little if any bond to that person; to enhance the strength of your relationship, you would have to alter the nature and extent of your interactions.

Sometimes, in an effort to get to know another person quickly, we may discuss topics at a depth that would normally be reserved for those with whom we are more intimate. When such disclosures occur too rapidly or prematurely in the development of a relationship, they may create a feeling that something is wrong, a signal that one participant was not ready for the relationship to progress that quickly or to be that intense. For example, employees in one company complained when a supervisor discussed personal aspects of his marriage with them during the business day; noting that hearing such intimate disclosures made them feel uncomfortable, they requested that he limit the depth and scope of his communications with them.

When interactants are ready to deepen a relationship, they see increases in breadth and depth as a natural and comfortable development.

Together, the nature and the amount of information we share with another person affect the strength and the quality of our interpersonal relationship. When we deliberately reveal information about ourselves to another person, information that we consider significant and would otherwise not be known to that person were it not for our purposeful intervention, we take steps to increase both the breadth of information people have about us and the depth of understanding they have for what makes us tick. **Self-disclosure** is the voluntary, purposeful revealing of confidential personal information about us that others would not otherwise have access to. The amount of disclosing we do with another person usually is a gauge of how close we feel to the person or how close we desire to become. On the other hand, when a relationship begins to wane, usually there are decreases in the breadth as well as the depth of our disclosures. We refrain from talking about some topics, and we discuss the topics we do talk about in less depth. Such changes signal that we are becoming less personal or intimate and have begun the depenetration, or pulling-away, process. Thus, self-disclosure reflects the health of a relationship. When disclosure between relationship partners is reciprocal and honest, partners feel more secure in the relationship. They become comfortable sharing their humanness.

How do you feel when someone reveals more to you than you are ready for? Have you ever made anyone feel uncomfortable by revealing too much too quickly? What prompted you to do it? How did the other person react?

self-disclosure

the process of revealing to another person information about the self that he or she would not otherwise know

"Let's go someplace where I can talk."

DEVELOPMENT AND ANALYSIS OF RELATIONSHIPS

Relationships can be analyzed with reference to their stages, costs and benefits, or dialectical perspectives. As you read about each stage, consider how it applies to a close relationship of yours.

Stages of Relationships: From Beginning to Ending to Beginning . . .

All relationships we share are complex (each of us is a unique bundle of experiences, thoughts, fears, and needs) and ever-changing (as we change, our relationships change—they grow stronger or weaker over time). Relationships pass through a number of stages as they strengthen, stabilize, or dissolve.[38] We will explore them now.

STAGE 1: INITIATING

Initiating involves the things that happen when we first make contact and look for signals that either lead us to begin a conversation or tell us that we have nothing to gain by conversing. If we decide to converse, we search for an appropriate conversation opener—for example, "Nice to meet you" or "What's happening?"

initiating
the relationship stage during which contact is first made

What happens when we can't find an appropriate opener? The following passage from *Conversationally Speaking* by Alan Garner describes one such possibility:

> I decided to marry her. Courtship would be a mere formality. But what to say to begin the courtship? "Would you like some of my gum?" sounded too low-class. "Hello," was too trite a greeting for my future bride. "I love you! I am hot with passion!" was too forward. "I want to make you the mother of my children," seemed a bit premature.
>
> Nothing. That's right, I said nothing. And after a while, the bus reached her stop, she got off, and I never saw her again.
>
> End of story.[39]

STAGE 2: EXPERIMENTING

Once we initiate contact, we try to find out more about the other person; we begin to probe the unknown. This is the stage of **experimenting.** In an effort to get acquainted, we exchange small talk, such as telling the other where we're from and whom we know. Although many of us may hate small talk, or cocktail party chatter, according to Mark Knapp it serves several useful functions:

1. It provides a process for uncovering integrating topics and openings for more penetrating conversations.
2. It can serve as an audition for a future friendship or a way to increase the scope of a current friendship.
3. It provides a safe procedure for indicating who we are and how the other person can come to know us better (reduction of uncertainty).
4. It allows us to maintain a sense of community with our fellow human beings.[40]

In an article on small talk, Michael Korda notes: "The aim of small talk is to make people comfortable—to put them at their ease—not to teach, preach, or impress. It's a game, like tennis, in which the object is to keep the ball in the air for as long as possible."[41]

At this stage, our relationships lack depth; they are quite casual and superficial. The vast majority of them never progress beyond this point.

STAGE 3: INTENSIFYING

When a relationship progresses beyond experimenting, it enters the third stage, **intensifying.** During this stage, people become good friends—they begin to share things, disclose more, become better at predicting each other's behavior, and may even adopt nicknames for each other or exhibit similar postural or clothing cues. In a sense, they are beginning to be transformed from an "I" and an "I" into a "we."

STAGE 4: INTEGRATING

The fusion of "I" and "I" really takes place in stage 4, **integrating.** We now identify two individuals as a team, a pair, a couple, or "a package." Interpersonal synchrony is heightened; the two people may dress, act, and speak more and more alike or share a song ("our song"), a savings account, or a project.

STAGE 5: BONDING

In stage 5, **bonding,** two people announce that they are formalizing their commitment to each other. They institutionalize their relationship with a formal contract—a wedding license or a business contract, for example. The relationship

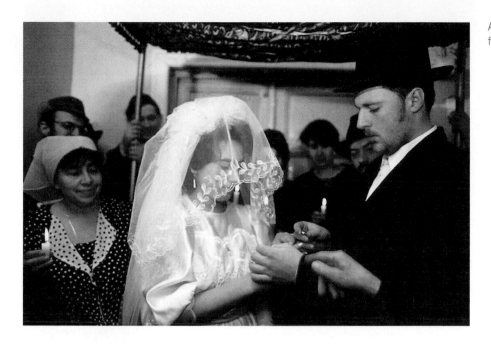

A wedding signifies the formal bonding of a couple.

takes on a new character. It is now guided by specified rules and regulations. Sometimes this alteration initially causes discomfort or rebellion as the two people attempt to adjust to the change.

STAGE 6: DIFFERENTIATING

In stage 6, **differentiating,** instead of continuing to emphasize "we," the two people involved attempt to reestablish an "I" orientation, to regain a unique identity. They ask, "How are we different?" "How can I distinguish me from you?" During this phase, previously designated joint possessions take on a more individualized character; "our friends" become "my friends," "our bedroom" becomes "my bedroom," "our child" becomes "your son" (especially when he misbehaves). Although an urge to differentiate the self from the other is not uncommon (we need to be individuals as well as members of a relationship), if it persists, it can signal that the relationship is in trouble or that the process of uncoupling has begun.

differentiating
the relationship stage in which two people identified as a couple seek to regain unique identities

STAGE 7: CIRCUMSCRIBING

In stage 7, **circumscribing,** both the quality and the quantity of communication between relationship partners decreases. Sometimes a careful effort is made to limit areas open for discussion to those considered safe. Other times there is no actual decrease in breadth of topics, but the topics are no longer discussed with any depth. In other words, fewer and less intimate disclosures are made, signaling that one or both partners desires to withdraw mentally or physically from the relationship.[42] Dynamic communication has all but ceased. A lack of energy, shrinking interest, and a general feeling of exhaustion characterize the relationship.

circumscribing
the relationship stage in which both the quality and the quantity of communication between two people decrease

STAGE 8: STAGNATING

When circumscribing continues, the relationship stagnates. In stage 8, **stagnating,** the two parties feel that they no longer need to relate to each other because they know how the interaction will proceed; they conclude that it is better to say

stagnating
the relationship stage during which communication is at a standstill

nothing. Communication is at a standstill. Only the shadow of a relationship remains: The two mark time by going through the motions while feeling nothing. In reality, they are like strangers inhabiting the hollow shell of what once was a thriving relationship. They still live in the same environment, but they share little else.

STAGE 9: AVOIDING

avoiding
the relationship stage during which the participants intentionally avoid contact

During the stage of **avoiding,** the participants actually go out of their way to be apart; they avoid contact with each other. Relating face-to-face or voice-to-voice has simply become so unpleasant that one or both can no longer continue the act. Although communicated more directly at some times than at others (sometimes the "symptom" is used as a form of communication; at other times an effort is made to disconfirm the other person), the dominant message is "I don't want to see you anymore; I don't want to continue this relationship." At this point, the end of the relationship is in sight.

STAGE 10: TERMINATION

termination
the relationship stage during which the relationship ends

At stage 10, **termination,** the bonds that used to hold the relationship together are severed; the relationship ends. Depending on how the participants feel

"I've been thinking, Neil, I'd really like to get to know you less."

(whether or not they agree on termination), this stage can be short or drawn out over time and can end cordially (in person, over the telephone, with an e-mail or legal document) or bitterly. All relationships eventually terminate (by the death of one participant if not before), but this does not mean that saying good-bye is easy or pleasant.[43]

SUMMARY

A relationship may stabilize at any one of the stages. Many relationships never proceed beyond the experimenting stage; others stabilize at the intensifying stage, the bonding stage, and so on. When the participants disagree about the point of stabilization, difficulties can arise. Movement through the stages may be forward or backward. For instance, we may advance and then retreat, deciding that a more superficial relationship is what we really desire. Additionally, we proceed through the stages at our own pace. Some relationships, especially those in which time is perceived to be limited, develop more quickly than others; the rate at which the participants grow together or apart, however, usually depends on their individual needs. What is important to remember is that many relationships do not arrive at a stage and simply stay there. Rather, they can be recursive. Relationships may even terminate and then begin anew.

Identify relationships in your own life that have stabilized at one or more of Knapp's "coming together" stages: initiating, experimenting, intensifying, integrating, bonding.

A Special Case: Relationship Termination Caused by Death

What happens when death takes a loved one or a relationship partner away? When this occurs, many of us experience feelings of loneliness and social isolation. Actually, the **grief process** (see Figure 8.3) entails a number of stages: The first stage is denial—we deny what has happened. Denial diminishes as we acknowledge the impact of our loss and the feelings that accompany it. The second stage is anger—feeling helpless and powerless, we strike out and rail against the loss. The third stage is guilt—we turn our anger against ourselves. We feel bad about things we have said or done to hurt the person who has died. We find ourselves left with a sense of unfinished business. In the fourth stage, depression, we feel that nothing will be right again. Looking forward feels impossible. We feel lonely, empty, and isolated. The fifth stage is acceptance—while things will not be the same, we believe that we will make it through and be able to go on with life.[44] The question is, How do we get to stage 5?

grief process

a mourning process composed of five stages: denial, anger, guilt, depression, and acceptance

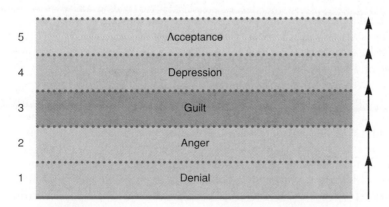

FIGURE 8.3
The Grief Process.

The tendency in those who are closest to someone who has suffered a loss is to try to protect the person and shield him or her from sadness. Instead of trying to suppress and walk around sadness, however, we should work to help mourners experience it. For example, even though the death of a family member might make a family turn inward, for the person(s) grieving, expressing feelings to friends who are not directly affected by the loss can help.

Even very young children grieve, although their grief may be different from the grief experienced by adolescents and adults. With help and support, however, people of all ages can handle rather than submerge grief and, as a result, recover from grief's effects and go on with their lives. Part of the process involves constructing an image of the deceased loved one that the bereaved can take with them into their continuing lives.[45] It is the processing of feelings that appears to be key.

Research reveals that we do not simply replace a former partner but, rather, remain loyal to the deceased partner in almost all new relationships that we form, whether the relationship takes the form of a consummate partner, less intimate steady companion, or service provider. Still, reengagement in consummate partnerships and steady companionship is effective in reducing loneliness and helping us fulfill our relational needs.[46]

Personalization has hit the casket industry. You can now purchase a casket adorned with scenes of the last supper, your favorite flag, or your favorite musical group. Some critics see these "art caskets" as an expression of self-absorption and narcissism, while others see it as a meaningful way to have the last word in self-expression. What do you think?

Men and women handle the death of a partner differently, especially when they are older. The myth is that, in widowhood, women grieve while men replace. Despite the fact that a significant percentage of men and women aged 50 and over attain new partner relationships after divorce or widowhood, older widowed men are more apt to remarry than are older widowed women. For some widows, particularly those who, as a result of their partner's death, are living by themselves for the first time, being alone actually provides a sense of liberation. These women do not want to give this up or use it as trade-off for companionship and caring responsibilities. As a result, some establish living apart together (LAT) relationships, relationships that offer a fulfilling intimate relationship but also ensure a significant degree of autonomy and avoid the unequal demands of caring for a partner that may have previously been experienced. In contrast, widowers view the loneliness they experience after the death of a partner as a sense of deprivation, especially after a life of being cared for by a woman in whom they had entrusted their emotional existence.[47]

Cost–Benefit/Social Exchange Theory and Relationship Development

Though relationships may proceed through stages, they are not always predictable. No relationship is foreordained in heaven or hell for success or failure. Rather, our relationships develop as a consequence of the energy we commit to them and as a result of what we do with and for one another.

cost–benefit/social exchange theory

the theory that we work to maintain a relationship as long as the benefits we receive outweigh the costs

Unless the people who share a relationship continue to grow together and adapt to their continually changing environment, the relationship may begin to deteriorate at any point. According to **cost–benefit/social exchange theory,** we work to maintain a relationship only as long as the benefits we perceive for ourselves outweigh the costs.[48] These benefits include feelings of self-worth, a sense of personal growth, a greater sense of security, additional resources for accomplishing tasks, and an increased ability to cope with problems. In comparison, costs include the time spent trying to make the relationship work, psychological and physical stress, and a damaged self-image. We enter our relationships with a **comparison level** in mind; we have a general idea, standard, or expectation of the kinds of rewards and profits that we believe we ought to get out of the relationship. When the rewards we receive equal or surpass our comparison level, we usually feel satisfied with the relationship. However, we also have a **comparison level for alternatives;** we compare the rewards we get from a current relationship with the ones we think we are able to get from an alternative relationship. If we believe that present relationship rewards are below those we could receive from an alternative relationship, then we might decide to exit our present relationship and enter a new one.

In general, however, when we think of a relationship in economic terms, the greater our rewards or profits and the lower our costs, the more satisfying a relationship will be. Each relationship partner acts out of a self-oriented goal of profit taking.[49] When costs begin to outweigh benefits, we are more and more likely to decide to terminate the relationship. In contrast, when benefits outweigh costs, the relationship will probably continue to develop. Cost–benefit/social exchange theory predicts that the worth of a relationship influences its outcome. Positive relationships will probably endure, whereas negative relationships will probably terminate.

comparison level
an expectation of the kinds of rewards and profits we believe we ought to derive from a relationship

comparison level for alternatives
the comparing of rewards derived from a current relationship with ones we expect to get from an alternative relationship

Relational Dialectics Theory

According to relational dialectics theorists, relationships are not linear but, rather, consist of the oscillation between contradictory goals or desires. During relationship development, communicators seek to meet important goals, some of which may be incompatible. When opposing goals meet, they create **dialectical tensions.** Three central relational dialectical tensions exist between connection and autonomy, predictability and novelty, and openness and privacy.[50] Let us explore each in turn.

dialectical tensions
tensions that occur when opposing goals meet

CONNECTION VERSUS AUTONOMY

We desire to be independent of our significant others and to find intimacy with them. We want to be close as well as separate. Perhaps you have found yourself saying the following about a partner. "He barely spent any time with me." "I have no time for myself." "She made me feel trapped." "He just wouldn't commit to being an 'us.'" "I need my freedom." If any of these statements sound familiar, then you and a partner had conflicting desires for connection and independence. Since we want to establish more intimate connections with others we care about, we cherish the sharing of experiences. At the same time, however, we need to preserve an independent identity. We do not want our relationships to destroy our individuality. Some relationships do not survive the connection–autonomy negotiations; instead of working out an acceptable balance that preserves individuality while creating intimacy, partners break up. On the other hand, as a result of resolving their connection–autonomy disagreements, relationship partners can redefine their relationship and become even closer.[51]

PREDICTABILITY VERSUS NOVELTY

We desire the excitement of change and the comfort of stability. We want both a routine and spontaneity. Too much routine becomes boring. Perhaps these words sound familiar: "We always do the same things." "I want to do something different." "I know everything there is to know about her." Variety adds spice to normal routines. The challenge for relationship partners is to find the right mix between the desire for predictability and the need to keep the relationship fresh and interesting.

OPENNESS VERSUS PRIVACY

We wrestle with tensions between dislosure and silence or concealment. For many of us, complete openness is intolerable to contemplate. While we want to share our inner selves with people we care deeply about, there are times when we do not feel like sharing and desire the preservation of privacy instead. Desiring privacy some of the time does not mean a relationship is on the rocks. Our desires for openness and closedness wax and wane. We go through periods of disclosing and periods of withholding.[52] During every stage of our relationship, our desires for openness and privacy can fluctuate.

RESOLVING DIALECTICAL TENSIONS

When a relationship is successful, partners are able to manage the dialectical tensions by using a number of different strategies. First, they can negotiate a balance between connection and autonomy, predictability and novelty, and openness and closedness. Second, they can choose to favor one dialectic and ignore the other. Third, they can segment each of the dialectics by compartmentalizing different areas of their relationship and assigning each dialectic to different times or spheres. Fourth, they can reframe the dialectics by defining them as not contradictory at all.[53] One ineffective way of handing dialectical tensions is to deny that they exist. Instead of confronting the challenges that face the relationship, the partners ignore them.

DECEPTION AND RELATIONSHIPS

Are we living in the age of deception?[54] Over the past few years, photos have been digitally altered to influence or mislead readers or viewers; major corporations, such as Enron, Global Crossing, and Arthur Andersen, have been charged with deceiving stockholders and the public; news reporters have staged stories; and the entertainment industry has based the outcomes of a number of new programs on the ability of participants to lie.

Lying and Relationship Development

While most of us would condemn lying, during the course of a typical week, nearly every one of us lies. How do you explain this?

Consider your feelings about lying. How do you define the word lie? To whom would you lie? What kinds of situations call for a lie? How many times in the past month have you lied to someone with whom you share a relationship? How many times were you caught? What happened as a result?

A lie is the deliberate presentation of information you know not to be true. You can lie by omission or commission. When you lie by omission, you deliberately withhold relevant information, thereby causing people to draw an erroneous conclusion. When you lie by commission, you make a statement you know to be false. Although at times the motivation for lying is to avoid a confrontation or increase one's social desirability, there is no question that the speaker's intention is to deceive one or more receivers when a lie is told.[55]

While women appear to be more sensitive than men to relational deception, and develop more negative attitudes to the deceiver than do men, exposed instances of deception cause members of either sex to view the target significantly less favorably.[56]

Lying appears to be commonplace in our society. Some 91 percent of Americans confess that they regularly do not tell the truth; 20 percent admit they cannot get through a day without telling a conscious, premeditated lie. Approximately a quarter of all serious lies are told to cover up an affair.[57] Thus, we lie not only to strangers but also to those we care about.

When we lie to someone, we do not merely deliver wrong information; we also intentionally seek to deceive him or her. Sissela Bok, the author of *Lying,* says that, when we lie, it is both our hope and our expectation that we will succeed in making the target of our efforts believe something we do not believe.[58] This description is supported by the communication theorists Steven A. McCornack and Timothy R. Levine, who note: "Deception is the deliberate falsification or omission of information by a communicator, with the intent being to mislead the conversational partner."[59]

It is rare to tell someone only one lie. To sustain our original lie, we usually need to tell more lies. As Bok writes, "The liar always has more mending to do." And the liar has to expend a great deal of energy remembering to whom he or she told what and why.

Why do people lie? Of course, the reasons are as numerous as the situations that precipitate a need to lie in the first place. However, two reasons appear to dominate: Most people lie to gain a reward or to avoid punishment. What kinds of reward are we after in our relationships, and what kinds of punishment are we trying to avoid?

According to some researchers, we lie to continue to satisfy the basic needs fulfilled by our relationships, to increase or decrease desired and undesired affiliations, to protect our self-esteem, and to achieve personal satisfaction.[60] Most often, when we lie, we benefit ourselves, although a percentage of our lies are designed to protect the person or persons we are lying to, and an even smaller percentage benefit a third party.

In fact, sometimes we **equivocate** (use purposefully vague language to finesse a response) in an effort to avoid having to tell the unvarnished and unpleasant truth. Being deliberately vague helps us spare another's feelings and/or relieves us of having to confront our anger. For example, if asked how we like a gift given to us, we might reply, "It's really special," when what we really think is that it is tasteless. Or if asked how we like someone's hairstyle, we might say, "It's really you," when we believe it detracts from the person's appearance. Equivocating takes the teller off the hot seat. It also helps the receiver save face. While people believe equivocating is better than lying, when asked, they still say that they prefer to be told the truth.[61] Do you believe them?

Are we good at detecting lies? Research says we are not. In one study, a researcher had subjects watch their romantic partners describe another person as attractive or unattractive. Other subjects who did not know the romantic partner also watched the interaction. Results revealed that the subjects with the romantic attachment were considerably worse at spotting their partners' lies than were the strangers. If the romantic partners were asked indirect questions, however, such as how suspicious they were or if they received enough information from their partners, the answers indicated that at some level they had picked up the deception, and picked it up better than strangers did. It seems, without being asked such questions, they were reluctant to call their partner a liar.[62]

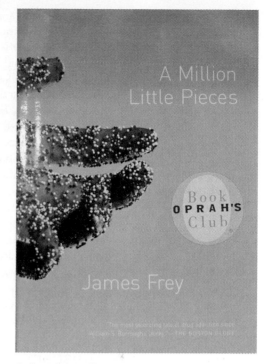

Author James Frey apologized to Oprah Winfrey for deceiving her and readers for writing a memoir that contained fabrications. Would you have forgiven him?

Why are you lying to me who are my friend?

—Moroccan proverb

equivocate

use purposefully vague language to finesse a response

In Tennessee Williams's play A Streetcar Named Desire, *one of the characters— Blanche DuBois—says, "I don't tell the truth. I tell what ought to be truth." Does this practice help or hinder the development of relationships? Why?*

How is a liar like a counterfeiter?

Focus on Service Learning

Speak at a local meeting of parents and teachers about the importance of honesty in relationships. You can limit your topic by focusing on the role of honesty in online interaction, parent–child interaction, teacher–child interaction, parent– teacher interaction, or friendship. For help in completing this assignment, in addition to consulting research articles and books, you may want to visit Web sites such as www.coping.org.

How does a lie affect our relationships once it is uncovered? Imagine sharing a relationship, no matter how ideal in other aspects, in which you could never rely on the words or gestures of the other person. Information exchanged in that relationship would be virtually worthless, and the feelings expressed would be practically meaningless. No one likes to be duped. No one likes to appear gullible. When someone does deceive us, we become suspicious and resentful; we are disappointed both in the other person and in ourselves.

As Sissela Bok observed, people who discover they have been lied to "are resentful, disappointed and suspicious. They feel wronged; they are wary of new overtures." Further, Bok notes, people "look back on their past beliefs and actions in the new light of the discovered lies." While bending the truth to sustain a relationship may be a common practice, unless trust and truthfulness are present, it is only a matter of time before the relationship will die. Lying is likely to precipitate a relationship crisis. Many relationship breakups are attributed directly to the discovery of a major deception.

Quite simply, lies are fundamentally destructive and often kill a relationship. Few factors have more influence on a relationship than trust. In fact, the reason most commonly cited for terminating a relationship is a loss of trust in one's partner. And nearly all breakups due to deception are reported to be initiated by the recipient of the lie.[63]

Trust and Relationship Development

Trust gives us the ability to rise above our doubts.

—John K. Rempel,
John G. Holmes

There is potential for trouble in any relationship. As we saw in the previous section, one cause of trouble is lying. Another, equally important, cause is the undermining of trust. Trust is an outgrowth of interpersonal communication. It is a reflection of how secure we are that a person will act in a predicted and desirable way. When we trust another person, we have confidence that he or she will behave as we expect and that the person will not use whatever personal information we have confided to him or her to harm us. Some of us are more trusting than others. How trusting are you? Whether or not you trust another person depends on whether prior relationships have reinforced trusting behavior or consolidated your fears about the risks of exhibiting trusting behavior. Trust creates a paradox: To be able to trust, we must be willing to take the risk of trusting. When we take the risk, we risk being wrong. If we fail to take the risk, however, we can never be right.[64] The degree of trust you place in another person to accept information you disclose to him or her without hurting you or the relationship is your **tolerance of vulnerability.** Your tolerance of vulnerability varies from person to person, topic to topic, and situation to situation.

Researcher William Rawlins designed a matrix, shown in Figure 8.4, that we can use to analyze the amount of trust we place in different people at different times in a relationship's development. We can also use this matrix to determine which of our relationships have more stability or staying power than others. A relationship in which the partners have difficulty trusting one another is a troubled relationship.

tolerance of vulnerability

the degree of trust you place in another person to accept information you disclose without hurting you or the relationship

hurtful messages

messages designed to upset or to cause emotional pain that further hampers trust

Troubled relationships often involve the sending of **hurtful messages** (messages designed to upset or to cause emotional pain that further hampers trust). If the hurtful messages are intense, making it difficult for their target to ignore or forget them, they poison the relationship, making it impossible to sustain closeness in or derive satisfaction from it.

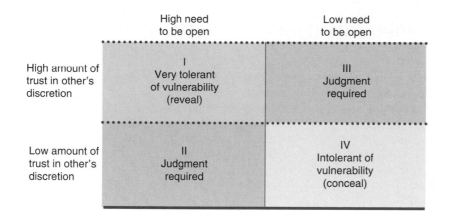

FIGURE 8.4

Rawlins's Trust Matrix.

Source: Matrix created by William K. Rawlins from "Openness as Problematic in Ongoing Friendships: Two Conversational Dilemmas," by W. K. Rawlins, *Communication Monographs* 50 (March 1983), p.11. Reproduced by permission of Taylor & Francis Group, LLC, www.taylorandfrancis.com.

How do you respond when you are the target of a hurtful message? Are you likely to respond actively by mounting a counterattack, defending yourself, or seeking reasons that explain why the other person acted hurtfully toward you in the first place? Would you acquiesce by apologizing or becoming emotional? Or do you ignore or laugh at the hurtful messages in an effort to shrug them off and prove your invulnerability to the sender? According to researchers Vangelisti and Crumly, the more emotional pain hurtful messages cause, the greater is the likelihood that we will respond by acquiescing. The less they hurt us, the more probable it becomes that we will seek to communicate our invulnerability instead. The healthier and more satisfying a relationship, the more likely it becomes that we will respond actively when we are the target of hurtful messages.[65]

Exploring Diversity

Does the Truth Lie?

1. Interview three people from cultures different from your own regarding their experiences of being lied to and of lying to someone else.

   a. Have them identify who lied to them, the nature of the lie, and their reactions upon discovering that they had been lied to.

   b. Ask them the nature of the lie they told to someone else, their reason for telling the lie, and the other person's reaction upon discovering he or she had been lied to.

   c. Whether they were the ones lying or being lied to, ask them the specific effect the lie had on their relationship with the other person.

2. People belonging to Asian cultures are likely to value social harmony more than telling the truth. In these cultures a person is expected to tell another person what that person wants or needs to hear. Compare and contrast that orientation with the desire that members of Western European cultures have to determine the truth. Could the differences in orientation be reflective of one culture's emphasis on collectivism and the other culture's preference for individualism? Which orientation do you believe helps preserve relationships? Which do you believe is more sociable?

3. Could telling someone the truth ever undermine trust the way lying does? Explain your answer with reasons.

Ethics & Communication

What Shames Us? From Reality TV to the Workplace, What Are We Learning about Ourselves and Relationships?

1. On shows such as *How Clean Is Your House? Trading Spouses,* and *The Swan,* people "put it all out there," parading their flaws before millions of viewers just to have the opportunity to have personal and family problems solved for free. In effect, they literally and figuratively air their dirty laundry for all to see.

Are we a nation of exhibitionists, unafraid to speak about things or behave in ways that at one time would have caused us to be ashamed? Do we like to watch others who behave or live in ways we consider shameful so that we can tell ourselves that we would not do or say what they do? To what extent do you believe that shows like these desensitize us to the problems they expose, even normalizing some of the coarser behaviors featured?[66]

2. What do you perceive to be the advantages and disadvantages of workplace romances? How do you feel about entering into a romantic relationship with a co-worker or boss? Would you be ashamed to admit the relationship to others? How do you imagine the relationship you shared would affect others who work with you? How do you imagine it would affect you and your career?

What if you were not the person having such a romantic relationship? What if it were your boss and another co-worker? Or what if it were two of your co-workers? Do you think either relationship would affect you and your chances for career success? Which do you think would affect you more?

LAUGHTER AS AN INTERPERSONAL TOOL

Like trust, laughter is an interpersonal tool. Every day we give and receive social laughter while interacting with friends, co-workers, and lovers. Laughter punctuates our conversations so regularly that we are apt not to think about or notice it. However, if laughter disappeared from any of our important relationships, we would miss it.

In the section "A Special Case: Relationship Termination Caused by Death," we discussed the grief that accompanies the death of someone we love. Even in grief, however, humor can play a part. Humor can help us cope with anything. Once you are able to laugh again, you know that you are regaining control. Laughter helps reduce our stress by releasing our excess energy. Like other interpersonal competencies, it also helps us develop fresh perspectives on events large and small by freeing us of anxious feelings or frustrations.

According to Dr. Robert R. Provine, laughs are rhythmic bursts of social glue.[67] He reports that much of what we laugh at in life is predominantly the stuff of social banter, not necessarily particularly funny or clever. Laughter, however, is contagious. When we hear laughter, we usually start laughing ourselves. Its infectious nature can have dramatic effects on our relationships. We, not only our relationship partners, laugh at what we say; in fact, the average speaker laughs 46 percent more frequently than do those listening to him or her. While laughter does not intrude on speech, it does provide its punctuation. It helps us synchronize our moods and perhaps our actions. As such, it may also help solidify our relationships.

Like any relationship tool, laughter has a downside too. The opposite of joyful laughter is jeering, malicious laughter, laughter that is designed to punish, belittle, or exclude rather than include another. In this case, laughter, rather than expressing our sociability, signals our disdain for and power over another person.

When it comes to the use of humor in our relationships, there are wide laughter variations based on sex. A man talking with a male listener laughs only marginally more than his interaction partner. A woman talking with a woman listener laughs somewhat more than her partner. And a male speaker with a female listener laughs less often than does the woman. However, when a woman speaks to a man, she laughs much more than her male partner.[68] Why do you think that is so?

Laughter is a relationship tool. What role does it play in the relationship you share?

TECHNOLOGY AND OUR RELATIONSHIPS

Technology and the Internet are enabling men and women alike to initiate, sustain, and end relationships in new ways. We now have different options when it comes to developing or terminating our relationships. In fact, while we still have singles bars, singles cruises, parties, and personal ads, many friendships and romantic relationships now begin on the Internet. In addition to an abundance of chat rooms, there are many commercial Web sites focused on helping people meet. The online dating business is booming, with revenues surpassing $300 million.[69] The popularity of sites such as Match.com and Yahoo Personals is a testament to the fact that online services are changing the way people find others today. Such sites are especially popular with busy people who do not have to leave home to develop relationships that gel.[70]

In addition, newsgroup users form friendships or relationships with persons they meet online. Approximately 25 percent of the people in one newsgroup study reported that they communicated with their partners a minimum of three or four times weekly.[71] While women are more likely than men to form personal relationships online, persons of both sexes establish both friendships and romantic relationships in cyberspace.[72] Although the computer probably will not replace face-to-face interaction, the relationships begun in cyberspace may transfer to real space. In fact, a number of relationships begun in cyberspace develop into extended friendships, romances, and marriage.[73] Thus, the computer presents us with different options when it comes to developing or terminating our relationships.

A number of key differences between face-to-face and online communication can impede relationship development. First, unless we exchange photographs or video, the person with whom we are connected in cyberspace remains invisible to us. Second, since we cannot see most of the nonverbal behavior that accompanies another person's message, we may misinterpret the message's meaning. Third, because we control the pace of online interaction, some of the spontaneity as well as the immediate feedback that characterize face-to-face communication and make it interesting are missing. Fourth, because we do not have access to as much information (verbal and nonverbal) as face-to-face interaction provides, we may find it even more difficult to decide if we can trust the person with whom we are relating.

Despite these drawbacks, for many users, being able to develop relationships online complements face-to-face relationships and has certain benefits. One teenager even notes that it is easier to begin a relationship online: "It's easier to talk to girls on the Internet than in school. Sometimes I can't talk well in person. It doesn't come out like I want it."[74]

According to Sherry Turkle, author of *Life on the Screen: Identity in the Age of the Internet,* when people are online, they tend to express different aspects of themselves in different settings. They find ways to conceive of themselves not as single and unitary but, rather, as having many aspects. As people form new relationships, they come to see themselves as the sum of their distributed presence on the windows they open on their screens.[75]

In addition, as more and more people make their way online, they are discovering that the anonymity that characterizes cyberspace enables those who communicate on the Internet to disregard gender, race, and appearance. Instead, whether or not an online relationship continues depends on the ability to build rapport. At least until people meet face-to-face, looks are placed on the back burner.

On the other hand, simply because of the inelasticity of time, Internet use may substantially reduce face-to-face interpersonal interaction and communication, contributing to our sense of alienation.[76] Indeed, some observers note that heavy Internet users become alienated from normal social contacts, even cutting off such traditional interactions as the Internet becomes the predominate social factor in their lives. As a result, they believe that increased Internet use will ultimately lead to loneliness. In contrast, others counter that it is those people who are already lonely who spend the most time online.[77] What do your experiences with the Internet tell you?

Adding to this debate are those who wonder if e-mail makes contact less of an intrusion. For example, when compared with an e-mail, a telephone call may be perceived as an outright invasion. Now, rather than calling another person and wondering if it is a good time for that person to talk to us, we can send an e-mail and that person can get back to us when it is convenient.[78]

Many believe that e-mail, chat rooms, instant messages, and the Internet, in addition to enabling us to connect with our friends, are also strengthening family connections by facilitating our contact. They enable us to engage in **distance relating** with family members who live far away. Online Web logs (blogs) for example, are a popular means of keeping in touch with family and friends or others who share our interests. Users post such things as photos, stories, and links they like on their personal sites. Similar to journals, blogs are a favorite pastime for some users, an obsession for others. When blogging becomes an obsession, however, instead of linking family and friends in a virtual world, blogs may cause users to neglect family, friends, and jobs in the real world.[79] Problems can develop when

distance relating
relating with persons via e-mail, chat rooms, and instant messages

the low-quality relationships we nurture in virtual reality replace our higher-quality, real-world relationships.

On the other hand, social networking online serves a number of prosocial functions. The Internet is helping the homebound overcome conditions that make them feel isolated and lonely. While the homebound may not be able to meet in person with others because of their situation, they are now able to initiate and sustain a number of surrrogate online contacts.

Online relationships also have a dark side. Sometimes when clicking their way into online relationships and support groups, the people in need elicit outpourings of sympathy not only from the compassionate and from fellow sufferers but also from incorrigible fakes who lie their way into networks of people with real troubles who have come to care about one another. For example, teenagers present themselves as adults, poor people present themselves as wealthy, and some adults who want to have relationships with children or teens present themselves as members of these groups.[80] Because persons met online may be concealing their true identities, it is wise to proceed cautiously, being careful not to reveal personal

"You can access me by saying simply 'Agnes.'
It is not necessary to add 'dot com.'"

information that could compromise personal security. Children are especially vulnerable to online solicitations, making it necessary for parents to monitor their online usage. Unfortunately, in addition to the relational benefits it presents, the Internet also lends itself to personal misrepresentation and deception.[81]

The Pew Internet and American Life Project reports that approximately 40 percent of American adults say they are not connected to the Internet. A large percentage of these (20 percent) identify themselves as "Net evaders": people living in Internet-connected homes where others go online. Reasons given for remaining offline include limited free time, fear that it will take over their lives, and a desire for face-to-face contact. According to the Pew study, 17 percent of nonusers are Net dropouts, persons who became disillusioned with the online world.[82] Are you a member of either of these two groups?

IMPROVING YOUR RELATIONSHIP SATISFACTION

Our relationships contribute to feelings of happiness or unhappiness, elation or depression. While they can enrich and stimulate us, they can also limit and harm us. To enhance your ability to develop relationships that satisfy, follow these guidelines.

Actively Seek Information from Others and Reinforce Others Attempting to Seek Information from You

People who fail to initiate contacts or fail to reinforce the conversational attempts of others are less likely to build stable foundations for effective relationships. Passive, restrained communicators are simply more likely to remain chronically lonely. Although we all experience short-term loneliness from time

Our relationships can contribute to our feelings of happiness.

Thinking Critically

Reflect and Respond

Using yourself or someone you know as an example, agree or disagree with the following statement by interpersonal communication theorist Steve Duck. Supply reasons and examples that support your stance.

Unfortunately, the evidence is that some people are not good at this basic human activity [conducting close personal relationships] . . . . Relationships do not conduct themselves in the ways that common sense often supposes.[83]

to time, sustained chronic loneliness leads to social apathy, which in turn increases loneliness.

Recognize the Characteristics of Friendship

People who share effective **friendships** report that the following qualities are present: enjoyment (they enjoy each other's company most of the time), acceptance (they accept each other as they are), trust (both assume that one will act in the other's best interest), respect (each assumes that the other will exercise good judgment in making life choices), mutual assistance (they are willing to assist and support each other), confidences (they share experiences and feelings with each other), understanding (they have a sense of what the other thinks is important and why the other behaves as he or she does), and spontaneity (they feel free to be themselves).[84]

friendships
relationships characterized by enjoyment, acceptance, trust, respect, mutual assistance, confidences, understanding, and spontaneity

Recognize That Relationships Evolve

Ours is a mobile and increasingly technological society in which each change we experience has the potential to bring us different relationships. Be prepared for changes in relationships; recognize that in our lives we are likely to experience a certain amount of turnover and change. As we grow and develop, so will our relationships.

Know When to Sever a Relationship

While one party to a relationship may desire to sustain it, not all relationships or connections are meant to continue. When a relationship is draining our energies and our confidence, or when it becomes unhealthy, we need to extricate ourselves from it before it destroys us.

Recognize That Communication Is the Lifeblood of a Relationship

Without communication, relationships shrivel and die. Any relationship that is worth your time and energy depends on effective communication to sustain and nourish it. Your desire and motivation to communicate are key ingredients in the establishment and growth of a relationship.[85]

Revisiting Chapter Objectives

1. **Explain why we need interpersonal relationships.** Communication is one variable common to all relationships. As a result of communication, we establish and nurture or withdraw from and end our relationships. Relationships play many roles in our lives. They fulfill our needs for inclusion, control, and affection.

2. **Define and discuss the following terms: *inclusion, control, and affection.*** We need to feel that others take an interest in us, that they view us as capable of exerting control over our lives, and that we are lovable. It is through conversation that we establish, maintain, and end our relationships.

3. **Explain and distinguish among social penetration theory, cost–benefit/social exchange theory, and relational dialectics theory.** Every relationship we share is unique and varies in breadth (how many topics we discuss with the other person) and depth (how much we are willing to reveal to the other person about our feelings). Most relationships develop according to a social penetration model, beginning with narrow breadth and shallow depth; over time, some relationships increase in breadth and depth, becoming wider, more intimate, or both. Cost–benefit/social exchange theory holds that we work to maintain those relationships that yield the greatest personal profits and fewest costs. Relational dialectics explores the oscillation that occurs between conflicting relationship goals.

4. **Identify and describe the 10 stages of relationships.** Researchers have identified a number of stages our relationships may pass through: initiating, experimenting, intensifying, integrating, bonding, differentiating, circumscribing, stagnating, avoiding, and termination. Note that a relationship may stabilize at any stage. When the participants disagree about the point of stabilization, problems are likely to arise.

5. **Discuss how deception, gender, and technology affect interpersonal communication.** Relationships are also affected by gender and cultural preferences, lies or deception, vulnerability and trust, and even technological innovations.

6. **Identify ways to enhance your satisfaction with your relationships.** It is important to recognize that how we communicate plays a key part in determining whether our relationships are as effective and rewarding for us as they could be.

Resources for Further Inquiry and Reflection

To apply your understanding of how the principles in Chapter 8 are at work in our daily lives, consult the following resources for further inquiry and reflection. Or, if you prefer, choose any other appropriate resource. Then connect the ideas expressed in your chosen selection with the communication concepts and issues you are learning about both in and out of class.

Listen to Me

"You'll Think of Me" (Keith Urban)
"Crash into Me" (The Dave Matthews Band)
"Don't Know Why" (Norah Jones)
"She's Leaving Home" (The Beatles)
"Your Song" (Elton John)
"You've Got a Friend" (James Taylor)
"Fifty Ways to Leave Your Lover" (Paul Simon)

These songs explore close relationships. Choose one and discuss the speaker's beliefs about his or her role in the relationship.

 ## View Me

Elizabethtown   *Unfaithful*
Shopgirl   *Sweet November*
Prime   *Secrets and Lies*
The Boiler Room   *When Harry Met Sally*
Wall Street

These films explore the stages of relationships and why we maintain or end a relationship, as well as the role honesty and deception play in relationship building or termination. Choose one film and use it to discuss the factors just identified.

 ## Read Me

Candace Bushnell. *Lipstick Jungle*. New York: Hyperion, 2005.

Lauren Weisberger. *The Devil Wears Prada*. New York: Broadway Books, 2004.

Edward Albee. *Who's Afraid of Virginia Woolf?* New York: Dramatist Play Service, 1962.

Robert Harling. *Steel Magnolias*. New York: Dramatist Play Service, 1998.

William Shakespeare. *The Taming of the Shrew*. Edited by Robert Heilman. New York: Penguin Books, 1998.

Tennessee Williams. *A Streetcar Named Desire*. New York: New American Library, 1947.

These works explore the nature of friendships and/or intimate relationships. Choose one and use it to describe how the nature of the communication shared by people contributes to the health or toxicity of their relationship.

 ## Tell Me

Share with the class the insights you gained from your chosen Listen to Me, View Me, or Read Me selection.

In a brief presentation, respond to the following questions: What do you consider the most acceptable rationale for lying? Do you think it is more acceptable to lie if the lie will benefit you or if the lie will save others from hurt?

Key Chapter Terminology

Use the Communication Works CD-ROM and the Online Learning Center at www.mhhe.com/gamble9 to further your knowledge of the following terminology.

affection 212
autistic society 210
avoiding 220
bonding 218
breadth 215
circumscribing 219
comparison level 223
comparison level for alternatives 223
control 212

cost–benefit/social exchange theory 222
depth 215
dialectical tensions 223
differentiating 219
distance relating 230
experimenting 218
equivocate 225
friendships 233
gossip mill 213

Communication Works

online learning center

www.mhhe.com/gamble9

Idioms in Translation

adds spice—adds interest

bond—connection

breadth of topics—number of topics

break up or sever the bonds of a relationship—end a relationship

connect with—communicate with

depth of topics—how much you reveal

dissolve a relationship—end a relationship

small talk—superficial conversation

what makes us tick—what makes us who we are

Communication
Works

online learning center

www.mhhe.com/gamble9

Test Your Understanding

Go to the *Self Quizzes* on the Communication Works CD-ROM and the book's Online Learning Center at www.mhhe.com/gamble9.

Notes

1. Jeanne McDowell. "When You Wish upon TV." *Time*, June 13, 2005, pp. 48–50.
2. Virginia Satir. *The New Peoplemaking*. Palo Alto, CA: Science and Behavior Books, 1998, p. 51.
3. John L. Locke. *The De-Voicing of Society: Why We Don't Talk to Each Other Anymore*. New York: Simon & Schuster, 1998.
4. Bruce Headlam. "Awash in All These Words, Will We Forget How to Talk?" *The New York Times*, December 17, 1998, p. G-12.
5. John Naisbitt. *Megatrends*. New York: Warner, 1984, pp. 35–52.
6. See Debra Lynn Veal. "Electric Friendship, Information—Even Love." *Sunday Record*, April 3, 1994.
7. See Duane Stoltzfus. "Meeting á la Modem: Personal Computer Goes Interpersonal." *Sunday Record*, December 19, 1993.
8. Catherine Greenman. "From Yakety-Yak to Clackety-Clack." *The New York Times*, November 5, 1998, pp. G-1, G-7.
9. See Judy Jeannin. "Sister Can You Spare a Moment?" *Sunday Record*, January 30, 1994.
10. J. O'Neil. "Help Others for a Longer Life." *The New York Times*, November 12, 2002, p. F6.
11. William C. Schutz. *The Interpersonal Underworld*. Palo Alto, CA: Science and Behavior Books, 1966, pp. 18–20.
12. Steve Duck. *Human Relationships*, 3rd ed. Thousand Oaks, CA: Sage, 1999, p. 57.
13. *Time*, December 20, 1993, p. 15.

14. See, for example, Robert A. Bell. "Conversational Involvement and Loneliness." *Communication Monographs* 52, 1985, pp. 218–235.

15. Robert A. Bell and Michael Roloff. "Making a Love Connection: Loneliness and Communication Competence in the Dating Marketplace." *Communication Quarterly* 39:1, winter 1991, pp. 58–74.

16. Anna Quindlen. "The Human Touch." *The New York Times,* May 14, 1994, p. 21.

17. Schutz, p. 24.

18. Andrea Heiman. "Flirting Still Has Its Attractions." *Sunday Record,* March 20, 1994.

19. Robert E. Nofsinger. *Everyday Conversation.* Newbury Park, CA: Sage, 1991, p. 1.

20. See Deborah Cameron. *Good Talk? Living and Working in a Communication Culture.* Thousand Oaks, CA: Sage, 2000.

21. Anita L. Vangelisti and Mary A. Banski. "Couples' Debriefing Conversations: The Impact of Gender, Occupation, and Demographic Characteristics." *Family Relations* 42:2, April 1993, pp. 149–157.

22. Karen Shafer. "Talk in the Middle: Two Conversational Skills for Friendship." *English Journal* 82:1, January 1993, pp. 53–55.

23. B. Smith. "Care and Feeling of the Office Grapevine." *Management Review* 85, February 1996, p. 6; and L. Hilton. "They Heard It through the Grapevine," *South Florida Business Journal* 21, August, 2000, p. 53.

24. R. Westen. "The Real Slant of Gossip." *Psychology Today,* July 17, 1996, p. 44.

25. M. M. Turner, M. A. Mazur, N. Wendel, and R. Winslow. "Relational Ruin or Social Glue? The Joint Effect of Relationship Type and Gossip Valence on Liking, Trust, and Expertise." *Communication Monographs* 70, June 2003, pp. 129–141.

26. William B. Gudykunst. *Bridging Differences: Effective Intergroup Communication,* 3rd ed. Thousand Oaks, CA: Sage, 1998.

27. Tamar Lewin. "Poll of Teen-Agers: Battle of the Sexes on Roles in Family." *The New York Times,* July 11, 1994.

28. Heiman.

29. Heiman.

30. Julia T. Wood and C. Inman. "In a Different Mode: Recognizing Male Modes of Closeness." *Journal of Applied Communication Research,* August 1993.

31. Julia T. Wood. *Gendered Lives,* 3rd ed. Belmont, CA: Wadsworth, 1999, p. 201.

32. Deborah Tannen. *The Argument Culture: Moving from Debate to Dialogue.* New York: Random House, 1998, pp. 186–187.

33. J. D. Ragsdale. "Gender, Satisfaction Level, and the Use of Relational Maintenance Strategies in Marriage." *Communication Monographs* 63, 1996, pp. 354–369.

34. See M. Hecht, S. Ribeau, and J. Alberts. "An Afro-American Perspective on Interethnic Communication." *Communication Monographs* 56, 1989, pp. 385–410; and M. Hecht, S. Ribeau, and M. Sedano. "A Mexican-American Perspective on Interethnic Communication." *International Journal of Intercultural Relations* 14, 1990, pp. 31–55.

35. H. C. Triandis. *Culture and Social Behavior.* New York: McGraw-Hill, 1994, p. 30.

36. M. J. Collier. "Communication Competence Problematics in Ethnic Friendships." *Communication Monographs* 63, 1996, pp. 314–336.

37. I. Altman and D. A. Taylor. *Social Penetration: The Development of Interpersonal Relationships.* New York: Holt, Rinehart & Winston, 1973.

38. Mark L. Knapp and Anita L. Vangelisti. *Interpersonal Communication and Human Relationships,* 2nd ed. Boston: Allyn & Bacon, 1992, p. 33.

39. Alan Garner. *Conversationally Speaking.* New York: McGraw-Hill, 1981, p. 69.

40. Knapp and Vangelisti.

41. Michael Korda. "Small Talk." *Signature,* 1986, p. 78.

42. See Lawrence B. Rosenfield and Daniella Bordaray-Sciolino. "Self-Disclosure as a Communication Strategy during Relationship Termination." Paper presented at the national meeting of the Speech Communication Association, Denver, CO, November 1985.

43. Rosenfield and Bordaray-Sciolino.

44. See, for example, H. S. Kushner. *When Bad Things Happen to Good People*. New York: Schocken Books, 1981.

45. Erica Goode. "Experts Offer Fresh Insights into the Mind of the Grieving Child." *The New York Times*, March 28, 2000, pp. F7, F12.

46. N. Stevens. "Re-engaing: New Partnerships in Late-Life Widowhood." *Aging International* 27:4, spring 2003, pp. 27–43.

47. See J. De Jong Gierveld. "The Dilemma of Repartnering: Considerations of Older Men and Women Entering New Intimate Relationships in Later Life." *Aging International* 27:4, spring 2003, pp. 61–79; S. G. Karlsson, and K. Borell. "Intimacy and Autonomy, Gender and Ageing: Living Apart Together." *Aging International* 27:4, spring 2003, pp. 11–27; and K. Davidson. "Gender Differences in New Partnership Choices and Constraints for Older Widows and Widowers." *Aging International* 27:4, spring 2003, pp. 43–61.

48. J. W. Thibaut and H. H. Kelly. *The Social Psychology of Groups*. New York: Wiley, 1959.

49. See Richard West and Lynn H. Turner. *Introducing Communication Theory: Analysis and Application*. Mountain View, CA: Mayfield, 2000, pp. 180–190.

50. L. A. Baxter and B. M. Montgomery. *Relating: Dialogues and Dialectics*. New York: Guilford, 1996; and L. A. Baxter. "Dialectical Contradictions in Relationship Development." *Journal of Social and Personal Relationships* 7, 1990, pp. 69–88.

51. See also Sandra Petronio, ed. *Balancing the Secrets of Private Disclosures*. Mahwah, NJ: Erlbaum, 1999.

52. C. A. VanLear. "Testing a Cyclical Model of Communicative Openness in Relationship Development." *Communication Monographs* 58, 1991, pp. 337–361.

53. J. T. Wood, L. Dendy, E. Dordek, M. Germany, and S. Varallo. "Dialectic of Difference: A Thematic Analysis of Intimates' Meanings for Differences." In K. Carter and M. Presnell, eds. *Interpretive Approaches to Interpersonal Communication*. New York: State University of New York Press, 1994, pp. 115–136.

54. See, for example, L. Anolli, M. Balconi, and Rita Ciceri. "Deceptive Miscommunication Theory (DeMIT): A New Model for the Analysis of Deceptive Communication." In A. Luigi, R. Ciceri et al. eds. *Say Not to Say: New Perspectives on Miscommunication*. *Studies in New Technologies and Practices in Communication*. Amsterdam, Netherlands Antilles: IOS Press. pp. 73–100.

55. See J. F. Roiger. "Using Expectations and Causes of Behavior: Naïve Perceptions of Differing Acts of Deception." Paper presented at the annual meeting of the National Communication Association, New Orleans, LA, November 2002.

56. See Erica Goode. "To Tell the Truth, It's Awfully Hard to Spot a Liar." *The New York Times*, May 11, 1999, pp. F-1, F-9; and William G. Powers. "The Effects of Gender and Consequence upon Perceptions of Deceivers." *Communication Quarterly* 41:3, summer 1993, pp. 328–337.

57. Goode; Janny Scott. "Bright, Shining or Dark: American Way of Lying." *The New York Times*, August 16, 1998, p. WK-3; and Bernice Kanner. "Americans Lie, or So They Say." *The New York Times*, June 2, 1996, p. 43.

58. Sissela Bok. *Lying*. New York: Pantheon, 1978. See also Sissela Bok. *Secrets*. New York: Random House, 1989.

59. Steven A. McCornack and Timothy R. Levine. "When Lies Are Uncovered: Emotional and Relational Outcomes of Discovered Deception." *Communication Monographs* 57, June 1990, p. 119.

60. C. Camden, M. T. Motley, and A. Wilson. "White Lies in Interpersonal Communication: A Taxonomy and Preliminary Investigation of Social Motivations." *Western Journal of Speech Communication* 48, 1984, pp. 309–325.

61. See, for example, J. B. Bavelas, A. Black, N. Chovil, and J. Mullett. *Equivocal Communication*. Newbury Park, CA: Sage, 1990, p. 171.

62. Goode.

63. For an extended discussion of deception, see Dariusz Galasinski. *The Language of Deception*. Thousand Oaks, CA: Sage, 2000.

64. J. K. Rempel and J. G. Holmes. "How Do I Trust Thee?" *Psychology Today*, February 1986.

65. A. L. Vangelisti and L. P. Crumley. "Reactions to Messages That Hurt: The Influence of Relational Contexts." *Communication Monographs* 65, 1998, pp. 173–196.

66. Virginia Rohan. "Have We No Shame?" *The Record*, September 26, 2004, pp. E1, E4.

67. Natalie Angier. "Laughs: Rhythmic Bursts of Social Glue." *The New York Times*, February 27, 1996, pp. C-1, C-5.

68. Angier. Also see Regina Barreca. *They Used to Call Me Snow White . . . but I Drifted: Women's Strategic Use of Humor.* New York: Penguin Books, 1991.

69. Patricia Winters Lauro. "Online Dating." *The New York Times*, January 27, 2003, p. C9.

70. Karen S. Peterson. "Dating Game Has Changed." *USA Today*, February 11, 2003, p. 9D.

71. M. R. Parks and K. Floyd. "Making Friends in Cyberspace." *Journal of Communication* 46, winter 1996, pp. 80–97.

72. Parks and Floyd; and M. L. Nice and R. Katzev. "Internet Romantics: The Frequency and Nature of Romantic On-line Relationships." *CyberPsychology and Behavior* 1, fall 1998, pp. 217–233.

73. A. N. Markham. *Life Online: Researching Real Experience in Virtual Space.* Walnut Creek, CA: AltaMira, 1998.

74. Scott McCartney. "Society's Sub Cultures Meet by Modem." *The Wall Street Journal*, December 8, 1994, p. B1.

75. Sherry Turkle. *Life on the Screen: Identity in the Age of the Internet.* New York: Simon & Schuster, 1995; and Katie Hafner. "At Heart of a Cyberstudy, the Human Essence." *The New York Times*, June 18, 1998, p. G-9.

76. N. H. Nie. "Sociability, Interpersonal Relations, and the Internet: Reconciling Conflicting Findings." *American Behavioral Scientist* 45:3, November 2001, pp. 420–426.

77. Y. Amichai-Hamburger and E. Ben-Artzi. "Loneliness and Internet Use." *Computers in Human Behavior* 19:1, January 2003, pp. 71–81.

78. See, for example, Esther Dyson. *A Design for Living in the Digital Age.* New York: Broadway Books, 1998.

79. Katie Hafner. "For Some, the Blogging Never Stops." *The New York Times*, May 27, 2004, pp. G1, G7.

80. See, for example, M. Lewis. "Faking It." *New York Times Magazine*, July 15, 2001, pp. 32–37, 44, 61–63.

81. Denise Grady. "Faking Pain and Suffering in Internet Support Groups." *The New York Times*, April 23, 1998, pp. G-1, G-7.

82. Katie Hafner. "Eluding the Web's Snare." *The New York Times*, April 17, 2003, pp. G1, G5.

83. Steve Duck. *Understanding Relationships.* New York: Guilford, 1991, pp. 1–2.

84. Keith E. Davis. "Near and Dear: Friendship and Love Compared." *Psychology Today*, February 1985, pp. 22–30.

85. For a discussion of how to enhance the teaching of relationships in the basic course, see Diane Tkinson Gorcyca. "Enhancing the Instruction of Relationship Development in the Basic Communication Course." Paper presented at the annual meeting of the Speech Communication Association, Miami Beach, FL, November 18–21, 1993.

CHAPTER 9

Person to Person: Relationships in Context

After finishing this chapter, you should be able to

1. Identify and distinguish among the following relationship life contexts: acquaintanceship, friendship, and romantic, family, and work relationships.

2. Define and distinguish among the following terms: *emotional intelligence*, *emotion state*, and *emotion trait*.

3. Explain how attraction, proximity, reinforcement, similarity, complementarity, and the suppression and disclosure of feelings can affect the development of relationships.

4. Define *assertiveness*, *nonassertiveness*, and *aggressiveness*, and explain how feelings can be handled effectively during conflicts.

5. Identify behaviors that foster or impede the development of a relationship based on assertiveness.

6. Draw and explain a relationship window.

7. Create and explain a DESC script.

There are no empty people, only people who have deadened their feelings and feel empty.

—Theodore Isaac Rubin

For years, many of us have watched MTV's *The Real World,* a reality-type program in which a number of strangers relocate into a comfortable home or apartment, agreeing to live there together for a period of time. A camera follows their every move as they get to know one another and establish a variety of interpersonal relationships. Some form real friendships. Some date and end up lovers. Others dislike each other intensely and find themselves enemies. We observe as their layers of anonymity are peeled away, and we listen as the "houseguests" share some rather raw, emotionally intense interactions. We imagine what it would be like to be them. More recently, we viewed two other reality-type programs, *Wife Swap* and *Trading Spaces: Meet Your New Mommy.* In these, parents or other adults trade families, sharing their lives with other people's spouses and children. Can you imagine agreeing to trade relationships with a stranger? Can you see yourself sharing your life and personal relationships with millions of unknown viewers? The people in these shows did just that—displaying their conflicts and emotions for us to judge.

Over time, some participants demonstrate that they can handle their emotions, while others act more like very young children, revealing an inability to control their emotions and a general lack of emotional intelligence. **Emotional intelligence**, a relatively recent concept, includes the ability to motivate oneself, to control impulses, to recognize and regulate one's moods, to empathize, and to hope.[1] Our success in our relationships depends to a great degree on how emotionally intelligent or mature we are. If, for example, we can understand and manage our emotions, such as anger and jealousy, and be sensitive to others' feelings as well, then we can also improve our ability to get along with a broad array of people in diverse contexts.

Thus, while this chapter explores relationships in context, it is also about emotions and feelings—your emotions and feelings and the emotions and feelings of people with whom you share relationships.

In successful relationships we communicate clearly and effectively about our feelings.[2] Relationships involve a huge amount of emotional work.

■ ■ ■

RELATIONSHIP CONTEXTS: FROM FRIENDSHIP TO ROMANCE TO FAMILY TO WORK

Relationships are colored by the life contexts in which they occur. By exploring the different kinds of relationships we share, we can learn how to strike a balance between intimacy and distance with the people we interact with regularly, whether

emotional intelligence
the ability to motivate oneself, to control impulses, to recognize and regulate one's moods, to empathize, and to hope

that interaction occurs with friends, lovers, family members, or persons with whom we work. We will see how we have been socialized to express or limit our expression of emotions about relationships, depending on the relational context we find ourselves in.

Relationships, Uncertainty Reduction, and Predicted Outcomes

No matter how close we eventually become with another person, we start out as strangers. What is your goal when you meet someone for the first time? According to uncertainty reduction theory, when we initially meet someone, uncertainty characterizes our relationship.[3] Because we prefer the known to the unknown, our communication goal is to reduce the uncertainty we have about that person.[4] To create understanding, we need to gain knowledge. We desire to find out what the other person is like and we want to figure out how to act. Do you agree? If so, how do you accomplish your objectives?

We rely on three key strategies to reduce uncertainty and increase predictability during an interpersonal relationship: (1) passive strategies, during which we unobtrusively observe the other person while he or she is engaged in doing something, preferably interacting with others; (2) interactive strategies, during which we communicate directly with the other person, asking probing questions that encourage the person to talk about himself or herself; and (3) active strategies, during which we get information about this person from a third party, manipulate a situation that enables us to observe another person, or set up a situation in which we can have someone else observe us as we talk with the other person. The more we interact with and converse with another person, the more our uncertainty decreases. The more we discover that we and the other person share things, the more our uncertainty wanes. The more we and the other person share a communication network—that is, interact with the same people—the more uncertainty is reduced. Since interpersonal ignorance is uncomfortable, the urge to reduce uncertainty motivates communication. If we are able to reduce uncertainty to the point that we become comfortable in the situation, our interaction will increase and the relationship may continue. Just as reducing uncertainty acts as a bridge to relational development, so it can also be used to bridge some culture gaps.[5]

Another factor that affects relationship development is the predicted outcome value of the potential relationship. Researchers believe that we formulate a personal hypothesis regarding whether or not a given relationship will be rewarding. Because we typically have limited information at the outset of a relationship, our initial judgment may be based on a person's physical appearance, the behaviors we observe, or the information we obtain from others.[6] As we reduce our uncertainty, our ability to make accurate predictions about a relationship's future increases. How accurate have you been at predicting the success of relationships at a first meeting?

Acquaintanceships

acquaintanceships
relationships with persons we know by name and with whom we converse when the chance arises

We have **acquaintanceships** with people we know by name, with whom we converse when the chance arises, but with whom our interaction is usually limited in scope and quality. Unless we want to turn an acquaintance into a friend, we rarely go out of our way to see that person, preferring instead to leave our meeting each other to chance.

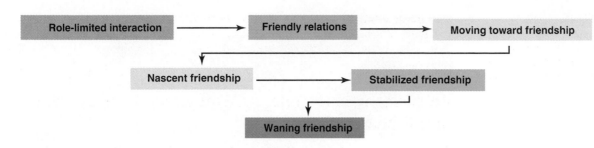

FIGURE 9.1   Rawlins's Six-Stage Model of Friendship.

Friendships

A number of our acquaintanceships develop into friendships. Friends, in contrast to acquaintances, seek each other out, like being with each other, and exhibit a strong mutual regard. Friends accept each other, confide in each other, trust each other to keep any confidences disclosed confidential, provide each other with emotional support, share interests, and expect their relationship to last.[7]

Of course, we might grow closer to some friends than others. It is to our very closest friends that we usually confide our most private thoughts and feelings. We share a greater degree of intimacy with the friends we feel closest to.

As friendships develop and become closer, we begin to increase our knowledge of and trust in each other, and both the breadth and depth of our relationship are enhanced. Bill Rawlins's six-stage model explains how friendships develop.[8] (See Figure 9.1.)

ROLE-LIMITED INTERACTION

According to Rawlins, friendships begins with **role-limited interaction,** during which two individuals make initial contact in some context. Someone we meet at work, in a restaurant, on an airplane, or at a sports event can develop into a friend. The first stage of our potential friendship occurs when we first meet. At this point, we are unclear whether our relationship will develop, and we act tentatively in relating to each other. We lack personal knowledge about each other, and we are hesitant to reveal personal information. Typically, we trade polite exchanges and rely on standard scripts when conversing.

FRIENDLY RELATIONS

The next interaction stage, **friendly relations,** finds us exploring whether we have enough in common to continue building a relationship. We engage in more small talk in an effort to see if our interest is reciprocated. We drop our guard somewhat and become more expressive, as we seek to discover if the other person is interested in us as well.

MOVING TOWARD FRIENDSHIP

During the **moving toward friendship** stage, we step beyond conventional social rules and role playing and make small personal disclosures as a means of indicating that we'd like to expand our friendship. We invite the other person to interact with us in a context outside those that happen serendipitously. We might, for example, ask if the person might like to go out for a cup of coffee, to the movies,

What is a Friend? I will tell you. It is a person with whom you dare to be yourself.

—Frank Crane

Do you agree with Frank Crane's definition of friendship?

role-limited interaction
the beginning stage of friendship

friendly relations
the friendship stage in which we explore whether we have enough in common to continue building a relationship

moving toward friendship
the friendship stage in which we make small personal disclosures demonstrating the desire to expand our relationship

During the nascent friendship stage, friends may run together. What kinds of activities do you get together with your friends for?

or to the library. Once in a different setting, we can reveal more of our attitudes, beliefs, and values to each other.

NASCENT FRIENDSHIP

nascent friendship
the friendship stage that finds us considering each other friends

As the other person echoes our moves toward friendship, we enter the **nascent friendship** stage and begin to consider each other friends. We substitute our own rules in place of the social stereotypes and standards that regulated our interactions to this point. For example, we might decide to get together every Sunday afternoon to run in the park or every Friday night for a movie or to have dinner. We plan the activities we will share together. Our interactions become more regular.

STABILIZED FRIENDSHIP

stabilized friendship
the friendship stage in which we decide that our friendship is secure and will continue

We enter the **stabilized friendship** stage once we decide that our friendship is secure and will continue. We now count on the other person to be there without our specifically planning to meet. We trust each other and respond to each other in ways that display our trustworthiness. We get together more frequently across a greater number of settings. We share more intimate information and reveal the fears and vulnerabilities that we keep hidden from most other people.

WANING FRIENDSHIP

waning friendship
the friendship stage during which friends begin to drift apart

When friends begin to drift apart, they enter the **waning friendship** stage. Sometimes this happens when friends take their friendship for granted. Other times, for one reason or another, one or both make less of a personal effort to keep the friendship going. Perhaps career, personal, or family obligations get in the way. Perhaps a trust is violated or one person develops new interests that the other person does not share. Since friendships do not maintain themselves, when one or more of the preceding situations occur, the friendship may dissolve.

Romantic Relationships

Romantic love is different from the kind of love we feel for our friends or family members. Although statistics reveal that over half of all marriages in the United States ultimately fail, when we enter into marriage or a civil union, we expect it to last. In fact, it is the expectation of permanence that helps distinguish a romantic relationship from other kinds of relationships.

Three additional characteristics unique to romantic relationships are commitment (the intention to remain in the relationship even if trouble occurs), passion (intensely positive feelings of attraction that make you want to be with the other person), and intimacy (sustained feelings of closeness and connection). Although any one of these can exist without the others, all three are essential to a romantic relationship.[9]

Romantic relationships, like friendships, develop in stages that reflect each party's perception of the amount of self-disclosing that is occurring and the kind of intimacy shared.

According to social historian and co-director of the National Marriage Project at Rutgers University, Barbara Dafoe Whitehead, we face "a contemporary crisis in dating and mating."[10] Most young men and women today want to be established in a career before they start looking for love. When ready for a true romantic relationship, they are not sure how to find it. The fast pace of our society leads some of us to expect instant relationships.

Not all romantic relationships are healthy. Some turn dark and become destructive. When a romantic relationship becomes dysfunctional, it is characterized by **toxic communication,** which includes the consistent use of verbal abuse and/or physical or sexual aggression or violence. Although spousal abuse is all too common, the highest incidence of violence occurs among unmarried cohabiting couples.[11] Relationship well-being is higher if a relationship we share develops in the way we think it should.[12]

Like romantic relationships, dysfunctional relationships move through a series of stages. During the first stage, relational tensions build in the abuser, who blames a partner for problems and seeks an excuse to vent anger. In the second stage, the tensions erupt into violence. In the third stage, the abuser apologizes and promises to make it up to the victim, assuring the victim that it will never happen again. In the fourth stage, there is a lull in violent activity, during which the victim again feels loved. Ultimately, however, relational tensions again build, and the cycle of abuse continues.[13]

toxic communication
the consistent use of verbal abuse and/or physical or sexual aggression or violence

Family Relationships

Most of our earliest relationships occurred within our family. Family members mutually influence each other as they work out the nature of their relationships. They are also expected to play certain roles in relation to each other and to the family as a whole. Among the roles family members perform are wage earner, homemaker, financial manager, and child care provider. These roles may be shared or may be the prime responsibility of a single family member. In healthy families, role relationships evolve as family members grow, develop, and enter different life stages.

Family members also have expectations for each other. They expect to receive emotional support from one another. They expect members to pull together to preserve the family unit. The rules that guide family interaction help

MediaWise

regulate the behavior of family members. They reveal how family members divide tasks—who is in charge of what and the like. To thrive in a family, you need either to follow or to successfully renegotiate the rules that prescribe member behavior.

When a family practices healthy communication, members offer emotional and physical support to each other, reveal their feelings and thoughts to each other, meet each other's needs, and display flexibility and a willingness to adapt to change. On the other hand, when a family's communication practices become dysfunctional—that is, when they prohibit members from adequately expressing their feelings or needs or contain messages that are physically, sexually, or emotionally abusive—then family relationships suffer and deteriorate.[14]

Work Relationships

Friendships affect the well-being of both individuals and organizations. Even at work, we develop friendship networks that benefit us both in and out of the office.[15] When we work in an organization, we share interdependent relationships with the other people who work in the organization. When we are knowledgeable about how to build person-to-person on-the-job relationships, we put ourselves in a better position to nurture both our personal growth and the organization's growth. The notion of the rugged individual in the organization appears to be passé; replacing the rugged individual is the team player—a person who is effective working with one or more other employees both within and between groups. Team players realize the potential to work together to develop meaningful partnerships with many others in the organization.[16]

The relationship level is where most of the work of the organization gets done; it is also where many of the organization's difficulties are encountered.

In any organization, we find relationships in which some people are leaders and others are team members. Leaders and team members spend much of their time interacting. As with other relationships, when interactions are perceived as supportive, open, and honest; when people operate in a climate that is trusting and confirming; when they feel part of a participative organization; and when leaders have a high tolerance for disagreement, job satisfaction is usually high. These aspects of communication will be discussed in greater depth in Part Three of this book.

EMOTIONS IN RELATIONSHIPS: FACTORING IN FEELINGS

Emotions play a role in all relationships. When a relationship is healthy, relational partners understand how their emotions affect their relationship and how the relationship affects their emotions. How well are you able to read and express feelings in the relationships you share? For example, can you tell and react appropriately when a friend, family member, or co-worker is feeling happy, grows sad, becomes angry, or experiences jealousy? Can your relational partners do the same for you?

Distinguishing between Emotion States and Traits

Whether you realize it or not, at any given time, you are experiencing some emotion to some degree. In any particular context with any particular people, you will almost certainly have certain thoughts or attitudes about the situation. These thoughts or attitudes will give rise to a particular emotion state. According to theorist Carroll E. Izard, an **emotion state** is a particular emotional process of limited duration, lasting from seconds to hours and varying from mild to intense. One example is a state of sadness. Izard notes that "chronically intense emotions, or frequent episodes of intense emotion, may indicate psychopathology."[18] Thus a person who always feels an emotion intensely—who is always in an extreme state of joy, depression, or anger—is unusual.

emotion state
a particular emotional process of limited duration

In addition to emotion states (such as sadness), people may also exhibit **emotion traits**—that is, the tendency to experience specific emotions when interacting with others. For instance, if you were described as exhibiting a sadness trait, this would indicate that you had a tendency to experience sadness frequently in your daily interactions.[19]

emotion traits
the tendency to experience specific emotions when interacting with others

What emotion traits have you experienced or observed in others in the past 24 hours? Does any particular emotion trait punctuate either your own interpersonal behavior or the behavior of those with whom you habitually relate?

Not everyone experiences an emotion or expresses their feelings in the same way. Your ability to accept the reactions of other people indicates your awareness that they may experience responses to events and situations that are separate and distinct from your own. As Carroll Izard observes, "The joyful person is more apt to see the world through 'rose colored glasses,' the distressed or sad individual is more apt to construe the remarks of others as critical, and the fearful person is inclined only to see the frightening object (tunnel vision)."[20] Feelings are our reaction to what we perceive; they define and color our relationships and image of the world. Whether we are at work or at home, with a friend or significant other; whether we want to create liking, build trust, engage in self-disclosure, influence others, resolve conflicts, or handle anger, we need to be in touch with and communicate feelings.

WORKING THROUGH FEELINGS IN RELATIONSHIPS

Feelings are at the heart of our relationships. A key step in the study of how feelings affect and color relationships is to recognize what causes us to seek out some people as relational partners, but not others.

Factors in Attraction

Why are we attracted to one person and not to another? Why do we develop a positive attitude toward one person and a negative attitude toward another? A number of researchers have identified variables that influence how attracted people feel toward one another.[21] Attractiveness (not surprisingly), proximity, similarity, reinforcement, and complementarity are consistently named as determiners of attraction.

ATTRACTIVENESS

The first kind of information we process when we interact with someone is that person's outward attractiveness. We tend to like physically attractive people more than physically unattractive people, and we tend to like people who exhibit pleasant personalities more than those who exhibit unpleasant personalities. Of course, judgments of what is physically attractive and what constitutes a pleasant personality are subjective.[22] However, whatever we perceive as pleasing functions as an important element in creating and sustaining interpersonal attraction.

PROXIMITY

Proximity is the second factor influencing attraction. We usually find that, for the most part, we enjoy interacting with people with whom we work or with people who live close to us. Apparently, physical nearness affects the amount of attraction we feel. Living physically close to another person or working near another person gives us ample opportunity to interact, talk, share similar activities, and thus form an attachment. For these reasons, the closer two people of the opposite sex are geographically, the more likely it is that they will be attracted to each other and marry. In all fairness, however, we should examine an opposite effect of proximity. According to Ellen Berscheid and Elaine Walster, the authors of *Interpersonal Attraction*, the closer people are located, the more likely it is that they can come to dislike each other. Berscheid and Walster note: "While propinquity may be a necessary condition for attraction, it probably is also a necessary condition for hatred."[23] What do you think?

REINFORCEMENT

Explore relationships you shared with a person who was critical of you, one who praised you, one who cooperated with you, and one who competed with you. Which relationship caused the most problems? Which was the most satisfying? Which was the most productive?

Reinforcement is the third factor appearing in practically all theories of interpersonal attraction. We will feel positive about people who reward us or who are associated with our experiences of being rewarded, and we will feel animosity or dislike for people who punish us or are associated with our experiences of punishment. Thus, we are likely to like people who praise us, like us, and cooperate with us more than people who criticize us, dislike us, and oppose or compete with us. Of course, reinforcement can backfire: If people become overzealous in their praise and fawn over us too much, we will question their sincerity and motivation. But in general, as social psychologist Eliot Aronson notes, "We like people whose behavior provides us with a maximum reward at minimum cost."[24]

SIMILARITY

Similarity also affects our attraction to others. We are attracted to people whose attitudes and interests are similar to our own and who like and dislike the things we like and dislike. We usually like people who agree with us more than we like those who disagree with us, especially when we are discussing issues we consider salient or significant. In effect, similarity helps provide us with social validation:

It gives us the evidence we need to evaluate the "correctness" of our opinions or beliefs. We also expect people who hold attitudes similar to our own to like us more than people who hold attitudes that are dissimilar to ours. Perhaps if we believed that everyone we met could not help liking us, we would more readily associate with unfamiliar people who held attitudes different from our own. By seeking the company of "similars," we play it safe.

COMPLEMENTARITY

Not all the evidence suggests that we seek to relate only to carbon copies of ourselves, however. In fact, **complementarity**—the last of the factors influencing interpersonal attraction—suggests just the opposite. Instead of being attracted to people who are similar to us, we frequently find ourselves attracted to people who are dissimilar in one or more ways. Both psychologist Theodore Reik and sociologist Robert Winch note that we often tend to fall in love with people who possess characteristics that we admire but do not ourselves possess. Thus, a dominant woman might seek a submissive man, and a socially awkward man might seek a socially poised woman.

complementarity
the attraction principle which states that opposites attract

Can You Feel What I Feel?

Our relationships with most of the people we contact in the course of a lifetime will be transitory and will not amount to much. At times, however, we find that our interchanges continue; then it becomes quite important to be able to determine what the person with whom we are communicating is feeling. At that point, it is just as necessary for us to understand the world of the other person as it is for us to understand ourselves.

Feelings by themselves are not inherently good or bad. Feelings as such do not disrupt relationships, build walls, or add problems to your life. Rather, it is what you think and how you act when experiencing feelings that can affect a relationship for better or worse. For example, anger and fear are not necessarily harmful. As Izard notes, "Anger is sometimes positively correlated with survival, and more often with the defense and maintenance of personal integrity and the correction of social injustice."[25] Fear may also be associated with survival and at times helps us regulate destructive aggressive urges. Thus, it is not any emotion itself that is an issue but, rather, how you deal with the emotion and the effect it has on you and on those who are important to you.

ANGER'S EFFECTS

Why do you become angry with another person? Most typically, anger results from interference with the pursuit of a goal. Being either physically or psychologically restrained from doing what you would like to do can produce anger. So can being personally insulted

Learning to express anger constructively is a valuable skill.

Media Wise

Rants and Revelations

On radio and television talk shows, on MTV, in blogs, in political and self-help columns, and in books, we find people ranting, engaging in name-calling, venting, delivering tirades, and also revealing their innermost secrets. Listening and reacting to extremely angry or confessional human beings are new entertainment forms.[30]

Song lyrics, Internet sites, and blogs contain frequent references to anger and/or the private thoughts of their authors or creators. Talk show hosts and guests spew hate across the airwaves and cable, probe for and reveal new depths of intimacy, and confess to having dark thoughts or desires. Is cacophony in media driving out

reason? Are public, personal confessions making personal disclosures less meaningful?

Consider these questions:

1. What functions do you think mediated rants serve? Do we need to take steps to restore civility into the common discussion of social problems? If you think no steps are necessary, why not? If you think they are, what are they?

2. With respect to public disclosures of private matters, are we creating a new type of online intimacy? And if we are, are we making intimacy in the real world less important?

or rejected. Thus an action that shows someone's disregard for our feelings and needs may anger us.

Anger, like its close cousin, hostility, is a potentially damaging state. According to psychiatry professor Redford Williams, strong evidence exists that hostility alone damages the heart: "It isn't the impatience, the ambition or the work drive. It's the anger. It sends your blood pressure skyrocketing. It provokes your body to create unhealthy chemicals. For some hostile people, anger is poison."[26] Research suggests that genes may account for 27 to 40 percent of a person's tendency toward anger.[27] Some people have free-floating hostility, meaning that they are usually angry, often without real cause. These people are the most at risk. This is not to suggest that all expression of anger is unhealthy. Indeed, for people who express some anger, versus a lot of anger, the risks of disease may be lower than for persons who express little or no anger. In fact, moderate expressions of anger, when compared with low expressions of anger, decrease the risk for heart attack and stroke by about 50 percent.[28] Unexpressed anger can lead to passive–aggressive behavior and the development of a negative and hostile personality. Consequently, demonstrating anger management—that is, learning to express anger constructively by expressing angry feelings in an assertive, not aggressive, way, redirecting anger, and calming oneself down—is a valuable skill.

Anger management has entered the technology age. Some e-mail programs use a screening device, MoodWatch, software that analyzes incoming and outgoing messages for sentence structure and word usage that looks offensive or aggressive. By warning a receiver of a potentially anger-arousing message that could ruin the day, it allows the receiver to delete the e-mail before reading it.[29] Would you use such a screening aide to avoid arousing your anger?

EMOTIONAL CREATION AND CONTAGION

Have you ever put on a happy face? What happened? Did you discover that smiling actually made you feel happy? What effect did your smile have on

We unconsciously mirror and imitate the moods and emotions of individuals with whom we interact.

people around you? Putting on a sad, happy, or frightened face can produce the feeling that the expression represents. Facial expressions in and of themselves elicit feelings; they are not simply the visible sign of an emotion.[31] Thus, while emotions may influence facial expressions, facial expressions may similarly influence emotions.

Our moods may also be contagious. If you have ever started your day in a great mood, gone to class, and then ended up in a bad mood, you may want to consider that someone gave you that nasty mood. The more empathetic we are, the more apt we are to be susceptible to **emotional contagion** and to catch someone else's mood. According to psychologist Elaine Hatfield, we do this by unconsciously mirroring and/or imitating the moods and emotions of those with whom we interact.[32]

emotional contagion
the catching of another person's mood

Ethics & Communication

Emotional Contagion

Emotional Intelligence author Daniel Goleman, psychoanalyst Carl Jung, and psychologist Elaine Hatfield each contend that our moods can be contagious. In fact, the more emotionally expressive people are, the more likely they are to transmit their moods when they talk with another person. The transmission of emotion appears to occur both instantaneously and unconsciously.

If we assume this phenomenon is true, should a person who is experiencing a bout of sadness or a similar depressive emotion be kept isolated from others so as not to "infect" them with the same feeling? What do you think? Would we be better off if we were exposed only to people who were in good moods? Why or why not?

SHARING FEELINGS IN RELATIONSHIPS

Our feelings tell us about our needs and about the state of our relationships.[33] People who share healthy relationships are able to pay direct attention to the emotional reactions that occur during their interactions. They take time to become aware of these emotions by periodically asking themselves, "What am I feeling?" Once the feeling has been identified, their next step is to estimate its strength: "How strong is this feeling?" Next, they ask, "How did I get to feel this way?" "Where did the feeling come from?" "How did I contribute?" In healthy relationships, an emotion is reported as experienced—for instance, "I'm getting angry, and I'm beginning to say things I really don't mean."

Healthy relationships do not consist totally of positive feelings. Other feelings are also important. Unfortunately, many of us lack the commitment, courage, and skill needed to express our own feelings—particularly when those feelings are not positive—or to allow other people to express their feelings to us. Many people are reluctant to work their feelings through; instead, they ignore or deny a feeling until it eventually becomes unmanageable.

Thus, we often keep our feelings too much in check or, when we do express them, we express them ineptly and incompletely. Did you know that the majority of people who are fired from their jobs are asked to leave not because of incompetence but because of personality conflicts? Many of the problems we have with friends, parents, or employers are due to the inability to express or accept messages about feelings. Efforts to sacrifice or disregard feelings inevitably lead to problems with relationships or failures of relationships. In the next section we will examine how this happens.

Suppression and Disclosure of Feelings

Sometimes the way we handle feelings impedes our relationships with others.[34] For example, in any relational context, we may bury our real feelings, hesitate to express them, or unleash them uncontrollably.

CENSORING YOUR FEELINGS

Feelings are not the enemy of healthy human relationships, yet at times we are taught to act as if they were. As a result, many of us grow up afraid of feelings.

Have important people in your life ever expressed sentiments similar to the following to you?

"You shouldn't feel depressed about what happened."

"If you can't tell me you're pleased with the way it looks, then don't say anything."

"Don't you scream at me! You have no right to get angry with me!"

"There's nothing to be afraid of! Why are you such a baby?"

As these examples imply, feelings and emotions are frequently perceived as dangerous, harmful, and shameful. When this is the case, we censor our feelings and become overly hesitant to express them to others or to let others express their feelings to us. We exhibit only socially approved feelings for fear of being considered irrational or emotionally volatile. This leads to communication that is shallow, contrived, and frequently inappropriate.

Often, so as not to make waves or alienate others, both males and females act the part of the nice guy. At times people desperately want others to like them and so are willing to pretend to feel, or not feel, a particular emotion. People may also become what Theodore Isaac Rubin calls **emotional isolationists.**[35] That is, they may try to protect themselves from any exchange of feelings by minding their own business and avoiding entanglements or involvements. Or they may overintellectualize every experience in an attempt to render their emotions impotent. Each of these techniques is counterproductive and can ultimately cause problems with relationships.

emotional isolationists
persons who seek to avoid situations that may require the exchange of feelings

DISPLAY RULES

Various types of unwritten laws, or display rules, guide us in deciding when or when not to show our emotions. For instance, when we are young, we may be told not to cry at school, not to yell in front of strangers, or not to kiss in public. As adults, we may be advised not to flirt at office parties, not to display anger when disciplined, or not to be too outspoken during a meeting.

One determinant of display rules is gender. Although feelings do not discriminate between the sexes, and although members of both sexes obviously are equally capable of emotions of all kinds, our society for some reason deems it appropriate for men and women to behave differently with regard to their emotions. Theodore Isaac Rubin, author of *The Angry Book*, gives the following examples of confused ideas about anger:

Big anger displays are not feminine.

Big anger displays are only feminine and are not masculine.

Gentlemen simply don't show anger.

Ladies must not get angry at gentlemen.

Gentlemen must not get angry at ladies.

Very loud anger displays are evidence of homosexuality.[36]

As Rubin observes, "members of both sexes get equally angry" and "are equally expressive"; nevertheless, different rules and taboos regarding the expression of anger, and other emotions, have been internalized by males and females.

The two sexes may handle anger and aggression in strikingly different ways. While men and women are equally likely to experience anger, women are far more likely to suppress, repress, and deny it.[37] Only 9 percent of women report that they deal with anger by directly confronting the person who caused it, and 25 percent insist that they wouldn't express anger to a family member.[38] Instead, they keep it bottled up by enacting a "no anger" script.

In our society, men are generally viewed as more rational, objective, and independent than women. Women are perceived to be more emotional, subjective, and dependent than men. Women are also supposed to do more disclosing than men. When asked, people typically indicate that the "male" traits are more desirable than the "female" traits. But Kay Deaux notes in *The Behavior of Women and Men* that the supposedly female characteristics are not all seen as bad:

There is a cluster of positively valued traits that people see as more typical of women than men; these traits generally reflect warmth and expressiveness. Women are described as tactful, gentle, aware of the feelings of others, and able to express tender feelings easily. Men in contrast are viewed as blunt, rough, unaware of the feelings of others, and unable to express their own feelings.[39]

"Do you know how masculine it is to risk crying?"

For the most part, women are perceived as warm and men as competent. Which do you feel is the more desirable trait? In general, because of the sharing of feelings and amount of disclosing involved, female friendships are perceived to be deeper and more enduring than the friendships of men. In addition, while women's willingness to verbalize their feelings is believed to improve their mental and physical health, prolonged ruminating about feelings can deepen depression and lead to anxiety and anger.[40]

The second important determinant of display rules is culture. For example, in some African societies, people will assume that you are friendly until you prove to them that you are not. When they smile, it means that they like you; if they don't smile, it means that they distrust you. The Japanese, on the other hand, often laugh and smile to mask anger, sorrow, or disgust. People from Mediterranean countries often intensify emotions such as grief, sadness, and happiness, whereas the British deintensify, or understate, these emotions.

To whom do you feel free to say, "I'm frightened of that," or "What you just did disappointed me," or "I really care about you"?

The third determinant of display rules is personal values. In effect, we decide for ourselves under what conditions and with whom we will freely share or inhibit our emotional expressions. You might, for instance, feel it inappropriate to show anger before a parent, but you might readily reveal it to a boyfriend, girlfriend, or spouse. You might hesitate to express your innermost fears to an instructor or employer, but you might readily disclose them to a close friend.

Our personal display rules might also cause us to develop a characteristic style of emotional expression.[41] We might become *withholders* and try never to show how we feel, or we might become *revealers* and try always to show how we feel. Or we might become what Paul Ekman and Wallace V. Friesen call unwitting expressors, blanked expressors, or substitute expressors.[42] *Unwitting expressors* reveal their feelings without being aware that they have done so. (They then wonder how someone could read their emotions.) *Blanked expressors* are certain that they are communicating feelings to others but, in fact, are not. (They are then confused or upset when people fail to pick up on their cues.) *Substitute expressors* substitute the appearance of one emotion for another emotion without realizing they have done so. (They then cannot

Exploring Diversity

Culture, Gender, and Emotional Displays

When it comes to the display of emotion, our culture and our gender appear to compel us to act in accordance with societal norms. For example, Asians are less likely than Americans to express negative emotions publicly, and men generally tend to be more reticent in expressing emotions such as sympathy, sadness, and distress, while women are more inhibited when it comes to expressing anger and sexuality.

How are these cultural and gender expression differences sustained? Parents and society, in general, reinforce them. For example, recent studies reveal that, in the United States, we still treat boys and girls differently when it comes to their emotional lives. According to psychologist Virginia O'Leary, "The stereotypes of emotionality for men and women are as strong as ever, in spite of two decades of efforts to break them down." Some of the most compelling laboratory research shows, for instance,

that when provoked, men and women have equivalent reactions in terms of heart rate and other physiological responses, but, when questioned, men usually say they are angry, while women usually say they are hurt or sad.

In another study, men and women viewed scenes of accidents and their victims. Although physiological measures indicated that both the men and women were equally affected by the scenes, the men's faces showed no expression, while the women's faces expressed sympathy.

Consider the following questions:

1. To what extent does your own behavior confirm or contradict the preceding observations? Explain.
2. How might the different messages that men and women send about their emotions affect their ability to communicate honestly and effectively with each other?

understand why people react in unexpected ways.) Thus, personal display rules sometimes work to impede interpersonal relationships.

EFFECTS OF SUPPRESSED FEELINGS ON RELATIONSHIPS

As Jerry Gillies, the author of *Friendship*, writes, "You are not making contact if you are not putting out what you really are."[43] Interpersonal communication theorist Sidney Jourard noted that dissembling, concealing, and being hesitant to reveal feelings are "lethal" habits for men.[44] Jourard believed that men, because they are not as apt to express their feelings as are women, encounter stresses that actually cause them to have a shorter life span than women. Now that women are assuming what were traditionally male roles, will they, too, feel more compelled to keep their feelings to themselves? Whatever the answer, it is acknowledged that all people are likely to experience personal and interpersonal difficulties when they try to repress or disguise their feelings.

According to communication expert David Johnson, many people mistakenly assume that all we need to ensure the development of effective interpersonal relationships is rationality, logic, and objectivity. "To the contrary," writes Johnson, "a person's interpersonal effectiveness increases as all the relevant information (including feelings) becomes conscious, discussable, and controllable."[45] Thus, he holds, suppression of feelings results in ineffective interpersonal behavior. Psychologist Thomas Gordon notes that, besides reducing your interpersonal effectiveness, continually bottling up your feelings can cause you to develop ulcers, headaches, heartburn, high blood pressure, a spastic colon, and various psychosomatic problems.[46] There is also evidence linking emotion, disease, and the immune system. Researchers have found that strong emotional responses may bolster the immune system. For example, cancer patients who openly showed that they were upset and who exhibited a fighting spirit seemed able to marshal stronger immune defenses than patients who suppressed their feelings.[47] David Viscott, a medical doctor, states, "When we lose touch with our feelings, we lose touch with our most human qualities. To paraphrase Descartes, 'I feel, therefore, I am.'"[48]

If either person in a relationship attempts to suppress his or her feelings, one or more of the following consequences may result. First, it may become increasingly difficult to solve interpersonal problems. Research reveals that, in a relationship, the quality of problem solving improves when the participants feel free to express both positive and negative feelings. When the participants feel inhibited, the quality of communication is diminished. Second, unresolved feelings foster a climate in which misinterpretation, distortion, and nonobjective judgments and actions can thrive. Unresolved feelings create or enlarge blind spots in our interpretation of people and events. Third, repression of emotions can lead to serious conflicts and blowups. Intense feelings that are not dealt with fester beneath the surface until they erupt as a result of mounting internal (self) and external (other) pressures. (Holding in such feelings can make it impossible for participants to think clearly.) Fourth, maintaining an effective relationship means that participants are honest with each other. To penalize or reject a person for expressing emotions honestly is to tell that person that you deny him or her the right to reveal an authentic self. You also deny yourself the ability to know the person. Finally, continued repression of feelings can in time cause you to obliterate your capacity to feel anything.

EFFECTS OF DISCLOSED FEELINGS ON RELATIONSHIPS

Certainly, there are people to whom you may not choose to reveal your feelings, and there are situations in which you decide that disclosure of your feelings would be inappropriate. Nevertheless, when you take the risk of revealing your feelings to others, your relationship is likely to reap definite benefits.

First, by honestly revealing your feelings, you make it less threatening for the other person to reveal his or her feelings. You demonstrate that you care enough to share your feelings; thus, risk taking becomes a reciprocal process. Second, you acknowledge that emotions are acceptable. You do not censor the feelings the other person experiences, nor do you decide which feelings he or she may and may not feel. You express an interest in the whole person; instead of using emotions as weapons, you show that you are willing to use them as tools. Third, by describing your feelings and by sharing your perceptions with others, you become more aware of what it is you are actually feeling. Fourth, you give yourself the opportunity to resolve difficulties and conflicts in a productive way. Fifth, by revealing your feelings, you can indicate to others how you want to be treated. In contrast, by keeping quiet—by saying nothing—you encourage others to continue behavior of which you may disapprove. Feelings, when respected, are friendly, not dangerous.

CONFLICTS AND RELATIONSHIPS

conflict

perceived disagreement

Conflict, or perceived disagreement about views, interests, and goals, is a part of every relationship. It is not so much the conflict or disagreement that creates problems in our relationships but the way we approach and handle it. Thus, while disagreements are normal and their presence does not signal relationship trouble, how we choose to manage conflict with another is an indicator of a relationship's health.

Managing Conflict: Handling Feelings during Conflict

One of our objectives in this chapter is to investigate conflict to see how we can learn to handle it effectively. You have been, and will continue to be, faced with conflicts all your life. Observing your own conflicts and giving more thought to them can be a positive experience.

Conflict develops for a multitude of reasons and takes a multitude of forms. It can arise from people's different needs, attitudes, or beliefs. Conflict tests each relationship we share with another person and in so doing helps us assess the health or effectiveness of the relationship. Handled well, conflict can help each participant develop a clearer picture of the other; thus, it can strengthen and cement a relationship. Handled poorly, conflict can create schisms, inflict psychological scars, inflame hostilities, and cause lasting resentments. Thus, conflicts can produce highly constructive or highly destructive consequences.[49]

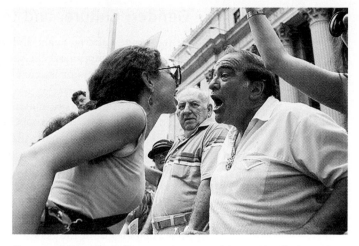

How we approach conflict can create problems. Handled poorly, conflict can destroy relationships and inflame hostilities.

Every relationship worth maintaining, every relationship worth working at, is certain to experience moments of conflict. As David Johnson notes, "A conflict-free relationship is a sign that you really have no relationship at all, not that you have a good relationship."[50] To say there should be no conflict amounts to saying that we should have no relationships. If a relationship is healthy, conflicts will occur regularly. If a relationship is healthy, conflicts will also be handled effectively. A survey by *Redbook* magazine suggests that how people express themselves in conflict situations is frequently more important than what they disagree about.[51] *Redbook* asked female readers how they were most likely to behave when displeased with their husbands and how their husbands were most likely to behave when displeased with them. Readers were asked whether they were most apt to "say nothing, brood about it, hint they were unhappy, express their feelings, or start an argument." They were also asked how they handled themselves when they did argue with their spouses. For instance, were they most likely to "leave the room, sulk, sit in silence, swear, shout, hit out, cry, or break things"? The results indicated that the most happily married women were those who said that both they and their husbands were able to reveal displeasure, discuss it, and try to resolve the problem calmly and rationally. They also noted that they rarely if ever felt compelled to resort to active aggressive fighting (swearing, shouting, hitting out, crying, or breaking things) or to passive–aggressive fighting (leaving the room, sulking, or keeping silent). Thus, it appears that avoiding conflicts, trying to settle them prematurely, or prohibiting the discussion of differences can lead to serious problems.[52]

Research also indicates that how your parents handled conflict may have influenced your early academic achievement and emotional well-being.[53] There is evidently a link between the emotional lives of your parents and your own emotional health.[54]

What conflicts have you been involved in recently—in class, at work, or at home? Why did you define each situation as a conflict?

Gender, Culture, and the Handling of Conflict

When women and men, and individuals from diverse cultures, communicate, they carry their assumptions, beliefs, and perceptions of each other with them. What soon becomes apparent is that the sexes, and different cultures, approach conflict in different ways.

From childhood on, males are typically more competitive and aggressive, while females adopt more cooperative behaviors. Since most males are more concerned with power, they tend to make demands, while most females, more concerned with relationship maintenance, tend to make proposals. Males often fail to provide rationales for positions, while females freely offer reasons.

As with men and women, different cultures socialize their members to behave in different ways when faced with conflict. Whereas members of individualistic cultures, such as exists in the United States, are likely to exhibit a direct approach that emanates from the belief that individuals have a right to defend themselves, members of collectivistic cultures believe that such behavior is out of place or rude. Instead, they tend to value harmony, restraint, and nonconfrontation.[55] Hesitant to refuse a request directly, the members of a collectivistic culture might say, "Let me think about that" in place of "No."

My idea of an agreeable person is a person who agrees with me.

— Benjamin Disraeli

By becoming sensitive to such differences, and recognizing the assumptions on which they are based, we can work toward developing a clearer understanding of how conflicts can be resolved.[56]

Reexamine your personal conflict inventory to identify your style of managing conflict. Do you or people you know use any ineffective methods of dealing with conflicts? Do you feel a need to deny that a conflict exists, withdraw, surrender, placate, or distract by introducing irrelevancies? Do you intellectualize, blame, find fault, or force the other person to accept your ideas by physically or emotionally overpowering him or her? Why? What elements of your relationship elicit irrational responses instead of a rational discussion of the disputed issues?

Of the strategies available, only discussion, or leveling, can break impasses and solve difficulties. Thus, the fate of any conflict is related to the communication strategies employed. Conflict forces people to select response patterns that will forge an effective network of communication. We can choose either disruptive or constructive responses.

Can you think of situations in your own life that illustrate the four values of conflict discussed here?

We see that, in any situation, problems can develop if we fail to deal with conflict appropriately. We can also see that there are certain definite benefits to be derived from handling conflict effectively. Alan Filley, in the book *Interpersonal Conflict Resolution*, identifies four major values arising from conflict. First, many conflict situations can reduce or even eliminate the probability of more serious conflict in the future. Second, conflict can foster innovation by helping us acquire new ways of looking at things, new ways of thinking, and new behaviors. Third, conflict can develop our sense of cohesiveness and togetherness by increasing closeness and trust. Fourth, it can provide us with an invaluable opportunity to measure the strength or viability of our relationships.[57] Conflict, after all, is a natural result of diversity.

How Conflict Arises: Categorizing Conflicts

We have examined what conflict is and how we feel about it. Now let us explore how and why it arises. Conflict is likely to occur wherever human differences meet. As we have seen, conflict is a clash of opposing beliefs, opinions, values, needs,

Skill Builder

Tied in Knots

This exercise was suggested by an experience included in Virginia Satir's book *Peoplemaking*.

1. Think of some idea, belief, value, need, or goal that has involved you in a conflict situation.

2. Identify the relevant aspects of yourself or the other person or persons involved. Briefly summarize each position.

3. Choose class members to play the parts of those you perceived yourself to be in conflict with.

4. Cut heavy twine or rope into 10-foot lengths, one for each player. Also cut a number of 3-foot lengths to tie

around each player's waist, including your own. Next, tie your 10-foot lead rope to the rope around your waist. Then, hand your rope to the person with whom you perceive yourself to be in conflict, who will also hand his or her rope to you.

5. While tied to each other, begin to talk about the issue that is the cause of conflict.

Source: Virginia Satir. *Peoplemaking*. Palo Alto, CA: Science and Behavior Books, 1988.

---

assumptions, and goals. It can result from honest differences, from misunderstandings, from anger, or from expecting either too much or too little from people and situations. Note that conflict does not always require two or more people; you can sometimes be in conflict with yourself. **Self-conflict** occurs when we find ourselves having to choose between two or more mutually exclusive options—two cars, two classes, two potential spouses, two activities; the internal struggle in such a situation is called **intrapersonal conflict.** In contrast, **interpersonal conflict** is the same type of struggle between two or more people. Interpersonal conflict can be prompted by differences in perceptions and interests; by a scarcity of resources or rewards, such as money, time, and position; or by rivalry—situations in which we find ourselves competing with someone else. Those involved in an intrapersonal or interpersonal conflict usually feel pulled in different directions at the same time.

Consider the Skill Builder "Tied in Knots." How did that experience feel? Of course, when engaged in conflict, you do not have real ropes tugging at you, but you sometimes feel as if you do. When you are able to handle a conflict, the ropes do not get in the way. At other times, however, a conflict escalates out of control. Before you know it, you are tied up in knots and unable to extricate yourself. Those who see themselves in conflict with each other are interdependent and have the power to reward or punish one another. Thus, whenever two or more people get together, conflicts serious enough to damage their relationship may develop.

We can categorize conflict in different ways. First, we can classify the goal or objective about which a conflict revolves. Goals or objectives can be nonshareable (for example, two teams cannot win the same basketball game) or shareable (your team can win some games and the other team can win some). Or they can be fully claimed and possessed by each party to the conflict. (You can each win everything—members of the rival Teamsters and Independent Truckers unions all get raises.)

Second, conflicts can be categorized according to their level of intensity. In a **low-intensity conflict,** the persons involved do not want to destroy each other; they devise an acceptable procedure to help control their communications and permit them to discover a solution that is beneficial to each. In a **medium-intensity conflict,** each person feels committed to win, but winning is seen as sufficient.

self-conflict
the type of conflict that occurs when a person has to choose between two or more mutually exclusive options

intrapersonal conflict
internal conflict

interpersonal conflict
conflict between two or more people

low-intensity conflict
a conflict in which the persons involved work to discover a solution beneficial to all parties

medium-intensity conflict
a conflict in which each person feels committed to win, but winning is seen as sufficient

high-intensity conflict

a conflict in which one person intends to destroy or seriously hurt the other

pseudoconflict

the situation that results when persons mistakenly believe that two or more goals cannot be achieved simultaneously

content conflict

a disagreement over matters of fact

value conflict

a disagreement that arises when persons hold different views on an issue

ego conflict

a disagreement in which persons believe that winning or losing is tied to their self-worth, prestige, or competence

When evaluating a conflict, Americans tend to see one side as right and the other as wrong. In contrast, the Chinese are more likely to see the validity of both sides. What do you see as the benefits and drawbacks of each orientation?

No one feels that the opposition must be destroyed. In a **high-intensity conflict,** one person intends to destroy or at least seriously hurt the other. In high-intensity conflicts, winning as such is not necessarily sufficient; to mean anything, victory must be total.

A conflict can also be classified as a pseudoconflict, a content conflict, a value conflict, or an ego conflict. A **pseudoconflict** (as the term implies) is not really a conflict but gives the appearance of a conflict. It occurs when a person mistakenly believes that two or more goals cannot be simultaneously achieved. Pseudoconflicts frequently revolve around false either–or judgments ("Either I win or you win") or around simple misunderstandings (failing to realize that you really agree with the other person). A pseudoconflict is resolved when the people realize that no conflict actually exists.

A **content conflict** occurs when people disagree over matters of fact: the accuracy or implications of information, the definition of a term, or the solution to a problem. If the interactants realize that facts can be verified, inferences tested, definitions checked, and solutions evaluated against criteria, they can be shown that a content conflict can be settled rationally.

A **value conflict** arises when people hold different views on a particular issue. As an example, consider the American welfare system. A person who values individual independence and self-assertiveness will have opinions about public welfare very different from those of someone who believes that we are ultimately responsible for the well-being of others. The realistic outcome of such a conflict would be that the interactants would disagree without becoming disagreeable—that is, they would discuss the issue and learn something from one another, even though they might continue to disagree. In effect, they would agree that it is acceptable to disagree.

Ego conflicts have the greatest potential to destroy a relationship. An **ego conflict** occurs when the interactants believe that winning or losing is a reflection of their own self-worth, prestige, or competence. When this happens, the issue itself is no longer important because each person perceives himself or herself to be on the line. Thus, it becomes almost impossible to deal with the situation rationally.

At this point, you should understand that conflict can develop for a number of different reasons, and you should be aware of the types of disagreements and problems that can arise during intrapersonal and interpersonal conflict. Particular conflict-generating behaviors affect each of us differently.

Some of us perceive ourselves to be involved in a conflict if we are deprived of a need; others do not. Some of us perceive ourselves to be involved in a conflict if someone impinges on our territory or disagrees with us about the way we define a role; others do not. Take some time to discover your own sources of conflict. Making such observations will help you understand the types of issues that draw you into disharmony with yourself and others. It will also let you see how you tend to respond when faced with a conflict situation. We will now examine constructive and destructive ways of handling conflict in greater detail.

Resolving Conflict: Styles of Expression

As we have seen, our emotions and how we handle them can make or break the relationships we enter into. In other words, we can make our feelings work for or against us. There are three basic ways of handling emotionally charged or conflict-producing situations: nonassertively, aggressively, and assertively.

NONASSERTIVENESS

Have there been moments in your life when you believed you had to suppress your feelings to avoid rejection or conflict, or when you felt unable to state your feelings clearly? Are you ever afraid to let others know how you feel? If you have ever felt hesitant to express your feelings to others, intimidated by another person, or reluctant to speak up when you believed you were being treated unfairly, then you know what it is to exhibit **nonassertiveness.** When you behave nonassertively, you force yourself to keep your real feelings inside. Frequently, you function as a weather vane or change colors as a chameleon does in order to fit the situation in which you find yourself. You become an echo of the feelings around you. Unfortunately, nonassertive people rarely take the steps needed to improve a relationship that is causing problems; as a result, they frequently end up with something they don't really want. With so much at stake, why do people refrain from asserting themselves?

nonassertiveness
the hesitation to display one's feelings and thoughts

Experience shows that we hesitate to assert ourselves in our relationships for a number of reasons. Sometimes inertia or laziness is a factor; the easiest response is simply no response at all. (After all, assertion can be hard work.) At other times, apathy leads us to be nonassertive; we simply do not care enough to become actively involved. Frequently, fear can lead to nonassertiveness. In particular, we may fear that rejection might result from active self-assertion. (We become convinced that speaking up may make someone angry.) Or we may simply feel we lack the interpersonal skills needed for assertiveness.

Why might you hesitate to protect your rights; that is, why would you be reluctant to assert yourself? Under what circumstances would nonassertiveness be most likely to occur?

Another important cause of nonassertiveness is shyness. Each of us feels inadequate from time to time. We may feel exploited, stifled, or imposed upon. These feelings manifest themselves in a variety of ways—as depression, as weakness, as loneliness—but most of all, according to psychologist Philip G. Zimbardo, as shyness. Shyness is embarrassment in advance. It is created by the fear that our real self will not match up with the image we want to project.[58]

According to Zimbardo and Shirley L. Radl, coauthors of *The Shyness Workbook*, few shy people consider their shyness a positive trait; they see it as evidence that something is wrong with them. Zimbardo and Radl note: "Shyness is not a permanent trait but rather is a response to other people evoked by certain situations. The unpleasant feelings of shyness come from having low self-esteem and worrying about what other people will think of you."[59]

Which situations and people in your life make you feel shy? What are the consequences of your shyness?

According to Lynn Z. Bloom, Karen Coburn, and Joan Pearlman, authors of *The New Assertive Woman*, in our society shyness or nonassertiveness is often considered an asset for women but a liability for men.[60] To what extent do your experiences support this? Do you think women gain more from being nonassertive than men lose? Why?

There are many degrees of shyness. For example, shyness can take the form of mild bashfulness, or it can simply cause you to increase the distance you like to keep between yourself and others. Unfortunately, extreme shyness can make you fear all social relationships and can prevent you from expressing or even acknowledging your emotions.

AGGRESSIVENESS

Unlike nonassertive people, who often permit others to victimize them and are reluctant to express their feelings, persons who display **aggressiveness** insist on standing up for their own rights to the point at which they ignore and violate the rights of others. Although some people deliberately defy pushy people, in general, aggressive people manage to have more of their needs met than nonassertive peo-

aggressiveness
the expressing of one's own thoughts and feelings at another's expense

Describe an interpersonal situation in which someone took advantage of you and you permitted it. What do you believe motivated the other person? What motivated you? Describe a situation in which you took advantage of someone else. Why do you believe the other person allowed you to victimize him or her?

ple do. Unfortunately, they usually accomplish this at someone else's expense. The aggressor always aims to dominate and win in a relationship; breaking even is not enough. The message of the aggressive person is selfish: "This is the way I feel. You're stupid if you feel differently. This is what I want. What you want doesn't count and is of no consequence to me." In contrast to the nonassertive person, who ventures forth in communication hesitantly, the aggressive person begins by attacking, thereby precipitating conflict. It is therefore not surprising that a conversation with an aggressive person will often escalate out of control: The target of the aggressor frequently feels a need to retaliate. In such situations, no one really wins, and the result is a stalemated relationship.

People feel a need to act aggressively for a number of reasons. First, according to two assertiveness counselors, Arthur J. Lange and Patricia Jakubowski, we tend to lash out when we feel ourselves becoming vulnerable; we attempt to protect ourselves from the perceived threat of powerlessness.[61] Second, emotionally volatile experiences that remain unresolved may cause us to overreact when faced with a difficulty in a relationship. Third, we may firmly believe that aggression is the only way to get our ideas and feelings across to the other person. For some reason, we may think that people will neither listen to nor react to what we say if we take a mild-mannered approach. Fourth, we may simply never have learned to channel or handle our aggressive impulses. (In other words, we may not have mastered a number of necessary interpersonal skills.) Fifth, aggression may be related to a pattern of repeated nonassertion in the past; the hurt, disappointment, bewilderment, and sense of personal violation that resulted from nonassertion may have risen to the boiling point. No longer able to keep these feelings inside, we abruptly vent them as aggressiveness.

Damaged or destroyed relationships are a frequent result of aggression. Neither the nonassertive nor the aggressive person has many meaningful relationships. For this reason, we need to find a middle ground, or golden mean, between the extremes of nonassertion and aggression.

ASSERTIVENESS

Go to the Online Learning Center at www.mhhe.com/gamble9 and answer the questions in the *Self Inventory* to evaluate your understanding of assertiveness.

assertiveness

the expressing of one's thoughts and feelings while displaying respect for the thoughts and feelings of others

The intent of nonassertive behavior is to avoid conflict of any kind; the intent of aggressive behavior is to dominate. By contrast, the intent of assertive behavior is to communicate honestly, clearly, and directly and to support your beliefs and ideas without either harming others or allowing yourself to be harmed. If we can assume that both nonassertion and aggression are due at least partly to having learned inappropriate ways of reacting in interpersonal encounters, we should be able to improve our interpersonal relationships if we work to develop appropriate ways of reacting. Understanding the nature of assertiveness will help us accomplish this goal.

When you display **assertiveness,** you protect yourself from being victimized; you meet more of your interpersonal needs, make more decisions about your own life, think and say what you believe, and establish closer interpersonal relationships without infringing on the rights of others. To be assertive is to recognize that all people have the same fundamental rights and that neither titles nor roles alter this fact. We all have the right to influence the way others behave toward us; we all have the right to protect ourselves from mistreatment. Furthermore, we all have the right to accomplish these objectives without guilt.

Assertive people have learned how to stop themselves from sending inappropriate nonassertive or aggressive messages. Thus, assertive people announce what they think and feel without apologizing but without dominating. This involves learning to say "no," "yes," "I like," and "I think." In this way, neither oneself nor the other person is demeaned; both are respected.

FIGURE 9.2
Relationship Window.

The focus of assertiveness is negotiation. Assertive people try to balance social power to equalize the relationships they share. Whereas aggressive people often hurt others and nonassertive people often hurt themselves, assertive people protect themselves as well as those with whom they interact. This means attending to feelings and using specific verbal and nonverbal skills to help solve interpersonal problems.

Remember that being assertive does not mean being insensitive, selfish, stubborn, or pushy. It does mean being willing to defend your rights and communicate your needs, and it does mean being willing to attempt to find mutually satisfactory solutions to interpersonal problems and conflicts. It is up to you to decide whether you would like to redefine some of the ways you relate to others. It is up to you to determine whether you need to shake off any inappropriate and unproductive ways of behaving in favor of assertiveness.

You may, of course, encounter difficulties as you attempt, through assertiveness, to promote more successful and open communication with others. Most assertion situations fall into at least one of four categories: (1) an interaction with a stranger, in which you are requesting something; (2) an interaction with a friend or an intimate, in which you are requesting something; (3) an interaction with a stranger, in which you are refusing something; (4) an interaction with a friend or an intimate, in which you are refusing something.[62] These situations may be represented as a relationship window (see Figure 9.2).

Most people will experience the majority of their difficulties with assertiveness in one or more of the quadrants shown in Figure 9.2. For example, some people may find it easy to refuse a stranger's request but difficult to deny that of a friend. For others, refusing close friends or strangers alike may pose few problems; instead, they may experience great anxiety when making requests of others. Where do you experience the most difficulty?

At one time or another, we will all have some difficulty in at least one of the quadrants. Once you have identified your own problem areas, however, you can begin to examine your behavior more closely. You can begin to recognize when you feel a need to fight, when you feel a need to flee, and when you feel a need to assert yourself. Fighting or fleeing makes sense for animals and is therefore characteristic of their behavior. These alternatives do not necessarily make sense for human beings in dealing with one another; still, we sometimes flee from each other, and we sometimes fight with each other. Sometimes we display these behaviors because we want to, sometimes because we feel we must, and sometimes because we don't know what else to do or may think we lack the social skills to do anything else. What we can do, however, is use our problem-solving ability to develop assertive ways to handle interpersonal difficulties. We can learn to be socially adept.

For any relationship to grow, the participants need to demonstrate at least a minimal level of assertiveness in their communication with each other. The important thing is to try to let your actions be dictated by the circumstances and the people. There is no single right way to act in every interpersonal encounter, and the choice of how you act should be your own. In general, however, we can all increase our feelings of self-worth by learning to be more assertive.[63]

In a cyberaffair, one person carries on an interpersonal relationship that is not necessarily physical or intimate with another person online. In cybersex, which is anonymous and built on fantasy, persons talk about having sex, describing various sexual acts, with an online partner. If your significant other were to have a cyberaffair or engage in cybersex, would you consider him or her to be guilty of infidelity? Why or why not? What relational factors do you believe lead someone to have a cyberaffair and/or engage in cybersex?

TECHNOLOGY, RELATIONSHIPS, AND THE COMMUNICATION OF EMOTION

By using the Internet, we bring another social world into our offline lives, one in which we communicate with and maintain ties with people who live at a distance, some of whom we may never meet face-to-face.[64] How successful are we at managing the integration of this new world of relationships into our existing world? To what extent does our involvement with persons in cyberspace affect the relationships we already share with friends, family members, and people at work? Do you feel successful managing multiple interpersonal worlds?

The Internet has the potential to expand our relationship reach. The Net, in many ways, is the ultimate *noncontact* person-to-person network. For this reason, despite the fact that millions of people use Internet dating sites, unless they progress beyond the use of computers, cyber-relationships cannot become the developmental equivalents of real friendships or romances.[65] On the other hand, the Internet can be used to strengthen existing relationships and increase interaction with relatives and friends.

For some of us, the computer has freed us to express feelings and emotions we would be hesitant to express publicly. For example, e-mail and online chat groups are enabling shy persons to come out of their shells and interact with others. In addition, they allow those who are bedridden or isolated from others to find emotional support from online sources. They are also enabling those of us who have had limited contact with or experience interacting with persons from different backgrounds to have such opportunities. In the process, we are able to practice handling the conflict that can result when we converse with people who have different values or think differently than we do.

In addition to exposing us to differences, the bulletin boards we frequent can also function as electronic soapboxes, which we or others use to sound off or to vent our feelings. Chat rooms and e-mail may even function as virtual hotel rooms for friendly get-togethers into which you and one or more others may check into on a whim and interact.[66] When interacting online, in addition to interacting pleasantly, individuals can hurl insults, or **flames,** that feed interpersonal conflict. In fact, some people send computer-assisted messages to persons that they would never dare send if they were face-to-face with those individuals. Because there is neither rootedness to place nor danger of physical contact while interacting via computer, but there is the potential for anonymity, certain persons may even allow themselves the freedom to become verbally abusive or aggressive. How you react when you are the target of such flaming or verbal abuse is revealing. Some who are flamed withdraw, sit on the side, or turn away, while others counter the personal attack by replying immediately to the same audience. As with speech, the tone we imagine other persons to be using as they type their computer-mediated messages to us often becomes more important than what they actually write.[67]

flames

online insults

We also use online journals and blogs to communicate. With these new media, used primarily as vehicles for pouring out emotions, we can inwardly focus as we publish journal entries or read and comment on the entries of friends and other journal keepers.[68] Some researchers believe that pouring out painful traumas on a computer screen also improves health and increases self-insight.[69]

Others, however, believe that use of the medium is isolating, severely limits face-to-face interactions, and shields the social lives of users from their parents or other people who love them. They also fear that because the Internet connects users to the impersonal world at large, it fosters a "put it all out there" orientation that encourages emotionally detached people to think they are going places together when they are going nowhere, because they do not even leave the confines of their own rooms. Transforming a virtual relationship into a real-world one can be difficult.[70] Posts are neither private nor only for friends. Some are primarily bids for attention. Others are painfully emotional, revealing the journal keeper's innermost insecurities to strangers.[71]

In addition to changing the media we use to interact with each other, new technologies are redefining how and where we work. Greater and greater numbers of us spend significant parts of our day in front of computers (desk or laptop), on cellular telephones, and in general, less tied to the notion of a traditional office. For many of us, the office is a relic. We telecommute, linked with others by a computer network. We have more virtual contact and less and less face-to-face contact. To combat the dearth of face-to-face interaction workers have with each other, some employers go out of their way to arrange opportunities for employees to meet face-to-face for casual exchanges.

New technologies are also changing how the boss delivers both good and bad news to workers. According to one study, people are more honest when using e-mail to communicate bad news than they are with other methods, such as phone or personal delivery. When negative feedback is delivered via e-mail, it contains less sugarcoating. According to managers, e-mail also lets them dole out praise more quickly. Managers now give workers virtual pats on the back.[72]

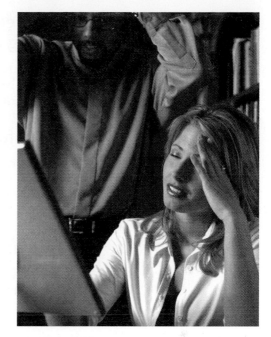

Can you read the emotions of people you interact with online? What cues do you use?

Are online journals or blogs appropriate places to make personal disclosures? Do you think it is possible to learn things online about people with whom you share relationships that would be difficult to learn offline? How do you prefer to disclose your thoughts and feelings to others, on- or offline? Why?

HANDLING FEELINGS EFFECTIVELY IN RELATIONSHIPS

Many of us have trouble expressing our feelings in person and online. Either we behave nonassertively and keep our emotions too much in check, or we behave aggressively and become excessively demanding or belligerent. The result is that our emotions impede the development of healthy relationships and foster the development of unhealthy relationships.

It is sad that we are rarely, if ever, taught to reveal our emotions in ways that will help our relationships. The key to using our feelings to promote effective relationships is learning to express them effectively. The following guidelines should help you communicate feelings in positive ways and thereby enrich the quality of your interpersonal encounters and relationships.

Work on Feelings You Have Difficulty Expressing or Handling

By now you should have a good idea of what feelings you have trouble expressing or responding to. Now concentrate on expressing or responding to these feelings when they arise. A first step is to let others know what feelings cause problems for you.

Stand Up for Your Emotional Rights

When we sacrifice our rights, we teach others to take advantage of us. When we demand rights that are not ours, we take advantage of others. Not revealing your feelings and thoughts to others can be just as damaging as disregarding the feelings and thoughts of others.

Check Your Perceptions

So far we've discussed *your* feelings, but what about the other person's feelings? Sometimes our interpretations of another person's feelings are determined by our own. Checking your perceptions requires that you express your assessment of others' feelings in a tentative fashion. You want to communicate to other people that you would like to understand their feelings and that you would like to refrain from acting on the basis of false assumptions that you might later regret. Sample perception checks include the following:

> "Were you surprised at what Jim said to you?"
>
> "Am I right in thinking that you feel angry because no one paid attention to your ideas?"
>
> "I get the feeling that what I said annoyed you. Am I right?"
>
> "I'm not certain if your behavior means you're confused or embarrassed."

Show Respect for Feelings

Don't try to persuade yourself or others to deny honest feelings. Comments like "Don't feel that way," "Calm down," and "Don't cry over spilt milk" communicate that you believe the other person has no right to a particular feeling. (You should avoid advising yourself or others to repress or ignore feelings.) Feelings are potentially constructive and should not be treated as destructive.

Use a Script to Handle Feelings Assertively

DESC script
an acronym for *describe, express, specify,* and *consequences;* a system for expressing one's feelings and understanding the feelings of another

In their book *Asserting Yourself,* Sharon Bower and Gordon Bower present a technique you can use to handle interpersonal dilemmas effectively.[73] The approach utilizes what is called a **DESC script** (*DESC* stands for *describe, express, specify, consequences*). A script contains characters (you and the person with whom you are relating), a plot (an event or a situation that has left you dissatisfied), a setting (the time and place the interaction occurred), and a message (the words and nonverbal cues of the actors).

You begin the script by describing, as specifically and objectively as possible, the behavior of another person that troubles you and makes you feel inadequate. By describing the bothersome occurrence, you give yourself a chance to examine the situation and define your personal needs and goals. Once you have identified what it is about the other person's behavior that you find undesirable, you are in

Thinking Critically

Reflect and Respond

Agree or disagree with the following quotation. Supply reasons and examples from a number of relationship contexts to support your stance.

In a sense we have two brains, two minds—and two different kinds of intelligence: rational and emotional. How we do in life is determined by both—it is not just IQ, but emotional intelligence that matters.[74]

a better position to handle it. Use simple, concrete, specific, and unbiased terms to describe the other's actions. For example, instead of saying, "You're always overcharging me, you dirty cheat!" try, "You told me the repairs would cost $50, and now you're charging me $110." Instead of saying, "You're ignoring me; you don't care about me," say, "You avoid looking at me when we speak." Instead of guessing at motives and saying, "You resent me and want Lisa," say, "The last two times we've gone out to eat with Jack and Lisa, you've criticized me in front of them."

After you have written a direct description of a behavior that bothers you (identifying the characters, the plot, and the setting), next add a few sentences expressing how you feel and what you think about the behavior. To do this, get in touch with your emotions and use personal statements. Using personal statements makes it clear that you are referring to what you are feeling and what you are thinking. The distinguishing feature of a personal statement is a pronoun such as "I," "me," or "my"; for example, use "I feel," "I believe," "my feelings," "it appears to me." Thus, when hurt by the behavior of an unthinking friend, you might say, "I feel humiliated and demeaned when you make fun of me." Realize that there are a number of ways feelings can be expressed. You can name a feeling: "I feel disappointed." "I feel angry." You can use comparisons: "I feel like a weeping willow" or "I feel like a rose whose petals have been ripped off, one by one." Or you can indicate the type of action your feelings are prompting you to exhibit: "I feel like leaving the room" or "I feel like putting cotton in my ears." By disclosing such feelings tactfully, you can make your position known without alienating the other person.

Once you have described the bothersome behavior and expressed your feelings or thoughts about it, your next step is to write down your request for a specific different behavior. That is, you specify the behavior you would like substituted. In effect, you are asking the other person to stop doing one thing and start doing something else. As before, make your request concrete and particular. It would be more effective to say, "Please stop playing the drums after 11 p.m." than to yell, "Stop being so damn noisy!"

Finally, note possible consequences—positive and negative—in terms of your own and the other person's behavior and feelings. Then review your script and rehearse it until you feel that your verbal and nonverbal cues support your goal.

Focus on Service Learning

Run a seminar on emotional intelligence or anger management for a local organization. Design your seminar by using the material contained in this chapter, researching scholarly and popular articles on your selected seminar topic, and visiting Web sites such as eqi.org/ or ei.haygroup.com/resources/default_ieitest.htm, or www.apa.org/pubinfo/anger.html. Before offering your seminar, rehearse it by presenting it to a campus group.

Practice Four Basic Assertive Behaviors

Practice the following assertive behaviors:

1. Stop automatically asking permission to speak, think, or behave. Instead of saying, "Do you mind if I ask to have this point clarified?" say, "I'd like to know if . . ." In other words, substitute declarative statements for requests for permission.

2. Establish eye contact with people with whom you interact face-to-face. Instead of looking down or to the side (cues that imply uncertainty or insecurity), look into the eyes of the person you are speaking to. This lets people know you have the confidence to relate to them honestly and directly.

3. Eliminate hesitations and fillers ("uh," "you know," "hmm") from your speech. It is better to talk more slowly and deliberately than to broadcast the impression that you are unprepared or lack self-assurance.

4. Say "no" calmly, firmly, and quietly; say "yes" sincerely and honestly; say "I want" without fear or guilt.

The Wrap Up

Revisiting Chapter Objectives

1. **Identify and distinguish among the following relationship life contexts: acquaintanceship, friendship, and romantic, family, and work relationships.** Our relationships occur in various life contexts. Among the different kinds of relationships we share are acquaintanceships, friendships, romantic relationships, family relationships, and work relationships. While interaction with acquaintances is usually limited in scope and quality, some do develop into friendships. As friendships become closer, relationship breadth and depth are enhanced. The expectation of permanence distinguishes romantic relationships from other relationship types. We play roles in both family and work relationships. In families that practice healthy communication, family members pull together to preserve the family unit. Members of an organization who are "team players" also recognize their interdependence.

2. **Define and distinguish among the following terms: *emotional intelligence, emotion state,* and *emotion trait.*** We are experiencing some emotion to some degree at any given time. Our emotional intelligence, the ability we have to motivate ourselves, to control our impulses, to recognize and regulate our moods, to empathize, and to hope, determines how effective we are at handling feelings in our relationships. A temporary emotional reaction to a situation is an emotion state; a tendency to experience one particular emotion repeatedly is an emotion trait.

3. **Explain how attraction, proximity, reinforcement, similarity, complementarity, and the suppression and disclosure of feelings can affect the development of relationships.** Feelings are at the heart of our important interpersonal relationships. Our moods may also be contagious. Among the factors that can cause us to establish relationships with some people but not others are attractiveness (we favor people who are physically attractive and who have pleasing personalities), proximity (we are more apt to interact with people whom we live near or work with), reinforcement (we like being around people who reward us), similarity (we enjoy being with people whose attitudes and interests are similar to ours), and complementarity (sometimes we find ourselves attracted to people who are dissimilar to us). How we deal with our emotions can influence a relationship's course. When we censor or fail to disclose our feelings, our interactions may become shallow and less fulfilling. Concealing,

not expressing feelings honestly, or uncontrollably unleashing them can impede relationships.

4. **Define *assertiveness, nonassertiveness,* and *aggressiveness,* and explain how feelings can be handled effectively during conflicts.**   There are three ways of expressing feelings in emotionally charged or conflict-producing interpersonal situations: assertively (we express our feelings and thoughts honestly without infringing on the rights of others), nonassertively (we fail to express our real feelings), and aggressively (we stand up for our rights by ignoring or violating the rights of others).

5. **Identify behaviors that foster or impede the development of a relationship based on assertiveness.**   Being insensitive, selfish, stubborn, or pushy impedes relationship development by infringing on the rights of others. When we display assertiveness, we meet our interpersonal needs, make our own decisions, and think and say what we believe without infringing on others' rights. Only the assertive style enables us to express our beliefs and ideas without harming others or being victimized ourselves.

6. **Draw and explain a relationship window.**   We can use a relationship window—a model that analyzes how we interact with strangers, friends, and intimates—to identify the kinds of interactions in which we find it most difficult to be assertive.

7. **Create and explain a DESC script.**   We can analyze and learn to handle a typical situation by using a DESC script. DESC is an acronym for *describe, express, specify,* and *consequences.*

Resources for Further Inquiry and Reflection

To apply your understanding of how the principles in Chapter 9 are at work in our daily lives, consult the following resources for further inquiry and reflection. Or, if you prefer, choose any other appropriate resource. Then connect the ideas expressed in your chosen selection with the communication concepts and issues you are learning about both in and out of class.

 Listen to Me

"Emotion" (Destiny's Child)
"Emotions" (Mariah Carey)
"Happy Together" (The Turtles)
"Song Sung Blue" (Neil Diamond)
"You Can't Hurry Love" (The Supremes)
"What's Love Got to Do with It?" (Tina Turner)

Discuss the lessons the selected song teaches about how people's feelings affect their relationships.

 View Me

A History of Violence   *Disclosure*
Wedding Crashers   *Jungle Fever*
Just Friends   *Parenthood*
The Story of Us   *Anger Management*
A River Runs through It

These films explore relationships in a specific context. Choose one film and discuss the relationship's context, what we learn from the film about the effective and/or ineffective handling of emotions, how the suppression or expression of feelings affects relationships, and how conflict can influence a relationship's course.

Read Me

Janet Evanovich. *Metro Girl*. New York: HarperTorch, 2005.

Anita Shreve. *Light on Snow*. Boston: Little, Brown, 2005.

Judith Guest. *Ordinary People*. New York: Viking Press, 1976.

Jacqueline Mitchard. *The Deep End of the Ocean*. New York: Viking Press, 1996.

These books are about families in crisis. Discuss how the untimely death or disappearance of a child affects family members. Identify the problems family members face as they try to cope with their tragedy. What, if anything, do family members do to improve their communication climate and get in touch with their emotions?

 Tell Me

Share with the class the insights you gained from your chosen Listen to Me, View Me, or Read Me selection.

Discuss your opinion regarding one of the following positions: Computer-mediated communication within virtual communities is a means of widening our social relationships. Computer-mediated communication within virtual communities is a means of diminishing the need for in-person relationships.

Key Chapter Terminology

Communication
Works

online learning center

www.mhhe.com/gamble9

Use the Communication Works CD-ROM and the Online Learning Center at www.mhhe.com/gamble9 to further your knowledge of the following terminology.

acquaintanceships 242
aggressiveness 261
assertiveness 262
complementarity 249
conflict 256
content conflict 260
DESC script 266
ego conflict 260
emotion state 247
emotion traits 247
emotional contagion 251
emotional intelligence 242
emotional isolationists 253
flames 264
friendly relations 243

high-intensity conflict 260
interpersonal conflict 259
intrapersonal conflict 259
low-intensity conflict 259
medium-intensity conflict 259
moving toward friendship 243
nascent friendship 244
nonassertiveness 261
pseudoconflict 260
role-limited interaction 243
self-conflict 259
stabilized friendship 244
toxic communication 245
value conflict 260
waning friendship 244

Idioms in Translation

be outspoken—talk bluntly

come out of a shell—emerge from shyness

don't cry over spilt milk—don't worry about what has already been done

echo feelings—replicate emotions

lash out—attack

pouring out—revealing

read emotions—decipher feelings

stalemated relationship—a relationship going nowhere

strike a balance—work things out

Test Your Understanding

Go to the *Self Quizzes* on the Communication Works CD-ROM and the book's Online Learning Center at www.mhhe.com/gamble9.

Communication
Works

online learning center

www.mhhe.com/gamble9

Notes

1. Daniel Goleman. *Emotional Intelligence*. New York: Bantam, 1995, p. 34.

2. See, for example, Julie Yingling. *A Lifetime of Communication*. Mahwah, NJ: Lawrence Erlbaum Associates, 2004.

3. Charles Berger. "Uncertainty and Information Exchange in Developing Relationships." In Steve Duck, ed. *Handbook of Personal Relationships*. New York: Wiley, 1988, p. 244.

4. C. R. Berger and R. J. Calabrese. "Some Explorations in Initial Interactions and Beyond: Toward a Developmental Theory of Interpersonal Communication." *Human Communication Research* 1, 1975, pp. 98–112.

5. See, for example, W. Gudykunst. "Uncertainty and Anxiety." In Y. Y. Kim and W. Gudykunst, eds. Theories in Intercultural Communication. Sage: Newbury Park, CA: 1988, pp. 123–156.

6. M. Sunnafrank. "A Communication-Based Perspective on Attitude Similarity and Interpersonal Attraction in Early Acquaintance." *Communication Monographs* 51, 1984, pp. 372–380.

7. See, for example, Keith E. Davis. "Near and Dear: Friendship and Love Compared." *Psychology Today* 19, 1985, pp. 22–30; and Rosemary Blieszner and Rebecca G. Adams. *Adult Friendship*. Newbury Park, CA: Sage, 1992.

8. W. K. Rawlins. "Friendship as a Communicative Achievement: A Theory and an Interpretive Analysis of Verbal Reports." Doctoral dissertation, Temple University, Philadelphia, 1981.

9. Robert J. Sternberg. "A Triangular Theory of Love." *Psychological Review* 93, 1986, pp. 119–135; and Robert L. Sternberg. *The Triangle of Love: Intimacy, Passion, Commitment*. New York: Basic Books, 1988.

10. Karen S. Peterson. "Dating Game Has Changed." *USA Today*, February 11, 2003, p. 9D.

11. See Sally A. Lloyd and Beth C. Emery. *The Dark Side of Courtship: Physical and Sexual Aggression*. Thousand Oaks, CA: Sage, 2000; and J. D. Cunningham and J. K. Antill. "Current Trends in Nonmarital Cohabitation: The Great POSSLQ Hunt Continues." In Julia Wood and Steve W. Duck, eds. *Understanding Relationship Processes, 6: Off the Beaten Track: Understudied Relationships*. Thousand Oaks, CA: Sage, 1995, pp. 148–172.

12. D. Holmberg. "So Far So Good: Scripts for Romantic Relationship Development as Predictors of Relational Well-Being." *Journal of Social and Personal Relationships* 19:6, December 2002, pp. 777–796.

13. Julia T. Wood. *Gendered Lives*, 3rd ed. Belmont, CA: Wadsworth, 1999, p. 340.

14. Virginia Satir. *The New Peoplemaking*. Mountain View, CA: Science and Behavior Books, 1988, p. 79; and D. Olson and H. McCubbin. *Families: What Makes Them Work*. Beverly Hills, CA: Sage, 1983.

15. D. Gibbons and P. M. Olk. "The Individual and Structural Origins of Friendship and Social Position among Professionals." *Journal of Personality and Social Psychology* 84:2, February 2003, pp. 340–352; and "The Power of Nice," *Workforce* 82:1, January 2003, pp. 22–24.

16. See, for example, Susan A. Wheelan. *Creating Effective Teams: A Guide for Members and Leaders*. Thousand Oaks, CA: Sage, 1999; and James R. Barker. *The Discipline of Teamwork: Participation and Concertive Control*. Thousand Oaks, CA: Sage, 1999.

17. See, for example, Gabriel Weimann. *Communicating Unreality: Modern Media and the Reconstruction of Reality*. Thousand Oaks, CA: Sage, 1999.

18. Carroll E. Izard. *Human Emotions*. New York: Plenum, 1977, p. 5.

19. Izard.

20. Izard, p. 10.

21. For example, Ellen Berscheid and Elaine Hatfield Walster. *Interpersonal Attraction*, 2nd ed. Reading, MA: Addison-Wesley, 1978.

22. Emily Prager. "The Science of Beauty." *The New York Times*, April 17, 1994.

23. Berscheid and Walster.

24. Eliot Aronson. *The Social Animal*, 3rd ed. San Francisco: Freeman, 1980, p. 239.

25. Izard.

26. Earl Ubell. "The Deadly Emotions." *Parade*, February 11, 1990, pp. 3–5; and Jane E. Brody. "Controlling Anger Is Good Medicine for the Heart." *The New York Times*, November 20, 1996, p. C-15.

27. See *The Record*, June 20, 1994, p. B-1; and Thomas Sancton. "Oedipus, Schmoedipus." *Time*, December 9, 1996, p. 74.

28. E. Nagourney. "Blow a Gasket, for Your Heart." *The New York Times*, February 11, 2003, p. F6.

29. "Flame Retardant for Hot E-Mail Messages." *Newsweek*, August 28, 2000, p. 62.

30. Emily Nussbaum. "My So-Called Blog." *The New York Times Magazine*, January 11, 2004, pp. 33–37.

31. See Daniel Goleman. "A Feel-Good Theory: A Smile Affects Mood." *The New York Times*, July 18, 1989, C1, p. 9.

32. Ellen O'Brien. "Moods Are as Contagious as the Office Cold." *The Record*, November 15, 1993, p. B-3.

33. John Powell. *Why Am I Afraid to Tell You Who I Am?* Niles, IL: Argus, 1969.

34. Sandra Petronio, ed. *Balancing the Secrets of Private Disclosures*. Mahwah, NJ: Erlbaum, 1999.

35. Theodore Isaac Rubin. *The Angry Book*. New York: Macmillan, 1970; and Theodore Isaac Rubin. *Emotional Common Sense*. New York: Harper & Row, 1986.

36. Rubin. *The Angry Book*.

37. Marilyn Elias. "The Traits of Wrath in Men and Women." *USA Today*, August 11, 1994, p. 1D.

38. Elias, p. 2D.

39. Kay Deaux. *The Behavior of Women and Men*. Belmont, CA: Brooks/Cole, 1976.

40. Carol Tavis. "How Friendship Was 'Feminized.'" *The New York Times*, May 28, 1997, p. A-21.

41. See, for example, Michael Ryan. "Go Ahead—Cry!" *Parade*, January 5, 1997, p. 22.

42. Paul Ekman and Wallace Friesen. *Unmasking the Face*. Los Angeles: Consulting Psychology, 1984. For an intercultural perspective, see Stella Ting-Toomey. *The Challenge of Facework*. Albany: State University of New York Press, 1994.

43. Jerry Gillies. *Friendship: The Power and Potential of the Company You Keep*. New York: Coward-McCann, 1976.

44. Sidney Jourard. *The Transparent Self*. New York: Van Nostrand, 1971; and Sidney Jourard and Ted Landsman. *Health Personality*. New York: Macmillan, 1980.

45. David Johnson. *Reaching Out: Interpersonal Effectiveness and Self-Actualization*. Englewood Cliffs, NJ: Prentice-Hall, 1972.

46. Thomas Gordon. *Parent Effectiveness Training*. New York: Plume, 1988.

47. Daniel Goleman. "Strong Emotional Response to Disease May Bolster Patients' Immune System." *The New York Times*, October 22, 1985.

48. David Viscott. *The Language of Feelings*. New York: Pocket Books, 1976, p. 54.

49. See, for example, Denise H. Cloven and Michael E. Roloff. "The Chilling Effect of Aggressive Potential on the Expression of Complaints in Intimate Relationships." *Communication Monographs* 60:3, September 1993, pp. 199–219.

50. Johnson.

51. *Redbook*, June 1976.

52. See Bonnie Burman et al. "America's Angriest Home Videos: Behavioral Contingencies Observed in Home Reenactments of Marital Conflict." *Journal of Consulting and Clinical Psychology* 61:1, February 1993, pp. 28–39.

53. Susan Chira. "Study Finds Benefits in Emotional Control." *The New York Times*, May 26, 1994.

54. See Myra Warren Isenhart and Michael L. Spangle. *Collaborative Approaches to Resolving Conflict.* Thousand Oaks, CA: Sage, 2000.

55. Also see J. W. Pennebaker, B. Rime, and V. E. Blankenship. "Stereotypes of Emotional Expressiveness of Northerners and Southerners: A Cross-Cultural Test of Montesquieu's Hypotheses." *Journal of Personality and Social Psychology* 70, 1996, pp. 372–380.

56. For additional information, see J. D. Pearson. *Gender and Communication*, 2nd ed. Dubuque, IA: Brown, 1991, pp. 183–184; and Stella Ting-Toomey. "Managing Intercultural Conflicts Effectively." In Larry A. Samovar and Richard E. Porter. *Intercultural Communication: A Reader*, 7th ed. Belmont, CA: Wadsworth, 1994, pp. 360–372.

57. Alan C. Filley. *Interpersonal Conflict Resolution.* Glenview, IL: Scott, Foresman, 1975.

58. Philip Zimbardo and Shirley L. Radl. *The Shyness Workbook.* New York: A&W, Visual Library, 1979.

59. Ibid.

60. Lynn Z. Bloom, Karen Coburn, and Joan Pearlman. *The New Assertive Woman.* New York: Dell, 1975.

61. Arthur J. Lange and Patricia Jakubowski. *Responsible Assertive Behavior.* Champaign, IL: Research Press, 1976.

62. Sherwin B. Cotler and Julio J. Guerra. *Assertive Training.* Champaign, IL: Research Press, 1976, pp. 15–22.

63. For exercises related to the topics covered, see Danny Saunders. "Exercises in Communicating." *Simulation/Games for Learning* 21:2, June 1991, pp. 186–200.

64. M. M. Kazmer and C. Haythornthwaite. "Juggling Multiple Social Worlds: Distance Students Online and Offline." *American Behavioral Scientist* 45:3, November 2001, pp. 510–530.

65. See, for example, K. Y. A. McKenna and A. S. Green. "What's the Big Attraction? Relationship Formation on the Internet." *Journal of Social Issues*, 2002; and M. Orecklin. "Are You with Anyone?" *Time*, February 5, 2001, pp. 31–35.

66. See, for example, Clifford Stoll. *Silicon Snake Oil: Second Thoughts on the Information Highway.* New York: Anchor Books, 1995, p. 219.

67. See Nicholas Negroponte. *Being Digital.* New York: Vintage Books, 1995.

68. David F. Gallagher. "A Site to Pour Out Emotions, and Just about Anything Else." *The New York Times*, September 5, 2002, p. G6.

69. Marilyn Elias. "You've Got Trauma, but Writing Can Help." *USA Today*, July 1, 2002, p. 6D.

70. S. B. Barnes. *Computer-Mediated Communication: Human-to-Human Communication across the Internet.* Boston: Allyn & Bacon, 2003.

71. See Keith Ablow. "Speaking in the Third Person, Removed from Reality." *The New York Times*, November 1, 2005, p. F5; Brent Staples. "What Adolescents Miss When We Let Them Grow Up in Cyberspace." *The New York Times*, May 29, 2004, p. A14; and Nussbaum.

72. Stephanie Armour. "Boss: It's in the E-Mail." *The Wall Street Journal*, April 10, 1999, p. B3.

73. Sharon Bower and Gordon Bower. *Asserting Yourself.* Reading, MA: Addison-Wesley, 1977.

74. Goleman, *Emotional Intelligence*, p. 28.

CHAPTER 10

Person-to-Person: Interviewing

After finishing this chapter, you should be able to

1. Define *interview*.

2. Identify six types of interviews and the kind of information shared by participants in each type.

3. Describe the stages of an interview.

4. Formulate closed, open, primary, and secondary questions.

5. Compare and contrast the roles and responsibilities of interviewer and interviewee.

Dear_____:

We enjoyed having you visit us here (last week) (last month) (recently). Everyone who talked with you was most impressed, and I personally feel that you are one of the most promising young (men) (women) I've seen in a long time. We all wish we could make you an offer at this time. However, . . .

—From a corporation's form letter

Twenty years from now, the typical American worker will have changed jobs four times and careers twice and will be employed in an occupation that does not exist today.

—Jeffrey Hallet

What does a job interview have to do with interpersonal communication? A lot. In fact, when it comes to the kinds of skills that job recruiters look for, 89 percent of those surveyed say that *communication and interpersonal skills* are "very important," making those skills the most important factors in getting a job.[1] An employment interview is like Match.com. However, instead of two people seeking to determine if they have what it takes to make a love connection, during the job interview both the job candidate and the employer try to find out if they are a match when it comes to the organization's corporate culture and needs, and the applicant's values and skills. Culture clash or a mismatch is one of the biggest reasons new hires fail or find their jobs a struggle.[2]

During the course of our lives we all take part in interviews—sometimes as interviewee and other times as interviewer. Whichever side of the desk we find ourselves on, the interview incorporates many of the characteristics and principles of communication we have already discussed. Culture, self-concept, perception, listening and feedback, nonverbal cues, language and meaning, and assertiveness have parts to play in determining an interview's success. Let us explore the interview process and what you can do to succeed as either interviewer or interviewee.

■ ■ ■

THE INTERVIEW: BEYOND CASUAL CONVERSATION

Like other forms of communication, interviews usually involve face-to-face interaction. Unlike informal person-to-person communication, however, interviews go beyond talking for enjoyment. Instead, the conversations that occur during interviews tend to be planned and designed to achieve specific objectives. Thus, we define the **interview** as the most common type of purposeful, planned, decision-making, person-to-person communication. Interviewer and interviewee are involved in a process of personal contact and behavior exchange as they give and receive information in order to make educated decisions.

MediaWise

Piquing Career Interest

Have you found that you and/or your friends are taking more of an interest in criminal justice and forensics? If so, you are not alone. Even a large number of universities report having increased the scope of courses they offer in criminal justice. To what is this surge in interest attributed? Many believe it is due to television.

The public appears fascinated with investigation and the justice system, as evidenced by the popularity of television shows such as *Crossing Jordan, Law and Order, Without a Trace,* and *CSI.* Their popularity has spilled over into the real world, sparking an increasing interest in criminology careers. Even the Nevada law enforcement agency Field Services Division has responded to popular interest in forensic science, changing its name to Crime Scene Investigations.[3]

In your opinion, to what extent, if any, is the portrayal of criminology careers on television and film contributing to unrealistic career expectations in those who now seek to become criminologists? For example, most of the crimes featured on *CSI*-type shows are solved in an hour, while they might take months or even years to solve in the real world. In addition, the programs on television rarely show the boring days, they reveal the staff working with state-of-the-art equipment that many cities cannot afford, and they have a crimes-solved rate that actual criminologists could never attain.

Programs like *CSI* have sparked interest in criminology careers.

---

interview

the most common type of purposeful, planned, decision-making, person-to-person communication

Types of Interviews: Purposes and Goals

Interviews serve a variety of purposes. People engage in interviews to gather information (the information-gathering interview), to participate in an evaluation (the appraisal interview), to change someone's attitudes or behavior (the persuasive interview), to determine why someone is leaving a position (the exit interview), to provide guidance (the counseling interview), and to gain employment or select the right person for a job (the hiring or selection interview). Each of these types is characterized by different goals on the part of the participants.

INFORMATION-GATHERING INTERVIEW

In an information-gathering interview, the interviewer's goal is to collect information, opinions, or data about a specific topic or person. It is the interviewer's job to ask the interviewee questions designed to add to the interviewer's knowledge—questions about the interviewee's views, understanding, insights, predictions, and so on. Examples are interviews conducted with experts to complete an assignment

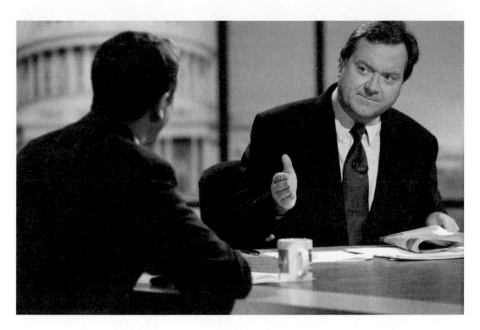

The interview is a popular format used by the media.

and interviews conducted for the popular media. Whether the interviewer is Tim Russert, Oprah Winfrey, or you, the aim is to gather information from someone who has knowledge that you do not yet have.

APPRAISAL INTERVIEW

In an appraisal interview, the interviewer, usually from management, assesses the performance of the interviewee. The goal is to evaluate what the interviewee is doing well and what he or she could do better. Through this means, expectations and behaviors are brought closer together. Interviewees gain perspective on how others view their work, and they reveal how they see themselves performing. In addition to reviews by supervisors, businesses also sometimes use a 360-degree assessment. This means that employees are rated not only by their superiors but also by their peers and subordinates. In addition, some companies separate the performance review from the salary review process.[4]

PERSUASIVE INTERVIEW

The goal of the interviewer in a persuasive interview is to change the interviewee's attitudes or behavior. The hope is that, as the interview progresses, the interviewee will come to a desired conclusion or give a desired response. Salespeople typically conduct persuasive interviews with customers to close a sale.

EXIT INTERVIEW

An exit interview is often conducted when an employee leaves an organization; it is an effort to determine why the match between employer and employee did not work or why the employee has decided to leave. Employers use the information obtained during an exit interview to refine the hiring process, to help prevent other employees from leaving, or merely to make the departure a more pleasant experience.

What types of information have you shared during interviews? What information have you received from the other participant in interviews? How do you think the information exchanged affected the decision-making process?

COUNSELING INTERVIEW

A counseling interview is usually conducted by someone trained in psychology and is designed to provide guidance and support for the interviewee. Counseling interviews help people solve problems, work more productively, interact with others more effectively, improve relationships with friends and family members, and cope more successfully with daily life.

HIRING OR SELECTION INTERVIEW

A hiring or selection interview is conducted to fill an employment position. The interviewer is an agent of the employer—perhaps a member of the personnel or human resources department or perhaps the person who would actually be the interviewee's supervisor. The interviewee, of course, is the person applying for the job. Because the hiring interview is experienced so commonly—and because it is so important—we will explore it in depth.

HOW DO YOU FEEL ABOUT INTERVIEWS? ASSESSING YOUR INTERVIEW ANXIETY

How do you feel about interviews? Are you more comfortable as interviewer or interviewee?

In the following list of fears commonly expressed by interviewers, circle the number beneath each statement that most accurately reflects your own level of apprehension: 0 = completely unconcerned; 1 = very mild concern; 2 = mild concern; 3 = more apprehensive than not; 4 = very frightened; 5 = a nervous wreck.

Go to the Online Learning Center at www.mhhe.com/gamble9 and answer the questions in the *Self Inventory* to evaluate your understanding of interview apprehension.

Interviewer

1. I won't be able to think of good questions to ask.

   0   1   2   3   4   5

2. I will appear very nervous.

   0   1   2   3   4   5

3. I will give the interviewee too little or too much information.

   0   1   2   3   4   5

4. I will not be considered credible.

   0   1   2   3   4   5

5. I will be asked questions about the company that I can't answer.

   0   1   2   3   4   5

6. I will be a poor judge of character.

   0   1   2   3   4   5

7. I will have poor rapport with the interviewee.

   0   1   2   3   4   5

8. I will not appear organized.

   0   1   2   3   4   5

9. I will be ineffective at probing for more information.

0   1   2   3   4   5

10. I will not hire the right person for the job.

0   1   2   3   4   5

Total the numbers you circled to arrive at your "interviewer's anxiety" score.

The following are some fears frequently expressed by interviewees. Circle the numbers that most accurately reflect your own level of apprehension: 0 = completely unconcerned; 1 = very mild concern; 2 = mild concern; 3 = more apprehensive than not; 4 = very frightened; 5 = a nervous wreck.

Interviewee

1. I will be asked questions I cannot answer.

0   1   2   3   4   5

2. I will not dress properly for the interview.

0   1   2   3   4   5

3. I will appear very nervous.

0   1   2   3   4   5

4. I will not appear competent.

0   1   2   3   4   5

5. The interviewer will cross-examine me.

0   1   2   3   4   5

6. I will be caught in a lie.

0   1   2   3   4   5

7. I will talk too much or too little.

0   1   2   3   4   5

8. I will have poor rapport with the interviewer.

0   1   2   3   4   5

9. I will undersell or oversell myself.

0   1   2   3   4   5

10. I won't be hired.

0   1   2   3   4   5

Total the numbers you circled to arrive at your "interviewee's anxiety" score.

Your scores indicate how frightened you are of assuming the role of interviewer or interviewee. If you accumulated 45 to 50 points, you are a nervous wreck; if you scored 35 to 44 points, you are too frightened; if you scored 20 to 34 points, you are somewhat apprehensive; if you scored 11 to 20 points, you are too casual; if you scored 0 to 10 points, you are not at all concerned—that is, you simply do not care.

Contrary to what you might assume, not being concerned at all about participating in an interview is just as much of a problem as being a nervous wreck, and being too casual can do as much damage as being too frightened. An interviewer or interviewee should be apprehensive to a degree. If you are not concerned about what will happen during the interview, then you will not care about making a good impression and, as a result, will not perform as effectively as you could.

THE HIRING OR SELECTION INTERVIEW

Some interviews are over before they begin. Why? Because the interviewer asks a question that he or she thinks is easy but that the interviewee cannot answer. For example, on being asked what she had to offer the company, all one interviewee could respond was, "Hmmmmm, that's a toughie." Then she added, "I was more wanting to hear what you could do for me." The candidate did not get the job.[5] How would you have replied to that question?

The hiring or selection interview is among the best known and most widely experienced type of interview and probably is the next major interview you will face. In addition, the vast majority of organizations use the hiring interview as a primary tool for selecting employees.[6]

It is as a result of a hiring or selection interview that we find ourselves accepted or rejected by a prospective employer—an individual, a small business, a large corporation, and so on. The employment interview offers a unique opportunity for the potential employer and employee to share meaningful information that will permit each to determine whether their association would be beneficial and productive. It gives both participants a chance to test each other by asking and answering relevant questions. Employers hope to gather information about you during the interview that your résumé, references, and any personality tests you may have been asked to take do not provide. They also believe the person-to-person approach is an effective way to sell their organization to you. As an applicant, you seek information about the employer and the job during the interview. You can deduce from your interaction with the interviewer what your long-term relationship might be and what life in that organization might be like if you are hired.

The better prepared you are for an employment interview, the better your chances will be of performing effectively and realizing your job objectives. Remember, an interview is not "just talk."[7] Both the interviewer and the interviewee must plan and prepare to participate in one. Only with planning and preparation will important questions and answers be shared and interview anxiety reduced. Let us begin by familiarizing ourselves with some important aspects of the hiring or selection interview, most of which are also aspects of interviews in general.

The hiring interview is the primary tool for selecting employees. Both interviewer and interviewee gain information during the interview.

Preliminary Tasks: Preparing the Cover Letter and Résumé

The job of the applicant is to prepare fully for the interview. By completing two documents—a cover letter and a résumé—that are well written and register a positive impression, you provide the interviewer with a preview of who you are and why you are qualified for the position.

Keep a number of facts in mind as you do this. When asked how much time they spend reviewing résumés, 56 percent of executives surveyed admitted to reviewing them for five minutes or less.[8] Thus, you need to work to capture the attention of the person to whom you send your résumé.

THE COVER LETTER

The cover letter introduces you to the interviewer. It is a brief (usually one-page), well-written letter that fulfills the following six criteria: (1) It expresses your interest in a position; (2) it tells how you learned of the position; (3) it reviews your primary skills and accomplishments; (4) it explains why these qualify you for the job; (5) it highlights any items of special interest about you that are relevant to your ability to perform the job; and (6) it contains a request for an interview. A résumé is always included with a cover letter. Figure 10.1 presents a sample cover letter.

THE RÉSUMÉ

The résumé summarizes your abilities and accomplishments. It details what you have to contribute that will meet the company's needs and help solve the employer's problems. Although formats differ, the résumé typically includes the following:

1. contact information—your name, address, telephone number, and e-mail address
2. job objective—a phrase or sentence that focuses on your area of expertise
3. employment history—your job experience, both paid and unpaid, beginning with the most recent
4. education—schools attended, degree(s) completed or expected, dates of completion, and a review of courses that relate directly to your ability to perform the job
5. relevant professional certifications and affiliations
6. community service
7. special skills and interests you possess that are revelent to the job

1616 River Road
New Milford, NJ 07646
June 10, 2006

Ms. Kelly Ames
Vice President, Human Resources
Stars and Strategies
1850 Broadway
New York, NY 10023

Dear Ms. Ames:

Your advertisement for a client representative in sports management appearing in last Sunday's *New York Times* immediately caught my attention and piqued my interest. My education and training uniquely qualify me to assist you in taking Stars and Strategies to the next level.

According to your advertisement, the job includes "assisting in the coordination and implementation of client services, as well as assisting in the identification and opening of new markets." It occurs to me that my background and experience in sports marketing parallel your needs. In addition, I am a highly motivated individual and a self-starter, with the following special qualifications to offer:

Four years of formal training in marketing
   and entrepreneurial studies
Proficiency in computers and Web site design

Once you have examined the enclosed résumé, I would like to talk with you about how I can put my skills and abilities to work for Stars and Strategies. I hope to have the opportunity to discuss in depth how my educational background and professional experience can contribute to your company's growth.

Sincerely,

John P. Garcia

John P. Garcia
Enclosure

8. references—people who agree to elaborate on your work history, capabilities, and character; reveal only that references are available on request unless you are asked to provide specific references at the time you submit your résumé

Figure 10.2 presents a sample résumé.

Structure: Stages of the Interview

Most effective interviews have a clear structure that includes a beginning, a middle, and an end. The beginning, or opening, is the segment of the process that provides an orientation to what will come. The middle, or body, is the longest segment and the one during which both parties really get down to business. The end, or close, is the segment during which the participants prepare to take leave of one another.

Just as the right kind of greeting at the start of a conversation can help create a feeling of friendliness, so the opening of an interview can help establish rapport between interviewer and interviewee.[9] The primary purpose of the opening is to

FIGURE 10.2
Sample Résumé.

In your résumé, do you have the most important information first?

JOHN P. GARCIA

1616 River Road
New Milford, New Jersey 07646
201-836-4444
jpg@aol.com

EDUCATION
School of Management, Syracuse University
Bachelor of Science in Management, May 2006; GPA: 4.0
Concentration in Marketing and Entrepreneurial Studies

HONORS
Golden Key National Honor Society
Dean's List 2002–2006
President, Investment Club

EXPERIENCE
Steiner Sports Marketing, New York, New York
(Summer 2005, 2004) Marketing Intern
Assisted in the management of client relations
Solved client and customer problems
Represented the company at numerous special events

Shearson Lehman Brothers, Stamford, Connecticut
(Summer 2003) Investment Intern
Assisted financial consultants
Analyzed trades
Evaluated financial securities options

KPMG, Montvale, New Jersey
(Summer 2002) Accounting Intern
Assisted in analysis of weekly financial reports
Prepared daily cash activity records
Conducted interviews with clients to determine level of satisfaction

COMPUTER SKILLS
Proficient in HTML and Web site creation
Experienced in using Lotus, WordPerfect for Windows, Excel, PowerPoint,
Quark Express, and PageMaker
Adept at mastering new programs and applications

ACTIVITIES
Student Council Representative, 2002–present
Peer Tutor, 2002–present
Orientation Leader, 2003–2006
Soccer Team, 2002–present

REFERENCES
Available upon request

make it possible for both parties to participate freely and honestly by creating an atmosphere of trust and goodwill and by explaining the purpose and scope of the meeting. Conversational icebreakers and orientation statements perform important functions at this stage. Typical icebreakers include comments about the weather, the surroundings, and current events—or a compliment. The idea is to use small talk to

Ethics & Communication

Résumé Padding and Résumé Poaching

1. Résumé padding has been around for a long time. Would you lie on your résumé to get your foot in the door? Would you "fix up" your résumé to help you look better on paper than you really are?

Not too long ago, Notre Dame's football coach, George O'Leary, had to step down from his head coach position after admitting that he had falsified the academic and athletic credentials listed on his résumé. In your opinion, should O'Leary have been fired for his résumé misrepresentations? Why or why not?

2. It is not merely some résumé writers who are ethically challenged. So are some recruiters. In fact, résumés posted on Internet job boards are not necessarily private or restricted to recruiters and other employers who pay a fee for access. While some sites may sell their résumés, résumé poaching also threatens the privacy of job seekers. The employees of competitive sites have been known to pose as recruiters in order to download thousands of résumés without permission. Persons who post their résumés on supposedly secure sites find themselves harassed by readers who object to their professions. For example, one job seeker in chemistry found herself harassed by activists against animal research.[10] In your opinion, should Internet job search sites be billboards for all to see, or should they be kept private, with recruiters and employers being adequately screened before being given access?

"It has come to my attention, Pickarell, that you may have been somewhat less than forthcoming in your résumé."

For the next few days, keep track of the verbal and nonverbal messages people use when they say hello or good-bye. Which beginnings and endings were particularly communicative? Which were ineffective? Did you observe any false starts or false endings? How could they have been avoided?

help make the interview a human encounter rather than a mechanical one. Typical orientation remarks include an identification of the interview's purpose, a preview of the topics to be discussed, and statements that motivate the respondent and act as a conduit, or transition, to the body of the interview.

In the body of the interview, the parties really get down to business. At this point, the interviewer and interviewee might discuss work experiences, including the applicant's strengths, weaknesses, major accomplishments, difficult problems tackled in the past, and career goals. Educational background and activities or interests are relevant areas to probe during this phase of the interview. Breadth of knowledge and the ability to manage time are also common areas of concern.

During the close of the interview, the main points covered are reviewed and summarized. Since an interview can affect any future meetings the parties may

Skill Builder

Wake-up Calls

1. According to one résumé expert, "The biggest mistake that people are making is that their résumés have no real impact.... A good résumé won't get you a job, but it will get you in the door."[11]

Look at the cartoon that appears in this box. What steps can you take to ensure that your résumé doesn't end up as origami? Describe how you would market yourself so that the person who receives your résumé actually opens it and spends some time reading it. For example, one applicant for a marketing position included her résumé in a package of gourmet coffees that she sent to the potential interviewer with the slogan

"Lindsay will wake up your marketing" affixed to the package. Do you think the interviewer read her résumé?

2. Once your résumé gets you in the door, give yourself an interview wake-up call. By exhibiting the following behaviors during your interview, you can help ensure you make the final cut: (1) Refer to the company you are interviewing with by name; (2) make it clear that you have researched the company; (3) respond enthusiastically to information the interviewer shares; (4) back up your answers to questions you are asked with specific examples; (5) use questions to demonstrate your knowledge of the industry and the company.

To assure that her resume stood out among hundreds of others, Sheila coated it with a mild adhesive.

---

have, care must be taken to make the leave-taking comfortable.[12] Expressing appreciation for the time and effort given is important; neither interviewee nor interviewer should feel discarded. In other words, the door should be left open for future contacts.

Questions: The Heart of the Interview

How many times a day are you asked questions? How many times a day do you ask questions? Questions are obviously a natural part of our daily discourse.

> *The only way to get the accurate answers is to ask the right questions.*
>
> —Kevin J. Murphy,
> *Effective Listening:*
> *Your Key to Career Success*

Questions asked in the course of typical, everyday interpersonal encounters perform a number of functions. They help us find out needed information, satisfy our curiosity, demonstrate our interest, and test the knowledge of the person we are questioning; at the same time, they permit the person we are questioning to reveal himself or herself to us.

For these reasons, questions are the primary means of collecting data in an interview. Not only do questions set the tone for an interview, but they also determine whether the interview will yield valuable information. Asking the right questions opens the window into the personality of both the interviewer and the interviewee.[13]

The effective interviewer, like the effective newswriter, can benefit from this famous verse by Rudyard Kipling:

> I keep six honest serving-men
> (They taught me all I know).
> Their names are what and why and when
> And how and where and who.

Using the interrogatives *what, where, when, who, how,* and *why* throughout an interview lays a foundation of knowledge on which to base decisions or conclusions.

During the course of an interview, closed, open, primary, and secondary questions may all be used, in any combination.[14] **Closed questions** are highly structured and answerable with a simple yes or no or in a few words. Following are examples of closed questions:

Where do you live?

What schools did you attend?

Did you graduate in the top quarter of your class?

Would you accept the salary offered?

What starting salary do you expect?

Open questions are broader than closed questions and are less restricting or structured; hence, they offer the interviewee more freedom with regard to the choice and scope of an answer. Following are examples of open questions:

Tell me about yourself.

What are your perceptions of our industry?

How do you judge success?

Why did you choose to interview for this job?

What are your career goals?

Describe a time you failed.

Describe a time when you failed to solve a conflict.

Open questions give interviewees a chance to express their feelings, attitudes, and values. Furthermore, they indicate that the interviewer is interested in understanding the interviewee's perspective. For example, let's consider the first question above. "Tell me about yourself" is not a request for your life story. The interviewer is really asking, "Why should I hire you?" Thus, your task when answering a question like this is to showcase your communication skills by crafting a statement shorter than two minutes, or about the length of an elevator ride, that lets the interviewer know more about you and what you can do for the company, that is, the benefits you will bring to your employer.[15]

Each party has questions in the interview—both you and the employer. The essence of the interview is to find out the answers to those questions.

—Richard N. Bolles

closed questions

highly structured questions answerable with a simple yes or no or in a few words

open questions

questions that offer the interviewee freedom with regard to the choice and scope of an answer

Open and closed questions may be either primary or secondary. Interviewers use **primary questions** to introduce topics or to begin exploring a new area. "What is your favorite hobby?" and "Tell me about your last job" are examples of primary questions—the first is closed; the second is open. A smart interviewer will prepare a list of primary questions before going to the interview, and smart interviewees will anticipate the primary questions they may be asked.

Interviewers use **secondary questions**—sometimes called probing questions—to follow up primary questions. They ask for an explanation of the ideas and feelings behind answers to other questions, and they are frequently used when answers to primary questions are vague or incomplete. Following are examples of secondary questions:

> Go on. What do you mean?
>
> Would you explain that further?
>
> Can you give me an example?
>
> What did you have in mind when you said that?

"Uh-huh" and "Hmm" are typical comments to the answers produced by secondary questions. The effective use of secondary questions distinguishes skilled from unskilled interviewers.[16]

To ask effective follow-up questions, you need to be an effective listener. You must be sensitive to and on the lookout for an interviewee's feelings and attitudes, in addition to the facts and opinions he or she states. You need to develop techniques that will permit you to see the world through the other person's eyes.

The key to the success of professional interviewers, such as Diane Sawyer and Larry King, is their ability to listen.[17] Of course, the interviewee must also be an effective listener.

primary questions

questions used to introduce topics or explore a new area

secondary questions

probing questions that follow up primary questions

Objectives: Roles and Responsibilities

Let us now examine the roles and responsibilities of each participant in an interview.

Both interviewer and interviewee come to the interview with certain goals in mind. Interviewers usually have a threefold objective: They hope to (1) gather information that will enable them to evaluate the interviewees' probable performance accurately, (2) persuade applicants that the business or organization is a good one to work for, and (3) ascertain whether the applicants and the people with whom they will work will be compatible. Interviewers also want to keep their own jobs. Remember that a company invests both time and money in hiring and training a new employee. If the employee does not work out, the investment is sacrificed, and some of the blame falls on the original interviewer.

To fulfill their objectives, interviewers need to master the art of structuring a successful interview, use effective questioning techniques, and approach each interview with flexibility and sensitivity. Good interviewers work hard during an interview. They wear three hats: information seeker, information giver, and decision maker (see Figure 10.3). They recognize good answers, are aware of word choices, and pick up on silences and hesitations. They are active, not passive, participants as they seek to differentiate what is real from what is make-believe. They need to be patient observers and search for the inner truth that lies beneath the surface of a candidate.

You might be in demand for a job. And the potential employer might even be looking for someone with just your skills. But you still have to demonstrate that

According to Mimi Collins, spokesperson for the National Association of Colleges and Employers, employers often cite good communication skills, both oral and written, as important. Honesty and integrity are second, teamwork skills are third, interpersonal skills fourth, and strong work ethic fifth. How do you evaluate yourself against these criteria?

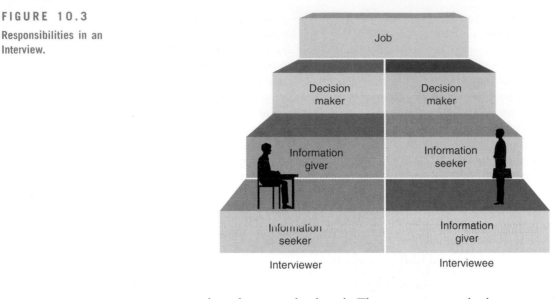

you are the right person for the job. Thus, interviewees also bear responsibility during an interview. They, too, need to speak and listen, provide information, and at the same time collect information that will help them decide whether or not to accept the job. To accomplish these goals, interviewees need to research the organization to which they are applying and try to anticipate the questions they will be asked. They also need to plan to ask questions themselves. It is unfortunate and unproductive when only the interviewer gains information from an interview. The interviewee can often learn much about work conditions and the prospects for advancement by asking questions and probing for answers. To the extent that interviewees have a right to share the control of the interview, they can affect its direction and content. Like interviewers, interviewees need to be good listeners. They, too, must be adaptable and sensitive to the image they project.

Effective interviewees work hard at self-assessment. In effect, they take stock of themselves to determine who they are, what their career needs and their goals are, and how they can best sell themselves to an employer.

As a prospective interviewee, you will find it useful to prepare by thinking about and answering the following questions:

1. For what types of positions has my training prepared me?
2. What has been my most rewarding experience?
3. What type of job do I want?
4. Would I be happier working alone or with others?
5. What qualifications do I have that make me feel I would be successful in the job of my choice?
6. What type or types of people do I want to work for?
7. What type or types of people do I not want to work for?
8. How do I feel about receiving criticism?
9. What salary will enable me to meet my financial needs?
10. What salary will enable me to live comfortably?
11. What will interviewers want to know about me, my interests, my background, and my experiences?

In addition to conducting a self-survey, the interviewee needs to work to withstand the pressure of the interview situation. Are you prepared to maintain your composure while being stared at, interrupted, spoken to abruptly, or asked difficult questions? Have you practiced enough to keep cool when on the interview hot seat?[18] How do you think you would react if you were asked tough questions? The following questions are favorites among interviewers.[19] How would you answer them?

1. Tell me about yourself.
2. What do you think you're worth?
3. What are you good at?
4. If we hired you, what about this organization would concern you most?
5. What attributes do you think an effective manager should possess?
6. What are your short-term goals? How are they different from your long-term goals?
7. How has your background prepared you for this position?
8. What are your major strengths and weaknesses?
9. How would a former employer or instructor describe you?
10. Why did you leave your last job?
11. What do you consider your greatest accomplishment?
12. What's wrong with you?
13. What would you do if I told you that I thought you were giving a very poor interview today?
14. How long do you plan to remain with us if you get this job?
15. What would you like to know about us?

Some interviewers prefer to ask even more searching questions, such as the following:

Tell me about how you handled the last mistake you made.

Are there things at which you aren't very good?

At your weekly team meetings, your boss unexpectedly begins aggressively critiquing your performance on a current project. What would you do?

You're in a situation in which you have two very important responsibilities that both have deadlines that are impossible to meet. You cannot accomplish both. How do you handle that situation?[20]

Practice in answering questions like these—under both favorable and unfavorable conditions—is essential.[21] It is important that you know what you want to say during the interview and that you use the questions you are asked as an opportunity to say it. Along the way, you can flatter the interviewer by offering comments such as "I think you've touched on something really important."

The interviewer can, of course, consult a résumé to ascertain information about the applicant—about educational background and previous positions held, for example. However, gathering enough information to evaluate the personal qualities of an applicant is more difficult. Following is a list of personal qualifications, with the questions interviewers typically ask to evaluate them:

1. *Quality:* Skill in managing one's own career
   Question: What specific things have you done deliberately to get where you are today?

What other qualities do you believe interviewers look for in interviewees? If you were an interviewer, what questions would you ask to determine if a person possessed those qualities?

2. *Quality:* Skill in managing others
   Question: What are some examples of things you do and do not like to delegate?
3. *Quality:* Sense of responsibility
   Question: What steps do you take to see that things do not fall through the cracks when you are supervising a project?
4. *Quality:* Skill in working with people
   Question: If we assembled in one room a group of people you have worked with and asked them to describe what it was like to work with you, what would they be likely to say? What would your greatest supporter say? What would your severest critic say?

When it comes to answering questions about items listed on your résumé, one career coach suggests using the acronym S.T.A.R. (situation, task, action, result) as a guide. For example, let's say your résumé notes that you turned around a sales territory in decline, ultimately increasing sales by 10 percent in your first year. The interviewer asks: "How did you do that?" Your job is to walk the interviewer through the process by revealing the situation you faced, how you assessed your task, the action you took, and the result you achieved.[22]

Most employment interviews can be grouped into one of three categories: the behavioral, the case, and the stress interview. In the **behavioral interview,** an employer is looking for specific examples from the prospective employee of times when he or she has exhibited specific skills. When asked a question such as "Tell me about a time you acted in a leadership role," the interviewee might respond, "I was the director of a fund-raising group," or "I was an officer in Women in Communication." In the **case interview,** a company presents the interviewee with a business case and asks for him or her to work through it. To help prepare yourself for such an interview, check out the company Web site beforehand. Some companies post sample cases on their sites. The third type of interview, the **stress interview,** typically includes more than one interviewer firing questions at the interviewee to see how that person handles himself or herself during a stressful situation.

Because the interview is a conversation and not an interrogation, during the course of the interview, the interviewee should ask questions of the interviewer as a means of demonstrating interest in the job and the company.[23] When the interviewee asks questions, the interview becomes more balanced. What kinds of questions should you ask when in the interviewee role? You should not ask questions that you can answer easily by visiting the company's Web site. You should, however, ask questions that seek clarification; for example: "I read on your site that you will be introducing new products. Could you tell me more about how you plan to roll them out?"

In general, interviewees ask questions about the company and corporate culture (rather than about salary or benefits), the industry, the position, and the people in the company. Following are some examples:

Why is this position open?
What would you say are the main challenges of this job?
What will be the priorities in the first 90 days?
With whom will I be working?
How is the department organized, and what will my role be?

---

behavioral interview

an employment interview in which an employer looks for the employee to provide specific examples of specific skills

case interview

an employment interview in which the interviewee is presented with a business case by the employer and asked to work through it

stress interview

an employment interview in which more than one person fires questions at an interviewee

Skill Builder

Let's Get Tough

Human relations consultant and interviewer trainer Justin Menkes helps employment recruiters learn how to gather a lot of information in a brief period of time. To accomplish this, he suggests they ask questions like those identified in the text. Try your hand at answering one of those questions: You have two very important responsibilities that both have deadlines that are impossible to meet. You cannot accomplish both. How do you handle that situation?

Which of the following possible responses does your answer most resemble?

1. I'd focus on the project I'm most comfortable with and give it my all.

2. I'd plan carefully, assign segments of the project to others, and multitask so that I could complete both.

3. I'd ask my supervisor which project is most important to the company.

According to Menkes, the first response suggests that the interviewee's focus is on himself or herself, the second response does not answer the question asked, and the third response reveals an interest in the needs of the company and an interest in developing a collaborative relationship.[24]

How will performance be measured and evaluated?

How are conflicts resolved?

How are decisions made?

Why do you like working here?[25]

To be effective, both interview participants need to work hard. Questioner and respondent constantly exchange information. While one speaks, the other conveys nonverbal information through posture, facial expression, gestures, and so on. You may stop talking during an interview, but that does not mean that you stop communicating. Know what you want to accomplish with your verbal and nonverbal messages.

Impression Management: Effective Interviewing

How well do we need to know someone before we believe we understand him or her? Experience says not very long. According to psychologists Nalini Ambady and Frank Bernieri, the power of first impressions arms us with a kind of prerational ability or intuition for making judgements about others that color the other impressions we gather over time.[26] It becomes a self-fulfilling prophecy. We assume that the way someone behaves in an interview is indicative of the way that person always behaves.

As an interviewee, what first impressions do you make? How do you know?

The adage that first impressions count apparently holds true for job interviews.[27] In fact, the word *interview* is derived from the French word *entrevoir*, meaning "to see one another" or "to meet." What happens when an interviewer and an interviewee meet for the first time? What variables influence the impressions the interviewer forms of the interviewee? Most interviewers make their decisions about an applicant during the actual course of the interview. In fact, although most decide in the last quarter of the interview whether or not to invite the applicant back, a bias for or against the candidate is established earlier in the interview, often during the first four to six minutes.

Exploring Diversity

Voices and Impression Management

People from different cultures use their voices differently, a fact that could lead to misunderstandings between interviewers and interviewees. People from the Middle East, for example, tend to speak louder than Westerners, causing Westerners to perceive them as overly emotional.

In contrast, the Japanese tend to be much more soft-spoken, leading Westerners to believe that they are extremely polite and humble.

How could such habitual ways of speaking affect the interview process? What can interviewers and interviewees do to diminish such perceptual barriers?

In *Your Attitude Is Showing*, Elwood N. Chapman notes:

> First impressions are important because they have a lasting quality. People you meet for the first time appear to have little radar sets tuned into your attitude. If your attitude is positive, they receive a friendly, warm signal, and they are attracted to you; if your attitude is negative, they receive an unfriendly signal, and they try to avoid you.[28]

Apparently, once interviewers form an initial impression, they selectively pick up on whatever information supports that impression. In effect, interviewers make self-fulfilling prophecies.

According to researcher Lois Einhorn, how much of the time allotted for an interview is actually used also sends an important message.[29] She found that interviewees who were not hired had participated in interviews shorter than those of successful applicants. She also found that successful interviewees spoke a greater percentage of the time than their unsuccessful counterparts. In fact, the successful applicants spoke for some 55 percent of the total interview time, whereas the unsuccessful applicants spoke only 37 percent of the time. Seeming to control the interview also leaves an impression. In Einhorn's research, successful applicants initiated 56 percent of the comments made during their interviews, whereas unsuccessful applicants were viewed as followers—they initiated only 37 percent of the comments. It is important for an interviewee to send messages that he or she is active, not passive.

THE JOB APPLICANT

Believe in yourself.

—The Wizard of Oz, to Dorothy

As a job applicant, you will have to work to manage the initial impression you give. You will be evaluated on how you come across and present yourself during the interview. What you say and how you say it are your basic resources—the key tools you have to work with. In effect, you are your own marketing manager; therefore, it is up to you to sell yourself to the interviewer. How you communicate your assets, your values, your attitudes, and your overall credibility will determine whether or not you are hired.

Of necessity, interviewers need to find out a great deal about you in a short period of time. They want to evaluate your strengths as a communicator, your general personality, your social effectiveness, and your character. The interviewer also wants to determine your needs and wants—including your career and educational goals, interests, and aspirations. Interviewers will assess your appearance, your ability to use body language effectively, and your ability to maintain control during the interview.

The interviewer's assessment of you will determine whether or not you get the job. The following are some of the negative factors that turn off the interviewer and lead to applicant rejection:

arrogance

lack of motivation or enthusiasm

immaturity

poor communication skills

unclear goals

unwillingness to relocate or travel

deficient preparation for the interview

lack of experience

too sloppy or too slick an appearance.[30]

Among the factors leading to your receiving job offers are the following:

a pleasant personality (likableness)

enthusiasm

interpersonal skills

ability to function as part of a team

knowledge of the field

computer literacy

creativity

clear purpose and goals

flexibility and the ability to handle change

confidence in what you are doing and who you are

integrity and moral standards

global perspective

sense of humor[31]

Interviewers will use dress and appearance in their assessment of you. If you were the interviewer, how would you assess the dress of these two candidates?

1. *Enumerate the qualities and skills that would make you a good investment for an employer.*
2. *Enumerate the qualities and skills you need to develop further and plan how to do this.*
3. *Compose a "Position Wanted" advertisement for yourself.*

Interviewers will also judge you on the basis of the nonverbal cues you send. Interviewers consistently give higher general ratings to applicants who score high in nonverbal expression than to applicants who score low. A highly rated non-verbal presentation includes (1) maintaining comfortable eye contact with the interviewer rather than looking away; (2) varying the pitch and volume of your voice rather than speaking in a monotone, whispering, or shouting; (3) eliminating hesitations ("uhs" and "ums"); (4) leaning forward from the trunk rather than slumping in your seat; and (5) communicating a high level of energy supported by smiles, hand gestures, and appropriate body movements. In like fashion, the avoidance of tightly held hands, twitching feet or fingers, and various other signs of physical tension will influence the interviewer positively.

Obviously, appropriate dress is also important to the impression you make during the interview. Most job applicants are aware that casual dress is out and conservative styles are in at job interviews. Ultraconservative is becoming the norm and the color gray, with its connotation of rock-solid dependability, the color of choice.[32] Consultant John Molloy reports that, when you interview for a job, it is advisable to dress as if you were a candidate for a position one or two steps higher

What type of clothing would you consider inappropriate for a job interview? What type of clothing would you wear to a job interview?

Would you send your thank-you via e-mail or letter? Demonstrating a mindfulness of etiquette can go a long way in your job search. A recent survey of hiring managers by CareerBuilder.com found that 15 percent would reject a job candidate who neglected to send a thank-you letter after the interview; 32 percent reported that they would still consider the applicant but that their opinion of him or her would decline. Some 23 percent of the managers prefer handwritten thank-yous, while 21 percent expect a typed hard copy, and 19 percent want e-mail thank-yous followed up with a letter.

than the one for which you are actually applying.[33] Why is there so much concern with dress? When all else is comparable—education, aptitude, experience—appearance may well be the deciding factor. The candidate who looks the most professional, competent, and confident will probably be the one who is hired.

You can cement a positive image in two ways. First, do not ask about vacation, company benefits, and personal days during your first interview.[34] Work instead to display your knowledge of the company and to understand its goals and how you can fit in. Ask questions that touch on strategic and tactical issues. Second, be sure to send a brief thank-you note to the person or persons who interviewed you. Richard Bolles, an interview specialist, writes: "This is one of the most essential steps in the whole job-seeking process—and the one most overlooked by job-seekers."[35] In fact, one of the authors was actually told that a person who interviewed her for a teaching position had recommended her because she was the only applicant to send him a thank-you note after the interview.[36]

THE INTERVIEWER

In any interview, the interviewer who judges is also judged by the interviewee. To the extent that this judgment is favorable, the interviewer can elicit the interviewee's fullest cooperation in accomplishing the aims and objectives of the interview.

The interviewer's ability to set the tone by reducing the interviewee's initial anxiety is an extremely important factor in the interviewee's first impression. During the body of the interview, the interviewer must work to (1) maintain control of the interchange, (2) deliver information so that it is clearly understood, (3) listen for both facts and feelings, (4) build trust, and (5) distinguish relevant from irrelevant information. Finally, at the conclusion, it is up to the interviewer to explain to the applicant the next course of action to be taken and to terminate the encounter smoothly and graciously.

Like interviewees, interviewers must be adept at using nonverbal cues. They must know when to pause and when to speak. For example, three- to six-second silences by interviewers have been found effective in getting interviewees to provide more in-depth information; this is one way the interviewer can increase the amount of time an applicant spends answering a question. Another way to increase the length of an applicant's response is for the interviewer to murmur "Mm-hmm" while nodding affirmatively. In fact, answers to questions posed by interviewers who say "Mm-hmm" have been found to be as much as two times longer than answers given to interviewers who offer no "Mm-hmms." When interviewees give a high rating of the interviewer's vocal communication and ability to listen, they tend to enjoy the interview more and rate the interviewer favorably in general.

DIVERSITY AND THE INTERVIEW

Culture influences how we conduct ourselves during interviews. For example, in collectivistic cultures such as those in China, Japan, and Korea, interviewees habitually display modesty. If Americans, who are used to stressing their positive qualities, were interviewing in any of those countries, they could be perceived as arrogant and self-centered. On the other hand, if persons from a collectivistic culture were to interview in the United States, they could be perceived as unassertive, lacking in confidence, and unprepared to assume leadership. While Western culture encourages people to be assertive and showcase strengths, Eastern culture traditionally teaches members to be more modest and humble about their personal achievements, qualifications, and experience. Similarly, Native American culture teaches that cooperation is a benefit and that one leads through deeds, not words. Thus, not wanting to appear boastful, Native Americans could also be hesitant to discuss their personal strengths.[37]

There are gender differences in what employees seek in a job. Survey results reveal that most men value compensation above all else, while most women put employee benefits first. Compensation is ranked third on most women's list, after opportunities for skill development.[38]

Age also correlates with what employees want most in a job. In contrast with all other groups, the under-thirties do not even rank benefits among their top five concerns. What is important to most persons in this age bracket are opportunities to develop skills, chances for promotion, compensation, vacations, and an appealing culture and colleagues.[39]

Interviewers need to be sensitive to and demonstrate their respect for all cultures. Not hiring someone on the basis of age, sexual preference, national origin, or religion is illegal. Despite this, many Muslim workers report having thought about changing their last names to avoid alienating potential employers.[40] Would you ever change your name if you thought doing so would help you get the job you want? Why or why not?

TECHNOLOGY AND THE JOB SEARCH

The Web continues to change the way we find jobs. Persons with online savvy can gain unexpected advantages over the competition because job openings are often posted online before they appear in newspapers.[41]

Applicants should use a company's home page to get background information on the organization or to e-mail a résumé and cover letter. A company's Web site is a good place to learn about the company's culture. Many sites provide an overview of work-related policies and perks, including whether the firm encourages job sharing or telecommuting.[42] In addition, many companies post job openings on their own sites as well as on recruitment sites such as Monster.com. Following are some Web sites you can consult for information on companies and jobs:

Company Information
www.wsj.com
www.nytimes.com
www.bizweb.com

The Web is revolutionizing the job search. Monster.com is a job search site. Log on and see if you can find a job opening of interest to you.

Reprinted with permission from Monster.com.

Job Information

http://stats.bls.gov   The Bureau of Labor Statistics Web site, which offers information on positions by state, listing the average salary being paid per position

www.careerbuilder.com

www.NowHiring.com

www.monster.com

Usenet newsgroups, and listserv mailing lists, and blogs are three other Internet resources you can use to learn about employment possibilities and company cultures. Of the three, blogs are becoming increasingly popular in electronic recruiting, functioning as a prime means that applicants use to find out about companies. Often they contain information such as what it is like to work at a company as well as what is going on in an industry.[43]

Job seekers also create their own home pages, featuring both their online résumé and business card.[44] A variety of online resources and computer programs exist to help you prepare your résumé. Many provide you with templates that you can complete as is or customize. You can also post your résumé on the Net by e-mailing it to a server.

In fact, more and more companies now request that potential employees submit an electronic résumé (a résumé that is obtained and analyzed electronically by the employer).[45] An electronic résumé includes keywords that describe the person's competencies and skills. Once the employer scans the résumé into the company's computer tracking system, when a job becomes available, the employer can efficiently search the résumés contained in the database by the keywords that describe the characteristics a person qualified for the position should have. Electronic résumés require standard formats and block letters that are plain and simple. A résumé that is going to be scanned should not use boldface type, underlining, or bullets, because these special effects interfere with the scanning process. To facilitate the initial résumé screening, which will be done by a bias-free computer, an electronic résumé typically contains a block paragraph of keywords, which immediately follows the identification information centered above it. Unlike your traditional résumé, which probably contains action verbs such as *communicates well*, your electronic résumé should contain nouns, such as *organizational skills*. A number of Internet sites can help you prepare an electronic résumé. By posting your résumé on a home page, you increase the likelihood that an employer looking for someone with your background and qualifications will access your résumé and contact you directly.

Employers also use computers to add flexibility to currently available interviewing channels. By conducting a computer-assisted interview, for example, employers are able to conduct preliminary conversations with people geographically dispersed from them. In increasing numbers, in addition to telephones and videoconferences, employers are also conducting interviews via e-mail and chat groups. Although these channels do not enable interviewer and interviewee to shake hands with each other, and despite the fact that such interviews will probably not replace face-to-face interviews, they do expand the information resources used by organizations and can be used to supplement face-to-face interviews.[46]

You will want to avoid the following five blunders commonly made by people who use the Internet to search for a job:[47]

1. *Mismerged cover letters.* The interviewee sends a letter that expresses the desire to put skills to work for one company when applying for a job with another company.

2. *Goofy personal e-mail addresses.* Using a name like Snickerdoodle @pastrylover.com or egotisticalking@sold.com can make you look like a less than serious candidate. Use a business-sounding e-mail address instead.

3. *Fun with fonts.* It is a mistake to use bright colors and exotic fonts in résumés or e-mails. Use a plain-text format instead.

4. *Playing out of your league.* Because the Internet makes applying for a job so easy, many applicants apply for jobs for which they are not qualified.

5. *Thinking Send is the end.* Your work is not done when you click Send. Networking and follow-up remain essential components of any job search. Indeed, 61 percent of people surveyed report that networking and referrals remain the best sources for new jobs.[48]

Getting a job today has much in common with reality-show contests. Hundreds of job candidates compete, but there will be only one winner.

LOOKING AT THE LAW: ILLEGAL QUESTIONS IN INTERVIEWS

While we have seen that some interview questions are tough and probing, others concerning age, race, marital status, and other personal characteristics are protected under antidiscrimination statutes and are illegal to ask. The Equal Employment Opportunity Commission (EEOC) is the arm of the federal government responsible for monitoring discriminatory practices in hiring decisions. More than three decades ago, the EEOC initially issued employment interview guidelines. Over the years, these guidelines have been updated, and the laws of the EEOC apply in all 50 states.

According to the EEOC, criteria that are legally irrelevant to job qualifications are discriminatory. Interviewees in all states are protected from answering questions about race, ethnicity, marital status, age, sex, disability, and arrest records. It is important for both interviewers and interviewees to realize which questions are legally impermissible in employment interviews. Both parties to the interview have to be well versed in their rights to be able to protect them. The determining factor in whether a question is lawful is simple: Is the information sought relevant to your ability to perform the job? The following are among the most commonly asked illegal questions:

1. Are you physically disabled?
2. How old are you?
3. Are you married?
4. Do you have or are you planning to have a family?
5. What political party do you belong to?
6. Have you ever served time in prison?
7. Is English your native language?
8. What is your religion?
9. Will you need to live near a mosque?
10. Is it hard for you to find child care?
11. Are you a United States citizen?
12. Where were your parents born?
13. Who lives with you?
14. When did you graduate from college?
15. What was the date of your last physical exam?
16. To what clubs or social organizations do you belong?
17. Have you had any recent or past illnesses or operations?
18. How is your family's health?
19. Have you ever been arrested?
20. If you have been in the military, were you honorably discharged?

On the other hand, it is legal to ask the following questions:

1. Are you authorized to work in the United States?
2. What languages do you read or speak fluently (if relevant to the job)?
3. Are you over 18?
4. Would you relocate?
5. Would you be willing to travel as needed?
6. Would you be able and willing to work overtime as necessary?
7. Do you belong to any groups that are relevant to your ability to perform this job?
8. What education do you have?
9. Have you ever been convicted of [fill in the blank]? (The crime must be reasonably related to the performance of the job.)
10. In what branch of the armed forces did you serve?[49]

What if an interviewer asks you an illegal question? You can object diplomatically and remind the interviewer that the question is inappropriate. Doing so, however, can make that interviewer defensive and less willing to select you for the job. Another option is to respond to the illegal question with only information that the interviewer could have legally sought from you. That is, you handle the question by answering the part you do not object to without providing any information you do not wish to provide. For example, if the interviewer asks whether English is your native language, you can respond, "I am fluent in English." If he or she asks whether you belong to a political group, you can respond, "The only groups with which I affiliate that are relevant to this job are the Public Relations Society of America and the American Society for Training and Development."

GUIDELINES FOR INCREASING YOUR EFFECTIVENESS IN INTERVIEWS

As you can see, an interview, like any other interpersonal relationship, requires the cooperation, skill, and commitment of both participants to be effective. Both interviewees and interviewers can benefit from the following guidelines:

1. *Be prepared.* Understand the purpose of the interview; plan or anticipate the questions you will ask and be asked; understand your goals; and be able to communicate those goals clearly.

2. *Practice sending and receiving messages.* By its very nature, an interview demands skill at sending and receiving verbal and nonverbal messages. Not only must the parties clearly encode their messages, but they must also be skilled at reading the reactions and checking the perceptions of the other.

3. *Demonstrate effective listening skills.* Problems occur in interviews when either the interviewer or the interviewee fails to listen closely to what the other is saying. As is noted in John Brady's *The Craft of Interviewing*, if participants listen carefully—rather than thinking about what they plan to say next—the interview has a better chance of being productive.[50]

4. *Have conviction.* Ask and answer questions and express your opinions with enthusiasm. If you are not excited by your ideas, skills, and abilities, why should anyone else be?

5. *Be flexible.* Do not overprepare or memorize statements. Think things through thoroughly, and be prepared to handle questions or answers you did not anticipate. Be able to adjust to the other person's style and pace.

6. *Be observant.* Pay attention to the nonverbal signals sent to you and by you. Be sure that the signals you send are positive, not negative. Give the other person your total attention.

7. *Consider the offer.* Both interviewer and interviewee need to consider the ramifications of a job offer. A typical 40-hour-a-week job done for approximately 50 weeks a year adds up to 6,000 hours in only three years. Be sure that your choice is one both you and the organization can live with.

Focus on Service Learning

Using information provided on the EEOC's (Equal Employment Opportunity Commission's) Web site, www.eeoc.gov, and other Web sites, such as www.resumagic.com/ interviewspreparation.html, share with persons currently unemployed your understanding of how to conduct yourself during interviewing, including how to manage illegal questions.

8. *Chart your progress.* Each time you participate in an interview, fill out a copy of the following evaluation. Circle the number that best describes your response to each question.

a. How prepared were you for the interview?

Not at all prepared   1   2   3   4   5   Fully prepared

b. What kind of climate did you help create?

Hostile climate   1   2   3   4   5   Friendly climate

c. Were the questions you asked clear?

Not clear   1   2   3   4   5   Clear

d. Were the responses you offered complete?

Incomplete   1   2   3   4   5   Complete

e. How carefully did you listen to the other person?

Not at all   1   2   3   4   5   Very carefully

f. How carefully did you pay attention to nonverbal cues?

Not at all   1   2   3   4   5   Very carefully

g. To what extent were you distracted by external stimuli?

Very much   1   2   3   4   5   Not at all

h. How self-confident were you during the interview?

Not at all   1   2   3   4   5   Very confident

i. How flexible were you during the interview?

Not flexible   1   2   3   4   5   Very flexible

j. Would you like to change or improve your behavior for your next interview?

Very much   1   2   3   4   5   Little, or not at all

If your answer to the last question is 1, 2, 3, or 4, consider how you would like to change.

Thinking Critically

Reflect and Respond

Agree or disagree with each of the following statements. Supply reasons and examples that support your stance.

Interviewers care less about what you say than how you say it.

The hiring process is a negative process. The goal of the interviewer is to find out what's wrong with you.

What do your responses tell you about how you feel about and approach interviews?

Looking Back and Ahead
Consider This Case: Breaking Up Is Hard to Do

"Hey, Hiroko, what's up?" Nick slung his backpack to the floor in Starbucks and dragged an empty chair next to his friend. "You look pretty glum."

"Nick! Hey." Hiroko made room on the table for Nick's coffee. "Good to see you. Kathy's here too." He nodded in the direction of the counter where a young woman was collecting her order. "We're both feeling down."

"What's happening?" Nick said, shrugging out of his coat.

"Casey's moving out." Casey was one of Hiroko and Kathy's housemates in their residence near campus.

"Wow, that's too bad. How come?"

"Her mom is pretty sick, so Casey's moving back home to help her dad take care of her two little brothers. She's going to have to commute to school for a while."

Kathy sat down with them and nodded a hello at Nick. "We're pretty bummed," she confirmed. "None of us knew about her mom, and we had no clue anything big like this was coming. We're drowning our sorrows in latte, right, Hiroko?"

"Latte! No way," said Hiroko. "Black coffee for me."

"Well," said Nick, "I'm sorry to hear about Casey's mom. But Casey'll still be around school, right? And all you have to do is advertise for another housemate. How about me?" he grinned.

"Funny, Nick," said Hiroko dourly. Nick had one of the few single dorm rooms on campus and treasured his privacy. "It's not that easy. I'm really worried about what losing Casey is going to mean for us."

Kathy sipped her drink and nodded. "She's so cheerful all the time, Nick. I don't know whether I can explain. When you're sitting there feeling sorry for yourself because you're the only one home on a Friday night, or you're dragging yourself off to an early class or worrying about an exam or

something, Casey can just walk into the room and suddenly . . . ," she shrugged, looking for words, "suddenly, you feel better. She knows how you feel; she knows what to say to you."

Hiroko nodded. "Not only that," he said, "but she's our peacemaker. She hates it when any of us have conflicts." He turned to Kathy. "Remember when Zack and I got into that stupid thing about who was supposed to clean up after his birthday party?" Zack was another housemate of theirs. "Remember how he invited all those extra people? I was furious at him, and he didn't even care, but Casey fixed it up between us," he said with admiration. "I don't know how, but she did it. Zack and I are cool with everything now."

"She makes our household *work*," Kathy sighed. "Everything's different when she's there. We're going to be lost without her." There was silence for a minute while Nick watched Kathy and Hiroko, who were staring into their drinks.

"Hey, come on, you two!" Nick finally said with a laugh. "You shouldn't feel so down about this! I bet you can find another housemate with no problem. Advertise, interview a few candidates, pick the most cheerful one." He reached under the table for his backpack and got ready to get up. "What's so hard about that?"

Kathy and Hiroko stared at him in disbelief.

DISCUSSION QUESTIONS

1. What are some of the interpersonal communication skills that Casey seems to have? Do you think she uses them well? Why or why not?
2. What do you think Kathy and Hiroko are feeling right now? Why?
3. How well have Kathy and Hiroko expressed their feelings to Nick?
4. What are Nick's perceptions about the housemates' situation? Is he accurately interpreting their words, their feelings, both, or neither? Explain your answer.
5. What can the housemates do to ensure that their interpersonal relationships survive Casey's departure?

Revisiting Chapter Objectives

1. **Define *interview*.** During the course of our lives, we all take part in a number of different types of interviews, as either interviewee or interviewer. The interview is the most common type of purposeful, planned, decision-making, person-to-person communication.

2. **Identify six types of interviews and the kind of information shared by participants in each type.** We explored six different types of interviews: the information-gathering interview (designed to collect information, opinions or data), the appraisal interview (designed for evaluation purposes), the persuasive interview (designed to influence attitudes or behavior), the exit interview (designed to determine why someone is leaving a position), the counseling interview (designed to provide guidance), and the hiring or selection interview (designed to select the right person for a job).

3. **Describe the stages of an interview.** Effective interviews are well-structured interactions. They have a beginning, which provides an orientation to what is to come; a middle, when the participants get down to business; and an end, when the main points are reviewed and the participants take leave of one another.

4. **Formulate closed, open, primary, and secondary questions.** Questions are the heart of the interview and the primary means of collecting data. Four basic types of questions are asked in an interview: closed, open, primary, and secondary. Closed questions are highly structured and can be answered with a simple yes or no or in a few words; open questions are broader and offer the interviewee more freedom in responding. Primary questions introduce topics or begin exploring a new area; secondary questions (probing questions) follow up primary questions by asking for further information. Whatever the type of question, an interviewee must maintain honesty in answering.

5. **Compare and contrast the roles and responsibilities of interviewer and interviewee.** Good interviewers and interviewees work hard during an interview, functioning simultaneously as information seekers, information givers, and decision makers. To be a successful interviewee requires specific preparation. Honest self-assessment, practice in answering typical questions, and mastery of the techniques of impression management are of prime importance. To avoid misunderstanding, both interviewer and interviewee need to be aware of how cultural differences can affect the interview.

Resources for Further Inquiry and Reflection

To apply your understanding of how the principles in Chapter 10 are at work in our daily lives, consult the following resources for further inquiry and reflection. Or, if you prefer, choose any other appropriate resource. Then connect the ideas expressed in your chosen selection with the communication concepts and issues you are learning about, both in and out of class.

Listen to Me

"Working Girls" (10cc)
"From 9 to 5" (Dolly Parton)
"Let the River Flow" (Carly Simon)
"Working Class Hero" (John Lennon)

Each of these songs revolves around the world of work. What do the attitudes expressed in the song suggest about our eagerness and/or preparedness to interview for a job?

 View Me

A Few Good Men   Kramer vs. Kramer
Bowling for Columbine   Roger and Me
Goodnight and Good Luck   The Smartest Guys
Kinsey   in the Room
Disclosure

Interviews play a key role in each of these films. How does the knowledge gleaned through one or more interviews advance the plot?

 Read Me

Moises Kaufman. *The Laramie Project*. New York: Dramatists Play Service, 2001.
Studs Turkel. *Working*. New York: Avon Press, 1992.
John Patrick Shanley. *Doubt*. New York: Theatre Communication Group, 2005.

Interviews play a key role in each of these works. Identify the kinds of questions raised by the interviewer(s) that elicited the most useful information from the interviewee(s).

 Tell Me

Share with the class the insights you gained from your chosen Listen to Me, View Me, or Read Me selection.

Discuss the most unusual thing that you are aware of happening during an interview to either the interviewer or the interviewee.

Key Chapter Terminology

Use the Communication Works CD-ROM and the Online Learning Center at www.mhhe.com/gamble9 to further your knowledge of the following terminology.

behavioral interview 290

case interview 290

closed questions 286

interview 276

open questions 286

primary questions 287

secondary questions 287

stress interview 290

Communication
Works

online learning center

www.mhhe.com/gamble9

Idioms in Translation

a toughie—something difficult

cover letter—the letter that precedes a résumé

door should be left open—possibility should be kept open

get you in the door—get you an appointment

provide a platform—give a public forum

telecommute—work from home using a computer or other technology

things do not fall through the cracks—things are not forgotten or overlooked

to roll them out—to introduce [new products]

touched on something—spoke about something

walk the interviewer though—explain to the interviewer

Test Your Understanding

Go to the *Self Quizzes* on the Communication Works CD-ROM and the book's Online Learning Center at www.mhhe.com/gamble9.

Communication
Works

online learning center

www.mhhe.com/gamble9

Notes

1. Ronald Alsop. "How to Get Hired." *The Wall Street Journal*, September 22, 2004, p. R8.
2. Erin White. "Savviest Job Hunters Research the Cultures of Potential Employers." *The Wall Street Journal*, March 29, 2005, p. B1.
3. Rick Bentley. "Interest in Forensic Science Has Surged during 'CSI.'" *heraldonline*, January 12, 2002, www.heraldonline.com.
4. Linda Martin. "Room with a Review." *The New York Times*, March 31, 2002, p. 13.
5. Melinda Ligos. "Young Job Seekers Need New Clues." *The New York Times*, August 8, 2001, p. G1.
6. William G. Kirkwood and Steven M. Ralson. "Inviting Meaningful Applicant Performances in Employment Interviews." *Journal of Business Communication* 36:1, January 1999, pp. 55–76.
7. For example, Lois J. Einhorn reports in "An Inner View of the Job Interview: An Investigation of Successful Communicative Behavior." *Communication Education* 30, 1981, pp. 217–228, that successful candidates were able to identify with the employer, support their arguments, organize their thoughts, clarify their ideas, and speak fluently.
8. "Résumés Get Only a Glance." *USA Today*, March 8, 2001, p. B1.
9. Leonard Zunin and Natalie Zunin. *Contact: The First Four Minutes*. Los Angeles: Nash, 1972, pp. 8–12.
10. Adam Geller. "Problem Postings." *The Record*, March 17, 2003; and Kris Maher. "Résumé Rustling Threatens Online Job Sites." *The Wall Street Journal*, February 25, 2003, pp. B1, B10.
11. David Koeppel. "On a Résumé, Don't Mention Moon Pies or Water Cannons." *The New York Times*, November 24, 2001, Section 10, p. 1.
12. See Mark L. Knapp, Roderick P. Hart, Gustav W. Friedrich, and Gary M. Schulman. "The Rhetoric of Goodbye: Verbal and Nonverbal Correlates of Human Leave-Taking." *Speech Monographs* 40, 1973, pp. 182–198.
13. Herbert M. Greenberg and Patrick J. Sweeney. *HR Focus* 76:10, 1999, p. 6.
14. Charles J. Stewart and William B. Cash, Jr. *Interviewing: Principles and Practices*, 6th ed. Dubuque, IA: Brown, 1991.
15. Arlene Hirsch. "'Tell Me about Yourself' Doesn't Mean 'Tell It All.'" *The Record*, November 28, 2004, pp. J1, J2; and Anthony DePalma. "Preparing for 'Tell Us about Yourself.'" *The New York Times*, July 27, 2003, p. NJ1.
16. Stewart and Cash.
17. David Bianculli. "Nice Guys Can Interview, but 'Naturals' Get Results." *Baltimore Sun*, May 19, 1984, p. E3.
18. Amy Joyce. "Career Track: How to Keep Cool on the Interview Hot Seat." *Washington Post*, June 21, 1999, p. FO-8.
19. See also Joan E. Rigdon. "Careers: Starting Over." *The Wall Street Journal*, February 27, 1995, p. R13.
20. Malcom Gladwell. "What Do Job Interviews Really Tell Us?" *New Yorker*, May 29, 2000, p. 84.
21. Ibid.

22. Eli Amdur. "Train Yourself to Be a S.T.A.R. during the Job Interview." *The Record*, September 4, 2005, p. J1.

23. Eli Amdur. "An Interview Is a Two-Way Deal, So Ask Questions." *The Record*, April 17, 2005, pp. J1, J2.

24. For a study confirming that employers use a candidate's speech characteristics to judge competence and likability, see Robert Hopper. "Language Attitudes in the Employment Interview." *Speech Monographs* 44, 1974, pp. 346–351.

25. Eli Amdur. "Be the Person Companies Will Want to Hire." *The Record*, October 24, 2004, pp. J1, J2.

26. Gladwell, pp. 68–86.

27. "Initial Minutes of Job Interview Are Critical." *USA Today*, January, 2000, p. 8.

28. Elwood N. Chapman. *Your Attitude Is Showing*. Chicago: Science Research Associates, 1987; see also Elwood N. Chapman. *I Got the Job!* Los Angeles: Crisp, 1988.

29. Einhorn.

30. Rachel Emma Silverman and Kemba J. Dunham. "Even in a Tight Market, Job Hunters Can Blunder." *The Wall Street Journal*, June 20, 2000, p. B12.

31. Also see Gladwell, pp. 68–72, 84–86; and C. J. Stewart and W. B. Cash, Jr. *Interviewing Principles and Practices*, 7th ed. Dubuque, IA: Brown, 1994.

32. Francine Parnes. "New Interview Uniform: Gray Means Business." *The New York Times*, January 19, 2003, Section 10, p. 1.

33. See John T. Molloy. *Dress for Success*. New York: Warner, 1977; and John T. Molloy. *The Woman's Dress for Success Book*. New York: Warner, 1977.

34. Jay Levin. "Unforgettable Interviews." *The Record*, June 16, 1997, pp. H-8, H-12.

35. Richard Nelson Bolles. *The 1997 What Color Is Your Parachute?* Berkeley, CA: Ten Speed Press, 1997.

36. See Joan E. Rigdon. "Talk Isn't Cheap." *The Wall Street Journal*, February 27, 1995, p. R13.

37. See, for example, F. Mahoney. "Adjusting the Interview to Avoid Cultural Bias." *Journal of Career Planning and Employment* 52, 1992, pp. 41–43.

38. Mary Williams Walsh. "Money Isn't Everything." *The New York Times*, January 30, 2001, p. 10.

39. Ibid.

40. "More Moslems Claim Job Bias." *The Wall Street Journal*, April 15, 2003, pp. B1, B8.

41. N'Gai Croal. "Want a Job? Get Online." *Newsweek*, June 9, 1997, pp. 81–82.

42. Maria Mallory and Margaret Steen. "Two-Way Interview: It's for You and the Employer." *Atlanta Journal*, April 2, 2000, p. R1.

43. Kris Maher. "Blogs Catch On as Online Tool for Job Seekers and Recruiteers." *The Wall Street Journal*, September 28, 2004, p. B10.

44. For a discussion of online search techniques, see Cynthia B. Leshin. *Internet Investigations in Business Communication*. Saddle River, NJ: Prentice Hall, 1997, pp. 95–134.

45. See Zane K. Quible. "Electronic Résumés: Their Time Is Coming." *Business Communication Quarterly* 58, September 1995, pp. 5–9.

46. Wallace V. Schmidt and Roger N. Conaway. *Results-Oriented Interviewing: Principles, Practices and Procedures*. Boston: Allyn & Bacon, 1999, p. 11.

47. Mark Cenedella. "Top 10 Blunders of Online Job Hunters." *The Record*, September 5, 2004, p. J1.

48. David Koeppel. "Web Can Help, but a Job Hunt Still Takes Lots of Hard Work." *The New York Times*, September 12, 2004, pp. MB 1, 3.

49. From David Kirby, "Selling Yourself: There Are Questions You Shouldn't Answer." Adapted from *The New York Times*, January 30, 2001, p. 2. Copyright © 2001 by the New York Times Co. Reprinted with permission.

50. John Brady. *The Craft of Interviewing*. New York: Vintage, 1977.

CHAPTER 11

Groups and Teams: Strategies for Decision Making and Problem Solving

After finishing this chapter, you should be able to

1. Define *group*.

2. Provide examples of how a group's climate affects its operations.

3. Enumerate the advantages and disadvantages of group decision making and problem solving.

4. Define and distinguish among task, maintenance, and self-serving group roles.

5. Explain and provide examples of how cooperation versus competition and a defensive versus a supportive climate affect the interactions of group members.

6. Compare and contrast various decision-making methods.

7. Apply the reflective-thinking framework to increase your effectiveness at problem solving.

8. Describe and use brainstorming.

Talented administrators know that they do not know all there is to know.

—Anonymous

Not even computers will replace committees, because committees buy computers.

—Edward Shepperd Mead

When it comes to your future, teamwork is one of the most important communication skills you can master.[1] Do you think that you could learn team-building skills by taking cooking classes? A number of companies, such as Sun Microsystems, Viacom, and Bank One Corp., think so. They have invested thousands of dollars in cooking classes for executives. The thinking is that since a lot of things can go wrong in the kitchen, it is a good place to improve teamwork. Either "cooks" cooperate or they get in trouble.[2]

Many contemporary organizations focus on team building as a means of improving the functioning of regular work groups.[3] A team is a group of people with a strong sense of their collective identity, acting collaboratively. The members agree on their need for each other if they are to accomplish their goals. Unlike other groups, teams by definition are composed of people who have *diverse skills* and bring *different resources* to a problem or task. Teams depend on members' pooling their abilities, knowledge, and insights to solve problems and make better decisions than any single individual in the team could do acting alone. All teams are groups. However, because not every group has members contributing specialized knowledge or different resources, not every group is a team.[4] (See Figure 11.1 for a look at the differences in behavior the members of nominal (in name only) and real (functioning) teams exhibit.)

We profit from working together in groups and teams. Research suggests that teamwork can be its own reward. Researchers note that, just as desserts and money cause many of us to experience delight, so does cooperating with each other to achieve a goal. Using magnetic resonance imaging (MRI) to take portraits of the brain, researchers have shown that humans derive pleasure when they choose to forego immediate personal gain and opt instead to cooperate with others for the long-term common good.[5]

■ ■ ■

GROUPS, TEAMS, AND YOU

How important are groups and teams in your life? Try to visualize what your personal and professional life would be like if you belonged to no groups or teams. What would you miss? Some of the groups we belong to, such as the group of friends who meet for dinner once a week, are social. Some are more formally

FIGURE 11.1

Key Dimensions of Teams.

Groups vary on each dimension from one extreme to the other. How would you describe a group you currently belong to? Is your group a real team?

Nominal Team		Real Team
Functional Group	**Identification**	Team
Independence	**Interdependence**	Interdependence
High	**Power Differentiation**	Low
Distant	**Social Distance**	Close
Forcing, Accommodating, Avoiding	**Conflict Management Tactics**	Confronting, Collaborating
Win-Lose	**Negotiation Process**	Win-Win

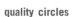

online learning center

Go to the Online Learning Center at www.mhhe.com/gamble9 and answer the questions in the *Self Inventory* to evaluate your understanding of group interactions.

quality circles

small groups of employees who meet regularly to discuss organizational life and the quality of their work environment

organized, such as the Parent–Teacher Association. Some, such as the Rotary Club, serve both public and private purposes. Others exist primarily to meet the needs of the organizations in which we work. Thus, groups provide much of the social fabric of our lives. In addition, they are also the basic building blocks of organizations, and when it comes to the world of work, team management is fast becoming the norm.

Over two-thirds of United States companies use formal work teams to accomplish their objectives.[6] Workers now participate in more groups and teams and attend more meetings than ever before. It is commonplace for committees of employees to make the kinds of decisions that "dictatorial" executives once handled. According to researchers, the majority of a manager's time is spent in meetings of one kind or another.[7] Thus, today's workers and managers are experienced at participating in different kinds of groups. **Quality circles,** for example, are small groups of employees who meet regularly to discuss organizational life and the quality of their work environment. During these meetings, employees make recommendations for improving products and

Employees spend extensive amounts of time in meetings.

work procedures. **Self-directed teams** are autonomous groups in which employees are empowered to make decisions and even supervise themselves. Among the major companies championing such approaches are Xerox, Procter & Gamble, and General Motors.[8] Do you feel prepared to become part of such groups?

You already spend a great deal of time in groups. A large part of your socialization—your adaptation to society—occurred in your family group. Much of your leisure time is spent in the company of groups of friends. If you attend a religious service, you become part of a group. If you participate in student government, a study group, or sports, you are part of a group. As a class member, you belong to a group. Thus, from your earliest days, you have been a member of a variety of groups.

CHARACTERISTICS AND COMPONENTS OF GROUPS

While defining a group can be tricky business,[9] identifying the characteristics groups have in common will help you understand how to behave more effectively when part of one. As we see, groups are everywhere. They help define us. The groups to which you belong or aspire to belong tell you about your own preferences and goals. The groups you refuse to join tell you about your dislikes, fears, and values. Groups have a great impact on your daily life, and you need to belong to a number of them to survive in today's world.[10]

Some of your most important communication will take place in one group or another. Estimates are that over 11 million meetings are held each day. At least 40 percent of your work life will be spent attending group meetings and conferences. A recent survey showed that the typical executive spends about 700 hours per year interacting in groups. That is the equivalent of two of every five days on the job.[11] Thus, knowing how to relate to others in a group setting is vital if you are to attain not only personal but also professional success.[12] For this reason, although we realize that social groups are important, in these chapters we will focus on the work-related decision-making, problem-solving group, also called the task group.

By the time you conclude your study of small-group communication, you will have the information you need to understand the forces that shape and modify group behavior, and the skills you need to improve the quality of interactions in task groups. The knowledge and abilities you gain will be transferable to other areas of your life. We begin by looking into the nature of group membership.

Group Membership

A **group** is a collection of people. But it is not just a random assemblage of independent individuals; rather, it is composed of individuals who interact verbally and nonverbally, occupy certain roles with respect to one another, and cooperate to accomplish a definite goal. The members of a group recognize the other individuals who are part of the activity, have certain kinds of attitudes toward these people, and obtain some degree of satisfaction from belonging to or participating in the group. They acknowledge the do's and don'ts of group life, the norms that specify and regulate the behavior expected of members. Furthermore, communication within a group involves more than the casual banter that occurs between strangers at bus stops or in department stores.

---

self-directed teams
autonomous groups of employees empowered to make decisions and supervise themselves

Most of us belong to a number of different groups. Are you currently a member of two groups? Ten groups? Twenty groups? Take a moment to assess the nature of your group membership.

Our world contains over 6 billion individuals. It also contains hundreds of millions of formal and informal groups. How do the groups you belong to influence you as an individual?

Compile a list of groups to which you belong, groups to which you aspire to belong, and groups to which you would refuse to belong. Give your reasons for accepting, seeking, or refusing membership.

group
a collection of individuals who interact verbally and nonverbally, occupy certain roles with respect to one another, and cooperate to accomplish a goal

The fact that a number of people are present in a particular space at the same time does not mean that a group exists. For example, under ordinary conditions, passengers in a train or an elevator are not a group. (However, should the train or elevator break down or experience some other difficulty, they might become a group to meet the demands of the new situation.) Rather, the members of a group consistently influence each other and are influenced by each other; that is, interaction in the form of mutual influence occurs. The individual members affect the character of the group and are affected by it.[13]

Group Size

While most group theorists and practitioners set the lower limit of group size at three members, researchers have found that, for most tasks, groups of five to seven people work best. This size enables members to communicate directly with each other as they work on a common task or goal, such as solving problems, exchanging information, or improving interpersonal relationships.

What is the optimal size for a group? In task-oriented groups, it is the smallest number of people capable of handling the assigned task.[14] The larger the group, the more difficult it becomes to schedule meetings, share information, and equalize opportunities for participation.

Group Goals, Structure, and Climate

group goals

a group's motivation for existing

group structure

group member positions and roles performed

group patterns of communication

patterns of message flow in a group

group norms

informal rules for interaction in a group

group climate

the emotional atmosphere of a group

Every group establishes its own **group goals** (motivation for existing, the end state desired), **group structure** (member positions and roles), **group patterns of communication** (patterns of message flow), **group norms** (informal rules for interaction), and **group climate** (emotional atmosphere). Every participant in the group usually has a stake in the outcome, develops relationships with the other members of the group, and assumes roles and relationships that relate to group tasks and either foster or impede the group's effectiveness. Thus, the members' styles of interaction have an impact on the kind of atmosphere, or climate, that develops in the group. Conversely, the climate affects what members say to each other and how they say it. For example, have you ever belonged to a group that had too "hot" a climate—one in which members were intolerant of each other and tempers flared? Have you ever belonged to a group that had too "cold" a climate—one in which members were aloof, sarcastic, unconcerned about hurting one another's feelings, or too self-centered to notice that the needs of others were not being adequately met?

A group's climate tends to persist. If the group climate is cold, closed, mistrustful, or uncooperative, individual members frequently react in ways that perpetuate those characteristics. In contrast, if the group climate is warm, open, trusting, and cooperative, members usually react in ways that reinforce those characteristics. In the book *Communication within the Organization*, Charles Redding suggested that an effective climate is characterized by (1) supportiveness, (2) participative decision making, (3) trust among group members, (4) openness and candor, and (5) high performance goals.[15] The healthier the group climate, the more cohesive the group.

Group climate affects group norms—the explicit and implicit rules that members internalize concerning their behavior. In some groups, members exhibit certain behaviors that they would not dare exhibit in others. For example, in which groups that you belong to do you feel free to ask a question that might be considered "dumb," interrupt someone who is talking, express disagreement with another member, openly express support for an unpopular position, point out that someone is not making sense, offer a comment unrelated to the topic, or simply not attend a meeting? In some groups, interaction is formal and stuffy; in others, it is informal and relaxed. Groups invariably create standards that they expect members to live up to. In this way, a group is able to foster a certain degree of uniformity.

In Chapter 12 we will take a closer look at leadership behaviors, conflict resolution, and problems that develop in groups. For now, let us recognize that certain attributes facilitate the group process, whereas others work against it. Douglas McGregor, an expert in organizational communication, summarizes the characteristics of an effective and well-functioning group as follows:

1. The atmosphere tends to be informal, comfortable, and relaxed.

2. There is a lot of discussion in which virtually everyone participates, but it remains pertinent to the task.

3. The task or objective is well understood and accepted by the members. There will have been free discussion of the objective at some point, until it was formulated in such a way that the group members could commit themselves to it.

4. The members listen to each other. Every idea is given a hearing. People do not appear to be afraid of being foolish; they will offer a creative thought even if it seems fairly extreme.

5. There is disagreement. Disagreements are not suppressed or overridden by premature action. The reasons are carefully examined, and the group seeks to resolve disagreements rather than dominate dissenters.

6. Most decisions are reached by a kind of consensus in which it is clear that everyone is in general agreement and willing to go along. Formal voting is at a minimum; the group does not accept a simple majority as a proper basis for action.

7. Criticism is frequent, frank, and relatively comfortable. There is little evidence of personal attack, either overt or hidden.

8. People are free to express their feelings and their ideas about the problem and the group's operation.

9. When action is taken, clear assignments are made and accepted.

10. The chairperson of the group does not dominate it, nor does the group defer unduly to him or her. In fact, the leadership shifts from time to time, depending on the circumstances. There is little evidence of a struggle for power as the group operates. The issue is not who controls but how to get the job done.

11. The group is self-conscious of its own operation.[16]

The Dynamics of Group Development

Once in place, a group's development occurs in stages. According to researchers, the key stages that a group moves through are forming, storming, norming, performing, and adjourning.[17] (See Figure 11.2.)

Select two groups you have belonged to that represent what you consider effective and ineffective climates. For each group, identify the types of behavior exhibited by members. How did each climate affect your participation in the group? How did each climate affect your relationship with other group members?

random thoughts by archy
i have noticed that when chickens quit quarreling over their food they often find that there is enough for all of them i wonder if it might not be the same way with the human race

—Don Marquis,
archy's life of mehitabel

FIGURE 11.2
Stages of Group Development.

Trace the development of a group to which you belong. Has it passed through each of the stages identified here?

Upon joining a new group, we may experience some initial confusion or uncertainty, resulting in our experiencing *primary tension.* We are unsure about how to behave or interact with others and unclear about the roles that we will have in the life of the group. We need to figure out who is in charge and why we were brought together. Thus, in the *forming stage* of a group, our primary objective is to fit in and be perceived as likable. We also make an effort to find out about other group members and the group's task. Once we feel valued and accepted, we begin to identify with the group.

Invariably, members experience some conflict as they determine how to work together. Typically, groups experience both task and relational conflicts. During the *storming stage,* the group's members experience *secondary tension*—tension that results from members' disagreeing and/or struggling to exert leadership as they work to clarify goals and the roles members will have in the life of the group. During this stage, rather than being concerned with fitting in, members now focus on expressing their ideas and opinions and securing their place in the group power structure.

Over time, a clear group structure emerges. Members firm up roles, and a leader or leaders emerge. During the *norming stage,* the group solidifies its behavioral norms, especially those relating to conflict management. In addition, the group forms a sense of identity as member awareness of interdependence and the need to cooperate with each other increases.

The emphasis of the group then switches to task accomplishment. During the *performing stage,* often perceived as the most important stage of group development, members combine their skills, knowledge, and abilities to overcome obstacles and reach the group's goals. Group members focus on problem solving.

Finally, during the *adjourning stage,* members review and reflect on their accomplishments or failures and determine how or whether to end the group and the relationships that have developed. Ending a group can involve having a party or simply saying good-bye to each other, or it can be more complicated and prolonged, with some groups opting to continue working together on a new or different task, and some members choosing to continue relationships that developed during the group's life.[18]

How a group develops through each of these stages determines how effectively it is able to function.

If, as the saying goes, "a camel is a horse designed by a committee," why do we do so much of our work in groups?

USING GROUPS TO MAKE DECISIONS AND SOLVE PROBLEMS

We form small groups to share information we require to solve common problems and make decisions about achieving certain identified common goals. But why use a small group instead of a single person? Working in groups is both frustrating and rewarding; groups can facilitate or limit problem-solving effectiveness.

Advantages of the Small Group

In many ways, using a group to solve a complex problem is more logical than relying on one individual. Group problem solving offers a number of important advantages.

First, it permits a variety of people with different information and different points of view to contribute to the problem-solving, decision-making process. That is, a small group facilitates the pooling of resources. The broader the array of knowledge that is brought to bear on any problem, the more likely an effective solution becomes. Second, participating in a group apparently increases individual motivation. Group efforts often lead to greater commitment to finding a solution and then to greater commitment to that solution. Third, group functioning makes it easier to identify other people's mistakes and filter out errors before they can become costly or damaging. Groups are frequently better equipped than individuals to foresee difficulties, detect weaknesses, visualize consequences, and explore possibilities. As a result, they tend to produce superior decisions and solutions. Fourth, the decisions or solutions of a group tend to be better received than those of an individual. As the adage says, "There is strength in numbers." The person or persons to whom a group solution is reported will tend to respect the fact that a number of people working together came to one conclusion. Fifth, working as part of a group is generally more pleasant and fulfilling than working alone. The group provides companionship, a chance to affirm ideas and feelings, and an opportunity for self-confirmation. It is rewarding to know that others respect us enough to listen and react to what we have to say. It is even more rewarding to have our thoughts and concerns accepted by others. (These advantages are summarized in Figure 11.3.)

Disadvantages of the Small Group

This is not to suggest that using a group does not have potential drawbacks. Group problem solving has several disadvantages.

First, when we are working with a number of other people, it sometimes becomes very tempting to let someone else handle the duties and responsibilities. A lazy group member can maintain a low profile and simply coast along on the efforts of others. Second, personal goals sometimes conflict with group goals. As a result, people may try to use the group to achieve self-oriented objectives that might interfere with or even sabotage group objectives. Third, the decision-making, problem-solving process may be dominated by a few forceful, persistent

You know . . . everybody is ignorant, only of different subjects.

—Will Rogers

There is a tendency to define one's own group positively in order to evaluate oneself positively.

—John C. Turner

Give an example of how you have enacted the above quotation.

As a new employee, what problems might you experience when interacting with others in a problem-solving group?

Advantages	Disadvantages
Varied resources can be pooled.	Laziness is encouraged.
Motivation and commitment are increased.	Personal goals may conflict with group goals.
Errors are easier to identify.	A few high-status members may dominate.
Decisions are better received.	Stubbornness leads to deadlock.
Rewards of working with others are provided.	Riskier decisions are made.
	Reaching a decision takes longer.

FIGURE 11.3

Why Use Teamwork?

members who do not take the time to ensure that all members have a chance to speak and be heard. Actual or perceived status plays a part here. Group members may be hesitant to criticize the comments of high-status people, and low-status people may be reluctant to participate at all. Consequently, position and power can affect whether ideas are offered, listened to, or incorporated into group decisions. Fourth, certain people who are set on having their ideas and only their ideas accepted may be unwilling to compromise. When this happens, the group decision-making machinery breaks down, and frequently no solution can be agreed on. In other words, the group becomes deadlocked. Fifth, the decisions reached and the actions taken after a group discussion are often riskier than the decisions individuals would have made or the actions individuals would have taken. This phenomenon is known as the risky shift. Sixth, it often takes longer to reach a group solution than an individual decision. In business and industry, where time is frequently equated with money, the group can be a costly tool. (See Figure 11.3 for a summary of these drawbacks.)

In a group decision, risk is inescapable. How does calculating the risk increase your chances of making a good choice?

When to Use a Group for Decision Making and Problem Solving

In view of these pros and cons, we ask: When does it make sense to use a group? At what point do the advantages outweigh the possible disadvantages?

Experience suggests that we use a group rather than an individual to make decisions and solve a problem if the answer to most of the following questions is yes:

Groups can bring out the worst as well as the best in human decision making.

— Irving Janis

1. Is the problem complex rather than simple?
2. Does the problem have many parts, or facets?
3. Would any one person be unlikely to possess all the information needed to solve the problem?
4. Would it be advisable to divide the responsibility for problem solving?
5. Are many potential solutions desired, rather than just one?
6. Would an examination of diverse attitudes be helpful?
7. Are group members more likely to engage in task-related than non-task-related behavior?

In these complex times, it often makes sense for individuals of varied expertise to pool their knowledge and insight to solve problems. Group effort is futile if the members pool only ignorance and obstinacy. The more information the members can gather and share, the more likely they are to rid themselves of bias, and in turn, the more objective their work becomes.[19]

UNDERSTANDING THE ROLES GROUP MEMBERS PLAY

Roles are patterns of behavior. There are roles that we expect group members to play (functional roles) because they contribute to the group's effectiveness, and roles we expect group members to refrain from playing (dysfunctional roles) because of their harmful effects on the group.

Even though their **group role-classification model** was formulated almost a half century ago, the system proposed by Kenneth Benne and Paul Sheats is still commonly used today. It describes the functions participants should seek to assume—and the functions they should avoid—during the life of a group.[20] Benne and Sheats considered goal achievement (completing the task) and group maintenance (building relationships) the two basic objectives of any group. They further reasoned that eliminating self-serving roles (nonfunctional behaviors) is a requirement or condition that must be met if the preceding goals are to be realized. Guided by these assumptions, Benne and Sheats identified three categories of roles:

1. task-oriented roles
2. maintenance-oriented roles
3. self-serving roles

group role-classification model
a model that describes functions participants should seek to assume and to avoid in groups

Task-Oriented Roles

The following are among the **task roles** that help the group realize its goals:

Initiating. The member defines a problem; suggests methods, goals, and procedures; and starts the group moving along new paths or in different directions by offering a plan.

Information seeking. The member asks for facts and opinions and seeks relevant information about the problem.

Opinion seeking. The member solicits expressions of feeling and value to discover the values underlying the group effort.

Information giving. The member provides ideas and suggestions and supplies personal experiences as well as factual data.

Opinion giving. The member supplies opinions, values, and beliefs and reveals his or her feelings about what is being discussed.

Clarifying. The member elaborates on the ideas of others, supplies paraphrases, offers examples or illustrations, and tries to eliminate confusion and increase clarity.

Coordinating. The member summarizes ideas and tries to draw various contributions together constructively.

Evaluating. The member evaluates the group's decisions or proposed solutions and helps establish standards for judgment.

Consensus testing. The member checks on the state of group agreement to see if the group is nearing a decision.

task roles
group roles designed to help the group achieve its goals

maintenance roles
group roles designed to ensure the smooth running of a group

Maintenance-Oriented Roles

The following **maintenance roles** help the group run smoothly:

Encouraging. The member is warm, receptive, and responsive to others and praises others and their ideas.

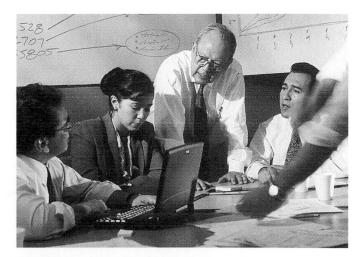

Members in a group perform different roles. Which roles do you perform regularly?

Gatekeeping. The member attempts to keep communication channels open; he or she helps reticent members contribute to the group and works to keep the discussion from being dominated by one or two members.

Harmonizing. The member mediates differences between participants and attempts to reconcile misunderstandings or disagreements; he or she also tries to reduce tension by using humor or other forms of relief at appropriate junctures.

Compromising. The member is willing to compromise his or her position to maintain group cohesion; he or she is willing to admit error and modify beliefs to achieve group growth.

Standard setting. The member assesses whether group members are satisfied with the procedures being used and indicates that criteria have been set for evaluating group functioning.

Self-Serving Roles

self-serving roles

group roles that impede the functioning of a group by preventing members from working together effectively

Self-serving roles prevent the group from working effectively:

Blocking. The member is disagreeable and digresses in an effort to ensure that nothing is accomplished.

Aggression. The member criticizes or blames others and works to deflate the egos of other group members in an effort to enhance his or her own status.

Recognition seeking. The member attempts to become the focus of attention by boasting about his or her own accomplishments rather than dealing with the group task; he or she may speak loudly and exhibit behavior that is unusual.

Withdrawing. The member appears indifferent, daydreams, is lost in thought, or sulks.

Dominating. The member insists on getting his or her own way, interrupts others, and gives directions in an effort to run or control the group.

Which roles do you find yourself performing most frequently? What conditions in the group, or what personal needs, do you think precipitate such behavior on your part?

Joking. The member appears cynical or engages in horseplay or other inappropriate or irrelevant behaviors.

Self-confessing. The member uses other group members as an audience and reveals personal feelings or insights that are not oriented toward group concerns.

Help seeking. The member tries to elicit sympathy or pity from other members.

Ethics & Communication

The Social Loafer

A common complaint expressed by students who have to work is groups is that some members end up having to do the work of other members who do not share a comparable level of commitment to the group or its task. Upon joining a group, members who function as social loafers reduce their work effort, miss meetings, or engage in otherwise dysfunctional behavior.

Why do you think that social loafers tend to be more prevalent in groups in individualistic cultures than in collectivist cultures? What steps should a group take to reduce the impact a social loafer has on other members and the group?

UNDERSTANDING GROUP MEMBER RELATIONSHIPS AND INTERACTION

In addition to the various roles played by group members, the nature of the relationships shared by the members is also highly significant in determining whether the group will operate effectively. For this reason, the following questions deserve our attention: To what extent do members of a group cooperate or compete with one another? To what extent do the members foster a defensive or a supportive environment?[21]

Cooperation versus Competition

Obviously, the personal goals of each member have an impact on the operation of a group. If individual members view their goals as congruent or coinciding, an atmosphere of cooperation can be fostered. However, if individual members see their goals as contradictory, a competitive atmosphere will develop. Too frequently, group members attempt to compete with one another when cooperating would be more beneficial to the group. Psychologists Linden L. Nelson and Spencer Kagen believe that it is irrational and self-defeating to compete if cooperating makes better sense.[22] When a group experience develops into a dog-eat-dog situation, all the members may go hungry.

Few factors do more to damage a group's ability to maintain itself and complete a task than competition among members, yet highly competitive individuals do belong to groups and do, in fact, affect the group's communication climate and emergent goal structure. The term *goal structure* describes the way members relate to each other. Under a **cooperative goal structure,** the members of a group work together to achieve their objectives, and the goals of each person are perceived as compatible with or complementary to those of the others. Group members readily pool resources and coordinate their efforts to obtain what they consider common aims. In contrast, when a group develops a **competitive goal structure,** members do not share resources or coordinate efforts. Consciously or unconsciously, individuals work to hinder one another's efforts to obtain the goal. According to psychologist Morton Deutsch, group members who have a competitive orientation believe that they can achieve their goals only if other members fail to do so.[23]

Certain requirements need to be met if the members of a group are to cooperate with each other. First, the members need to agree that each has an equal right to satisfy needs. Second, conditions must be such that each person in the group is able to get what he or she wants at least some of the time. Third, members avoid plays for power that rely on techniques such as threatening, yelling, or demanding. Finally, members do not attempt to manipulate each other by withholding information or dissembling. Consequently, when you cooperate as a group member, you do not aim to win or to beat or outsmart others. Unlike competition, cooperation does not require gaining an edge over the other members of your group; for this reason, unlike competition, cooperation does not promote defensiveness.

Supportiveness versus Defensiveness

Defensive behavior occurs when a group member perceives or anticipates a threat. When you feel yourself becoming defensive, you may experience one or more of the following symptoms: a change in voice tone (as you become nervous, your

How do you act in group situations you define as cooperative? In situations you define as competitive? To what extent does the sex of the other group members appear to make a difference?

cooperative goal structure
a goal structure in which the members of a group work together to achieve their objectives

competitive goal structure
a goal structure in which members hinder one another's efforts to obtain a goal

defensive behavior
behavior that occurs when one perceives a threat

When was the last time you behaved defensively in a group? What precipitated such a response from you? How did your response affect others?

throat and vocal mechanism grow tense and your vocal pitch tends to rise), a tightening of your muscles and some degree of rigidity throughout your body, and a rush of adrenaline accompanied by an urge to fight or flee. Now let us examine the behaviors that can precipitate such reactions.

In general, we tend to become defensive when we perceive others as attacking our self-concept. In fact, when we behave defensively, we devote a great amount of energy to defending the self. We become preoccupied with thinking about how the self appears to others, and we become obsessed with discovering ways to make others see us more favorably. When a member of a group becomes overly concerned with self-protection, he or she may compensate either by withdrawing or by attacking the other members. When this happens, the conditions necessary for the maintenance of the group begin to deteriorate. In short, defensive behavior on the part of one group member gives rise to defensive listening in others. The postural, facial, and vocal cues that accompany words can also raise the defense level. Once the defensiveness of a group member is aroused, that person no longer feels free to concentrate on the actual meaning of messages others are trying to send. Instead, the defensive member feels compelled to distort messages. Thus, as group members become more and more defensive, they become less and less able to process each other's emotions, values, and intentions accurately. For this reason, the consequences of defensiveness include destroyed or badly damaged individual relationships, continuing conflicts and increased personal anxiety within the group, wounded egos, and hurt feelings.

Before we can work to eliminate or even reduce defensiveness in our group relationships, we must understand the stimuli that can cause us to become defensive in the first place. Sociological researcher Jack R. Gibb identified six behaviors that cause defensiveness and six contrasting behaviors that allay or reduce the perceived level of threat (see Table 11.1).[24]

Gibb's first pair of contrasting behaviors is evaluation versus description. Group relationships can run into trouble if a member makes judgmental or evaluative statements. As Gibb notes in the article "Defensive Communication," "If by expression, manner of speech, tone of voice, or verbal content the sender seems to be evaluating or judging the listener, then the receiver goes on guard."[25] Far too often, we offhandedly label the actions of others "stupid," "ridiculous," "absurd," "wonderful," or "extraordinary" because we simply are predisposed to use judgmental terms. Although it is true that some people do not mind having their actions praised, it is also true that most of us do mind having our actions condemned; moreover, whether judgment is positive or negative, the anticipation of

TABLE 11.1 Behaviors Characteristic of Defensive and Supportive Climates	
Defensive Climate	**Supportive Climate**
1. Evaluation	1. Description
2. Control	2. Problem orientation
3. Strategy	3. Spontaneity
4. Neutrality	4. Empathy
5. Superiority	5. Equality
6. Certainty	6. Provisionalism

judgment can hinder the creation of an open communication climate. In contrast to evaluative statements, descriptive statements recount particular observable actions without labeling those behaviors as good or bad, right or wrong. When you are descriptive, you do not advise changes in behavior. Instead, you simply report or question what you saw, heard, or felt.

Gibb's second pair is control versus problem orientation. Communication that group members see as seeking to control them can arouse defensiveness. In other words, if your intent is to control other group members, to get them to do something or change their beliefs, you are likely to evoke resistance. How much resistance you meet depends on how openly you approach these people and on whether your behavior causes them to question or doubt your motives. When we conclude that someone is trying to control us, we also tend to conclude that he or she considers us ignorant or unable to make our own decisions. A problem orientation, however, promotes the opposite response. When senders communicate that they have not already formulated solutions and will not force their opinions on us, we feel free to cooperate in solving the problems at hand.

Gibb's third pair is strategy versus spontaneity. Our defensiveness increases if we feel that another group member is using a strategy or is trying to put something over on us. No one likes to be conned or to be the victim of a hidden plan. We are suspicious of strategies that are concealed or tricky. We do not want others to make decisions for us and then try to persuade us that we made the decisions ourselves. Thus, when we perceive ourselves as being manipulated, we become defensive and self-protective. In contrast, spontaneous behavior that is honest and free of deception reduces defensiveness. Under such conditions, the receiver feels no need to question the motivations of the sender, and trust is engendered.

Gibb's fourth pair is neutrality versus empathy. Neutrality is another behavior that increases defensiveness in group members. We need to feel that others empathize with us, like us, and see us as worthwhile and valued. We need to feel that others care about us and will take the time to establish a meaningful relationship with us. If, instead of communicating empathy, warmth, and concern, a group member communicates neutrality or indifference, we may well see this as worse than rejection. We feel that he or she is not interested in us; we may even conclude that he or she perceives us as a nonperson.

Gibb's fifth pair is superiority versus equality. Our defensiveness is aroused if another group member communicates feelings of superiority about social position, power, wealth, intelligence, appearance, or other characteristics. When we receive such a message, we tend to react by attempting to compete with the sender, by feeling frustrated or jealous, or by disregarding or forgetting the sender's message altogether. On the other hand, a sender who communicates equality decreases our defensive behavior. We perceive him or her as willing to develop a shared problem-solving relationship with us, as willing to trust us, and as feeling that any differences between us are unimportant.

Gibb's sixth pair is certainty versus provisionalism. The expression of absolute certainty or dogmatism on the part of a group member will probably succeed in making us defensive. We are suspicious of those who believe they have all the answers, view themselves as our guides rather than our fellow travelers, and reject all information that we attempt to offer. In contrast, an attitude of provisionalism or open-mindedness encourages the development of trust. We perceive people who communicate a spirit of provisionalism—instead of attempting to win arguments, to be right, and to defend their ideas to the bitter end—as flexible and open.

DECISION MAKING IN GROUPS: REACHING GOALS

Thus far, we have established what a group is, the stages groups pass through during their development, and when and why it makes sense to use a group. In the process, we noted that every group member performs roles, and every group has a goal—a reason for existing. We turn now to examining how groups reach their goals.

Identify the methods of decision making that are used most often in your class, at home, and at work. Are you satisfied with them? Why?

In our society, we usually relegate critical decisions to groups. Depending on the group, a wide variety of decision-making strategies or approaches may be used. In this section, we investigate the diverse methods members can adopt to arrive at a decision, as well as the advantages and disadvantages of each approach. Let's start by considering these questions: How do the groups to which you belong make decisions? Do different groups use different strategies? Why? Does the method any one group uses change from time to time? Why? Are you happy with each group's approach?

 # Ethics & Communication

Avoiding Problems

Group members face a number of problems that can influence the effectiveness of the decisions they make. How would you respond when faced with each of the following situations? What do your responses reveal about the nature of groups?

1. What consequences might your group face if instead of handling a problem, the members opted to run away from the problem, rationalize it, or otherwise avoid confronting it directly? Is running away from a problem ever a viable alternative to solving the problem?

2. Put yourself in the place of the character, Jim, in the following situation. What advice would you offer Jim?

Jim is, at heart, an investigative journalist who has considerable talent but who has been earning a living by writing restaurant reviews for a major magazine, which pays him very well, enabling him to support his wife and three young children. Despite this, Jim longs to return to his real vocation. Recently, he was offered a freelance position with a well-known newspaper, which asked Jim to resign from his present position and go undercover in an effort to determine if there is collusion between U.S. government agencies and major companies that seek to influence policy decisions being made by the administration. If Jim is successful in his investigation, it could make his journalistic career. If he is unsuccessful, however, he will have expended considerable time and energy, possibly ruining his reputation and ending his journalistic career. Should Jim give up his current job to take the new assignment? Check the lowest probability that you would consider acceptable for Jim to take the new assignment:

___ 1 in 10		___ 6 in 10	
___ 2 in 10		___ 7 in 10	
___ 3 in 10		___ 8 in 10	
___ 4 in 10		___ 9 in 10	
___ 5 in 10		___ 10 in 10	

PEANUTS reprinted by permission of United Features Syndicate, Inc.

Strategies: Methods of Decision Making

Before we examine the different methods that groups use in making decisions, consider the following list to decide which decision-making strategy or strategies a group you belong to would employ most often if you had your way. Do this by ranking the possibilities from 1 (your first choice) to 8 (your last choice).

____ Ask an expert to decide.

____ Flip a coin.

____ Let the majority rule.

____ Let the group leader decide.

____ Stall until a decision no longer needs to be made.

____ Let the minority rule, because that is sometimes fair.

____ Determine the average position, since this is least likely to be offensive to anyone.

____ Reach a **decision by consensus;** that is, be certain all have had input into the discussion, understand the decision, can rephrase it, and will publicly support it.

Then consider the implications of your ranking.

According to Malcolm Gladwell, the author of Blink, *snap decisions (rapid cognitions) can be valid, useful, and often better than those based on prolonged, rational analyses. In your opinion, do snap decisions help or impede group problem solving?*

decision by consensus

a decision that all members understand and will support, reached as a result of members' voicing feelings and airing differences

---

(Place a check next to 10 in 10 if you think Jim should take the new assignment only if it is certain that his investigation will be a success.)

After reaching your own decision, discuss the dilemma in a group. Determine if your group is likely to take a greater risk, be more cautious, or stay the same.

While some believe that groups are more cautious than individuals, in practice, the opposite actually is true. Decisions made in a group are usually riskier. This phenomenon is dubbed the *risky shift.* How do you imagine the risky shift phenomenon might affect the deliberations of juries? Business or military leaders?

3. There is another tendency in decision making that involves a movement toward *group polarization,* in which discussion is found to strengthen the average inclination of group members. For example, when business students were asked to imagine themselves having to decide whether to invest more money in the hope of preventing losses in various failing projects, individually 72 percent chose to reinvest money, while in groups 94 percent came to that decision.[26] Discussion with like-minded people strengthens existing views. How might such a trend influence the beliefs of prejudiced and unprejudiced persons when it comes to issues involving racial profiling, affirmative action, and those responsible for increases in crime? How might it influence the thinking of like-minded terrorist groups?

4. Look at the following cartoon. On the basis of your understanding of group polarization, would you agree with the advice the older sheep is giving the younger one? Why or why not?

"Now remember, 'just because everybody else is doing it' is a plenty good enough reason."

© Six Chix–Ann Telnaes. King Features Syndicate. Reprinted with permission.

A Japanese firm made the decision to turn over its $20 million art collection to Christie's auction house for sale after Christie's defeated its rival Sotheby's in the game of rock–paper–scissors. Is that any way to make a decision?

As the preceding list suggests, the methods used by groups to make decisions include (1) decision by an expert, (2) decision by chance, (3) decision by the majority, (4) decision by the leader, (5) total deferral of decision, (6) decision by the minority, (7) decision by averaging individual decisions, and (8) decision by consensus. Each method has certain advantages and is more appropriate and workable than others under certain conditions. An effective group bases its decision-making strategy on a number of variables, including (1) the nature of the problem, (2) the time available to solve the problem, and (3) the kind of climate in which the group is operating or would prefer to operate.

Experience reveals that methods of group decision making vary considerably in their effectiveness. Majority vote is the method used most frequently. Most elections are decided and many laws are passed using this approach, and a large number of other decisions are made on the basis of the vote of at least 51 percent of a group's members. Lest we overlook the importance of the minority, however, we should note that it, too, can carry weight. Think of how often committees subdivide responsibilities, with the result that subgroups actually end up making the key recommendations and thus the key decisions.

Another popular decision-making strategy is averaging, by which the most popular decision becomes the group's decision.

Letting the expert member decide what the group should do is also fairly common. In this case, the group simply defers its decision-making power to its most knowledgeable member.

In many groups the leader retains all the decision-making power. Sometimes this is done after consultation with group members; at other times it is done without consultation.

Although each of these methods has been used successfully by a variety of groups, the most effective decision-making strategy is decision by consensus. When a group achieves consensus, all members agree on the decision. Even more important, all of them help formulate the decision by voicing their feelings and airing their differences of opinion. Thus, they all understand the decision and will support it.

The greater the involvement of members in the decision-making process, the more effective the decision will be. Of course, decisions by a leader, by an expert, or by a majority or minority vote all take less time than consensus; however, it is the group that will usually be responsible for implementing the decision. If members disagree with a decision or do not understand it, they may not work very hard to make it succeed. A leader may make routine decisions or may be called on to make decisions when little time is available for a real discussion of the issues; under most circumstances, however, one person cannot be the best resource for all decisions. A drawback of the decision-by-expert method is that it is sometimes difficult to determine who the expert is. Also, decision by an expert—like decision by a leader—fails to involve other group members. Decision by averaging, on the whole, is superior to either decision by a leader or decision by an expert. With averaging, all members can be consulted and individual errors will cancel each other out, and an average position will usually not dissatisfy anyone too much. On the other hand, an average position usually does not satisfy anyone very much; thus, commitment to the decision tends to be rather low.

Under most circumstances, the quality of decision making and the satisfaction of the participants are higher when a group seeks consensus. Consensus puts the resources of the entire group to effective use, permits discussion of all issues and alternatives, and ensures the commitment of all members. It is not the decision alone that is important in group interaction; also of concern are the reactions and feelings of group members.

Questions for Decision Makers: Facts, Values, and Policies

The actual content of decision making is based on three key kinds of questions: questions of fact, questions of value, and questions of policy.

Questions of fact focus on the truth or falsity of a statement. Existing information may be inconsistent or contradictory, and group members try to ferret out the truth. For example, a group might seek to determine whether evidence proved beyond a doubt that Scott Peterson was involved in the murder of his wife, Laci, or that former president Richard Nixon was taking mind-altering drugs without a prescription while in office. We might phrase questions of fact like this: "What evidence supports the guilt or innocence of _____?" Similarly, a group might wrestle with questions like these: "What is the likelihood that a comet will hit the earth?" "What are the effects of depletion of the atmospheric ozone layer?" As you can see, answering questions like these requires that a group examine and interpret the available data carefully.

questions of fact
questions involving the truth or falsity of a statement

In contrast, **questions of value** are not factual; they involve subjective judgments. "Who was the best president to serve in the past 100 years?" is a question of value. So are the following: "To what extent is a college education valuable to all Americans?" "How desirable are physical fitness programs?" "To what extent, if any, is the use of laboratory animals for scientific research justified?"

questions of value
questions involving subjective judgments

Questions of policy help us determine what future actions, if any, we should take. In fact, the key word in a question of policy is the word *should*: "What should colleges do to prevent student suicides?" "What should the United States do to discourage terrorism?" "What should federal policy be regarding the sale of semi-automatic military-style weapons to the general public?"

questions of policy
questions designed to help determine future actions

A Framework for Decision Making: Reflective Thinking

The quality of a group's decisions depends at least partly on the nature of its decision-making system. There is a generally agreed-upon structure, consisting of several stages, which, if used properly, can increase the problem-solving effectiveness of most groups. This is called the **reflective-thinking framework.** It was first proposed by John Dewey in 1910. It is probably still the sequence most groups commonly use.[27]

reflective-thinking framework
a system for decision making and problem solving that is designed to encourage critical inquiry

The reflective-thinking framework has six basic components:

1. What is the problem? Is it clearly defined? Do we understand the general situation in which it is occurring? Is it stated so as not to arouse defensiveness? Is it phrased so as not to permit a simple yes or no answer? (For example, "What should the college's policy be toward final exams for seniors?" instead of "Should the college stop wasting the time of its seniors and eliminate final exams?" and "What should the government's policy be toward gun control?" instead of "Should the government restrain trigger-happy hunters?")

2. What are the facts of the situation? What are its causes? What is its history? Why is it important? Whom does it affect, and how?

3. What criteria must an acceptable solution meet? By which and whose standards must a solution be evaluated? What are the principal requirements of the solution? How important is each criterion?

4. What are the possible solutions? How would each remedy the problem? How well does each satisfy the criteria? What are the advantages and disadvantages of each?

5. Which is the best solution? How would you rank the solutions? Which offers the greatest number of advantages and the smallest number of disadvantages? Would some combination of solutions be beneficial?

6. How can the solution be implemented? What steps need to be taken to put the solution into effect?

To make this framework function, every member of the group must suspend judgment. Group members must be open to all available ideas, facts, and opinions. They must guard against early concurrence, which could force them to conclude the discussion prematurely. All data and alternative courses of action must be appraised thoroughly. Instead of insisting on your own position and closing yourself to new information, you need to explore all the major variables that contributed to the problem and investigate all the major issues that may be involved in producing a workable solution.

As you make your way through the framework, ask yourself if (1) the resources of all the group members are being well used, (2) the group is using its time to advantage, (3) the group is emphasizing fact-finding and inquiry, (4) members are listening to and respecting one another's opinions and feelings, (5) pressure to conform is being kept to a minimum while an honest search for diverse ideas is

 ## Exploring Diversity

Culture, Gender, and Global Teams

Not only do we need to be able to work in teams in United States corporations, but because of the prevalence of multinational corporations and our developing global workforce, we also must prepare ourselves to work in global teams in which diversity will be a given. For example, some members of the global team may believe in individualism and loyalty to the individual, while others may believe in collectivism and loyalty to the group. Some may believe that status is inherited, while others may believe it is achieved. Some may believe that members may confront one another when a disagreement occurs, while others may believe that a disagreement should never be discussed in front of others. Some may be monochromic, doing only one thing at a time and paying strict attention to deadlines and schedules, while others may be polychromic, doing many things at a time and not worrying about deadlines and schedules, believing that people are more important than work. Some may want a decision that delivers a quick payoff, while others may defer gratification in pursuit of long-term goals.

What do you believe you would need to learn and understand about yourself and others to function effectively as a member of a mixed-sex, global work team comprising persons from the United States, Britain, Japan, Indonesia, and Saudi Arabia, whose cultures cause them to adhere to contradictory values? What specific problems would you need to overcome for the global team to become a productive unit? What steps would you take to find something that works for everyone on the team? Finally, is it possible for a group of such diverse individuals to become a collaborative team?

made, and (6) the atmosphere is supportive (noncritical), trusting (nonthreatening), and cooperative (noncompetitive). Remember, if group members are afraid to speak up, closed-minded, reluctant to search for information, or unmotivated, they will not perform effectively.

The Search for Better Ideas: Brainstorming

According to Jay Cocks, a business theorist and writer, "In an era of global competition, fresh ideas have become the most precious raw materials."[28] Where do fresh ideas come from? Betty Edwards, author of *Drawing on the Right Side of the Brain*, believes that fresh ideas come from developing creative problem-solving skills, as well as from encouraging creativity in the workplace.[29] To prepare students to meet the demands of the twenty-first century, colleges and universities across the country are offering entire courses on creativity. According to instructional technologist Jeff DeGroff, "The lesson of the twentieth century is that people must change patterns of thinking."[30] Thus, if you can come up with creative solutions, you may find yourself of great value to the companies and corporations of today and tomorrow. **Brainstorming** is one key technique used to thaw frozen patterns of thinking and encourage creativity. What is brainstorming?

A number of researchers suggest that the best way to have a good idea is to have lots of ideas. Frequently, however, instead of suspending judgment and permitting ideas to develop freely, problem solvers tend to grasp at the first solution that comes to mind. Recognizing that this practice inhibits the search for new avenues of thought, Alex Osborn devised a technique called brainstorming.[31] This method is used primarily to promote a free flow of ideas and can be incorporated into the problem-solving process. For instance, although groups use brainstorming most frequently when members are attempting to identify a solution, it can also be used to help identify the factors causing a problem, the criteria that a solution should meet, and ways to implement the solution.

To ensure that brainstorming sessions are successful, group members need to adhere to certain guidelines:

1. Temporarily suspend judgment. That is, do not evaluate or criticize ideas. Instead, adopt a "try anything" attitude. This will encourage rather than stifle the flow of ideas.

2. Encourage freewheeling. The wilder the ideas that are offered, the better. It is easier to tame a wild idea later than it is to replace or invigorate an inert idea. At this point, the practicality of an idea is not of primary importance.

3. Think of as many ideas as you can. At this stage, it is the quantity—not the quality—of ideas that is important. The greater the number of ideas, the better the chance of finding a good one. Thus, in a brainstorming session, no self-censorship or group censorship is permitted. All ideas should be expressed.

4. Build on and improve or modify the ideas of others. Work to mix ideas until they form interesting combinations. Remember, brainstorming is a group effort.

5. Record all ideas. This ensures that the group will have available all the ideas that have been generated during the session.

6. Only after the brainstorming session is finished should group members evaluate the ideas for usefulness and applicability.

Life is the sum of all your choices.

— Albert Camus

brainstorming
a technique designed to generate ideas

I had an immense advantage over many others dealing with the problem inasmuch as I had no fixed ideas derived from long-established practice to control and bias my mind, and did not suffer from the general belief that whatever is, is right.

— Henry Bessemer (discoverer of a new way of making steel)

Brainstorming is effective because it lessens the inhibitions of members and makes it easier for them to get their ideas heard; it promotes a warmer, more playful, enthusiastic, and cooperative atmosphere; and it encourages each individual's potential for creativity. But the unique aspect of brainstorming—and perhaps its most important benefit—is suspended judgment.

Too often, one or two group members stifle the creative-thinking effort of a brainstorming group. Despite the lip service they may pay to suspending judgment, they have come to the problem-solving experience with an evaluative mind-set. According to consultant Sidney Parnes, who studies creative thinking, this attitude surfaces in the form of **killer phrases,** like the following: "That won't work," "We tried that idea before," "You've got to be joking!" Comments like these stop the flow of ideas.[32]

This practice strikes at the heart and nature of brainstorming. It replaces the green light of brainstorming not so much with a yellow light of criticism or thoughtful evaluation as with a red light of frozen judgment. Killer phrases are often accompanied (or replaced) by **killer looks**—looks that discourage or inhibit the generation of ideas. (How often do killer phrases or looks intrude upon your group experiences?) By gaining insight into these types of killers and their effects, you can increase your ability to analyze your own behavior and change it if necessary.

The following example describes how to foster creativity in the workplace:

> Pamela Webb Moore, director of naming services (she helps companies figure out good names for their products at Synectics, a creativity consulting firm), uses a number of techniques to encourage creativity.
>
> One technique she uses to limber up the minds of tightly focused corporate managers is "sleight of head." While working on a particular problem, she'll ask clients to pretend to work on something else. In one real-life example, a Synectics-trained facilitator took a group of product development and marketing managers from the Etonic shoe corporation on an "excursion," a conscious walk away from the problem—in this case, to come up with a new kind of tennis shoe.
>
> The facilitator asked the Etonic people to imagine they were at their favorite vacation spot. "One guy," Moore says, "was on a tropical island, walking on the beach in his bare feet. He described how wonderful the water and sand felt on his feet, and he said, 'I wish I could play tennis barefoot.' The whole thing would have stopped right there if somebody had complained that while his colleague was wandering around barefoot, they were supposed to come up with a shoe. Instead, one of the marketing people there was intrigued, and the whole group decided to go off to play tennis barefoot on a rented court at 10 at night."

killer phrases

comments that stop the flow of ideas

killer looks

looks that discourage or inhibit the generation of ideas

Do you see a problem as a game or as work? According to Mary Ann Glyn, who teaches organizational behavior at Yale University, people who see problems as games come up with more creative solutions than those who consider the same problems work.

Skill Builder

Problem Solving in Organizations

While work groups use a variety of problem-solving methods, including reflective thinking, three other frequently employed techniques include the nominal group technique, the Delphi method, and quality circles. How might your college use each of the following methods to solve a particular problem it faces? Be specific. Which method do you think you would find the most satisfying?

The nominal group technique uses limited discussion, reaching a group decision by secret vote. Especially valuable when group members are reluctant to voice their opinions, perhaps because the issue under discussion is extremely controversial and they do not want their idea attacked, this method enables each group member to contribute equally. The system involves a series of steps that alternates individual work and discussion. (1) The problem is defined for group members. (2) Without having any discussion, every group member writes down ideas for possible solutions to the problem. (3) Going in round-robin sequence, each member, in turn, offers one idea on his or list. The offered ideas are recorded in order on a flip chart or an overhead, so that everyone can see them, until all ideas are exhausted. Duplicate ideas on the list are eliminated. Overlapping ideas on the list are combined. (4) Members clarify ideas. (5) Privately and in writing, every member ranks the listed suggestions. (6) Member rankings are combined to produce a group ranking. (7) Discussion, clarification, and reordering, if necessary, ensue. (8) The ideas with the highest rankings are put into practice.

The Delphi method depends for its effectiveness on a selected group of experts, who do not communicate directly with each other but, instead, respond to a series of questionnaires. It is especially useful when you want to involve all members in finding a solution, when you want to prevent a dominant member from unduly influencing other members, and/or if it would be inconvenient or impossible to get participants physically together in the same location. It, too, contains a series of steps. (1) The problem is defined and the contribution needed from each member is specified. (2) Each member contributes ideas in writing. (3) The ideas provided by all members are combined and redistributed to the members. (4) Members choose the three or four best ideas. (5) Another list is created, using these contributions, and is distributed to members. (6) Members select and submit one or two ideas from the new list. (7) Using these responses, another list is created and distributed to members. (8) The solutions are identified and shared with all members.

A quality circle is a group of employees, often with different areas of expertise and from different levels in an organization's hierarchy, whose task it is to explore and make recommendations for improving the quality and usually the profitability of an organizational function. They use any problem-solving technique they desire to achieve their goal. At the same time, by becoming involved in the decision-making process, workers feel more empowered, bond to the organization, and develop better morale. The goal of any organization should be continual improvement.

While the Etonic people played tennis, the facilitator listed everything they said about how it felt. The next morning, the group looked at her assembled list of comments, and they realized that what they liked about playing barefoot was the lightness of being without shoes, and the ability to pivot easily on both the ball of the foot and the heel. Nine months later, the company produced an extremely light shoe called the Catalyst, which featured an innovative two-piece sole that made it easier for players to pivot.[33]

Brainstorming is also related to what researcher Rosabeth Moss Kanter calls **kaleidoscope thinking.** According to Kanter,

A kaleidoscope takes a set of fragments and forms them into a pattern. But when the kaleidoscope is twisted or approached from a new angle, the same fragments form a different pattern. Kaleidoscope thinking, then, involves taking existing data and twisting it or looking at it from another angle in order to see and analyze the new patterns that appear.[34]

kaleidoscope thinking
the taking of existing data and twisting it or looking at it from another angle

FIGURE 11.4

Fishbone Technique.

Groups use the fishbone technique to identify the possible causes of a problem however remote they may seem. How can such brainstorming help in the search for an effective solution?

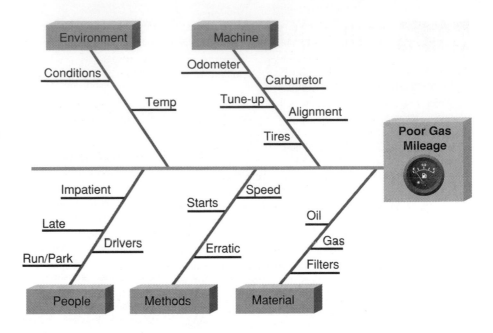

Fishboning is a structured brainstorming technique groups use to aid the search for solutions to problems such as poor gas mileage. When using this technique, group members first create a diagram that resembles a fishbone. Two other names for fishbone diagrams are *cause-and-effect diagrams* and *Ishikawa diagrams* (after Kaoru Ishikawa, who created the system). As shown in Figure 11.4, the problem or effect is placed at the fishbone's head, or right side of the diagram, and the problem's possible cause or effects in their order of probable occurrence or significance are positioned as if growing out the fishbone's spine. Subcauses are also shown as contributors to the primary causes.

GENDER, CULTURE, AND GROUP INTERACTION

The gender and the cultural backgrounds of a group's members provide a set of unstated assumptions and rules that guide their behavior and affect the group.[35]

Gender and Group Member Behavior

When working in groups, men and women are likely to focus on different aspects of the group's life. They also perceive and use power differently. While women tend to pay more attention to the relationships among group members, men tend to focus more on the group's task-related matters.[36] Similarly, women display more signs of liking or immediacy toward each other, while men display more signs of power or potency.[37]

When it comes to the exercise of power in groups, in contrast to most men, who perceive power as finite, something to be guarded for oneself and used to enhance personal status, most women perceive power as unlimited, as something to share, and as a resource for empowering others.[38] Almost without exception, the male members of groups speak more often and longer than do the female members. Even the longest speaking turns of women are likely to be shorter than the shortest turns of men. Men also interrupt the speech of other members more than women, using their interruptive behavior to gain conversational control.[39] Given this finding, how do you explain the stereotype that women talk too much and interrupt others frequently?

As to problem analysis, women tend to analyze problems holistically, whereas men to analyze problems in a more linear fashion, looking for cause-and-effect relationships. Studies of mixed-sex groups indicate that because men and women contribute in unique ways to a group, having them work together enhances group productivity.[40]

Culture and Group Member Behavior

The cultural backgrounds of group members similarly affect the nature of communication in the work group or team. The good news is that increasing group member diversity leads to more effective problem solving and also enhances the satisfaction of members.[41]

When working in a diverse group, members need to understand how cultural factors influence behavior. For example, since African-American culture in the United States is an oral culture, both verbal inventiveness and playfulness are highly valued. As a result, African Americans rely on back-channel responses (saying things such as "That's right" or "Go on" to indicate their interest and involvement in the discussion). Because European Americans do not tend to use back-channel responses as frequently, African Americans may perceive them as underreactive in the group's communication. In contrast, European Americans may perceive the African Americans as overreactive.

Persons from collectivistic cultures, such as those of Japan, China, and Pakistan, tend to be more conforming in groups than do persons from individualistic cultures, such as those of the United States, Great Britain, Australia, and Canada, who place a greater value on competition and dissent. In Japan, for instance, an organization's members have been taught to feel a sense of obligation to those who provide them with security, care, and support. When paired with the sense of dependency, a force called *on* results. *On* links persons in the group forever because the Japanese believe obligation continues throughout life. Hence, because nothing can be decided without a consideration of how the outcomes will influence everyone involved, consensus seeking, although not time efficient, becomes a priority.[42] Since collectivists use group norms rather than individual goals to guide their participation, they are also likely to be group players, and stress harmony and cooperation.[43] Individualists, on the other hand, are more apt to dominate group discussions and more prone to want to win in decision making. They are more likely to voice their disagreement, unlike collectivists, who prefer to slowly assess the feelings and moods of group members without verbalizing their objections or doubts. Consensus seeking does not come as easy to individualists as it does to collectivists.[44]

The makeup of a group also influences the nature of the group's goals and whether they will be short- or long-term in nature. Members of Western cultures tend to focus on short-term goals that deliver more immediate payoffs whereas members of East Asian cultures are more patient and willing to defer gratification and thus more likely to seek long-range goals. Group members need to work out their differences in goal orientation to work together harmoniously.

TECHNOLOGY AND GROUPS: GROUPS IN CYBERSPACE

The Internet is host to a plethora of virtual groups whose members interact with one another online without necessarily ever meeting face-to-face. Like groups that meet in real spaces, groups that meet in cyberspace fulfill both social and professional needs and functions. There are numerous online forums and message board discussions for cancer survivors, parents who have suffered the loss of a child, persons in recovery, running enthusiasts, and political activists, to name just a few.

Those desiring real-time interaction can participate in chat groups. Chat group discussion groups are called channels. Communication in chat groups ranges from random chatter to a serious exchange of information and ideas. Whatever the nature of group member conversation, for trust to develop among chat room members, numbers must be limited. After all, for the chat room to have a community touch, it should not be turned into a railroad station.[45]

Chat room participants are free to talk about many subjects—even those they would hesitate to talk about with others when face-to-face. Because rank is virtually invisible in cyberspace groups, a leveling of status differences tends to occur. In cyberspace, groups of people can chat and not have gender, race, appearance, age, vocal qualities, or fear of how others are going to respond influence member interaction. Though cyberspace groups are proliferating and becoming staples of group interaction around the world, Internet analyst Clifford Stoll is critical of them because a number of popular online discussion groups revolve around sex, bondage, and pornography.[46]

Networked communities provide an environment that offers a sense of neighborhood to those who frequent them. When visiting a site, individuals may play roles as they create a virtual community, sharing, collaborating, and fantasizing with others who are also part of the interactive role game. Since no one is certain of anyone else's identity, participants interact with online personae. Online communities, as we have seen, serve purposes beyond game playing.

The members of cyberspace groups perform roles much as real-space group members do. Included among the roles online group members perform are hackers, phreakers, moderators, and Net police. The rules that guide the group are part of the group's netiquette, or standards of conduct. The absence of physical proximity and traditional nonverbal cues tends to make members less inhibited in expressing themselves. Group members can reproach a member who consistently violates the group's standards and practices, even depriving the person of access to the group. Group members can be reproached for violating ethical standards (revealing personal information about another member without his or her permission); using inappropriate language (language that demeans, insults, or is sexist); and wasting bandwidth (failing to edit a message judiciously).[47]

Businesses in increasing numbers hold virtual conferences, enabling people separated by great distance to interact with each other in real time. Whether the discussion is via teleconferencing, which relies on telephones and speakerphones to connect people in different locations; via videoconferencing, which enables people in different locations to see one another; or via interactive computer conferencing, technology is increasing accessibility and reconfiguring the meeting landscape for groups.

Unlike groups that meet in real space, groups meeting in cyberspace experience continuous membership evolution. Thus, they are not as likely to maintain

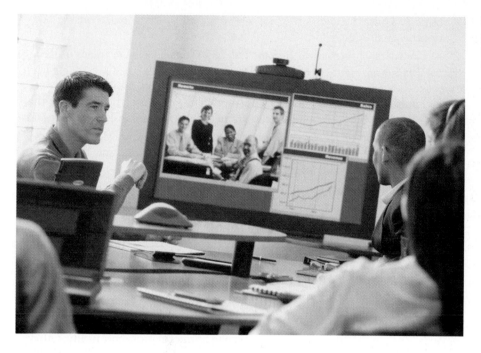

Getting together with group or team members is more easily and quickly accomplished online.

themselves with the same group membership over sustained periods of time as are traditional groups. Despite their increasing prevalence, online groups still do not experience the same levels of effectiveness, efficiency, and member satisfaction as traditional groups.[48]

HOW TO IMPROVE GROUP MEMBER COMMUNICATION

If a problem-solving group is to be effective in a real or an online setting, certain characteristics need to be present, and concerned members must work to develop these qualities. By becoming aware of the difference between optimal problem-solving behaviors and the actual behaviors you and your fellow group members exhibit, you can begin to improve your group's method and style of operation.

An effective group exhibits the following characteristics:

1. *Group goals are clearly understood and cooperatively formulated by the members.* Goals are not merely imposed. If group members are confused about the nature of a problem, they will not be able to solve it. (As theorists Bobby R. Patton and Kim Giffin stress, "If we aim at nothing, we are pretty apt to hit it."[49])

2. *All members of the group are encouraged to communicate their ideas and feelings freely.* Ideas and feelings are valued; they are neither ignored nor suppressed. Keynote phrases are "I think," "I see," and "I feel." These phrases reveal a personal point of view and indicate that you recognize that someone else may feel, think, or see differently than you do.

3. *Group members seek to reach a consensus when the decision is important.* Input from all members is sought. Each member's involvement is considered

critical. Thus, the decision is not left to an authority to make on the basis of little or no discussion.

4. *Consideration is given to both the task and maintenance dimensions of the problem-solving effort.* Members look at the progress the group as a whole makes toward achieving its goal, as well as how successful members are at maintaining themselves as a group. In other words, both the quality of the decision and the well-being of the group members are considered important.

5. *Group members do not set about problem solving haphazardly.* A problem-solving framework is used, and an outline is followed that aids the group in its search for relevant information.

6. *Motivation is high.* Group members are eager to search for information, speak up, listen to others, and engage in an active and honest search for a better solution. They neither jump impetuously at the first solution that presents itself nor prematurely evaluate and criticize ideas.

7. *An effort is made to assess the group's problem-solving style.* Group members identify and alleviate factors that impede the group's effectiveness as well as identify and foster factors that enhance its effectiveness.

8. *The environment is open and supportive.* Group members feel free to contribute ideas and feelings. They also believe that others will listen to their ideas. When members feel free to exchange information and feelings, they are more likely to achieve their objectives. It is only through the transmission and accurate reception of task- and maintenance-related content that groups progress toward their goals. Experienced group members realize how essential it is to elicit contributions from all members and to encourage communication among all members.

9. *The climate is cooperative.* A competitive goal structure can impede effective group interaction. Members of a cooperative group deal honestly with each other, while members of a competitive group sometimes begin to dissemble and deliberately mislead each other. To guard against destructive competition and foster a cooperative orientation, members need to work to demonstrate mutual trust and respect. Participative planning is essential. Coordination, not manipulation, is key.

10. *The group encourages continual improvement.* Group members pay careful attention to how their behavior affects others and how the behavior of others affects them. They continually make the effort to improve and facilitate effective group interaction.

Focus on Service Learning

To apply what you now know about problem solving and working in groups, select a worthy project such as First Night, which protests the prevalence of alcohol at events and designs programs to keep young people alcohol free, or Take Back the Night, which protests the prevalence of sexual violence. After selecting your project and identifying and visiting relevant Web sites, such as www. alcoholpolicysolutions.net or www.redbankfirstnight.com for First Night, or www. campusoutreachservices.com or www.womentakebackthenight. org for Take Back the Night, develop strategies to successfully attract media attention, help raise funds, or raise awareness on campus for the project.

Thinking Critically

Reflect and Respond

Agree or disagree with the following statement attributed to businessperson Arthur Jensen. Supply reasons and examples to support the position you take.

Most of the decisions that affect our lives are not made by individuals, but by small groups of people in executive boardrooms, faculty meetings, town councils, quality circles, dormitory rooms, kitchens, locker rooms, and a host of other meeting places.

Revisiting Chapter Objectives

1. Define *group*.   In communication theory, a group is defined as a collection of people who interact verbally and nonverbally, occupy certain roles with respect to one another, and cooperate with each other to accomplish a definite goal. Some of our most important communication experiences take place in small groups. Today, groups are used, both online and offline, to solve common problems and make decisions by sharing information.

2. Provide examples of how a group's climate affects its operations.   To operate effectively, group members need to be supportive; exercise participative decision making; show trust, openness, and candor; and set high performance goals. The healthier the group climate, the more cohesive the group. Keep in mind that in group meetings, men tend to speak more often, and longer, than women. Thus, women should make an effort to take the initiative, and men should give women the opportunity to air their views.

3. Enumerate the advantages and disadvantages of group decision making and problem solving.   The advantages of using a group instead of an individual are that resources can be pooled, motivation is increased, errors are more likely to be detected, decisions are more readily accepted by those outside the group, and group members can enjoy the companionship and rewards of working with others. There are, however, potential disadvantages to group problem solving: It may encourage laziness among some members; conflict may arise between personal and group goals; the group may be dominated by a few; one or two stubborn members may create a deadlock; the group may make an excessively risky decision; and the decision itself usually takes longer to reach.

4. Distinguish among task, maintenance, and self-serving roles.   Group members perform specific group roles. We contribute to the group's objective when we assume a task-oriented role (behaving in a way that promotes the accomplishment of the task) or a maintenance-oriented role (helping maintain the relationships among group members). However, we can undercut the group's effectiveness by playing a self-serving role—seeking to satisfy only our own needs or goals.

5. Explain how cooperation versus competition and a defensive versus a supportive climate manifest themselves in a group's interaction.   A group benefits from cooperation and a lack of defensiveness among members. Sharing resources and working together to achieve objectives help the group maintain itself while competition and power plays hinder group functioning and promote defensiveness in members.

6. Compare and contrast various decision-making methods.   Groups use a number of methods to make decisions—decision by an expert, by chance, by majority, by the leader, by the minority, by the average of individual decisions, and by consensus—or the group can defer a decision entirely. Making decisions by consensus is considered the most effective strategy. When a group achieves consensus, all members have helped formulate the decision, all have agreed on it, and all will support it.

The Wrap Up

7. **Apply the reflective-thinking framework to increase your effectiveness at problem solving.** Most groups can improve their problem-solving effectiveness by using the reflective-thinking framework, a systematic six-step approach to decision making.

8. **Describe and use brainstorming.** A technique that is useful in some situations is brainstorming, which encourages each member's potential for creativity. Brainstorming can help you change your patterns of thinking and find new solutions.

Resources for Further Inquiry and Reflection

To apply your understanding of how the principles in Chapter 11 are at work in our daily lives, consult the following resources for further inquiry and reflection. Or, if you prefer, choose any other appropriate resource. Then connect the ideas expressed in your chosen selection with the communication concepts and issues you are learning about both in and out of class.

 Listen to Me

"Where Is the Love" (Black Eyed Peas)
"We Can Work It Out" (The Beatles)
"We Are the World" (Stevie Wonder)
"Peace on Earth" (U2)

How can problem-solving skills be put to work to resolve the problems identified in one of these songs?

 View Me

Munich	March of the Penguins
ANTZ	The Full Monty
The Italian Job	12 Angry Men

All of these films focus on the role of the group in problem solving. Identify the decision-making and problem-solving lessons you learned from viewing any one of them.

 Read Me

Jim Collins. *Good to Great*. New York: HarperCollins, 2001.
Patrick Lencioni. *The Five Dysfunctions of a Team*. San Francisco: Jossey-Bass, 2002.
George Orwell. *Animal Farm*. New York: Harcourt Brace, 1954.
Robert D. Putnam. *Bowling Alone: The Collapse and Revival of American Community*. New York: Simon & Schuster, 2000.

How do groups contribute to the establishment of a sense of community? What happens when the sense of community is stifled or disappears? What factors lead a group to destruction? Choose one of these books to use when answering these questions.

 Tell Me

Share with the class the insights you gained from your chosen Listen to Me, View Me, or Read Me selection.

Agree or disagree with this statement, with reasons: The major difference between a group meeting and a funeral is that the purpose of a funeral is perfectly clear.

Key Chapter Terminology

Use the Communication Works CD-ROM and the Online Learning Center at www.mhhe.com/gamble9 to further your knowledge of the following terminology.

brainstorming 325
competitive goal structure 317
cooperative goal structure 317
decision by consensus 321
defensive behavior 317
group 309
group climate 310
group goals 310
group norms 310
group patterns of communication 310
group role-classification model 315
group structure 310

kaleidoscope thinking 327
killer looks 326
killer phrases 326
maintenance roles 315
quality circles 308
questions of fact 323
questions of policy 323
questions of value 323
reflective-thinking framework 323
self-directed teams 309
self-serving roles 316
task roles 315

www.mhhe.com/gamble9

Idioms in Translation

decision-making machinery—decision-making methods
gaining an edge—gaining an advantage
horseplay—rowdy behavior
pooling their abilities—combining their abilities
pros and cons—benefits and drawbacks
round-robin sequence—one-after-another sequence

Test Your Understanding

Go to the *Self Quizzes* on the Communication Works CD-ROM and the book's Online Learning Center at www.mhhe.com/gamble9.

Notes

1. See, for example, C. C. Dubois. "Portrait of the Ideal MBA." *The Penn Stater*, September–October 1992, p. 31; and J. Vice. "Developing Communication and Professional Skills through Analytical Reports." *Communication Quarterly* 64, 2001, pp. 84–93.

2. Eileen Daspin. "Memo to the Team: This Needs Salt!" *The Wall Street Journal*, April 1, 2000, pp. B1, B14.

3. See P. M. Senge, A. Kleiner, C. Roberts, R. B. Ross, and B. J. Smith. *The Fifth Discipline Fieldbook: Strategies and Tools for Building a Learning Organization*. New York: Doubleday, 1994, p. 354.

4. See, for example, G. Lumsden and D. Lumsden. *Communicating in Groups and Teams*, 4th ed. Belmont, CA: Wadsworth, 2004.

5. Natalie Angier. "Why We're So Nice: We're Wired to Cooperate." *The New York Times*, July 23, 2002, pp. F1, F8.

6. See, for example, H. Lancaster. "That Team Spirit Can Lead Your Career to New Victories." *The Wall Street Journal*, January 14, 1996, p. B1; and "Work Week." *The Wall Street Journal*, November 28, 1995, p. A1.

7. Robert Gebeloff. "Oh No, Not Another Meeting." *The Record*, June 20, 1994, pp. C1, C4.

8. See M. A. Verspej. "When You Put the Team in Charge." *Industry Week*, December 1990, pp. 30–32; A. Versteeg. "Self-Directed Work Teams Yield Long-Term Benefits." *Journal of Business Strategy*, November/December 1990, pp. 9–12; and R. S. Wellins, C. W. Byham, and J. M. Wilson. *Empowered Teams: Creating Self-Directed Workgroups That Improve Quality, Productivity, and Participation*. San Francisco: Jossey-Bass, 1991.

9. Different texts offer different definitions. See, for example, Lumsden and Lumsden, 4th ed., and Thomas E. Harris and John C. Sherblom. *Small Group and Team Communication*. Boston: Allyn & Bacon, 1999.

10. See, for example, Robert D. Putnam. *Bowling Alone: The Collapse and Revival of American Community*. New York: Simon & Schuster, 2000.

11. Cheryl Hamilton and Cordell Parker. *Communicating for Results*. Belmont, CA: Wadsworth, 1990, p. 259.

12. Vincent DiSalvo. "A Summary of Current Research Identifying Communication Skills in Various Organization Contexts." *Communication Education* 29, 1980, pp. 281–290.

13. See, for example, J. K. Brilhart and G. J. Galanes. *Effective Group Discussion*, 9th ed. Madison, WI: Brown & Benchmark, 1998.

14. J. Hackman. "The Design of Work Teams." In J. Lorsch, ed. *Handbook of Organizational Behavior*. Englewood Cliffs, NJ: Prentice-Hall, 1987, pp. 315–342.

15. Charles Redding. *Communication within the Organization*. New York: Industrial Communication Council, 1972.

16. Douglas McGregor. *The Human Side of Enterprise*. New York: McGraw-Hill, 1960.

17. B. Tuchman. "Developmental Sequencer in Small Groups." *Psychological Bulletin* 63, 1965, pp. 384–399; and S. A. Wheelen and J. M. Hockberger. "Validation Studies of the Group Development Questionnaire." *Small Group Research* 27:1, 1996, pp. 143–170.

18. See, for example, J. Keyton. "Group Termination: Completing the Study of Group Development." *Small Group Research* 24, 1993, pp. 84–100.

19. See, for example, Marshall Scott Poole. "Do We Have Any Theories of Group Communication?" *Communication Studies* 41:3, 1990, p. 237.

20. Kenneth Benne and Paul Sheats. "Functional Roles of Group Members." *Journal of Social Issues* 4, 1948, pp. 41–49.

21. For a discussion of supportive leadership, see Peter G. Northouse. *Leadership: Theory and Practice*, 2nd ed. Thousand Oaks, CA: Sage, 2001.

22. Linden L. Nelson and Spencer Kagen. "Competition: The Star-Spangled Scramble." *Psychology Today*, September 1972, pp. 53–56, 90–91.

23. Morton Deutsch. "A Theory of Cooperation and Competition." *Human Relations* 2, 1949, pp. 129–152.

24. Jack R. Gibb. "Defensive Communication." *Journal of Communication* 2, 1961, pp. 141–148.

25. Gibb.

26. See Y. Otsubo, A. Masuchi, and D. Nakanishi. "Majority Influence Process in Group Judgment: Test of the Social Judgment Scheme Model in a Group Polarization Context." *Group Process and Intergroup Relations* 5:3, July 2002, pp. 249–262; and D. G. Meyers. *Social Psychology*, 7th ed. New York: McGraw-Hill, 2002, pp. 302–303.

27. John Dewey. *How We Think*. Boston: Heath, 1910.

28. Jay Cocks. "Let's Get Crazy!" *Time*, June 11, 1990, p. 40.

29. Betty Edwards. *Drawing on the Right Side of the Brain*. New York: St. Martin's, 1979.

30. Jeff DeGroff. In Maryanne George. "Grab Your Textbook and Your Poker Cards." *The Record*, January 28, 1991.

31. A. F. Osborne. *Applied Imagination*. New York: Scribner's, 1957.

32. Sidney Parnes. *A Source Book for Creative Thinking*. New York: Scribner's, 1962.

33. Leslie Dorman and Peter Edidin. "Original Spin." *Psychology Today*, July 8, 1989, p. 46.

34. Rosabeth Moss Kanter. "How to Be an Entrpreneur without Leaving Your Company." *Working Woman*, November 1988, p. 44. See also Rosabeth Moss Kanter. *When Giants Learn to Dance*. New York: Touchstone, 1990.

35. G. Hofstede. *Culture and Organizations: Software of the Mind*. New York: McGraw-Hill, 1997.

36. John E. Baird. "Sex Differences in Group Communication: A Review of Relevant Research." *Quarterly Journal of Speech* 62, 1986, pp. 179–192.

37. L. P. Stewart, A. D. Stewart, S. A. Friedley, and P. J. Cooper. *Communication between the Sexes: Sex Differences and Sex Role Stereotypes*, 2nd ed. Scottsdale, AZ: Gorsuch Scarisbrick, 1990.

38. S. Helgesen. *The Female Advantage: Women's Use of Leadership*. New York: Doubleday, 1990.

39. For a discussion of gender and group behavior, see T. Gamble and M. Gamble. *The Gender Communication Connection*. Boston: Houghton Mifflin, 2003.

40. Julia T. Wood. *Gendered Lives*. Belmont, CA: Wadsworth, 1994, p. 277.

41. See, for examples, S. B. Paletz, K. Peng, M. Erez, and C. Maslach. "Ethnic Composition and Its Differential Impact on Group Processes in Diverse Teams." *Small Group Research* 35, 2004, pp. 128–157.

42. Delores Cathcart and Robert Cathcart. "The Group: A Japanese Context." In Larry A. Samovar and Richard E. Porters, eds. *Intercultural Communication: A Reader*, 8th ed. Belmont, CA: Wadsworth, 1997, pp. 329–339.

43. Harry C. Triandis, Richard Brislin, and C. Harry Hul. "Cross-Cultural Training across the Individualism–Collectivism Divide." *International Journal of Intercultural Relations* 12, 1988, pp. 269–289.

44. Cathcart and Cathcart.

45. Leslie Miller. "Chat Not Enough for Community Touch." *USA Today*, August 1, 2000, p. 3D.

46. Clifford Stoll. *Silicon Snake Oil: Second Thoughts on the Information Highway*. New York: Anchor Books, 1995, p. 57.

47. See, for example, Steven G. Jones. *Cybersociety: Computer-Mediated Communication and Community*. Thousand Oaks, CA: Sage, 1995, pp. 95–101.

48. B. B. Baltes, M. W. Dickson, M. P. Sherman, C. C. Baver, and J. S. LaGanke. "Computer-Mediated Communication and Group Decision Making: A Meta-Analysis." *Organizational Behavior and Human Decision Processes* 87:1, January 2002, p. 156.

49. Bobby R. Patton and Kim Giffin. *Decision Making: Group Interaction*. New York: Harper & Row, 1978.

CHAPTER 12

Leading Others and Resolving Conflict

After finishing this chapter, you should be able to

1. Define *leadership* and distinguish among various leadership styles: type X, type Y, autocratic, laissez-faire, and democratic.

2. Describe how trait theory, situational theory, functional theory, and transformational leadership contribute to our understanding of leadership.

3. Define *conflict* and explain how you feel when involved in a group conflict.

4. Define *groupthink* and explain its consequences.

5. Distinguish between competitive and cooperative conflict orientations.

6. Identify how to use the conflict grid and describe the benefits and problems that can result from effective and ineffective handling of group conflict.

7. Identify behaviors that can be used to resolve conflicts effectively.

Man is the only animal that can remain on friendly terms with the victims he intends to eat until he eats them.

—Samuel Butler

You can't eat your friends and have them too.

—Budd Schulberg

Leadership and conflict management are key variables in a team's or a group's success or failure. In 2006 at least one newspaper dubbed the Olympic Games "The Individual Games," as a result of conflict that surfaced among individual U.S. athletes. When individual achievements trump team outcomes, a team suffers. When an athlete's flamboyance takes precedence over team member camaraderie and the individual sees him- or herself as more important than the team, the team faces a crisis. When coaches (team leaders) fail in their efforts to build teams that survive the competition for attention that individuals seek, then individual rivalries combine to create intragroup conflicts that render teamwork an inoperative concept and have the potential to tear the team apart.[1]

Our focus in this chapter is on the variables of leadership and the management of conflict. By gaining insights into how both affect group performance, we prepare ourselves to analyze and improve our own leadership and conflict-resolution behavior in groups.

■ ■ ■

APPROACHES TO LEADERSHIP: THE LEADER IN YOU

What is leadership? What qualities does a good leader possess? Are effective leaders born or made?[2] What sets leaders apart from the pack? Why should anyone be led by you?[3]

What Is Leadership?

Leadership is the ability to influence others. Thus, every person who influences others can be said to exert leadership.[4] Leadership can be either a positive or a negative force. When its influence is positive, leadership facilitates task accomplishment by a group. But if its influence is negative, task accomplishment is inhibited. Every group member is a potential leader.[5] Whether this potential is used wisely or is abused—or whether it is used effectively or ineffectively—depends on individual skills, personal objectives, and commitment to the group.

Groups, especially problem-solving groups, need effective leadership to achieve their goals. Effective leadership can be demonstrated by one or more of the members. Note that there is a difference between being appointed a leader—that is, serving

leadership
the ability to influence others

designated leader
a person given the authority to exert influence within a group

achieved leader
a person who exhibits leadership without being appointed

Go to the Online Learning Center at www.mhhe.com/gamble9 and answer the questions in the Self Inventory to evaluate your understanding of conflict.

Explore what leadership means to you by completing these sentences:

A leader is a person who . . .
I like a leader who . . .
I am a leader when . . .
It is essential for a leader to . . .
I possess the following leadership skills: . . .
I lack the following leadership skills: . . .

as a designated leader—and exhibiting leadership behaviors. When you function as a **designated leader,** you have been selected to be the leader; this means that an outside force has given you the authority to exert your influence within the group. When you engage in effective leadership behavior without being appointed or directed to do so, you function as an **achieved leader;** that is, you are automatically performing roles that help a group attain task or maintenance objectives.

Effective leaders perform combinations of the task and maintenance roles introduced in Chapter 11; they demonstrate role versatility. Such leaders help establish a group climate that encourages and stimulates interaction; they make certain that an agenda is planned for a meeting; they take responsibility for ensuring that group communication proceeds smoothly. When group members get off the track, this type of leader asks relevant questions, offers internal summaries, and keeps the discussion going. This is also the kind of leader who encourages continual evaluation and improvement by group members.

Leadership Styles

Theorists have identified a number of leadership styles. Among them are type X, type Y, autocratic, laissez-faire, and democratic leadership.

TYPE X AND TYPE Y LEADERS

The assumptions we make about how people work together influence the type of leadership style we adopt. The following are eight assumptions that a leader might make about how and why people work. Choose the four with which you are most comfortable.

1. The average group member will avoid working if he or she can.
2. The average group member views work as a natural activity.
3. The typical group member must be forced to work and must be closely supervised.
4. The typical group member is self-directed when it comes to meeting performance standards and realizing group objectives.
5. A group member should be threatened with punishment to get him or her to put forth an adequate effort.
6. A group member's commitment to objectives is related not to punishment but to rewards.
7. The average person prefers to avoid responsibility and would rather be led.
8. The average person not only can learn to accept responsibility but actually seeks responsibility.

type X leader
a leader who does not trust group members to work and is unconcerned with the personal achievement of group members

type Y leader
a leader who displays trust in group members and is concerned with their sense of personal achievement

If you picked mostly odd-numbered items in the preceding list, you represent what management theorist Douglas McGregor calls a **type X leader.** In contrast, if you checked mostly even-numbered items, you represent what McGregor calls a **type Y leader.**[6] The type Y leader is more of a risk taker than the type X leader. Y leaders are willing to let each group member grow and develop to realize his or her individual potential. X leaders, however, do not readily delegate responsibility; unlike Y leaders, X leaders are not concerned with group members' personal sense of achievement. (Are you satisfied with the set of assumptions you chose? What consequences could they have?)

Media Wise

Shakespeare et al. on Leadership

A number of the plays of Shakespeare offer insightful explorations of leadership. The lessons contained in them are as relevant in the twenty-first century as they were in the sixteenth century. For example, from the works of Shakespeare, we learn the importance of timing in achieving goals, the value of courage in facing challenges, the value of determination, and the need for establishing a firm, clear vision. While the artifacts of twenty-first-century corporate life are increasingly high-tech—dominated by cell phones, the Internet, and e-mail—the essence of leadership remains remarkably constant. The effectiveness of corporate teams and groups depends in large measure on the strengths or failings of the corporation's leadership, just as in Shakespeare's day it depended on the strengths or failings of the king.[7]

While not up to the standard set by Shakespeare's plays, contemporary media offerings such as *24* and *Survivor* also explore different types of leaders. As we recognize the types of leaders presented to us, we come to understand them and may even learn to deal with them more effectively.

Pick a recent film or television show. Identify and discuss one or more leadership lessons you learned from viewing the selected film or program, and explain how one or more of the characters in the film or program deepened your awareness of the people you work with or interact with every day.

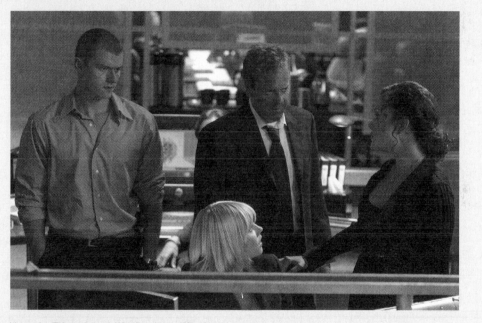

How do TV and real-life leaders differ?

AUTOCRATIC, LAISSEZ-FAIRE, AND DEMOCRATIC LEADERS

In most discussions of leadership styles, three categories in addition to type X and type Y usually come up: the autocratic leader (the "boss"), the democratic leader (the "participator"), and the laissez-faire leader (the "do your own thing" leader).[8] Let's examine each briefly.

Though it was only his second day on the job, employees were already getting bad vibes about the new division chief.

autocratic, or authoritarian, leaders
directive leaders

laissez-faire leader
a nondirective leader

democratic leaders
leaders who represent a reasonable compromise between authoritarian and laissez-faire leaders

The successful organization has one major attribute that sets it apart from unsuccessful organizations: dynamic and effective leadership.

—P. Hersey and K. Blanchard

Autocratic, or authoritarian, leaders are dominators who view their task as directive. In a group with an autocratic leader, the leader determines all policies and gives orders to the other group members. In other words, one boss typically assumes almost all leadership roles; in effect, this person becomes the sole decision maker. Although such an approach may be effective and efficient during a crisis, the usual outcome of this behavior is low group satisfaction.

The opposite of the autocratic leader is the **laissez-faire leader.** This type of leader adopts a "leave them alone" attitude. In other words, this person diminishes the leadership function to the point where it is almost nonexistent. The result is that group members are free to develop and progress on their own; they are indeed free to do their own thing. Unfortunately, the members of a laissez-faire group often are distracted from the task at hand and lose their sense of direction, with the result that the quality of their work suffers.

The middle leadership position—and the one that has proved most effective—is that of **democratic leaders.** In groups with democratic leadership, members are directly involved in the problem-solving process; the power to make decisions is neither usurped by a boss nor abandoned by a laissez-faire leader. Instead, the leader's behavior represents a reasonable compromise between those two extremes. Democratic leaders do not dominate the group with one point of view, but they do attempt to provide direction to ensure that both task and maintenance functions are carried out. The group is free to identify its own goals, follow its own procedures, and reach its own conclusions. Most people prefer democratic groups. Morale, motivation, group-mindedness, and the desire to communicate all increase under the guidance of a democratic leader.

Although democratic leadership is traditionally preferred, all three leadership styles can be effective under the appropriate conditions. Thus, when an urgent decision is required, the autocratic style may be in the group's best interest. When a minimum of interference is needed for members to work together effectively, the laissez-faire style may be more effective. When commitment to the group decision is of greatest importance, the democratic style should be practiced.

Theories of Leadership

Where does leadership ability come from? Why do some people exert more leadership than others? Why are some people more effective leaders than others? Are some people born to be leaders? Or does every situation create its own leader? Or is leadership a matter of learned abilities and skills? Over the years, theorists have given various answers to these questions.

TRAIT THEORY

The earliest view of leadership was trait theory. According to **trait theory,** leaders are people who are born to lead.[9] (Do you know any men or women who seem to have been born to lead?) Trait theorists also believed there are special built-in, identifiable leadership traits. Accordingly, attempts were made to design a test that could predict whether a person would become a leader.

After many years of research, proof of trait theory is still lacking. Personality traits are not surefire predictors of leadership. For one thing, no one set of characteristics is common to all leaders, and leaders and followers share many of the same characteristics. Also, the situation appears, at least in part, to determine who will come forward to exert leadership. This is not to suggest, however, that trait research did not yield valuable findings. In fact, while the statement "Leaders must possess the following personality traits . . ." is not valid, the research does enable us to note that certain traits are indeed more likely to be found in leaders than in nonleaders.

Use the scale in Table 12.1 to assess the extent to which you possess leadership attributes. Calculate your leadership score by adding up the numbers you have

Divide into groups. Create a problem-solving situation and explain how an authoritarian, a laissez-faire, and a democratic leader might handle it. For example, imagine that a corporation needs to purchase data-processing equipment. What behaviors might each type of leader exhibit in a group discussion on this topic? In turn, each group will role-play each leadership style.

trait theory
the theory of leadership asserting that certain people are born to lead

Describe a person who you believe was born to be a leader. What attributes do you believe destined this person to lead?

TABLE 12.1 Evaluating Your Leadership Traits				
Trait	Low			High
Dependability	1	2	3	4	5
Cooperativeness	1	2	3	4	5
Desire to win	1	2	3	4	5
Enthusiasm	1	2	3	4	5
Drive	1	2	3	4	5
Persistence	1	2	3	4	5
Responsibility	1	2	3	4	5
Intelligence	1	2	3	4	5
Foresight	1	2	3	4	5
Communication ability	1	2	3	4	5
Popularity	1	2	3	4	5

chosen. Next, use the scale to evaluate a person you definitely perceive as a leader. Finally, use the scale to evaluate a person you definitely do not perceive as a leader. To what extent did you see yourself as having leadership traits? The highest possible score is 55. Such a score probably indicates strong leadership potential and means that a person perceives himself or herself as a leader or is so perceived by others. How does your total score compare with that of the person you considered a leader? With that of the person you considered a nonleader? If you are interested, you can compute an average score for men and women.[10] Which sex do you think would score higher? Why do you think each set of results turned out as it did?

According to researcher Marvin Shaw, the characteristics identified in Table 12.1 indicate leadership potential. Shaw notes that a person who does not exhibit these traits is unlikely to be a leader.[11] Of course, having leadership potential does not guarantee that you will actually emerge as a leader. A number of group members may have the qualities of leadership, but the final assertion of leadership will depend on more than potential.

SITUATIONAL THEORY

situational theory
the theory of leadership asserting that leadership depends on the situation

The second theory of leadership is **situational theory.** According to this theory, whether an individual displays leadership skills and behaviors and exercises actual leadership depends on the situation.[12] The development and emergence of leadership can be affected by such factors as the nature of the problem, the social climate, the personalities of the group members, the size of the group, and the time available to accomplish the task. As organizational behavior theorist Keith Davis notes in *Human Relations at Work,* leader and group "interact not in a vacuum, but at a particular time and within a specific set of circumstances."[13] A leader is not necessarily a person "for all seasons."

Fred Fiedler's contingency theory and Paul Hersey and Ken Blanchard's readiness theory are both situational theories. Fiedler's theory contends that predicting a group's leader is contingent upon three situational factors: leader–member relations, task structure, and position power.[14] Hersey and Blanchard's theory contends that the readiness level of a group (the degree that members are willing and skilled enough to perform a task) determines the degree of task or relationship behavior a leader needs to emphasize.[15] Thus, the relationship behavior, task behavior, and maturity of the group members all come into play as a leader determines the style called for. For example, when groups are new, a *telling* style of leadership may be effective. The leader needs to provide direction, training, and instructions. When a group has some confidence in its skills, a *selling* style of leadership, one in which the leader uses both task and relational behavior to persuade members to accomplish tasks, is called for. In contrast, when group members take on more responsibility and become more independent, the leader becomes more equal to other group members. In this case, the leadership style of *participating* is used and decision making is shared. Finally, when the group is ready to provide its own leadership, a *delegating* style is appropriate.

FUNCTIONAL THEORY

functional theory
the leadership theory suggesting that several members of a group should be ready to lead because various actions are needed to achieve group goals

The third theory of leadership is **functional theory.** In contrast to trait theory and situational theory, which emphasize the emergence of one person as a leader, functional theory suggests that several group members should be ready to lead because various actions are needed to achieve group goals.

Ethics & Communication

Keeping Down with the Competition

What problems are encountered when a group aspires to produce not the best work it possibly can but, rather, work that is only as good as that produced by competing groups?

Is a group as good as its strongest member? As bad as its weakest member? More than the sum of its parts? Explain.

"That's settled, then. We'll lower our standards to meet the competition."

Functional theorists believe that any of the task or maintenance activities can be considered leadership functions. In other words, when you perform any needed task or maintenance function, you are exercising leadership. Thus, according to functional theory, leadership shifts from person to person and is shared. Of course, sometimes one or two group members perform more leadership functions than others do. Consequently, one member might become the main task leader, whereas another might become the main socioemotional leader. However, the point is that we can enhance our leadership potential by learning to perform needed group functions more effectively.[16]

From the functional viewpoint, then, leadership is not necessarily a birthright; nor is it simply a matter of being in the right situation at a critical juncture. Instead, we are all capable of leadership, and what is required is that we have enough self-assertion and sensitivity to perform the functions that are needed as they are needed. In effect, this theory is asserting that good membership is good leadership. And the converse is also true: Good leadership is good membership.

Skill Builder

Thinking about the Culture of a Group

A group's culture is "the pattern of values, beliefs, norms, and behaviors that are shared by group members and that shape a group's individual 'personality.'"[17] The culture of a group provides the foundation for the rules followed, standards of behavior adhered to, actions undertaken, and behaviors exhibited or prohibited by group members. Organizational theorists believe that every organization evolves a unique group culture, which guides its behavior and the behavior of its members.

Describe the culture of an organization in which you would like to work. What makes the organization's culture and, especially, its norms attractive to you? How do employees use communication to perform the culture? For example, if a person wants to be successful in this organization, what should he or she do? What should he or she not do? What specifically does this organization make possible for its members?

TRANSFORMATIONAL LEADERSHIP

transformational leader

a leader who gives a group a new vision, strengthening its culture or structure

A **transformational leader** transforms a group by giving it a new vision, strengthening its culture or structure. The transformational leader does not merely direct members, elicit contributions from members, or wait for members to catch up with his or her thinking. Instead, the transformational leader helps group members imagine and visualize the future they can build together. Transformational leaders inspire, motivate, and intellectually stimulate group members to become involved in achieving the group's goals. They function as the group's guiding force.[18]

LEADING THE WAY THROUGH CONFLICT MANAGEMENT

How a group handles conflict, which can occur at any point in the group's existence and which can be started by any member of the group, makes a difference in member satisfaction as well as in the decision-making and problem-solving effectiveness of the group. A conflict can originate within a single group member (opposing or contradictory forces within us create inner, or intrapersonal, conflicts), or between two or more group members (the seemingly incompatible views, interests, or goals of group members create external, or interpersonal, conflicts).

How we feel about conflict and whether we view it positively or negatively reveals how we might act when facing one. The following test will help you assess your personal attitudes toward conflict.

1. State your personal definition of *conflict*, and indicate how you feel when involved in a conflict.
2. Next, use the scale in Table 12.2 to assess the extent to which you consider conflict in a small group positive or negative. For each item, circle the number that best reflects your attitude.
    a. Total your circled numbers. If your score is 10 to 14, you believe that conflict is definitely positive. If your score is 15 to 20, you believe

TABLE 12.2 Conflict: Positive or Negative?

Good	1	2	3	4	5	Bad
Rewarding	1	2	3	4	5	Threatening
Normal	1	2	3	4	5	Abnormal
Constructive	1	2	3	4	5	Destructive
Necessary	1	2	3	4	5	Unnecessary
Challenging	1	2	3	4	5	Overwhelming
Desirable	1	2	3	4	5	Undesirable
Inevitable	1	2	3	4	5	Avoidable
Healthy	1	2	3	4	5	Unhealthy
Clean	1	2	3	4	5	Dirty

that conflict can be helpful. If your score is 21 to 30, you do not like to think about conflict; you have very ambivalent feelings. If your score is 31 to 40, you believe that conflict is something to try to avoid. If your score is 41 to 50, you believe that conflict is definitely negative.

b. Determine the average scores for men and for women in the class. How do they compare? If they differ, what do you believe causes the difference? How does your score compare with the average for your sex?

c. Compute the average score for your class as a whole. How does your score compare with the class average?

3. Complete these sentences:

a. The time I felt worst about dealing with conflict in a group was when . . .

b. The time I felt best about dealing with conflict in a group was when . . .

c. I think the most important outcome of group conflict is . . .

d. When I am in conflict with a group member I really care about, I . . .

e. When I am in conflict with a group member I am not close to, I . . .

f. When a group member attempts to avoid entering into a conflict with me, I . . .

g. My greatest difficulty in handling group conflict is . . .

h. My greatest strength in handling group conflict is . . .

The dictionary defines *conflict* as "disagreement, . . . war, battle, and collision." These definitions suggest that conflict is a negative force that of necessity leads to undesirable consequences. To what extent does your score suggest that you support this premise? To what extent do you believe that conflict is undesirable and should be avoided at all times and at all costs? Do you feel that conflict is taboo? Why? Unfortunately, many of us have been led to believe that conflict is evil— one of the prime causes of divorce, disorder, and violence—and that to disagree, argue, or fight with another person will either dissolve whatever relationship exists or prevent any relationship from forming. Somehow, many of us grow up thinking that nice people do not fight, do not make waves. Some believe that if they do not smile and act cheerful, other people will not like them and they will not be accepted or valued as group members.[19]

Former Supreme Court Justice Arthur Goldberg is credited with saying, "If Columbus had an advisory committee he would probably still be at the dock." How has conflict among group members impeded the decision making and action taking of a group you have been in?

What high school groups did you belong to? Were you and your group(s) part of the in-group? In your opinion, might the presence of in- and out-groups in high school contribute to the kind of atmosphere that provides the context for school violence, such as the massacre that occurred at Columbine High School?

How would being in conflict with others affect your ability to function on the job?

AVOID GROUPTHINK: A DETERRENT TO MAKING GOOD DECISIONS

Agree or disagree; state your reasons: The group is dumber than its smartest members.

A body of research suggests that "smart people working collectively can be dumber than the sum of their brains."[20] This theory seems to have been at work in the tragedy involving the space shuttle *Columbia*. Investigators questioned the quick analysis by Boeing engineers that NASA used to conclude early in space shuttle *Columbia*'s mission that falling foam did not endanger the shuttle's safety. The conclusion reached by the engineers reveals that the culture of decision making at NASA was indicative of groupthink. This was not the first time NASA was accused of exhibiting a predilection toward groupthink. The agency suffered from the same criticism in 1986 after the loss of space shuttle *Challenger* and its crew on January 28 of that year. The official inquiry into that disaster revealed that the direct cause was a malfunction of the O-ring seal on the solid rocket booster that caused that shuttle to explode 73 seconds after it was launched. It seems that concerns about the O-rings had circulated within the agency for quite a while prior to the accident but that nothing was done about them. Groupthink has also been targeted as a cause of numerous other fiascos, including the sinking of the *Titanic*, the surprise attack on Pearl Harbor, the foiled Bay of Pigs invasion of Cuba, and the escalation of the Vietnam War.

groupthink

An extreme means of avoiding conflict that occurs when groups let the desire for consensus override careful analysis and reasoned decision making

What is **groupthink?** How does it come about? According to Irving Janis, author of *Victims of Groupthink*, it occurs when groups let the desire for consensus override careful analysis and reasoned decision making.[21] In effect, then, groupthink is an extreme way of avoiding conflict. While cohesiveness is normally a desirable group characteristic, when carried to an extreme, it can become dysfunctional or even destructive.

Are you a groupthinker? To find out, answer yes or no to each of the following questions and explain your answers.

In groups characterized by groupthink, members try to maintain harmony by forgoing critical decision making. Did you or anyone you know ever feel a need for self-censorship at a meeting because it seemed dangerous to challenge the leader or boss? Did you ever feel the need to twist facts to please a boss or leader or to agree with whatever he or she said? If so, how did this influence the course of the meeting? If not, why not?

1. Have you ever felt so secure about a group decision that you ignored all warning signs that the decision was wrong? Why?
2. Have you ever been party to a rationalization justifying a group decision? Why?
3. Have you ever defended a group decision by pointing to your group's inherent sense of morality?
4. Have you ever participated in feeding an "us versus them" feeling—that is, in depicting those opposed to you in simplistic, stereotyped ways?
5. Have you ever censored your own comments because you feared destroying the sense of unanimity in your group?
6. Have you ever applied direct pressure to dissenting members in an effort to get them to agree with the will of the group?
7. Have you ever served as a "mind guard"? That is, have you ever attempted to preserve your group's cohesiveness by preventing disturbing outside ideas or opinions from becoming known to other group members?
8. Have you ever assumed that the silence of other group members implied agreement?

Each time you answered yes to one of these questions, you indicated that you have contributed to an illusion of group unanimity. In effect, you let a tendency to agree interfere with your ability to think critically. In so doing, you became a groupthinker. Groupthink impedes effective group functioning; when all group members try to think alike, no one thinks very much.

*"**We're** looking toward the Pacific Rim, Greenfield. What the hell are **you** doing?"*

Groupthink is the triumph of concurrence over good sense. It is the primacy of authority over expertise. To prevent the flawed group dynamics that characterize decisions made when in a groupthink mode, group members would be well served to consider the merit of ideas rather than the titles of persons who express ideas. They should encourage critical evaluation, even assigning a devil's advocate, an individual who argues against a widely held position, to spur the airing of differences. Group members should also welcome critiques from persons both inside and outside the group. They should reward independent, critical thinking. The goal is to ensure that all the pros and cons of proposed solutions are considered, conflicting opinions are given a voice, and lingering doubts are aired.

Conflict as such is neither a positive nor a negative phenomenon. For this reason, we will not discuss how to avoid it. However, how you view conflict and how you handle it in any group to which you belong will determine the nature of the group's experience and your satisfaction with it. Conflict can be productive if you meet its challenge, but it can be counterproductive if you deal with it improperly. In other words, whether a group conflict is helpful or harmful, destructive or facilitative, depends on how constructively you cope with it.

Gender, Leadership, and Conflict: Comparing Approaches

Who would you rather have as the leader of your group, a man or a woman? While responses to the question vary, men usually come out ahead. However, there is a greater likelihood today that you will be working with members of both sexes in

Exploring Diversity

The 20 Percent Solution

It has been found that discrimination in groups decreases when minorities and women constitute at least 20 percent of a group's members.[22] If increasing the representation of women and ethnic minorities can reduce the bias against persons in these groups, including whether they have a chance to be chosen or emerge as a leader in major corporations, organizations, and government agencies, what steps should be taken to sensitize persons to the need for greater diversity, and what should be done to help women and minorities improve their chances to occupy such leadership positions?

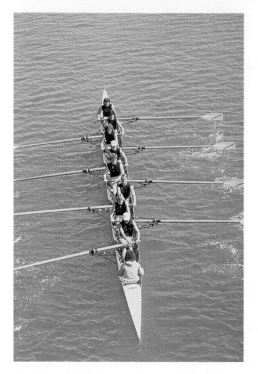

Who would you rather have as the leader of your group or team, a man or a woman? Why?

Have you ever observed gender differences during conflict? Do you think you handle conflict more like the typical man or the typical woman? Why?

the workplace. And when it comes to leadership, while both men and women enjoy being leaders, when part of a group, women are often more motivated to help others than are men and thus exhibit a much more personal leadership approach.[23] Women are also more likely to employ a more participatory or collaborative communication style; men, in contrast, display a more directive style.[24] Thus, women tend to excel at relationship building and participative leadership, while men exhibit more work-directed and assertive behaviors.

Research reveals that sex-role stereotypes influence how the behaviors of leaders are perceived. The same messages are evaluated differently, depending on whether they are delivered by a male or a female. For this reason, while women delivering some messages are considered bossy or emotional, men delivering the same messages are seen as responsible and as exercising leadership. Too frequently, the leadership efforts of women are misinterpreted.[25]

Women and men also have been socialized to approach conflict differently. While most males have been socialized to be demanding and competitive, females have been taught to practice cooperativeness, compromise, and accommodation instead. While males tend to become verbally aggressive and adopt a fight mentality, women are more likely to engage in protracted negotiation in an attempt to avoid a fight.[26] Males are apt to give orders and assert themselves, while females are more prone to make proposals, give reasons for their positions, and attempt to resolve disagreements nonaggressively. When asked to describe how their style of handling conflict differed from that of men, women noted that men are overly concerned with power and content issues and underconcerned with relational issues. When compared with men, women place more emphasis on preserving their relationships during conflict; instead of focusing on content, they focus on feelings.[27]

Men, however, are more likely to withdraw from a conflict situation than are women. Researchers believe this may occur because men become substantially psychologically and physiologically aroused during conflict and may opt to withdraw from the conflict rather than risk further arousal.[28] Women, in contrast, prefer to talk about conflict in an effort to resolve it.[29] Women, when compared with men, are more likely to reveal their negative feelings and become emotional during conflict. Men, on the other hand, are more apt to keep their negative feelings to themselves and argue logically instead.[30]

Culture, Leadership, and Conflict: Comparing Views

Your culture influences the way you communicate when you are part of a group. While cultural variations can enhance a group's operation, at times cultural clashes can impede it. For example, when Corning and the Mexican company Vitro made a cross-border alliance, their communication efforts were hurt by cultural misunderstandings. According to business leaders, problems developed in the relationship because of stereotypes as well as different decision-making and work-style approaches employed by the two companies. While the Americans were accustomed to eating during meetings, the Mexicans were used to going out for leisurely meals. The Mexicans typically put in much longer workdays because of their longer lunches and conducted evening meetings, whereas the Americans wanted to hold business to daytime hours. The Mexicans saw the Americans as too direct, while the Americans viewed the Mexicans as too polite. The decision-making methods of the two companies posed the toughest problem: Because Mexican businesses tend to be much more hierarchical, the decisions were made by the top executives, which slowed down the decision-making process. The Mexicans, unlike the Americans, displayed an unwillingness to criticize. As a result, their conversations were more indirect.[31]

Like the Mexican style, the Japanese decision-making style differs from the American approach. While Americans tend to value openness in groups, the Japanese value harmony. While Americans emphasize individual responsibility, the Japanese stress collective responsibility.[32] Thus, there is a tendency among the Japanese to lose individual identity within the group.[33] While Americans believe that the individual is the most important part of a group, that the individual is free to choose the roles he or she will perform in a group, and that it is an individual's right to remain as part of a group, the Japanese believe in the submergence of the individual within the group and demand complete loyalty. Group orientation is so pervasive that members do not usually assume self-serving roles, such as blocker or recognition seeker, because to do so would jeopardize the success of the group. To leave a group in Japan is to risk losing one's identity. Since Japan is a collectivistic culture, the group, not the individual, is the significant entity. In individualistic cultures such as the United States, the individual group member is accorded significant importance.

Native Americans, like the Japanese, refrain from competing publicly with others in a group for fear of causing embarrassment. Humiliating a fellow group member to prove a point is alien to them.

Even though group membership and group identity are highly valued in collectivistic cultures, participating in decision-making groups does not appear to give group members actual decision-making power. In one study of 48 Japanese organizations, while members were encouraged to contribute ideas, the decision-making power remained with the CEO and managers high in the organization hierarchy.[34] Thus, culture influences both membership and leadership style.

Cultural values also influence attitudes toward conflict. In cultures that value individualism (such as the United States and Australia), the importance of the individual over the group is emphasized; conflict is viewed as a way of airing differences. As a result, conflict is usually not repressed but is handled openly and directly. In contrast, in cultures that value collectivism (such as Japan and Korea), the importance of group unity over individual desire is stressed; group conflict is perceived as a threat, and efforts are made to suppress it in public.[35]

The Japanese, for example, are apt to reveal false fronts, or *tatemae,* when interacting in meetings. This helps all participants save face. The importance of saving face is revealed in the following example. For years the automaker Mitsubishi hid complaints about defects in a file known to workers as "H," for the Japanese word for "secret" or "defer." The defects, including failing brakes, fuel leaks, malfunctioning clutches, and fuel tanks prone to falling off, were fixed on a case-by-case basis to avoid any humiliating recalls.[36]

In general, members of African-American and Asian-American cultures are also more collective than are members of the European-American culture—

Exploring Diversity

Win–Win

A new teacher—let's call her Mary—arrived at a Navaho reservation. Each day in her classroom, something like the following would occur. Mary would ask five of her young Navaho students to go to the chalkboard and complete a simple mathematics problem from their homework. All five students would go to the chalkboard, but not one of them would work the problem as requested. Instead, they would all stand, silent and motionless.

Mary, of course, wondered what was going on. She repeatedly asked herself if she might be calling on students who could not do the assigned problems. "No, it couldn't be that," she reasoned. Finally, Mary asked her students what the problem was. Their answer displayed an understanding not many people attain in a lifetime.

Evidently, the students realized that not everyone in the class would be able to complete the problems correctly. But they respected each other's uniqueness, and they understood, even at their young age, the dangers of a win–lose approach. In their opinion, no one would win if anyone was embarrassed or humiliated at the chalkboard, and so they refused to compete publicly with each other. Yes, the Navaho students wanted to learn—but not at the expense of their peers.

Where do you stand? Would typical American schoolchildren behave similarly? Why or why not? Should they behave like the Navahos?

---

especially male members.[37] In fact, for African Americans, success in mixed-race groups is more related to building and maintaining relationships than it is for European Americans.[38]

While individualistic cultures view conflict as a step along the problem-solving path, collectivistic cultures see it as dysfunctional, distressing, and dangerous. The Japanese proverb "The nail that sticks out shall be hammered down" contrasts sharply with "Do your own thing," a well-known motto of American society. Consequently, while individualists see the potential for conflict to yield positive results, collectivists instead visualize the time that experiencing conflict will require them to invest in face-saving work.[39] As a result, collectivists refuse to put their personal interests before those of other group members, believing instead that the team's collective state of mind is what is crucial.

THE LEADER'S ROLE IN RESOLVING CONFLICT

Like it or not, you are a negotiator. Negotiation is a fact of life. . . . Everyone negotiates something every day.

—Roger Fisher and William Ury,
Getting to Yes

Conflict must be managed effectively if a group is to benefit from it. Whether conflict facilitates or debilitates group functioning depends directly on the orientations leaders and members bring to the conflict situation and how they define it.

Cooperative versus Competitive Conflict: Win–Win or Win–Lose

A lion used to prowl about a field in which four oxen dwelled. Many a time he tried to attack them; but, whenever he came near, they turned their tails to one another, so that whichever way he approached them he was met by the horns of one of them. At last, however, they fell a-quarreling among themselves, and each

Skill Builder

Conflict Corner: Can You See It My Way?

Choose a current issue that is significant and controversial (for example, abortion, global warming, capital punishment, nuclear energy). You will be assigned to defend or oppose it. Defenders and opposers will have a chance to meet and prepare their cases. Each defender (A) will be paired with an opposer (B). Person A will have five minutes to present the defense's position to person B.

Person B then will have five minutes to present the opposition's position to person A.

Players will then switch roles, so that B presents A's case and A presents B's case.

1. To what extent did reversing roles help you understand and appreciate another point of view?
2. How could such a procedure help a person change from a win–lose orientation to a win–win orientation?

---

went off to the pasture alone in a separate corner of the field. Then the lion attacked them one by one and soon made an end to all four.[40]

How does this story from *Aesop's Fables* apply to our study of conflict? Unlike the oxen, you can learn to handle your conflicts constructively; you can learn to disagree without becoming disagreeable. To do this, you need to put conflict into a mutual, noncompetitive framework. Unfortunately, sometimes this is more easily said than done. In many conflict situations, we are too quick to view our own position as correct or true while condemning and misperceiving the other person's position. Also, besides causing us to be too hasty in defending our own position and condemning someone else's, conflict in and of itself can make us compete when we should cooperate. When a conflict first develops, one of the key variables affecting the outcome is whether the participants' attitudes are cooperative or competitive. Will one person achieve victory by destroying the positions of others? Will the participants argue to a draw? Or will they share the goal?

In general, we can say that people enter a conflict situation with one of two orientations, or perspectives: competition or cooperation. People who have a **competitive set** perceive a conflict situation in all-or-nothing terms and believe that, to attain victory, they must defeat the other participants. They do not believe that their own interests and those of others are compatible. By contrast, people with a **cooperative set** believe that a way to share the rewards of the situation can be discovered.

If people bring a competitive orientation to a conflict, they will tend to be ego-involved and will see winning as a test of personal worth and competence. In contrast, if people bring a cooperative orientation to a conflict, they tend to look for a mutually beneficial way to resolve the disagreement.

For a conflict to be defined as cooperative, each participant must demonstrate a willingness to resolve it in a mutually satisfactory way. In other words, each person must avoid behaving in any way that would escalate the conflict. If the people involved in a conflict are treated with respect by all the others involved, if they are neither demeaned nor provoked, and if communication is free and open instead of underhanded and closed, the disagreement may be settled amicably.

competitive set
a readiness to perceive a conflict in all-or-nothing terms

cooperative set
a readiness to share rewards to resolve conflicts

With whom have you had to negotiate recently: friend, spouse, co-worker, boss? Over what: money, goods, services, information, rules, prestige? What was the outcome?

If a conflict is defined as competitive, the participants become combatants: they believe that, to attain victory, they must defeat the other side. Unfortunately, competing with or defeating another person with whom we are interacting is characteristic of encounters in our society. Many phrases we use reflect this orientation: We speak of "outsmarting" others, of putting people "in their place," of getting ourselves "one up" and someone else "one down."

We can define a conflict as a win–lose situation, or we can define it as a win–win situation. If we define it as win–lose, we will tend to pursue our own goals, misrepresent our needs, attempt to avoid empathizing with or under-standing the feelings of others, and use threats or promises to get others to go along with us. If we define a conflict as win–win, we will tend to view it as a common problem, try to pursue common goals, honestly reveal our needs to others, work to understand their position and frame of reference, and make every effort to reduce rather than increase defensiveness.[41]

Interview a manager. Ask about the nature of a conflict he or she had to resolve and the strategies he or she used to handle it.

To transform a conflict from competitive to cooperative, you must use effective communication techniques.[42] You can discover workable strategies and practice them until you can use them for yourself. You should aim to become a conflict processor and develop the ability to view a conflict from the standpoint of other people.

role reversal

a strategy in which persons in conflict act as each other in order to understand each other's position

Role reversal—that is, acting as if you were the person(s) with whom you are in conflict—can help people involved in a conflict understand each other, find creative ways to integrate their interests and concerns, and work toward a common goal. Reversing roles helps you avoid judging others by enabling you to see things from their perspective. Once you can replace a statement like "You're wrong" or "You're stupid" with one like "What you believe is not what I believe," you will be on your way to developing a cooperative orientation.

GOALS AND STYLES: A CONFLICT GRID

A number of paradigms, or models, have been proposed to represent the ways we try to resolve conflicts. Among them is Robert Blake and Jane Mouton's **conflict grid** (see Figure 12.1).[43] This grid has two scales. The horizontal scale represents the extent to which a person wants to attain personal goals. The vertical scale represents the extent to which the person is concerned for others. The interface between the two scales indicates how strongly the person feels about these concerns—that is, how his or her concern is apportioned.

conflict grid

a model portraying the styles individuals use to resolve conflicts

Both scales range from 1 (low) to 9 (high), representing increasing importance of personal goals ("concern for production of results") and of other people ("concern for people"). On the basis of this measure, Blake and Mouton identified five main conflict styles. As you consider their grid and the following descriptions of their five styles, try to identify your own conflict style.

avoider

a person who, when faced with a conflict, uses the unproductive strategy of mentally or physically fleeing the situation

A person with a 1/1 conflict style can be described as an **avoider;** the avoider's attitude can be summed up as "lose and walk away." If you have a 1/1 style, your goal is to maintain neutrality at all costs. You probably view conflict as a useless and punishing experience, one that you would prefer to do without. Rather than tolerate the frustrations that can accompany conflict, you physically or mentally remove yourself from the conflict situation.

accommodator

a person who, when faced with a conflict, overvalues the maintenance of relationships and undervalues the achievement of his or her own goals

A person with a 1/9 style is an **accommodator,** whose attitude is "give in and lose." If you are a 1/9, your behavior demonstrates that you overvalue the

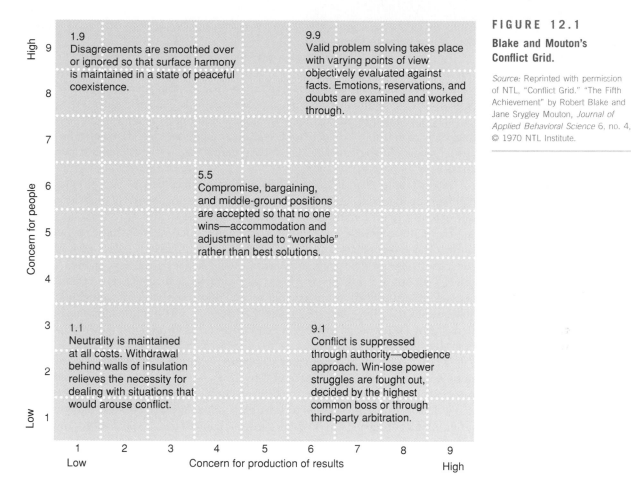

FIGURE 12.1

Blake and Mouton's Conflict Grid.

Source: Reprinted with permission of NTL, "Conflict Grid." "The Fifth Achievement" by Robert Blake and Jane Srygley Mouton, *Journal of Applied Behavioral Science* 6, no. 4, © 1970 NTL Institute.

maintenance of relationships and undervalue the achievement of your own goals. Your main concern is to ensure that others accept you, like you, and coexist in peace with you. You are afraid to make others angry, and you will do anything to avoid being perceived as a troublemaker. Although conflicts may exist in your world, you refuse to deal with them. You feel a need to maintain the appearance of harmony at all costs. This discrepancy leads to an uneasy, tense state characterized by a great deal of smiling and nervous laughter.

A person with a 5/5 style is a **compromiser,** whose attitude is "find a middle ground." If you are a 5/5, your guiding principle is compromise. Thus, you work to find a way to permit each participant in a conflict to gain something. Compromise is, of course, a valid strategy in some cases. But it can be a problem if you always settle for a workable solution because you are afraid the conflict may escalate if you try to find the best solution. It is undeniable that "half a loaf is better than none," and this conflict style will leave participants half satisfied, but it can also be said to leave them half dissatisfied. Thus, compromise is sometimes referred to as the lose–lose approach.

A person with a 9/1 style is a **competitive forcer,** who takes a win–lose attitude. If you are a 9/1, attaining your personal goals is far more important to you than concern for other people. You have an overwhelming need to win and

Why would people who are competitors (9/1) enjoy being surrounded by "yes people" (1/9)? What dangers can such a mix pose?

compromiser

a person who, when faced with a conflict, tries to find a middle ground

competitive forcer

a person who, when faced with a conflict, adopts a win–lose orientation in which the attaining of personal goals is paramount

problem-solving collaborator

a person who, when faced with a conflict, adopts a win–win orientation, seeking to satisfy his or her own goals as well as those of others

Which conflict-resolving strategies do you use? Why?

In the parable of the Abilene paradox, a family is contentedly playing dominoes when one member comes up with the idea of going to Abilene for dinner. Since everyone thinks all the others believe it's a good idea, no one voices any objections, and they go on the long, dusty trip to get lousy food. What does this suggest about each member's role in a group?

dominate others; you will defend your position and battle with others, whatever the cost or harm to them.

A person with a 9/9 style is a **problem-solving collaborator,** who takes a win–win attitude. If you are a 9/9, you actively seek to satisfy your own goals (you are results-oriented) as well as those of others (you are also person-oriented). This, of course, is the optimum style when you are seeking to reduce conflict. As a problem solver, you realize that conflicts are normal and can be helpful; you also realize that each person in a conflict holds legitimate opinions that deserve to be aired and considered. You are able to discuss differences without making personal attacks.

According to Alan Filley, effective conflict resolvers rely to a large extent on problem solving (9/9) and smoothing (1/9), whereas ineffective conflict resolvers rely extensively on forcing (9/1) and withdrawal (1/1).[44]

If we are to develop and sustain meaningful group relationships, we need to learn to handle conflicts constructively. A conflict has been productive if all the participants are satisfied with the outcomes and believe they have gained something.[45] In other words, no one loses; everyone wins. In contrast, a conflict has been destructive if all the participants are dissatisfied with the outcomes and believe that they have lost something. Perhaps one of the most important questions facing each of us is whether we can turn our conflicts into productive rather than destructive interactions.

We will be most likely to create constructive rather than destructive interactions if our conflicts are characterized by cooperative problem-solving methods, attempts to reach mutual understanding, accurate and complete communication, and a demonstrated willingness to trust each other. We will be most likely to fail if our conflicts become win–lose encounters characterized by misconceptions and misperceptions; inaccurate, sketchy, and disruptive communication; and a demonstrated hesitancy to trust each other. It is apparent that in a conflict situation the best approach to a constructive resolution is cooperation.

LEADING GROUPS AND HANDLING CONFLICTS IN CYBERSPACE

Web conferencing, teleconferencing, and videoconferencing enable corporations to hold virtual meetings, linking participants in remote locations. For many, it is becoming the daily business tool that enables corporate leaders to bring more people to a meeting than would otherwise be feasible, save time and money, and increase productivity.[46]

Aside from business, people engage in online discussions for other reasons, seeking people who share their personal and professional interests. Some sites, such as MySpace and Facebook, are all about building a cyberspace community.[47] For people who do not have a real-world support community, logging on to find or create one is the alternative.[48]

Electronic discussion groups also exist for virtually all academic subjects and topics of interest. Often, leaders or facilitators function as moderators. They often double as the persons responsible for judging the appropriateness of messages and for keeping the contentiousness of some of the group's members under control. On the Net, when persons are involved in newsgroups in which controversial issues surface and are discussed, the conflict that almost inevitably results among group members sometimes gets out of hand and escalates into an attack called a **flame war.**

Not all flame wars are fought over major issues. Some are fought over relatively minor ones, such as spelling, semantics, or grammar disagreements. Whatever their source, however, flames tend to be directed at specific persons, are usually argumentative or vituperative in tone, and frequently develop into disagreements that are unrelated to the original controversies that provoked them. Because flames are extremely personal, persons who are flamed may react reflexively by encoding insults that are even more offensive than the ones that initially elicited a disruptive response from them. Group members who are flamed perceive their reputations to be on the line and feel a need to defend them.[49]

Flame wars that get out of hand end up interfering with the discussion of persons who are not involved in them. Thus, if not extinguished quickly, flame wars can reduce the usefulness of the Usenet or newsgroup discussion itself. Sometimes group members decide to take their flame war to a conflict room—a place where they can participate in a flame war without disrupting the discussions of others in the group. Thus, when in the midst of a conflict, someone writes, "Let's take this discussion to 'alt. flame,'" that is what they are suggesting.[50]

Online conflicts also result because of spamming—the sending of repeated unsolicited e-mail or posting of the same message on numerous bulletin boards even though the message is inconsistent with the focus of the group. Spamming causes its recipients to consume valuable time and energy reading something they never wanted to receive. It also clogs systems and slows them down.

flame war
a conflict that occurs in cyberspace groups

In what ways, if any, is online conflict different from face-to-face conflict?

THE ETHICAL MANAGEMENT OF CONFLICT: SKILLS AND STRATEGIES

Conflict can be resolved productively by applying the principles of effective communication. When you use effective communication techniques, you reduce the likelihood that your comments will escalate a conflict by eliciting angry, defensive, or belligerent reactions. Learning to handle conflict successfully is an attainable goal that can lead to increased self-confidence, improved relationships, and a greater ability to handle stressful situations. All that is required is a commitment to practice and apply the necessary skills. Anyone who is willing can learn creative and effective ways of managing conflict—ways that will increase the likelihood of future harmony and cooperation.

Let us now examine the behaviors that can turn conflict situations into problem-solving situations. The following suggestions are a basic guide to conflict resolution.

Recognize That Conflicts Can Be Settled Rationally

A conflict stands a better chance of being settled rationally if you avoid certain unproductive behaviors, such as the following:

pretending that the conflict simply does not exist

withdrawing from discussing it

What does this photo suggest to you regarding the handling of conflict? Why is President Bush pointing at both other participants?

placating or surrendering to the people with whom you are in conflict

trying to create distractions so that the conflict will not be dealt with

overintellectualizing the conflict or rationalizing the conflict

blaming or finding fault with the other people

attempting to force the others to accept your way of seeing things

Recognizing unproductive behaviors is a first step in learning to handle conflicts more effectively. Being willing to express your feelings openly, directly, and constructively without resorting to irrational techniques that destroy trust and respect is a prerequisite for becoming a productive conflict manager. Thus, instead of insulting or attacking others or withdrawing from a conflict, be willing to describe whatever action, behavior, or situation you find upsetting. Do this without evaluating other people negatively or causing them to become defensive. Focus on issues, not personalities. Be willing to listen to and react to what the other person is saying.

Conflicts can be settled rationally if you act like a capable, competent problem solver and adopt a person-to-person orientation.

Define the Conflict

Once you have recognized that conflicts can be handled rationally, you are ready to ask, "Why are we in conflict? What is the nature of the conflict? Which of us feels more strongly about the issue? What can we do about it?" Here again, it is crucial to send "I" messages ("I think it is unfair for me to do all the work around here"; "I don't like going to the library for everyone else") and to avoid sending blame messages ("You do everything wrong"; "You are a spoiled brat"; "You'll make us fail"). Be very clear that you would like to join with the other group members in discovering a solution that will be acceptable and beneficial for all of you—a solution whereby none of you will lose and each will win.

Check Your Perceptions

A situation is a conflict when it is perceived as a conflict. In conflict-ripe situations, we often distort the behavior, position, or motivations of the other person involved. We prefer to see one set of motivations rather than another because it meets our own needs to interpret the situation that way. When we do this, we deny the legitimacy of any other position. Thus, it is not uncommon for each person in a conflict to believe, mistakenly, that the other person is committing underhanded and even vicious acts. It is not extraordinary for each person to make erroneous assumptions about the other's feelings, nor is it unusual for people to think they disagree with each other simply because they have been unable to communicate their agreement. For these reasons, it is important for each person to take some time to explain his or her assumptions and frame of reference to the others. It is also important for all the people involved to feel that their contributions are listened to and taken seriously.

After each of you has identified how you feel, it is time to determine whether you understand one another. This calls for active, empathic listening. Each of you should be able to paraphrase what the other has said in a way the other finds satisfactory. Doing this before you respond to the feelings expressed can help avert escalation of the conflict. Along with active listening, role reversal can help people in conflict understand one another. Like active listening, role reversal permits you to see things as others in the group see them. If you are willing to listen to and experience another person's point of view, that person will be more likely to listen to and experience yours.

Suggest Possible Solutions

The goal during the "possible solutions" phase is for group members to put their heads together and come up with a variety of solutions. Most important, neither you nor anyone else in the group should evaluate, condemn, or make fun of any of the suggestions. You must suspend judgment and honestly believe that the conflict can be resolved in a variety of ways.

 Thinking Critically

Reflect and Respond

On the basis of your understanding of leadership and the value of conflict and conflict management, agree or disagree with this excerpt from Deborah Tannen's *Talking from 9 to 5*. Supply reasons and examples from both research and your own life that support the stance you are taking.

When decisions are made by groups, not everyone has equal access to the decision-making process.

Those who will take a position and refuse to budge, regardless of the persuasive power or intensity of feeling among others, are far more likely to get their way. Those who feel strongly about a position but are inclined to back off in the face of intransigence or very strong feeling from others are much less likely to get their way.[51]

Focus on Service Learning

Using resources on conflict management and resolution, such as www.campus-adr.org/ or www.conflictresolution.uiuc. edu/mediation/, develop a plan to address a campus conflict such as how to resolve disagreements between dorm and apartment mates. Lead a team in executing your plan, creating press releases for the campus paper, and working with residence hall and student life counselors to develop a workshop based on your plan to present on campus.

Assess Alternative Solutions and Choose the One That Seems Best

After possible solutions have been generated, it is time to see which solution each person considers best. It is legitimate to try to determine which solutions will let one side win at the other's expense, which will make everyone lose, and which will let everyone win. Your objective is to discover which solutions are totally unacceptable to each side and which are mutually acceptable. (It is crucial to be honest during this stage.) Once all the solutions have been assessed, you are in a position to determine if one of the mutually acceptable solutions is clearly superior to all the others—that is, if it has the most advantages and the fewest disadvantages. Also, be sure to explore whether it is the most constructive solution.

Try Your Solution and Evaluate It

During the "tryout" stage, we see how well the chosen solution is working. We try to ascertain who is doing what, when, where, and under what conditions, and we ask how all this is affecting each person in the group. We want to know if the people involved were able to carry out the job as planned, whether the solution we adopted has solved the problem, and whether the outcome has been rewarding to everyone. If not, we know it is time to begin the conflict resolution process again.

Looking Back and Ahead
Consider This Case: Sorry, Wrong Number

"Your participant code has been accepted," said the automated voice on the phone. "The conference has begun; please hold while we connect you."

Relieved, Sam heard a couple of clicks and the familiar musical tone, and then the voice of his boss, Karen, saying, "Hello?" Karen, customer relations manager for a small manufacturer of healthy snack foods, including veggie chips and salt-free dip, worked at company headquarters about 100 miles away. Sayid and Jennifer, two of his co-workers, were located at a branch office about halfway between Sam and Karen. Asher, the fifth member of the department, worked at headquarters and was Karen's assistant.

Sam, the newest employee, worked from his home office, traveling to headquarters once a

month. Sayid and Jennifer visited headquarters once a month as well, and the three of them and Asher usually spent the day working with Karen, bringing her up to date on their progress and getting feedback from her about their job performance. Sam's responsibility was to answer the company's toll-free number and respond to customer e-mails sent to the corporate Web site. Customer communications that called for refunds or replacement products, or that required any kind of investigation, were passed along to Sayid and Jennifer for resolution.

"Hi, Karen, it's me, Sam," he said.

"Sam! I've been waiting for you to call in!" Karen's annoyance came through clearly over the phone.

Sam checked his watch. "Am I late?" he asked anxiously. This week had been his turn to send everyone an e-mail confirming their regular weekly conference call, and he was sure that when he set it up, he'd accounted for the fact that Karen's location was in a different time zone from everyone else's. He'd sent the agenda, too, he remembered—the agenda items were their weekly status reports, the new customer complaint form that headquarters wanted them to fill out, and their vacation schedules.

"No, you're not late," Karen snapped. "Asher's late. But I think there's been a mix-up with the conference call. Sayid just sent me an IM—he and Jennifer are already waiting for us on a different line, wondering where we are. Why are they calling in on a different number?"

"I don't know," said Sam nervously. "Hang on a minute." He clicked open the e-mail he'd gotten from the phone company and checked the call-in number he'd sent everyone. Sure enough, it was a different number from the one they usually used.

"Um, I'm sorry, Karen. It looks like the phone company did give us a different number this week for some reason, and that's what I put in the e-mail—that's the number you and I are talking on now. But I guess Sayid and Jennifer dialed the old one by mistake, and that's why we've got two conference calls going on instead of one. What do you think we should do? Should we hang up and call the other number?"

"Sayid and Jennifer should hang up and call back so they can join us here," said Karen. "You contact the two of them, and I'll keep this line open while I go try to find out where Asher is."

"OK," said Sam. "Again, I'm sorry about the mix-up."

"Well, don't worry about it now," said Karen with a sigh. "Sayid and Jennifer should have read your memo more carefully. The thing is, we're losing time here, and I need to talk to all of you about our department's new goals before I leave for the airport. So let's get everyone on the same page right away, all right?"

"Sure," said Sam, torn between embarrassment at his own error and irritation at Sayid and Jennifer. It was their failure to read his memo carefully that had made him look bad in front of his boss, he reasoned. Even Karen thought so. Why couldn't those two pay more attention?

Cradling the receiver between his ear and his shoulder, he started typing a message to Sayid and Jennifer. Suddenly he took in what Karen had just said. She wanted to talk about goals—why hadn't he put that on the agenda? Desperately, he tried to remember whether Karen had sent him any input about the agenda. Had he remembered to ask her for it? Would Asher, Sayid, and Jennifer blame him if they were caught unprepared for that part of the call?

Suddenly, Sam heard the musical tone that signaled another party joining the call. "Hey, Sam!" said Asher. "Where's Karen? How come you're not in the conference call with Jenn and Sayid?"

DISCUSSION QUESTIONS

1. How could Sam have prevented the problems in this phone call?
2. What can you deduce about Karen's leadership style in this situation?
3. What difference do you think it made to Karen and Sam's conversation that there was no nonverbal component for either of them to interpret?
4. What conflict-resolution style is Sam using? Do you think it's the most effective one to use in this situation? Why or why not?
5. What are some of the advantages and disadvantages of online communication that Sam's experience with Sayid, Asher, and Jennifer reveals?

The Wrap Up

Revisiting Chapter Objectives

1. **Define *leadership* and distinguish among various leadership styles: type X, type Y, autocratic, laissez-faire, and democratic.**   To achieve their objectives, groups need effective leadership. Leadership is simply the ability to influence others, and there are many leadership styles. A type X leader believes group members need to be closely controlled and coerced to work. A type Y leader believes members are self-directed and seek responsibility as well as opportunities for personal achievement. The autocratic leader dominates and directs all the other members of the group, whereas the laissez-faire leader lets them do their own thing. In most situations, the democratic leader, who encourages all the members to be involved constructively in decision making and problem solving, is preferred.

2. **Describe how trait theory, situational theory, functional theory, and transformational leadership contribute to our understanding of leadership.**   There are four principal explanations of how people become leaders. Trait theory holds that some men and women are simply born to lead. Situational theory holds that the situation itself—the nature of the problem and the characteristics of the group—determines who assumes leadership. Functional theory holds that a number of group members can and should share the various leadership functions that need to be performed if the group is to achieve its goals. A transformational leader helps group members imagine and visualize the future group members can build together, strengthening the group's culture.

3. **Define *conflict* and explain how you feel when involved in a group conflict.**   Conflict is an inevitable part of the life of any group. A group experiences conflict whenever a member's thoughts or acts limit, prevent, or interfere with his or her own thoughts or acts or with those of another member.

4. **Define *groupthink* and explain its consequences.**   Conflict is not always a negative force. In fact, the absence or avoidance of conflict can result in groupthink, a problem that occurs when a group allows the desire for consensus to override careful analysis and reasoned decision making.

5. **Distinguish between competitive and cooperative conflict orientations.**   When a conflict is handled constructively, no one loses and everyone wins. A conflict can be destructive if all the participants are dissatisfied with its outcomes and believe they have lost something. Using cooperative problem-solving methods instead of competitive orientations, which create win–lose encounters, facilitates constructive conflict resolution.

6. **Identify how to use the conflict grid and describe the benefits and problems that can result from effective and ineffective handling of group conflict.**   Whether a conflict helps or hinders a group's operation depends on how the members react to it. If they resort to strategies such as blaming, withdrawing, intellectualizing, distracting, and forcing, their effectiveness will be impaired. However, if they discuss the issues calmly, they can break impasses and solve difficulties. Various styles of handling conflict can be plotted on Blake and Mouton's conflict grid. The most effective style is that of the problem-solving collaborator, who takes a win–win approach and has high concern both for results and for the feelings of other people. It is essential to take into account

the various cultures that people may reflect in their approaches to conflict and conflict resolution.

7. Identify behaviors that can be used to resolve conflicts effectively. A number of communication techniques can help us resolve conflicts that occur both online and offline. The first step is simply to recognize that conflicts can be settled rationally—by focusing on the issues, not on personalities. Next, we should define the conflict and check the accuracy of our perceptions, using "I" messages, empathic listening, and role reversal, as appropriate. Then, we should suggest and assess a variety of solutions to the conflict, choose the best one that is mutually acceptable, and try it.

Resources for Further Inquiry and Reflection

To apply your understanding of how the principles in Chapter 12 are at work in our daily lives, consult the following resources for further inquiry and reflection. Or, if you prefer, choose any other appropriate resource. Then connect the ideas expressed in your chosen selection with the communication concepts and issues you are learning about both in and out of class.

 Listen to Me

"Sometimes You Can't Make It on Your Own" (U2)
"The In Crowd" (Ramsey Lewis Trio)
"Leader of the Pack" (The Shangri-Las)

Each of these songs explores the nature of a hero or a leader. What leadership and conflict-resolution concepts does any one of these songs illustrate?

 View Me

Apollo 13   Glory Road
Titanic   Lord of the Flies
Mutiny on the Bounty   Hotel Rwanda

These films explore how leadership can impede and/or foster group effectiveness, including the handling of group conflict. Choose one film and use it to discuss the nature of leadership, dangers of groupthink and/or effective conflict management techniques.

 Read Me

Tom Wolfe. *The Right Stuff*. New York: Bantam Books, 1983.
David Halberstam. *The Education of a Coach*. New York: Hyperion, 2006.
Herb Cohen. *Negotiate This!* New York: Warner Business Books, 2003.
Rudolph Giuliani. *Leadership*. New York: Hyperion, 2002.
William Golding. *Lord of the Flies*. New York: Penguin Books, 1999. (Original work published 1954.)
Irving Janis. *Victims of Groupthink: A Psychological Study of Foreign Policy Decisions and Fiascos*. Boston: Houghton Mifflin, 1972.

These books explore the nature of leadership or conflict resolution. Choose one and discuss the leadership and/or conflict management lessons contained in it that you consider the most important.

 Tell Me

Share with the class the insights you gained from your chosen Listen to Me, View Me, or Read Me selection.

Agree or disagree with the following statement, with reasons: Truth springs from conflict.

Communication Works

online learning center

www.mhhe.com/gamble9

Key Chapter Terminology

Use the Communication Works CD-ROM and the Online Learning Center at www.mhhe.com/gamble9 to further your knowledge of the following terminology.

accommodator 354	functional theory 344
achieved leader 340	groupthink 348
autocratic, or authoritarian, leaders 342	laissez-faire leader 342
avoider 354	leadership 340
competitive forcer 355	problem-solving collaborator 356
competitive set 353	role reversal 354
compromiser 355	situational theory 344
conflict grid 354	trait theory 343
cooperative set 353	transformational leader 346
democratic leaders 342	type X leader 340
designated leader 340	type Y leader 340
flame war 357	

Idioms in Translation

a body of research—numerous research studies

a host of—numerous

alien to them—unknown to them

deepened your awareness—increased your awareness

devil's advocate—person who argues against what others believe

for all seasons—for all time

never made it up the chain of command—never got to the person in charge

Communication Works

online learning center

www.mhhe.com/gamble9

Test Your Understanding

Go to the *Self Quizzes* on the Communication Works CD-ROM and the book's Online Learning Center at www.mhhe.com/gamble9.

Notes

1. Tim Reed, "Olympic Spirit Lacking from U.S. Team at Turin games," mercurynews.com, February 23, 2006.
2. For a creative idea on how to use film to better understand leadership, see Roy V. Leeper. "Mutiny on the Bounty: A Case Study for Leadership Courses." Paper presented at the joint meeting of the Southern States Communication Association, Lexington, KY, April 14–18, 1993.

3. Paul B. Brown. "What Sets Leaders Apart from the Pack?" *The New York Times*, February 5, 2006, p. BU8.

4. For a historical perspective and a summary and critique of 114 studies on small groups, focusing on leadership, discussion, and pedagogy, see John F. Cragan and David W. Wright. "Small Group Communication Research of the 1970s: A Synthesis and Critique." *Central States Speech Journal* 31, 1980, pp. 197–213; and Michael S. Frank. "The Essence of Leadership." *Public Personnel Management* 22:3, fall 1993, pp. 381–389.

5. For a discussion of how to develop leadership skills, see Stephen S. Kaagan. *Leadership Games*. Thousand Oaks, CA: Sage, 1999.

6. Douglas McGregor. *The Human Side of Enterprise*. New York: McGraw-Hill, 1960.

7. Norman Augustine and Kenneth Adelman. *Shakespeare in Charge*. New York: Hyperion, 1999.

8. For a classic study on leadership style, see K. Lewin, R. Lippit, and R. K. White. "Patterns of Aggressive Behavior in Experimentally Created Social Climates." *Journal of Social Psychology* 10, 1939, pp. 271–299.

9. For an early study on trait theory, see Frederick Thrasher. *The Gang: A Study of 1313 Gangs in Chicago*. Chicago: University of Chicago Press, 1927.

10. For more information on this topic, see Nancy A. Nichols. "Whatever Happened to Rosie the Riveter?" *Harvard Business Review* 7:4, July–August 1993, pp. 54–57, 60, 62.

11. Marvin Shaw. *Group Dynamics: The Psychology of Small Group Behavior*, 3rd ed. New York: McGraw-Hill, 1981.

12. See Fred Fiedler. *A Theory of Leadership Effectiveness*. New York: McGraw-Hill, 1967.

13. Keith Davis. *Human Relations at Work*. New York: McGraw-Hill, 1967.

14. See, for example, F. E. Fiedler. "Personality and Situational Determinants of Leadership Effectiveness." In D. Cartwright and A. Zander, eds. *Group Dynamics: Research and Theory*, 3rd ed. New York: Harper & Row, 1968, pp. 389–398.

15. P. Hersey and K. Blanchard. *Management Organizational Behavior: Utilizing Human Resources*. Englewood Cliffs, NJ: Prentice Hall, 1988.

16. See Stephen R. Covey. *The 7 Habits of Highly Effective People*. New York: Simon & Schuster, 1989.

17. J. K. Brilhart, G. J. Galanes, and K. Adams. *Effective Group Communication Theory and Practice*, 10th ed. New York: McGraw-Hill, 2001, p. 124.

18. See, for example, M. Z. Hackman and C. E. Johnson. *Leadership: A Communication Perspective*, 4th ed. Long Grove, IL: Waveland, 2004.

19. For an interesting discussion of how conformity pressures can hamper decision making, see Russel F. Proctor. "Do the Ends Justify the Means? Thinking Critically about 'Twelve Angry Men.'" Paper presented at the annual meeting of the Central States Communication Association, Chicago, April 11–14, 1991.

20. John Schwartz and Matthew L. Wald. "NASA's Curse?" *The New York Times*, March 9, 2003, p. WK5.

21. Irving Janis. *Victims of Groupthink: A Psychological Study of Foreign Policy Decisions and Fiascos*. Boston: Houghton Mifflin, 1972.

22. T. Pettigrew and J. Martin. "Shaping the Organizational Context for Black American Inclusion." *Journal of Social Issues* 43, 1987, pp. 41–78.

23. P. W. Lunneborg. *Women Changing Work*. Westport, CT: Glenwood, 1990.

24. J. Rosener. "Ways Women Lead." *Harvard Business Review*, November–December 1990, pp. 119–125.

25. D. Butler and F. L. Geis. "Nonverbal Affect Responses to Male and Female Leaders: Implications for Leadership Evaluations." *Journal of Personality and Social Psychology* 58, 1990, pp. 48–59.

26. Deborah Tannen. *The Argument Culture: Moving from Debate to Dialogue*. New York: Random House, 1998, pp. 170, 194.

27. J. F. Benenson, S. A. Ford, and N. H. Apostoleris. "Girls' Assertiveness in the Presence of Boys." *Small Group Research* 29, 1998, pp. 198–211.

28. See, for example, Daniel Canary, William R. Cupach, and Susan J. Messman. *Relational Conflict.* Thousand Oaks, CA: Sage, 1995.

29. Marjaana Lindeman, Tuija Harakka, and Liisa Keltikangas-Jarvinen. "Age and Gender Differences in Adolescents' Reactions to Conflict Situations: Aggression, Prosociality, and Withdrawal." *Journal of Youth and Adolescence* 26, 1997, pp. 339–351.

30. Canary, Cupach, and Messman.

31. Anthony De Palma. "It Takes More Than a Visa to Do Business in Mexico." *The New York Times,* June 26, 1994.

32. Lea P. Stewart. "Japanese and American Management: Participative Decision Making." In Larry A. Samovar and Richard E. Porter. *Intercultural Communication: A Reader.* Belmont, CA: Wadsworth, 1985, pp. 186–189.

33. Delores Cathcart and Robert Cathcart. "Japanese Social Experience and Concept of Groups." In Larry A. Samovar and Richard E. Porter, *Intercultural Communication: A Reader.* Belmont, CA: Wadsworth, 1994, pp. 293–304.

34. Marie Brennan. "Mismanagement and Quality Circles: How Middle Managers Influence Direct Participation." *Employer Relations* 13, 1991, pp. 22–32.

35. See Stella Ting-Toomey, C. Gab, P. Trubisky, Z. Z. Yang, H. S. Kim, S. L. Lin, and T. Nishida. "Culture, Face Maintenance, and Styles of Handling Interpersonal Conflict: A Study in Five Cultures." *International Journal of Conflict Management* 2, 1992, pp. 275–296.

36. Yuri Kageyama. "Mitsubishi Admits Coverup." *The Record,* August 23, 2000, pp. B1, B3.

37. See, for example, Anita K. Foeman and Gary Pressley. "Ethnic Culture and Corporate Culture: Using Black Styles in Organizations." *Communication Quarterly* 35, fall 1987, pp. 293–307.

38. Hal Lancaster. "Black Managers Often Must Emphasize Building Relationships." *The Wall Street Journal,* March 4, 1997, p. B1.

39. P. Trubisky, S. Ting-Toomey, and S. L. Ling. "The Influence of Individualism-Collectivism and Self-Monitoring on Conflict Styles." *International Journal of Intercultural Relations* 15, 1991, pp. 65–84.

40. Adapted from Aesop's Fables.

41. See, for example, Larry K. Leslie. *Mass Communication Ethics: Decision Making in Post Modern Culture.* Boston: Houghton Mifflin, 2000, pp. 263–266; Barbara Ehrenreich. "In Defense of Talk Shows." *Time,* December 4, 1995, p. 92; and Howard Kurtz. *Hot Air.* New York: Basic Books, 1997.

42. For a description of how to promote a win–win approach to conflict, see Deborah Weider-Hatfield. "A Unit in Conflict Management Communication Skills." *Communication Education* 30, 1981, pp. 265–273; Joyce L. Hocker and William W. Wilmot. *Interpersonal Conflict,* 3rd ed. Dubuque, IA: Brown, 1991; and Herb Cohen. *Negotiate This!* New York: Warner Business Books, 2003.

43. Robert Blake and Jane Mouton. "The Fifth Achievement." *Journal of Applied Behavioral Science* 6, 1970, pp. 413–426.

44. Alan Filley. *Interpersonal Conflict Resolution.* Glenview, IL: Scott, Foresman, 1975.

45. Morton Deutsch. "Conflicts: Productive and Destructive." *Journal of Social Issues* 25, 1969, pp. 7–43; H. Whitteman. "Group Member Satisfaction: A Conflict-Related Account." *Small Group Research* 22, 1992, pp. 24–58; and R. C. Pace. "Personalized and Depersonalized Conflict in Small Group Discussion: An Examination of Differentiation." *Small Group Research* 21, 1991, pp. 79–96.

46. Barbara De Lollis. "Talking Heads Are Catching On as Web Meetings Take Off." *USA Today*, September 7, 2004, p. 7B.

47. David Brooks. "Bondage and Bonding Online." *The New York Times*, January 8, 2006, p. WK 14.

48. Olivia Barber. "Web Spins Personal Laundry." *USA Today*, August 1, 2005, p. 1D, 2D.

49. Steven G. Jones. *Cybersociety: Computer-Mediated Communication and Community*. Thousand Oaks, CA: Sage, 1995, pp. 129–131; and Tannen, pp. 238–240.

50. Tannen, p. 130.

51. Deborah Tannen. *Talking from 9 to 5*. New York: Morrow, 1994.

CHAPTER 13

The Speaker and the Audience: The Occasion and the Subject

After finishing this chapter, you should be able to

1. Approach public speaking systematically.

2. Identify the characteristics of effective public speakers.

3. Explain how the nature of the occasion influences a speech.

4. Formulate clear and precise purpose statements for yourself and behavioral objectives for your audience.

5. Formulate the thesis statement.

In the United States there are more than twenty thousand different ways of earning a living, and effective speech is essential to every one.

—Andrew Weaver

Public speaking can be a horror for the shy person, but it can also be the ultimate act of liberation.

—Susan Faludi

Violence is, essentially, a confession of ultimate inarticulateness.

— *Time* magazine

Can you stand before an audience without fear? Can you personalize a message, win the ears of receivers, and draw them into your message? Can you organize a message and stay on course without getting unnerved or derailed? Can you deliver a message so that audience members leave the experience richer for having listened to you? And can you have fun doing it? Even in our technologically rich environment with its e-mail, voice mail, personal digital assistants, beamed messaging, and instant messaging, we still turn to public speaking as a key means of sharing ideas, expressing concerns, and making our voices heard.

In our age of electronic connections, public speaking is booming. Membership in the National Speakers Association, a professional speakers trade group, continues to grow. In addition, the number of platforms available for speakers has also increased. Everyone seems to want a speaker these days.[1] Perhaps because now more than ever, everyone needs to be a speaker. In some ways, public speaking functions as a form of currency, only instead of providing its users with access to the marketplace of goods and services, it provides access to the marketplace of ideas. Becoming effective at communicating ideas in a public forum is a skill that is equally important for women and men to develop. Public speaking is sure to play an important role in your future. Are you prepared for the challenge?

■ ■ ■

PUBLIC SPEAKING DEFINED

Public speaking—these are two seemingly harmless words. **Public speaking** is the act of preparing, staging, and delivering a presentation to an audience. We speak every day. Under ordinary circumstances, we rarely give speaking, or our skills in speaking, a second thought—that is, until we are asked to deliver a speech or simply to speak in public. Once we know that is what we are going to have to do, if we are like most Americans, we fear it more than we fear bee stings, accidents, heights, or our own death.[2]

Just as we can learn to handle ourselves more effectively in our interpersonal and group relationships, if we take the time that is needed to analyze and practice successful behaviors, we can also learn to handle ourselves more effectively as

public speaking

the act of preparing, staging, and delivering a presentation to an audience

online learning center

Go to the Online Learning Center at www.mhhe.com/gamble9 and answer the questions in the *Self Inventory* to evaluate your understanding of public speaking.

public speakers. With practice, we can develop the understanding and master the skills that will make us articulate speakers who are organized, confident, and competent, and can communicate ideas in such a way that others will be interested in them and persuaded by them.

When you assume the role of speaker, you have the potential to effect change in the members of your audience, and when you are in the role of audience member, others have the ability to effect change in you. Thus, while the abilities to (1) organize your ideas logically, (2) encode or express them clearly, (3) analyze and adapt to receivers readily, and (4) think critically and make ethical decisions about messengers and their messages are skills needed in all types of communication, they are particularly relevant in public speaking.

Unfortunately, far too few of us ever bother to analyze our effectiveness in speaking until after we have stepped into the spotlight. It is time to correct this error. With that end in mind, the chapters in Part Four help you gain the understanding and master the skills you need to speak like a pro and to feel like a winner after addressing an audience.

APPROACHING SPEECH MAKING SYSTEMATICALLY

People respond to the challenge of public speaking in a variety of ways. Some believe that speech making is an inborn skill: "I talk a lot, so this public speaking business poses no difficulty for me." Others view it as torture: "I'm scared stiff! This will be traumatic!" These attitudes represent two extremes, and both can cause problems. Overconfident people run the risk of being inadequate speakers because they conduct little research and thus are ill prepared. People who are overly anxious or fearful may find it terribly trying and nerve-racking to stand before an audience and deliver a talk. The most effective speakers are those who display a healthy respect for the challenges involved in speaking before others and who work systematically to create, prepare, and deliver an admirable presentation.

How can you become an effective speaker? You must work at it. To help you, this chapter will put the entire speech-making process into a logical format that you can examine and follow in detail. The process should serve as a road map—one you can use to prepare every public presentation you will ever make.

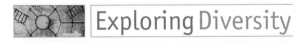

Exploring Diversity

Report Talk and Rapport Talk

According to researcher Deborah Tannen, men are more comfortable speaking in public than women are, while women are more comfortable speaking in private. Tannen finds that men excel at "report talk," while women excel at "rapport talk."

Do your experiences confirm or contradict this? If this disparity exists, what, if anything, do you think should be done to change it?

HOW TO PREPARE FOR YOUR FIRST SPEECH

Most likely, you will be assigned a speech before you have had the chance to finish reading and applying all the relevant information contained in subsequent chapters, so here we offer a preview of the speech preparation you need as you get ready to speak before your class for the first time.

The staircaselike chart in Figure 13.1 reveals a systemic, step-by-step approach. As you make your way up the staircase, you move from one speech-making phase into another. There is a logical order to speech making that reduces the process

There is just no way around it—you have to do your homework. A speaker may be very well informed, but if he hasn't thought out exactly what he wants to say today, to this audience, he has no business taking up other people's valuable time.

—Lee Iacocca, *Iacocca: An Autobiography*

FIGURE 13.1

Systematic Speaking Process.

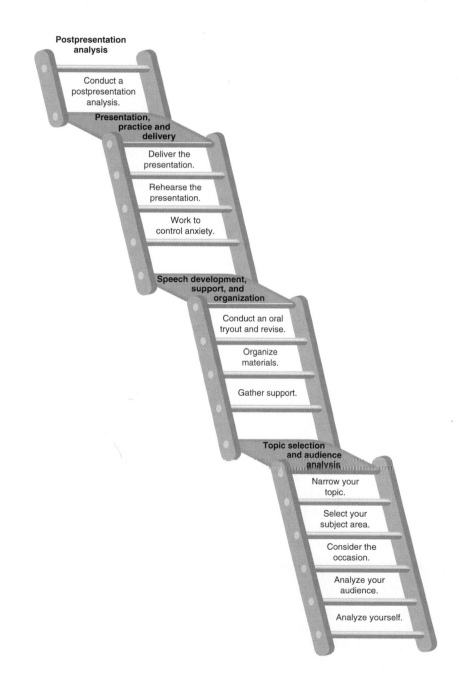

to four landings: (1) topic selection and audience analysis; (2) speech development, support, and organization; (3) presentation practice and delivery; and (4) postpresentation analysis. Before we look at these phases, let us remind you that the staircase is only as strong as its foundation. Each time you speak, ask yourself: Are you handling your topic as *ethically* as possible? Are you applying principles of *critical thinking*? Are you as sensitive as you can be to the challenges posed by the *diversity* inherent in receivers?

Step 1. Select the topic
During the first phase of speech preparation, your focus is on topic selection. To choose an appropriate topic, you need to do five things: (1) Analyze yourself to identify your interests, concerns, and areas of special knowledge; (2) analyze your audience to identify ways their interests, needs, and knowledge could affect your selection; (3) identify the occasion for speaking, including any special requirements assigned by your instructor or the nature of the event that calls for the speech; (4) choose a general subject area; and (5) concentrate on making that subject increasingly specific, narrowing its scope so you can cover it in the allotted time.

Step 2. Develop the speech
During the second phase of speech preparation, you research and gather supporting materials to clarify the purpose of your speech. Organize the material you have gathered into a logical sequence that facilitates the communication of your message.

Prepare a clear thesis statement (a one-sentence speech summary) and a preview that lets receivers know what you are going to share with them, a body that explains the meaning of each main point and ties them together with transitions, and a conclusion that restates the thesis—reviewing what you have shared and providing a sense of closure.

Then outline your speech. By examining your outline and reading it aloud, you can assess whether your speech will achieve the response you seek from your audience, whether your main points support your central idea or proposition (the thesis), and whether your subpoints explain or prove your main points.

As you deliver your presentation, you will need to support, clarify, and explain your ideas with language that expresses your ideas clearly, connects with receivers, avoids bias, and creates vivid pictures—helping you increase the clarity and impact of your ideas.

Step 3. Rehearse and deliver the presentation
During the third phase of speech preparation, you concentrate on making every effort to ensure that you deliver your speech as effectively as possible. Rehearse your presentation, revise it, rehearse it again, and revise it again until it flows, has maximum impact, and is readily comprehensible. You should also anticipate and prepare for questions audience members may ask and reactions they may have. You can then focus the energy produced by any anxiety you may be experiencing and put it to work for you during the actual delivery of your speech.

Step 4. Conduct a postpresentation analysis
After delivering your speech, compare and contrast your expectations with what you actually experienced during the delivery of your speech.

Effective speakers critique their performances. They know that they and their receivers will be changed in some way by every speech event; they know that their words, once spoken, leave an indelible impression, and they want to be certain that they learn as much as possible from the experience so that they can apply the lessons learned to the next speech.

The speech-making staircase is one you will climb again and again, working your way from one speech experience to the next. In time, you will master the ins and outs of public speaking. Answering questions such as the following can help prepare you to work your way systematically through the speech-making process:

What kind of presentation are you going to make? _____

What will be its central message? _____

Why are you giving it? _____

Where and when will you deliver it? _____

How much time will you have? _____

Who and how many people will be in your audience? _____

How much do audience members know about your topic? _____

What do you want your audience to think, do, feel, or remember? _____

What are your speech-making goals? _____

What will you do to capture the audience's attention? _____

What will you include in the presentation's body? _____

How will you close? _____

Let us continue our climb up the ladder together.

CONSIDERING THE SPEAKER

When you listen to a speaker—either in person or through the media—how do you expect him or her to behave? What do you want the speaker to do for you? It is helpful to view the process of speech making from the standpoint of the listeners. After all, without listeners, we would be speaking to ourselves—and that is not what public speaking is all about.

Speech . . . preserves contact—it is silence which isolates.

—Thomas Mann

Expectations for Speech Makers: Criteria

Good speakers have certain characteristics, which you may want to keep in mind as you prepare your own presentations. First, good speakers have insight. They know their own strengths and limitations. They understand and have considered the reservoir of experience on which they may draw. Second, good speakers know their audiences. They work to understand the nature and concerns of the people they have been called on to address. They are able to feel the pulse of this public, to stand in the shoes of the audience members, and to view the event or occasion through the audience's eyes so that they are able to share something that will be of value. Third, good speakers believe that what they are doing is important; they know why they are speaking, and they know what they hope to accomplish by speaking. They are clear about their purpose and about the main ideas they want to communicate. In addition, they are adept at formulating and delivering a message that is organized to support their purpose. Fourth, good speakers always practice. They conduct dry runs of the presentation, adapting it to potential changes in the audience and the audience members' needs. They also prepare well for questions audience members may ask. Fifth, good speakers think of the speech as if it is a performance. They know that they will need to work hard to keep the audience interested in what they have to say; they understand the essential fickleness of audiences, so they make it easy and pleasurable for listeners to stay tuned to their ideas. Finally, good speakers make a critique, or postpresentation analysis, of the speech. They know that there is much to learn from each experience, much that they may be able to apply the next time they are in the spotlight.

As a result of the media explosion, our society has grown accustomed to high-quality speeches. Talk shows, television news programs, and entertainers bring professional speech making into our homes every day. Newscasters, for example, have had years of training and practice in speaking. Public relations practitioners are often carefully schooled in public speaking to ensure that they know how to communicate a positive image to an audience. Many corporate executives employ speechwriters and speech coaches to help them communicate with diverse audiences. The need to deliver a high-quality presentation creates a difficult, though not an impossible, task for the student who is about to step into the spotlight. The communication environment you find yourself in is challenging. You need to add the skills of sharing information and convincing audiences of your credentials, for only then will you have the expertise to communicate effectively in our multifaceted environment. From the classroom to the corporation, from the boardroom to the television studio, from the steps of city hall to the podium in a local auditorium, your challenge is to develop the skills and confidence you need to deliver—clearly and persuasively—the messages that are important to you and important to the people you represent.

Self-Analysis: You and Your Topic

Thorough self-analysis is a prerequisite for effective speech making. Although at times topics may be assigned, under many circumstances the choice will be left to you, the speaker. Even when a topic is specified, it is recommended that you conduct a self-analysis to help you uncover aspects that you may find particularly interesting or appealing. Such an analysis can also become the basis for personal stories or anecdotes that can eventually be integrated into your presentation.

Skill Builder

From the Listener's Point of View

1. Describe the behaviors exhibited by the most effective speaker you have had the good fortune to hear.

2. Contrast that description with a description of the most ineffective speaker you ever had the misfortune to hear.

There are more topics for speeches than you could possibly exhaust in a lifetime.[3] Still, "I just don't know what to say" is an all-too-familiar lament.

> But where was I to start? The world is so vast, I shall start with the country I know best, my own. But my country is so very large. I had better start with my town. But my town, too, is large, I had best start with my street. No: my home. No: my family. Never mind, I shall start with myself.[4]

At the outset of your preparation, you should take some time for what corporate trainers call a front-end analysis—a preliminary examination of possibilities. Following are five useful forms that a front-end analysis can take.

REVIEW YOUR LIFE: YOUR AUTOBIOGRAPHY

You can begin by reviewing your life in terms of potential topics:

1. Divide your life (thus far) into thirds: early, middle, more recent. Compose one sentence to sum up what your life consisted of during each segment (for example, "I lived in Gary, Indiana, with my two brothers and mother, and went to elementary school").

2. Under each summary statement, identify your main interests and concerns at that time of your life.

3. Examine the interests and concerns you listed. Which of them recur? Which have you left behind? Which have you developed only recently?

CONSIDER THE MOMENT: THIS MOMENT

A second approach is to consider this very moment as a source of potential topics:

1. On the left side of a sheet of paper, list sensory experiences; that is, list everything you are able to see, hear, taste, smell, or touch from your present vantage point.

2. When you have listed 10 to 15 items, go back over the list and note topics that might be suggested by each observation or experience. Arrange these in a corresponding list on the right side of the paper. For example, if you list "passing train" in the left column, you might enter "mass transportation" in the right column. Note: If you are not satisfied with the topics you have identified, move to another location and begin the process again.

SEARCH THE NEWS: NEWSPAPERS, NIGHTLY NEWS, AND NEWSMAGAZINE SHOWS

A third approach is to work with a newspaper to find potential topics:

1. Take today's newspaper and, beginning with the front page, read a story and compile a list of topics suggested by it.

2. Do not prejudge your ideas. Simply work your way through the paper, looking for possibilities. For example, the January 15, 2006, issue of the *New York Times Magazine* was devoted to the coverage of a living wage. What potential speech topics does such a subject area suggest to you? A speech on what a living wage is? The growing gap between the rich and the poor? Why we need labor unions? The relationship between education and wages?[5]

A variation on this approach calls on you to view a nightly local or national news broadcast or newsmagazine program with pen and paper in hand. Divide the paper into two columns. Label the first column "Stories Presented." Label the second column "Ideas Generated by This News Story." Work your way through the program, looking for possibilities. The same methodology will work for newsmagazine programs such as *60 Minutes*, *20/20*, and *Nightline*.

USE AN ONLINE TOPIC GENERATOR

A number of Web sites can help with topic generation. Try using the following topic generators:

www.yukoncollege.yk.ca/~agraham/guides/tpgen.htm

www.lib.odu.edu/research/idca/index.htm

CONSIDERING THE AUDIENCE

Make a list of 10 subjects you believe would be inappropriate for delivery to your class. Discuss how each topic might be approached to make it appropriate.

Having conducted a search of yourself, it is now time to determine where your audience fits in. A pitfall for many speakers is speaking to please themselves—approaching speech making with only their own interests and their own points of view in mind and neglecting the needs and interests of their audience. These speakers will often choose an inappropriate topic, dress improperly, or deliver a presentation that is either too simple or too technical for the audience. We have all heard medical experts address general audiences using such complex language that their listeners were baffled and bored. We have also heard speakers address highly educated groups in such simple language and about such mundane topics that everyone was not only bored but insulted. There is a catchy acronym for describing speeches that bore or confuse audience members; it is **MYGLO,** for "my eyes glaze over"—which is exactly what happens when you lose the audience's attention.[6]

MYGLO

an acronym for "my eyes glaze over"

Your focus during the initial stages of speech preparation should not, therefore, be solely on yourself. Be prepared to consider a potential topic from the point of view of your audience. Just as you bring your own background and experiences

Poor preparation may cause audience members to stop paying attention—a direct result of MYGLO—"my eyes glaze over."

to a presentation, the audience members will bring theirs. Thus, it is important to consider what your listeners are thinking about, what their needs and hopes are. You may start by considering where you are, but you must not be so self-centered as to stop there. Successful communicators, in a sense, enlarge the area of the spotlight to include the audience.

To pay proper attention to your audience, you must know something about it. For example, how familiar are the audience members with what you are going to talk about? What is their attitude toward your topic? What are they anxious about? What would they like to know? What are their expectations? If you do not find out the answers to questions like these, you run the risk of having your words fall on deaf ears. Unfortunately, of all the steps in the process of public speaking, audience analysis is most often overlooked. Speaking to hear yourself speak is a trap you will want to take steps to avoid every time you must speak before others. Making a speech without considering the audience is like talking to yourself. It is from behind the eyes of your audience that you must approach speech making.

Beginning Your Audience Analysis: Who Are They?

How can you know, or how can you try to determine, precisely who will attend your presentation? For example, can you expect certain interested groups or individuals to come? Will others whom you do not expect surprise you by showing up?

THE MAKEUP OF YOUR AUDIENCE

Finding information about the people you will be speaking to can often seem difficult or even impossible. Nevertheless, it is important to make educated guesses about the makeup of your intended audience. Actually, this is a simple task. What you are doing at this stage of the process is creating a mental picture of the people to whom you are going to speak.[7] Once you have created such an image, or snapshot, for yourself, you will be better able to continue planning your presentation.

Ethics & Communication

The Magic Bullet of Speech Making

What is the magic bullet of speech making? Practitioners and consultants offer varied answers to this question. George W. Bush, for example, believes a speech has to involve receivers on an emotional level. When reading and reworking the drafts of speeches presented to him by his staff of speechwriters, the president makes comments and notes including such thoughts as "tugs at heartstrings" and "an emotional call to arms."[8]

On the other hand, Roger Ailes, president of Fox News, says that being likable is the magic bullet of communication. Ailes writes: "With it, your audience will forgive just about everything else you do wrong. Without it,

you can hit every bull's-eye in the room, and no one will be impressed."

What do you think the magic bullet is? Is it being emotionally involving, likable, or something else? Is being able to emotionally arouse receivers more or less important than having something significant to say? Should it be? Is being likable more or less important than giving receivers information they need to have but may not enjoy hearing? Should it be? What happens when you have something significant or necessary to say but you fall short when it comes to involving receivers or motivating them to like you? What hurdles does a speaker whom you dislike have to overcome or who fails to involve you emotionally have to overcome?

SOURCES OF AUDIENCE INFORMATION

Information about your audience should come from two key sources:

1. your personal experience with the group
2. original research

Let's consider each of these.

Personal Experience   The best source of information about your audience is your personal experience with the group—either as a speaker or as an audience member. If you have attended several functions or are a member of the class or organization you are expected to address, you have personal knowledge of the audience members. Thus, you will probably be able to formulate reasonably accurate predictions about the appropriateness of your material for that group.

Research   What if you have had no previous contact with the group you are to address? If that is the case, you might ask the program planner to provide you with relevant information. For instance, if you have been asked to speak at a professional convention, you would be concerned with specific information about the makeup of the audience: How many will attend the lecture? Will there be students present? These and other factors would have to be taken into account in preparing and customizing the presentation.

Another way to gather information about a group is to obtain copies of public relations material. Recent news releases highlighting the organization may help put you on the same track as your audience. Corporate newsletters and websites can also be valuable, as can a trip to the local library for information describing the organization.

Original research often takes the form of discussions with members of the potential audience. Robert Orben, a speech consultant and writer for former president Gerald Ford, tells the following story.[9] A presidential address had been planned for a college campus in Minnesota. The speechwriters knew that many of the students were not supporters of the president. They therefore spent a great deal of time on the telephone with students and school officials in an effort to obtain specific bits of information that could be included in the speech to help create a bond between the president and his audience. Finally, a somewhat disgruntled student provided the writers with the "gem" they felt they needed. They completed the speech, confident that they had done their job well—and they had. Ford began his address by saying, "Washington may have the new subway, Montreal may have the monorail, but this campus has the Quickie!" The students in the audience laughed and applauded warmly. Why? The drinking age was 21 in Minnesota but 18 in a neighboring state. And the 15-mile trip students often took to get to the first bar across the state line was known as "the Quickie." In this instance, talking at length to potential members of the audience provided information that helped establish an atmosphere in which the listeners, although not necessarily in agreement with the speaker, were at least rendered friendly enough to listen to his views.

Demographics of Audiences: What Are They Like?

Since the background and composition of your audience are important factors to consider in planning a speech, every effort must be made to determine audience demographics: age, gender, family orientation, religion, cultural background, occupation, socioeconomic status, educational level, and additional factors (such as membership in organizations). Despite the fact that no one audience will be entirely uniform in all these categories, you should consider each one during your initial planning sessions.

AGE

Would you give precisely the same presentation to a group of children that you would give to your class? Almost certainly not. How might your presentations differ? Could you even deal with the same subject? The adult students would bring many more years of experience to your presentation than the children would. Adults may have been through economic hassles and even a war, for instance—experiences that children have probably not yet faced. Of course, the maturity of the two audiences would also differ. These contrasts may seem obvious, but age is a factor often overlooked in planning speeches. You might choose to speak on abortion or birth control to a college audience, but you might fail to realize that the same material would probably have less intrinsic appeal to an audience of senior citizens.

It's also wise to consider how your own age will affect your presentation. How close are you to the mean, or average, age of your anticipated listeners? If you are about the same age as the audience members, your job may be a little easier. If you are much older or much younger than the audience members, you will need to attempt to see your topic through their eyes and adjust it accordingly.

Your goal is to be sensitive to the references you employ, the language you use, and the rate at which you speak so that you shrink rather than enlarge the age gap that may exist between you and your receivers. Only if the receivers are able to comprehend your words, identify with your examples and illustrations, and recognize the persons and events you refer to will they be in a position to respond as you hope. When you close whatever age gap exists, you increase the

Choose a topic of current interest. How would you approach the topic for a presentation to people your own age? How would you change your approach to appeal to an older or a younger audience?

The background and composition of the audience need to be taken into account when planning a speech.

likelihood of audience understanding. The point is that the average age of your audience matters. Research shows that, while younger listeners are more open to new ideas, older ones are less receptive to change. You can use information like this to judge how difficult it will be for you to attain your speech-making goal.[10]

GENDER

Gender can also influence an audience's reaction to your speech. There are, admittedly, some myths and misconceptions about the effects of gender. (For example, in the past, researchers believed that women could be more easily persuaded than men.[11] Do you think this is a valid viewpoint today?) Still, you need to consider gender differences, especially if you speak to an audience composed entirely or mainly of one sex. Study your potential audience before drawing any conclusions. Although the same topics may appeal to both men and women, gender may affect the ways male and female audience members respond. For example, a discussion of rape may elicit a stronger emotional reaction from the women in your class, whereas a discussion of vasectomy may elicit a stronger response from the men. Be aware, though, that the so-called traditional roles of men and women are changing and that stereotypes once attributed to both groups are crumbling.

FAMILY ORIENTATION

Are most of the members of your audience single? Married? Divorced? Widowed? From one-parent or two-parent homes? These factors might influence your audience's reactions to your presentation. The concerns of one group are not necessarily the concerns of another.

RELIGION

If you are speaking to a religious group with which you have little familiarity, make a point of discussing your topic in advance with some group members. Some groups have formulated very clear guidelines regarding issues such as divorce, birth control, and abortion. It is important for you to understand the audience and its feelings if you are to be able to relate effectively to its members.

CULTURAL BACKGROUND

Use your knowledge of an audience's culture and mind-set to create a bond with your listeners. Because our society is becoming increasingly multicultural, it is more important than ever that you attune yourself to beliefs held by audience members.[12] As you plan your speech, keep in mind how potential misunderstandings can result from racial, ethnic, religious, or cultural differences. Once you are aware of the makeup of your audience, you will be in a better position to predict how audience members will feel about your topic or the position you are advocating. Take time to consider how the presence or absence of receiver diversity might influence the reaction both to you and to your speech.

OCCUPATION

People are interested in issues that relate to their own work and the work of those important to them. Consequently, if possible, relate your subject to the occupational concerns of your audience. Also, if you are speaking before an audience whose members belong to a particular occupational group, you must attempt to find or create examples and illustrations that reflect their concerns.

On the Web site www.greatspeaking.com, accessed on May 20, 2003, it was suggested that, to appeal to the diverse backgrounds and interests of receivers, the speaker might "bounce around" rather than spend too much time catering to the interests and concerns of any one type of audience member. The subtext was that if a speaker spent too much time attempting to involve only one audience member type, he or she would lose the interest of all the others in the audience. To what extent, if any, do you agree with such advice? On the other hand, do you see any potential dangers in bouncing around?

SOCIOECONOMIC STATUS

Researchers have found that there are psychological as well as economic differences among different socioeconomic classes. Having or lacking discretionary income, power, and prestige evidently influences our attitudes and beliefs. Since our society is socially mobile, with a "move-up" philosophy, as a speaker, you can usually assume that your audience members want to get ahead and improve their position in life, and you can adjust your presentation to appeal to that desire.

EDUCATIONAL LEVEL

Although it is important to determine your listeners' educational level, you cannot let your findings trap you into making unwarranted assumptions—either positive or negative—regarding their intellectual ability. Still, in general, you will probably find that the higher people's level of education, the more general their knowledge and the more insightful their questions. In addition, the more knowledgeable members of your audience may have specific data to dispute your stand on controversial issues. An educated and sophisticated audience may be far more aware of the impact of various political and social programs than, say, a group of high school dropouts. A less educated audience may need background information that a more educated audience may consider superfluous.

Whatever the educational level of your listeners, the following are three precepts to keep in mind:

1. Don't underestimate the intelligence of your listeners; don't speak down to them.
2. Don't overestimate their need for information; don't try to do too much in the time that is available to you.
3. Don't use jargon if there's a chance that your listeners are unfamiliar with it; listeners will quickly tune out what they don't understand.

ADDITIONAL FACTORS

You may find that you need to consider several additional variables as you prepare your presentation. For example, if your audience is your class, do class members belong to a particular campus organization? Do members of the class involve themselves in any particular types of projects? Do the interests of the class relate in any way to your speech? Do class members have any identifiable goals, fears, frustrations, loves, or hates that could be tied in? How has their environment influenced their perception of key issues?

SUMMARY

If used wisely, your knowledge of audience demographics can help you achieve your purpose as a speech maker. It can permit you to draw inferences about the predispositions of audience members and their probable responses to your presentation. Thus, when planning your next presentation, fill out a chart like the one in Table 13.1.

Attitudes of Audiences: What Do They Care About?

Once you have considered audience demographics, your next step is to try to predict the attitudes your listeners will have toward you and toward your presentation. You should consider whether or not the audience members are required to

TABLE 13.1 Audience Demographics

Age of audience members: _____

Gender makeup: _____

Family orientation: _____

Religious preference: _____

Cultural background: _____

Occupation: _____

Socioeconomic status: _____

Educational level: _____

Additional relevant factors: _____

My topic: _____

Ways to use the demographic information: _____

_____

_____

attend, whether the audience is homogeneous or heterogeneous, and whether the audience members favor your stand or are actively opposed to it.[13]

MOTIVATION: IS ATTENDANCE OPTIONAL OR REQUIRED?

People may attend a presentation because they want to (that is, they do so willingly), because they have to (they are required to do so), or simply because they are curious. You might attend a town council meeting because a proposed increase in property taxes is being considered, or you might attend a parents' meeting at school out of a sense of duty or because your spouse insisted that you go.

Try to rate your audience on the following scale with respect to audience members' overall motivation:

Required to attend   1   2   3   4   5   Strongly desire to attend

Since the audience's willingness to attend can affect how your presentation is received, it is important to make an educated guess regarding its probable level of enthusiasm. (Of course, it is also important to remember that, just because audience members want to attend your talk, they will not necessarily agree with what you have to say.)

VALUES: IS THE AUDIENCE HOMOGENEOUS OR HETEROGENEOUS?

A second factor for consideration is the degree of homogeneity—that is, the extent to which everyone in the audience has similar values and attitudes. Of course, it is easier to address a homogeneous audience than a heterogeneous one. In addressing heterogeneous groups, speakers need to vary their appeals to ensure that all segments of the audience spectrum are considered.

Use the following scale to measure the extent to which the members of your audience share similar characteristics and values:

Homogeneous   1   2   3   4   5   Heterogeneous

LEVEL OF AGREEMENT: DOES THE AUDIENCE AGREE WITH YOUR POSITION?

Whatever your topic, you must attempt to predict your audience members' reaction to the stance you take. For example, they may oppose you, they may support you, or they may be neutral or uninterested. The accuracy of your prediction will determine to some extent how your presentation is received.

Use the following scale to help you assess your audience's position in terms of its similarity or dissimilarity to your own:

Agrees with me   1   2   3   4   5   Disagrees with me

Your objective when speaking to an audience that agrees with your position is to maintain its support. Your objective when speaking to a neutral audience is to gain your listeners' attention and show them how your presentation can be of value to them. When facing an audience that disagrees with you, you need to be especially careful and diplomatic in your approach. In this case, your objective is to change your listeners' minds—to move the audience closer to the "agrees with me" side of the continuum. This task becomes easier if you establish a common ground with audience members   that is, if you first stress values and interests that you share. Keep in mind that your goal is to increase the likelihood that a voluntary audience will attend to your message and that a captive audience will give you a fair hearing.

LEVEL OF COMMITMENT: HOW MUCH DO THEY CARE?

Finally, you need to consider how much the audience members care about your topic. Is it very important to them? Do they feel strongly enough to be moved to action? Or are your concerns irrelevant to your listeners?

Use the following scale to represent your audience's commitment:

Passive   1   2   3   4   5   Active

Together, the four attitudinal scales will indicate how much background and motivational material you need to include in your presentation.

Predicting the Audience's Reaction

Once you have completed your audience research, you will be in a position to predict your listeners' reception of any topic you select. Consider the following questions:

1. What do the audience members now know about my topic?
2. To what extent are they interested in my topic?
3. What are their current attitudes toward this topic?

As you develop your presentation, you must keep in mind the audience's knowledge of, interest in, and attitude toward the subject matter. These important factors will help you select and shape material specifically for the audience members. If you have been unsuccessful at gathering information about how your

We like to hear what makes us feel comfortable and self-assured. Yet this is exactly what we have no need of hearing; only those who disturb us can improve us.

—Sydney J. Harris

audience feels about your topic, you may find it helpful to take the pulse of public opinion, in general, by familiarizing yourself with the results of several public opinion polls on your chosen subject. Log onto a Web site that features public opinion polls, such as www.gallup.com or www.washingtonpost.com, in an effort to get the information you seek.

In addition to focusing on yourself and your receivers, whenever you give a speech, you should also have a clear idea of the nature of the speech-making occasion and how your topic relates to it. Both the occasion and your subject will affect the way you develop your presentation, stage it, and deliver it. We focus on these considerations next.

CONSIDERING THE OCCASION

If asked to speak before a group—including your own class—your first response might well be "Why? What's the occasion?" Identifying the occasion and your role in it is also an essential step in the process of preparing a speech. Fortunately, much, if not all, of what you need to know about the occasion is relatively easy to determine. Essentially, only the following need to be specified:

> date and time of the presentation
> length of the presentation
> location of the presentation
> nature of the occasion
> size of the audience

Date and Time: When and How Long?

Date and time are the most obvious—and among the most important—bits of information you need to acquire. On some occasions, student speakers and professional speakers have arrived an hour early, an hour late, and even a day early or a day late.

Timing can influence a speaker's effectiveness. For example, one well-known speaker arrived late at a New York college and found a hostile audience that had waited nearly an hour. Some professional speakers schedule their engagements so close together—two or three a day—that they must rush out the door rudely, almost before they have completed their talks. In a situation like that, the audience may react angrily.

The length of the presentation can also influence its effectiveness. For instance, one student speaker was supposed to deliver a 10-minute informative speech, "The History of the Corvette." Although it was suggested that he limit his consideration of the topic to two or three major model changes, he attempted to discuss every minute body and grill alteration in the Chevrolet Corvette from 1954 to the present. The instructor made several attempts to stop him, but 40 minutes into the speech he was still going strong. At this point, the instructor announced a class break. The student responded, "That's fine. I'll just continue." And he did—although the majority of his audience had departed.

Are you able to plan a presentation to ensure that you will not run over or under your time limit?

Location and Participants: Where and Who?

Reminding yourself of the location of your presentation and of the people directly connected with it is an important aspect of preparing a speech. This may seem obvious, but it is sometimes neglected, with absurd and embarrassing results. For example, at a speech by a world-famous psychologist whose audience consisted of members of the host college and the surrounding community, early in his speech, the eminent Dr. M_____ mumbled what seemed to be the name of another college, although most of his listeners failed to notice. The second time, however, he clearly announced how happy he was to be at X_____, mentioning the wrong college again. (Doubly unfortunate was the fact that college X was a rival of the host college.) By then, some members of the audience appeared embarrassed for the speaker, and others appeared hostile. The third time, the psychologist mentioned not only the wrong school but the wrong town as well. At this point, there was sufficient commotion in the audience for him to realize his error, and in evident confusion he turned to the college president to ask where he was.

How can you avoid such a problem? The minister who officiated at this book's authors' marriage had a possible solution. During the wedding rehearsal, a page in his Bible was marked with a paper clip that held a slip of paper, and later we asked him about it. The minister showed us that it had our names clearly written on it. He explained that, because he was somewhat nervous when conducting a wedding, he frequently tended to forget the names of the bride and groom, even if they had belonged to the congregation for years. The slip of paper provided an unobtrusive reminder. Taking our cue from this experience, we now attach a slip of paper to the first page of our notes whenever we address a group. The slip bears the name of the organization, its location, the name of the person introducing us, the names of the officers, and other important information. Thus, we have at our disposal the data we need, to be integrated as appropriate. You may also want to adopt this simple procedure to avoid unnecessary embarrassment or loss of credibility.

Type of Occasion: Why and How Many?

Why have you been asked to speak? Although every occasion is unique, you can ask some general questions to clarify the situation in your own mind. For example, is it a class session? Right now it probably is, but in the future it could well be a sales meeting, a management planning session, a convention, or a funeral. Is your presentation part of the observance of a special event? For example, is the occasion in honor of a retirement? A promotion? Is it some other type of recognition? Who else, if anyone, will be sharing the program with you? Factors like these can affect the nature of your presentation. An appropriate topic for a retirement party, for instance, might be considered inappropriate for a more formal occasion.

Determining how many people will show up to listen to any particular presentation is difficult. In a classroom situation, for example, on one day the room may be filled, but on another day a speaker may arrive and find that a number of students are out sick or off on a special project for another course. The same problem confronts the professional speaker. It is a good idea to multiply and divide the sponsor's estimate by 2. Thus, you can be prepared to speak to a small group—that is, possibly 20—if 40 are expected—or to a large group—possibly 100—if 50 is the estimate.

Since you are not likely to have an advance person at your disposal when preparing to deliver your presentation—at least not yet—you must do all the

Speakers need to be prepared to address sales meetings and management planning sessions.

advance thinking for yourself. Make it a habit to complete an analysis of both your audience and the occasion before completing work on any presentation. The predictions you make will serve you well as you continue preparing your speech.

CONSIDERING THE TOPIC

To continue preparing your speech without having selected a subject—on the basis of self-analysis, audience analysis, and occasion analysis—would be like trying to buy an airline ticket without knowing your destination.

Selecting a Topic: Criteria

You must carefully examine the list of possible topics you generated during the self-analysis and audience-analysis phases of your preparation. During this examination, you evaluate your ideas according to specific criteria: (1) apparent worth, (2) appropriateness, (3) interest, and (4) availability of material. When you keep these criteria in mind, selecting a topic will be easier—if only because few of your choices will meet each of the criteria equally well with regard to the needs of particular audiences.[14]

IS THE TOPIC WORTHWHILE?

You need to determine if the topic is important to you and to the people who will listen to you. Many speakers—including college students and businesspeople—often fall into the trap of choosing topics that are of little value to the audience. One of the authors recalls a time in a military training institute when he heard one colonel tell another, "After 25 years as an officer, I'm expected to waste my time

Skill Builder

Topic Evaluation Time

1. Working individually or in groups, develop a list of criteria by which you believe a topic for a class speech should be assessed.
2. Share your criteria with others. Which criteria seem to be most important in the selection process? Which appear to be least important? Why?
3. Compare the criteria you developed with those identified in the text. How are they similar or different?

hearing how to inspect a fork!" To that audience of high-ranking officers, the topic "Fork Inspection Techniques" was clearly trivial. You may also find that some topics chosen by others are trivial from your perspective. They may be so common-place—how to set a table, for example—that they do not merit the time and energy you must expend in listening to them. Many subjects that are acceptable for interpersonal discourse may be inconsequential when presented in a public setting where the speaker's purpose is to inform or persuade. Which topics do you judge to be worth your time? Which, in your opinion, are unworthy of consideration?

IS THE TOPIC APPROPRIATE?

We have already discussed how important it is to determine if a topic is appropriate to you and your personal interests. Two additional facets of this criterion must also be considered: (1) Is the topic appropriate to the audience? (2) Is it appropriate to the occasion? Let's examine each in turn.

By this time, you should have developed an audience profile. That is, you have either determined precisely or made educated guesses about the age, gender, and educational level of the majority of the people who are going to hear your speech. It then becomes imperative for you to ask which of your possible topics is most appropriate for such a mix of people. Sometimes this determination is easy. For instance, you would not ordinarily give a talk about the evils of television to a group of network representatives. Nor, ordinarily, would you opt to speak on the advantages of a women's college to an audience already attending a women's college. Every subject area must be seen through the eyes of its intended audience. Just as an automobile is customized for a particular owner, so a subject area must be customized to reflect the needs of a particular group of listeners. Just as the automobile is painted, detailed, and upholstered with an owner or a type of owner in mind, so you as a speaker must "outfit" your topic to appeal to the audience members you hope to reach. This takes work, but it can be done.

The appropriateness of the topic to the occasion must also be considered. For example, you can probably think of any number of occasions on which a humorous topic would be ill-conceived. Can you think of occasions when a humorous topic would be an asset? For example, a humorous topic would be inappropriate for an event commemorating servicemen and -women who have given their lives for their country, whereas it would be welcomed at a roast.

IS THE TOPIC INTERESTING?

Speech makers often make the mistake of selecting topics they think they should speak about rather than topics they want to speak about. Student speakers, for instance, will sometimes turn to a newspaper or newsmagazine and, without further thought, select a story at random as the basis for a speech. One student insisted on talking about labor–management relations. Why? He thought it sounded like an important subject. Unfortunately, he had spent little time in the labor force and no time in management. And because he did not care enough to do much—if any—research, the entire subject remained foreign to him. Not surprisingly, the speech he delivered was dull and disjointed.

John Silverstein, a spokesman for General Dynamics, put it this way: "You need to believe in your idea. This is very important. What a listener often gauges is how convinced the speaker is. If he has lived it, breathed it, and is himself really sold on it, it generally is enough to sell the argument."[15] Of course, selecting a topic that is appealing to you is a personal matter and can be relatively simple, but determining what will interest your audience can be somewhat more challenging.

Here, students have an advantage. As a student, you know your fellow students, and you should be able to identify topics that will interest them. When addressing less familiar audiences, however, you should feel free to return to your audience analysis and make some educated guesses. Determining an audience's interests is a never-ending challenge—one that some unadventurous speech makers prefer not to tackle. One corporate executive, for example, once delivered a speech that was gratifyingly well received. Unfortunately, he then delivered essentially the same speech for the next five years, although times and needs kept changing. Needless to say, his current audiences are not interested in his topic. Topics must be updated to match the moods, needs, and concerns of listeners; only by updating can you ensure that your topic treats an issue of interest to your audience.

When considering the interests of your audience members, ask yourself how your subject relates to them. Ask yourself what they stand to gain from listening to you. Create an inventory for each of your possible subjects. If you are unable to identify significant ways your audience will benefit from hearing about a topic, there is good reason for you not to speak on that topic.

IS SUFFICIENT RESEARCH MATERIAL AVAILABLE?

Before choosing a topic, be certain that material on the subject exists and that you can find it readily—on the Internet, in a library, or somewhere else. Many speakers fall into the trap of requesting material that is unavailable in a school or local library, only to have it arrive too late or turn out to be unpromising. Such an experience can cause last-minute panic, and the result is an inadequately prepared speech maker and an inadequate presentation. Avoid this pitfall by giving careful attention to your library and other nearby sources during the selection phase of your preparation.

Narrowing the Topic

It is essential to consider how much time is available for your speech. For example, an army chaplain more than once demonstrated how adept he was at handling time constraints. The chaplain's job was to address groups of recruits during basic training, and on each occasion he was given only three minutes to get his message across. One day his objective was to persuade soldiers not to use foul language. (It was his belief that such a practice degraded both individuals and the service.) Realizing that he could accomplish only so much in the time permitted, he chose to focus on a single word—the particular word that he found most

FIGURE 13.2
Ladder Technique for
Narrowing a Topic.

offensive. During his three-minute talk, he suggested that the troops avoid using just that one term. By doing this, the chaplain demonstrated that he understood how important it is to narrow a topic to manageable proportions and, incidentally, succeeded in realizing his objective. (After his speech, the abused word was heard much less frequently around the base.)

Far too many speakers attempt to give audiences "the world" in five minutes. It is essential to narrow your topic to fit the constraints imposed by the situation. Do not try to take on too much. Five minutes is not sufficient time to discuss the history of Russia, the industrial revolution, or even pedigreed dogs.

There is a strategy you can use to avoid biting off more than you can chew— or talk about. Select a topic and place it at the top of a "ladder." Then subdivide the topic into constituent parts; that is, break it down into smaller and smaller units, as shown in Figure 13.2. The smallest unit should appear on the lowest step of the ladder. This process is like whittling or carving a stick of wood. The more you shave off, the narrower the topic becomes. Like the carver, you decide what shape to give your topic and when to stop shaving.

Let's say that you want to speak on the need to save the rain forest. One way to narrow your topic would be to focus on how indigenous people can save the rain forest. Your topic could be focused even further. You might explore how their harvesting of native plants can stop deforestation or, more specifically, how their harvesting of fruit can help preserve the ecological balance. Here's another example: If you want to talk on the current technology revolution, you might focus on how the use of multimedia has revolutionized education or, more specifically, on how computers are used to teach writing skills.

Formulating a Purpose Statement and Behavioral Objectives

Once you have identified a topic and narrowed its scope, reexamine exactly why you are speaking. What is your purpose? What do you hope to accomplish?[16] What kind of response would you like from your audience? What do you want your listeners to think or do as a result of your presentation? What is your ultimate objective?

Most speakers have one of two general objectives when they prepare to deliver a speech: They aim either to inform listeners (to share new information or insights with the audience) or to persuade listeners (to convince audience members to believe in or do something). However, in actual speaking situations, the purpose is not always so clear. Persuasive speeches usually contain informative material, and informative speeches may sometimes include elements of persuasion.

THE INFORMATIVE SPEECH

If your purpose is to inform, your primary responsibility is to relay information to your audience in an interesting, well-organized, and professional manner. Informative speakers may explain something, demonstrate how something functions, or describe how something is structured. When speaking informatively, you hope to provide a learning experience for your listeners, sharing information they did not possess before your talk. In other words, if your main goal is to inform an audience, you must be certain that the data you provide will enhance your listeners' understanding, and you must find ways to help the audience remember what you say.

To ensure that your purpose is clear—initially to yourself and ultimately to your listeners—you will find it helpful to develop a purpose statement. What this means is that you commit to writing a summary of what you want to accomplish; you describe what you hope to do with your speech. The purpose statement of an informative speech often contains such words as *show, explain, report, instruct, describe,* and (not surprisingly) *inform.* The following are examples of purpose statements for various kinds of informative speeches:

> To explain how selected Chinese character letters evolved
>
> To describe how a tornado forms
>
> To instruct class members on how to reduce personal debt
>
> To report on efforts to prevent human cloning

Notice that each example takes the form of an infinitive verb phrase; thus, each begins with *to.* Notice also that each statement contains only one idea and that it is written from the speaker's perspective.

Sometimes, in addition to developing a purpose statement, it is helpful to view the speech from the perspective of the listeners. To facilitate this process, you can formulate behavioral objectives. Objectives identify what you want the audience to take away after hearing your presentation; that is, they describe the behavior or response you want the audience to exhibit as a result of listening to your speech. For instance, you may want your listeners to be able to list, explain, summarize, state, or apply certain information. The following are examples of behavioral objectives:

> After listening to this speech, the audience will be able to name three kinds of questions that are unlawful in employment interviews.
>
> After listening to this presentation, the audience will be able to discuss the three main reasons college students fail to graduate.

THE PERSUASIVE SPEECH

The same principles used for an informative speech may be applied in formulating a purpose statement and behavioral objectives for a persuasive speech. In a persuasive speech, your main goal is to reinforce or change an audience's beliefs or to make the audience behave in a certain way. The words *convince, persuade, motivate,* and *act* commonly turn up in purpose statements for persuasive speeches. The following are some examples:

> To motivate listeners to contribute money to the American Cancer Society
>
> To persuade class members to become actively involved in the conservation of global resources
>
> To convince class members that racist speech should be exempt from First Amendment protection

With regard to behavioral objectives, you might want your audience to support a plan or take an overt action. The following are examples of behavioral objectives:

> After listening to my presentation, audience members will write their representatives, asking them to seek legislation that bans the sale and manufacture of air guns that shoot projectiles at speeds greater than 350 feet per second.[17]
>
> After listening to my presentation, students will sign up to will their eyes to an eye bank.
>
> After listening to my speech, students will boycott stores that sell products made using child labor.

In summary, formulating precise purpose statements and behavioral objectives makes good sense. Both can help you focus your efforts and clarify your goals.

Formulating the Thesis Statement

In recent years, public speaking theorists have begun to look more closely at guidelines for writing. As a result, speakers are now often encouraged to develop theses for their speeches, just as writers do for papers. A thesis simply divides a topic into its major components. Thus, once you have formulated a specific purpose, the next step is to prepare a declarative sentence that summarizes the thesis of your speech. When your speech is an informative one and not intended to persuade, the thesis statement is phrased in a relatively objective and neutral manner and is sometimes referred to as the central idea or topic statement of your speech. Its focus is on what you want audience members to understand or learn—for example, "Nuclear power plants have three major parts: the reactor core, vessel, and control rods." When your speech is persuasive, it is simply called the thesis statement or the claim. A thesis for a persuasive speech expresses an arguable opinion or point of view; for example, a thesis for a persuasive speech against the use of nuclear energy plants might be, "Nuclear power plants should be decommissioned." Whether your speech is informative or persuasive, the thesis statement can be a powerful rhetorical device for setting your agenda as a speaker.

The thesis statement is the core idea or bottom line of your speech; it is your speech in a nutshell. It is a statement of the overriding concept of your speech that all the facts, quotations, and ideas in your speech are designed to support. In effect, the specific statement is the steering wheel of your speech; it directs the course of your speech and determines the content in it. The thesis helps you derive the main ideas or major propositions your speech will explore. Everything you say should support the thesis. In and of itself, the thesis statement does not present all the information you will offer in your speech; instead, it efficiently focuses that information into a brief summarizing statement.

An effective thesis statement fulfills three guidelines. First, it is a single sentence that conveys the essence of the speech. Second, it focuses the attention of the audience members on what they should know, do, or feel after experiencing your speech. Third, it supports the specific purpose. The following are examples:

> Thesis: Sleep deprivation costs business billions of dollars a year in employee accidents and avoidable mistakes.
>
> Thesis: Criminalizing eating when driving will decrease accidents and save lives.
>
> Thesis: Getting a good night's sleep will enhance your personal and professional life in four key ways.
>
> Thesis: Community efforts to censor the books we read are an infringement of our individual right of freedom of expression and will limit our ability to think critically about important issues.
>
> Thesis: Decreases in state funding to colleges will result in cuts in educational programs, extracurricular offerings, and financial aid.

As you can see from these examples, the thesis brings you a step closer to the structure of the speech itself.

TECHNOLOGY AND TOPIC SELECTION

search engine

a program that allows you to look through an entire database of information quickly

Usenet newsgroups

a conference system of computer bulletin boards devoted to different topics, in which people with similar interests across the world can interact with each other

The Internet is a huge, rich source of information and an excellent resource for speakers and speech critics alike. A multitude of online services currently exist on virtually any subject. You can find just about anything you want on the Net—if you know how to use it. By using a **search engine,** a program that allows you to look through an entire database of information quickly, such as "Google," or "Yahoo!" you can probe for and find information on selected topics easily and quickly. The results of the search will be a set of links to all the Web pages in that database that match the key word(s) you selected.

In addition, the Net has thousands of mailing lists, forums for the discussion of particular topics. Once you subscribe to a mailing list, the messages posted to the list are sent to your mailbox, too.

Usenet newsgroups are another resource. These constitute a huge conference system of computer bulletin boards devoted to different topics in which people with similar interests across the world can interact with each other.[18]

 Thinking Critically

Reflect and Respond

Agree or disagree with the following statement; supply reasons and examples that support your stance.

Effective public speaking is nothing more than one side of an extended conversation. With the exception of preparation time, public speaking and conversation demand the same skills.

One group of students decided to see what information they could find on infant mortality rates. Entering this subject produced hundreds of articles. The Division of Vital Statistics, for example, produced infant mortality rates from around the world. An accompanying abstract summarized the major conclusions observers could draw from the data, including the fact that over half of all infant deaths in the United States each year are attributed to sudden infant death syndrome. Another group decided to investigate day care for young children. An examination of the National Public Radio (NPR) site provided several features about day care—including one on the subject of Chinese day care in the United States. It appears that many young Chinese couples send their children back to China to be with their grandparents.[19] The NPR site is particularly interesting because the features contained in it are available in downloadable audio formats.

Accessing the online sites of major and local newspapers can also be worthwhile. Thus, logging onto www.washingtonpost.com, www.usatoday.com, www.nytimes.com, or the Web site of your local paper can facilitate the research process.

Speakers use the Internet as a resource. How have you used the Net to facilitate your speech research?

USING ANALYSIS EFFECTIVELY

Effective speech makers do not approach their task haphazardly. As we have seen, careful thought precedes the actual speech. Every speaker, from novice to professional, can benefit from following these suggestions:

1. *Focus your attention on the characteristics of people you consider good speakers.* Assess the extent to which you measure up to the standards they represent. Begin to identify ways of improving your speaking skills.

2. *Conduct a systematic self-analysis as a preparation for speech making.* Take the time you need to survey your own likes, dislikes, and concerns. Effective speakers know themselves well. They know what they care about, and they know what ideas they would like to share with others.

3. *Analyze your audience.* Effective speakers adapt their ideas to reflect the needs and interests of their listeners. Speeches are delivered with the specific purpose of informing or persuading others—of affecting others in certain specific ways. The degree to which you will succeed is directly related to how well you know your listeners and how accurately you are able to predict their reactions.

4. *Analyze the occasion.* It is essential that you learn why, when, where, and for how long you are expected to speak. Without this information, your preparation will be incomplete and insufficient.

Focus on Service Learning

Using a variety of research sites, including www.NPR.org and www.cdc.gov/flu/avian/, explain how you can apply what you have learned in this chapter to help a community group share its understanding of avian (bird) flu with an audience of senior citizens.

5. *Determine if your topic is supported by your own interests, your audience's interests, and the demands of the occasion.* Be certain to evaluate your subject according to the following criteria: Is the topic worthwhile? Is the topic appropriate? Is the topic interesting? Is sufficient research material available? Have I sufficiently narrowed my focus?

The Wrap Up

Revisiting Chapter Objectives

1. **Approach public speaking systematically.**   There is a logical order to speechmaking that speakers follow: (1) Topic selection and audience analysis; (2) Speech development, support, and organization; (3) Practice and presentation; and (4) Postpresentation analysis.

2. **Identify the characteristics of effective speakers.**   Public communication, unlike interpersonal communication, occurs in a somewhat formal setting and requires the communicator to be well prepared. Effective speakers understand the challenges involved in speaking before others. They know their strengths and limitations, know their audiences, believe in their message, practice, think of their speech as a performance, and critique it.

3. **Explain how the nature of the occasion influences a speech.**   Identifying the occasion and your role in it is another essential step in the process of preparing a speech. Once you have determined the date, time limit, and location of the speech, as well as the nature of the occasion and the audience, you can start thinking about a suitable topic. Choosing a topic usually involves two steps: selecting a general subject and narrowing it down to a manageable topic. You can evaluate your topic by answering the following questions: Is the topic worthwhile? Is it appropriate for the intended audience? Is it interesting? Is sufficient research material available? Will there be enough time to cover the topic adequately?

4. **Formulate a clear and precise purpose statement for yourself and behavioral objectives for your audience.**   After you have chosen your topic, you need to reexamine your purpose for speaking. Most speakers have one of two general objectives when they prepare to deliver a speech: to inform listeners (to share new information or insights) or to persuade listeners (to convince audience members that they should believe or do something). To ensure that your purpose is clear, you should formulate a purpose statement—a summary of what you want to accomplish, expressed as an infinitive phrase. For example, you may want to inform your audience about something, to describe something, or to explain how something is done. You can also list behavioral objectives—abilities you want the audience to have internalized after listening to your presentation.

5. **Formulate the thesis statement.**   The thesis statement is the central idea or claim of your speech. It is your speech in a nutshell. A declarative sentence, the thesis statement directs the course of your speech, helping you determine the main ideas or major propositions your speech will explore.

Resources for Further Inquiry and Reflection

To apply your understanding of how the principles in Chapter 13 are at work in our daily lives, consult the following resources for further inquiry and reflection. Or, if you prefer, choose any other appropriate resource. Then connect the ideas expressed in your chosen selection with the communication concepts and issues you are learning about both in and out of class.

 Listen to Me

"What's Going On?" (Marvin Gaye)
"We Didn't Start the Fire" (Billy Joel)
"Wake Me Up When September Ends" (Green Day)
"Born in the USA" (Bruce Springsteen)
"Know your Rights" (The Clash)

What speech subjects come to mind as you listen to each recording?

 View Me

The Boiler Room   *Patch Adams*
Ransom   *The Yes Men*

How does the sales manager in The Boiler Room apply lessons relevant to speech topic selection, development, presentation, and evaluation when making his pitch to the members of his sales team? How does Patch Adams use his knowledge of the audience to reach a group of terminally ill patients? What audience is Tom Mullen addressing in *Ransom* when he appears on a newscast? How do the yes men use their knowledge of receivers to attains their goal?

 Read Me

To what extent, if any, does the cartoon below reflect your feelings about public speaking before reading this chapter? After reading this chapter? Explain.

 Tell Me

Share with the class the insights you gained from your chosen Listen to Me, View Me, or Read Me selection.

The National Opinion Research Center (NORC) and the Gallup Poll are two well-known and respected polling organizations. Both conduct polls on a broad array of topics, from attitudes toward the presidency and government to attitudes toward the trustworthiness of the press and the military. To access NORC, go to www.norc.uchicago.edu/. To access the Gallup Poll, go to www.gallup.com/poll/index/ asp. In your opinion, should speakers use public opinion polls such as these solely to find out valuable information about audience attitudes prior to developing their own speeches? Or should they use them to decide what topics to speak on or what opinions to support when preparing to speak before audiences, because that way at least they know they'll receive a favorable hearing?

Communication
Works

online learning center

www.mhhe.com/gamble9

Key Chapter Terminology

Use the Communication Works CD-ROM and the Online Learning Center at www.mhhe.com/gamble9 to further your knowledge of the following terminology.

MYGLO 376

public speaking 370

search engine 392

Usenet newsgroups 392

Idioms in Translation

audience makeup—audience composition

booming—popular

feel the pulse—understand the mood

in the spotlight—onstage

magic bullet—secret

nerve-racking—upsetting

wins the ears of—interests

Communication
Works

online learning center

www.mhhe.com/gamble9

Test Your Understanding

Go to the *Self Quizzes* on the Communication Works CD-ROM and the book's Online Learning Center at www.mhhe.com/gamble9.

Notes

1. Leslie Wayne. "Leaping to the Lectern." *The New York Times,* September 8, 1995, p. D-1.

2. David Wallechinsky, Irving Wallace, and Amy Wallace. *The Book of Lists.* New York: Morrow, 1977, p. 469.

3. For an overview of the speech selection process, see Teri Gamble and Michael Gamble. *Public Speaking in the Age of Diversity,* 2nd ed. Boston: Allyn & Bacon, 1998; and Stephen Lucas. *The Art of Public Speaking,* 7th ed. New York: McGraw-Hill, 2001.

4. Elie Wiesel. *Souls on Fire.* New York: Summit, 1982.

5. See, for example, *New York Times Magazine,* January 15, 2006.

6. See Charles Francis. "How to Stop Boring Your Audience to Death." *Vital Speeches of the Day,* February 15, 1996, p. 283.

7. The following sources expand on our discussion of audience analysis: Bruce Gronbeck, Douglas Ehninger, and Alan Monroe. *Principles of Speech Communication,* 12th ed. New York: Harper-Collins, 1995; and Steven R. Brydon and Michael D. Scott. *Between One and Many.* Mountain View, CA: Mayfield, 1994.

8. D. T. Max. "The Making of the Speech: The 2988 Words That Changed a Presidency: An Etymology." *New York Times Magazine,* October 7, 2001, p. 36.

9. Robert Orben. "Speech Writing for Presidents." Presentation delivered to the Speech Communication Association in Washington, DC, April 1983.

10. W. McGuire. "Attitudes and Attitude Change." In G. Lindsley and E. Aronson, eds. *The Handbook of Social Psychology,* Vol. 2. New York: Random House, 1985, pp. 287–288.

11. Thomas M. Scheidel. "Sex and Persuasability." *Speech Monographs* 30, 1963, pp. 353–368.

12. W. A. Henry. "Beyond the Melting Pot." *Time,* April 9, 1990, p. 29.

13. See Lawrence R. Wheeless. "The Effects of Attitude Credibility and Homophily on Selective Exposure to Information." *Speech Monographs* 41, 1974, pp. 329–338.

14. For a look at the topics recently treated in public speeches by the leaders of the largest corporations in the United States, see 2004–2006 issues of *Vital Speeches of the Day.*

15. Thomas Leech. *How to Prepare, Stage and Deliver Winning Presentations.* New York: Amacom, 1982, p. 11.

16. For a step-by-step explanation of how to establish your purpose, see Leon Fletcher. *How to Design and Deliver a Speech,* 5th ed. New York: HarperCollins, 1995.

17. See Avril Johnson. "Air Guns: Weapons or Toys?" *Winning Orations,* 1993, pp. 87–89.

18. For additional information on Internet resources, see Carol Clark Powell. *A Student's Guide to the Internet,* 2nd ed. Upper Saddle River, NJ: Prentice Hall, 1998; and Randy Reddick and Elliot King. *The Online Student.* Fort Worth, TX: Harcourt Brace, 1996.

19. Jennifer Ludden. "Chinese Daycare." WBUR, Boston, (www.npr.org), 2000.

CHAPTER 14

Developing Your Speech: Supporting Your Ideas

After finishing this chapter, you should be able to

1. Identify and use the various online and offline research resources available to you.

2. Conduct an informal survey and a personal interview.

3. Identify various types of supporting material, including definitions, statistics, examples, illustrations, and testimonials.

4. Use comparison and contrast, repetition and restatement.

5. Explain how visual and audio aids can enhance a presentation.

Research is the process of going up alleys to see if they are blind.

—Marston Bates

The world is already full of speakers who are too busy to prepare their speeches properly; the world would be better off if they were also too busy to give them.

—William Norwood Brigance

Basic research is what I am doing when I don't know what I am doing.

—Wernher von Braun

Now that you have considered your choice of subject from both your point of view and the point of view of your audience, and you have taken the nature of the speech-making occasion into account, it is time for you to focus on researching and developing support for your speech topic. In fact, your first step in the topic development stage of speech preparation is to gather material, such as illustrations, statistical evidence, expert opinions, and quotations, to integrate into your speech. Why do you do this? You do it to help answer the questions of audience members. As you deliver your speech, audience members listen, silently asking themselves, What do you mean? Why should I accept what you say? Why should I care? If you research and develop your speech with care, you will make the answers to these questions clear to receivers.

If you're like many people in America today, you are likely fascinated with crime scene investigation (CSI) television programs and films that demonstrate the painstaking effort that goes into solving crimes. Like forensic pathologists, whose task it is to take nothing for granted and to leave no stone unturned in the search for clues and the analysis of evidence, so the public speaker also needs to investigate a topic very carefully in an effort to discover appropriate supporting material with which to build the substance of a speech.

■ ■ ■

RESEARCHING YOUR TOPIC

If you are like most other people, when you want to see a movie or try a new restaurant, you might start by checking the movie listings of your local newspaper or accessing Fandango online. Or you might decide to drive by the theater to see what films appear on its marquee. When it comes to choosing a new restaurant, you might ask your friends for their advice, peruse a guide such as *Zagat*, or review restaurant home pages on the Internet. What does this have to do with public speaking? The research we do when preparing to speak in public is much like the personal research we conduct daily. However, because a speech is likely to be shared with others in a somewhat more formal setting, we use a more formal research approach.

Research sources available to you include published works, other people, and of course, yourself. If you are discussing some aspect of sports medicine, for instance, you may rely on your experience of being injured when playing a sport. If your topic has to do with business or technology, you may use examples from your work in an industry that relates directly to your topic. Far too often, speakers fail to realize that they can use their personal experiences to establish credibility and add interesting and pertinent examples.

Go to the Online Learning Center at www.mhhe.com/gamble9 and answer the questions in the *Self Inventory* to evaluate your understanding of investigation.

Conducting Online and Offline Research

Suppose you were going to speak on the role of spin in our society, and you wanted to focus on how both government supporters and dissenters used spin during the waging of the war on terror. Where would you go for information? What sources would you turn to in order to learn what spin is, how it functions, why it is used, what its effects are, and whether it is ethical and/or legal, as well as to find examples of spin in action? For example, both adherents of the Iraqi war effort and those opposed to it spun their stories of the war's successes and failures. Would these stories serve as good examples to use in your speech? Through conducting research, you become able to answer such questions.

Libraries contain information storage and retrieval systems—resources that are invaluable for every type of research. The library is one of the few real bargains left in our society. A huge array of material is available free; other materials and services (those available through a variety of photographic and electronic systems) are yours for only a minimal cost. In addition, every academic and public library has on its staff knowledgeable people who have been trained to aid you with your investigative work. In addition to your college library, you can also consult the following Internet libraries: the Internet Public Library (www.ipl.org), the Library Spot (www.libraryspot.com), and the Reference Desk (www.refdesk.com).

When you begin library research, consult an array of reference sources to compile a preliminary bibliography. Your first stop may well be the library's electronic catalog. Next, you may move on to a variety of newspaper, magazine, and journal indexes. Depending on your subject, you may also consult bibliographical sources, encyclopedias, and almanacs. And you will almost certainly use computer-assisted searches.

USING THE LIBRARY'S ONLINE CATALOGS

In lieu of the card catalog system, now banished from most libraries, today's libraries usually contain a computerized catalog. Libraries, in increasing numbers, now offer computer or online catalogs that enable you to run more productive Boolean searches. When you run a **Boolean search,** instead of needing to know a specific author or title, you can merely enter two or three keywords into the computer and it will search the library's collection for you. No longer do you need to go from card catalog drawer to card catalog drawer, searching for source materials. The computer makes the search process much more efficient.

Boolean search

a keyword search

USING REFERENCE WORKS

Since magazines, newspapers, and scholarly periodicals may contain information valuable to you, indexes are critical resources. One of the first indexes you will consult will probably be the *Reader's Guide to Periodical Literature*. It can lead you to a variety of popular, mass-distribution magazines, including *Time, Newsweek,* and *U.S. News & World Report*, all of which may contain information relevant to your subject. The *New York Times Index* and the *Wall Street Journal Index* are also high on the list of indexes you should consider. If your topic warrants it, you may also need to explore issues of *Education Index*, *Psychological Abstracts*, and *Sociological Abstracts*. These sources will offer you leads to articles that have appeared in a number of scholarly journals.

The *World Almanac*, *Statistical Abstract of the United States*, and *Information Please Almanac* are only three of many such reference works that can provide the speech maker with interesting factual and statistical evidence. Multivolume encyclopedias, such as the *Britannica* and the *Americana*, and one-volume versions, such as the *Random House Encyclopedia* and the *Columbia Encyclopedia*, may also be consulted. Specialized encyclopedias, such as the *McGraw-Hill Encyclopedia of Science and Technology*, may be useful for technologically oriented topics.

Biographical materials can be located in the *Dictionary of National Biography*, the *Dictionary of American Biography*, and even the *New York Times Obituary Index*. Similarly, *Current Biography* can help you research the lives of contemporary public figures.

COMPUTER-AIDED AND ONLINE SEARCHES

Were it not for online catalogs, libraries would find it difficult, if not impossible, to process all the materials that need to be cataloged. The library research you conduct today can be done electronically rather than manually as in years past. What is required is that you master the proper commands that enable you to conduct an online subject search or author and title search so that you will be able to locate the information you are seeking.

A variety of reference tools, such as the *Reader's Guide to Periodical Literature*, *Facts on File*, and a number of encyclopedias, are now available online. *Magazine Index* (a database that indexes hundreds of American and Canadian magazines) and *InfoTrac* (a resource covering general publications and government documents) are available on laser disk. See Figure 14.1 for a sample search using Google, an online database. *Business Index*, another computerized resource, indexes the *New York Times* financial section and the *Wall Street Journal*.

There are also more sophisticated databases that you can consult via computer. Among them are *ERIC*, a comprehensive research system that indexes published and unpublished materials on a wide array of educational topics, and

Skill Builder

CSI: It's Your Turn

1. Working individually within groups, choose one well-known criminal case to investigate. Possibilities for investigation include the Jeffrey Dahmer, Scott Peterson, Mumia Abu-Jamal, Natalee Holloway, and JonBenet Ramsey cases.

2. Using the resources available in the local or college library, compile a bibliography of relevant materials.

3. Rank the entries in your bibliography:
   1 (what seems to be the most useful source),
   2 (the next most promising source), and so on.

4. Compare your list with the lists developed by the other members of your group. Discuss the number of sources cited by each individual in your group, the most unusual material located, and the decisions you made in ranking your references.

FIGURE 14.1

Sample Google Search.

Source: Reprinted with permission from Google.com.

ASI *(American Statistics Index).* Since many of these searches require the payment of a fee, you'll want to be certain of your topic and of the specific information you need before using them.

You can also use the Internet as a well-equipped international library of information resources.[1] Among the major Internet resources you will want to use when researching a speech are e-mail, newsgroups, and the World Wide Web.

E-Mail You can use e-mail to write to knowledgeable potential sources, a group, or a **listserv,** an e-mail list of several to over hundreds of people who have interest in and knowledge of a particular topic—potentially one that you are researching. Go to www.liszt.com, a directory containing information about numerous listservs and whether new members are welcomed, to explore potentially useful listservs. Before joining a listserv, try to identify the types of messages members send and their usefulness to you. Also read the frequently asked questions (FAQ) file so that you do not ask questions that have already been answered.

Using e-mail, you can also create a listserv for your class. Once you have one in place, you can use it to ask your potential audience members to fill out questionnaires that reveal their attitudes toward your chosen topic. You can also use the class listserv to seek and receive feedback after your speech.

Newsgroups Newsgroups facilitate the exchange of ideas on a broad array of topics through discussion forums. The Internet contains a multitude of newsgroups, also known as Usenet. In a newsgroup, you can post messages, read the posts of others, and respond to them. Like listservs, newsgroups bring together people interested in sharing ideas about a topic. As with a listserv, before joining a newsgroup, be sure you read through the FAQ file; doing so will ensure you receive maximum benefits from the newsgroup.

---

listserv

an e-mail list of people who have interest in and knowledge of a particular topic

Skill Builder

Ask.com

One way to research a potential topic is to access www.ask.com to research your topic. Based on the information you seek, you will receive a series of sources and Web sites to check out. In your opinion, is it ethical to have Ask.com do your legwork? If Ask.com locates sources, what is left for you to do? The answer is to separate the wheat from the chaff—that is, the useful and relevant from the useless and irrelevant. As you evaluate each potential source, answer the following questions:

1. Who wrote the material? Is the author a qualified and reliable source?

2. Who is the site's sponsor? To what sites, if any, is this site linked? What is the connection between the site and the links? What clues does the Internet address of the site provide? Is it, for example, a military site, a college or university, a business or commercial enterprise, a government agency, or someone's personal page?

3. How recent is the Web page? How often is information on it updated?

4. Why is the site on the Web? Is its primary purpose to provide information or to sell something?

You can use a search engine such as Deja News to search newsgroups for information on requested topics. Newsgroups that receive news feeds from news services such as the Associated Press are especially useful. You can also use the newsgroup to ask questions and poll people for opinions for a speech.

World Wide Web Almost any kind of content you can find in print is also available on the World Wide Web. The World Wide Web links all the individual Web sites and contains a vast collection of written, graphic, audio, and video documents. Just as a library offers you books, periodicals, news, and so forth, so does the Web. You can subscribe to various special interest groups or use a search engine to browse for information on your selected topic. A search engine is a program that makes it possible for you to search a database or index of Internet sites for information on topics of interest to you. Popular Internet browsers, such as Netscape and Internet Explorer, include search functions as a part of their home pages, thereby providing ready links to popular search engines and directories. While browsing, you might visit CNN or the Associated Press online, peruse copies of historical documents or the *Congressional Record*. With the Internet, you have easy access to the information that exists on numerous campuses and every continent.[2]

Among search engines are Google (www.google.com), the most popular search engine; Yahoo! (www.yahoo.com), the next most popular; MSN Search (www.msn.com); AltaVista (www.altavista.digital.com); and Terra Lycos (www.terralycos.com).[3] These, together with Excite (www.excite.com), Infoseek (www.infoseek.com), and HotBot (www.hotbot.com), are search engines as well as directories. Newer in the search engine arena are Alltheweb (www.alltheweb.com), Teoma (www.teoma.com), and Wisenut (www.wisenut.com).

Which search engine is your personal favorite? Why?

It is becoming easier to predict the Web site addresses of potential sources. When you know an address, or a uniform resource locator (URL), you are able to access the Web site by simply entering it in your Web browser. Corporate Web sites, for example, usually accessed by www.nameofcorporation.com, will provide you with access to annual reports, copies of speeches, and other information. You can also save your favorite sites as bookmarks, a Web browser feature that allows you to save your favorite links in a file to facilitate future access.

As you would do with all other research, consider your source when conducting research over the Internet. Check the independence of the information you discover.

While the information contained in traditional research sources, including books, magazines, and journal articles, is typically reviewed and checked by others before being published, virtually anyone can post information in a Web site or to a newsgroup. Thus, verifying and thinking critically about the quality of the information you find online is a serious responsibility. As you decide what and what not to include in your speech from your Web search, ask yourself who a site's sponsor is. For example, CNN, MSNBC, and Fox are established news organizations, and you can weigh the information you find on their sites in the same way as you would weigh the information you use from their cablecasts. The same goes for major newspapers that also operate Web sites. As you evaluate Web-based information from other sources, it is important to determine if the source has an apparent or hidden bias. Ask yourself if postings are specific or general. Do the claims they make seem justifiable? Do not value a source simply because it is published on the Internet. Seek out confirming sources for what you discover.

Conducting Primary Research

You may also want to use primary information to support or flesh out your presentation. Three primary research techniques are (1) personal observation and experience, (2) informal surveys, and (3) interviews.

PERSONAL OBSERVATION AND EXPERIENCE

One of the best ways to research a topic is to examine what you know about it. Search your own background and experiences for materials you might want to integrate into your presentation.

If your topic is one for which direct observation of an event, a person, or a stimulus would be appropriate, then by all means go out and observe. An observational excursion might take you to a biology laboratory, an airport, a supermarket, or a construction site, for example. When conducting a direct observation, be sure to take careful notes. If possible, ask the interviewee's permission to arrive at the location with tape recorder or video recorder in hand. Sit down immediately after the experience and record your thoughts and feelings. File your firsthand notes with the materials gathered during your library research.

INFORMAL SURVEYS

Developing a reliable scientific survey instrument is complicated. However, informal surveys can be used to provide the speech maker with useful and often entertaining information. Let's say you are investigating the possibility of adding online courses to the curriculum; a survey at your school may produce data you can use. (For instance, you may be able to discover the percentage of students interested in enrolling in such courses.)

Informal surveys normally consist of no more than 5 to 10 questions. To conduct an informal survey with a prospect, you need to identify yourself first and state the purpose of your

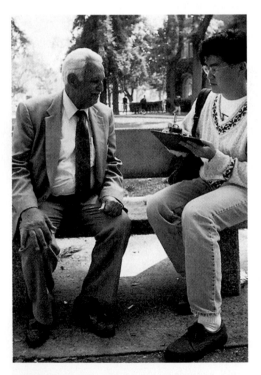

Informal surveys and formal interviews provide a speaker with statistical information, testimonials, and examples to use in his or her speech.

survey: "Hello, I'm _____. I'm investigating the feasibility of incorpo-rating online courses into the regular curriculum of the college." The survey can be conducted either orally, in writing, or over the Internet. A sample of 25 to 50 people and some simple mathematical calculations should provide adequate statistical information to integrate into your presentation. When you conduct an informal survey, you may gain more than expected. While running the survey or examining the results, you may find interesting off-the-cuff remarks to incorpo-rate in your speech.

INTERVIEWS

An interview is similar to a survey except that it is usually more detailed and assumes that the person being interviewed is in some way an expert on the topic under consideration. On your campus, in your community, or in an online Usenet discussion group, you will probably find knowledgeable people to interview about current issues and many other topics. Political, business, and religious leaders, for instance, can often be persuaded to talk to student speakers. And, of course, fac-ulty members of a college are often eager to cooperate.

Be sure to record accurately the information gathered during an interview. Take careful notes and repeat or verify any direct quotations you intend to use in your presentation. Also be certain during the speech to credit the interviewee as your source, unless he or she has asked not to be mentioned by name.

A Note on Recording Information

It is important to organize the information you collect so that it is easily retriev-able and usable. Buy a pack of 5- by 8-inch note cards to record the information you gather. You might record the source of your data at the top of the card and write below it a direct quotation or summary of the information gathered. This procedure can be used for material derived from print, nonprint, survey, and inter-view sources. Also, since it is impossible to "make appointments" with ideas, you should plan to record any of your own thoughts in the same way. For instance, an idea about a possible format for your speech may occur to you. If so, write it down. Do not rely on your memory.

INTEGRATING YOUR RESEARCH: TYPES OF SUPPORTING MATERIAL

Taken together, your research and your experiences should yield a wealth of infor-mation to integrate into your presentation. But making your research and experi-ences come to life for an audience is not an easy task; in fact, it is a key chal-lenge facing the speech maker. Following are some major ways to make research and experience understandable and believable for an audience.[4]

Definitions

It is especially important to use **definitions** when your listeners are unfamiliar with terms you are using or when their associations for words or concepts might differ from yours. Only if you explain how you are defining a term can you hope to share

definitions
explanations of what a stimulus is or what a word or concept means

your meanings with your listeners. Thus, the purpose of a definition is to increase the audience's understanding.

Choose a word for which people have different associations—for example, an abstract concept such as honesty, jealousy, freedom, justice, or love. Write your own definition and share it with the class.

For example, in a famous speech, "On Woman's Right to Suffrage," Susan B. Anthony took pains to define what she believed was meant by "we, the people": "It was we, the people, not we, the white male citizens; nor yet we the male citizens; but we, the whole people who formed the union."[5]

In a speech on post-traumatic stress disorder and soldiers serving in Iraq and Afghanistan, speaker Megan Solan defined *psychological injury* as "that which soldiers suffer when they lose their peace of mind, their ability to function in society and their belief in the existence of human virtues."[6] The student went on to flesh out this definition with specifics: "soldiers learn skills such as the art of deception; the capacity to respond instantly with violent, lethal force; and the suppression of such emotions as compassion, horror, guilt, tenderness, grief, and disgust, all necessary skills for combat, but all skills with dangerous potential within civilian society and severe consequences for the human psyche."[7]

Statistics

Statistics are simply facts expressed in numerical form. They may be cited to explain relationships or to indicate trends. To be used effectively as support, statistics must be honest and credible. If used appropriately, they can make the ideas you are presenting memorable and significant.

In a speech on the danger of tattoos, student Chandra Palubiak of Berry College used a series of statistics to make the point that "adding a little artwork" to one's epidermis can be dangerous to one's health: "The *Milwaukee Journal Sentinel* says getting a tattoo could cause Hepatitis C, the most widespread chronic viral illness touching almost 2 percent of the United States population. Two percent doesn't seem that significant until you realize that it is nearly 4,500,000 people in the U.S. . . . 33 percent of those with tattoos contract Hepatitis C, which is nearly one in every three people."[8]

statistics
facts expressed in numerical form

In a speech on the importance of learning to speak a second language, student Ann Marie Ursini noted: "Students are not taking advantage of the resources available to them. Unfortunately, undergraduate enrollment in language classes is less than eight percent according to the National Foreign Language Center."[9]

Examples and Illustrations

Examples are representative cases; as such, they specify particular instances.[10] **Illustrations,** on the other hand, tell stories and thus create more detailed narrative pictures. Both examples and illustrations may be factual or hypothetical.

Solomon D. Trujillo, chairman, president, and CEO of US West, Inc., used a series of examples to demonstrate for audience members that one idea can make a difference:

examples
representative cases

illustrations
stories; narrative pictures

> We've seen how the idea that all people are created equal can find expression in an African-American woman on a bus in Alabama, or [in] a student on a soda-fountain stool in North Carolina, or even in a young Hispanic businessman in Cheyenne, Wyoming.
>
> A few weeks back, I was at the University of Colorado talking to a group of business students, and I told them that I would not be in the job I have were it not for Affirmative Action.

When I joined the old Bell system, AT&T had just entered into a consent decree with the government. Before I joined the company, people like me . . . for some reason . . . weren't likely to get hired. Those who were hired . . . for some reason . . . weren't in management jobs.

But people with courage and foresight knew that our nation's promise of freedom and justice for all was an empty one if you had the wrong color of skin, if you were female, if you spoke with an accent, or if your last name ended in a "z" or a vowel.[11]

University of South Dakota student Tony Martinet used a series of brief examples to add impact to a speech on the extent of incivility by parents of children participating in organized sports games:

A book entitled *The Dark Side of Youth Sports* by sports psychologist Shane Murphy offers three examples of emotional abuse that almost everyone has witnessed:

- A mortified child whose mother is screaming at the referee about a "blown call"
- The embarrassed child whose dad is yelling at the coach about "getting my kid into the game"
- The despondent child who is being verbally attacked by their parent or coach for a perceived lack of effort or for making a "dumb" mistake.[12]

Testimony

Whenever you cite someone else's opinions or conclusions, you are using **testimony,** or a testimonial. Testimony gives you an opportunity to connect the ideas in your speech with the thoughts and attitudes of respected and competent people. The testimony you include in a presentation need not be derived exclusively from present-day sources; words of people from the past may also be used to tie today and yesterday together. When using testimonials, be sure to consider whether the people you cite as authorities are credible sources, whether their ideas are understandable, and whether their comments are relevant to your purpose.

testimony
someone else's opinions or conclusions

In a speech on the implication of the Patriot Act, Newman University student Stacy Champagne used an unusual mixture of testimony sources to make a point about the act's dangers:

The . . . *Baltimore Sun* points out, "Anti-terrorism legislation passed by the House as the 'Patriot Act' and in the Senate as the 'Uniting and Strengthening Act' implying that opponents to the legislation are unpatriotic or opposed to uniting America." Chilling! Perhaps Hitler's second in command, Hermann Goering, explained it best in the Nuremberg Trials when he said, "The people can always be brought to do the bidding of the leaders. That is easy. All you have to do is tell them they are being attacked, and denounce the pacifist for lack of patriotism and exposing the country to danger."[13]

As we see, testimony reinforces a speaker's claims. It may be quoted directly, as in the preceding example, or it may be paraphrased, as illustrated by Theresa McGuiness in her speech advocating that fraternities be abolished:

Bernice Sandler, executive director of the Project on the Status and Education of Women at the Association of American Colleges, said that 90 percent of the gang rapes reported to her office involved fraternity members. According to Sandler, fraternity members have a word for gang rape: they call it "pulling train."

Exploring Diversity

Experts and Cultural Groups

If the testimony of others influences us in making decisions and assessing situations, then an audience's judgments about a public speaker—and about his or her speech—ought to be influenced by people the speaker quotes or refers to, who presumably have special knowledge or experience relevant to the topic.

Does it matter whether a speaker uses experts from the same cultural group as the audience, or would experts from other cultural groups serve just as well in adding strength and impact to the speaker's ideas? Explain your position.

She adds that charts of how many beers it took to seduce sorority women are common in fraternity houses. And if a woman actually does press charges against a fraternity, Sandler says, "Their excuse is, 'she asked for it'—even if she was unconscious."[14]

Use direct quotations when you believe that the language and the length of an expert's remarks are appropriate for your audience. Use a paraphrase when you need to summarize an expert's opinion in fewer words, or when you need to simplify its language.

Comparisons and Contrasts

Comparisons stress similarities between two entities; contrasts stress differences. Both are employed by speakers to help audiences understand something that is unknown, unfamiliar, or unclear.

William L. Laurence combined comparison and contrast when he described the atomic bombing of Nagasaki:

> As the first mushroom floated off into the blue, it changed its shape into a flower-like form, its grand petals curving downward, creamy white outside, rose-colored inside. . . . Much living substance had gone into those rainbows. The quivering top of the pillar was protruding to a great height through the white clouds, giving the appearance of a monstrous prehistoric creature with a ruff around its neck, a fleecy ruff extending in all directions, as far as the eye could see.[15]

Which of the kinds of support mentioned in this chapter appeal most to you? Do you think that men and women are equally attracted to each kind of support? Why?

William D. Novelli, CEO of AARP, used comparison and contrast to make his point about the need to transform our current health care system, noting: "We might compare fixing our health-care system to wrestling an octopus: Two arms are hugging you, two arms are trying to strangle you, and God knows what the other four arms are doing. Every time you think you're making headway, another arm reaches out and grabs you and pulls you back."[16]

Repetition and Restatement

When a speaker uses repetition, the same words are repeated verbatim. When a speaker uses restatement, an idea is presented again, but in different words. If used sparingly, these devices can add impact to a speech maker's remarks and thereby increase memorability.[17]

One of the most famous examples of successful use of repetition is the speech delivered by Martin Luther King, Jr., in 1963 at the Lincoln Memorial:

> I say to you today, my friends, so even though we face the difficulties of today and tomorrow, I still have a dream. It is a dream deeply rooted in the American dream. I have a dream that one day this nation will rise up . . . live out the true meaning of its creed—we hold these truths to be self-evident, that all men are created equal. . . .
>
> I have a dream that my four little children will one day live in a nation where they will not be judged by the color of their skin but by the content of their character. I have a dream today. . . .
>
> I have a dream that one day every valley shall be exalted, and every hill and mountain shall be made low, the rough places shall be made plain, and the crooked places shall be made straight and the glory of the Lord will be revealed and all flesh shall see it together.[18]

ILLUSTRATING YOUR RESEARCH: PRESENTATION AIDS

The first question to ask yourself about audio and visual aids is, Do I need them? Many speakers make the mistake of not using such aids when the content really demands them. Other speakers use too many audio and visual aids; they clutter the content so much that the presentation becomes confusing and loses momentum. Of late, visual aids have become a weapon of choice of speakers in the public arena. In fact, at congressional hearings, it is common for senators and representatives to use poster board aids that show text in letters large enough to be seen by the cameras.

In this section, we consider (1) how you can determine whether your presentation can be improved by audio and visual aids and (2) how you can select and prepare such aids when they are needed.

Why Use Presentation Aids?

Presentation aids have several functions. Ideally, they make it easier for the audience to follow, understand, respond to, and remember your speech. Thus, when deciding whether to use an audio or visual aid, begin by asking yourself if it will serve at least one of those purposes.

If your presentation contains highly technical information, an appropriate aid may help reduce your listeners' confusion. If the presentation needs additional impact, an audio or visual aid can help increase listeners' motivation. If you want to highlight an important point, an audio or visual aid can add emphasis. A three-dimensional model of the molecular structure of a virus, for instance, might evoke more interest than would words alone. The damage smoking does to a human lung can be depicted with visuals to capture the attention of smokers and nonsmokers alike. Audio and visual aids can also help an audience remember what you have said. A chart can dramatize statistical data, indicating, for instance, the number of infants who

Visual aids reinforce a speaker's spoken message. A visual that is tangible can add drama to a presentation.

fall prey to sudden death syndrome each year or symbolizing a decline in real income. By providing your audience with an additional channel, audio and visual aids give needed reinforcement to key points and ideas.[19]

Selecting and creating materials to help accomplish your speech-making goals is not easy.[20] Once you decide to use audio or visual aids, you have to make a number of serious decisions. Initially, you will need to identify precise points in your presentation when aids will be effective. One way to prepare yourself to make such judgments is to examine how producers of newscasts select audio and visual aids to complement the work of on-camera reporters. After all, in many ways you are the "producer" of your speech.

Another strategy is brainstorming. Examine the information you have and repeatedly ask yourself the following question: Which specific pieces of information could be improved with audio or visual aids? Keep a record of each idea that comes to mind, being sure to indicate how the audio or visual support would actually be used.

Once you have analyzed your needs for audio and visual reinforcement, it is time to reconsider the possibilities you have identified.

Visual Aids

Is it sufficient if all a visual aid does is jog the memory of audience members? Why?

One of the prime reasons for using visual aids is to increase audience comprehension and retention. Visuals reinforce and help communicate the speaker's spoken message, enabling receivers to understand what words alone cannot transmit.

TYPES OF VISUAL AIDS

Let's now examine a sampling of the types of visual aids at your disposal.

Objects and Models   In your brainstorming session, you may have decided that you would like to use an object to illustrate a certain concept. The object you choose can be the real thing—for example, a set of earphones, a food processor, or a computer.

However, using an actual object is often impractical: Objects like automobiles are obviously too large, and objects like microelectronic chips may be too small. In such cases, it may be necessary to use a model instead. A model can be made of clay, papier-mâché, wood scraps, or other materials. If used creatively, inexpensive materials can serve your purpose very well. Your aim is simply to make a reasonable facsimile of the object—something that will enable you to share information more meaningfully.

The accompanying photographs show celebrity spokespersons Sean "P. Diddy" Combs and Avril Lavigne using themselves as models and wearing the message they both sought to share with receivers. Do you think a speaker's dress should become part of the speaker's message?

Objects and models make it easier for you to pull your audience into your speech. Since they are tangible, they can make your points more realistic, and they can add drama to your presentation.

pie, or circle, graph
a circle with the various percentages of the whole indicated by wedges; a means of showing percentage relationships

Graphs   You can use graphs to make an effective presentation even more successful. The most commonly used graphs are pie, or circle, graphs; bar graphs; line graphs; and pictographs.

A **pie, or circle, graph** is simply a circle with the various percentages of the whole indicated by wedges. By focusing on relationships, pie graphs show how

Both Sean "P. Diddy" Combs and Avril Lavigne are wearing a message they want others to accept.
In your opinion is wearing a message an effective means of communicating? Why or why not?

items compare with each other and with the whole. Since the entire circle represents 100 percent, the pie graph is an effective way to show percentage relationships or proportions. In a speech on how to use the Web to find romance, one student used a pie graph to provide a snapshot of persons in various age groups who are using online personal ads to look for love (see Figure 14.2).[21]

If your goal is to show the performance of one variable over time, a **bar graph** might be appropriate. A bar graph is used to compare quantities or magnitude. In a speech on cell phone addiction, a student used the bar graph in Figure 14.3 to compare and contrast inventions we hate most but cannot seem to live without.[22] A bar graph can also be used to show the performance of one variable over time.

bar graph
a graph used to show the performance of one variable over time or to contrast various measures at a point in time

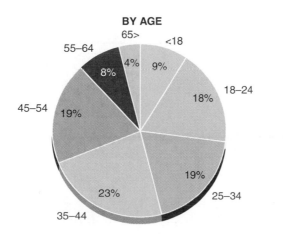

BY AGE

65> 4%
<18 9%
55–64 8%
45–54 19%
18–24 18%
35–44 23%
25–34 19%
19%

FIGURE 14.2

Pie Graph.

Who is using online personal ads to find romance?

Source: "Who Is Using Online Personal Ads?" from *Newsweek*, May 12, 2003, p. E20. Copyright © 2003 Newsweek, Inc. Reprinted by permission.

Inventions we hate most but can't live without

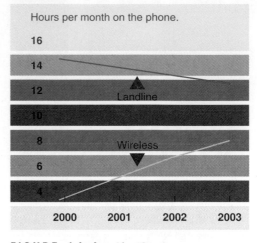

Cellphone	30%
Alarm clock	25%
Television	23%
Shaving razors	14%
other	8%

FIGURE 14.3   Bar Graph.

Source: 2004 Lemelson-MIT Invention Index, http://mit.edu/invent/

Talking

Hours per month on the phone.

16

14

12
Landline

10

8
Wireless

6

4

2000   2001   2002   2003

FIGURE 14.4   Line Graph.

Source: Adapted from *Wall Street Journal,* January 26, 2004. Copyright 2004 by Dow Jones & Co. Inc. Reproduced with permission of Dow Jones & Co. via Copyright Clearance Center.

line graphs

graphs used to illustrate trends, relationships, or comparisons over time

Like bar graphs, **line graphs** can illustrate trends, relationships, or comparisons over time. In the speech on cell phone addiction referred to earlier, the student also used a line graph to make the point that wireless phones will soon replace landline phones (see Figure 14.4).[23] This line graph, in addition to showing the number of hours per month we spend talking on phones, also illustrates a perceptible trend in decreased landline use and increasing cell phone use. Also note how the lines in Figure 14.4 are color-coded for clarity. When well designed, the line graph is one of the easiest types for audiences to read and follow.

pictographs

graphs that use sketches to represent concepts

Pictographs use sketches of figures to represent concepts (see Figure 14.5). During your research, you may discover sketches or pictures that could be integrated into a pictograph to help vitalize your content.

FIGURE 14.5

Pictograph.

Source: New York Times, August 18, 1994. Based on data from the United Nations Population Fund. Copyright © 1994 The New York Times Co. Used by permission of The New York Times Graphics.

DEMOGRAPHICS

Global Population

1994
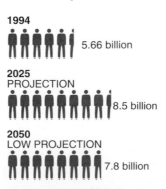
5.66 billion

2025
PROJECTION
8.5 billion

2050
LOW PROJECTION
7.8 billion

2050
MEDIUM PROJECTION

10 billion

2050

12.5 billion

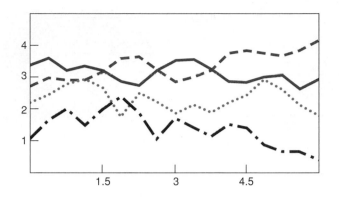

FIGURE 14.6
Poorly Designed Line Graph.

The general rule to follow in making and using graphs is that a single graph should be used to communicate only one concept or idea. Consider the line graph in Figure 14.6. This graph is far too cluttered for an audience to read easily and quickly. Your goal in devising a graph is to eliminate extraneous information and to focus, rather than diffuse, the audience's attention. Emphasize the essentials.

Photographs and Drawings   Drawings, like photographs, can help generate a mood, clarify, or identify. In explaining a sequence of plays that led to a success for his football team, one speaker used a drawing like the one in Figure 14.7. Would you recommend simplifying this sketch?

You may find photographs or drawings that can add interest to your presentation and provide greater reality. For example, one student juxtaposed a photograph of deceased gymnast Chrisy Heinrich (taken from an article in a national weekly magazine) with one of her own sister to illustrate that anorexia nervosa is a disease afflicting both famous and ordinary people. Another used drawings taken from *The Wall Street Journal* to help illustrate her speech on how a tsunami forms (see Figure 14.8).[24]

If possible, use a variety of dark, rich colors, such as red, black, blue, and green, to add contrast to a drawing. But remember, unless a drawing is large enough to be seen, it will not increase your audience's attention or strengthen your presentation.

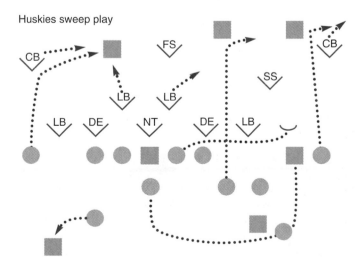

FIGURE 14.7
Drawing.

Where two plates meet on the sea floor...

...one plate dives beneath the other. Above where the ocean floor has deformed, an immense column of water falls...

...and rises, as the ocean tries to regain equilibrium.

Waves radiate away from the fault; two major waves are formed. One tsunami travels toward the closest coast, and the other heads out into the open ocean.

Near the origin of the tsunami, the wave is long and flat–several feet high and tens to hundreds of miles long. Sailors might not even notice.

As the tsunami hits shallower coastal waters, it slows and gets taller and narrower, and carries even more destructive power.

Shoreline

At the shore, the tsunami arrives as a drastic rise in sea level; the wall of water can flood hundreds of yards inland past the average high-tide level, sweeping away sand and trees, people and homes.

Wall of Destruction

How an earthquake caused the giant waves that devastated Southeast Asia yesterday.

FIGURE 14.8

Drawings.

How a tsunami forms.

Source: Wall Street Journal, December 27, 2004, with data from the U.S. Geological Survey, University of Washington. Copyright 2004 by Dow Jones & Co. Inc. Reproduced with permission of Dow Jones & Co. via the Copyright Clearance Center.

Computer Graphics   Advances in computer technology have made it possible for speech makers to use computer-generated visual aids. Most college speakers have traditionally used poster board and marking pens to enlarge charts and graphs so that they can be seen easily, but now computer graphics hardware and software are making it easier for students to develop professional-looking charts and graphs.

To prepare a computer graphic, begin by organizing your data. Then select the type of graphic you want—for example, pie chart, bar chart, or some other graphic. Many programs automatically generate legends for the visual.

The leading graphics program available is PowerPoint. Figure 14.9 shows a sample of a computer-generated graph. You can use PowerPoint to produce such

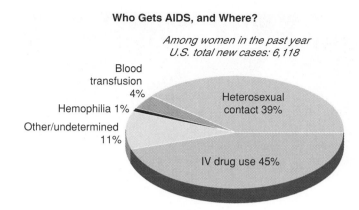

Who Gets AIDS, and Where?

*Among women in the past year
U.S. total new cases: 6,118*

- Blood transfusion 4%
- Hemophilia 1%
- Other/undetermined 11%
- Heterosexual contact 39%
- IV drug use 45%

FIGURE 14.9
Computer-Generated Graph.

a graph. When using PowerPoint to strengthen or help communicate ideas, the presenter is free to select or create backgrounds, colors, formats, layouts, and sounds. The speaker can also animate text and graphics to fade in or out or to dissolve, as he or she desires. In addition, the presenter can scan in other appropriate photographs or relevant visuals, including film clips. (We discuss Power-Point-assisted presentations in greater detail a little later in this chapter). You can also use graphics generated by a professional, as one student did when delivering a speech on dyslexia (see Figure 14.10), and as another student did when explaining how the Ebola virus works (see Figure 14.11).[25]

GUIDELINES FOR USING VISUAL AIDS

Speakers can justify the use of visual aids by showing how they contribute to audience understanding of the message.

Criteria   When evaluating visuals, remember that they must be appropriate to the audience, the occasion, the location, and the content of your speech—and to you yourself.

A BAD CONNECTION
Dyslexics may have an abnormality in the brain's medial geniculate nucleus, which relays sound signals to the cortex. The MGN has too few of the neurons that "hear" staccato consonants like "ka."

- Medial geniculate nucleus
- Auditory cortex

FIGURE 14.10
Computer-Generated Image.

Source: Howard Sochurek-Medichrome-stock shop.

FIGURE 14.11

Speakers Often Use Professional Graphics.

The Ebola virus at work.

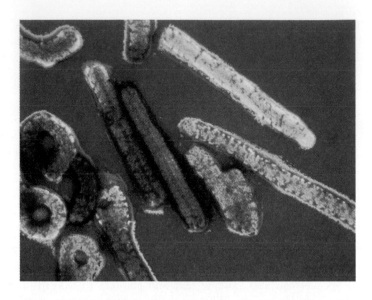

In your mind, what is the difference between a visual aid and visual notes?

In developing visual materials, keep three criteria in mind: (1) simplicity, (2) clarity, and (3) visibility. *Simplicity* means that the visuals should be as transportable as possible (so that you can easily take them with you to the presentation) and as easy as possible to use. Give careful consideration to the size and weight of large items. Ask yourself if a visual can be displayed without disrupting the environment. Ask yourself if it can be set up and taken down in a minimal amount of time. With regard to clarity, remember that the purpose of a visual aid is to enhance understanding, not to cause confusion. Ideally, each visual should depict only one idea or concept, or at least should be displayed so that only the relevant portions are visible at the appropriate point in your speech. Visibility is the third criterion. Since a visual aid obviously serves no purpose if it cannot be seen and read, you must determine if your audience will be able to see and read it. Make sure that the lettering is tall enough (3 by 4 inches high or larger) and that photographs or pictures are large enough.

Methods and Equipment One way to present flat visuals is to display them on a chart board or on oaktag. With variously colored markers, a yardstick, and a little time, you should be able to create appealing and functional visuals. You may also use more sophisticated equipment to present visuals—overhead projectors, film, videotape, and 35 mm slides. Overhead projectors are often used by training professionals and salespeople. Transparencies can be created from almost any 8½- by 11-inch original of a photograph, an illustration, or a graph. Then the image can be projected onto a screen or a light-colored wall (if no screen is available). The room need not be completely darkened to use an overhead projector, but you should rehearse with transparencies to be sure they are clearly visible. (Setup time is about 10 minutes.)

Film clips can also be used to add life and motion to a presentation. For film, you need a screen or light-colored wall in a room that can be darkened. It will take about 15 minutes to prepare the room and equipment. Without adequate setup time, a film clip can become more of a hindrance than a help.

Slides are easier to use than film. However, unless you have been trained in multimedia or multi-image production, the number of slides you use should be kept to a minimum. (Also, be prepared to deal with jammed slide trays and burned-out bulbs.)

DVD recorders have improved greatly in recent years and are easy for speakers to use. Video stores have many DVDs that can be used to arouse an audience's interest. One speaker used a clip of Abbott and Costello's "Who's on First?" routine to introduce the topic of language. A company president regularly uses clips from the various *Rocky* films to motivate the sales force. The cable channel C-Span makes it convenient to incorporate current events into speeches. If your topic is current, check the C-Span listings—if C-Span is available in your area—to determine if and when the topic will be covered. Then, in addition to quoting a public official, you can actually have him or her as a video guest to briefly illustrate a point.

When using DVDs, cue up the DVD before you begin the speech. Far too many speakers press the Play button only to find that they have no picture or sound on the monitor. One speaker had scarcely begun his presentation before he had to call a coffee break while repairs were done on the video equipment. Audiences today are simply not willing to sit while you and others tinker with electronic gadgetry. Prepare it carefully in advance, and rehearse.

Audio Aids

Audiotape is readily available and easy to use as an accompaniment to a speech. Cassette and CD players come in a variety of forms and sizes, many of which are easily portable. Since speech makers often find it advantageous to integrate a brief excerpt from a song or a segment from an interview or a newscast into their presentations, audiotape has become a popular support medium. One student, for example, reinforced an informative presentation entitled "The Speech Capabilities of Dolphins" with a few moments of dolphin sounds that she had recorded during a visit to an aquarium. Another added impact to a speech called "Teenage Runaways" by using a segment of the Beatles' now-classic song "She's Leaving Home."

If you decide to use audiotape, cue the tape to the precise point at which you want to begin. Do this before you arrive at the front of the room, so that finding the right spot on the tape will not bring your presentation to an untimely halt.

What is this cartoon suggesting about the use of visuals?

Visuals should enhance a presentation.

Skill Builder

The Proper Prop

Read this article by media relations practitioner Merrie Spaeth.

"Prop" Up Your Speaking Skills

When Moses came down from the mountain with clay tablets bearing the Ten Commandments, it was perhaps history's first example of a speaker using props to reinforce his message. It wouldn't have had the same impact if Moses had simply announced: "God just told me 10 things, and I'm going to relay them to you."

Props can be an invaluable tool in business presentations. They drive home the point in ways words alone cannot. A partner from a Big Six accounting firm showed clients an article criticizing executive compensation. "We're going to see more and more of this," he said, "and that's why it's important to look at how you executives stack up against industry standards." Seeing the article dramatized the topic's importance.

President Reagan loved to use letters as props. Once, at a briefing for editors of women's magazines, he was emphasizing that overregulation is a women's issue. He held up a letter from a small-business woman that described the burden of time and money that Occupational Safety and Health Administration rules imposed on her. It made his message credible and underscored his interest in women.

Pictures or illustrative objects make great props. A Texas banker was speaking to potential clients—treasurers of companies that were doing business in dozens of countries—about his bank's expertise in foreign exchange. He held up various foreign bills. Most of the treasurers recognized Dutch guilders, French francs and German marks, but were at a loss to identify currencies from places like Liberia and Turkmenistan. The bank, he made clear, had specialized knowledge that could help improve its clients' profits.

Props make a wonderful tool to introduce humor, especially if you aren't naturally funny. To point out how difficult it is for executives to juggle all their responsibilities, one CEO juggled three small bean-bags. He got them going, looked up to acknowledge the applause—and lost his rhythm. As he grabbed for the beanbags, he said, "I said it was hard. Now, I proved it."

The new CEO of a large insurance company used props to make a vivid statement of his commitment to change. At his first speech to 250 top managers and agents, he eschewed traditional black-and-white overheads in favor of a variety of props—from a McDonald's bag to a large garbage can. He began by discussing how industries had changed. Holding up the McDonald's bag, he commented that the fast-food industry, which didn't exist until a few decades ago, had thrived because it met the needs of its customers. He talked about what new technology was going to mean for the agent on the street. He dragged the trash can to center stage and threw in a pile of receipts and bookkeeping forms. He got a standing ovation.

Even a seemingly outlandish prop can succeed in lightening a tough message. Three years later, that same CEO needed to get across the point that his agents weren't adapting quickly enough. He began by holding up a lobster. When the colonists arrived, he said, lobsters were plentiful: "No longer." The environment had changed, but lobsters hadn't. The audience leaned forward in their seats as he plopped the lobster into a pot of boiling water. Pacing up and down the stage, he explained how the business environment had changed—and periodically checked the pot. At the end of his speech, he hoisted aloft the now-cooked lobster, and said that companies and people who resist change are destined to become someone's lunch. "But we will change," he announced. Long pause: "Ladies and gentlemen, let's have lunch." All adjourned for lobster bisque.

The audience loved it. More important, the message that came through was a positive one: Change means opportunity. Speeches in which management must convey to employees that "you're not doing it right" or "you're not doing enough" are among the hardest to deliver successfully. The message is intimidating unless the tone is just right. In this case levity made a tough speech into a morale builder.

The use of props isn't without its pitfalls. For one, a prop that doesn't really relate to what's being said only makes the speaker look foolish. One CEO, talking about lousy industry conditions, took a rubber chicken and threw it into the audience. Get it? Neither did the audience.

And if you don't rehearse, the best-conceived idea can go wrong. You don't want to be the executive whose letter gets stuck in his lapel pocket, or who pulls out a picture upside down, or who can't get the whip to crack. Executives don't practice enough, and we always hear the same excuse: "I don't have enough time."

But if you do make time for props, you'll likely find that they're an inexpensive and effective way of ensuring that the audience remembers your message.

Now, using the following general speech topics, identify props you might use to ensure the audience remembers your speech:

cell phones and public places

privacy and the Internet

getting out the vote

product safety

automatic external defibrillators (AEDs)

Finally, what lesson about props and speech making is contained in the following cartoon?

Source: From "'Prop' Up Your Speaking Skills" by Merrie Spaeth in *The Wall Street Journal*, July 1, 1996, p. A14. Copyright © 1996 Dow Jones & Co. Reprinted by permission of Dow Jones & Co. via Copyright Clearance Center.

"Thank you, Barbara. Next, David Lombardo will give his presentation on the ancient city of Pompeii."

Computer-Assisted Presentations: PowerPoint

Of all the visual aids mentioned, computerized presentations are increasing the most in popularity.[26] You can not only create various types of charts but also build effective online slide shows from your speech outline. You can also use a computer to display video clips, text, photographs, drawings, and charts. PowerPoint, for example, contains a clip art library that enables you to select images that enhance the meaning of your words. It also allows you to generate backgrounds, formats, layouts, and colors that you believe best reflect the purpose of your presentation. The computer-generated visuals you create can be run directly from a computer projector, converted to 35 mm slides, printed out in handout form, or blown up for display to the audience. (See the sample computer-assisted slide presentation on page 421.)

When planning a PowerPoint presentation, you need to think in bullets (see sample slide presentation). Supporting your spoken speech, PowerPoint slides illustrate your talk. Pictures and charts, as well as animated graphics and talking points, are projected onto a screen, which both you and receivers use.

Although computerized presentations are rapidly becoming the standard in business and education, you do need to be selective when deciding whether or not to create one. If not prepared with care or if allowed to upstage the speaker and overpower the message, computer presentations can drain a speech of its vitality.[27] Reflecting the growth in PowerPoint presentations, the current chairman of the Joint Chiefs of Staff issued the following order, although not in these exact words, to U.S. military bases around the globe: "Enough with the bells and whistles—just get to the point."[28] To what extent do you agree or disagree with this advice? Whatever your position, the point is that a piece of technology that is supposed to facilitate communication should not be used in such a way that it becomes an obstacle to it.

One fear is that dazzling PowerPoint presentations can be used to cover up weak content.[29] Another is that the number of words and slides used will be out of control. In fact, one U.S. computer company has distributed guidelines to its employees about PowerPoint presentations that require them to adhere by the "Rule of Seven": seven bullets or lines per slide, seven words per line.[30] On the other hand, MIT psychology professor Steven Pinker notes that PowerPoint gives visual shape to an argument. Says Pinker, "Language is a linear medium: one damn word after another. But ideas are multidimensional . . . . When properly employed, PowerPoint makes the logical structure of an argument more transparent. Two channels sending the same information are better than one."[31]

Sample Computer-Assisted Slide Presentation

Here is a speech that is supported by a computer slide program.

1. The first slide introduces the topic to the audience. Speakers usually keep the title slide simple but provocative to draw receivers into the presentation. The speaker's task is to find a background for the slide that reflects the tone of the presentation. What do you think of the background provided here?

1. **Whirlwinds**

Tornadoes in Your Life

2. **What Is a Tornado?**

The National Weather Service defines a tornado as a violently rotating column of air in contact with the ground. It is a pendent from a thunderstorm.

3. **How Tornadoes Work**

■ Vortex of air rises into a cloud.
■ Vortex becomes a funnel.
■ Vortex wind speed can reach 300 mph.

4. **Tornado Warnings**

■ A major storm approaches.
■ The atmosphere feels unsettled.
■ Wind becomes more and more violent.

2. The second slide introduces the first main point of the speech. The speaker uses the slide to ask and answer a question, clarifying the subject for receivers. How did the speaker add credibility to the definition provided? In your opinion, should the speaker have done more to orient receivers visually to the topic prior to defining this key term?

3. The third slide introduces the second main point of the speech by summarizing how tornadoes work. In your opinion, will this slide help sustain receiver interest? Why or why not?

4. The fourth slide introduces the third point of the speech by revealing the warning signs of an approaching tornado.

5. **The Fujita Scale**
Wind Speed

■ F0–Up to 72 mph. Broken tree limbs and signs.
■ F1–Up to 112 mph. Trailer homes flipped.
■ F2–Up to 157 mph. Roofs torn off; trailer homes demolished.

6. **The Fujita Scale**
Wind Speed

■ F3–Up to 206 mph. Roofs and walls torn down; trains thrown from tracks.
■ F4–Up to 260 mph. Frame homes leveled.
■ F5–Over 260 mph. Homes and buildings completely destroyed.

7. **How Large Are Tornadoes?**

■ Average 500 feet in width
■ Travel 5 miles on ground
■ Last only a few minutes

8. **Where Do Tornadoes Occur Most Often?**

■ South in early spring
■ Midwest in May
■ The Texas and Oklahoma Panhandles are sometimes known as Tornado Alley in the spring and early summer.
■ Later in the summer, tornadoes are found in the eastern part of the country.

5. In the fifth, sixth, and seventh slides, the speaker develops the fourth main point of the speech by describing how tornadoes are rated, explaining the size of the average tornado, and offering dramatic examples of tornado damage.

6. In the eighth and ninth slides, the speaker develops the fifth main point of the speech by summarizing where and when tornadoes are likely to occur and the kind of people who track them. In your opinion, are these slides too wordy? What should the speaker do to enhance receiver involvement in this phase of the speech?

7. The tenth and eleventh slides focus on the speaker's last main point— what receivers can do to protect themselves from tornadoes.

9. **Who Chases Tornadoes?**

■ People who work for the National Weather Service
■ Tourists
■ A travel agency in Amarillo, Texas, plans two-week tours every summer for amateur tornado chasers.

10. **Protection from Tornadoes**

■ Listen to weather reports.
■ Get inside a building away from glass.
■ Basements are the safest places.

11. **AVOID!**

■ TRAILER HOMES
■ OVERPASSES ON THE HIGHWAY
■ TRYING TO CHASE A TORNADO

12. **WHIRLWINDS**

DON'T LET THEM CAUSE TURBULENCE IN YOUR LIFE!

8. The final slide wraps up the speech by supporting the speaker's concluding words. It also provides a sense of closure by reflecting the first slide the speaker used in the presentation. In your opinion, did the speaker need to use a slide prior to this one, summarizing what the speech had accomplished? If so, what should that slide have contained?

9. Are there any other slides you think the speaker should have added to this presentation, or are there any that you feel the speaker could have done without?

10. How many slides did the speaker use that you believe contain too many words or bullets? Shorten these slides to make them more effective.

Ethics & Communication

Diversity and the Visual

The following commentary on the retouching of a visual for a university's recruiting brochure appeared in *The Record*. Explain the extent to which you agree or disagree with the position taken by the article's author.

A University's Awkward Effort to Do Better

The University of Wisconsin found itself embroiled in controversy last week when graphic artists used computer technology to alter a photo in an attempt to make the school appear racially diverse.

The photo—used on the cover of the 2000 undergraduate application form—features a crowd of white football fans. An image of a black student was digitally inserted into that scene, creating the impression that he was also in the stands at that 1993 Badgers game.

Moral watchdogs took umbrage at this manipulation of history.

"They cheated!" shouted one newspaper headline this week. "A lie is a lie" clucked a Chicago Tribune *editorial Friday. "Tsk, tsk," fumed one radio commentator, who wondered whether the university's research could be trusted and used the gaffe as yet another example of how society has lost its way.*

Spare me the hand-wringing. The university may be guilty of clumsiness, but moral bankruptcy? Not even close.

The flap made me realize how far we've come since I was a features editor at the Gary Post-Tribune *in the mid-1980s. Before my arrival, it was standard practice to replace the city wedding announcements with pictures of white couples for suburban zones because "people who live outside of Gary don't want to see black faces." All that color, an editor thought, might scare off white advertisers.*

I wonder whether those editors, stripping and sanitizing the paper because "it's good business," could have envisioned a world so dramatically changed that future editors would add minorities instead of hiding them?

To me, the inevitable backlash about academic integrity is much ado about nothing. Just as a newsroom has different standards than the advertising department, a university uses a different measure for a promotional brochure than for a medical journal. For starters, if this controversy were really about journalistic accuracy, the university wouldn't be using an image from seven years ago—but nobody is complaining about that.

Flip through any college recruiting material (or corporate report, for that matter) and you will see a black, a white, and an Asian together—preferably in autumn, when the campus is dappled in sunlight. No one sports a Mohawk, tattoo, or triple piercing. Every dorm room is worthy of Martha Stewart, and

TECHNOLOGY AND SPEECH RESEARCH: THE DANGERS OF INFORMATION OVERLOAD AND THE ETHICS OF VISUAL MANIPULATION

How much information is too much information? How do we avoid being overwhelmed with information or overwhelming others with information? What steps can we take to minimize the effects of information overload or "data smog"?[32]

The temptation the Internet creates to keep piling on more and more information is something we have to watch out for. According to David Shenk, author of *Data Smog: Surviving the Information Glut,* "With a majority of American workers now paid to churn out data, we have generated a morass of expert information that has started to undermine logical approaches to deliberation and problem solving."[33] For example, more than 100,000 studies have been done on depression. What this produces is an overabundance of information

cafeteria food is just one star short of the Michelin guide.

Anyone who thinks that recruiting publications are not carefully staged is naive, said Alan Cubbage, vice president of university relations at Northwestern University: "High school juniors understand that they are being marketed to . . . . This is about an institution wanting to put its best face forward."

It was a sentiment echoed throughout the Big Ten. Other calls to administrators revealed that they manipulate images, too, whether it's zapping a trash bin out of a landscape or showcasing a female professor at the front of a crowded lecture hall.

"We all struggle with striking the right balance," Cubbage conceded. "It is important to show diversity to convey that this is a place that is welcoming and inclusive, but if you do, you are accused of a setup, of tokenism."

Clearly, Wisconsin was more interested in projecting its hopes for the future than documenting the present. The 40,000-member student body is 10 percent minority but only 2 percent African-American, lagging behind other Big Ten schools. (Michigan leads the pack with 8 percent, followed by Illinois and Northwestern at 7 percent).

Is it unethical? Wisconsin's graphic manipulation is different than if it ha been done by, say, the University of Vermont, which has no black students at all, according to one college guide. And its motive is certainly different than the thinking behind Time magazine's digital darkening of the image of O.J. Simpson on its cover, which made him appear more ominous and sinister.

To me, the most troubling result of Wisconsin's tweaking is that the "doctored" student, senior Diallo Shabazz, will now know that whatever else he accomplished in his four years at Madison, he was most prized for his pigmentation.

The university has apologized to Shabazz and recalled the brochures. Even without that mea culpa, though, I was willing to cut the Badgers some slack—unlike the mail-order retailer that delivered a jacket that looked nothing like the one in the catalog or the frozen-foods company that sold me a lasagna that bore no resemblance to what was in the box.

The goal here is so much loftier than merely boosting sales and pleasing stockholders. It's about an institution, and a society, aspiring to be better than they were before. Along the way, there are bound to be missteps. But considering that, not so long ago, rows of beaming black brides were perceived as a threat, this digital dust-up is a small price to pay for progress.

Source: Bonnie Miller Rubin. "What's Wrong with This Picture?" September 24, 2000, 1C. Copyright 2000 Chicago Tribune. Reprinted with permission.

Thinking Critically

What do the experts think? Is nuclear power safe or unsafe? Does affirmative action work or not? Do vitamins prevent cancer? Using one of the preceding controversial issues or another of your choice, surf the Internet in search of studies and arguments on both sides of the question. Does your search lead you to agree or disagree with The New York Times, *which noted that the "volleys of data" result in endless argumentation but no decision? Explain.*

How can the public speaker solve such a dilemma?

and so many competing expert opinions that it becomes virtually impossible to draw a conclusion, which leads one to suffer the consequences of "paralysis by analysis."

When it comes to deception, computer graphics now make it possible for us to distort actual images. Unethical speakers can manipulate what receivers see by altering their visuals to conform to the point they are seeking to make. For example, because it was seeking an image of diversity in its recruitment literature, the University of Wisconsin at Madison admits to making an "error in judgement" when it doctored a photo on a brochure cover by inserting a Black student in a crowd of White football fans.[34] Because presenters now have the technological ability to doctor their visuals to make their points, the question that cries to be answered is the following: At what point does the touching up or retouching of a visual put you onto ethical thin ice? Just because a visual you have doctored works does not mean it is ethical to use that visual.

IMPROVING YOUR ABILITY TO SUPPORT YOUR IDEAS

A speech devoid of support is like a skeleton; the structure is there, but the flesh is missing. By developing an understanding of the way support functions to flesh out ideas, you increase your chances of becoming a proficient speaker. Speakers who are adept at finding and using support realize the following:

1. *Support rarely, if ever, surfaces on its own.* You need to search for it by examining yourself, other people, and published materials.

2. *For ideas to affect listeners, the audience's imagination must be stirred.* Supportive devices can serve this function. Definitions, statistics, examples and illustrations, testimonials, comparison and contrast, and repetition and restatement can all be used to make spoken words more understandable and more believable, as well as to give them greater impact.

3. *Audio and visual aids can also be used to enhance the effectiveness of a presentation.* If appropriately designed and integrated, they will increase listeners' comprehension, retention, and motivation.

Focus on Service Learning

Using information contained in your text and in Web sites such as http://marketingtoday. com/presentations/why_a_ speech.htm, work with a community group such as Big Brothers Big Sisters or Habitat for Humanity to create a visually effective presentation designed to help the group raise funds. Be sure to learn as much as possible about your chosen group before beginning your work.

IMPROVING YOUR ABILITY TO EVALUATE SUPPORTING MATERIALS

How credible is the support you include in your speech? The following supporting material analysis system is a tool you can use to test the effectiveness of the information/evidence you use to build your speech. Simply ask yourself each of the following questions about the materials you incorporate:

1. How recent is the information/evidence?
2. How accurate is the information/evidence?
3. How reliable is the information/evidence?
4. How sufficient is the information/evidence?
5. How appropriate is the information/evidence?

To assess recency, ask yourself when the information/evidence was written or produced. While some topics require you to locate very recent sources, others are not time-based and allow for more flexibility.

Ask the following questions to assess accuracy: Do other sources contain similar data? Does the source of this information provide specific information, or does he or she make unsupported claims?

When assessing reliability, determine if the information cited appeared in a major book, newspaper or news show, magazine, or Web site. If, for example, the source is a Web site, determine who is responsible for information that appears on that site. Your goal is to determine if the site's administrators or founders are biased or unbiased, supportive of particular social or political agendas or neutral.

When assessing the sufficiency of your information, determine whether or not you have enough data to support the point(s) you are making.

Finally, when assessing appropriateness, evaluate whether the information you offer is supportive of your topic and used in good taste.

Revisiting Chapter Objectives

1. **Identify and use the various online and offline research resources available to you.** The first step in the development stage of preparing a speech is to gather a variety of effective research materials to integrate into your presentation. The materials you gather may come from online or offline sources. For example, when working offline, you may consult published works, including books, journals, magazines, and newspapers available in the library. When working online, you have the Internet and its many resources, including e-mail, listservs, newsgroups, and the World Wide Web at your disposal.

2. **Conduct an informal survey and a personal interview.** In addition to online and offline resources, you may be able to draw on your personal observations and experiences. You can, for example, conduct informal surveys and/or personal interviews. Informal surveys consist of approximately 5 to 10 questions that you ask people affected by or familiar with your topic. Interviews are similar

The Wrap Up

to surveys except that they are more detailed and assume that the persons whom you interview are experts on your topic.

3. **Identify various types of supporting material, including definitions, statistics, examples, illustrations, and testimonials.** You can make your research interesting and understandable to audience members by using a variety of verbal support: definitions (an explanation of what a word or concept means), statistics (facts expressed in numerical form), examples (representative cases), illustrations (stories and narrative pictures), and testimonials (someone else's opinions or conclusions; quotations).

4. **Use comparison and contrast, repetition and restatement.** You can also increase the impact and memorability of your speech by using comparisons that express similarities and contrasts that express differences, as well as repetition (the same words repeated verbatim) and restatement (the same idea in different words).

5. **Explain how visual and audio aids can enhance a presentation.** Many speeches can be enhanced with visual and audio support. Objects, models, graphs, photographs, drawings, slides, videotapes, and audiotapes can be incorporated into the presentation to reinforce, clarify, and dramatize concepts. Computer graphics programs are now making professional-looking graphics available even to student speakers.

Resources for Further Inquiry and Reflection

To apply your understanding of how the principles in Chapter 14 are at work in our daily lives, consult the following resources for further inquiry and reflection. Or, if you prefer, choose any other appropriate resource. Then connect the ideas expressed in your chosen selection with the communication concepts and issues you are learning about both in and out of class.

Listen to Me

"Fight," "Have You Seen Me?" and "The Morality Squad" from *Live from Antarctica* (GWAR)
"Stupid Girls" (Pink)
"Scenes from an Italian Restaurant" (Billy Joel)

What topics are explored in the music of GWAR, Pink, and/or Billy Joel? For example, how does the explicitness and threatening nature of the band's rhetoric affect you? What meanings do receivers derive from the violent language and profane imagery contained in GWAR's songs? What means of support are used to target the central negative force in the band's message? How does Pink support her premise of "stupid girls"? What organizational pattern does Billy Joel use to convey the nature of the relationship between Brenda and Eddie?

View Me

Other People's Money
The Net
Syriana

What means of support does Danny DeVito's, Sandra Bullock's, or George Clooney's character use to make his or her case?

Read Me

David Slayden and Rita Kirk Whellock, eds. *Soundbite Culture: The Death of Discourse in a Wired World*. Thousand Oaks, CA: Sage, 1999.

James Risen. *State of War*. New York: Free Press, 2006.

Peggy Noonan. *We Will Prevail*. New York: National Review, 2003.

What do the insights provided by the author(s) of any chapter in these books reveal about the state of reasoned discourse and use of evidence in our society?

 Tell Me

Share with the class the insights you gained from your chosen Listen to Me, View Me, or Read Me selection.

Imagine that you have started late on preparing a speech on the topic of affirmative action. Because time is of the essence, you ask a friend if you can borrow a research paper that your friend wrote on the same subject. You reason that it probably contains the kind of research you would find if you only had the time to investigate the topic yourself. Explain why you would or would not use the paper your friend provides. Also indicate, if you decide to use it, whether you consider your use of your friend's paper to be plagiarism.

Key Chapter Terminology

Use the Communication Works CD-ROM and the Online Learning Center at www.mhhe.com/gamble9 to further your knowledge of the following terminology.

bar graph 411

Boolean search 400

definitions 405

examples 406

illustrations 406

line graphs 412

listserv 402

pictographs 412

pie, or circle, graph 410

statistics 406

testimony 407

Communication
Works

online learning center

www.mhhe.com/gamble9

Idioms in Translation

being drawn into—being fascinated by or interested in

blown call—wrong call

driving blind—being without direction

flesh out—develop

leave no stone unturned—thoroughly research

piling on—adding

snapshot of persons—quickview of persons

touching—affecting

Test Your Understanding

Go to the *Self Quizzes* on the Communication Works CD-ROM and the book's Online Learning Center at www.mhhe.com/gamble9

Communication
Works

online learning center

www.mhhe.com/gamble9

Notes

1. See Ted Spencer. "The Internet Comes of Age for 1997." *Spectra*, January, 1997, p. 5.

2. Randy Reddict and Elliot King. *The OnLine Student*. Fort Worth, TX: Harcourt Brace College, 1996, p. 3. Information on conducting research, pp. 161–179, is particularly valuable.

3. Jeffrey Graham. "Thrill of Hunt Lures Google Competitors." *USA Today*, May 13, 2002, p. 4D.

4. For a more comprehensive treatment of supporting materials, see Teri Gamble and Michael Gamble. *Public Speaking in the Age of Diversity*, 2nd ed. Boston: Allyn & Bacon, 1998, chaps. 7 and 8.

5. See Jack Selzer, *Argument in America: Essential Issues, Essential Texts*. Boston: Longman, 2004.

6. Megan Solan. "Serving Those Who Serve." *Winning Orations 2004*. Mankato MN: Interstate Oratorical Association, 2005.

7. Solan.

8. Chandra Palubiak. "To Tattoo or Not to Tattoo." *Winning Orations*. Mankato: MN: Interstate Oratorical Association, 2002, pp. 11–13.

9. Ann Marie Ursini. "Subtitle Nation." *Winning Orations 2004*. Mankato MN: Interstate Oratorical Association, 2005.

10. For a discussion of the power of examples in public speaking, see Gamble and Gamble; and Scott Consigny. "The Rhetorical Example." *Southern Speech Communication Journal* 41, 1976, pp. 121–134.

11. Solomon D. Trujillo. "Two Lives: The One We Make Defines Our Legacy." *Vital Speeches of the Day* 66:6, January 1, 2000, p. 169. Reprinted with permission.

12. Tony Martinet. "Parents: Poor Losers." *Winning Orations*. Mankato, MN: Interstate Oratorical Association, 2002, pp. 77–79. Reprinted with permission.

13. Stacy Champagne. "The Patriot Act—Enduring Freedom?" *Winning Orations*, Mankato: MN: Interstate Oratorical Association, 2002, pp. 29–31. Reprinted with permission.

14. Theresa McGuiness. "Greeks in Crisis." *Winning Orations*. Mankato, MN: Interstate Oratorical Association, 2000, p. 75. Reprinted with permission.

15. William L. Laurence. "Eyewitness Account: Atomic Bomb Mission over Nagasaki," *The New York Times*, Sept. 9, 1945.

16. William D. Novelli. "Wrestling the Octopus." *Vital Speeches of the Day*, October 1, 2005, p. 745.

17. The power of repetition and restatement is stressed in most books on public speaking, including Gamble and Gamble.

18. "I Have a Dream" by Martin Luther King, Jr. Reprinted by arrangement with the Estate of Martin Luther King, Jr., c/o Writers House as agent for the proprietor, New York, NY. Copyright © 1963 Dr. Martin Luther King, Jr., copyright renewed 1991 Coretta Scott King.

19. V. Johnson. "Picture-Perfect Presentations." *Training and Development Journal* 1989, pp. 43, 45.

20. C. Wilder. *The Presentation Kit*. New York: Wiley, 1990.

21. "Romance on the Web." *Newsweek*, May 12, 2003, p. E20.

22. See "Addicted to Cellphones." *The Record*, January 27, 2004, p. L14.

23. *The Wall Street Journal*, January 26, 2004, p. B1.

24. Sharon Begley and Gautam Naik. "The Science of Tsunamis." *The Wall Street Journal*, December 27, 2005, pp. B1, B4.

25. *Discover*. June 2003, pp. 42–47.

26. W. I. Ringle and W. D. Thompson. *TechEdge: Using Computers to Present and Persuade*. Needham Heights, MA: Allyn & Bacon, 1998.

27. L. Zuckerman. "Words Go Right to the Brain, But Can They Stir the Heart?" *New York Times*, April 17, 1999, pp. A-17–A19.

28. Greg Jaffe. "What's Your Point, Lieutenant? Just Cut to the Pie Charts." *The Wall Street Journal*, April 26, 2000, pp. A1, A6.

29. June Kronholz. "PowerPoint Goes to School." *The Wall Street Journal*, November 12, 2002, pp. B1, B6.

30. Jan Parker. "Absolute PowerPoint." *New Yorker*, May 28, 2001, pp. 76–87.

31. Parker.

32. See David Shenk. *Data Smog: Surviving the Information Glut*. San Francisco: Harper Edge, 1997.

33. Shenk, p. 93.

34. "College Faked Photo in Pitch for Diversity." *The Record*, September 21, 2000, p. A-13.

CHAPTER 15

Designing Your Speech: Organizing Your Ideas

After finishing this chapter, you should be able to

1. Identify main and subordinate ideas.

2. Create a full sentence outline.

3. Identify five methods of ordering ideas.

4. Use internal summaries and transitions effectively.

5. Develop an effective introduction and conclusion.

6. Use a tryout to refine a speech.

*Every speech ought to be put together like a living creature, with a body
of its own, so as to be neither without head nor without feet, but to
have both a middle and extremities, described proportionately to each
other and to the whole.*

—Plato

Tell me to what you pay attention and I will tell you who you are.

—José Ortega y Gasset

Our lives are so busy and cluttered that many of us obsess about the need for order.[1]
We hire closet experts to organize our closets. We use handheld computers, more
commonly known as personal digital assistants (PDAs), to organize our day. Organization is important to the speaker as well. You can have the best ideas in the world
and the most impressive and eye-opening support, but if you are unable to organize your ideas and integrate your support so that the audience can follow what you
are trying to communicate, you might as well not speak at all. Organization is one
of the main challenges you will face as a speech maker. It is the second step in
the topic development stage of preparing a speech.

What is your goal when you are organizing ideas? Primarily, you want to order
your materials so that you facilitate communication with your audience. How can
you accomplish this? You must plan. Just as an architect develops a plan for a
building, so you must develop a plan for your speech. Your plan shows the structure you will adhere to—the developmental sequence you think will work best. Of
course, just as an architect considers numerous designs before selecting one, you
should test potential patterns to determine which one will best clarify and amplify
your ideas. Fortunately, you do not have to grope your way through a thicket of
possibilities. Communication theorists have developed guidelines to help you with
this phase.

■ ■ ■

BUILDING THE OUTLINE: A SPEECH FRAMEWORK FOR SUCCESS

An audience has to be able to follow your speech for it to be effective. Without
good organization, a speech's message remains fuzzy and hard to follow. Since
receivers rarely interrupt speakers during a speech to seek clarification, and because
they do not usually have access to transcripts or tapes of presentations, speakers
need to organize the ideas of their speeches so that receivers comprehend them
the first time they hear them. Receivers have no rewind button to push if they
become distracted or confused. Thus, speakers must structure their messages so
that confusion is kept to a minimum.[2]

FIGURE 15.1

Framework for a Speech.

| Introduction |
| Body |
| Conclusion |

Go to the Online Learning Center at www.mhhe.com/gamble9 and answer the questions in the *Self Inventory* to evaluate your understanding of speech outlining.

speech framework

a skeleton for speech development

As we saw in Chapter 7, not everyone is a skillful listener. For this reason, you should base your organization on the *principle of redundancy*. In other words, to ensure comprehension, you will need to build a certain amount of repetition into your speech. Only if this is done will listeners be able to follow your ideas easily. This basic developmental principle is often expressed as follows: *Tell them what you are going to tell them, then tell them, and finally, tell them what you have told them.*

One of the best ways to organize a speech is the introduction-body-conclusion format (see Figure 15.1), called a **speech framework** because it provides a frame, or skeleton, on which any speech or other formal presentation can be built.

Any speech you develop should be organized according to this framework. Your introductory remarks and your concluding statements should each take up approximately 10 to 15 percent of the total presentation. That leaves 70 to 80 percent of your time for developing the ideas contained in the body of your speech. Since the body will be the main portion of your presentation, it is often advisable to begin by preparing this part of the speech; once the body is set, you can move on to develop the introduction and the conclusion. Let's consider the three key parts of a speech in that order: body, introduction, and conclusion.

ORGANIZING THE BODY OF YOUR PRESENTATION

As you begin to outline the body of your speech, you will want to build a suitable structure onto which you can place your ideas. You develop this structure in stages. During the first stage of outline development, you create a *preliminary working outline*. This sparse outline has points containing one or two words that eventually will achieve fuller form in the second stage, the full sentence outline. You develop the *full sentence outline* only after you have researched and fully developed the ideas of your stage. Ultimately, during the third stage of outline preparation, you will transform your full sentence outline into an *extemporaneous outline, or speaker's notes*, that you will then use as your guide when you deliver your speech.

Outlining Principles: Identifying Main and Subordinate Ideas

Let's imagine that you have created the following working plan, or outline, for a speech about affirmative action:

I. Definition
II. Purposes
III. Outcomes
IV. Why under attack

Your next task is to develop those topics. As you begin the development process, keep in mind that your audience is unlikely to recall a long, wandering, unstructured collection of data. Thus, after you have conducted your research, you will need to develop a full sentence outline that distinguishes between your **main ideas**—your speech's subtopics that directly support your thesis—and your **subordinate ideas**—those ideas that function as support or amplification for your main ideas or subtopics.

In many ways, subordinate ideas are the foundation on which larger ideas are constructed (see Figure 15.2). Consequently, you should begin the organizational process by arranging your materials into clusters of main and subordinate ideas. As you do this, you will be able to determine which evidence supports the main ideas and which supports the subordinate ideas. Your main ideas will be, say, two to five major points that you want the audience to remember.

If you are developing a speech on affirmative action programs, you might begin as follows:

Purpose: To inform the audience about affirmative action

Behavioral objective: After listening to my speech, audience members will be able to define affirmative action, identify its uses and results, and explain why it is a policy under fire.

Thesis: The definition, uses, and results of affirmative action have contributed to its being a policy under fire. (See Figure 15.3.)

You are now off to a good start. Next, you need to develop these major points into complete sentences using parallel structure—that is, using sentences with similar or matching styles.

main ideas
the main points of a speech; the subtopics of a speech

subordinate ideas
ideas that amplify the main ideas or subtopics of a speech

FIGURE 15.2
Construction of an Idea.

FIGURE 15.3

Dividing a Thesis into Major Points.

I. Affirmative action can be defined as any action taken to ensure or affirm equal opportunity for oppressed or previously disadvantaged groups.

II. Affirmative action is used in hiring and college admissions decisions.

III. Affirmative action has benefits and drawbacks.

IV. Affirmative action is under fire for being reverse discrimination.

Many people find it helpful to pull together clusters of information that support their main ideas, as follows:

I. Main idea
   A. Subordinate idea
      1. Support for subordinate idea
      2. Support for subordinate idea
   B. Subordinate idea
      1. Support for subordinate idea
      2. Support for subordinate idea

When you take the time to prepare an easy-to-follow structure for your speech, in addition to enhancing receiver perceptions of your competence and adding to the personal credibility you have in their eyes, your efforts also help fulfill receiver expectations. That is, the main points of a speech alert receivers to listen for supporting information. Because they are not struggling to give order to a disordered array of information, they can focus instead on the thesis of your speech and the support you offer to build your presentation. Taking time to develop an outline has a third benefit, as well. Because you know what information you are using to support each main point of your speech, your delivery of the speech will be improved. Since your ideas are carefully laid out before you, instead of having to concentrate on what to say next, you free yourself to focus on establishing a good relationship with your receivers.

If you have taken notes on cards, you can lay out or pattern the body of your speech in the following way:

Purpose:
I. Main idea
   A. (Supports I)   B. (Supports I)
      1. (Supports A)   1. (Supports B)
      2. (Supports A)   2. (Supports B)
      3. (Supports A)
II. Main idea
   A. (Supports II)
   B. (Supports II)

Notice that the outline you develop indicates the relative importance of each item included in it. The main points—roman numerals I, II, III, and so on—are the most important items you want your audience to remember. Your subpoints—capital letters A, B, C, and so on—are supportive of but less important than the main points. Likewise, items beginning with arabic numerals 1, 2, 3, and so on are supportive of but less important than subpoints. Remember to line up the entries in your outline correctly. Locate the main ideas closest to the left margin. The subpoints underlying the main points should begin directly underneath the first letter of the first word of each main point. Keep in mind that a traditional rule of outlining is that at least two subpoints must support every main point.

Items that support the subpoints begin directly underneath the first letter of the first word of each subpoint. Indicate the supporting materials for these with lowercase letters (a, b, c, and so on). In this way, the full sentence outline functions as a visual representation of the supportive underpinnings for ideas. In general, there should be at least a 3 to 1 ratio between the number of words in your speech and the number of words in your outline.

An outline on avian flu, using the symbols and indentions just discussed, might be built as follows:

Purpose: To inform audience members about the fears and questions
concerning the H5N1 avian flu (bird flu)

I. Several fears about H5N1 avian flu are prevalent in society today.
II. Many questions remain regarding future efforts to protect against a pandemic strain of avian flu.

Looking at this example, we have in plain sight the central features of what will become a speech. Because the speaker identifies two aspects of the subject, there will be two main points in the speech. It is important for the ordering of main points to flow logically if receivers are going to be able to follow the presentation easily. In this speech, to guide the receiver in processing the speech, the speaker chose to first confront existing fears about the avian flu, and then to discuss the questions revolving around the disease's control and potential treatment should it develop into a pandemic. Here is how the speaker developed the speech's main points:

I. Several fears concerning the H5N1 avian flu are prevalent in society today.
   A. Many people fear that H5N1 avian flu is the next pandemic.
      1. Cases of human infection of H5N1 avian flu have been reported in a number of countries, including China, Cambodia, Turkey, and Iraq, among people who handled infected birds.
      2. There is concern that the H5N1 avian flu virus will mutate spontaneously, giving it greater ability to jump from human to human.
      3. There is concern that travel, especially by air, will accelerate transmission of the disease around the world.
   B. Currently, chances of contracting H5N1 avian flu are small for people who do not have intimate contact with birds.
      1. Not a single bird in the United States has been found to suffer from avian influenza.
      2. Casual contact with birds will not spread flu because of the species barrier.

II. Many questions remain regarding future efforts to protect against a pandemic strain of avian flu.

    A. Developing a vaccine to attack a pandemic avian flu virus is problematic.

        1. Whether Tamiflu and Relenza will be effective against the pandemic version of the avian flu virus is unclear.

        2. Because scientists do not know what the pandemic flu virus will look like, a vaccine cannot yet be made.

        3. Scientists hope that the H5N1 vaccines now in trials will provide at least some protection in a pandemic.

    B. Improving international cooperation is critical.

        1. We need to increase awareness of the threat.

        2. We need to improve surveillance and diagnosis of the disease in birds.

    C. Biosecurity is key.

        1. The president signed an executive order adding pandemic influenza to the list of quarantinable diseases.

        2. The N95 mask provides aerosolization protection from the droplets that spread the virus.

        3. Discouraging personal stockpiling, the government is calling for the maintenance of national and regional supplies.

Giving Order to Your Ideas Using Traditional and Nontraditional Formats

Do you prefer listening to speeches that are organized using traditional or nontraditional formats? Why?

Speeches have either a linear or a nonlinear format. Western cultures favor a linear organization, while non-Western cultures favor organizational nonlinear formats. As Richard Nisbett notes, there appears to be a geography of thought when it comes to both the development of a worldview and the frameworks of thinking that support it.[3] In his book *The Geography of Thought: How Asians and Westerners Think Differently . . . and Why,* Nisbett notes that human cognition and reasoning preferences differ, depending on whether you were brought up in a Western or an Eastern culture. According to Nisbett, East Asians are more holistic and contextual in their perceptions, while Westerners have more of a tunnel-vision perceptual style that depends more on identifying with what is prominent in a situation and remembering it. Persons from Eastern cultures tend to tolerate subtleties and deal in relationships (the stress is placed on intuitive thinking and informal logic, not the use of categories—for example, the practice of feng shui is not atomistic but extraordinarily complex). On the other hand, persons from Western cultures tend to be analytic, prefer absolutes, and deal in categories (the stress is placed on categorization and rational, logical thinking—for example, delivering a speech entitled "Six Ways to Increase Your Self-Esteem"). East Asian persons start out by focusing on the context, not zeroing in on an object of interest. Westerners begin by focusing on a central object.

These preferences affect how persons from Eastern and Western cultures prefer to organize their ideas. According to Nisbett, in the West, we start out with a general statement and give suggested solutions. We present the evidence in favor of our position. We argue against the reasons that others might not accept the position we have taken. We summarize and offer a conclusion. In the East, they do not do it this way. Instead, they cycle back into the same topic from different directions.[4] Nisbett suggests that the following example—offered by an English professor, which focuses on writing but could equally focus on public speaking— reveals this difference in methodology:

> I was surprised when one of my students who had been a teacher in China before coming here told me that she didn't understand the requirements of essay structure. I told her to write a thesis statement and then prove its three points in the following paragraphs. She told me if she wrote this way in China she would be considered stupid. "In China," she said, "essays were written in a more circular fashion moving associated ideas closer and closer to the center."[5]

While we need to be cautious about overgeneralizing, especially since persons from one culture who spend time in another culture tend to tune their thinking style into the culture in which they are interacting, we will see these differences surface as we explore both linear and nonlinear organizational formats. You need to order the ideas in your speech in a way that will make sense to your audience.

TRADITIONAL ORGANIZATIONAL FORMATS

Traditional organizational formats display a linear logic and are typical of the prototypes many North American speakers use to make sense of information. A speech has a linear organization if its main points develop and relate directly to the thesis or topic sentence that comes early in the presentation. We will look at five traditional approaches to ordering material: (1) chronological, or time, order; (2) spatial order; (3) cause-and-effect order; (4) problem-and-solution order; and (5) topical order. Before doing this, let us examine some pointers to keep in mind when drafting an outline for any of these traditional approaches.

Tips for Drafting the Body of the Outline The body is the part of the speech that develops and explains the key ideas you have gathered in support of your topic or thesis. Your first task in drafting an outline is to identify potential main points for use in your speech. Once you have done this, you need to select the main ideas (usually between two and five) that are most important to the success of your presentation; the ideas you select are the ones you believe will be most useful to you in fulfilling your primary purpose for speaking.

Each main point in the outline you develop should be a sentence that summarizes your supporting material. Main points should be similarly constructed. They should exhibit parallel structure. For example, if your first main point uses a subject and verb construction, so should each of your other main points. Main points should also contain vivid and descriptive language designed to interest receivers. For example, the following set of main ideas does not contain parallel structure or effective use of language:

> Few breeds of dogs are as intelligent as poodles.
> Poodles like to explore their environment.
> Have one, and you'll find that these dogs like human contact.

In contrast, the sentences in the next set have parallel structure and make better use of descriptive language:

Poodles are one of the most intelligent breeds of dogs.

Poodles are naturally curious and creative as they explore their environment.

Poodles make wonderful pets because they thrive on human contact.

chronological, or time, order

an organizational format that develops an idea using a time order

Chronological Order   **Chronological, or time, order** involves developing an idea or a problem in the order it occurs or occurred in time.

One student, for example, used chronological order to describe the events that resulted in the elephant's becoming an endangered species:

Purpose: To explain why the elephant is becoming an endangered species

I. Until the early 1900s, elephants had little reason to fear people.
II. During the 1920s, elephants were slaughtered as the demand for ivory products increased in the United States and Europe.
III. Within the past 20 years, products made from ivory have also come to be prized in the Far East.

As you can see, this student has considered the steps leading to the present situation in the order they occurred. In addition, each main point the speaker used covers a particular time period. Since the main points describe a sequence of happenings, they help the audience keep track of where the speaker is in time.

Another student used chronological order for a speech on the insanity defense:

Purpose: To examine the history of the insanity defense in criminal jurisprudence

I. In the seventeenth and eighteenth centuries, belief in witchcraft influenced popular legal conceptions of mental disorder.
II. The nineteenth-century showcase for the insanity defense was the trial of Daniel M'Naghten, a political assassin.
III. Not until 1954 did the courts begin to acknowledge that a wide variety of diseases or defects may impair the mind.
IV. As we begin the twenty-first century, the legacy of the Jeffrey Dahmer case again raises questions regarding our attitude toward crime, punishment, and personal responsibility.

Think of three topics you could develop using chronological order. Why do they lend themselves to that arrangement?

Any event that has occurred in time can be examined chronologically. With a time-ordered presentation, it is up to you to decide where to begin and end your chronology and what events to include. As you might expect, time order is used most often in informative speeches.

spatial order

an organizational format that describes an object, a person, or a phenomenon as it exists in space

Spatial Order   **Spatial order** describes an object, a person, or a phenomenon as it exists in space. An object, for example, might be described from

top to bottom.

bottom to top.

left to right.

right to left.

inside to outside.

outside to inside.

With spatial order, you must select one orientation and carry it through.

One student used spatial order to explain the appearance and functioning of a beehive:

I. Outside the hive

II. Inside the hive

Another student used a spatial pattern to discuss the different kinds of natural disasters that plague different sections of the United States:

I. States along the East Coast of the United States are hurricane-prone.

II. States in the central region of the United States are tornado-prone.

III. States along the West Coast of the United States are earthquake-prone.

Like chronological order, spatial order is used most frequently in informative speeches.

Visuals can be used effectively to reinforce information contained in a spatially ordered presentation—whether you intend to discuss the components of a computer, the terrain of a national park, the design of a new car, or the floor plan of a presidential library. Using spatial order involves organizing your ideas according to an area concept, which should be reflected in the main points of the outline.

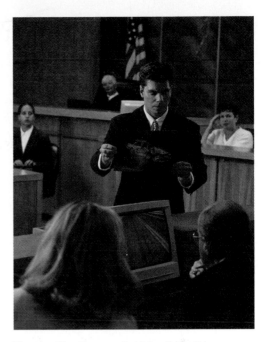

Visuals, like the one held by this attorney, reinforce presented information—would you find this visual effective if you were on the jury?

How could you use spatial order to describe yourself? (For practice, try it.)

Cause-and-Effect Order Cause-and-effect order requires you to categorize your material into things related to the causes of a problem and things related to its effects. It is then up to you to decide which aspect you will explore first. Thus, in a speech on drunk driving, you might begin by discussing the percentage of drivers during a certain period who were drunk when involved in car accidents (cause). You might then discuss the number of deaths each year that are attributed directly to drunk driving (effect).

cause-and-effect order

an organizational format that categorizes a topic according to its causes and effects

Skill Builder

Speaker's Choice

1. Find a rock, a shell, a piece of driftwood, or some other natural object.

2. Describe the object to a partner, a group of students, or the entire class, using spatial order.

3. Explain why your spatial ordering took the form it did.

4. Would approaching the object from a different angle have altered your audience's understanding and appreciation? How?

Ethics & Communication

Sound Bites

Are sound bites—public presentations of positions that usually last no more than 90 seconds—an effective way of informing the electorate? Why or why not?

How organized must a speaker be to present ideas or urge action in this manner? What organizational format do you believe lends itself best to this type of presentation? Is 90 seconds or less enough time to deliver a message designed not just to inform but also to influence? Explain your position.

"Hey, do you want to be on the news tonight or not? This is a sound bite, not the Gettysburg Address. Just say what you have to say, Senator, and get the hell off."

You can vary this approach by discussing the effect before the cause. In the following example, a student used effect-and-cause order to reveal the causes of excessive stress among students:

I. The number of students suffering from stress-related ailments is increasing at an alarming rate.

II. Experts on such ailments have identified four major explanations for this increase.

Cause-and-effect order and effect-and-cause order are quite versatile. They are used in both informative and persuasive speeches.

Problem-and-Solution Order Problem-and-solution order requires you to (1) determine what problems are inherent in a situation and (2) present a solution to remedy them. Thus, you might discuss the problems that develop when many students entering college are deficient in writing skills. The second portion of your speech can then suggest a number of ways the identified problem might be alleviated (perhaps, for example, by expanding tutoring programs or offering noncredit remedial courses).

One student used problem-and-solution order to argue that her state should drop the legal definition of intoxication to a blood alcohol level of 0.08:

I. The problems caused by intoxicated teenagers are increasing.

II. Lowering the legal definition of intoxication to a 0.08 blood alcohol level will do much to alleviate the situation.

When using a problem-and-solution format, you may discuss the advantages of the solution as well. In that case, the body of the speech would include three main points:

I. The problem

II. The solution

III. The advantages of adopting the solution

The following example demonstrates how to develop the problem-and-solution format.

Purpose: To convince my audience that we should act now to revise the way we report poverty statistics

Thesis: We should act now to solve the problem caused by the way we currently report poverty statistics.

I. The poverty level is currently understated to keep people off welfare rolls.
   A. Poverty levels for families of four are absurdly low.
   B. Poverty levels for single-parent families are even more outrageous.

II. Minimally acceptable income levels must be raised.
   A. Government levels must be raised for families.
   B. Additional help must be given for single parents.

III. These increases will solve some of the problems of the poor.
   A. They will make life easier for families.
   B. Additional aid to single parents will help them help themselves and their children.

How could you use cause-and-effect order to explain a recent disagreement you had with an instructor, an employer, a friend, or a family member?

problem-and-solution order
an organizational format that identifies the problems inherent in a situation and presents a solution to remedy them

Problem-and-solution order is most frequently employed in persuasive speeches.

Topical Order   At times, a speech may not fit neatly into any of the patterns previously described. When this happens, you may choose to develop or cluster your material by arranging it into a series of appropriate topics. This is **topical order.** Examples of topical order include the following categorical arrangements: advantages and disadvantages of a proposal; social, political, and economic factors that contribute to a problem; perceptions of upper-class, middle-class, and lower-class people on an issue. When you use topical order, you may find that you can intermingle cause-and-effect, time, problem-and-solution, or spatial order within the topical order.

A student used topical order to argue in favor of active euthanasia (mercy killing):

   I. Euthanasia is merciful.
   II. Euthanasia is death with dignity.

Because of its wide applicability, topical order is used very frequently.

Support All Main Points   While each example in the previous sections contained only main points, in a developed outline, each of these points should be supported by information, including examples, definitions, and visual aids, that pertain to the subject in the main point they support and enable the audience to understand why the main point is true. Usually, two to four subpoints are offered in support of a main point.

NONTRADITIONAL FORMATS

In developing an outline, you can use a number of organizational patterns in place of a linear framework. You should use one of the nontraditional patterns discussed in this section if you believe the cultures and dispositions of the persons in your audience warrant it. While a number of us prefer to use **linear logic** to develop our ideas, others of us—including some persons from Native American, Asian-American, or Latino cultures—do not. As we deduce from the preceding prototypes, linear logic develops ideas step-by-step, relying on facts and data to support each main point. In contrast to formats that depend on linear logic are formats that are more indirect and less explicit in offering hard evidence and proof in defense of a point. These patterns are called **configural formats.**

Instead of previewing, spelling out, and discussing each key point, one at a time, persons who prefer configural thinking approach their subject from a variety of perspectives and rely on examples and stories to carry the crux of their message; they also rely on receivers to understand the messages implied by the examples and stories used. Because they believe the explicit stating of a message is unnecessary, speakers who use a configural style do not bluntly tell receivers their conclusion or call on them to make a specific response; instead of ensuring that the conclusion is obvious to receivers, the speakers lead them to their conclusion indirectly and by implication. Thus, configural frameworks require receivers to do more work.

While persons in cultures who favor the use of configural patterns might not categorize them in this way, Westerners do identify three kinds of configural systems of organization. First is the *deferred-thesis pattern,* in which the main points of a speech gradually build to the speaker's thesis, which he or she does not indicate until the speech is nearly over. Second is the *web pattern,* in which threads of thought refer back to the speaker's central purpose; while to Western ears the

topical order

an organizational format that clusters material by dividing it into a series of appropriate topics

For practice, for each of the main points in the preceding examples, conduct research in an effort to identify two to four subpoints to support each main point.

linear logic

the step-by-step development of ideas; the reliance on facts and data to support main points

configural formats

organizational patterns that are indirect and inexplicit

Can you think of speech topics that lend themselves to these kinds of configural systems of organization?

speaker may seem to be "off topic" at points, to receivers in other cultures the tangents the speaker explores are connected to the speaker's topic and make it more meaningful. Third is the *narrative pattern*, in which the speaker tells a story without stating a thesis or developing it with main points. When using this pattern, the speaker may only "discover" the main point via a series of illustrations and parables.

The following speech outline is organized configurally. As such, it requires the audience to participate more actively in interpreting what the speaker implies.

> *Purpose:* To persuade my audience that E. coli presents problems for our food supply
>
>   I. A hypothetical food worker, Jake, who is employed in a meat-packing plant, inadvertently infects the plant's meat supply with E. coli.
> II. Jake's carelessness contributes to the infection of a number of persons in an array of cities across the United States.
> III. The plant is closed because of E. coli contamination.
> IV. Today, members of the families of those who were sickened by E. coli ask the federal government, "How can our food supply be made safe?"

As the speaker embellishes each of the ideas identified in the outline during his or her presentation, it is up to the receivers to interpret the meaning of the speaker's narrative from the stories, examples, and testimony offered. The speaker will not state directly what receivers should think or do but will rely on them to draw their own conclusions and come up with their own solutions.

You'll recall from Chapter 2 that members of low-context cultures, such as the United States, are usually more direct in how they convey information to others than are members of high-context cultures, such as Latin America, Japan, and Saudi Arabia. To low-context receivers, the speaker from a high-context culture may come off as vague or deceptive because of his or her reluctance to be direct, explicit, or obvious. In contrast, high-context receivers prefer to receive information through examples, illustrations, and other indirect means of expression.[6]

Should speakers match the organizational format they use to the preferred perceptual system of the receivers?

Connecting Your Ideas: Internal Summaries and Transitions

To transmit your ideas to an audience with clarity and fluidity using linear logic, you will need to use internal summaries and transitions to move from one idea to the next.

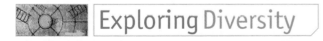

Exploring Diversity

Is Paying Attention Cultural?

Edward T. Hall suggests that "culture . . . designates what we pay attention to and what we ignore." If this is so, how can speakers ensure that audience members who belong to other cultural groups will pay attention to the right things? In other words, how can speakers target crucial ideas and emphasized points? How can a speaker be sure that listeners are not paying attention to the wrong thing and screening out what they should be concentrating on?

Source: Edward T. Hall. *The Hidden Dimension.* New York: Doubleday, 1966.

internal summaries
rhetorical devices designed
to help listeners remember
content

transitions
connective words and
phrases

*While few in number,
transitions help the audience
follow a speech. Do you
consciously plan good
transitions?*

The body of a speech organized according to linear logic contains brief **internal summaries;** these are designed to help listeners remember the content. The following are examples: "Thus far we have examined two key housing problems. Let us now consider a third." "The four characteristics we have discussed thus far are . . . ." Besides helping the audience recall the material, **transitions**—connective words and phrases—facilitate the speaker's movement from one idea to another; in effect, they bridge gaps between ideas so that there are no abrupt switches.[7]

To indicate that additional information is forthcoming, you might use such transitional words and phrases as *equally important, next, second, furthermore, in addition,* and *finally.* To signal that you will be discussing a cause-and-effect relationship, you can use the expressions *as a result* and *consequently.* To indicate that there is a contrasting view to the one being elaborated, you could use phrases such as *after all, and yet, in spite of,* and *on the other hand.* To indicate that you are summing up briefly, you can say *in short.* Expressions such as *likewise* and *similarly* signal that a comparison will be made. The phrases *for example* and *for instance* let the listeners know that a point will be illustrated.

BEGINNINGS AND ENDINGS

Once you have outlined the body of your speech and considered the need for transitional devices, you are ready to "tell them what you are going to tell them" and "tell them what you have told them." In other words, it is time to develop your introduction and conclusion.[8]

The Introduction

All too frequently, the introduction is overlooked or neglected because speakers are in too much of a hurry to get to the heart of the matter. However, in public speaking, just as in interpersonal communication, first impressions count. Thus, it is essential that you make the first few minutes of your speech particularly interesting.

FUNCTIONS OF THE INTRODUCTION

The functions of your introduction are to gain the attention of the audience members, to make them want to listen to your speech, and to provide them with an overview of the subject you will be discussing. The art of designing introductions is much like any other art; that is, it requires creative thinking. You will need to examine your purpose, the speech itself as you have developed it, your analysis of the audience, and your own abilities.

The opening moments of contact, with one person or with a multitude, can affect the developing relationship either positively or negatively. Unquestionably, the first few moments of your speech—the introduction—will affect your audience's willingness to process the remainder. It is at this point that people will decide whether what you have to say is interesting and important or dull and inconsequential. If your introduction is poorly designed, your audience may tune you out for the remainder of your speech. On the other hand, a well-designed introduction can help you develop a solid rapport with the audience and thus make it easier for you to share your thoughts.

The material you include in your introduction must be selected with care. Since in all likelihood your listeners have not been waiting in line for several days

In the introduction, one of the speaker's goals is to build rapport with the audience.

to hear you speak, you will need to work to spark their interest; you will need to motivate them to listen to you. Student speakers sometimes go overboard in trying to accomplish this objective. Some have been known to yell or throw books across the room. Such devices are certainly attention-getters, but startling an audience can turn your listeners against you. Other speakers look for a joke—any joke—to use as an attention-getter. Unfortunately, a joke chosen at random is seldom related to the topic and thus can confuse or even alienate listeners rather than interest and involve them. (A well-chosen anecdote, however, can be very effective.) Some speakers insist on beginning with statements like "My purpose here today is . . . ." or "Today, I hope to convince you . . . ." Such openings suggest mainly that the speech maker has forgotten to consider motivation and attention.

Years ago, television shows began simply by flashing the title of the program onto the screen. Today, however, it is common to use a teaser to open a show. The teaser usually reveals segments of the show designed to arouse the interest of potential viewers—to encourage them to stay tuned. Without this device, many viewers would probably switch channels. Your listeners, of course, cannot switch speakers, but they can decide not to listen actively to what you have to say. Therefore, you, too, must design a teaser to include in your introduction—material that will interest and appeal to your audience.

Use brainstorming to devise a number of ways you could introduce yourself to a group of people you don't know.

TYPES OF INTRODUCTIONS

Effective speech makers begin in a number of different ways. They may relate an unusual fact, make a surprising statement, or cite shocking statistics. Or they might ask a question, compliment the audience, or refer to the occasion. Sometimes they use a humorous story or an illustration as a lead-in. Sometimes they rely on a suspenseful story or a human interest story to capture their listeners' attention.

Audiences respond to stories about people. For this reason, the plight of a family left homeless by a fire might be used effectively to open a speech on fire prevention, and a description of people severely injured in an automobile accident might introduce a speech supporting the use of air bags. If you have selected a topic because you have a personal interest in it, you can use a personal anecdote to begin your presentation. Let us examine a few examples of these approaches.

Some of the most effective introductions use *humor*, as in the following example from a speech by Tim Norbeck of the Connecticut State Medical Society, speaking to a medical association gathering.

> Bethel, Connecticut–born P. T. Barnum, the great showman, used to exhibit what he advertised as a "happy family." This family consisted of a lion, a tiger, a wolf, a bear, and a lamb, all in one cage.
>
> "Remarkable," said a visitor to Mr. Barnum. "How long have these animals lived together this way?" "Eight months," Barnum replied. "But occasionally we have to replace the lamb."
>
> There can be no lambs in this, the belligerent cradle of the insurance industry called Connecticut.
>
> Health care delivery in Connecticut has become a war zone—our state is indeed a true microcosm of America.[9]

Examples also make effective introductions. One student, Ajay Krishnan of Rice University, used the following example to begin his speech on automobile repair fraud:

> On September 28 of last year, 34-year-old Mark Hartman took his car to the local Econo Lube 'n Tire in Tucson, Arizona, for its regular oil change. While he was waiting, the manager asked him over to the service bay, and told him the shocking truth about his 1990 Chevy Corsica. Using a large chart, the manager pointed out that new cars should have red transmission fluid, whereas Mr. Hartman's transmission fluid was brown, meaning that the car was on the verge of a $3,500 breakdown. Unsure of what to do, Mr. Hartman desperately turned to his owner's manual to try to learn anything at all about his car's transmission. If nothing else, the manual made one fact abundantly clear: the manager was lying. Nothing was wrong with Mark Hartman's car.[10]

When used in introductions, *illustrations* can add drama, as is seen in the following introductory remarks of Erin O'Dell of Kansas State University.

> When Susan and Gary Wilson bought their new home, they thought their dreams came true. They moved into a wonderful, upper-class neighborhood, with wonderful upper-class neighbors. One such neighbor, Steven Glover, was entrusted to watch over the family's home while the family was away on vacation. Glover had been a longtime friend and a member of the clergy at the Wilsons' church, but when months later Glover started commenting on how Susan was doing her hair in the bathroom, and making comments on other parts of their private lives, the Wilsons became suspicious. What they eventually found shocked them. Glover had secretly placed cameras in the Wilsons' bathroom, and above their bed, and was watching them in their most intimate moments.[11]

Students Erin Gallaher and Adrienne Hallett both used *suspense* to make their points. Which of the introductions do you think is more effective? Erin's speech began this way:

> Flip through any furniture catalog, and you'll be sure to note descriptions of color, style, fabric, and texture. When deciding to purchase a new sofa or

armchair, most likely you'll carefully weigh options like "to recline or not to recline"—that is the question.

But there is something that most people never even consider when they're shopping for upholstered furniture. What is this hidden feature? It's the extremely flammable polyurethane foam found in the cushions of virtually every piece of upholstered furniture in your home.[12]

Adrienne's speech began this way:

He showed all of the classic symptoms. His response time was slowed, his judgement was impaired, but he thought he could handle it. As he drove home along the Interstate, his car swerved onto the shoulder of the road, running over and killing a man who was trying to change a flat tire. When the police questioned him later, he didn't remember a thing. What caused this Ohio man's actions is something we have all been guilty of, yet we won't readily admit it. Although the U.S. Department of Transportation estimates that it kills 13,000 people annually, no one will be taking the keys, calling a cab or taking a stand on this issue. Whenever we get into the driver's seat, we must be prepared for the risk presented by an impaired driver— surprisingly, not from alcohol but from a lack of sleep.[13]

Another student began a speech by asking a rhetorical question:

Do you know who you voted for in the last presidential election? I bet you don't. I bet you think you voted for the Democratic, Republican, or Independent candidate. But you didn't. You voted to elect members of the electoral college. In the course of my speech, I will explain why this practice is undemocratic, un-American, and unacceptable.

Another student used *frightening facts* to jolt her audience:

In the time it takes me to complete this sentence, a child in America will drop out of school. In the time it takes me to complete this sentence, a child in this country will run away from home. Before I finish this presentation, another teenage girl will have a baby.

We have a country [that] is gripped by a lost generation. This is an invisible group of kids lost and alone on the streets. On their own, they are hungry, sick, and scared. They are victims of our society. They are victims who desperately need help.

In this presentation I will show you how we can all help these kids.

Finally, many speakers use *startling statistics* to capture the audience's interest. The following example is from a speech entitled "Homeless Gay and Lesbian Youth: Confronting an Unseen Problem," by Daniel Roth:

Handcuffed to a chair, packed in a room in a family court holding tank with two dozen other children, Max, 15, began to think about his recent past. Max left his mother's New York apartment a month before because he could no longer take the beating from his mother's boyfriend. He had lived in a "squat house" for three weeks, until the cops came down on him and bolted him to the chair. Max had told his mother and her boyfriend he was gay the month before, which was when the beatings began. Even though the United States Declaration of Independence claims all men are created equal, Max was discovering the United States has declared a state of inequality for hundreds of thousands of American youth like him.

That night, Max was transferred to a group home with eight teenage boys who beat him nearly unconscious. The adults at the small residence failed to respond to his screams. The adults solved the problem by giving Max $2, and at 4 a.m., showing him the door. That night Max became one of the 42 percent of homeless youth who are gay and lesbian. In order to stop this injustice, we must first better understand the problems that force gay youth onto the streets so that we know what we can do to help them.[14]

The Preview

If your speech is organized in a linear fashion, after you have used your introduction to spark interest and motivate your audience to continue listening, it is necessary for you to preview your speech. That is, you need to let your audience know what you will be discussing. Consider the following examples of previews by student speakers:

> There are three "weight classes" of people in our society: the overweight, the underweight, and those who are the right weight. Unfortunately, many people fail to understand the role weight plays in their lives. Your weight affects how your body functions. Let's explore how.

> People have traditionally relied on oil or gas to heat their homes. Today, solar energy is gaining favor as an alternative. However, I believe there are four good reasons why it is inappropriate to consider installing a solar energy system in your home at this time.

Your preview should correspond to your purpose statement. It should let your audience know what to listen for. Additionally, by presenting it after you have gotten your listeners' attention and motivated them to continue paying attention, you ensure that your purpose statement will get a fair hearing.

The Conclusion

The conclusion summarizes the presentation and leaves your listeners thinking about what they have just heard. It provides a sense of completion.

FUNCTIONS OF THE CONCLUSION

The conclusion's summary function may be considered a preview in reverse. During your preview, you look ahead, revealing to your listeners the subject of your efforts. During the summary, you review for them the material you have covered. For example, a summary might begin, "We have examined three benefits you will derive from a new town library." During the remainder of this summation, the three benefits might be restated, to cement them in the minds of the listeners.

Inexperienced speech makers sometimes say that the summary appears to be superfluous ("After all, I've just said all of that not more than two minutes ago"). However, it is important to remember that you are speaking for your listeners, not for yourself. The summary provides some of the redundancy mentioned earlier; it enables audience members to leave with your ideas freshly impressed on their minds. In addition to refreshing your listeners' memory, the conclusion can help clarify the issues or ideas you have just discussed.

Besides serving as a summary, your conclusion should be used to heighten the impact of the presentation. You can do this in a number of ways. One popular technique is to refer to your introductory remarks; this gives your speech a sense of closure. If, for example, you are speaking about child abuse and you begin your presentation by showing pictures of abused children, you might paraphrase your opening remarks and show the pictures again, to arouse sympathy and support. Quotations and illustrations also make effective conclusions. For example, if you

An effective conclusion heightens the impact of a presentation.

are speaking about the problems faced by veterans of the war in Iraq, you could provide a moving conclusion by quoting some veterans or retelling some of the challenges they face. You are also free to draw on your own experiences when designing a conclusion. Keep in mind that, as they do with introductions, audiences respond to conclusions that include personal references, surprising statements, startling statistics, or relevant humor.

TYPES OF CONCLUSIONS

Let's examine how some conclusion techniques work in practice. One student, for example, used an *illustration* to end a speech called "The Nature of AIDS":

> I take their hand and talk to them. I tell them I was happy I could make things easier. Then I say, "Thank you for letting me work for you." But every night before Jerry Cirasulolo goes to sleep, he also recites a little prayer: "Please God, give me the strength to keep on caring. And please don't let me get AIDS."[15]

In a speech on identity theft, speaker R. J. Holmes concluded with a set of *startling statistics*:

> Today, we have become more and more careless about how we handle our money and the responsibilities associated with it. After identifying the problem, realizing the dangers, and looking at ways to take back who we are as consumers, we can understand that identity theft is an issue which cannot be ignored. It may not seem like such a big problem to our generation, but with 74 percent of college students using one or more credit or charge cards, we are all the more vulnerable to becoming future victims of identity theft.[16]

Recognizing the effectiveness of statistics and *rhetorical questions*, Brian Swenson, a student at Dakota Wesleyan in South Dakota, ended a speech on guns and children with these words:

> Today we have looked at a few cases of child shootings, some facts and statistics about child shootings, and what you should do if you own a gun to prevent this

from happening to your children or other children. Now, maybe you still think that you don't need to lock up your gun and that this won't happen to you; but I have one more figure for you. One child is killed every day with a handgun, and for every child killed ten others are injured. Now, I have a question for you. Is your child going to be one of the ten that are injured, or is it going to be the one that is killed? The choice is yours.[17]

Quotations can increase the impact of a conclusion. Former attorney general Robert Kennedy often ended his speeches with the following words by the playwright George Bernard Shaw.

Some men see things as they are, and ask, "Why?" I dare to dream of things that never were, and ask—"Why not?"[18]

Humor, when used appropriately, can help keep people on your side. One student ended a speech directed at first-year students with the following "letter":

Dear Mom and Dad:

Just thought I'd drop you a note to clue you in on my plans.

I've fallen in love with a guy named Buck. He quit high school between his sophomore and junior years to travel with his motorcycle gang. He was married at 18 and has two sons. About a year ago he got a divorce.

We plan to get married in the fall. He thinks he will be able to get a job by then. I've decided to move into his apartment. At any rate, I dropped out of school last week. Maybe I will finish college sometime in the future.

Mom and Dad, I just want you to know that everything in this letter so far is false. NONE OF IT IS TRUE.

But it is true that I got a C in French and a D in math. And I am in need of money for tuition and miscellaneous.

Love, _____ [19]

In a speech on automobile insurance, one speaker included the following quotations from accident reports in his conclusion:

Coming home I drove into the wrong house and collided with a tree I don't have.

The other car collided with mine without giving warning of its intention.

I thought my window was down, but found it was up when I put my head through it.

I had been driving for 40 years when I fell asleep at the wheel and had an accident.[20]

A SAMPLE OUTLINE

The following is a student's full sentence outline, containing an introduction, body, transitions, and a conclusion. What do you think are its strengths and weaknesses?

GRANNY DUMPING

Specific purpose: To explore why "granny dumping" is on the rise

Thesis: Increased family stresses and a lack of government assistance are causing families to abandon their older relatives.

Would you have phrased the thesis similarly? Why or why not?

INTRODUCTION

I. Over 45 years ago playwright Edward Albee wrote *The Sandbox*, a play in which a family brings their grandmother to a playground and dumps her in a sandbox.

II. Over 45 years ago this idea was labeled as absurd.

III. Now this idea is all too real.

IV. Today, I would like to talk to you about the growing problem of granny dumping.

What do you think of the speaker's introduction?

(Transition: Let's begin by examining the plight of growing numbers of older Americans.)

Can you come up with an alternative transition?

I. Older Americans are being abandoned by their families.

   A. John Kingery, 82, was abandoned outside a men's room in Post Falls, Idaho.

      1. His clothes were stripped of their labels.

      2. An Alzheimer's sufferer, Kingery was not able to remember his name.

   B. Thousands of older Americans face similar situations.

      1. The American College of Emergency Physicians estimates that 70,000 people are abandoned each year.

      2. Most are from families that cannot pay for the necessary care.

What strategies did the speaker use to develop the first main idea?

(Transition: In addition to the pain that is being inflicted on the elderly, pain is also being inflicted on those who should care for them.)

How do you assess this transition?

II. Caregivers are overwhelmed by their responsibilities.

   A. Millions of Americans carry the burden of caring for one or more older adults.

      1. One in five families takes care of an older adult.

      2. Caregivers are besieged with bills.

      3. Caregivers receive little government assistance.

How did the speaker develop the second main idea?

(Transition: So much for the problem; what about solutions?)

What functions does this transition serve?

III. There are a number of solutions.

   A. Families themselves can work together more effectively.

      1. They can avoid placing all of the responsibilities on one person.

      2. Relatives can help out with the nonending stack of paperwork required by government agencies.

   B. The government needs to do more.

      1. Programs need to be added so that patients can be cared for outside the home at least part of the time.

         a. This would provide variety for the patient.

         b. Such programs would also give a rest to the family so they could avoid burnout.

      2. A holistic approach to elder care needs to be adopted.

         a. Caregivers need help in coping with the increased stresses that caring for an aged relative creates.

To what extent, if any, do you think the speaker developed the last main idea of the outline?

b. Patients need help so that they are treated with respect.

c. Both caregivers and patients need help to maintain their dignity.

Conclusion

I. We have seen that there is much that can be done to help people who must help their aging parent.

II. While Edward Albee's *The Sandbox* was labeled as an example of absurdism 45 years ago, granny dumping has become an all too real and all too tragic way of life for tens of thousands of American citizens.

BIBLIOGRAPHY

"Abuse Underreported in Many States," *USA Today*, April (from the society for the Advancement of Education) 2004, p. 3.

Edward Albee, *The Sandbox* (New York: New American Library, 1961).

Rachel Boax, "Why Do Some Caregivers of Frail Elderly Quit?" *Healthcare Financing Review* 30(2): winter 1991, pp. 41–47.

Robert Butler, "Health Care for All: A Crisis in Cost Access," *Geriatrics* 47(9), September 1992, pp. 34–48.

"Elder Abuse: A Hidden Tragedy," *Biotech Week*, October 20, 2004, p. 195.

Paul Krugman, "Does Getting Old Cost Society Too Much?" *New York Times Magazine*, March 9, 1997, pp. 58–60.

"Granny Dumping by the Thousands," *The New York Times*, March 29, 1992.

What functions does the conclusion serve?

What do you think of the outline's bibliography?

Focus on Service Learning

Locate a community agency that helps persons from another country acclimate to the United States. How can understanding the worldview of people new to the United States enable you to prepare a speech for delivery that uses an organizational framework favored by the members of this group? What would you teach these persons about your worldview so that they could organize a presentation for delivery to members of your culture? Use resources such as, but not limited to, www.idex.org, www.cyborlink.com/default.htm, and www.unbrokencircle.org to facilitate answering these questions. More specifically, what advice about organizational formats would you give a speaker from an Eastern culture who needed to address a predominantly Western audience and vice versa?

ANALYZING YOUR PRESENTATION: THE TRYOUT

In the theater, playwrights, producers, directors, and performers would never open an important show without first conducting a series of tryouts, or preview performances. These performances, often staged before invited guests or audiences who pay reduced prices, give the cast and backers an opportunity to experience audiences' reactions and, if necessary, make needed alterations. As a speech maker, you would be wise to give yourself the same advantage.

Once you've researched your topic, identified your supporting materials, and outlined your presentation, it is time to become your own audience—to explore the sound and feel of your speech. Three essential ingredients in your first tryout are your speech notes, a clock or wristwatch, and a tape or video recorder so that you can review the exact words you use to express your ideas. Before starting, check the time and turn on the recorder. You can then begin speaking. In effect, what you are doing is preparing an oral rough draft of your presentation.

What are you trying to determine? First, you want to know if your presentation consumes too much or too little time. If a run-through takes 25 minutes and your time limit is 5 minutes, you have serious revision ahead of you. If, on the other hand, you have designed a "60-second wonder," you may find that you need to go back to the library for more material. Second, as you actually listen to your speech, you should be alert for ideas that are not expressed as clearly as you would like. Third, you may find that the same thoughts are expressed again and again and again—more than is necessary for redundancy. Fourth, you may realize that the structure is confusing because of missing or inappropriate transitions. Fifth, you may have failed to develop an effective attention-getter. Sixth, the information in the body of your presentation

Thinking Critically

Reflect and Respond

Agree or disagree with each of the following quotations. Give reasons and examples that support the position you take.

A bad beginning makes a bad ending.
— Euripides

A speech is like a love affair. Any fool can start it, but to end it requires considerable skill.
— Lord Mancroft

---

may be too detailed or too technical for your audience. Seventh, your conclusion may not satisfy the psychological requirements you have established for it.

You can use the items on the following checklist to analyze the first tryout of your speech:

Topic
Date
Specific purpose
Length of presentation
Introduction
Attention-getter
Preview
 Most effective components
 Changes needed
Body
 Main points
 Support
 Most effective components
 Changes needed
Conclusion
 Summation function
 Psychological appeal
 Most effective components
 Changes needed

A modular approach is useful in making revisions. Electronic equipment is often designed with modules, which you can remove for repairs or replacement; similarly, you can extract selected modules from your outline to revise them, replace them, or delete them. For example, if you find that your main attention-getter is not as effective as it could be—improve it. If the supporting material under, say, the second main point in the body of your speech is confusing, rewrite it. If an illustration is too long and drawn out, shorten it. In other words, your goal during the tryout is to refine your speech until it is as close as possible to the one you will actually present. Once you reach that point, it is time to think about your delivery. Although we will consider delivery in depth in Chapter 16, before we do that, we need to discuss the importance of the preparation of an extemporaneous outline in your effectiveness as a speaker.

WORKING WITH AN EXTEMPORANEOUS OUTLINE

When you deliver an extemporaneous speech, instead of speaking from a script or word-for-word manuscript, you usually speak from brief notes. To be able to speak extemporaneously, you need to prepare an extemporaneous outline. Recall that an extemporaneous outline contains brief notes that remind the speaker of the key parts of the speech and make reference to the support the speaker will use to develop each point. The time for speakers to prepare an extemporaneous outline is after they have practiced delivering the speech a few times using a more detailed outline. Once speakers are comfortable and familiar with the speech, they are ready to rely on only the extemporaneous outline during their final practice sessions.

The extemporaneous outline should be prepared using regular 8½- by 11-inch paper, or notes should be entered on 5- by 8-inch note cards. Whatever format you opt to use, be sure to include the following: reminder phrases for the introduction; a statement of the central idea or thesis; brief notes on the main points and subpoints, including the complete names of sources or citations for references; transition reminders; and reminder phrases for the conclusion of your speech.

While the goal is to keep the extemporaneous outline as brief as possible so you will not be tempted to read your notes instead of maintaining eye contact with audience members, you will want to include a number of delivery cues in the card's margins, such as "emphasize" or "hold up the visual aid," much as an actor marks up a script, to facilitate your speaking smoothness.

For samples of both informative and persuasive outlines and speaker's notes, see Chapter 17, "Informative Speaking," and Chapter 18, "Persuasive Speaking."

The Wrap Up

Revisiting Chapter Objectives

1. **Identify main and subordinate ideas.** Organization is one of the main challenges facing the speech maker. Part of the organizational challenge is to distinguish between main and subordinate ideas. Main ideas are the primary points of a speech. Subordinate ideas amplify the main ideas.

2. **Create a full sentence outline.** One of the best ways to organize your speech is to build its framework and prepare a full sentence outline using the introduction-body-conclusion format. Since the body of the speech is the main part of your presentation, it should be prepared first.

3. **Identify five methods of ordering ideas.** There are five generally accepted ways based on linear logic to order the ideas in a speech: (1) chronological order, (2) spatial order, (3) cause-and-effect order, (4) problem-and-solution order, and (5) topical order. Speakers from a number of cultural groups prefer to use configural logic to structure their ideas.

4. **Use internal summaries and transitions effectively.** When you use linear logic, the body of your presentation must have internal summaries and transitions to help listeners recall the content. (Professional speakers today must be prepared to give very short synopses—sound bites—to the media if they want to appear on the air.)

5. **Develop an effective introduction and conclusion.** After you complete the body of the speech, you are ready to prepare the introduction and conclusion. The introduction should gain the attention of the audience members, make them want to listen to your speech, and provide them with an overview of the subject to be discussed. Devices used to enhance introductions include humor, illustrations, questions, surprising statements, and statistics.

    The purpose of the conclusion is to summarize the material covered, heighten the impact of the presentation, and enable the audience to leave the occasion with your ideas freshly impressed on their minds. Devices used to increase the effectiveness of conclusions include surprising statements, rhetorical questions, quotations, and humor.

6. **Use a tryout to refine a speech.** When you have completed the outline for the entire speech, you should become your own audience: Try out the speech and analyze the results. Be sure to take into account any cultural barriers that might affect your presentation to be sure that your presentation is clear to all members of your audience.

Resources for Further Inquiry and Reflection

To apply your understanding of how the principles in Chapter 15 are at work in our daily lives, consult the following resources for further inquiry and reflection. Or, if you prefer, choose any other appropriate resource. Then connect the ideas expressed in your chosen selection with the communication concepts and issues you are learning about both in and out of class.

 Listen to Me

"The Scientist" (Cold Play)
"Ode to Billie Joe" (Bobby Gentry)
"Cats in the Cradle" (Harry Chapin)
"Scenes from an Italian Restaurant" (Billy Joel)
"We Belong Together" (Mariah Carey)
"Since You've Been Gone" (Kelly Clarkson)
"You'll Think of Me" (Keith Urban)

What organizational schema does the speaker use to tell the song's story? Why do you think that this story structure was selected? Could the song have been organized using another approach? Why or why not?

 View Me

The American President	*Dave*
Mars Attacks!	*Independence Day*
The West Wing	*Commander-in-Chief*

Compare and contrast a key speech of the chief executive in each film or episode from the TV series. How does each commander-in-chief structure his or her address? Which do you evaluate as more effective and why?

Read Me

Jerome Lawrence. *Inherit the Wind*. New York: Random House, 1955.

How do both sides on the evolution–creationism debate begin, develop, and end their presentations to the court?

George Jonas. *Vengeance: The True Story of an Israeli Counter-Terrorist Team*. New York: Simon & Schuster, 2005.

How do the spokespersons for the Israelis and for the Palestinians use organization to advance their positions?

 Tell Me

Share with the class the insights you gained from your chosen Listen to Me, View Me, or Read Me selection.

Find examples that enable you to support or negate the following: It is equally effective to develop a speech using formal rules of logic as it is using a holistic approach.

Communication
Works

online learning center

www.mhhe.com/gamble9

Key Chapter Terminology

Use the Communication Works CD-ROM and the Online Learning Center at www.mhhe.com/gamble9 to further your knowledge of the following terminology.

cause-and-effect order 439

chronological, or time, order 438

configural formats 442

internal summaries 444

linear logic 442

main ideas 433

problem-and-solution order 441

spatial order 438

speech framework 432

subordinate ideas 433

topical order 442

transitions 444

Idioms in Translation

drafting an outline—creating an outline

get to the heart of the matter—make a point

off topic—lose focus

in plain sight—visible

jumping-off point—starting point

prototype—model

thicket of possibilities—array of choices

Communication
Works

online learning center

www.mhhe.com/gamble9

Test Your Understanding

Go to the *Self Quizzes* on the Communication Works CD-ROM and the book's Online Learning Center at www.mhhe.com/gamble9.

Notes

1. See, for example, Margaret J. Wheatley. *Leadership and the New Science*. San Francisco: Berrett-Koehler, 1994.

2. Several studies reveal how organization affects reception. For example, see Christopher Spicer and Ronald E. Bassett. "The Effect of Organization on Learning from an Informative Message." *Southern States Communication Journal* 41, 1976, pp. 290–299; and Johen E. Baird, Jr. "The

Effects of Speech Summaries upon Audience Comprehension of Expository Speeches of Varying Quality and Complexity." *Central States Speech Journal* 25, 1974, pp. 119–127.

3. Richard Nisbett. *The Geography of Thought: How Asians and Westerners Think Differently . . . and Why.* New York: Free Press, 2003.

4. National Public Radio. "Analysis: Geography of Thought." *Talk of the Nation* broadcast of interview of Richard Nisbett by Neal Conan, March 3, 2003. © 2003 National Public Radio, Inc. Used with permission.

5. National Public Radio.

6. Myron W. Lustig and Jolene Koester. *Intercultural Competence: Interpersonal Communication across Cultures*, 3rd ed. New York: Longman. 1999.

7. D. L. Thislethwaite, H. deHaan, and J. Kamenetsky suggest that a message is more easily understood and accepted if transitions are used; see "The Effect of 'Directive' and 'Non-Directive' Communication Procedures on Attitudes." *Journal of Abnormal and Social Psychology* 51, 1955, pp. 107–118. Also of value on this aspect of speech organization is E. Thompson. "Some Effects of Message Structure on Listeners' Comprehension." *Speech Monographs* 34, 1967, pp. 51–57.

8. For a more comprehensive treatment of introductions and conclusions, see Gamble and Gamble. *Public Speaking in the Age of Diversity*, 2nd ed. Boston: Allyn & Bacon, 1998, chap. 10.

9. Tim Norbeck. "The Patient Must Get Some Protection." *Vital Speeches of the Day* 66:12, April 1, 2000, p. 372. Reprinted with permission.

10. Ajay Krishnan. "Is Mr. Goodwrench Really Mr. Rip Off?" *Winning Orations*. Mankato, MN: Interstate Oratorical Association, 1998, p. 120. Reprinted with permission.

11. Erin O'Dell. Untitled. *Winning Orations*. Mankato, MN: Interstate Oratorical Association, 2000, p. 43. Reprinted with permission.

12. Erin Gallaher. "Upholstered Furniture: Sitting in the Uneasy Chair." *Winning Orations*. Mankato, MN: Interstate Oratorical Association, 2000, p. 99. Reprinted with permission.

13. Adrienne Hallett. "Dying in Your Sleep." Northfield, MN: Interstate Oratorical Association, 1995, p. 27. Reprinted with permission.

14. Daniel Roth. "Homeless Gay and Lesbian Youth: Confronting an Unseen Problem." *Winning Orations*. Mankato, MN: Interstate Oratorical Association, 2000, p. 108. Reprinted with permission.

15. From a student speech delivered at New York Institute of Technology.

16. R. J. Homes. "Other People's Money: The Problem with Identity Theft." *Winning Orations*. Mankato, MN: Interstate Oratorical Association, 1998, p. 39. Reprinted with permission.

17. Brian Swenson. "Gun Safety and Children." *Winning Orations*. Mankato, MN: Interstate Oratorical Association, 1990, p. 101. Reprinted with permission.

18. This Kennedy quote has been attributed to G. B. Shaw, as well as the poet Robert Browning.

19. From a student speech delivered at The College of New Rochelle.

20. Ibid.

CHAPTER

16

Delivering Your Speech: Presenting Your Ideas

After finishing this chapter, you should be able to

1. Assess your level of speech anxiety.

2. Use deep-muscle relaxation, thought stopping, visualization, and other techniques to reduce speech anxiety.

3. Discuss four styles of delivery: manuscript, memorized, impromptu, and extemporaneous.

4. Identify how the speaker can use visual and vocal cues to advantage.

5. Analyze a speech maker's performance (including your own) in terms of content, organization, language, and delivery.

The human brain is a wonderful thing. It operates from the moment you're born until the first time you get up to make a speech.

—Howard Goshorn

The greatest mistake you can make in life is to be continually fearing you will make one.

—Elbert Hubbard

Your research is finished. Your speech is organized. Your outline is prepared. You have an assigned presentation date. What happens next? If you're like most speakers, you shift your focus to thinking about delivering your presentation. As your focus shifts, you begin to feel more anxious. Maybe you feel tired or suffer from indigestion. Your back may hurt or you may feel a headache coming on. There are a host of ailments correlated with anxiety.[1] You feel so anxious that you wonder if you will really gather the courage to stand and speak before an audience. The answer is "Of course, you will!" You can overcome whatever anxiety you feel by understanding its sources, learning to cope with your fears, using strategies to handle both the physical and mental symptoms of anxiety, and finally, methodically rehearsing your presentation, because the greatest fear that many speakers have is forgetting what they are going to say.[2]

■ ■ ■

DEALING WITH ANXIETY AND SPEECH FRIGHT

One prominent motivational speaker begins his presentations as follows:

> I couldn't sleep last night. I finally got up at 4 this morning. I got dressed and went through this presentation 37 times. And guess what? You loved it. [Gentle laughter.] And let me tell you one thing I'll never forget about this group. That is, when I got introduced, everyone was standing. [More laughter.] Tell you what I'm going to do. I'm going to reintroduce myself, and what I want you to do is just give me the welcome you gave me this morning. Just pump it up, OK? Are you ready? [Music pulses.] Ladies and gentlemen, all the way from Atlanta, GA. If you forget everything I say, don't forget this. . . . You are the best at what you do because of one main thing: Attitude. [The audience stands and cheers.][3]

What attitude do you have toward speaking in public? Fear, or anxiety, is something that affects most public speakers.[4] It is so common that, when queried, many persons answer that they would rather be in the casket at a funeral than be delivering the eulogy. Thus, if you experience a certain amount of apprehension before, during, or after presenting a speech, rest assured that you are not alone.[5] Students sometimes allow their fears to get the better of them. Instead of using anxiety as a positive force, they let it overwhelm them. To combat this, in this chapter we will look at ways to make speech fright, or **speech apprehension** (fear of speaking to an audience), one form of **communication apprehension** (fear of communication, no matter what the context) actually work for you.

Rehearsal is an integral part of speech preparation. It also helps decrease anxiety.

speech apprehension
fear of speaking to an audience

communication apprehension
fear of communication, no matter what the context

We are largely the playthings of our fears.
—Horace Walpole

Approximately 20 percent of the U.S. population is "trait" communication apprehensive. This means that they exhibit a predisposition to being apprehensive and display escalated nervousness levels in most, if not all, communication situations. On the other hand, nearly all of us experience occasional "state" communication apprehension. This means that when facing a specific situation, such as public speaking, we display a somewhat elevated nervousness level.[6] To determine your communication apprehension score, you can take the self-analysis quiz included in the section "Self-Analysis: How Anxious Are You?" or access the Perceived Report of Communication Apprehension (PRCA) developed by James McCroskey, cited on his Web page (www.as.wvu.edu/~jmccrosk/jcmhp/html) under Publications.

Understanding Your Fears

SELF-ANALYSIS: HOW ANXIOUS ARE YOU?

How anxious are you about delivering a speech? Use the following inventory to find out. Although this inventory is not a scientific instrument, it should give you some indication of your level of fear. Note that you must display some level of anxiety to be categorized as "normal." If you had no anxiety about speaking in public, you would not be considered normal; what's more, you would probably not be a very effective speech maker.

For each statement, circle the number that best represents your response:

1. I am afraid I will forget what I have to say.
   Not afraid   1   2   3   4   (5)   Extremely afraid

2. I am afraid my ideas will sound confused and jumbled.
   Not afraid   1   2   3   4   (5)   Extremely afraid

3. I am afraid my appearance will be inappropriate.
   Not afraid   1   2   3   4   5   Extremely afraid

4. I am afraid the audience will find my speech boring.
   Not afraid   1   2   3   4   5   Extremely afraid

5. I am afraid people in the audience will laugh at me.
   Not afraid   1   2   3   4   (5)   Extremely afraid

Ethics & Communication

Is Compulsory Speech Making Fair?
Studies show that many people fear public speaking more than they fear death. Is it fair to demand that all students face up to their fear and take a course that requires them to deliver at least one speech? Are there other options that could provide the same skills without actually involving standing in front of an audience? Explain your opinion.

6. I am afraid I will not know what to do with my hands.

   Not afraid   1   2   3   4   5   Extremely afraid

7. I am afraid my instructor will embarrass me.

   Not afraid   1   2   3   4   5   Extremely afraid

8. I am afraid audience members will think my ideas are simplistic.

   Not afraid   1   2   3   4   5   Extremely afraid

9. I am afraid I will make grammatical mistakes.

   Not afraid   1   2   3   4   5   Extremely afraid

10. I am afraid everyone will stare at me.

   Not afraid   1   2   3   4   5   Extremely afraid

Next, add the numbers you chose and rate yourself as follows:

41–50 Very apprehensive   11–20 Overconfident
31–40 Apprehensive   10   Are you alive?
21–30 Normally concerned

online learning center

Go to the Online Learning Center at www.mhhe.com/gamble9 and answer the questions in the *Self Inventory* to evaluate your understanding of speech anxiety.

CAUSES OF SPEECH APPREHENSION

Before we can cope with our fears, we need to develop a clearer understanding of what causes them. Following are some of the more common causes of speech apprehension.

Fear of Inadequacy If adequacy is a state of feeling confident and capable, inadequacy is just the opposite—that is, feeling inferior and incapable. Feeling inadequate may cause us to assume that we will be unable to cope with writing or speaking. Do you fear to take risks because you imagine your performance will not be good enough or will be judged inadequate or not up to par? When you disagree with something you have read or heard, do you feel more comfortable swallowing hard and sitting quietly than you do speaking up for or writing about what you think is right? Is it easier for you to go along with a group than to write or speak your objections to other people's actions or words? If you feel inadequate, you probably prefer to play it safe; you do not want to put yourself in a position where you might feel even more inadequate.

Fear of the Unknown A new job may cause us to feel fearful because our co-workers, the situation, and our responsibilities are unfamiliar, unknown, or still unclear. We may fear delivering a speech for the same reasons. Each new event has a threatening, unknown quality—a quality that many people prefer not to deal with. When such an event involves speaking, we may be afraid because we do not know how people will react to what we say. Although we have a cognitive understanding of what is and is not likely to happen before an audience, we let our feelings take charge, causing us to react emotionally and behave irrationally.

Fear of Being Judged How sensitive are you to the judgment of others? Are you concerned about a friend's opinion of or judgment about you? An instructor's? Do you believe that what an audience, a reader, or an instructor concludes about you is necessarily true? Sometimes we become so sensitive to the judgments of others that we try to avoid judgment altogether. Public speaking is one situation in which such an attitude is common.

Fear of Consequences   Basically, one of two things can result from giving a speech: The audience may like it or may dislike it. That is, it will be a success or a failure. This basic result may then have further consequences. In the classroom, for example, an unsatisfactory speech may result in a failing grade. In a business situation, it may result in the loss of an important account. Whatever the consequences, the speaker needs to prepare to deal with them.

Learning to Cope with Your Fears: Controlling Anxiety

One of the best ways to cope with the fear of speech making is to design and rehearse your presentation carefully. The systematic approach suggested in this chapter covers both design and rehearsal and should—at least in theory—decrease your anxiety by increasing your self-confidence. However, theory and reality do sometimes diverge and, preparation notwithstanding, you may still find that you experience some anxiety about your speech. Let us now see how such anxiety can be controlled.

SYMPTOMS OF ANXIETY

The first thing you need to do is recognize the actual bodily sensations and thoughts that accompany and support your feelings of nervousness. Make a list of the physical symptoms and fear-related thoughts that contribute to your anxiety. Then examine the symptoms and thoughts that you and others in your class identified. Do the lists include any of these physical symptoms?

rapid or irregular heartbeat	stiff neck
stomach knots	lump in the throat
shaking hands, arms, or legs	nausea
dry mouth	dizziness

When people are asked about fear-related thoughts, they often make statements like the following. Were any of these included on your lists?

"I just can't cope."
"I'm under such pressure."
"This is a nightmare."
"I know something terrible is going to happen."

Once you have identified the physical and mental sensations that accompany fear, your next step is to learn how to control these reactions.[7] The next sections describe behavior modification techniques that can help you.

Deep-Muscle Relaxation: Overcoming Physical Symptoms

Muscle tension commonly accompanies fear and anxiety. However, a muscle will relax after being tensed. Deep-muscle relaxation is based on this fact.

Try this: Tense one arm. Count to 10. Now relax your arm. What feelings did you experience? Did your arm seem to become heavier? Did it then seem to

Skill Builder

Tense and Relax

1. Imagine that your body is divided into four basic sections:
   a. hands and arms
   b. face and neck
   c. torso
   d. legs and feet
2. Sit comfortably. In turn, practice tensing and relaxing each of these four sections of your body.
   a. *Hands and arms.* Clench your fists. Tense each arm from shoulder to fingertips. Notice the warm feeling that develops in your hands, forearms, and upper arms. Count to 10. Relax.
   b. *Face and neck.* Wrinkle your face as tightly as you can. Press your head back as far as it will go. Count to 10. Relax. Roll your head slowly to the front, side, back, and side in a circular movement. Relax.
   c. *Torso.* Shrug your shoulders. Count to 10 in this position. Relax. Tighten your stomach. Hold it. Relax.
   d. *Legs and feet.* Tighten your hips and thighs. Relax. Tense your calves and feet. Relax.

become warmer? Next, try tensing and relaxing one or both of your legs. When you examine what happens, you'll see why it is reasonable to expect that you can calm yourself by systematically tensing and relaxing various parts of your body in turn.

Try using the Skill Builder "Tense and Relax" several times before you actually present a speech. Many students report that butterflies or tensions tend to settle in particular bodily sections. Thus, it can be helpful to check the bodily sensations you feel when anxious, and personalize "Tense and Relax" to deal with your individual symptoms.

Thought Stopping: Overcoming Mental Symptoms

Anxiety is not simply a physical phenomenon; it also manifests itself cognitively—that is, in thoughts. Thus it is important to work to eliminate the thoughts associated with anxiety, as well as the bodily symptoms.

Many people use the word *relax* to calm themselves. Unfortunately, *relax* doesn't sound very relaxing to some people. You can substitute the word *calm.* Try the Skill Builder "Calm."

A variation on the "calm technique" is to precede the word *calm* with the word *stop.* When you begin to think upsetting thoughts, say to yourself, "Stop!" Then follow that command with "Calm"—for example,

"I just can't get up in front of all those people. Look at their cold stares and mean smirks."

"Stop!"

"Calm."

You may find that you can adapt this thought-stopping technique to help you handle symptoms of anxiety in interpersonal situations.

Think you can or think you can't; either way you will be right.

—Henry Ford

Skill Builder

"Calm"

1. Work through the procedure described in the text for releasing tension.
2. As soon as you experience the warm feeling throughout your body, say to yourself, "calm."

Try this several times, each time working to associate the "de-tensed" feeling with the word calm.

3. The next time you find yourself in a stress-producing situation, say "calm" to yourself and attempt to achieve the de-tensed state.

Visualization: A Positive Approach

Sports psychologists use a technique called visualization to help athletes compete more effectively. The athletes are guided in visualizing the successful completion of a play or a game. They are asked to imagine how they will feel when they win. Eventually, when they go out on the field to compete, it is almost as if they have been there before—and have already won.

You may want to try this technique to boost your confidence as a speaker. Sit in a quiet place. Picture yourself approaching the podium. See yourself delivering your presentation. Then hear your audience applaud appreciatively. After you have actually delivered the speech, answer these questions: Did the experience help you control your anxiety? Did it help you succeed?

Other Techniques

Speakers report that other techniques can also help reduce speech apprehension. Some try to include a bit of humor early in the speech to get a favorable response from the audience right away. They say that such a reaction helps them calm their nerves for the remainder of the presentation. Others look for a friendly face and talk to that person for a moment or two early in the speech. Others use charts, graphs, and other visuals to help them organize the material. In this technique, the visual shows the next major point to be covered, eliminating the necessity for the speaker to remember it or refer to notes. Still others report that they rehearse a speech aloud, standing in front of an imaginary audience and "talking through" the material again and again. What other techniques have you found helpful?

Remember, no matter how you choose to deal with it, fear is a natural response to public speaking and can probably never be eliminated completely. But you do need to learn to cope with fear; only in this way will you be able to deliver a successful, well-received presentation.

REHEARSING YOUR PRESENTATION

All speakers need to rehearse their presentations. The president of the United States, for example, practices by videotaping and reviewing the performance before delivering an address. Corporate leaders often spend hours rehearsing and refining the presentations they will deliver at sales meetings, stockholders' meetings, and so on. Actors, obviously, rehearse before a new play or production opens. It stands to reason that only the most foolhardy and unconcerned souls would undertake to deliver a speech that they have not adequately rehearsed.

By now, you have tried out your presentation orally at least once. During the tryout stage, your purpose was to analyze your speech to identify any major changes you needed to make. That done, you are now ready to begin rehearsing the speech.

Options for Delivery

There are four general styles of delivery available to you as a speech maker: (1) manuscript, (2) memorized, (3) impromptu, and (4) extemporaneous. We will briefly examine all four options.

MANUSCRIPT SPEECHES

A **manuscript speech** is written out word for word and then read aloud by the speech maker. Manuscript speeches are most common when it is imperative that precise language be used. For example, since presidential addresses are likely to be under close scrutiny not only in this country but also thoughout the world, they often are read from a typed page or a TelePrompTer. When corporate speakers are discussing matters with sensitive legal and commercial aspects, they may choose to deliver a manuscript speech.

Unfortunately, the use of a manuscript tends to reduce eye contact between speaker and audience. Furthermore, speakers reading aloud often sound as if they are reading to, rather than talking to, the audience, and thus it is difficult, if not impossible, to establish the much-needed conversational tone.

manuscript speech
a speech read from a script

MEMORIZED SPEECHES

A **memorized speech** is a manuscript speech that the speaker commits to memory. This delivery style frequently takes on a canned tone—often glaringly. Also, speakers who memorize their lines are less able to respond to audience feedback than they would be if they were working from notes. Additionally, of course, there is the problem of retention. Speech makers who insist on memorizing their presentations word for word often find themselves plagued by memory lapses, leading to long, awkward silences, during which they valiantly attempt to recall forgotten material. You may want to memorize certain key words, phrases, or segments of your speech, but at this point in your career there is little reason for you to commit the entire presentation to memory.

memorized speech
a manuscript speech committed to memory

IMPROMPTU SPEECHES

An **impromptu speech** is a speech you deliver spontaneously, or on the spur of the moment without formal preparation. An impromptu speaker often has no more than a few seconds or minutes to gather his or her thoughts. An impromptu speaking situation may arise, for example, when a boss unexpectedly asks an employee to discuss the status of a project that is still in its developmental stages. If you are faced with such a request, you will need to rely on what you have learned about patterning your ideas; using the introduction-body-conclusion format will facilitate your task.

impromptu speech
a speech delivered spontaneously, or on the spur of the moment

EXTEMPORANEOUS SPEECHES

An **extemporaneous speech** is researched, outlined, and then delivered after careful rehearsal. Extemporaneous speaking is more audience-centered than any of the

extemporaneous speech
a speech that is researched, outlined, and delivered after careful rehearsal

preceding options. Since the speaker prepares and rehearses in advance, she or he is free to establish eye contact with the members of the audience and to respond to feedback. In addition, because extemporaneous speakers may use notes, they are not constrained by a need to commit the entire presentation to memory. Nor are they handicapped by a manuscript that must be read word for word, inhibiting their adaptability.

Unfortunately, many speakers confuse manuscript, memorized, and impromptu speeches with extemporaneous speeches. Although asked to give an extemporaneous speech, they may insist on writing it out word for word and then either memorizing or reading it. Or they may spend too little time preparing the speech and deliver what is essentially a poorly developed impromptu presentation. Such misconceptions defeat the speakers' purpose and decrease their effectiveness as speech makers. The extemporaneous speech has been found most effective for most public speakers. Above all, do not turn extemporaneous speaking into something it is not.

REHEARSING: USING THE SPEAKERS' TOOLS

When we speak in public, we have three basic kinds of tools at our disposal: (1) visual, (2) vocal and (3) verbal. All three tools reinforce or detract from a speaker's message.

In addition to your ideas, what qualities in you do you want to communicate to an audience? If you're like most speakers, you want your audience to accept you as a credible source. As we will see in Chapter 18, this means that you want your listeners to consider you competent, trustworthy, and dynamic.

How is credibility communicated? Obviously, it is conveyed verbally, through the content and structure of language. However, far too frequently, speakers forget that credibility is also conveyed through visual and vocal cues. As we noted in Chapter 6, the nonverbal components of a message account for at least 65 percent of the total meaning transmitted to listeners. Thus, the visual and vocal dimensions of your speech merit careful attention.

Conduct a Visual Tune-up

Let's first consider visual cues. How do you think a speech maker should look standing before an audience? Close your eyes and picture his or her clothing, posture, gestures, movements and facial expressions, and use of eye contact.

CLOTHING

In deciding what to wear when you deliver your speech, you should consider the topic, the audience, and the occasion. Sometimes speakers make thoughtless errors in dress. For example, one student delivered a very serious tribute to a well-known leader while wearing a shirt emblazoned with a huge Mickey Mouse emblem. (When asked why he wore that shirt, he responded, "I didn't think anyone would notice.")

The clothing a speaker wears should reinforce, not detract from, the presentation.

The clothes you wear should not distract receivers from focusing on the ideas of your speech.

Be aware that it is up to you to choose what you will wear. Your clothing does not choose you.

POSTURE

As a public speaker, you will almost always be expected to stand when addressing your audience. Thus, unless you are physically challenged, you should expect to be on your feet. Although this may seem obvious, the problem is that standing is something many of us do not do very well. Your posture communicates; it sends potent messages to the audience. Speakers often seem to forget this, assuming a stance that works against them rather than for them. For example, some speakers lean on the lectern or actually drape themselves over it as if unable to stand without its assistance. Some perch on one foot like a crane. Some prop themselves against the wall behind them, giving the impression that they want to disappear into it.

To prepare yourself to stand properly in public, assume your natural posture and ask others to evaluate it. Are you too stiff? Do you slouch? Do you appear too relaxed? Feedback can help you put your best posture forward when you rise to speak.

GESTURES

As we noted in Chapter 6, gestures are movements of a speaker's hands and arms. The gestures you use when speaking in public may be purposeful, helping reinforce the content of your speech, or purposeless, detracting from your message. A problem most of us encounter is that we have certain favorite gestures that we are unaware of doing—things like scratching our neck, putting our hands into and out of our pockets, jingling our keys or jewelry, or smoothing our hair. Such mannerisms often become intensified when we find ourselves faced with a stressful situation such as speaking in public. In fact, when people are nervous, it is not unusual for them to add new gestures to their repertoire of annoying mannerisms. Speakers will sometimes tap a pencil or ring on the lectern or even crack their knuckles—things they would never do in normal circumstances.

Gestures can, however, serve a number of useful purposes. They can help you emphasize important points, enumerate your ideas, or suggest shapes or sizes. Thus, your job with regard to gestures is really twofold. First, you need to work to eliminate annoying gestures; second, you need to incorporate appropriate gestures that can be used to enhance the ideas contained in your speech.

MOVEMENTS AND FACIAL EXPRESSIONS

It is important to understand that your presentation begins as soon as you are introduced or called on to speak—that is, before you have spoken your first syllable. The way you rise and approach the speaker's stand communicates a first impression to your listeners. Similarly, your facial expressions as you complete your speech and your walk as you return to your seat also send important signals to your audience. Far too many speech makers approach the lectern in inappropriate ways. For example, they may walk in a way that broadcasts a lack of preparation. Some even verbalize this by mumbling something like "I'm really not

Stand up before the class and recite the alphabet. As you do so, make as many annoying gestures as you can. Then recite the alphabet a second time. During this second recitation, make gestures that are as appropriate as possible.

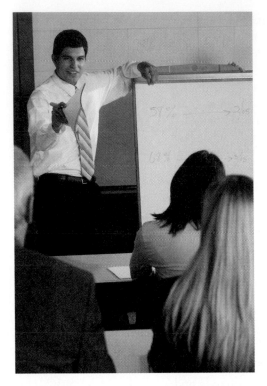

Eye contact draws receivers into a presentation.

ready. This will be terrible." Others apologize for a poor showing all the way back to their seats.

Consider carefully your way of moving to and from the speaker's stand. The way you move communicates whether or not you are in control. You may have noticed that confident people walk with head erect, follow a straight rather than a circuitous path, proceed at an assured rather than a hesitant or frenetic pace, and use open rather than closed arm movements.

EYE CONTACT

Eye contact also communicates. Unfortunately, some speakers "talk" to walls, chalkboards, windows, trees, or the floor rather than to their listeners. Some speakers seem embarrassed to look at any audience members; others seek the attention of one person and avoid looking at anyone else. Some student speakers avoid meeting the eyes of the instructor during a speech; others focus on him or her exclusively.

Be sure that your gaze includes all the members of the audience. Look at each individual as you deliver your speech. Such contact will draw even the most reluctant listeners into your presentation.

Conduct a Vocal Tune-up

Obviously, the voice is one of our main tools in speech making. Your voice is to your speech as the artist's brush is to a painting. The brush carries colors to the canvas just as your voice transmits ideas to your listeners. In Chapter 6, we considered four basic vocal dimensions: volume, rate, pitch, and quality. Review this material during your rehearsals, keeping in mind that your goal is to use your voice to reinforce the content of your speech.

To respond to your ideas, your audience must, of course, first hear them. Maintaining your voice at an appropriate volume is your responsibility. If you are to address a group in a large auditorium, a public-address system will probably be provided. If you are addressing a group in a smaller room, you will probably be expected to speak without amplification. By observing the people in the rear, you should be able to determine if you are speaking loudly enough for them to hear you easily. If you notice that any of the audience members look confused or upset, speak up. On the other hand, if your voice is normally loud and you notice that those seated nearest to you are cringing, turn down your volume a bit.

With regard to pitch, try not to fall into the monotone trap. If you maintain one predominant tone throughout your presentation, you will create a sense of boredom in the audience. Use pitch to reflect the emotional content of your material; use it to create interest.

Like volume and pitch, rate also communicates. Speaking too quickly or too slowly can impede understanding. Thus, respond to feedback from your audience and speed up or slow down your pace as appropriate.

Nonfluencies are a problem every public speaker needs to consider. "Uhs" and "ums" are normal in communication encounters, but they are not expected in speech making. During person-to-person conversations, we realize that people are thinking about or planning what they are going to say next. In contrast, we expect public speakers to have prepared their remarks carefully, and thus we are less tolerant of their nonfluencies. Attempt to eliminate nonfluencies from your delivery as much as possible.

Conduct a Verbal Tune-up

Although we have already focused on developing the verbal aspects of your speech (See Chapter 15), when rehearsing, be sure to use language that is clear and vivid.

As you rehearse your speech, ask yourself if it contains any unnecessary or confusing words or expressions. If so, eliminate them. For example, instead of saying "a sufficient supply of," say "enough." In general, choose simpler and more familiar words over those that could cause audience members difficulty in deciphering their meaning. Thus, say "plan" rather than "strategize." This especially holds true for idioms when addressing audiences composed of people from diverse cultures. Also remember to use transitions to guide your audience from one point to the next.

How do you make your words live in the minds of audience members? As you rehearse, ask yourself if your speech contains vivid words, including strong and active verbs, and figures of speech and images to enliven your presentation by helping audience members form mental pictures. Avoid using tired words such as "very interesting," or "world-class" or clichés such as "cool as a cucumber" or "sly as a fox." Phrases like these are used so often that audiences find them trite and meaningless. Language that helps audience members not only understand but also see, hear, and feel your message is your goal.

"It's a good speech—just a couple of points that need obfuscation."

Rehearsal Procedures: Communicating Confidence

Rehearsal—careful practice of your presentation—can help you acquire the confidence you need to deliver an effective speech. At this point, you have prepared an outline and appropriate visuals. Your task is to synthesize these ingredients into a polished presentation. Rehearsing will enable you to tell whether

- your speech takes the right amount of time or you need to add or delete material.
- the words of your speech flow smoothly or you need to work on phrasing.
- visual and audio aids are placed appropriately and smoothly integrated into your presentation or you need to rework them and troubleshoot technical problems.
- your confidence level and familiarity with the speech's content support your speech-making goals or you need to continue working on controlling your apprehensiveness and learning the speech.
- your manner of delivery is appropriate or you need to change it.

Although rehearsal is a highly individualized matter, you can follow these basic guidelines. Begin the rehearsal process by first reading through your outline several times, developing a list of key words and main points to be covered. These may become the basis of your delivery notes.

Second, learn your first and last sentences. Many speakers find it helpful to commit the first and last sentences of an address to memory. If you do not memorize your opening and closing sentences, you should at least become very familiar with them. (As one student put it, "That way I know that I'll be able to start and stop the speech.")

Third, conduct a preliminary auditory rehearsal. Stand up and face an imaginary audience. Present the entire speech. Time yourself. This will give you an idea of how the final address will sound.

Fourth, conduct additional rehearsals. Rehearse for several days, sometimes alone, at other times before a small group of friends or relatives. If you want, use an audio- or videocassette recorder.

When rehearsing, be sure to incorporate all your audio and visual aids into the presentation. Also, practice delivering the speech in several locations; this will help you get used to the foreign feel of the room where the speech will actually be presented. Your goal is to develop a flexible delivery—one that will enable you to meet the unique demands of the live audience.

GIVING THE SPEECH: SOME FINAL TIPS

If you follow the developmental plan outlined in this book, you should find yourself ready and eager to deliver your speech. Not only will you have carefully prepared and rehearsed your address, you will also have at your disposal tested techniques to help you control your nerves. At this juncture, you should need only a few additional pointers:

1. Arrive at your speaking location with ample time to spare. Be sure that you have prepared equipment to hold your notes and presentation aids.

2. If you are going to use a public-address system or other electronic equipment, test it so that you will not have to adjust the volume or replace bulbs or batteries unnecessarily during your presentation.

3. Give ample consideration to your clothing and appearance. Your confidence and believability will increase if you look the part. (But do not distract yourself with worries about your appearance while you are speaking.)

4. Let your audience know you are prepared by the way you rise when introduced and by walking confidently to the podium.

5. While speaking, work to transmit a sense of enthusiasm and commitment to your listeners.

6. Complete your speech before returning to your seat. You have worked hard to communicate your credibility to audience members; don't ruin it in the last few seconds. Last impressions, like first impressions, count.

AFTER THE SPEECH: EVALUATING YOUR EFFECTIVENESS

As soon as you have completed your presentation, the first question you will ask yourself is, How did I do? No doubt you will also want to know what your peers and your instructor thought of your performance.[8] You and your listeners can evaluate your speech by analyzing how effectively you were able to handle each of the following: content, organization, language, and delivery.

Content

Was the subject of your speech appropriate? Was it worthwhile? Was your purpose communicated clearly? Did you research the topic carefully? Were your audiovisual aids helpful? Did you use a variety of supports? Were your main points adequately developed? Were the main divisions of your speech effectively bridged by transitional words and phrases?

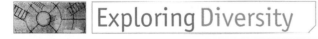 Exploring Diversity

Multicultural Communication Classes

Although made over two decades ago, the observations of communication scholar Dean Barnlund ring even more true today: Few communication classes are composed of students who are "cultural replicas" of each other. A number of students in your class may speak in different native tongues (English is their second language); they may also move at different paces, gesture in different ways, and respond to or seek different values.

What kinds of challenges do these differences pose for speakers and for listeners? Explain.

Should we expect that foreign students in the United States be cultural replicas of Americans? Why or why not?

Organization

How effective was your organizational approach? Did you begin with material that gained the attention of the audience? Did you preview each main point? Were your main points arranged in a logical sequence? Was the number of main points appropriate for the time allotted? Was your organizational design easily discernible? Did your conclusion provide a logical wrap-up of your main parts? Did it motivate listeners to continue thinking about your presentation?

Language

Did you use clear language to explain your ideas? Was it vivid? Did your speech sound as if it should be listened to rather than read? Could any of the words or phrases you used have been considered offensive to any audience members?

Delivery

Did you maintain effective eye contact with the members of the audience? Did you approach the speaking situation confidently? Were you able to use an extemporaneous style of delivery? Could you be heard easily? Was your speaking rate appropriate? Did you articulate clearly? Were you able to convey a sense of enthusiasm as you spoke? Did your gestures help reinforce your content?

TECHNOLOGY: AN AVENUE FOR REDUCING SPEECH-MAKING ANXIETY

The Internet is not just a resource for researching issues. It can also be used to collect and analyze information from persons representing virtually every imaginable point of view on every imaginable subject, including speaking anxiety. Using the Web, you can find information about relaxation techniques, share personal stories and experiences, or even use Internet or videophone to pretest the delivery of your speech and see how others unknown to you respond to it.

Among the Internet sites devoted specifically to public speaking are

http://www.school-for-champions.com/speaking/fear.htm
http://speeches.com
http://lrc.tridenttech.edu/pub-speak.htm

The first contains clues on how to overcome public speaking anxiety (PSA). The second contains excellent speechwriting resources that you can access for help in speech preparation. The site also offers a speech archive, links to speeches on the Web, and help in writing. The third is an online tutorial you can use to improve your speech-making skills.

Focus on Service Learning

Visit the Web sites listed on this page. How can you use them or similar sites, as well as what you know about speech apprehension, delivery, and credibility, to prepare a volunteer for a community group to take his or her message "on the road"?

A PERFORMANCE INVENTORY

When it is time for the audience members to comment on your presentation, they, like you, should consider the positive dimensions of your performance before making recommendations for improvement. Speaker and audience alike should remember that analysis is designed to be constructive, not destructive. It should help build confidence. It should not destroy the speaker's desire to try again.

Your instructor will probably provide you with a more formal analysis of your work, using an evaluation form similar to the one shown in Figure 16.1. Whether

FIGURE 16.1

Evaluation Form.

Name: _____ Speech: _____

Specific purpose: _____

1. Content
   ____ Based on accurate analysis of speaking situation.
   ____ Specific goal of speech was apparent.
   ____ Subject appropriate, relevant, and interesting to intended audience.
   ____ All material clearly contributed to purpose.
   ____ Had specific facts and opinions to support and explain statements.
   ____ Support was logical.
   ____ Handled material ethically.
   ____ Used audio and/or visual aids when appropriate.
   ____ Included a variety of data—statistics, quotations, etc.
   ____ Moved from point to point with smooth transitions.

2. Organization
   ____ Began with effective attention-getter.
   ____ Main points were clear statements that proved or explained specific goals.
   ____ Points were arranged in logical order.
   ____ Each point was adequately supported.
   ____ Concluded with memorable statement that tied speech together.

3. Language
   ____ Ideas were clear.
   ____ Ideas were presented vividly.
   ____ Ideas were presented emphatically.
   ____ Language was appropriate for intended audience.

4. Delivery
   ____ Was prepared to speak.
   ____ Stepped up to speak with confidence.
   ____ Maintained contact with audience.
   ____ Sounded extemporaneous, not read or memorized.
   ____ Referred to notes only occasionally.
   ____ Sounded enthusiastic.
   ____ Maintained good posture.
   ____ Used vocal variety, pitch, emphasis, and rate effectively.
   ____ Gestured effectively.
   ____ Used face to add interest.
   ____ Articulation was satisfactory.
   ____ On finishing, moved out with confidence.
   ____ Fit time allotted.

Additional comments:

or not your instructor uses the form in Figure 16.1, you will find it helpful as a personal guide.

Another means of evaluating your own effectiveness as well as the effectiveness of other speakers is to evaluate the credibility of the evidence included in a presentation. See the evaluation checklist at the end of Chapter 18.

DILBERT: © Scott Adams/Dist. by United Feature Syndicate, Inc.

Thinking Critically

Reflect and Respond

According to poet e. e. cummings, "Most people are perfectly afraid of silence." Do you agree with cummings? Provide reasons and examples to explain your position.

Which do you believe most people fear *more* and why—silence or speaking in public?

Finally, what do the quote by e. e. cummings and the following one, by Daniel Webster, have in common?

If all my talents and powers were suddenly taken from me by some inscrutable providence, and I were allowed to keep only one, I would unhesitatingly ask to be allowed to keep my power of speaking for with that one, I would quickly regain all the others.

Revisiting Chapter Objectives

1. **Assess your level of speech anxiety.** Anxiety, or fear, affects all speech makers. One of the best ways to cope with speech fright is to design and rehearse your presentation carefully. In addition, you should learn to recognize the causes of fear, as well as the physical and mental sensations that accompany it, so that you can learn to control your reactions with appropriate behavior modification techniques.

2. **Use deep-muscle relaxation, thought stopping, visualization, and other techniques to reduce speech anxiety.** Among the techniques you can use to reduce speech anxiety are deep muscle relaxing, thought stopping and visualization. These three techniques help eliminate the tension, thoughts and symptoms associated with fear—the first by eliminating stress, the second by stopping the fear-inducing process, the third by boosting confidence.

3. **Discuss four styles of delivery: manuscript, memorized, impromptu, and extemporaneous.** There are four general options for delivery: (1) A manuscript speech is written out word for word and then read aloud; (2) a memorized speech is a manuscript speech committed to memory; (3) an impromptu speech is delivered on the spur of the moment; (4) an extemporaneous speech is researched, outlined, and delivered after careful rehearsal.

4. **Identify how the speaker can use visual and vocal cues to advantage.** In delivering the speech, you have three basic kinds of tools at your disposal: verbal, visual, and vocal. Far too often, the verbal component is overemphasized, while the nonverbal aspects are underemphasized. Effective speech making requires that you pay attention to the visual aspects of your delivery, such as your clothing, posture, gestures, movements, and use of eye contact, and that your vocal cues including volume, rate, pitch and quality reinforce—rather than sabotage—the content.

5. **Analyze a speech maker's performance (including your own) in terms of content, organization, language, and delivery.** Careful rehearsal of your presentation can help you develop the confidence and competence required to deliver an outstanding speech. To ensure continued improvement, you should conduct postpresentation analyses focusing on content, organization, language and delivery which will enable you to profit from each speaking experience.

Resources for Further Inquiry and Reflection

To apply your understanding of how the principles in Chapter 16 are at work in our daily lives, consult the following resources for further inquiry and reflection. Or, if you prefer, choose any other appropriate resource. Then connect the ideas expressed in your chosen selection with the communication concepts and issues you are learning about both in and out of class.

Listen to Me

"Help!" (The Beatles)
"I Shall Believe" (Sheryl Crow)

How do the pleas of the speakers in the songs reflect your own when you are asked to give a speech? How can you use other people to help you improve both your speech-making effectiveness and readiness to speak?

 View Me

Dave   Maid in Manhattan
Bulworth   Anchorman: The Legend of Ron Burgundy

What lessons can you derive from the presentations of the title or supporting character? How would you evaluate the public performances of Dave, Bulworth, the 10-year-old son in *Maid in Manhattan*, or Ron Burgundy? Explain.

 Read Me

Philip G. Zimbardo. *Shyness*. New York: Jove, 1987.
Ron Huff. *I Can See You Naked*. Kansas City: Andrews & McMeel, 1992.

How can combating shyness prepare you to be a better speaker?

 Tell Me

Share with the class the insights you gained from your chosen Listen to Me, View Me, or Read Me selection.

Advertisements and public speakers have a number of characteristics in common. Both aim to inform as well as persuade. Their effectiveness depends on whether they are able to attract the interest of receivers, arouse their needs, and motivate them to listen and respond. The delivery of the characters in the ad, the images they project, together with the credibility of the spokespersons also affect an ad's overall impact. The same holds true for a speaker: delivery, image, and credibility interact to enhance or detract from the speaker's effectiveness. Those are the similarities. What differences do you see between public speakers and advertisements?

 Communication
Works

online learning center

www.mhhe.com/gamble9

Key Chapter Terminology

Use the Communication Works CD-ROM and the Online Learning Center at www.mhhe.com/gamble9 to further your knowledge of the following terminology.

communication apprehension 460	manuscript speech 465
extemporaneous speech 465	memorized speech 465
impromptu speech 465	speech apprehension 460

Idioms in Translation

not up to par—ineffective

play it safe—avoid taking a risk

stomach knots—tightness in your stomach

Test Your Understanding

Go to the *Self Quizzes* on the Communication Works CD-ROM and the book's Online Learning Center at www.mhhe.com/gamble9.

Notes

1. See, for example, "Ailments Correlated with Anxiety." *USA Today*, June 3, 2003, p. 1A.

2. J. B. Donovan. "Power to the Podium: The Place to Stand for Those Who Move the World." *Vital Speeches of the Day* 58, 1991, pp. 149–150.

3. Ellen Joan Pollock. "The Selling of a Golden Speech." *Wall Street Journal*, March 12, 1999, p. B1. The Wall Street Journal Eastern Edition by Robert L. Bartley. Copyright 1999 By Dow Jones & Co. Inc. Reproduced with permission of Dow Jones & Co. via the Copyright Clearance Center.

4. See, for example, Timothy L. Sellnow. "Controlling Speech Anxiety." Paper presented at the annual meeting of the Speech Communication Association, Chicago, IL, October 29– November 1, 1992; Marianne Martin. "The Communication of Public Speaking Anxiety: Perception of Asian and American Speakers." *Communication Quarterly* 40, summer 1992, pp. 279–288; and James McCroskey, Steven Booth Butterfield, and Steven K. Payne. "The Impact of Communication Apprehension on College Student Retention and Success." *Communication Quarterly* 37, spring 1989, pp. 100–107.

5. Eleanor Blau. "Taking Arms against Stage Fright." *New York Times*, September 20, 1998, p. AR-33.

6. J. D. Mladenka, C. R. Sawyer, and R. R. Behnke. "Anxiety Sensitivity and Speech Trait Anxiety as Predictors of State Anxiety during Public Speaking." *Communication Quarterly* 46, 1998, pp. 417–429.

7. For a more detailed guide to fear-control training, see Joe Ayres and Tim Hopf. "Visualization: Reducing Speech Anxiety and Enhancing Performance." *Communication Reports* 1:1, winter 1992, pp. 1–10.

8. See the published proceedings of the Speech Communication Association's Summer Conference on Assessment, Washington, DC, August 4–7, 1994. In addition, the 1994 meeting of the Speech Communication Association (New Orleans, November 19–22) featured a short course: "A Workshop on Assessing Interpersonal, Public Speaking, and Listening Competence in the Fundamentals Course."

9. A number of useful Internet sites are contained in Cynthia B. Leshin. *Internet Investigations in Business Communication*. Upper Saddle River, NJ: Prentice Hall, 1997.

Informative Speaking

After finishing this chapter, you should be able to

1. Define *informative speaking*.

2. Distinguish among four types of informative discourse.

3. Explain how to create information hunger and increase listeners' comprehension.

4. Develop and present an informative speech.

We now face the prospect of information obesity.

—David Shenk

There are things that are known and things that are unknown; in between are doors.

—Anonymous

We live in the age of information. While information is, of course, valuable, David Shenk, author of *Data Smog: Surviving the Information Glut,* notes: "Just as fat has replaced starvation as this nation's number one dietary concern, information overload has replaced information scarcity as an important new emotional, social, and political problem."[1] The real problem facing the public speaker today is how to make information understandable. With the sum of human knowledge increasing at an unparalleled rate, are you prepared to communicate what you know to others in a way that creates interest so that they will listen, explain it in a way that enhances receiver understanding, and discuss it in a manner that helps audience members remember it?

■ ■ ■

SPEAKING INFORMATIVELY

What's happening? How does it work? What's going on? What is it? What does it mean? These are the kinds of questions that an **informative speech** answers. Whenever you prepare an informative speech, your goal is to offer your audience members more information than they already have about a topic. Your objective is to update and add to their knowledge, refine their understanding, or provide background.[2]

How does the informative speech relate to your life? What informative messages have you received recently? Have you read an online survey? Listened to a televised news report? A radio commentary? Have you received instructions or directions from a friend, an employer, a co-worker, or an instructor? Our world is filled with informative messages that we depend on. Many of these messages are informal, but others are carefully planned, structured, and rehearsed to achieve maximum impact. In today's world, it is important to develop the ability to share information with other people. Some three-quarters of the U.S. labor force hold jobs that require the production, storage, and/or delivery of information. Educators in schools and businesses, sales professionals, medical practitioners, and consultants and managers in a wide array of fields depend on their skill in giving and receiving information for their livelihoods. They all share the need to make their messages clear, relevant, and useful to receivers.

The authors of this book once worked with a corporate vice president who—although he had a fine mind and excellent analytical abilities—considered the process of passing information on to people both above and below him in the organizational hierarchy a "deadly bore." He saw little need to inform others of his

How many people do you know whose job requires them to deliver speeches? What percentage of their time is devoted to preparing and delivering speeches?

Go to the Online Learning Center at www.mhhe.com/gamble9 and answer the questions in the *Self Inventory* to evaluate your understanding of speech topics.

activities or his accomplishments. Not surprisingly, he no longer holds his former position of power and influence. When his company merged with another organization, he lost his job—primarily because he was unable to explain his responsibilities and achievements to the new administration. Knowing how to design and deliver effective informative messages has important implications for our careers and our lives.[3]

TYPES OF INFORMATIVE PRESENTATIONS

Let's now consider four types of informative speeches: (1) messages of explanation (speeches of demonstration that explain the how or how-to of a subject), (2) messages of description (speeches that describe what a person, an object, or an event is like), (3) messages of definition (speeches that define what something is), and (4) narrative messages (speeches that tell a story).

Explanations

If your purpose is to explain how to do something (for example, how to motivate employees), how to make something (for example, how to make glass), how something works (for example, how a slot machine works), or how something develops or occurs (for example, how tornadoes form, how insider trading works), then you are preparing to deliver an explanation of a process. Your primary goal is to share your understanding of the process or procedure with your listeners and, in some instances, to give them the skills they need to replicate it.

When organizing a message of explanation, be especially careful to avoid overcondensing the data. It is not uncommon for an inexperienced speaker to recite a long list of facts that merely enumerate the steps involved in a process. This kind of perfunctory outline is hard for an audience to follow. Instead, use meaningful information groups. For example, grouping information under such headings as "Gathering Ingredients," "Blending Ingredients," and "Adding the Garnish" would be considerably more effective than simply relaying 15 steps involved in preparing a chocolate mousse. Besides facilitating understanding, this grouping system also helps the audience retain the material.

It is also important to consider the length of time it will actually take to accomplish your objectives in a process speech. Take a tip from televised cooking shows. Notice how an on-the-air chef always demonstrates some parts of the process live but has other parts of the dish prepared in advance to save time. This technique can be of great value to you, too.

What processes are you equipped to speak about?

What techniques is this coach using to share information with his players?

Descriptions

One of your responsibilities as a speaker is to be able to describe a person, place, or thing for your listeners. For instance, if you

Ethics & Communication

Assessing Informative Speaking Skills
People rely on informative speaking almost constantly when on the job; the need to inform others and be informed by others is experienced daily throughout life.

Should we, therefore, assess who has and who has not mastered the skills needed to deliver and process informative discourse on the job or in other settings?
If not, why not? If so, how?

were a site-location specialist for a fast-food chain, you would have to describe potential store locations to the management. If you were a spokesperson for a nuclear plant that had experienced a radiation leak, you would have to describe the location and extent of the mishap to the media. Whatever the nature of a descriptive message, your aim is to help your listeners form mental close-ups of places, people, or things. To do this, you need to find ways to describe condition, size, shape, color, age, and so on to make your subject come alive for your audience.

Speakers tend to use either a spatial or a topical organizational pattern when describing a person, place, or thing. Thus, a speaker might choose to use a spatial pattern when describing the Clinton Presidential Library, but opt to use a topical organization to describe the scientific contributions of Galileo.

Of course, visual aids are particularly relevant to a descriptive presentation. For example, photographs, maps, and drawings can make it easier for you to describe a significant archaeological dig, the pathos of a homeless person, the appearance of a high-tech artificial limb, or the blight of an inner-city slum.

Whatever your topic, you will want to ensure that the words and phrases you select will evoke the appropriate sensory responses in your listeners. To do this, you will need to communicate how your subject looks, tastes, smells, feels, and sounds. In a descriptive speech, you also paint with words.

Definitions

"What do you mean?" is a common question. In most cases, the questioner asks it when seeking clarification or elaboration of ideas from a speaker. Sometimes a satisfactory answer can be supplied in a sentence or two. At other times, however, it takes a speech, or even a book, to define a concept adequately. For example, books with titles such as *Data Smog*, *The Age of Paradox*, *Emotional Intelligence*, *Leader Effectiveness Training*, *The Age of Missing Information*, and *Happiness Is . . .* are actually extended definitions: The authors are discussing their meaning for a particular concept or idea. An informative speech of definition likewise provides an audience with an explanation of a term. "Shyness," "The Grief Cycle," "ESP," and "Muscular Dystrophy" are among the topics for which a definitional presentation would be appropriate.

Can you think of others? Many students find that topics such as "Racial Profiling," "The Meaning of Obscenity," "Prejudice," "Friendship," and "Sexual Harassment" give them the freedom they need to develop effective speeches of definition.

Skill Builder

What Does It Mean?

1. Working individually or in groups, list topics for a speech of definition.
2. Select five of the topics and develop purpose statements for them (see Chapter 13).
3. Design and present a three- to five-minute speech in which you define a concept or an idea. Organize it carefully and submit an outline.

Since many of the concepts you may choose to define will have connotative, or subjective, meanings not traditionally found in dictionaries, not all members of your audience will agree with the definition you present. On one television talk show, for example, two experts on shyness were unable to agree on what it means to be shy. It is necessary, therefore, to organize a definitional speech in a way that will be clear and persuasive. For example, how would you define *shyness?* To explain your meaning for the term, you might offer examples of what it feels like to be shy, describe how a shy person behaves, and then go on to discuss the consequences of shyness. Perhaps you would explain shyness by comparing and contrasting a shy person with an extrovert. Or you might choose to discuss the causes of shyness and then focus on different types or categories of shyness. No matter how you choose to order your ideas, your organization should be suggested by the topic and grow out of it.

Narratives

Extended stories, or narratives, function as "teaching moments" and are an alternative means of providing information. They are often more entertaining and involving than more traditional approaches to informative speaking. Speakers who use the narrative format need to convey clearly the message contained in the story they tell so that audience members perceive its relevance. "Post-Traumatic Stress Syndrome: A Soldier's Story," "The Story of My Brother's Death: My Travels through the Cycle of Grief," "My Adoption," and "How I Used a Defibrillator to Save a Life" are the titles of informative speeches in which speakers could benefit from using a narrative approach to tell audience members more about their subject. Speakers can use temporal, topical, and spatial patterns to develop informational personal narratives.

EFFECTIVE INFORMATIVE SPEECHES: INCREASING YOUR LISTENERS' INTEREST AND COMPREHENSION

An effective informative speech accomplishes several tasks: (1) makes your listeners want to learn more about the topic; (2) communicates the information clearly by providing information balance; (3) emphasizes key points; (4) involves audience members in your presentation; and (5) provides information in ways that make it memorable, perhaps through novelty, creativity, and audiovisuals. Let's look at these tasks.

Create Information Hunger

Your primary goal in an informative speech is to deliver a message of explanation, description, definition, or narrative, but it is equally important that audience members find your presentation interesting, intellectually stimulating, and relevant (that is, significant or personally valuable). In other words, you need to work to increase each listener's need to know and hunger to receive your message.

You will be more adept at creating information hunger if you have analyzed your audience carefully (see Chapter 13). Then, by using appropriate vehicles, you will be able to generate the interest that will motivate audience members to listen to the information you want to share. Remember to use the attention-getting devices discussed in Chapter 15. For example, you can relate your own experiences or the experiences of others; you can ask rhetorical questions; you can draw analogies for your listeners to consider. You can also arouse the audience's curiosity, and you can incorporate humor or use eye-catching visual aids.

Obviously, your effectiveness as a speaker will increase to the extent that you present your information creatively and succeed in arousing the desire and the need to know among audience members.

Seek Information Balance

Your speech will inform receivers only if they are capable of processing the information you deliver. A common danger in informative speaking is that the audience experiences information overload. **Information overload** occurs when (1) the speech maker delivers far more data about the topic than the audience needs or wants, confusing listeners and causing them to tune out what is being communicated; and (2) the speech maker presents ideas in words the listeners do not understand. Instead of using clear language and speaking at a level the audience comprehends, the speaker creates frustration among audience members by using unfamiliar jargon or words that soar beyond the reach of the listeners' vocabulary. Forgetting that an informative speech will fail if its ideas are superfluous or unclear, some speakers end up talking to themselves rather than to the audience. Remember, your speech must be understandable.

A speaker who tries to avoid information overload will often overcompensate and create a situation of information underload. **Information underload** occurs when the speaker underestimates the sophistication or intelligence of the audience members and tells them little that they do not already know.

As a speech maker, you need to strike a balance, providing neither too little information nor too much. As a rule, effective speech makers neither underestimate nor overestimate the capabilities of the audience. Instead, they motivate their listeners to want to fill in any information gaps.

Emphasize Key Points

As we discussed in Chapter 14, emphasis can be created through repetition (saying the same thing over again) and restatement (saying the same thing in another way). As long as you do not become overly repetitious and redundant, these devices will help your listeners process and retain the main points of your speech.

The organization of your speech can also reinforce your main ideas. Remember that you can use your introduction to preview ideas in your conclusion and

Focus on Service Learning

Develop a list of Web sites you could visit to prepare a presentation on the Medicare prescription drug plan or another topic of interest to senior citizens. Then using information provided on Web sites such as www.infolit.org/, www.noodletools.com, and www.medicare.gov, work with the leader(s) of a community group composed primarily of seniors to help the group's members deal more effectively with the challenges posed by the Medicare prescription drug plan (introduced in 2006) or the other topic of your choosing.

information overload
the situation that occurs when the amount of information provided by a speech maker is too great to be handled effectively by receivers

information underload
the situation that occurs when the information provided by a speech maker is already known to receivers

Exploring Diversity

Conveying Information across Cultures

Through informative presentations, speakers attempt to describe something, demonstrate how something works, or explain a concept. Their goal is to convey knowledge and understanding. For this goal to be realized, the information they want to share must be communicated clearly.

However, people who *seem* to speak the same language may in reality come from divergent backgrounds. How can such speakers hope to communicate clearly with each other? How can an appreciation of the communicative behavior of people from cultures different from your own facilitate this effort?

to help make those ideas memorable. Transitions and internal summaries also help create a sense of cohesiveness.

Involve Your Listeners

The relationship between audiences and speakers is changing. Contemporary audiences are restless. They are used to playing video games and talking back to small screens. Public speakers need to work to channel the nervous energy of their audience members.[4] People learn more if they become involved with the material that is being presented to them. Effective speech makers do not view the audience as a passive receptacle; rather, they work to find ways to let the audience take an active part in the presentation. For example, the audience may be called on to perform an activity during the presentation. If you are giving a speech on how to reduce stress, you might have your listeners actually try one or two stress-reducing exercises. Or if your speech topic is "How to Read an EKG," you might pass out sample EKGs for audience members to decipher.

Receivers learn more when directly involved in a presentation.

Provide Information Memorably

Remember that people want to understand and remember information that they perceive as relevant to their own lives. Few of us would have much interest in a speech on the development of bees. If, however, we found that the bees we are hearing about are a new species of killer bee that is extremely resistant to common insecticides, and that droves of these bees are on the way to our community and will arrive within the next two weeks, we would develop an intense interest very quickly.

Audiences also want to listen to new information. In this case, the term *new* means "new to them." A historical blunder may be new in this sense, and it may be relevant to a college or business audience today. The cable television industry has found that weather is worthy of its own channel; the weather forecast is constantly being updated and is therefore considered new.

Repetition can help as well; audiences respond to information that is repeated. Martin Luther King, Jr., understood the value of repetition in his "I have a dream" speech. Jesse Jackson uses repetition to foster his audiences' retention as well as their emotional involvement. As you prepare your informative speech, look for ways to let repetition augment your message.

NOVELTY AND CREATIVITY

An effective speaker looks constantly for ways to approach information from an unusual direction. If you are the fifth speaker that your audience will hear on the homeless, you must find a different slant or approach to the topic, or the audience may be bored from the outset. You might try taking a different point of view—through the eyes of a child, for example. Look for analogies that bring topics home to an audience: "The number of people entering teaching today is diminishing. The teaching profession is like a stream drying up." Try other ways to complete this analogy. As you prepare your presentation, remember that you are looking for creative ways of bringing your topic to life for the audience.

Take your mind out every now and then and dance on it. It is getting all caked up.

—Mark Twain

AUDIOVISUAL AIDS

You will want to include audiovisual aids in an informative presentation. Remember first, though, that you are your primary visual aid. The way you stand, walk, talk, and gesture is extremely important to the effectiveness of your presentation. Avoid hiding behind the lectern; avoid reading your notes. Move to the side. Use gestures to show the size and shape of objects.

Take objects, or make simple models if you cannot take the objects themselves. Use PowerPoint charts and graphs when appropriate. You can also have a graph converted to a transparency at a local copy shop so that you can use it with an overhead projector.

Also consider using video and audio clips to create interest. You can use camcorders to conduct interviews or show processes at work. One student, for example, interviewed other students about campus parking problems. Another showed a brief tape of a chemical reaction that could not have been demonstrated safely in the classroom.

The Internet is another source of visuals. On various Web sites, you will find images, charts, and graphs that you can incorporate into your presentation to help communicate your message.

TECHNOLOGY AND THE INFORMATIVE SPEAKER

Our society faces a knowledge gap. Because new communication technologies require that users have both the skill to use them and the money to afford them, specialized knowledge and wealth enable some people to acquire more information than those who are not as fortunate. Today, technological access and opportunities to gain knowledge go hand in hand. As researchers Jeanie Taylor and Cheris Kramarae note, "If the future of information is electronic, we need to ensure access for everyone, not just an elite. We imagine computer terminals connected to community systems in laundromats, homeless shelters, daycare centers, etc.—with sufficient support so that most people have access to the Internet." They continue by noting that poor is the "community that knowlingly allows whole segments of our real world to be excluded from the Internet."[5]

Significant efforts are being made to decrease the size of the knowledge gap. Once we have the technological access, we can use the information that is freely available on the Internet. There is a wide array of special interest lists where individuals can join a virtual community on a topic of interest and receive electronic mail in the form of a report, an article, an abstract, or a personal reaction. The following are two of the best resources for finding such mailing lists:

www.liszt.com

www.tile.net/tile/listserv/index.html

In addition, you can request information on listserv mailing lists for a particular subject by sending an e-mail message to LISTSERV@vm1.nodak.edu.

Usenet groups are similar to listserv groups, only larger. A Usenet group is a distributed bulletin board system (BBS) comprising thousands of specialized discussion groups. Once you subscribe to a newsgroup, you can scan the group's messages and send your own comments or questions.

When preparing an informative speech, you can use a search directory such as Google or Yahoo! to search for information on your chosen topic. You would then explore the links that seem to contain the most promising information. If you receive too much information—remember the dangers of information overload—narrow your search. If you receive too little information—remember the dangers of information underload—broaden your search.

Thinking Critically

Reflect and Respond

Agree or disagree with the following statement; supply reasons and examples that support your stance.

All information is persuasive. Thus, there is no such thing as an informative speech.

Then examine the sample informative speech outline and speech transcript that follow. Discuss how each sample can be used in defense of the position you have taken.

SAMPLE INFORMATIVE SPEECH OUTLINE

FULL SENTENCE OUTLINE

Topic:	Mad cow disease
Purpose:	To inform the class about the nature, causes, means of transmission, and symptoms of bovine spongiform encephalopathy (mad cow disease)
Central idea:	It is important for us to understand the facts about mad cow disease.

The purpose statement and central idea guide the speaker in developing the outline.

Introduction

I. A mad cow scare in the United States in December 2003 caused Japan to close its borders to U.S. beef. The ban on U.S. imports remained in effect for two years, not resuming until December 2005. Then just a short five and one-half weeks later, on January 21, 2006, Andrew Morton reported in *The Record* that after being shipped meat from the U.S. that they considered at risk for mad cow disease, the Japanese again abruptly slammed shut their doors to beef from the United States, asserting that it posed too many health risks.

The use of statistics, personalization, and a visual aid draw receivers into the speech.

II. Mad cow cases extend beyond the U.S. For example, on February 7, 2002, the *New York Times* reported that an Italian woman was afflicted with mad cow disease. That brought the number of human cases of the disease to over 100 worldwide. Among those concerned with this seemingly small number of human cases is McDonald's. McDonald's has seen its stock slide 40 percent as a direct result of MCD.

III. [Show McDonald's hamburger box visual.] Mad cow disease also threatens you and me.

IV. Today I would like to tell you about the nature, causes, means of transmission, and symptoms of bovine spongiform encephalopathy (mad cow disease).

The speaker reveals the speech's purpose.

Transition to main point I: First, let's explore what mad cow disease really is.

continued

The use of an actual McDonald's box enhanced the speaker's presentation.

The speech's body is organized into four main points, each with a number of subpoints. Note that every entry in the body is a complete sentence and contains only a single idea.

The speaker uses a definition, statistics, and a video to develop the first main point of the speech.

Body

I. Mad cow disease is a fatal disease.
  A. The disease enters and destroys the brains of cattle and other animals, including sheep, deer, and elk.
  B. Since 1986, over 200,000 cows worldwide have been diagnosed with the deadly disease.
  C. Recently the CBS program *60 Minutes II* showed what mad cow looks like in a dying cow. [Show video clip: *60 Minutes.*]

Transition to main point II: Now that we have seen the results of the disease, let's consider its cause.

II. According to Dr. Stanley Prusiner, the cause of mad cow disease is a deformed prion that kills the brain.
  A. The prion is a new infectious particle.
    1. The prion literally pokes holes in the brains of animals.
    2. Eventually the brain looks much like this piece of Swiss cheese. [Visual: samples of Swiss cheese.]
  B. According to Dr. Robert Gallo, MCD cannot be killed.
    1. Antibiotics are not effective.
    2. Cooking does not kill the disease.

The speaker uses a definition, a dramatic visual, and startling facts to develop the second main point of the speech.

Transition to main point III: Next, we need to examine how the disease is spread.

III. Mad cow disease spreads through infected feed.
  A. In the 1980s, cattle feed producers began feeding the ground-up parts of deceased animals to living cows.
    1. Healthy cows ate the remains of infected cows in a process called "rendering."

Testimony and imagery enable the speaker to develop the speech's third main point.

2. In Sheldon Rampton and John Stauberr's *Mad Cow USA,* Van Smith, a news reporter describes rendering: "A load of guts, heads, and legs recently retrieved from a local slaughterhouse sits stewing in one of the raw material bins at the plant's receiving bay. It will be fed into the hogger, a shredder that grinds up the tissue before it is deep fried in cookers charged with spent restaurant grease and blood."

B. The disease spreads to humans when they eat infected cows.

1. According to reporter Sandra Blakeslee, the human variant of mad cow disease, new variant Creutzfeld-Jacob disease (new variant CJD), first appeared in 1995 in young people in England.

2. The brains of new variant CJD victims are filled with holes—similar to the holes found in the brains of diseased cows.

3. CJD kills within 18 months.

C. Dietary supplements and vaccines may also spread CJD to humans.

1. Supplements such as Male Power and Brain Nutrition contain extracts from cattle organs.

2. The *New York Times* lists vaccines such as polio, diptheria, and tetanus as also containing ingredients from cows.

Transition to main point IV: Now that we have discussed how MCD can be transmitted, let's talk about its symptoms.

IV. Mad cow disease has a number of symptoms.

A. Cows lose weight, are skittish, behave belligerently, and appear confused.

B. People experience paranoia, suffer from lack of coordination, and lapse into a coma.

The speaker uses a series of dramatic images to develop the last main point of the speech.

Conclusion

I. Today we have explored the nature, causes, means of transmission, and symptoms of deadly mad cow disease.

II. It is possible that mad cow, a disease with no known cure, could be the plague of our time. Surveys reveal that around the world people still won't eat U.S. beef because of mad cow fears. Whereas the U.S. used to export beef to 119 countries, according to *Record* reporter Andrew Morton, it now exports beef to about 70. [Visual: Hold up the McDonald's fast-food container shown in the introduction.]

The speaker summarizes what the speech has accomplished and uses a visual that refers receivers to the speech's introduction, providing a sense of closure.

SAMPLE INFORMATIVE SPEECH

Topic:	Mad cow disease
Purpose:	To inform the class about the nature, causes, means of transmission, and symptoms of bovine spongiform encephalopathy (mad cow disease)
Central idea:	It is important for us to understand the facts about mad cow disease.

A mad cow scare in the United States in December 2003 caused Japan to close its borders to U.S. beef. The ban on U.S. imports remained in effect for two years, finally resuming in December 2005. Then just a short five and one-half weeks later, on January 31, 2006, Andrew Morton reported in *The Record* that after being shipped meat from the U.S. that they considered at risk for mad cow disease, the Japanese again abruptly slammed shut their doors to beef from the United States, asserting that it posed too many health risks.

Mad cow cases extend beyond the U.S. For example, on February 7, 2002, the *New York Times* reported that an Italian woman was afflicted with spongiform encephalopathy, better known as mad cow disease. That means that, to date, over 100 cases of this disease have been reported around the world. Among those especially concerned about this seemingly small number of cases of the disease is McDonald's. Why is McDonald's concerned? On January 25, 2002 [show McDonald's hamburger box visual], *Wall Street Journal* reporter Shirley Leung, in her article "McDonald's Net Sinks 40% on Fears over Slump, Mad-Cow Disease," noted that the net worth of the McDonald's corporation had shrunk 40 percent—in large part because of the threat posed by mad cow disease. Mad cow disease, however, doesn't only threaten McDonald's. It also threatens us. Today I would like to explain to you what mad cow disease is, how it is caused, its means of transmission, and what the symptoms of the disease are.

First, let's examine what bovine spongiform encephalopathy is.

Mad cow disease is a fatal disease that attacks the brains of cattle. It is one of a family of brain-destroying diseases that affect many species, including sheep, deer, elk, and humans. Mad cow disease made its first known appearance in cattle in England in 1984. It was diagnosed in 1986. Since then, over 200,000 cows have fallen ill with mad cow disease.

A few years ago, the CBS program *60 Minutes II* showed us what mad cow disease looks like in an afflicted cow. [Show video: Opening segment of the *60 Minutes II* presentation.]

What causes such a horrible disease? The cause of mad cow disease is a mutant protein, a prion, that kills the brain. CBS news correspondent Wyatt Andrews, in a report that aired January 31, 2001, revealed that, according to Dr. Stanley Prusiner, who won the Nobel Prize in medicine for his work with this prion, "The prion is a completely new infectious particle. It's not a virus, not a bacterium,

Does the speaker succeed in gaining your attention? Do you feel the topic of the speech has relevance?

Do you find the use of this visual effective? Is there any other visual you might have considered using in the introduction?

How effective do you find the speaker's orientation? Does it prepare you for what is to come?

Does this transition accomplish its purpose? Is it lengthy enough?

What is the speaker aiming to accomplish with the first main point? Even though you are not able to watch it, do you believe that the use of a brief video is appropriate and facilitative of the speaker's purpose?

not a fungus. It's a natural protein in mammals that can mysteriously deform itself, replicate, and concentrate in the brain." Thus, mad cow disease is composed of deformed prions, deadly variants of proteins that occur normally in nerve cells. According to the prion hypothesis, an abnormally shaped prion is eaten and absorbed into the bloodstream. It then crosses into the nervous system. The abnormally shaped prion changes normal prions into abnormal ones. The nerve cells try to get rid of the abnormal prions but can't. Because the nerve cells can't digest the abnormal prions, they accumulate and die. When the deadly prions enter the brains of animals, they literally poke holes in them. Over time, the brains become so filled with holes that they resemble this sample of Swiss cheese [show visual aid]. By this time, due to numerous nerve cell deaths, the brains can no longer function and the cows literally shake to death. Dr. Robert Gallo, a University of Maryland researcher who was also interviewed by Wyatt Andrews for CBS News, tells us that, unfortunately, nothing is as indestructible as a prion. Neither antibiotics nor heat is effective in killing a prion. A prion, it seems, can survive a temperature as high as 600 degrees Centigrade. Thus, cooking meat does not kill the prion.

Now that we know what mad cow disease is, let's consider how the disease is spread.

How did mad cow disease get into cattle in the first place? The theory is that mad cow disease got into cattle as a result of infected sheep that were ground up and added to the cattle feed. In the 1980s, producers of cattle feed (which often included ground meat and bone meal by-products from sheep) changed the way they processed feed. The change somehow enabled the scrappy disease agent to survive the cattle feed production process. As a result, contaminated food was fed to cattle.

Why were parts of dead animals fed to cattle in the first place? The answer is simple. In order to avoid waste, it was common for countries such as Great Britain to dispose of tons of animal waste by grinding the waste into meal and feeding it to cattle, unaware that the waste being used might contain the fatal brain-wasting disease. The process by which this is accomplished is called rendering. Over time, according to Sheldon Rampton and John Stauber, authors of the book *Mad Cow USA*, healthy cattle were fed contaminated feed that came from the waste of cows already infected with mad cow disease. In other words, healthy cows ate the remains of infected cows, caught the disease, and became sick. As reported in Rampton and Stauber's *Mad Cow USA*, Baltimore newspaper reporter Van Smith described the rendering process like this:

> A load of guts, heads, and legs recently retrieved from a local slaughterhouse sits stewing in one of the raw material bins at the plant's receiving bay. It will be fed into the hogger, a shredder that grinds up the tissue before it is deep fried in cookers charged with spent restaurant grease and blood. Suddenly a hot gust of wind blows droplets of it on us. As the bloated stomachs and broken body parts slide from the trailer bed to the bin, the workman shouts out, "Watch out for the splatter."

continued

Is the speaker's choice of expert appropriate? Is the speaker's explication easy to follow?

How do you respond to the speaker's choice of a visual aid? Does it advance the speaker's goal?

Would you change this transition in any way?

How do you respond to the speaker's use of rhetorical questions? Do you think the device is overused?

What does the speaker do to add credibility to the information being provided to receivers?

Can you imagine yourself reading this description? How could delivery be used to enhance impact?

It is the practice of rendering that researchers believe led to the spread of the disease. In effect, newly infected cows were slaughtered and then their brains and spinal cords were put back into animal feed. The feed was given to more cows, spreading the disease. Ultimately, human beings also ate the beef of cows that ate the feed containing the abnormal prions that cause mad cow disease. It was humans' eating the diseased meat of infected animals that enabled the disease to cross the species barrier.

How would you evaluate the speaker's use of research? In your opinion, does the research add to the speaker's credibility?

In 1995, the first case of a new form of Creutzfeld-Jacob disease, called new variant CJD, was diagnosed in Great Britain. Reporter Sandra Blakeslee, author of the article "On Watch for Any Hint of Mad Cow Disease," which appeared in the *New York Times* on January 30, 2001, tells us that, unlike traditional Creutzfeld-Jacob disease, a deadly illness due to genetic causes that affects about one in a million, typically older, people, new variant CJD also occurs in younger people, who, it is believed, get the disease by eating contaminated beef. The brains of new variant CJD human victims have prion-caused holes similar to those found in the brains of mad cow–infected cows. New variant CJD usually kills its human victims within 18 months from the onset of their symptoms.

This is not the whole story, however. The disease may be spread to humans in at least two other ways as well. Since 1991, the United States Department of Agriculture has prohibited the importation of the tissues and organs of cattle from countries that have been shown to have animals afflicted with mad cow disease. Most recently, the Agriculture Department forbid the importation of beef from Canada when a member of a cattle herd there was found to have died from mad cow disease. Unfortunately for us, these government regulations do not specifically apply to cosmetics or products used in dietary supplements. According to *USA Today* reporter Anita Manning, in an article titled "U.S. Supplements May Harbor Mad Cow Disease," issued on January 22, 2001, dietary supplements, including ones labeled "Male Power" and "Brain Nutrition," could contain imported extracts from brains, testicles, and other cattle organs. In addition, Melody Peterson and Greg Winter reported in their article, "5 Drug Makers Use Material with Possible Mad Cow Link," which appeared in the February 8, 2001, issue of the *New York Times,* that vaccines, including some given to millions of American children, such as polio, diphtheria, and tetanus, as well as the vaccine given to soldiers to protect against anthrax, could also contain ingredients from mad cow infected animals.

Now that we have discussed how mad cow disease can be transmitted, let's talk about its symptoms.

Is the speaker's description of symptoms vivid enough for you? If you were giving the speech, would you have included another visual aid prior to the speech's conclusion?

How can you tell when an animal or a human is infected with mad cow disease? Unfortunately, there is no current way to diagnose the disease before symptoms appear. The symptoms of the disease are horrific in both cows and humans. Cows lose weight, become skittish, act belligerently, appear confused, and suffer paralysis. People experience psychotic problems; become paranoid; suffer from a lack of muscle coordination; experience spasms, terrible tremors, and hearing and vision loss; and eventually suffer from dementia and lapse into a coma. There is no treatment or cure for the disease currently available. No one knows how many animals are harboring mad cow disease or how many people are infected with it.

Today we have explored the nature, causes, means of transmission, and symptoms of mad cow disease. The advent of mad cow disease and its human form, new variant Creutzfeld-Jacob disease, means that we may be living in a mad, mad, mad, mad world. If, like me and Nobel Prize–winning scientist Dr. Prousiner, you're wondering if mad cow disease could turn out to be the plague of the twenty-first century, consider this: 10 to 15 years or more can elapse from the time one eats meat from a mad cow–diseased animal until symptoms occur in a human. It was not that long ago, on Christmas Eve 2003, that the press reported the first case of mad cow in the U.S. A second case was discovered in Texas that June. Surveys reveal that around the world people still won't eat U.S. beef because of mad cow fears. Whereas the U.S. used to export beef to 119 countries, according to *Record* reporter Andrew Martin, it now exports beef to about 70. Thus, only time will tell if we have this disease. Hamburger anyone? [Hold up visual.]

Does the speaker effectively summarize the speech? What does the speaker do to give the speech a sense of closure? How else might the speaker have concluded the speech?

Works Consulted

Andrews, Wyatt. "The Science of Mad Cow Disease." *CBS News,* January 31, 2001.

Blakeslee, Sandra. "On Watch for Any Hint of Mad Cow Disease." *New York Times,* January 30, 2001, p. F3.

_____ "Study Lends Support to Mad Cow Theory," *New York Times,* July 30, 2004, p. A13.

"Italy: Mad Cow Disease Infects Woman." *New York Times,* February 7, 2002, p. A6.

Leung, Shirley. "McDonald's Net Sinks 40% on Fears over Slump, Mad-Cow Disease." *Wall Street Journal,* January 25, 2002, p. A16.

Manning, Anita. "U.S. Supplements May Harbor Mad Cow Disease." *USA Today,* January 22, 2001, p. 7D.

Morton, Andrew. "Japan Halts Imports of U.S. Beef over Error." *The Record,* January 21, 2006, pp. A1, A9.

Peterson, Melody, and Greg Winter. "5 Drug Makers Use Materials with Possible Mad Cow Link." *New York Times,* February 8, 2001, pp. C1, C5.

Rampton, Sheldon, and John Stauber. *Mad Cow, USA.* Monroe, ME: Common Courage Press, 1977.

Ridley, Matt. "Mad Cow Disease Is a Little Less Scarier." *New York Times,* May 25, 2003, p. wk3.

Wald, Matthew, and Eric Lichtblau. "U.S. Is Examining a Mad Cow Case, First in Country." *New York Times,* December 24, 2003, pp. A1, 19.

In your opinion, did the speaker provide you with information that you need and can use?

SAMPLE SPEAKER'S NOTES

Topic: Mad cow disease

Purpose: To inform the class about the nature, causes, means of transmission, and symptoms of bovine spongiform encephalopathy (mad cow disease)

Central idea: It is important for us to understand the facts about mad cow disease.

Introduction

I. January 2006, mad cow fears cause Japan to again ban U.S. beef imports.

II. Not long before, in February 2002, the *New York Times* reported the 100th case of MCD.

III. *Wall Street Journal* reporter Shirley Leung, "McDonald's net sinks 40% on fears over slump, Mad-Cow Disease." [Visual: McDonald's box]

IV. Today I would like to tell you about the nature, causes, means of transmission, and symptoms of MCD.

Body

I. What MCD is

Fatal

200,000 cows diagnosed

60 Minutes [video clip]

II. Cause

Mutant prion kills the brain.

Nobel Prize winner Dr. Stanley Prusiner: "The prion is a completely new infectious particle. It's not a virus, not a bacterium, not a fungus. It's a natural protein in mammals that can mysteriously deform itself, replicate, and concentrate in the brain." (CBS News, January 31, 2001)

Brain looks like a piece of Swiss cheese. [Visual: Swiss cheese]

Wyatt Andrews (CBS News): There's nothing as indestructible as a prion.

III. How MCD is spread

Ground-up sheep and cow parts fed to cattle

Through the rendering process

Described by Baltimore newspaper reporter Van Smith in *Mad Cow USA:* "A load of guts, heads, and legs recently retrieved from a local slaughterhouse sits stewing in one of the raw material bins at the plant's receiving bay. It will be fed into the hogger, a shredder that grinds up the tissue before it is deep fried in cookers charged with spent restaurant grease and blood. Suddenly a hot gust of wind blows droplets of it on us. As the bloated stomachs and broken body parts slide from the trailer bed to the bin, the workman shouts out, 'Watch out for the splatter.'"

Human form of mad cow disease, CJD

Reporter Sandra Blakeslee *NYT* report, January 30, 2001

Brains look like Swiss cheese, too.

    In cosmetics and dietary supplements, such as Male Power.

        USA Today Reporter Anita Manning Report, January 22, 2001

        Melody Peterson and Greg Winter Report, February 8, 2001

    IV. Symptoms: How do you know if a cow or human is infected?

    Cows lose weight, skittish, confused.

    People suffer lack of coordination and paranoia. There is no treatment.

Conclusion

    I. Today we have explored the nature, causes, means of transmission, and symptoms of MCD.

    II. Reference to Dr. Prousiner

   III. Reference to problems of 2003 and 2006.

    IV. It is possible that mad cow could be the plague of our times.

    V. Hamburger, anyone? [Visual: Fast-food hamburger box]

Revisiting Chapter Objectives

1. **Define informative speaking.** The goal of the informative speaker is to offer audience members more information than they presently have about a topic. Informative speaking aims to update and add knowledge, refine understanding, or provide background.

2. **Distinguish among four types of informative discourse.** Four kinds of informative speaking with which you need to be familiar are (1) messages of explanation, which explain the what or how-to of a subject; (2) messages of description, which describe what a person, an object, or an event is like; (3) messages of definition, which define what something is; and (4) narrative messages, which tell a story.

3. **Explain how to create information hunger and increase listeners' comprehension.** A primary goal of the informative speech is to increase each listener's need to know and hunger to receive a message. To do this, speakers need to analyze the audience and use appropriate attention-getting devices to generate receiver interest in their topics. At the same time that speakers work to create interest in receivers, they also need to avoid overloading or underloading receivers with information.

4. **Develop and present an informative speech.** Being able to design and deliver an effective informative speech has important implications for both your career and your life. An effective informative speech makes listeners want to learn more about the topic, communicates information clearly, involves audience members, and delivers information in a way that makes the speech memorable.

The Wrap Up

Resources for Further Inquiry and Reflection

To apply your understanding of how the principles in Chapter 17 are at work in our daily lives, consult the following resources for further inquiry and reflection. Or, if you prefer, choose any other appropriate resource. Then connect the ideas expressed in your chosen selection with the communication concepts and issues you are learning about both in and out of class.

 ### Listen to Me

"You Talk Too Much" (Joe Jones)
"The Wreck of the Edmund Fitzgerald" (Gordon Lightfoot)
"How to Dismantle an Atomic Bomb" (U2)

What lesson(s) can a speaker deduce from the laments of these songs' singers?

 ### View Me

Flight Plan	*Erin Brockovich*
Munich	*Silkwood*
All the President's Men	*My Cousin Vinnie*

To what extent did information hunger drive the investigation featured in each of the preceding films? What did the investigator do to enhance receiver comprehension of his or her discoveries?

 ### Read Me

Peter Morville. *Ambient Findability: What We find Changes Who We Become.* New York: O'Reilly Media, 2005.
David Shenk. *Data Smog: Surviving the Information Glut.* New York: HarperCollins, 1997.

Can we receive too much information? If yes, what are our options? If no, what steps should we take to facilitate our powers of information processing?

 ### Tell Me

Share with the class the insights you gained from your chosen Listen to Me, View Me, or Read Me selection.

Large quantities of spam, much of it with deceptive titles, are clogging the information arteries of our computers. In your opinion, should spam be regulated or censored to keep it out of our e-mail boxes? Should the sender of spam be assessed a fee?

What should we do to keep the information arteries of our mind clear of information clutter? With the voluminous amounts of information being created daily, what guidelines can we use to filter in, not out, what we need to know?

Communication
Works

online learning center

www.mhhe.com/gamble9

Key Chapter Terminology

Use the Communication Works CD-ROM and the Online Learning Center at www.mhhe.com/gamble9 to further your knowledge of the following terminology.

information overload 483	informative speech 480
information underload 483	

Idioms in Translation

bring topics home—find topics that interest

encyclopedic—voluminous

information balance—the right amount of information

strike a balance—achieve balance

Test Your Understanding

Go to the *Self Quizzes* on the Communication Works CD-ROM and the book's Online Learning Center at www.mhhe.com/gamble9.

Communication
Works

online learning center

www.mhhe.com/gamble9

Notes

1. David Shenk. *Data Smog: Surviving the Information Glut.* New York: HarperCollins, 1997, p. 29.

2. Although compiled years ago, a valuable source to consult is Charles Petrie. "Informative Speaking: A Summary and Bibliography of Related Research." *Speech Monographs* 30, 1963, pp. 79-91.

3. For a discussion on the informative speech, see Douglas Ehninger, Bruce Gronbeck, Ray McKerrow, and Alan Monroc. *Principles and Types of Speech Communication.* New York: HarperCollins, 1992.

4. See for example, Brendan Lemon. "Audiences Today Are Getting In on the Act." *The New York Times,* October 8, 2000, pp. AR-5, AR-22.

5. Quoted in Karen A. Foss, Sonja K. Foss, and Cindy L. Griffin. *Feminist Rhetorical Theories.* Thousand Oaks, CA: Sage, 1999, p. 51.

Persuasive Speaking

After finishing this chapter, you should be able to

1. Define *persuasive speaking*.

2. Define and distinguish between *attitudes* and *beliefs*.

3. Distinguish between logical and fallacious reasoning.

4. Explain the concept of credibility.

5. Develop and present a persuasive speech.

Man is the only animal that laughs and weeps; for he is the only animal that is struck with the difference between what things are and what they ought to be.

—William Hazlitt

It is not enough to identify the gene that predetermines the prospect of Alzheimer's disease if we go through the prime of life with a closed mind.

—Tom Brokaw

"Vote for me," the candidate advises. "Buy me," reads the ad. "Attend my rally," cries the advocate. "Support my cause," demands the lobbyist. "Give money to our movement," pleads the fund-raiser. Persuasion, the process of changing or reinforcing attitudes, beliefs, values, or behavior, is an integral part of our everyday activities. Advertisers, public relations professionals, politicians, religious leaders, and numerous others have the same primary goal—persuading you.

Our aim in this chapter is to increase your ability to prepare, present, and process persuasive speeches by showing you how to apply your general knowledge and skills to this special type of discourse.

■ ■ ■

SPEAKING PERSUASIVELY

When you deliver a **persuasive speech,** your goal is to modify the thoughts, feelings, or actions of your audience. You hope that your listeners will change attitudes or behaviors you do not approve of and adopt attitudes and behaviors that are compatible with your interests and the way you see the world. Persuasive discourse is becoming increasingly important; more than ever, we are concerned with being able to influence others.[1]

Today's communication environment demands effective persuasion skills. In fact, with the exception of class lectures, a majority of the presentations others direct at you are likely persuasive. So are the majority of presentations you make to others. When was the last time you tried to change someone's mind at home, at school, or at work? Maybe you wanted to be given the opportunity to improve a grade on a paper and had to develop reasons why your instructor should allow you a "do over." At work, you may have sought to persuade your employer to give you a raise or a more responsible position. Whatever your objective, it is the attitudes, beliefs, and values of the person(s) on the receiving end of your persuasive appeal that you use to frame and support your case. So, whether you are negotiating to buy property, arguing that the jury should acquit your client, working in support of Amnesty International, or making an appeal for any one of thousands of other causes, understanding your receivers enables you to decide how to approach persuasive discourse.

"I found the old format much more exciting."

persuasive speech

a speech whose primary purpose is to change or reinforce the attitudes, beliefs, values, and/or behaviors of receivers

proposition

a statement that summarizes the purpose of a persuasive speech

Go to the Online Learning Center at www.mhhe.com/gamble9 and answer the questions in the *Self Inventory* to evaluate your understanding of fallacious reasoning.

PURPOSES OF PERSUASION: THOUGHT AND ACTION

A speaker may believe that flying saucers exist, even though most of the audience may not; oppose bilingual education, while others support it; or want audience members to become organ donors, while audience members feel reluctant to make that commitment. The speaker's objective, sometimes referred to as the **proposition** of the speech, indicates what type of change the speaker would like to create in audience members. Typically, speakers want one or both of two general outcomes: They want to convince listeners that something is so (that is, to change the way audience members think), or they want to cause audience members to take an action (that is, to change the way they behave). Whatever the general nature of the proposition, it most likely will reflect at least one of the following persuasive goals: adoption, discontinuance, deterrence, or continuance.[2]

When your goal is *adoption*, you hope to persuade the audience to accept a new idea, attitude, or belief (for example, that genetically engineered food is hazardous to health), with the hope that in time, that belief will also be supported by action (your listeners will eliminate genetically engineered products from their diet). When your goal is *discontinuance*, you hope to persuade audience members to stop doing something they are now doing (stop drinking alcohol while pregnant, for example). When your goal is *deterrence*, you want to persuade the audience to avoid an activity or a way of thinking (for example, "If you believe that every woman has the right to exercise control over her own body, don't vote for candidates who would make abortions illegal."). Finally, if your goal is the *continuance* of a way of believing or acting, you want to encourage people to continue to think or behave as they now do (for instance, keep purchasing products made in the United States).

Adoption and discontinuance goals involve asking listeners to alter their way of thinking or behaving, whereas deterrence and continuance goals involve asking them not to alter the way they think or behave but, rather, to reinforce or sustain it. In general, persuaders find it easier to accomplish deterrence and continuance objectives. That does not mean, however, that accomplishing adoption or discontinuance goals is impossible. They may be more difficult to achieve, but if the speaker uses a variety of appeals and a sound organizational scheme and has credibility, these goals can also be realized.

Many theorists contend that, to persuade audience members to act differently, you must first persuade them to think differently. Do you agree?

To what extent do you think job effectiveness is related to the ability to influence others? Explain your answer.

TYPES OF PERSUASIVE SPEECHES

Persuasive speeches focus on questions of fact, value, or policy. Selecting which kind of speech you will present is among the first tasks you need to complete. By choosing one type over the others, the speaker formally decides to speak on what is or what is not (**proposition of fact**), how good or bad something is (**proposition of value**), or what ought to be (**proposition of policy**).

Propositions of Fact

The following are sample propositions of fact:

> DNA is the ultimate fingerprint.
> High-fiber diets prevent cancer.
> Internet use decreases interpersonal skills.
> The United States is addicted to oil.
> Torture is an ally in the fight against terrorism.
> Natalie Holloway was murdered in Aruba.

proposition of fact
a persuasive speech with the goal of settling what is or is not so

proposition of value
a persuasive speech that espouses the worth of an idea, a person, or an object

proposition of policy
a persuasive speech on what ought to be

The last example was a proposition of fact that consumed the attention of commentators on a number of 24-hour news channels, such as Fox News and MSNBC. Various "experts" appeared on network programs in the effort to convince viewers of the persuasiveness of their evidence.

Good propositions of fact cannot be resolved with just a yes or a no answer. Instead, they are open to debate, and settling them typically requires close examination and careful interpretation of evidence, usually from a number of documents or sources. When speaking on a proposition of fact, the speaker must provide enough evidence to convince receivers of the factual nature of the statement.

Propositions of Value

The following are examples of propositions of value:

> Same-sex high schools are better than co-ed high schools.
> Sex education belongs in school.

Using persons in developing nations as guinea pigs for drug testing is unethical.

The use of chemical weapons is immoral.

Grade inflation decreases the value of a college education.

Finding alternative sources of fuel is a worthwhile endeavor.

Propositions of value explore the worth of an idea, a person, or an object. Like questions of fact, they require more than a simple answer, or in this case, a true or false response. When speaking on a proposition of value, the speaker must convince receivers that the evaluation contained in the proposition is valid. This usually requires that the speaker also explore one or more propositions of fact. For example, you probably will not be effective advocating for the premise that fetal tissue research is morally justifiable until you establish that such research is necessary.

Propositions of Policy

The following are sample propositions of policy:

Gay and lesbian partners should be permitted to marry.

Embryonic stem cell research should receive the full support of the federal government.

Colleges should limit financial support for athletes.

The United States should encourage investment in alternative fuel sources.

Consumers should boycott companies who use children to manufacture products.

The U.S. government should repudiate torture as a means to fight terrorism.

Assisted suicide should be legal.

When speaking on a proposition of policy, the speaker goes beyond questions of fact or value. Instead, the speaker must demonstrate a need for the policy and earn audience approval and/or support for the policy in question. When you ask audience members to support a proposition of policy, you ask them to support a course of action. Such a request often needs to be supported with statements of fact and value as well.

PERSUADING RESPONSIBLY

Whenever we try to cause others to change their beliefs, attitudes, or behaviors, or whenever others try to influence us, we are participating in the persuasive process.[3] Understanding what persuasion *is not* will enable us to use it responsibly.

Persuasion Is Not Coercion

Imagine this: Someone puts a gun to your head and says, "Your money or your life." Such a person is acting illegally and coercively. You follow the individual's demands only because you fear for your life. Persuasion is different. When someone is successful at persuading you to do or believe what she or he asks, you choose to think or act differently because you *want to* not because you think you *have to*.

Persuasion Is Not Manipulation

When someone manipulates you to do or believe something, he or she usually uses unethical means to take advantage of you so that you do what is in *his or her* but not necessary *your* best interest. Ethical persuasion is honest and in the best interests of receivers. Its success does not depend on spreading false or misleading information. For example, one politician used deception to convince voters of his honesty by re-editing newspaper articles written about him so that receivers were manipulated into processing the information he presented about himself favorably, when in fact it was highly unfavorable.[4] When this unethical act was uncovered, it cast a cloud over the candidate.

PERSUADING EFFECTIVELY

Persuasion usually occurs in steps. Audience members do not usually surrender current ways of thinking and behaving easily or all at once. However, if you offer convincing arguments, solid evidence, and a clear message, in persuasive messages that you plan incrementally and deliver over time, receivers may gradually alter their positions.

Your persuasive goal needs to be based on an accurate analysis of the current beliefs and attitudes of receivers. For example, if your goal is to convince members of the National Rifle Association (NRA) that the nation's gun-control laws need overhauling, rather than advocating against the sale of all guns to the public, you might start your persuasive campaign by working to convince receivers that there are some problems with existing gun laws. Simply reducing the strength of their current stance on gun control would be a step forward that repeated persuasive efforts could then build on. Let's examine what you can do to increase your persuasiveness as a speaker.

Identify Your Goal

To be a successful persuader, you must have a clearly defined purpose. You must, in fact, be able to answer these questions:

> What response do I want from audience members?
> Would I like them to think differently, act differently, or both?
> Which of their attitudes or beliefs am I trying to alter? Why?

Unless you know what you want your listeners to think, feel, or do, you will not be able to realize your objective.

Know the Receivers You Are Trying to Reach

Your task is partly related to the extent and type of change you hope to bring about in people. The task is easier if you have some idea of how the audience members feel about whatever change you are proposing. To what extent do they favor the change? How important is it to them? What is at stake? The more ego-involved the members of your audience are, the more committed they will be to their current position; hence, the harder it will be for you to reach them.[5]

Acting on a good idea is better than just having a good idea.

—Robert Half

Understand the Factors Affecting Your Listeners' Attitudes

To be able to influence others, you need to understand the favorable and unfavorable mental sets, or predispositions, that audience members bring to a speech; that is, you need to understand **attitudes**—how they are formed, how they are sustained, and how they may be changed by you. The following forces or factors are among the most important influences on our attitudes.

FAMILY

If you say it enough, even if it ain't true, folks will get to believing it.

—Will Rogers

Few of us escape the strong influence exerted by our families. Many of our parents' attitudes are communicated to us and are eventually acquired by us. As communication theorists Scott Cutlip and Alan Center write, "It is the family that bends the tender twig in the direction it is likely to grow."[6]

RELIGION

Not only believers but also nonbelievers are affected by religion. In fact, the impact of religion is becoming ever more widespread as religious organizations strive to generate and guide attitudes on such social issues as abortion, civil rights, the death penalty, child abuse, and divorce.

EDUCATION

More people than ever are attending school; they start young (sometimes before the age of 5), and many attend until they are in or beyond their twenties. Moreover, the traditional role of the school has expanded, since large numbers of adults are now returning to complete their education, some by taking online courses. The courses taught, the instructors who teach them, the books assigned, and the films shown all help shape attitudes.

SOCIOECONOMICS

Economic status and social status also shape our attitudes. Our economic status helps determine the social arena we frequent. Our view of the world is likewise affected by the company we keep and the amount of money we have.

CULTURE

As seventeenth-century poet John Donne wrote, "No man is an island, entire of itself." From the crib to the coffin, we are influenced by others—in person and through the media. The groups we belong to, our friends, and the fabric of the society in which we find ourselves all help mold us. Our social environment contains ingredients that help determine our mental sets and, in turn, our attitudes. We shape our social institutions and are reciprocally shaped by them.

Understand Your Listeners' Beliefs

How do you react when someone questions your position on what you consider a critical issue? Why?

Your persuasive effectiveness will improve if you understand not only your listeners' attitudes but also their beliefs—and if you understand how audiences might respond when their important beliefs are challenged.[7]

Attitudes and beliefs are, of course, related—in fact, the two terms are sometimes used interchangeably—but they are not the same thing. We might say that attitudes and beliefs are related to each other as buildings are related to bricks, beams, boards, and so on. That is, in a sense, **beliefs** are the building blocks of attitudes. Whereas we measure attitudes on a favorable–unfavorable scale, we measure beliefs on a probable–improbable scale. Thus, if you say that you think something is true, you are really saying that you believe it. According to psychologist Milton Rokeach, your belief system is made up of everything you agree is true. This includes all the information and biases you have accumulated from birth. Your disbelief system, which is composed of all the things you do not think are true, develops along with your belief system. Together, the two significantly affect the way you process information.[8]

To your listener, some beliefs are more important than others. The more central or important a belief is, the harder audience members will work to defend it, the less willing they will be to change it, and the more resistant they will be to your persuasive efforts.

beliefs
confidence in the truth of something

Use Two Principles of Influence: Consistency and Social Proof

When you are speaking persuasively, you should be aware of two significant principles. First, we all have a desire to be consistent with what we have already done. In other words, once we take a stand, consistency theory tells us that our tendency is to behave consistently with that commitment.[9] Therefore, it is important to determine how your speech can engage this tendency toward **consistency**. If you can find a way to get audience members to make a commitment (to take a stand or go on record), you will have set the stage for them to behave in ways consistent with that stand.

Second, we all respond to **social proof.** That is, one method we use to determine what is right is to find out what other people think is right.[10] You can use the actions of others to convince your listeners that what you are advocating is right. As motivation consultant Cavett Robert notes: "Since 95 percent of the people are imitators and only 5 percent initiators, people are persuaded more by the action of others than by any proof we can offer."[11]

consistency
the desire to maintain balance in our lives by behaving according to commitments already formed

social proof
the determination of what is right by finding out what other people think is right

Reason Logically

Rational or logical proof (Logos) includes arguments, reasoning, and evidence that add substance to a claim. Evidence is quotations or testimony from authoritative sources, conclusions from relevant studies and reports (sometimes presented in the form of statistics), and examples and illustrations in support of a proposition. You increase your chances of persuading others if you offer logical reasons why they should support what you advocate. The most common forms of logical reasoning are deduction, induction, causal reasoning, and reasoning from analogy.

DEDUCTION

When we reason deductively, we move from the general to the specific. When using **deduction,** you present a major premise (a generalization) and a minor premise (a specific instance) that leads you to deduce a conclusion. The argument you make looks like this:

deduction
reasoning that moves from the general to the specific

Major premise: People who study regularly instead of cramming usually get better grades.

Minor premise: You want to get better grades.

Conclusion: Therefore, you should study regularly instead of cramming.

Wrong premises lead to faulty conclusions. For example:

All protestors are liberal.
Jerry Falwell is a protestor.
Jerry Falwell is a liberal.

If you choose to use deductive reasoning in support of your ideas, be sure your premises are true and defensible.

You can evaluate deductive reasoning by asking the following two questions:

1. Are the major premise and the minor premise (or minor premises) true?
2. Does the conclusion follow logically from the premises?

Be sure to give the necessary evidence to buttress your major and minor premises.

INDUCTION

induction

reasoning that moves from specific evidence to a general conclusion

When we reason inductively, we move from specific evidence to a general conclusion. Because we cannot examine the whole, we *sample* it by examining a number of specific instances and then drawing a generalization about them. The following is an example of **induction;** it moves from the specific to the general—from a series of facts to a conclusion:

Fact: After growing up on a diet of television violence, Ronnie Zamora committed a murder.

Fact: After watching the film *The Program,* a group of teenagers imitated a scene in the movie by lying down on the center line of a highway.

Fact: After two youths viewed an episode of *Beavis and Butthead,* 2-year-old Jessica Matthews died when her 5-year-old brother set the house on fire by playing with matches, as shown on the show.

Conclusion: Violence depicted on television and films is copied in real life.

Whenever speakers use what is true in particular cases to draw a general conclusion, they are reasoning by induction. For instance, we are reasoning inductively if we conclude that sexualized violence against women shown on MTV videos leads to acts of sexualized violence against women in real life because, in a number of cases, men have enacted in real life the situations they have seen on the videos.

You can evaluate inductive reasoning by asking the following two questions:

1. Is the sample of specific instances large enough to justify the conclusion drawn from them?
2. Are the instances cited representative, or typical, ones?

CAUSAL REASONING

causal reasoning

speculation about the reasons for and effects of occurrences

When we reason from causes and effects, we either cite observed causes and hypothesize effects or cite observed effects and hypothesize causes. We use **causal reasoning** every day. Something happens, and we ask ourselves, Why? Similarly, we speculate about the consequences of certain acts; that is, we wonder about what effects they have. The following statements illustrate causal reasoning:

Smoking cigarettes can cause cancer.
Smoking cigarettes can cause heart disease.

Smoking cigarettes can cause problems during pregnancy.

Cigarette smoking is hazardous to your health and should be eliminated.

To evaluate the soundness of causal reasoning, ask the following questions:

1. Is the presumed cause real or false?
2. Is the presumed cause an oversimplification?

REASONING FROM ANALOGY

To convince his audience what was wrong with our political environment, one speaker quoted this analogy saying:

> John Tierney, a political columnist, made the following observation in a column he wrote that appeared in the *New York Times* on February 4, 2006: "Take a good look during the Super Bowl at the Steeler fans with their Terrible Towels. Imagine what's happening inside their minds as they wave the gold rags. This is your brain on partisan politics."[12]

When we use **reasoning from analogy,** we compare like things and conclude that since they are alike in a number of respects, they are also alike in some respect that until this point has not been examined. For example, if you wanted to argue that the methods used to decrease the high school dropout rate in a nearby city would also work in your city, you would first have to establish that your city is similar to the other city in a number of important ways—number of young people, number of schools, skill of personnel, financial resources, and so on. If you said that the two cities were alike except for the fact that your city had not instituted such a program and that its dropout rate was therefore significantly higher, you would be arguing by analogy.

reasoning from analogy
reasoning by comparison

To check the validity of analogical reasoning, ask the following questions:

1. Are the two things being compared alike in essential respects? That is, do the points of similarity outweigh the points of difference?
2. Do the differences that do exist matter?

When you reason logically, you not only back up your persuasive arguments with solid evidence, but also cite your sources carefully. When quoting or using a source, share the source's credentials with audience members as did the student who quoted from the John Tierney op-ed piece above. Careful citation is critical to the development of well-reasoned arguments.

Reason Ethically

Ethical speakers do not employ logical fallacies. A fallacy is an error in logic; it is flawed reasoning. When a speaker attempts to persuade using flawed reasoning, in addition to misusing the reasoning process, he or she is also abusing the persuasion process. The following are among the most common fallacies that speakers should avoid. (Other logical fallacies are noted in Ethics & Communication, "Illogical Reasoning.")

ARGUMENTUM AD HOMINEM

When you present your audience with an **argumentum ad hominem,** you inject name-calling into your speech. It is literally an "argument against the man" (or woman). You appeal to receivers to reject an idea because of a flaw in a person

argumentum ad hominem
the use of name-calling in an argument

Ethics & Communication

Illogical Reasoning

When logic fails, speakers sometimes substitute logical fallacies in its place. Additional reasoning fallacies speakers may flaw their speeches with are the following:

The hasty generalization: being too quick to jump to a conclusion

The slippery slope: asserting that one action will set in motion a chain reaction

The appeal to tradition: telling receivers that things have always been done a certain way

Using the Internet, books of published speeches, or issues of *Vital Speeches of the Day,* locate examples of fallacious reasoning. Explain why you believe the logic is flawed in each example.

---

associated with that idea. You attack a person's character instead of his or her stand on an issue. "She's just a left-wing liberal" and "He's just a member of the radical right" focus attention on the person and not his or her ideas.

RED HERRING

red herring
a distraction used to lead the receiver to focus on an irrelevant issue

The term **red herring** derives its meaning from an act performed during English fox hunts, in which hunt masters would drag red herrings across trails in an effort to divert the hunting dogs from chasing the foxes. When you use a red herring in your speech, your goal is to send the audience on a wild goose chase. By causing receivers to focus on one or more irrelevant issues, you prevent them from considering the issue actually under discussion. For example, in an effort to negate the right of women to have abortions, one speaker attempted to deflect the focus of receivers by concentrating instead on the cost of health insurance.

FALSE DIVISION

false division
the polarization of options, when, in fact, many options exist

When you use a **false division** in your speech (a false dichotomy, dilemma, or either–or argument), you require audience members to choose between two options, usually polar opposites, when in reality there are many options in between. The following are examples of the false division at work: "If you believe in flag burning, you don't believe in the country." "If you don't like the policies of the United States, go back to your native country." "If you are not part of the solution, then you are part of the problem." "Either we eliminate gun control, or only outlaws will have guns."

POST HOC, ERGO PROPTER HOC (FALSE CAUSE)

post hoc, ergo propter hoc
the identification of a false cause

When your argument is based on the assumption of **post hoc, ergo propter hoc,** you identify a false cause; that is, you lead your receivers to assume mistakenly that one event causes another merely because they occur sequentially. For example, one speaker pointed out that a decrease in abortions in the United States began about the same time as increased opportunities in sports for women. While a causal link may exist, the speaker has to supply evidence to establish a definitive link between the two phenomena. Correlation is not causation.

ARGUMENTUM AD POPULUM (BANDWAGON APPEAL)

An **argumentum ad populum** is a bandwagon appeal—that is, an appeal to popular opinion. The speaker who uses such a fallacy tells receivers that, because "everyone is doing or supporting it," they should too. Widespread acceptance of an idea, however, does not mean the idea is sound. Rather than rush to judgment based on what everyone else is saying or doing, you should consider the facts carefully and decide for yourself.

ARGUMENTUM AD VERECUDIAM (APPEAL TO AUTHORITY)

When you inject an **argumentum ad verecudiam** fallacy into your speech, you use the testimony of someone who is not an expert on your subject and does not possess the credentials that would permit him or her to make a claim or endorsement. Name recognition and expertise are not synonymous. For instance, while the Foo Fighters may be well-known performers and experts on music, when it comes to talking about the foreign policy of the United States, their value as a source decreases.

The speeches of speakers from groups such as the Ku Klux Klan usually contain an array of logical fallacies.

Gain Your Listeners' Attention

Before you can persuade or convince other people, you must first get their attention. In his book *The Art of Persuasion*, Wayne Minnick relates how a 9-year-old girl succeeded in getting the undivided attention of a male guest at her party. It seems that all the boys had gathered at one end of the room, talking to each other and ignoring the girls. "But I got one of them to pay attention to me, all right," the little girl assured her mother. "How?" inquired the mother. "I knocked him down!" was the undaunted reply.[13]

You should not knock your listeners down to get their attention, but you will need to find ways to encourage them to listen to you. It is your responsibility to put them into a receptive frame of mind. You can do this in several ways. You can compliment your listeners. You can question them. You can relate your message directly to their interests, or you can surprise them by relating to them in an unexpected way. Once you have the attention of your listeners, you must continue to work to hold it.

argumentum ad populum
a bandwagon appeal; an appeal to popular opinion

argumentum ad verecudiam
an appeal to authority

To what extent must friends, co-workers, politicians, and advertisers compete to get your attention? Which strategies are the most effective? Why?

Make Your Listeners Feel As Well As Think

Appeals to emotion (pathos) add to a speech's impact. Following is an excerpt from a student's speech on the issue of Palestinians jailed without trial in Israel. In it, the student quotes from a letter written by a Palestinian prisoner to an Israeli officer who was sentenced to jail himself for refusing to serve as a jailer for the political detainees because of his belief that the practice of administrative detentions was wrong. Why do you think that the use of this passage in the student's speech is effective?

> Who are you, officer?
> I want to write to you, but first I have to know who you are. I have to know the reasons that moved you to act as you did. I have to know how you arrived at this principled decision of conscience; how you chose such a unique rebellion, so unexpected.

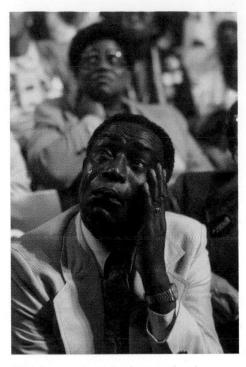

Effective speakers develop emotional appeals designed to make audience members feel.

What's your name? Where do you live? What do you do? How old are you? Do you have children? Do you like the sea? What books do you read? And what are you doing now in the cell where you are held? Do you have enough cigarettes? Is there someone who identifies with you over there? Do you ask yourself, "Was it worth paying the price?"

Can you see the moon and stars from the cell window? Have your ears grown accustomed to the jangle of the heavy keys, to the creak of the locks, to the clang of the metal doors? . . . Do you see in your sleep fields of wheat and kernels moving in the wind? Do you see expanses of sunflowers, and are your eyes filled with yellow, green and black hues, and the sun tans you, and you smile in your sleep, and the walls of the cell tumble and fall, and an unknown person waves his hand to you from afar? . . .

Don't you have regrets? Didn't you have doubts when they told you: "They're dangerous; they belong to Hamas, to Islamic Jihad and the Popular Front? Don't you trust our security services? Do you really believe that we are ready to throw innocent people in jail?"

Why do I feel as if I know you? . . .

Anonymous lieutenant, whatever your name is, sleep well; sleep the peaceful slumber of someone whose conscience is clear.

Many changes in human behavior have resulted from messages that combined emotional appeals with rational reasons. Since few people will change their attitudes or take action if they are unmoved or bored, effective speakers develop emotional appeals that are designed to make listeners feel.[14] Whether the feeling evoked is sadness, anger, fear, sympathy, happiness, greed, nostalgia, jealousy, pride, or guilt depends on the speaker's topic and the response desired.

As a speaker, you must appeal not just to your listeners' heads but also to their hearts. Thus, although your speech should be grounded in a firm foundation of logic and fact, it should also be built on feelings.

Evoke Relevant Needs and Issues

balance

a state of psychological comfort in which one's actions, feelings, and beliefs are related to each other as one would like them to be

Is it reasonable for speakers to cause receivers to experience dissonance to get them to believe something or do something? Is causing receivers to feel at risk, insecure, or vulnerable by manufacturing dissonance unethical? What if the speaker exaggerates the risk receivers face just to accomplish a goal? What if the risk is not really there at all?

Balance is a state of psychological health or comfort in which our actions, feelings, and beliefs are related to each other as we would like them to be. When we are in a balanced state, we are content or satisfied. Thus, we engage in a continual struggle to keep ourselves in balance. What does this imply for you as a persuasive speaker? If you want to convince your listeners to change their attitudes or beliefs, you must first demonstrate to them that a current situation or state of affairs has created an imbalance in their lives and that you can help restore their balance. The simple introduction of imbalance, or dissonance (whether that imbalance, or dissonance, is experienced by receivers for real or created vicariously by the speaker) motivates change in receiver thinking or behaving. Thus, speakers may deliberately create dissonance in receivers and then suggest what receivers need to think or do in order to be able to alleviate their dissonance and restore their sense of balance. It is our inner drive for balance that helps explain our positive responses to an array of persuasive appeals.

Remember that human behavior depends on motivation. If you are to persuade people to believe and do what you would like them to do, you must make your message appeal to their needs and goals.

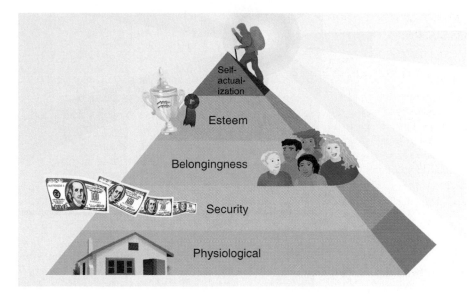

FIGURE 18.1

Maslow's Hierarchy of Needs.

From Abraham Maslow, *Toward a Psychology of Being.* Copyright © 1962. Reprinted by permission of John Wiley & Sons, Inc.

One popular device used to analyze human motivation is a schematic framework devised by famous psychologist Abraham Maslow.[15] In **Maslow's hierarchy of needs,** motivation is seen as a pyramid, with our most basic needs at its base and our most sophisticated needs at its apex (see Figure 18.1). Maslow defined survival needs as the basic necessities of life: shelter, food, water, and procreation. Safety needs include the need for security and the need to know that our survival requirements will be satisfied. At the third level are love and belonging needs. Once these are met, our esteem needs can be addressed. Esteem needs include self-respect and the respect of others. Our efforts to succeed are often attempts to satisfy our esteem needs, because success tends to attract respect and attention. At the peak of Maslow's hierarchy is the need for self-actualization. When we satisfy this, we have realized our potential; that is, we have become everything we are capable of becoming.

How does Maslow's hierarchy relate to you as a persuasive speaker? Find out by trying the Skill Builder "Climbing the Motivation Pyramid" on the next page. Remember that salient needs make salient motives. Your goal is to make your receivers identify your proposal with their needs. Whenever you attempt to do this, you will probably have to involve personal feelings.

Maslow's hierarchy of needs a model that depicts motivation as a pyramid with the most basic needs at the base and the most sophisticated at the apex

Promise a Reward

When you are speaking persuasively, demonstrate how your listeners' personal needs can be satisfied by your proposal. You should stress how your ideas can benefit the people you are trying to persuade. Make them believe that your proposal will supply a reward.

Remember, however, that different audiences value different types of rewards. For practice, think of three different types of audiences and identify the most important needs of each. Imagine that you are a salesperson trying to persuade each of those audiences to buy one of the following items: (1) guitar, (2) plant, (3) dog, (4) hat, (5) attaché case. Describe the strategies you would use with each

What are your own most important needs? How might someone use this information to persuade you to buy one of the items listed in the text?

Skill Builder

Climbing the Motivation Pyramid

For each of the following situations, identify the types of appeals you could use to persuade listeners to believe or behave as you would like them to. First, imagine a particular type of audience. Second, aim a part of your persuasive effort at each level of Maslow's hierarchy pyramid. Which level and which appeal do you think would be most effective? Explain your reasons.

1. You want to persuade someone to stop smoking.
2. You want to persuade someone to donate blood.
3. You want to persuade someone to support capital punishment.
4. You want to persuade someone to protest against using domestic animals for experimental research.

group. What adaptations would you make? To what extent would you display your awareness of individual differences?

It is important to remember that people are usually preoccupied with how something will benefit them personally. Your listeners, whoever they are, will want something in return for behaving as you would like them to behave.

MONROE'S MOTIVATED SEQUENCE: A FRAMEWORK FOR PERSUASIVE SPEAKING

Monroe's motivated sequence

a speech framework composed of five phases—attention, need, satisfaction, visualization, and action

One organizational framework that persuasive speakers have found particularly effective in motivating receivers to respond positively to their purpose is **Monroe's motivated sequence.**[16] Based on the psychology of persuasion, Monroe's framework is composed of five phases, which sequentially move receivers toward accepting and acting on a speaker's proposition. Its persuasive structure especially meets the needs of speakers who desire to move audience members to action.

Phase One: Attention. At the outset of a speech, the speaker's primary task is to gain the audience's attention. (In effect, you say, "Pay attention." Perhaps you enhance receivers' interest by asking a question, referring to their experiences, using an illustration or a dramatic story, supplying startling statistics, or providing an eye-catching visual. As a result of what you say or do, your audience members should realize why your message is important to them and why they should listen to what you have to say.)

Phase Two: Need. The speaker demonstrates for receivers that the present situation poses serious problems. He or she explicitly states the need and illustrates it with a variety of supporting materials. By revealing what is wrong to receivers and relating the need to their interests and desires, the speaker prepares them for the problem's solution. (In this stage, you say, "This is wrong, and here is what we need to do about it." In addition to identifying the problem or need, you illustrate it with specific examples. In addition, you support the need's existence with illustrations, statistics, testimony, or other forms of support. Your objective is to show how the identified need has an impact on the lives of audience members and how it affects their personal or professional goals, health, happiness, and/or financial security, for example.)

Phase Three: Satisfaction. Having shown the audience members that a need exists, the speaker's next task is to satisfy their desire for a solution. (Here, you tell receivers, "I have a way to solve the problem." You present your plan, explain it fully to receivers, and help them recognize that solving the problem will satisfy their interests and desires. By using examples and illustrations to flesh out what you want audience members to believe or do, and explaining why you are asking them to believe or do this, you help them understand how they can satisfy the need you described previously.)

Phase Four: Visualization. The speaker visualizes the plan's benefits for receivers, describing how things will improve when the plan is put into action. (In this phase, you say, "This is how my plan will meet your needs, alleviate the problems you face, and help make things better." You demonstrate the benefits audience members will receive once they act upon your ideas; if desired, you also explore the negative effects receivers will suffer if they fail to act on your plan.)

Phase Five: Action. The speaker's next task is to move receivers in a particular direction by telling them what they should do to ensure that the need is satisfied. In effect, the speaker asks receivers to support the policy and act on it. (In this phase, you say, "Here's what I would like you to do." You conclude with an appeal that reinforces their commitment to putting your solution to work. You are telling them to act.)

The following outline illustrates how the motivational sequence can be used to design a presentation advocating that we should not drive when drowsy.

Focus on Service Learning

Using information found on sites such as www.speech-topics-help.com/motivational-speech-topics.html, comm.colorado.edu/jjackson/1300/monroe.htm, and www.bluegrass.kctcs.edu/LCC/communications/monroe speecheval.doc, write a persuasive speech that supports the fund-raising efforts of your college or a local charity.

Introduction (Attention)	I. It was after midnight when six students walking to a fraternity party were killed when Brandon Kallmeyer fell asleep at the wheel of the pickup truck he was driving, veered off the road, and hit them.
	II. Over 100,000 accidents occur every year because drivers fall asleep at the wheel.
	III. The problem of people driving while drowsy is increasing.
	IV. Today I would like to explore why it is important to us to examine this problem, why it continues to escalate, and what steps we can take to help alleviate it.
Body (Need)	I. We have put sleep on the back burner.
	A. Everyone needs approximately eight hours of sleep a day to function effectively the next day, but we average only about six hours of sleep a day.
	B. The most important sleep hour is the REM stage, which occurs between the seventh and eighth hour.
	II. Sleep-deprived persons pose serious dangers on the road.
	A. Highway patrol officers report stopping motorists who appear drunk, only to discover they are fatigued.
	B. Drowsy driving is approaching a national epidemic.
	III. The drowsy driving problem can be alleviated once we fully understand its causes.

continued

(Satisfaction)   A. We are poor judges of our own sleeplessness.

B. Alcohol consumption contributes to becoming sleepy behind the wheel.

C. Comfortable drive is a contributing factor to becoming tired.

IV. Tragedy can be prevented if we take the proper steps.

(Visualization)   A. Imagine what would happen if the Federal Highway Administration added more rumble strips designed to wake us up when we began to veer off the road.

B. Imagine what would happen if cars were equipped with AutoVue cameras that emit rumble strip–like sounds when a driver drifts out of a lane.

V. There are some steps we can take personally to protect ourselves.

A. We can take naps to fight fatigue.

(Action)   B. We can sleep the recommended seven to eight hours a night.

Conclusion   I. Six innocent students were killed because someone didn't take action to avoid the tragedy.

II. It is time to get the sleep that could save our lives and the lives of others.[17]

BECOMING A MORE CREDIBLE PERSUADER

credibility

the receiver's assessment of the competence, trustworthiness, and dynamism of a speaker

According to attorney Gerry Spence, your success as a persuader will be determined in part by what your "targets" think of you—in other words, by your **credibility** (ethos).[18]

For some groups of people, the Dalai Lama is considered a highly credible speaker.

When we use the term *credibility*, we are talking not about what you are really like but about how an audience perceives you. If your listeners accept you as credible, they probably believe that you are a person of good character (trustworthy and fair) and are knowledgeable (trained, competent to discuss your topic, and reliable as source of information) and personable (dynamic, charismatic, active, and energetic). As a result, your ideas are more likely to get a fair hearing. However, if your listeners believe that you are untrustworthy, incompetent (not sufficiently knowledgeable about your topic), and passive (lacking in dynamism), they are less likely to respond as you desire.

It is entirely possible—even probable—that your listeners may consider you more credible about some topics than others. For example, the following are two pairs of imaginary statements. Which statement in each pair would you be more inclined to accept?

Exploring Diversity

Persuasion and Assumed Similarity

LaRay M. Barna, an intercultural communication theorist, points out that we are all influenced by our cultural upbringing, and, while we tend to assume that other people's needs, desires, and basic assumptions are the same as our own, often they are not. How can assumed similarity—the belief that we all have similar thoughts, feelings, attitudes, and nonverbal codes—cause problems for persuasive speakers? For example, while Americans tend to value materialism, success, and rationality, Arabs are more likely to value self-respect, courage, and honor. Arabs also value storytelling, eloquence, and the ability of words to spark emotional responses in others. To this end, they use emphatic assertions to convey their seriousness. When such assertions are missing, others may assume that an Arab speaker means the opposite of what was said.[19]

On the basis of this realization, is it more beneficial for a persuasive speaker to assume *differences* rather than similarity? Explain.

What should the speaker do if members of the audience come from a variety of cultures, some who expect a more formal style of delivery than the speaker is used to, some who expect the speaker to begin by humbling himself or herself and making respectful references to the audience, some who expect the speaker to be restrained rather than overly expressive, some who expect the speaker to rely on narratives rather than formal logic or standard inductive or deductive structures, and so on?

The United States must never negotiate with terrorists. Strength is the only language they will understand.

—Condoleeza Rice

The United States must never negotiate with terrorists. Strength is the only language they will understand.

—Madonna

****

The world of contemporary music has room in it for everyone. The message music sends is tolerance.

—Bono

The world of contemporary music has room in it for everyone. The message music sends is tolerance.

—Hillary Rodham Clinton

If you're like most people, you find the first statement in each pair more credible. The source cited for the first statement seems obviously more knowledgeable about the subject.

Regardless of the circumstances, however, it is up to you to build your credibility by giving audience members reasons to consider you competent, trustworthy, and dynamic.[20] To help them see you as competent, you can describe your own experiences with the subject and suggest why you feel you've earned the right to share your ideas. You can help receivers see you as trustworthy by demonstrating respect for different points of view and communicating a sense of sincerity. To help them see you as dynamic, speak with energy, use assured and forceful gestures, and create vocal variety.[21]

Note that the audience's assessment of your credibility can change during your presentation or as a result of it. Thus, we can identify three types of credibility:

Initial credibility is your credibility before you actually start to speak.

Derived credibility is your credibility during your speech.

Terminal credibility is your credibility at the end of your speech.

initial credibility
a measure of how an audience perceives a speaker prior to the speech-making event

derived credibility
a measure of a speaker's credibility during a speech-making event

terminal credibility
a measure of a speaker's credibility at the end of a speech-making event

Ethics & Communication

Big and Little Lies

What kinds of communication choices do you make when attempting to accomplish a goal? What would you do to get others to comply with your wishes? Would you lie? Would you cheat? Is it acceptable for a speaker to manipulate receivers?

Our society has been criticized for being a "culture of cheating."[22] From the school yard to the White House, from the boardroom to the war room, from the ball field to the farm field, cheating appears to go on everywhere. We saw it with the presentation of the reasons for going to war against Iraq, and we saw it with the alleged "rescue" of Private Jessica Lynch and the ensuing accusation that "the Pentagon tried to pull a fast one."[23] We saw it with Enron. We saw it with ImClone. We saw it with *A Million Little Pieces*. Politicians, CEOs, and some authors of books, such as James Frey, fudge statements, exaggerate the value of

evidence, and fabricate claims. Some lies are told "to protect national security," some to protect the president's skin; some are just boasting. What is more, it appears that the "cheaters prosper until they get caught."[24] Some, like Frey, prosper even after getting caught.

What damage, if any, do you believe is done to a speaker's credibility when receivers discover that he or she has lied to them? Is a speaker's tendency to exaggerate as harmful as committing a lie of omission or telling an outright lie? Do the ends ever justify the means? In other words, is it acceptable for a speaker to make up facts if his or her goal is a worthy one?

Would you ever lie to receivers? Would you make up statistics, pass off as true a narrative you knew to be hypothetical, or tamper with visuals if you knew that doing so would help you realize the objective(s) of your speech?

Of course, if your initial credibility is high, your task should be easier. But keep in mind that your speech can lower your initial credibility—and that it can also raise your initial credibility. What you say and how you say it are important determiners of credibility:

As Ralph Waldo Emerson wrote:

> The reason why anyone refuses his assent to your opinion, or his aid to your benevolent design, is in you. He refuses to accept you as a bringer of truth, because, though you think you have it, he feels that you have it not. You have not given him the authentic sign.

In brief, persuasive speaking involves more than simply communicating with others in a public setting. It includes your responsibility to familiarize yourself with the beliefs, attitudes, and needs of those you hope to persuade. Only by doing so will you be in a position to influence others—and to understand how they may try to influence you.

TECHNOLOGY AND THE PERSUADER

We live in an age when image manipulation is a reality. Today, it is increasingly difficult for us to know when something is real and when it is not. Currently, computer simulations are used in both news reports and live presentations. When speakers explained to the public the outcomes of battles fought during the first war in Iraq, for example, graphic models or simulations that represented the movement of tanks and the results of air strikes were used to enhance those reports.

Let us try to imagine how virtual reality might affect the audiences of public speakers in years to come. Vivid computer simulations will present receivers with a number of processing challenges. For example, is there such a thing as an objective simulation, or are simulations used by speakers to help internalize the reality

Thinking Critically

Reflect and Respond

Agree or disagree with the following statement; give reasons and examples that support your stance.

All persuasive speaking is informative. There is no such thing as a purely persuasive speech.

Then, using both the outline and transcript of the persuasive speech that follows in the text, provide examples from each that support the position you have taken.

that speakers would like receivers to support? And even if the image announces on its face that it is a simulation, doesn't it nonetheless by its very presence have persuasive impact? Is it possible that the speaker who can stage the most convincing persuasive simulations will succeed in having receivers think or do anything and win their minds and hearts?[25] In the future, when virtual reality is in full bloom, it may enable receivers to not just hear and see the speaker but also live the ideas expressed in the speech. The speaker's audience may be able to share more fully the dramatic moments or illustrations of a speech once they are transformed into multisensory stories. Audience members may be able to feel that they share a cardboard shelter with a homeless person or are in the middle of a rain forest. The sensory richness the speaker is able to provide may reduce the receiver's capacity to reason logically. In short, the emotional power of virtual reality may become a powerful, though ethically questionable, tool for persuasive speakers. As with any new communication medium, however, it is neither good nor bad in itself. How it will be used by speakers is what matters.

DELIVERING A PERSUASIVE SPEECH

As a persuasive speaker, you must show a great deal of interest in and enthusiasm for your topic. At the moment of presentation, it must become the most important issue in the world for both you and your listeners.

Be aware that audience members may object to what you say. As a persuader, you need to be able to handle objections in an effective manner. First, be prepared for opposing points of view. Anticipate your audience's concerns and rehearse possible answers. Second, consider the source of objections. For example, audience members may dispute your facts. If you make a statement about the number of millionaires in your state and an audience member has just completed a study on wealth in the United States and has up-to-date statistics, you will need to agree, restate your findings, or suggest that this is a good point, which you both should explore. An effective way to handle opposing views is to agree with them as much as possible. "I agree that life insurance may not be the best investment . . ." is a disarming technique often used by sales representatives to counter objections to purchasing insurance.

Answer any argument in a professional manner. Do not become angry that anyone would dare question your reasoning. Remember that your credibility is at stake while you are speaking in front of others. Respond to the question or objection in an authoritative manner and move on to other questions. Maintain control.

SAMPLE PERSUASIVE SPEECH OUTLINE

Full Sentence Outline

Topic: The Patriot Act[26]

Purpose: To persuade the audience that we need to work to restore the freedoms we lost as a result of passage of the Patriot Act

Thesis: The Patriot Act has trampled the freedoms of Americans.

By starting with a quotation from the Revolutionary War era and tying it to today, the speaker attempts to draw receivers into the speech.

Introduction

I. "They that would give up liberty just for a little safety deserve neither liberty nor safety." These words, delivered by Benjamin Franklin in 1778, ring true to our ears today, over 225 years later.

II. In October 2001, Congress passed the "Uniting and Strengthening America by Providing Appropriate Tools Required to Intercept and Obstruct Terrorism Act"—better known as the Patriot Act.

Having aroused the interest of receivers, and indicating that a problem exists, the speaker reveals the subject of the speech and specifically identifies the speech's objective.

   A. The focus of the bill is on safety, not liberty.

   B. Since 2001, Congress has passed limited extensions of the act while the Justice Department continues to advocate for its permanent renewal.

III. To understand the dangers inherent in the Patriot Act, we must first explore the root of the Patriot Act's flaws; second, examine the problems associated with this act; and third, look into some solutions to see what we can do to help restore the freedoms we have lost while continuing to ensure our safety.

The speaker identifies the first reason for the position taken in the speech and supports this reason with specific examples.

Body

I. The roots of the Patriot Act are flawed.

   A. The Patriot Act was passed out of fear.

      1. According to National Public Radio, because of fear, elected officials reached for a blanket of safety.

      2. The means devised to make us safe take away from us what we want to protect.

   B. The Justice Department stifled debate.

      1. Questioning the bill was labeled as "un-American."

      2. The stifling of debate is as heinous in the post–9/11 era as it was in the 1950s.

II. The Patriot Act has a number of problems.

   A. The Patriot Act is ineffective in fighting the war on terrorism.

The speaker uses dramatic statistical evidence and an emotionally charged illustration to support the second main point of the speech.

      1. According to *The London Daily Telegraph,* only 3 of the 700 suspected terrorists detained and the 300 arrested have been found guilty.

      2. Persons convicted under the Patriot Act have been low-level cell members.

      3. Consider the story of Vasilly Rajah, who was deported by the Justice Department, which declared him a risk to national security.

         a. Rajah was here legally.

         b. Rajah's wife died on 9/11 in Tower Two.

B. The Patriot Act infringes on the rights we cherish.
1. According to the *Washington Post* of November 19, 2002, the Patriot Act enables federal agencies to tap our phone lines and access our e-mail.
2. The Patriot Act is in conflict with the Fourth Amendment to the Constitution of the United States.
3. The Patriot Act invades our right to privacy.
   a. Federal agencies can access library records, including Internet usage.
   b. Federal agencies can investigate us because of the research we do.
   c. Persons seen as assisting an organization considered terrorist—even Greenpeace—may have their citizenship revoked.
   d. There is currently no right of appeal when the FBI makes demands for people's financial and other private records.

III. We must stand up for our civil liberties.
A. Research the Patriot Act.
B. Know what your civil liberties are.
1. Contact your local city council office.
2. ABC News notes that over 35 municipalities have chosen not to abide by the Patriot Act.
C. Alter your attitudes toward liberty and safety.
D. Remember the sacrifices of our nation's early patriots.

Conclusion
I. Khalid Sheik Mohammad was captured on March 1, 2003, without any use of the Patriot Act.
II. Let us not give away our freedoms.

Sources
The "Uniting and Strengthening America by Providing Appropriate Tools Required to Intercept and Obstruct Terrorism Act," also known as the Patriot Act, accessed at www.house.gov

"Debating the Patriot Act," www.npr.org/templates/story/story.php?storyId=4759727&sourceCode=gaw, accessed February 4, 2006.
London Daily Telegraph, February 10, 2003.
Washington Post, November 19, 2002.
Baltimore Sun, March 8, 2003.
ABC News.

The speaker also supports the second main point by supplying a litany of reasons with which receivers can identify.

The speaker involves receivers by telling them what they can do to help remedy the situation.

The speaker reminds receivers why they need to be vigilant.

The speaker uses an effective example to strengthen the position espoused by the speech.

SAMPLE PERSUASIVE SPEECH

Speech Title: The Patriot Act and Our Civil Rights[27]

Topic: The Patriot Act

Purpose: To persuade the audience that we need to work to restore the freedoms we lost as a result of passage of the Patriot Act

continued

Do you think that starting with a 225-year-old quotation is a good idea? Does the speaker's opening succeed in capturing your attention and motivating you to want to hear more? What other means might the speaker use to pull you into the speech? Could the speaker have benefited from the use of a visual aid?

How effective do you find the speaker's orientation? Does it help clarify the major parts of the speech?

How would you describe the basic speech-making structure of the speech?

Do you find the use of a National Public Radio transcript credibility-enhancing?

Does the speaker's use of another historical example and the indirect reference to the McCarthy era help advance the speech's purpose?

Does this transition facilitate the receivers' job?

Are the problems the speaker cites convincing? Does the speaker supply enough evidence to build a case?

Thesis: The Patriot Act has trampled the freedoms of Americans.

"They that would give up their liberty just for a little safety deserve neither liberty nor safety." These words, spoken by Benjamin Franklin warn of the loss of precious freedom out of fear. While Franklin first delivered his warning in 1778, this patriot's words still ring true over 225 years later.

On October 11, 2001, the United States Congress overwhelmingly approved the "Providing Appropriate Tools Required to Intercept and Obstruct Terrorism Act"—better known as the Patriot Act. At the time of the bill's introduction, the question was raised: "Which is more important: liberty or safety?"

And now more than 5 years since the bill was enacted, a new question has arisen: Is the sacrifice of liberty in the name of safety ever enough? *The Washington Post,* on February 8, 2003, reported that the Justice Department is currently considering expanding the Patriot Act beyond its already intrusive powers. The Patriot Act has trampled our American freedoms, and before we find these freedoms slipping even further from our grasp, we must address the issue.

In order to better understand the dangers that are inherent in the Patriot Act, we must first explore the roots of the Patriot Act's flaws, then examine the problems associated with the act, before finally looking into some solutions to see what we can do to help restore the freedoms we have lost while continuing to ensure our safety.

In a situation such as the one we face with the Patriot Act, we can pinpoint the Patriot Act's flaws without political bias. Our elected officials, regardless of political affiliation, did what any of us would have done in a time of such fear. They reached for the closest blanket of safety. However, it is the means by which some sought safety that contradicted the very essence of what we want to protect.

National Public Radio transcripts of February 9, 2003, report that, while the bill was passed in less than a month on the floor of Congress, during that time Justice Department officials effectively had all the debate stifled—not through any direct means but, rather, by implying that any questioning of this bill would be seen as "un-American," a term that was as heinous in the post–9/11 days as it was to be called a Communist during the 1950s. From this lack of discussion, the American system was cheated, diverted away from the intentions this nation was founded upon. But this diversion away from the Constitution would not be the last.

In our search for safety, we have seen several problems inherent with the Patriot Act, including the general ineffectiveness of the bill and the gross infringement of our civil liberties.

Primarily, the Patriot Act has yet to prove its worth in fighting the war on terrorism. *The London Daily Telegraph* of February 10, 2003, reports that in the United States there have been more than 700 detentions and 300 arrests of suspected terrorists. Of these, 3 have been found guilty. While certainly any convictions are helpful, the 3 who were convicted were admittedly lower-level cell members. Furthermore, when federal agencies decide to implement their strictest penalties, the chances of subduing a person who is a real risk are minimal at best. Consider the ironic story of Vasilly Rajah—a Russian immigrant who was recently deported after the Justice Department had him declared a risk to national security. Apparently Rajah's career as a computer software engineer raised a red flag on his record. His lack of a Green Card led to his being sent home. But Rajah wasn't living in America illegally. He was married to Tatiana Rajah, a Russian immigrant who had her nationalization papers. But when Tatiana died, Vasilly was no longer considered a conditional citizen. He was sent back to Russia without his now motherless children, who were born in the United States and therefore allowed to stay. The truly tragic twist in his story lies in the death of Tatiana, who was working in Tower Two of the World Trade Center on September 11th. Because of this legislation, passed as a result of September 11th, Vasilly Rajah, a man widowed by the attacks, was deported without ever being convicted of a crime. But having an ethnic-sounding name is not a prerequisite for being victimized by this bill.

Along with being generally ineffective, the Patriot Act is truly a misnomer. Certainly nothing that works to infringe on the rights of citizens can be considered the act of a patriot. *The Washington Post* of November 19, 2002, explains one of the greatest infringements on our civil liberties. The Fourth Amendment to the Constitution states that "the right of the people to be secure in their persons, houses, papers, and effects against unreasonable searches and seizures shall not be violated." However, using powers granted in the Patriot Act, federal agencies may now tap any individual's phone line and access any individual's e-mail content, using only the pretense of a suspicion of cooperating with terrorism as a reason. The Patriot Act is in conflict with a cornerstone of American democracy and, as such, works only to infringe on our civil liberties.

The Patriot Act also invades our right to privacy. One of the powers granted in the Patriot Act allows federal agencies to access public library records, as well as the records of Internet searches conducted in public libraries. These libraries include libraries located on campuses of public universities as well. In response, in February 2002, the American Library Association issued a newsletter warning its members to comply with any search request but to immediately seek legal counsel. To put this in another context, my own personal library records, just from researching this speech, could constitute my being seen as a threat to national security. Think about it. How many times have you researched an issue that could be considered questionable in the eyes of a federal agent?

Perhaps most shocking of all is a new provision being sought by the Justice Department. *The Baltimore Sun,* March 8, 2003, reports that, if the new Patriot II bill passes Congress, any individual seen as assisting an organization considered terrorist

Is the illustration the speaker provides effective? Do you think that the speaker needs to supply others?

In your opinion, does the speaker do a sufficient job of personalizing the problems with the Patriot Act for receivers? What proof does the speaker offer in support of the act's problems? Do you think the speaker ever gets overly dramatic?

continued

by nature may have his or her citizenship revoked. According to the article, using the wording of the bill, an action as passive as donating fifty dollars to Greenpeace could leave you without a country to call home. Ironically enough, with these newly proposed provisions you may no longer have to worry about infringements upon your rights as a citizen, because you may not be one.

There is currently no right of appeal when the FBI makes demands for people's financial and other private records. Banks, libraries, Internet service providers, and individuals should have the right to appeal when the FBI asks for the financial and other records of customers or individuals.

What do you think of the suggestions the speaker offers for action? Are the speaker's suggestions ones receivers can easily follow?

Before it is too late, we must stand up for our civil liberties. And only through personal resolve may we once again deserve both our liberty and our safety, for, as Thomas Jefferson said, "The people are the only sure reliance for the preservation of liberty."

Initially, in this fight to take back what is rightfully ours, we must arm ourselves with the strongest weapon democracy holds—knowledge. Research this issue for yourselves because I could not even read you the Patriot Act in 10 minutes. You can read the Patriot Act as well as the U.S. Constitution online at www.house.gov or in your local library. Don't worry. At least for now, reading the Constitution is still a protected right.

Knowing what your civil liberties are and knowing what rights are afforded you as a citizen is not just in your best interest; it is also your responsibility. But knowing what your civil liberties are is only the first step. Now you have to let your voices be heard. But you do not necessarily have to write to Washington just yet. You can just walk down to your local city council office, for, as ABC News points out, over 35 municipalities across the country—including Ann Arbor, Michigan; Oakland, California; and Madison, Wisconsin—have voted not to abide by the rulings of the Patriot Act. These cities have given their city workers, including their police forces, the option of not assisting any investigation that infringes on civil liberties.

In closing, does the speaker provide a sufficient summary of the speech for receivers?

Does the introduction of a new example in the conclusion help the speaker's case?

Most important, we have to alter our attitudes toward liberty and safety. After September 11th, we were all afraid for our national security and for our personal safety. Unfortunately, our officials were not immune from the same concerns. But the path they chose did more harm than good. We must remember the first patriots of this nation, who believed that our liberty and safety were not mutually exclusive ideas. Rather, they believed that we deserve not only to live, but to live free, and in their ultimate sacrifice, they ensured we would never have to endure infringement upon our liberties simply to be temporarily safe.

According to a 2006 report on NPR.org, the Justice Department credits the Patriot Act with helping it crack several cases, including facilitating the arrest of the Lackawanna Six, a group of Yemeni-Americans who trained in an al-Qaeda–affiliated camp near Kandahar. Critics, however, counter that the men were coerced into pleading guilty because the government threatened them with indefinite detention. In addition, on March 1st of 2003, the United States captured Khalid Sheik Mohammed, one of the top lieutenants in the al-Qaeda network. While this may prove to be a great step toward protecting our nation, it also teaches a very important lesson. Khalid Sheik Mohammed, to date the most noted arrest in the war on terrorism, was captured without any use of the Patriot Act.

Does the conclusion provide the speech with a sense of closure?

Our nation has already seen too much tragedy and felt too much sorrow. Let us not compound our regrets by giving away that one thing that truly makes us all Americans—our freedoms.

Were you the speaker, what would you do differently?

SAMPLE SPEAKER'S NOTES

Topic:	The Patriot Act[28]
Purpose:	To persuade the audience that we need to work to restore the freedoms we lost as a result of passage of the Patriot Act.
Thesis:	The Patriot Act has trampled the freedoms of Americans.
Introduction	I. "They that would give up liberty just for a little safety deserve neither liberty nor safety." These words, spoken by Benjamin Franklin, warn of the loss of precious freedom out of fear. While Franklin first delivered his warning in 1778, the patriot's words still ring true over 225 years later.
	II. In October 2001, Congress passed the "Providing Appropriate Tools Required to Intercept and Obstruct Terrorism Act"— better known as the Patriot Act.
	A. *Washington Post*, February 8, 2003—considering expansion of act
	B. Act tramples freedom
	III. In order to understand the dangers inherent in the Patriot Act, we must first explore the root of the Patriot Act's flaws, then examine the problems associated with the act before finally looking into some solutions to see what we can do to help restore freedoms we have lost, while continuing to ensure our safety.
Body	I. Patriot Act Flawed
	Passed out of fear
	Debate was stifled—National Public Radio, February 9, 2003
	II. Patriot Act Has Problems
	Ineffective
	London Daily Telegraph, February 10, 2003: Only 3 convictions out of 700 detained and 300 arrested
	Low-level cell members
	Story of Vasilly Rajah and wife Tatiana

continued

Patriot act infringes on rights: *Washington Post*, November 19, 2002.

Conflicts with Fourth Amendment

Phone and e-mail taps

Invades privacy, American Library Association, February 2002 newsletter

Danger of revocation of citizenship—*Baltimore Sun*, March 8, 2003, and Patriot II bill

No right to appeal

III. Stand up for civil liberties: Jefferson—"The people are the only sure reliance for the preservation of liberty."

Research and www.house.gov

Know civil liberties

Change attitudes about liberty and safety

Recall early patriot sacrifices

Conclusion   I. Capture of the Lackawanna Six and Khalid Sheik Mohammed

II. Don't give freedoms away.

EVALUATING THE PERSUASIVE SPEECH

While the evaluation form featured in Chapter 16 can be used to evaluate persuasive speeches, there are a number of criteria to keep in mind when evaluating persuasive discourse. Use the following checklist as a guide.

Rate the following criteria from 1 to 5; 1 represents "not at all" or "barely accomplished" and 5 represents "fully accomplished."

_____ Did the speaker's introduction fulfill its purpose?

_____ Was the speaker's proposition clearly understood?

_____ Were the reasons the speaker offered in support of the proposition clear?

_____ Was the speaker's use of testimony effective?

_____ Was the organizational pattern used by the speaker appropriate and easy to follow?

_____ Was the speaker's use of language vivid, appropriate, and motivating?

_____ Was the speaker effective in establishing his or her own credibility?

_____ Did the speaker's conclusion accomplish its purpose?

_____ Did the speaker conduct himself or herself ethically?

_____ Was the speaker's delivery effective?

Check *one* of the following:

The speech was _____ superior _____ above average _____ average _____ below average _____ poor

Looking Back and Ahead
Consider This Case: The Town Meeting Blues

"I don't know why you need to go through with this speech if it's making you so nervous," Mihwah said to her friend Daniel one evening.

"Because I really believe in what I'm going to say," said Daniel. "I just can't help being nervous about it, but I'm not going to let that stop me. At least, I'm going to try not to."

Mihwah and Daniel were housemates in a building near campus. Daniel was determined to speak at the upcoming town meeting in their community about an issue that was sure to be divisive. Mihwah had agreed to help him prepare and rehearse his speech, but as the day of the meeting drew closer, he was growing more apprehensive about his plan.

Daniel had been living off-campus for a year, and he'd become aware of a building boom that was taking place around the town. Private developers and contractors were busier than ever with home renovations and new commercial construction, and there was a shortage of workers for them to hire. At the same time, immigrants looking for work had begun gathering in the early morning hours, waiting on street corners for the contractors' trucks and vans to drive by. Often the contractors would stop, pick out a few men, hire them for the day, and drive on. An informal labor market had sprung up, and although it wasn't a perfect solution to the labor problem, or to the problems faced by the immigrant workers, it solved an immediate need, and local government hadn't made any attempt to interfere in it.

But a group of citizens had called a town meeting to try to force an end to the practice. They were mostly local business owners who claimed the small groups of men waiting for work were loitering in front of their stores, begging or scaring their customers away, and creating a public nuisance.

Daniel disagreed. As he'd explained to Mihwah, he believed the workers were sincerely looking for work. He'd never seen one of them begging, and he'd often observed how they kept quietly to themselves each morning until the contractors arrived. Anyone not hired for the day usually disappeared within a

few minutes, and no disruptions or disorderly behavior had ever occurred that he knew of.

Daniel believed that a solution to the shopkeepers' objections could be found. He planned to speak at the town meeting to propose his solution—designating a small park in the center of town as the accepted gathering place for the workers and contractors to meet each morning. It would mean the drivers would have to go a little out of their way to find the men, but it would keep the workers away from the storefronts and allow them to continue finding the work they needed. And the contractors would benefit too, by having continued access to the informal labor pool.

Daniel knew he would have to be very persuasive to convince the business owners to consider his proposal. He thought the contractors would agree to it because it would benefit them, too, but he wasn't sure. He was even less sure about what the local government would do if it were finally forced to make some kind of decision in the matter. And he wondered what any of the meeting participants would think about his speaking out. After all, he was only a student. He suddenly wondered whether anyone else would be speaking on behalf of the immigrant workers.

"Well," said Mihwah, breaking in on his thoughts. "Since you're determined to speak, let's go over your outline again. Ready?"

DISCUSSION QUESTIONS

1. How many diverse parties are involved in the situation Daniel has observed in town? Has he considered all their possible interests?
2. What should Daniel do to make himself a more credible speaker at the town meeting? What advantages and disadvantages does he have as an observer, not a participant, in the immigrant labor situation?
3. What does he need to find out about his audiences, and how can he research this?
4. What kind of supporting material do you think Daniel will need to make his speech a success?
5. What kinds of questions should Daniel anticipate being asked at the meeting, and how can he prepare himself to answer them?

The Wrap Up

Revisiting Chapter Objectives

1. **Define *persuasive speaking.*** Persuasive speaking is the means a speaker uses to modify the thoughts, feelings, or actions of receivers so that they change the attitudes or behaviors that the speaker does not approve and, instead, adopt attitudes and behaviors compatible with the speaker's interests and worldview. The proposition of the speech indicates the kind of change the persuasive speaker would like to create in receivers.

2. **Define and distinguish between *attitudes* and *beliefs.*** To influence receivers, speakers need to address their attitudes and beliefs. Attitudes are the mental sets, or predispositions, receivers bring to a speech. Beliefs are the building blocks of attitudes. A receiver's belief system is composed of everything the receiver believes to be true. Whereas attitudes are measured on a favorable–unfavorable scale, beliefs are measured on a probable–improbable scale. The more central a belief, the harder it is to change.

3. **Distinguish between logical and fallacious reasoning.** Speakers who give their receivers logical reasons to support their propositions improve their chances of realizing their speech-making goals. By using deductive and inductive reasoning, causal reasoning, and reasoning from analogy, speakers can build their case and earn receiver support. Ethical speakers do not rely on fallacious reasoning to win the support of receivers. Among the logical fallacies unethical speakers use are argumentum ad hominem, red herring, false division, false cause, the bandwagon appeal, and the appeal to authority.

4. **Explain the concept of credibility.** A speaker's success as a persuader is in part determined by his or her credibility—or how an audience perceives him or her. To find a speaker credible, receivers need to believe the speaker is a person of good character, is knowledgeable, and is personable. The assessment of a speaker's credibility can change during or as a result of a speech.

5. **Develop and present a persuasive speech.** The job of the persuader is to build an effective case, which includes well-supported reasons and appeals for accepting a speaker's proposition. The audience members must be drawn into the speech, sense the speaker's conviction and belief in the position he or she is advocating, and be reminded at the conclusion of the speech of what they need to believe and/or do.

Resources for Further Inquiry and Reflection

To apply your understanding of how the principles in Chapter 18 are at work in our daily lives, consult the following resources for further inquiry and reflection. Or, if you prefer, choose any other appropriate resource. Then connect the ideas expressed in your chosen selection with the communication concepts and issues you are learning about both in and out of class.

Listen to Me

"Boulevard of Broken Dreams" (Green Day)
"Burn" (Usher)
"Let It Be" (The Beatles)
"Truth No. 2" (Dixie Chicks)
"We Didn't Start the Fire" (Billy Joel)
"Let's Roll" (Neil Young)

Compare and contrast the attitudes toward persuasion and change expressed in any of these songs with your own attitudes. What does the song you chose suggest about potential subjects for a persuasive speech?

 ## View Me

North Country
The Constant Gardener
Syriana
Munich

Good Night, and Good Luck
Wall Street
Malcolm X
Bowling for Columbine

What do we learn about the ethics and persuasive approaches favored by featured characters from their own words and actions?

 ## Read Me

James Risen. *State of War: The Secret History of the CIA and the Bush Administration.* New York: Free Press, 2006.
Robert B. Cialdini. *Influence: The Psychology of Persuasion,* rev. ed. New York: Quill, 2000.
Anthony Pratkanis and Elliot Aronson. *Age of Propaganda: The Everyday Use and Abuse of Persuasion,* rev. ed. New York: Friedman, 2000.

In what ways, if any, do tactics of persuasion influence the susceptibility of receivers?

 ## Tell Me

Share with the class the insights you gained from your chosen Listen to Me, View Me, or Read Me selection.

Do you think the current U.S. president is an effective persuasive speaker? Explain why or why not.

Key Chapter Terminology

Use the Communication Works CD-ROM and the Online Learning Center at www.mhhe.com/gamble9 to further your knowledge of the following terminology.

argumentum ad hominem 507	initial credibility 515
argumentum ad populum 509	Maslow's hierarchy of needs 511
argumentum ad verecudiam 509	Monroe's motivated sequence 512
attitudes 504	persuasive speech 500
balance 510	post hoc, ergo propter hoc 508
beliefs 505	proposition 500
causal reasoning 506	proposition of fact 501
consistency 505	proposition of policy 501
credibility 514	proposition of value 501
deduction 505	reasoning from analogy 507
derived credibility 515	red herring 508
false division 508	social proof 505
induction 506	terminal credibility 515

Communication **Works**

online learning center

www.mhhe.com/gamble9

Idioms in Translation

building blocks—foundation

fight fatigue—become less tired

framing—shaping

move audience members—motivate audience members

targets—audience members

wild goose chase—futile pursuit

Test Your Understanding

Communication
Works

online learning center

www.mhhe.com/gamble9

Go to the *Self Quizzes* on the Communication Works CD-ROM and the book's Online Learning Center at www.mhhe.com/gamble9.

Notes

1. For an excellent explanation of why we study persuasion, see Deirdre D. Johnston. *The Art and Science of Persuasion.* Dubuque, IA: Brown & Benchmark, 1994. For an analysis of key theories of persuasion, see Dominick A. Infante, Andrew S. Rancer, and Deanna F. Womack. *Building Communication Theory*, 3rd ed. Prospect Heights, IL: Waveland, 1997. An interesting discussion also occurs in Jay A. Conger. "The Necessary Art of Persuasion." *Harvard Business Review* 76:3, May–June 1998, pp. 84–95.

2. See Wallace Folderingham. *Perspectives on Persuasion.* Boston: Allyn & Bacon, 1966, p. 33; and James Price Dillard. "Persuasion Past and Present: Attitudes Aren't What They Used to Be." *Communication Monographs* 60:1, March 1993, pp. 90–97.

3. For an interesting definition and discussion of persuasion, see Anthony Pratkanis and Elliot Aronson. *The Age of Propaganda,* rev. ed. New York: Freeman, 2000; and Robert B. Cialdini. *Influence: Science and Practice,* 4th ed. Boston: Allyn & Bacon, 2000.

4. Patrick D. Healy. "Weld Aides Find a Way to Deal with Negative Press: Re-edit It." *The New York Times,* February 4, 2006, pp. B1, B4.

5. For a discussion of now-classic studies, see M. Sherif and C. Hovland. *Social Judgment.* New Haven, CT: Yale University Press, 1961; and C. Sherif, M. Sherif, and R. Nebergall. *Attitude and Attitude Change.* Philadelphia: Saunders, 1965. For a very understandable explanation, see also E. Griffin. *A First Look at Communication Theory,* 4th ed. New York: McGraw-Hill, 2000.

6. Scott Cutlip and Alan Center. *Effective Public Relations.* Englewood Cliffs, NJ: Prentice-Hall, 1985, p. 122.

7. A framework for understanding the importance of beliefs is provided by Martin Fishbein and Icek Ajzen. *Belief, Attitude, Intention and Behavior: An Introduction to Theory and Research.* Reading, MA: Addison-Wesley, 1975. See especially Chapters 1 and 8.

8. Milton Rokeach. *The Open and Closed Mind.* New York: Basic Books, 1960.

9. Prominent theorists such as Leon Festinger, Fritz Hieder, and Theodore Newcomb consider the desire for consistency a central motivator of behavior. For a more contemporary discussion of the topic, see Robert B. Cialdini. *Influence.* rev. ed. New York: Quill, 2000.

10. Cialdini, p. 116.

11. Cialdini. See also Mike Allen. "Determining the Persuasiveness of Message Sidedness: A Prudent Note about Utilizing Research Summaries." *Western Journal of Communication* 57:1, winter 1993, pp. 98–103.

12. John Tierney. "Smells Like Team Spirit." *The New York Times,* February 4, 2006, pp. A13.

13. Wayne Minnick. *The Art of Persuasion.* Boston: Houghton Mifflin, 1968.

14. For a discussion of the role of affect, see, for example, Mary John Smith. *Persuasion and Human Action.* Belmont, CA: Wadsworth, 1982.

15. Abraham Maslow. *Motivation and Personality*. New York: Harper & Row, 1954, pp. 80–92.

16. Bruce E. Gronbeck, Raymie E. McKerrow, Douglas Ehninger, and Alan H. Monroe. *Principles and Types of Speech Communication*, 15th ed. New York, Allyn & Bacon, Boston, 2002.

17. Based on a speech by Amanda Taylor. "Drowsy Driving: A Deadly Epidemic." *Winning Orations*. Mankato, MN: Interstate Oratorical Association, 2000, pp. 12–15.

18. Credibility has received much attention from researchers. See, for example, James M. Kouzes and Barry Z. Posner. *Credibility*. San Francisco: Jossey-Bass, 1993.

19. J. W. Anderson. "A Comparison of Arab and American Conceptions of 'Effective' Persuasion." *The Howard Journal of Communications* 2:1, winter 1989–1990, pp. 81–114.

20. Speakers can establish credibility early in a speech. For example, see R. Brooks and T. Scheidel. "Speech as Process: A Case Study." *Speech Monographs* 35, 1968, pp. 1–7.

21. Nonverbal aspects of credibility are discussed in more detail in Chapter 16.

22. Bob Ivry. "From White Lies to the White House." *The Record*, June 8, 2003, pp. A-1, A-16.

23. Mark Bowden. "Sometimes Heroism Is a Moving Target." *The New York Times*, pp. WK1, WK4.

24. Bowden.

25. For a discussion of this issue, see Frank Biocca and Mark R. Levy, eds. *Communication in the Age of Virtual Reality*. Hillsdale, NJ: Erlbaum, 1995.

26. Developed as part of a class exercise by students in public speaking courses at the College of New Rochelle, New Rochelle, New York, and at New York Institute of Technology, New York City, New York, during the academic year 2002–2003.

27. Transcribed from a videotaped speech made by Paul Yeager. "The Patriot Act and Our Civil Rights," *Winning Orations*, Mankato, MN: Interstate Oratorical Association, 2003. Reprinted by permission.

28. Developed as part of a class exercise by students in public speaking courses at the College of New Rochelle, New Rochelle, New York, and at New York Institute of Technology, New York City, New York, using a transcript made of the videotaped speech by Paul Yeager. "The Patriot Act and Our Civil Rights." *Winning Orations*. Mankato, MN: Interstate Oratorical Association, 2003.

acceptance   the expression of a willingness to receive and respond to a message.

accommodation   the means by which co-culture members attempt to maintain their identity even while striving to establish relationships with members of the dominant culture.

accommodator   in a conflict, the person who gives in to the demands of another so that they are able to coexist in peace.

achieved leader   a person who displays effective leadership behavior without being appointed or directed to do so.

acquaintanceships   relationships with persons known by name but with whom interaction is usually limited in scope and quality.

affection   the need to express and receive love; the need to experience emotionally close relationships.

aggressiveness   the expression of one's own thoughts and feelings at another's expense.

aggressive stimulation theory   the contention that the watching of violence stimulates aggression in the viewer.

allness   the erroneous belief that a person can know all there is to know about everything.

allocentric   exhibiting a collectivistic orientation.

appreciative listening   listening for enjoyment or relaxation.

argumentum ad hominem   the use of name-calling in an argument.

argumentum ad populum   a bandwagon appeal; an appeal to popular opinion.

argumentum ad verecudiam   an appeal to authority.

artifactual communication   the use of personal adornments such as clothing, jewelry, makeup, hairstyles, and beards.

assertiveness   the honest, clear, and direct communication of one's thoughts and feelings while displaying respect for the thoughts and feelings of others.

assimilation   the means by which co-culture members attempt to fit in with members of the dominant culture.

attitudes   predispositions to respond favorably or unfavorably toward a person or subject.

attribution theory   a theory analyzing how we explain events and people.

audience adaptation   the process of adjusting one's speech to a particular audience.

audience analysis   the gathering of information about an audience that is relevant to the speech topic.

autistic society   a society at home with computers but disadvantaged when it comes to establishing human intimacy; the opposite of a high-tech–high-touch society.

autocratic, or authoritarian, leaders   directive leaders; leaders who dominate group decision making.

avoider   in a conflict, one who uses the unproductive conflict strategy of mentally or physically fleeing the conflict situation.

avoiding   the relationship stage that finds the participants seeking not to have contact with each other.

balance   a state of psychological comfort in which one's actions, feelings, and beliefs are related to each other as one would like them to be.

bar graph   a graph used to show the performance of one variable over time or to contrast various measures at a point in time.

behavioral interview   a hiring interview in which an employer seeks specific examples from prospects of specific skills.

beliefs   confidence in the truth of something.

blind area   the pane of the Johari window representing the part of the self known to others but not known to oneself.

blindering   the process by which one unconsciously adds restrictions that limit one's perceptual capabilities.

blogs   Web logs.

body   the main segment of a speech.

bonding   the commitment stage of a relationship, which involves the formal recognition of the relationship.

Boolean search   a keyword search.

brainstorming   a technique designed to generate ideas.

breadth   the number of topics you discuss with another person.

bridges   persons in groups who have intragroup contacts and who communicate with one or more persons in another group or clique.

bypassing   the pattern of miscommunication that occurs when individuals think they understand each other but actually miss each other's meaning.

case interview   a hiring interview in which the employer presents the interviewee with a business case to solve.

catalytic theory   the contention that, while the media may play a role in real-life violence, they will trigger it only if a viewer is predisposed to violence or particularly vulnerable.

catharsis theory   the contention that the viewing of violence makes one less apt to exhibit violence.

causal reasoning   speculation about the reasons for and effects of occurrences.

cause-and-effect order   an organizational format that categorizes a topic according to its causes and effects.

channels   media through which messages are sent.

chronemics   the study of the use of time.

chronological, or time, order   an organizational format that develops an idea using a time order.

circumscribing   the relationship stage that finds both the quality and quantity of communication between the parties decreasing.

civil inattention   the avoidance of sustained eye contact with strangers; the polite ignoring of others so as not to infringe on their privacy.

clique   a group of individuals who have a majority of their contacts with each other.

closed questions   highly structured questions that can be answered with a simple yes or no or in a few words.

closure   the tendency to fill in missing perceptual pieces to perceive a complete world.

co-cultures   members of the same general culture who differ in some ethnic or sociological way from the parent culture; groups of people who have a culture of their own outside the dominant culture.

cohesiveness   the property of togetherness; a measure of the extent to which group members stick and work together.

collectivistic cultures   cultures in which group goals are stressed.

communication   the deliberate or accidental transfer of meaning; that which occurs when someone observes or experiences behavior and attributes meaning to it.

communication apprehension   the fear of communicating.

comparison level   a measure of the rewards and profits individuals expect to gain from a relationship.

comparison level for alternatives   a comparison of the rewards attained from a present relationship with those expected to be derived from an alternative relationship.

competitive forcer   in a conflict, a participant who exhibits a win–lose attitude in which the attaining of personal goals is paramount.

competitive goal structure   a goal structure in which members hinder one another's efforts to obtain a goal.

competitive listening   the practice of manufacturing information to fill listening gaps.

competitive set   a readiness to perceive a conflict in all-or-nothing terms; the belief that to win, one must defeat others.

complementarity   the attraction principle stating that opposites attract.

comprehensive listening   listening to gain knowledge.

compromiser   in a conflict, a participant who seeks a middle ground.

computer graphics   computer-generated visual aids.

conclusion   the final segment of a speech.

configural formats   organizational patterns that are indirect and inexplicit.

conflict   perceived disagreement about views, interests, and goals.

conflict grid   a model portraying the styles individuals use to resolve conflicts.

connotative meaning   subjective meaning; one's personal meaning for a word.

consistency   the desire to maintain balance in our lives by behaving according to commitments already formed.

contact cultures   cultures that promote interaction and encourage displays of warmth, closeness, and availability.

content conflict   the type of conflict that arises when people disagree over matters of fact.

context   the setting of communication.

control   the need to feel we are capable and responsible and are able to exert power and influence in our relationships.

cooperative goal structure   a goal structure in which the members of a group work together to achieve their objectives.

cooperative set   the readiness to perceive a conflict situation in such a way that a means to share the rewards can be discovered.

cost–benefit/social exchange theory   the theory stating that we work to maintain a relationship only as long as the benefits we perceive for ourselves outweigh the costs.

credibility   the receiver's assessment of the competence, trustworthiness, and dynamism of a speaker.

critical listening   listening to evaluate the worth of a message.

critical thinking   the careful and deliberate process of message evaluation.

cultivation theory   a theory propounded by George Gerbner and colleagues focusing on the mass media's ability to influence users' attitudes and perceptions of reality.

cultural imperialism   the expansion of dominion of one culture over another culture.

culturally confused   lacking an understanding of cultural difference.

cultural nearsightedness   the failure to understand that we do not all attribute the same meanings to similar behavioral cues.

cultural pluralism   the adherence to the principle of cultural relativism.

cultural relativism   the acceptance of other cultural groups as equal in value to one's own.

culture   a system of knowledge, beliefs, values, customs, behaviors, and artifacts that are acquired, shared, and used by members during daily living.

cyberbole   exaggerated claims about the effects that new technologies have on society.

cyberspace   the digital world of computers and online communication.

decision by consensus a group decision reached and supported by all members of the group.

deduction reasoning that moves from the general to the specific.

deep-muscle relaxation a means of overcoming the physical symptoms of speech anxiety.

defensive behavior behavior that occurs when one perceives a threat.

defensive listening the practice of perceiving remarks made by another as a personal attack.

definitions explanations of what stimuli are or what words or concepts mean.

democratic leaders leaders whose leadership style represents a reasonable compromise between the authoritarian and laissez-faire styles.

demographics the social categories into which people can be grouped, including age, gender, family orientation, religion, cultural background, occupation, socioeconomic status, educational level, and membership in organizations.

denotative meaning dictionary meaning; the objective or descriptive meaning of a word.

depth a measure of how central the topics you discuss with another person are to your self-concept.

derived credibility a measure of a speaker's credibility during a speech-making event.

DESC script a system for expressing one's feelings and for understanding the feelings of another (*DESC* stands for *describe*, *express*, *specify*, and *consequences*).

designated leader a person given the authority by an outside force to act as leader.

dialectical tensions tensions that occur when relationship goals conflict; relationship differences that usually revolve around differences in the desires for connection and autonomy, predictability and novelty, and openness and privacy.

dialogic listening listening that focuses on what happens between people as they respond to each other, work toward shared understanding, and build a relationship.

differentiating the relationship stage in which two people reestablish their individuality.

digital divide information gap.

disclaimers remarks that diminish a statement's importance.

distance relating the use of e-mail, chat rooms, instant messages, and the Internet to facilitate relationships.

distinctiveness theory the theory stating that a person's own distinctive traits are more salient to him or her than are the more prevalent traits possessed by others in the immediate environment.

diversity the recognition of and valuing of difference.

dominant culture the culture in power; the mainstream culture.

effect the emotional, physical, and/or cognitive outcome of communication.

ego conflict the type of conflict that arises when individuals connect winning or losing with self-worth, prestige, or competence.

emblems nonverbal cues that directly translate words or phrases.

emoticons symbols that replace nonverbal cues during machine-assisted communication.

emotion the feeling one experiences in reaction to a person or situation.

emotion state a particular emotional process of limited duration and varying intensity.

emotion traits a tendency to experience a specific emotion when interacting.

emotional appeals appeals designed to evoke various feelings in receivers.

emotional contagion the catching of a mood from another person.

emotional intelligence the ability to motivate oneself, to control impulses, to recognize and regulate one's moods, to empathize, and to hope.

emotional isolationists persons who seek to avoid situations that may require the exchange of feelings.

emotive language words that reveal feelings.

empathic listening listening to help others.

empathy the ability to feel another's feelings.

essentials of communication those components present during every interpersonal, small-group, public, and mass communication event.

ethnocentrism the tendency to see one's own culture as superior to all others.

euphemism a pleasant term that is substituted for a less pleasant one.

evaluative feedback a positive or negative judgment.

evasive language words that disguise feelings.

examples representative cases.

exit interview an interview conducted when a person leaves an organization.

experimenting the relationship stage that involves the exchange of small talk to probe the unknown.

expert power power dependent on a person's knowledge.

extemporaneous outline, or speaker's notes an outline developed from a full sentence outline.

extemporaneous speech a speech that is researched, outlined, and delivered after a rehearsal period.

external feedback a communicative response from another.

facework   the means used to present a public image.

facial management techniques   the techniques used to attempt to conceal facial behavior, including emotion intensification, deintensification, neutralization, and/or masking.

fact   that which is known to be true on the basis of observation.

false division   the polarization of options, when, in fact, many options exist.

feedback   verbal and nonverbal cues sent out in response to another person's communication; information returned to a message source.

feminine cultures   cultures that value tenderness and relationships.

figure–ground principle   a strategy that facilitates the organization of stimuli by enabling us to focus on different stimuli alternately.

first impressions   initial judgments about people.

fixed-feature space   space that contains relatively permanent objects.

flame war   a conflict that occurs in cyberspace groups.

flames   insults delivered online.

formative feedback   a timed negative response, usually provided right before an activity is to be performed again.

fraudulent listening   pseudolistening.

friendly relations   the friendship stage involving small talk.

friendships   relationships that exist when persons seek each other out and exhibit a strong mutual regard for each other.

full sentence outline   an outline developed after researching a topic.

functional theory   the leadership theory suggesting that several members of a group should be ready to lead because various actions are needed to achieve group goals.

Galatea effect   the principle that we fulfill our own expectations.

gatekeeping   the filtering of messages from source to receiver.

geekspeak   online talk that disparages human beings and treats them like machines.

gender-lects   Deborah Tannen's term for language differences attributed to gender.

gossip mill   the network through which unverified information is spread.

grapevine   a type of informal, conversational network existing in an organization.

graph   a pictorial device used to present quantitative relationships.

grief process   a mourning process composed of five stages: denial, anger, guilt, depression, and acceptance.

group   a collection of individuals who interact verbally and nonverbally, occupy certain roles with respect to one another, and cooperate to accomplish a goal.

group climate   the emotional atmosphere of a group.

group communication   communication with a limited number of other persons during which information is shared, ideas developed, decisions made, and/or problems solved.

group conflict   conflict that occurs when a group member's thoughts or acts limit, prevent, or interfere with another group member's thoughts or acts.

group goals   a group's motivation for existing.

group norms   informal rules for interaction in a group.

group patterns of communication   the patterns of message flow in a group.

group role-classification model   the model proposed by Benne and Sheats describing functions participants should seek to assume and to avoid in groups.

group structure   member positions and roles performed.

groupthink   an extreme means of avoiding conflict that occurs when groups let the desire for consensus override careful analysis and reasoned decision making.

habitual pitch   the pitch (of the voice) one uses most often.

halo effect   the perceiving of qualities that are primarily positive.

haptics   the study of the use of touch.

hearing   the involuntary, physiological process by which we process sound.

hidden area   the pane of the Johari window representing the part of the self that contains information about the self known to oneself but hidden from or unknown to others.

high-context communication   a tradition-bound communication system that depends on indirectness; a culture whose members place less reliance on explicit verbal messages and more emphasis on the preservation of harmony.

high-intensity conflict   a conflict in which one party seeks to destroy or hurt the other party.

high power distance cultures   cultures based on power differences in which subordinates are quick to defer to superiors.

high self-monitors   people highly attuned to impression management efforts.

high-tech–high-touch society   a technologically oriented society whose members value personal contact; the opposite of an autistic society.

hiring interview   an interview conducted for the purpose of filling an employment position.

home page   the opening page of a Web site which details the structure and ordering of information in the site.

hyper-competitiveness   the contention that one needs to defeat another to achieve one's goals.

horn effect the perceiving of qualities that are primarily negative.

HURIER model a model of listening focusing on six skill areas or stages.

hurtful messages messages designed to upset or to cause emotional pain that further hampers trust.

idiocentric exhibiting an individualistic orientation.

illustrations stories; narrative pictures.

"I" messages messages that convey feelings about the nature of a situation without passing judgment on the actions of another.

impression management the creation of a positive image designed to influence others.

impromptu speech a speech delivered on the spur of the moment, with little or no preparation.

inclusion the need for social contact.

individualistic cultures cultures in which individual goals are stressed.

induction reasoning that moves from specific evidence to a general conclusion.

inference a conclusion that cannot be verified by observation; an assumption with varying degrees of accuracy.

informal space space that is highly mobile and can be quickly changed.

information-gathering interview an interview with the goal of collecting information, opinions, or data about a topic or person.

information overload the situation that occurs when the amount of information provided by a speech maker is too great to be handled effectively by the listeners; the speech maker may provide more data than is necessary or use unclear language or jargon.

information underload the situation that occurs when the information provided by a speech maker is already known by the listeners.

informative speech a speech whose primary purpose is to impart knowledge or to teach.

initial credibility a measure of how an audience perceives a speaker prior to the speech-making event.

initiating the first stage in a relationship; the point at which persons first make contact.

integrating the relationship stage when two persons are identified as a couple.

intensifying the relationship stage during which two persons become good friends.

intensional orientation the preoccupation with labels.

intercultural communication the process of interpreting and sharing meanings with individuals from different cultures.

interethnic communication the process of interpreting and sharing meanings with individuals of different ethnic origins.

internal feedback a response you give yourself as you monitor your own behavior.

internal summaries rhetorical devices designed to help listeners remember content.

international communication communication between persons representing different nations.

interpersonal communication communication with another; the relationship level of communication.

interpersonal conflict a struggle between two or more people.

interpersonal relationship a meaningful connection, such as friendship, between two persons.

interracial communication the process of interpreting and sharing meanings with individuals from different races.

interview the most common type of purposeful, planned, decision-making, person-to-person communication.

intimate distance a distance ranging from the point of touch to 18 inches from a person.

intracultural communication the process of sharing meaning with members of one's own racial or ethnic group.

intrapersonal communication communication with the self; communication that involves one person.

intrapersonal conflict an internal struggle.

introduction the initial segment of a speech.

isolates persons who do not feel well integrated into a group and have few, if any, contacts with others.

Johari window a model containing four panes (the open, blind, hidden, and unknown areas) used to explain the roles that self-awareness and self-disclosure play in relationships.

kaleidoscope thinking the taking of existing data and twisting it or looking at it from another angle.

killer looks looks that discourage or inhibit the generation of ideas.

killer phrases comments that stop the flow of ideas.

kinesics the study of the relationship between human body motion, or body language, and communication.

language a unified system of symbols that permits the sharing of meaning.

laissez-faire leader a nondirective leader.

leadership the ability to influence others.

legitimate power power by virtue of position.

liaisons persons who do not belong to any one group or clique but who link persons of one group with persons in another.

linear logic a step-by-step approach to developing ideas that relies on facts and data to support main points.

line graphs graphs used to illustrate trends, relationships, or comparisons over time.

linguistic determinism   the belief that language influences one's interpretation of the world.

linguistic prejudice   the use of prejudiced language.

linguistic relativity   the belief that persons who speak different languages perceive the world differently.

listening   the deliberate, psychological process by which we receive, understand, and retain aural (heard) stimuli.

listening level–energy involvement scale   a scale that describes energy expenditure during listening.

listserv   an e-mail list of people who share interests in and knowledge of a topic.

loneliness   a perceived discrepancy between desired and achieved social relationships.

low-contact cultures   cultures whose members value privacy and maintain distance when interacting.

low-context communication   a system that encourages directness in communication; a culture in which self-expression is valued.

low-intensity conflict   a conflict in which the persons involved seek solutions beneficial to all parties.

low power distance cultures   cultures that believe that power should be used only when legitimate.

low self-monitors   people who pay little attention to responses others have to them.

main ideas   the main points of a speech; the subtopics of a speech.

maintenance roles   group roles designed to ensure the smooth running of a group.

manuscript speech   a speech read from a script.

marginalized group   a group whose members feel like outsiders.

markers   items that reserve or set the boundaries of our space.

masculine cultures   cultures that value aggressiveness, strength, and material symbols of success.

Maslow's hierarchy of needs   a model that depicts motivation as a pyramid, with the most basic needs at the base and the most sophisticated needs at the apex.

mass communication   the process of transmitting messages that may be processed by gatekeepers before being transmitted to large audiences via a channel of broad diffusion, such as a print, an audio, or a visual medium.

media literacy   the ability to interpret mindfully the positive and negative meanings and effects one encounters in the media.

medium-intensity conflict   a conflict in which the parties are committed to winning but believe that winning is sufficient.

melting-pot philosophy   the philosophy advocating the assimilation of different cultures into the dominant culture.

memorized speech   a manuscript speech that the speaker commits to memory.

message   the content of a communicative act.

mixed message   an incongruent message that occurs when words and actions contradict each other.

monopolistic listening   the practice of defending one's right to speak while denying others the right to be listened to.

Monroe's motivated sequence   a speech framework composed of five phases—attention, need, satisfaction, visualization, and action—that sequentially moves receivers toward accepting and acting on a speaker's proposition.

moving toward friendship   the friendship stage involving personal disclosures; the stage during which individuals move beyond serendipitous encounters.

MUDs   online multiuser domains.

multiculturalists   persons respectful of and engaged with people from distinctly different cultures.

multitasking clothing   clothing with built-in electronic gadgetry.

MYGLO   acronym for "my eyes glaze over."

nascent friendship   the friendship stage during which individuals increase the regularity of their interactions and consider each other friends.

need for affection   the need to express and receive love; the need to experience emotionally close relationships.

need for control   the need to feel we are capable and responsible and are able to exert power and influence over our relationships.

need for inclusion   the need for social contact.

negative feedback   a communicative response that extinguishes behavior in progress.

netiquette   the rules of the Internet.

noise   anything that interferes with or distorts the ability to send and receive messages.

nonassertion   that which occurs when one hesitates to display one's feelings and thoughts.

nonassertiveness   a failure to stand up for one's rights; the suppression of one's thoughts or feelings as a result of fear or shyness.

nonevaluative feedback   a nondirective response.

nonfluencies   meaningless sounds or phrases that disrupt the natural flow of speech; hesitation phenomena.

nonverbal communication   the kinds of human messages and responses not expressed in words.

olfactics   the study of the sense of smell.

online, or machine-assisted, communication   communication via computers and the Internet.

onlinespeak   the informal communication style that marks electronic communication.

open area   the pane of the Johari window representing the part of the self containing information known both to the self and to others.

open questions   questions that offer the interviewee freedom with regard to the choice and scope of an answer.

paralanguage   the vocal cues that accompany spoken language.

paraphrasing   restating in your own words what another person has said.

perceived self   the self we believe ourselves to be.

perception   the process by which we make sense out of experience; the means by which we make experience our own.

perceptual constancy   the desire to perceive experience exactly as we have perceived it in the past.

perceptual sets   expectations that produce a readiness to process experience in a predetermined way.

personal distance   a distance ranging from 18 inches to 4 feet from a person.

persuasion interview   an interview with the goal of attitude and behavior influence.

persuasive speech   a speech whose primary purpose is to change or reinforce the attitudes, beliefs, values, and/or behaviors of receivers.

phatic communication   communication designed to open the channels of communication.

pictographs   graphs that use sketches to represent concepts.

pie, or circle, graph   a circle with the various percentages of the whole indicated by wedges; a means of showing percentage relationships.

pitch   the highness or lowness of the voice.

pop language   words and phrases used to sell oneself as hip or cool.

positive feedback   a communicative response that enhances behavior in progress.

post hoc, ergo propter hoc   the identification of a false cause.

prejudice   a biased, negative attitude toward a particular group of people; a negative or positive prejudgment based on membership in a social category.

prejudiced language   sexist, ageist, or racist language; language disparaging to the members of a co-culture.

preliminary working outline   a sparse outline containing only key words.

preview   the section of the speech that lets the audience know what the speaker will be discussing.

primacy effect   the tendency for a first impression to exert more influence than what comes later; the ability of one's first impression to color subsequent impressions.

primary questions   questions used to introduce topics or explore a new area.

probing   a nonevaluative response that asks for more information.

problem-and-solution order   an organizational format that identifies the problems inherent in a situation and presents a solution to remedy them.

problem-solving collaborator   in a conflict, a participant who exhibits a win–win attitude.

proposition   a statement that summarizes the purpose of a persuasive speech.

proposition of fact   a persuasive speech with the goal of settling what is or is not so.

proposition of policy   a persuasive speech on what ought to be.

proposition of value   a persuasive speech that espouses the worth of an idea, a person, or an object.

prosumers   consumers who produce the material of consumption themselves.

proxemics   the study of the use of space.

pseudoconflict   a situation with only the appearance of a conflict; results when parties mistakenly believe that two or more goals cannot be achieved simultaneously.

psychographics   categories into which persons may be grouped based on their attitudes, motivations, values, and level of information and commitment with respect to a topic.

public communication   communication designed to inform, persuade, or entertain the members of an audience.

public distance   a distance beyond 12 feet from a person.

public speaking   the act of preparing, staging, and delivering a presentation to an audience.

purpose statement   an infinitive phrase describing the goal of a speech.

Pygmalion effect   the principle that we fulfill the expectations of others.

qualifiers   words that lack certainty and make phrases tentative.

quality circles   small groups of employees who meet regularly to discuss organizational life and the quality of their work environment; recommendations for improving products and work procedures are made during these meetings.

questions of fact   questions concerned with the truth or falsity of a statement.

questions of policy   questions that help determine what future actions, if any, should be taken.

questions of value   questions that involve subjective judgments of worth.

racial code words   words that are discriminatory but not literally racist.

racist language   language that denigrates a person because of race.

rate   the speed at which one speaks.

reasoning from analogy   reasoning by comparison.

receivers   persons who receive, decode, and interpret messages.

reciprocal turn taking   the changing of the speaking and listening roles during conversation.

red-flag words   words that evoke emotional deafness, dropping listening efficiency to zero.

red herring   a distraction used to lead the receiver to focus on an irrelevant issue.

referent power   power dependent on one's desire to identify or be like another person.

reflective-thinking framework   a system for decision making and problem solving that is designed to encourage critical inquiry.

rejection   the expression of disinterest in communication; communication that indicates one's rejection of another's self-concept.

relational dialectics theory   the contention that relationships oscillate between contradictory goals or desires.

relationship   a meaningful connection with another person.

relationship level   the interpretation level of communication.

rhetorical question   a question asked for effect and without the expectation of an answer.

rigid complementarity   a relationship characterized by fixed, unchanging roles.

role-limited interaction   the beginning of friendship; the stage during which two individuals make initial contact.

role reversal   a conflict-resolution technique in which one acts as the person with whom one is in conflict.

romantic relationship   a relationship characterized by commitment, passion, intimacy, and the expectation of permanence.

Sapir–Whorf hypothesis   the belief that the labels we use help shape the way we think, our worldview, and our behavior.

search engine   a computer program that allows one to look through an entire database of information quickly.

secondary questions   probing questions that are used to follow up primary questions.

selective attention   the tendency to focus on certain cues and ignore others.

selective exposure   the selection of stimuli that reaffirm existing attitudes, beliefs, and values; the tendency to close oneself to new experiences.

selective listening   the practice of zeroing in on only the parts of a message of particular interest to the receiver.

selective perception   the means by which one interprets experience in a way that conforms to one's beliefs, expectations, and convictions; the inclination to distort one's perceptions of stimuli to make them conform to the need for internal consistency or closure.

selective retention   the tendency to remember those things that reinforce one's way of thinking and forget those that oppose one's way of thinking.

self-awareness   the ability to reflect on and monitor one's own behavior.

self-concept   everything one thinks and feels about oneself; one's self-evaluation.

self-conflict   the type of conflict that occurs when one person has to choose between two or more mutually exclusive options.

self-directed teams   autonomous work groups in which employees are empowered to make decisions and supervise themselves.

self-disclosure   the process of revealing to another person information about the self that he or she would not otherwise know.

self-efficacy   an optimistic belief in our own competence.

self-enhancement   the bolstering of one's self image.

self-esteem   how well one likes and values oneself.

self-fulfilling prophecy   a prediction or an expectation that comes true simply because one acts as if it were true.

self-image   the sort of person one perceives oneself to be.

self-serving bias   the overemphasis of external factors to explain our own behavior.

self-serving roles   group roles that impede the functioning of a group by preventing members from working together effectively.

semi-fixed-feature space   space in which objects are used to create distance.

senders   persons who formulate, encode, and transmit messages.

separation   the strategy co-culture members use to resist interacting with members of the dominant culture.

serial communication   a chain-of-command transmission.

sexist language   language derogatory to one sex.

silence   the absence of both paralinguistic and verbal cues.

situational theory   the theory of leadership asserting that leadership depends on the situation.

social distance   a distance ranging from 4 feet to 12 feet from a person.

social penetration theory   the theory stating that our relationships begin with relatively narrow breadth and shallow depth and develop over time.

social proof   the determination of what is right by finding out what other people think is right.

spatial order   an organizational format that describes an object, a person, or a phenomenon as it exists in space.

speech apprehension   fear associated with speaking in public.

speech framework   a frame, or skeleton, on which a speech is developed.

speech–thought differential   the difference between speaking rate and thinking rate.

stabilized friendship   the friendship stage that finds interactants sharing more intimate information because of the belief that the relationship is secure and will continue.

stagnating   the stage in a relationship that finds communication between the parties at a standstill.

statistics   facts expressed in numerical form.

stereotypes   generalizations about people, places, or events that are held by many members of a society.

stress interview   a hiring interview in which more than one interviewer fires questions at a single interviewee.

subordinate ideas   ideas that amplify the main ideas of a speech.

supportive feedback   a nonevaluative response that confirms the significance of a problem or situation.

symbol   that which represents something else.

tag questions   words that seek verbal confirmation; tags lie midway between outright statements and yes–no questions.

task roles   group roles designed to help the group realize its objectives.

technopoly   a culture in which technology monopolizes the thought-world.

terminal credibility   a measure of a speaker's credibility at the end of a speech-making event.

termination   the end stage of a relationship.

territoriality   the need to demonstrate a possessive or ownership relationship to space.

testimony   someone else's opinions or conclusions.

thought stopping   a means of overcoming the mental symptoms of speech anxiety.

time shifting   the ability to watch media offerings at a time convenient to you.

tolerance of vulnerability   a measure of the degree of trust you place in another person.

topical order   an organizational format that clusters material by dividing it into a series of appropriate topics.

toxic communication   the consistent use of verbal abuse and/or physical or sexual aggression or violence.

trait theory   the theory of leadership asserting that certain people are born to lead.

transformational leader   a leader who gives a group a new vision or culture.

transitions   rhetorical devices used to bridge ideas.

triangle of meaning   a model that explains the relationship that exists among words, things, and thoughts.

twenty-four seven   a reference to the ability to maintain contact 24 hours a day, 7 days a week.

type X leader   a leader who does not delegate responsibility because he or she does not believe in the abilities of group members; a leader who is unconcerned with the personal achievement of group members.

type Y leader   a leader who lets group members grow and develop; a leader concerned with the personal sense of achievement realized by group members.

understanding   a nonevaluative response that relies on the use of paraphrasing.

uniform resource locator (URL)   a Web page address.

unknown area   the pane of the Johari window representing the part of the self that is unknown to oneself and others.

Usenet newsgroups   a conference system of computer bulletin boards and discussion forums.

value conflict   the type of conflict that arises when people hold different views on an issue.

virtual neighborhoods and communities   online, surrogate communities.

virtual reality   an environment that exists as data in a computer system.

visual dominance   a measure calculated by comparing the percentage of looking while speaking with the percentage of looking while listening.

visualization   the picturing of experience in the mind; a technique used to help speakers imagine their own speech-making success.

volume   the degree of loudness of the voice.

waning friendship   the friendship stage during which friends drift apart.

"you" messages   messages in which a speaker denies responsibility for a situation by placing blame on another person; the opposite of "I" messages.

Photo Credits

Credits & Acknowledgments

C-1

The "n" in entries stands for "Note" and the number that follows is the footnote number that can be found on the page listed.